School Psychology: Essentials of Theory and Practice

School Psychology: Essentials of Theory and Practice

Cecil R. Reynolds

Department of Educational Psychology
Texas A&M University

Terry B. Gutkin

Department of Educational Psychology
University of Nebraska-Lincoln

Stephen N. Elliott

Department of Psychology
Louisiana State University

Joseph C. Witt

Department of Educational Psychology
University of Nebraska-Lincoln

JOHN WILEY & SONS

New York • Chichester • Brisbane • Toronto • Singapore

Copyright © 1984, by John Wiley & Sons, Inc.

All rights reserved. Published simultaneously in Canada

Reproduction or translation of any part of
this work beyond that permitted by Sections
107 and 108 of the 1976 United States Copyright
Act without the permission of the copyright
owner is unlawful. Requests for permission
or further information should be addressed to
the Permissions Department, John Wiley & Sons.

Library of Congress Cataloging in Publication Data:

Main entry under title:

School psychology.

Includes bibliographical references and indexes.
1. Educational psychology—Addresses, essays, lectures. I. Reynolds, Cecil R., 1952–
LB1055.S39   1984   370.15   83-21918
ISBN 0-471-08327-5

Printed in the United States of America

10 9 8 7 6 5 4 3 2 1

To Brenda, Barbara, Anita, and Larie, with love and appreciation for their patience and support.

The genesis of this book occurred at the University of Nebraska-Lincoln at which each of the authors served as a professor. The conceptual model presented herein reflects the training philosophy of that program.

Preface

The field of school psychology has emerged from its childhood and now is maturing rapidly. Presently, there are more than 200 graduate training programs in school psychology, and the field continues to grow rapidly. Two growing national organizations now represent the field: the American Psychological Association, Division of School Psychology (Division 16), and the National Association of School Psychologists (NASP). Nearly every state now has an active school psychology organization functioning either independently or as a division of a state psychological association.

Despite the emergence and subsequent growth of school psychology, the number and variety of texts in the discipline have remained quite limited. Although several major edited works have recently become available, the only major textbook in the field that is not a collection of readings was published in 1974. Much has happened in psychology and education since that time. Clearly, there is a need for an integrated, up-to-date discussion of the art and science of school psychology.

School Psychology: Essentials of Theory and Practice was written to reflect the current status of the field and to project a direction for its future development. To attain the first goal, the volume addresses the development of the discipline and provides in-depth treatment of core areas of day-to-day school psychological practice—consultation, assessment, and intervention. Our second goal, more complex and proactive in nature, is to provide integrated theoretical frameworks within which the practice of school psychology can best be understood and advanced. Emphasis is placed on examining service delivery models as a vehicle for conceptualizing current practice and for plotting the future course of school psychology. Bandura's (1978) model of reciprocal determinism and ecological perspectives of human behavior is proposed as a set of theoretical constructs that can, and should, shape the nature of school psychological services. A scientist-practitioner model of professional practice is espoused. By intertwining these and other related concepts throughout the text, we hope to foster a vision of school psychologists as problem solvers whose actions emanate from meaningful psychological theories and relevant empirical data.

We express our appreciation to our many colleagues who encouraged us in this venture and helped to sharpen our thinking. Special thanks go to Wayne Piersel for helping to conceptualize the project and for providing many insightful ideas and criticisms. Joseph French's detailed review of the entire manuscript was very helpful, as was Thomas Fagan's review of the historical sections. Finally, we acknowledge Alan S. Kaufman, E. Paul Torrance, Beeman Phillips, June Gallessich, James Carroll, and Lee Meyerson, who fostered in us the breadth of perspective we feel we have achieved with this volume. Several of our own graduate students read and commented on various aspects of the work in addition to doing a significant amount of the legwork at the library—to Julia Clark, Gloria Galvin, Ed Scholwinski, and Michael Stowe we also express our appreciation. Of course, without the support and patience of our families we could never have completed this project.

CRR
TBG
SNE
JCW

Contents

CHAPTER 1

School Psychology: The Development of a Professional Psychological Specialty

It is not too much to say that the improvement of mental health and mental hygiene in the United States rests in a major way upon the work of the schools and therefore in part upon the qualifications and training of those who become school psychologists.

Cutts, 1955, p. 7

School psychology, which has its developmental roots in the late 1800s, is presently one of the most vital and active disciplines in contemporary psychology. Since its inception, school psychology's major goals have been to provide direct and indirect psychological services to children and youth to improve their mental health and educational development. The means for accomplishing such major goals have necessitated a vast amount of knowledge and a diverse array of services that cut across specialties of applied psychology (i.e., clinical, counseling, and industrial/organizational), as well as several areas within education. Hence, today school psychology is a challenging and potentially rewarding profession for skilled *scientists* and *practitioners* of psychology.

The promise of school psychology as a means of high quality psychological services for children and youth has its conceptual origins in several domains of thought: namely, preventive and community mental health, special education, human development, and clinical psychology. Common assumptions, such as the sooner a problem is identified, the easier it is to remediate, or the closer an

1

Table 1.1   Major Published Works in School Psychology

Author(s)	Title	Date
Hildreth	*Psychological Services for School Problems*	1930
Symonds	*The School Psychologist* (entire issue of *The Journal of Consulting Psychology*)	1942
Cutts	*School Psychologists at Mid-Century*	1955
Mullen	*The Psychologist on the School Staff: Report of the Committee on Reconsideration of the Functions of the School Psychologist*	1958
White & Harris	*The School Psychologist*	1961
Eiserer	*The School Psychologist*	1963
Gottsegen & Gottsegen	*Professional and School Psychology*	1963
Gray	*The Psychologist in the Schools*	1963
Valett	*The Practice of School Psychology: Professional Problems*	1963
Reger	*School Psychology*	1965
Phillips	*Perspectives on School Psychology*	1966
Magary	*School Psychological Services in Theory and Practice: A Handbook*	1967 & 1972
Herron, Green, Guild, Smith, & Kantor	*Contemporary School Psychology*	1970
Holt & Kicklighter	*Psychological Services in the Schools: Readings in Preparation, Organization and Practice*	1971
Bardon & Bennett	*School Psychology*	1974
Fein	*The Changing School Scene: Challenge to Psychology*	1974
Meyers, Parsons, & Martin	*Mental Health Consultation in the Schools*	1979
Phye & Reschly	*School Psychology: Perspectives and Issues*	1979
Conoley	*Consultation in Schools: Theory, Research, Technology*	1980
Kratochwill	*Advances in School Psychology* (Vol. 1)	1981
	Advances in School Psychology (Vol. 2)	1982
Reynolds & Gutkin	*The Handbook of School Psychology*	1982
Hynd	*The School Psychologist: An Introduction*	1983

Note: This table is a modified version of one originally developed by T. R. Kratochwill, ''Advances in School Psychology: A Preview of the Contents and an Overview of the Chapters.'' In T. R. Kratochwill (Ed.), *Advances in School Psychology.* New York: Lawrence Erlbaum, 1981.

intervention is to the problem situation, the greater the opportunity for generalization of treatment, such assumptions are illustrative of the thinking that underlies the need for psychological services in educational settings. Thus, an educational system, a system which most children and youth are involved in for a significant time during the major formative periods of their lives, provides a setting and a vehicle for the delivery of psychological services. No other social system provides such a comprehensive opportunity to interact with children and families. Yet, no other social system seems to be open to as much public criticism and pressure as does education. Psychologists in schools and other educational settings, like educators, are very visable to the public and consequently are subject to the same detailed scrutiny as educators. Hence, the use of an educational system as a setting for the delivery of psychological services has been a two-edged sword for psychology. Although such a sword allows for effective service in experienced hands, it has liabilities in inexperienced (untrained) or careless hands.

The purposes of this book are to examine the profession of school psychology and its major conceptual and functional features within a service delivery system framework, and to acquaint readers with issues that have characterized the development of the profession. After completing this book, readers may find sources such as *The Handbook of School Psychology* (Reynolds & Gutkin, 1982) or the edited series *Advances in School Psychology* (Kratochwill, 1981, 1982) suitable complements. Other major works published during the past 50 years in the field of school psychology are listed in Table 1.1.

In the first chapter, we will examine the evolution of school psychology and its professional organizations with a primary focus on significant events during the past 35 years. For additional analyses of the history of school psychology, readers are referred to works by Bardon and Bennett (1974), Cutts (1955), and Farling and Agner (1979). Another emphasis of this first chapter will be to explore the various roles and functions assumed by school psychologists. Subsequent chapters will elaborate upon these roles and functions.

EVOLUTION OF THE DISCIPLINE OF SCHOOL PSYCHOLOGY

The history of psychology has been traced back to ancient Greece (Watson, 1971); however, its emergence as a distinct knowledge domain occurred during the last quarter of the nineteenth century (Schultz, 1975). Wilhelm Wundt (1832–1920) is generally credited with playing a major role in establishing psychology as a formal discipline for he was the first to apply experimental methods of natural science to the study of mental processes. Galton's (1869) work on the hereditary basis for intellectual superiority also played an instrumental role in stimulating thought and research about the psychology of individual differences.

The emergence of psychology coincided with a period of marked social and political reform. According to Levine and Levine (1970), the period between 1890 and 1920 was characterized by the decline of social Darwinism and a rise in beliefs that environmental factors greatly influenced an individual's life. Industrialization and urbanization also were on the increase in America. Consequently, the likelihood of extended families and homogeneous communities diminished and with them valuable support systems for individuals. The climate for the development of helping professions, like that of psychology, was right. Thus, the principles and methods utilized in experimental laboratories were beginning to be applied to solving the problems of adjusting to a more urbanized world.

The first psychological practitioners were persons trained or self-educated in the experimental psychology of the late 1800s. These practitioners relied chiefly on their knowledge of mental functioning and on psychophysical measures in order to understand and treat problems of adjustment and school learning difficulties. Many pioneering psychologists typically became involved in the provision of psychological services as a part-time function complementing their laboratory research (Murphy, 1929).

The Establishment of Psychological Clinics

Lightner Witmer was perhaps the most notable of the early American psychological practitioners who combined service and science. He was a student of both James McKeen Cattell and Wilhelm Wundt, studying first with Cattell at the University of Pennsylvania and then going to Leipzig for doctoral study with Wundt. After completing his doctorate, Witmer returned to the University of Pennsylvania to succeed Cattell as director of its Laboratory of Psychology. In 1896, he began to work in the laboratory with children who were having learning difficulties. Although Galton had established a similar laboratory or clinic in London nearly ten years earlier, Witmer's laboratory is usually referred to as the first child guidance clinic in America (Levine & Levine, 1970; Roback, 1964).

Witmer's clinic was the center of his teaching, research, and service functions at Pennsylvania. From its inception, the clinic was allied with education since one of Witmer's major goals was to train psychologists to help educators solve children's learning problems. Such training was enhanced by working directly with children who were referred to the clinic. Thus, psychologists received supervised training, while children, families, and educators received needed psychological services. In 1907, Witmer founded *The Psychological Clinic,* the first journal devoted to clinical psychology. The journal communicated about clients and services commonly seen at the clinic and had a masthead which described it as "A Journal for the Study and Treatment of Mental Retardation and Deviation." Witmer edited and wrote many of the articles in *The*

Psychological Clinic until 1935, when it ceased publication. In 1937, *The Journal of Consulting Psychology* was founded to carry on Witmer's important work; today, it is an American Psychological Association (APA) journal and is titled the *Journal of Consulting and Clinical Psychology.*

Witmer's contributions to applied psychology were significant; indeed, he is acknowledged as the founding father of both school psychology and clinical psychology. His work to develop psychological services for children may be his most noteworthy accomplishment. It was his clinic that served as a model for service delivery which other universities and school systems subsequently emulated (Cutts, 1955). Hence, psychological services to children and youth were beginning to be established for urban schools by 1910.

Witmer's contributions to school psychology were clearly seminal. Recognizing this, the Division of School Psychology (Division 16) of the American Psychological Association annually presents the "Lightner Witmer Award" to the outstanding young school psychologist in the Division.

Other Important Developmental Events in School Psychology

Other events coinciding historically with Witmer's work also influenced the development of school psychology. These include the work of Galton and Binet and his associates in individual measurement, the development of "special" classes for mentally handicapped children, and the mental health movement. Since each of these events has been written about in detail elsewhere, they will be reviewed here only briefly.

Measuring Individual Differences. The assessment of individual differences has its basis in the works of Sir Francis Galton and Alfred Binet. In the 1880s, Galton, stimulated by Darwin's work on heredity, began collecting data on human characteristics for the purpose of establishing similarities and differences among individuals. As a means of collecting information, he devised tests of vision, hearing, reaction time, and discrimination and persuaded school personnel to keep systematic records of how students performed on such tests (Anastasi, 1957). Some writers (White & Harris, 1961), in fact, point to Galton's work as the first example of school psychological services.

Although Galton devised and used tests to measure children's abilities in the 1880s, it was not until 1904 when French educators hired Alfred Binet and Theophile Simon to assess the learning potential of children that the testing movement really began. Binet and Simon designed a 30-item test based upon careful questioning of teachers to discern tasks which were sensitive to developmental differences in children. The Binet–Simon test, designed to measure mental processes and subsequently classify children, was quite successful, and after three revisions between 1905–1911, became the standard for a generation of test developers.

Lewis Terman of Stanford University became very interested in the Binet–Simon scales and was one of several psychologists (e.g., Goddard, Yerkes, Kuhlmann) who translated and adapted them for use in American schools. In 1916, the Stanford-Binet Intelligence Test, as Terman named it, was completed. It soon became widely used in public schools because it helped educators better understand children's learning aptitudes and achievement (Bardon & Bennett, 1974) and, though now quite dated, its influence is felt even today whenever an individual test of intelligence is administered (Kaufman & Reynolds, 1983).

The testing movement, which was originally given impetus by educators' desires for special classes for retarded children, served to promote major changes in educational practice (Murphy, 1929). Coupled with more humanitarian notions about mental retardation, the use of intelligence tests provided a means for diagnosing and classifying children and youth that had not existed previously. As a result, special education personnel eagerly elicited the assessment skills of psychologists. In fact, Arnold Gesell was hired as a school psychologist by the State of Connecticut in 1915 to travel about the state to test children for possible special class placement. Gesell is thought to be the first person to have the title of school psychologist (Cutts, 1955). The assessment role and relationship between school psychology and special education still exists today, and will be explored in detail later in this chapter.

Care and Treatment for the Disturbed. The mental health movement had its origins in the work of reformers such as Phillipe Pinel in France and Dorothea Dix in America (Reisman, 1976) and gained momentum from scholars of psychology such as Ernest Kraepelin and Sigmund Freud. The mental health movement crystallized, however, after the publication of Clifford Beers' (1908) work, *A Mind That Found Itself.* Beers was a former mental patient and was able to write effectively about the horrors of his commitment to a mental institution. He also worked to organize the National Committee for Mental Hygiene in 1909, which became an effective force in informing the public about mental health. This committee was also effective in establishing a number of child guidance clinics (Barker, 1918). Many of these early clinics focused on the prevention of juvenile delinquency (Lowry & Smith, 1933).

In the 1920s, many child guidance centers expanded their scope beyond the prevention of delinquency to serving children who evidenced many kinds of adjustment and developmental problems. A psychoanalytic orientation predominated most clinics' staffs which were composed of medical and psychological personnel. Schools began to work cooperatively with clinics; in fact, financial support for some clinics was assumed by schools. This relationship between clinics and schools, however, did not last more than a decade. Many educators became disenchanted with the therapies of the time and perceived clinic personnel as unsympathetic to the problems and constraints of schools. Clinic personnel were also disappointed for they perceived teachers as lacking knowledge or commitment. Educators began to look for other means of acquiring psychological services (Lowry & Smith, 1933).

The Development of Psychological Specialties: Clinical and School

Based on the previous overview of the history of psychology, it seems clear that applied psychology was established in America and abroad by the 1920s. Once established, specialization amongst practitioners began to occur. The American Association of Clinical Psychologists was founded in 1916. At approximately the same time, a section on Clinical Psychology was organized within the APA (Sundberg, Tyler, & Taplin, 1973). The term *clinical,* however, was used generically to refer to all of applied or service directed psychology. Early clinical psychologists worked primarily in academic or guidance clinic settings with children evidencing learning problems or youth who had violated the law. A handful were also employed by schools.

Over the course of four decades, 1910 to 1950, the world experienced two major wars and clinical psychology underwent significant changes, ultimately emerging as an independent professional specialty. Clinical psychologists began to affiliate less often with educational systems and more frequently with medical facilities, services were broadened from assessment to include therapeutic treatments, and the emphasis in service changed from community-based for children to individual-based for adults (Sundberg et al., 1973). Consequently, by 1945 the setting, the clientele, and the nature of services with which clinical or applied psychologists had been originally identified had changed noticeably. Psychologists employed by schools, however, continued to function as community-based providers of psychological services for children. According to Cornell (1942), by 1940 only 19 of the 745 clinics listed in the *Directory of Psychiatric Clinics in the United States* were directly under the auspices of a public school system. Thus, the number of practicing psychologists in the schools was apparently rather small.

School psychology is commonly conceptualized as an offshoot of the specialty of clinical psychology. However, given the development of the clinical psychological specialty, it is hard to view school psychology as an offshoot. Rather, as Harris (1980) put it, "In many respects it seems nearer to the truth to view school psychology as the offspring of applied psychology which 'stayed at home,' while clinical psychology moved on to new neighborhoods" (p. 15). Thus, psychologists working in schools or community-based clinics serving schools continued to pursue the goals of the founders and leaders in applied psychology. Whether by default or through proactive planning, a specialty in school psychology was soon to be identified.

The events surrounding the organization of a division of school psychology within the APA are not well documented. However, it is clear that sometime during mid-1946, Division 16 of APA became the Division of School Psychology. Harry J. Baker was elected as the division's first president for 1946–1947.

The examination of the 1946 volumes of the *American Psychologist,* the journal of the American Psychological Association, provides evidence of some of the confusion about the formalization of Division 16. For example, in the July 1946 issue (Vol. I, 7), the program for the 54th Annual Meeting of APA listed school psychology as a division. Yet, in the August 1946 issue (Vol. I, 8), Doll authored an invited article titled, "The Divisional Structure of the APA." In this article, Doll acknowledged apparent widespread dissatisfaction among APA members concerning a divisional structure recommended by the Intersociety Constitutional Convention (ICC) in 1943. School psychology was included only as a write-in under other divisions of the ICC's divisional structure. APA's Committee on Divisional Organization, which followed the ICC, suggested several modifications to the ICC plan of divisional structure. One of the recommendations was to make school psychology the 16th division in APA. Although Doll (1946, p. 339), a member of the Committee on Divisional Organization, wrote that a division of school psychology was unwarranted because of the small number of persons expressing interest in membership, it appears that the division was formalized at the annual meeting of APA in 1946. Ironically, the meeting was held at the University of Pennsylvania, the place where Witmer had begun delivering psychological services to school children nearly 30 years earlier.

Important Events in the Development of School Psychology

The creation of a division of school psychology within the American Psychological Association acknowledged both the relative importance and uniqueness of school psychological services. Initially, however, school psychology's identity was shaped by forces external to it. For example, schools and juvenile courts had demanded testing and social work, and clinical psychologists changed orientations and gained the "spotlight" by leaving the schools. Thus, although school psychology "stayed at home," it appeared to have initially lost some status in the eyes of its neighbors. Since the mid-1940s, however, numerous events and forces both internal and external have shaped the identity and functioning of school psychology. A selective review of major events over the past 35 years should provide important background for understanding the profession's development and current functioning.

The Boulder Conference. In psychology, the typical model for practitioner specialties has come to be known as the "Boulder Model." This model grew out of a conference on the training of clinical psychologists in Boulder, Colorado, in 1949 and defined the practicing psychologist as a scientist-practitioner (Raimy, 1950). A psychologist was a *scientist* in the sense that he or she should be a competent researcher and contributor of knowledge and a *practitioner* in that he or she applies knowledge and skills to daily problems experienced by individuals.

The Boulder Conference was precipitated by the Veterans Administration's demand for more clinical psychologists to work to improve the mental health of veterans of World War II. In order to accomodate the increased demand for clinical psychologists, university trainers needed to develop educational goals and policies, find and train additional faculty, and expand their training facilities. To facilitate coordination amongst trainers of clinical psychologists, the U.S. Public Health Service supported a two-week conference for 70 persons at Boulder. This conference, although specifically focused on clinical psychologists, had important ramifications for school psychologists because it established standards for the qualifications, training, and functioning of applied psychologists. In particular, the guidelines set at the Boulder Conference became the basis for the 4-year doctoral program in school psychology that balances training in research with field-based experiences. Additionally, the Boulder Conference served as a model for school psychologists wishing to further organize training and practice and thus led directly to the Thayer Conference.

The Thayer Conference. The lack of sufficient, well-trained personnel to provide school psychological services and the paucity of training programs in 1952 caused T. Ernest Newland of the University of Illinois to initiate discussions among his fellow school psychologists about the possibility of a conference, like the Boulder Conference, whereby issues of the qualifications and training of school psychologists would be studied. Subsequently, Division 16's committee on Certification and Training proposed such a conference and gained financial support form the Public Health Service in 1953.

The conference was held at the Hotel Thayer, West Point, New York, in August 1954. The objective of the conference was stated as the production of a definite statement about the functions, qualifications, and training of school psychologists. Responsibility for fulfilling this objective was given to a conference steering committee and 48 selected individuals who were involved in the delivery of or were consumers of school psychological services.

The entire conference has been summarized by Cutts (1955) in a volume titled ''School Psychologists at Mid-Century.'' Specific recommendations concerning the roles of school psychologists were as follows:

1. Assessing and interpreting intellectual, social, and emotional development of children.
2. Helping to identify exceptional children and collaborate with other professionals in developing individual educational programs.
3. Developing ways to facilitate the learning and adjustment of all children.

4. Encouraging and initiating research and interpreting research findings applicable to the solution of school problems.
5. Diagnosing educational and personal problems and recommending remediation programs.

Conference participants identified two levels of training and agreed that professional training of all psychological workers should be at the graduate level. In addition, training should involve both psychology and education coursework plus field experiences. With respect to levels of training, conference partcipants believed there was a need for both doctoral psychologists and individuals with less training. The title "school psychologist" was approved for the doctoral-level psychologist; however, participants were unable to recommend a suitable title for individuals trained at the subdoctoral level. In terms of graduate education, it was recommended that 2 years of study accompanied by a half-year internship was necessary as the entry level for the profession. Doctoral programs, the highest level of training, were described as 4 years of advanced study with a 1-year internship.

The Thayer Conference represented a significant milestone in the development of school psychology. For the first time, school psychologists had a document that represented a consensus concerning their major functions and means of training. The professional identity of psychologists working in schools was also enhanced greatly as the result of the conference. Thus, school psychology was showing positive developmental signs as a profession.

The Formation of a New Professional Organization. Growth in the number of training programs and practicing school psychologists was greatest during the 1960s (Tindall, 1979). Most of this growth involved subdoctoral training. Individuals without a doctorate could not gain full member status in APA, so consequently, many persons functioning as school psychologists had no professional organization to directly represent them.

A group of individuals within the Ohio School Psychologists Association believing that subdoctoral school psychologists were not well represented in APA nor were apt to be in the future planned a National Invitational Conference of School Psychologists to discuss alternative representation. The conference took place in Columbus, Ohio in March of 1968. The major resolution to come out of the National Invitational Conference was that "an unequivocal need existed for school psychologists to establish a national effort which would develop a more adequate definition of the profession of school psychology, obtain a strong professional identity at the national level, provide more effective means of communication across the country, and establish clearly identifiable and strong representation for legislative action" (Farling & Agner, 1979, p. 141).

According to Farling and Agner (1979), many participants at the Ohio conference considered APA to be unable to meet their needs; its membership policy effectively excluded nondoctoral individuals, and its academic orientation did not seem to relate well to the concerns of practitioners. Plans were laid for the formation of a new professional organization for school psychologists.

On March 15, 1969, the National Association of School Psychologists (NASP) was formed during a two-day convention in St. Louis. A tentative constitution was adopted and officers were elected; Pauline Alexander became the first NASP president. The founding of this new association for school psychologists was premised on four purposes: (a) to promote actively the interests of school psychology; (b) to advance the standards of the profession; (c) to help secure the conditions necessary to [promote] the greatest effectiveness of its practice; and (d) to serve the mental health and educational interests of all children and youth.

Since its inception, NASP's membership, largely nondoctoral and practitioner in nature, has grown from 400 to over 8,000 in 1983. Today, NASP has most of the hallmarks of a major professional organization. It holds an annual national convention, has a code of ethics, and has developed standards for training, credentialing, field placements, service delivery, and continuing education. A newsletter, the *Communique,* and a quarterly professional journal, the *School Psychology Review* (originally called the *School Psychology Digest*) are also published under the auspices of NASP.

The major issues which have divided most school psychologists and the two professional organizations representing them have involved contradictory positions about the nature of and the entry level for independent (unsupervised) practice in school psychology. Attempts to reconcile these differences between NASP and APA were begun in 1969, continued through the 1970s, and precipitated two major conferences in the early 1980s: Spring Hill and Olympia. However, before examining these two conferences, we will look at some of the significant events of the 1970s that influenced school psychology's development.

The Vail Conference. In July 1973, APA, with support of the National Institute of Mental Health (NIMH), held a conference in Vail, Colorado, to examine the widening split amongst psychological practitioners and scientists/academicians (Korman, 1974). Although clearly broader than school psychology, this conference dealt with a central issue that had contributed to division within the profession.

Unlike the previous conferences discussed, the Vail Conference was not limited in size and representation; it included various branches of psychology, civil rights groups, and interested consumer groups. Among the most important issue for school psychology was the endorsement of the professional training model (or PsyD degree, Doctor of Psychology) as an alternative to the traditional PhD degree. The endorsement of this model meant that APA recognized the importance of advanced practical training and considered it as equivalent to the more traditional, research-oriented training. In no way did endorsement of the PsyD degree suggest that APA was supportive of nondoctoral training, yet indirectly the endorsement seemed to buoy the NASP position that advanced "practical" training was a sufficient means of training psychologists. The issue of how much and what kind of "practical" training remained a point of disagreement.

Federal Legislative Influences on School Psychology. During the mid-1970s, many educators and legislators became concerned about appropriate education for handicapped individuals primarily due to the very effective lobbying efforts of the Council for Exceptional Children (CEC), a professional organization that is open to educators as well as parents of handicapped children. One significant outcome of this concern was federal legislation in the form of the Education for All Handicapped Children Act of 1975, better known as Public Law 94-142. This act was signed into law by President Gerald Ford in November of 1975 and was designed to assure all handicapped children a free and appropriate public education that emphasized special education and related services designed to meet their unique needs (Federal Register, 1977). This law, which will be examined in detail in Chapter 7, was intended for special education programs and also had a significant impact on the development of school psychology for it mandated related services including psychological services for handicapped children. The demand for school psychological services may have never been greater than in the late 1970s when school districts across the United States worked to implement P.L. 94-142.

The impact of P.L. 94-142 on school psychology has been perceived to be both positive and negative (Abramowitz, 1981). On the positive side, the law increased the visibility of school psychologists, provided funds for more positions, and helped to differentiate school psychologists from other pupil personnel specialists. On the negative side, the law was interpreted to effectively reinforce a testing role for school psychologists, a role that many school psychologists wanted to avoid or at least to reduce.

The ramifications of P.L. 94-142 and its corollary state mandates for the profession of school psychology have been multifaceted and pervasive. For example, a major outcome of P.L. 94-142 has been to draw school psychologists into a closer relation with special educators, a relationship that several authors have characterized as a "mixed blessing" (Buktenica, 1980; Miller & Dyer, 1980). More jobs were available for school psychologists, yet issues of role and professional identity became even more muddled as a result of these legally mandated relations with special education.

The Spring Hill Symposium. By the late 1970s, school psychologists were once again showing heightened concern about their roles and functions, and the future of the profession. Representation of the profession by two groups, APA and NASP who were not always in agreement, and increased involvement with special education apparently made it difficult for school psychologists to develop a stable identity. Several individuals, however, were concurrently seeking ways to clarify roles and improve relations amongst school psychologists.

The presidents of APA and NASP met at the 1978 APA annual convention to plan a series of cooperative activities including a national conference on the future of school psychology. Initially, unrelated to the plans for a national convention, was the development of a major project at the University of Minnesota under the direction of James Ysseldyke in partnership with APA and NASP. The project was called the National School Pyschology Inservice Training Network (Network). Once the Network was funded by the Bureau of Education for the Handicapped in 1978, it was decided that the Network was the ideal vehicle for planning a major cooperative conference on the future of school psychology. Ysseldyke and his associate, Richard Weinberg, decided that a preconference or small symposium should be held to provide a base upon which a major, national convention might be founded. Thus, after a year of planning, the Spring Hill Symposium on the Future of Psychology in the Schools was held in June of 1980, in Minnesota. The goal for the Spring Hill Symposium was to begin an intensive process of evaluating the status of school psychology and attending to its future. The symposium was therefore organized mainly to promote discussion and clarification of contemporary issues, not to make formal recommendations.

The major concerns of the 69 participants at Spring Hill were: (a) goals and roles for school psychology practice, (b) ethical and legal issues, (c) professionalization of school psychology, (d) content of training programs, and (e) accountability (Ysseldyke, 1982; Ysseldyke & Weinberg, 1981). Questions asked and issues which focused discussion at Spring Hill are outlined in Table 1.2.

In many ways, the issues that confronted school psychologists at Spring Hill in 1980 had not changed since the Thayer Conference. For example, opportunities for training, standards for certification, and accreditation of training programs were issues discussed at both conferences. Of course, they had taken on additional or new dimensions given significant changes in sociopolitical, economic, legal, and societal developments, plus the growth of the profession and governance by two organizations.

One of the most significant outcomes of the Spring Hill Symposium was that NASP and APA had engaged successfully in a process whereby issues internal and external to the profession of school psychology had begun to be examined cooperately. This spirit of cooperation, although formally initiated in 1978, when NASP and APA authorized an ongoing task force to study issues which had separated the two associations, had become very visible to individuals inside and outside of school psychology (see *School Psychology Review*, 1981, Vol. 10 for the entire proceedings of the Spring Hill Symposium). The work accom-

Table 1.2 Issues and Selected Questions Generated at the Spring Hill Symposium on the Future of Psychology in the Schools

Piaget has taught us that the kinds of questions children ask tell us a great deal about their cognitive development and the ways they view the world. In the same way, we believe that the questions raised about their profession by its members are indicative of the professional posture and issues that are important at a particular time. (Ysseldyke & Weinberg, 1981, p. 119)

What Are the Goals for the Practice of Psychology in the Schools?
What populations should be served (e.g., preschool, adult, special education, all children)?

Are psychological services being provided in the schools primarily by educators or psychologists?

To what extent should psychologists in the schools provide professional services to help staff members with personal problems that negatively affect their performance?

What Should Be the Role of Persons who Provide Psychological Services in Schools?
To what extent do school psychologists have control over their own professional destiny?

What essential competencies are required of psychologists who are employed in the schools? To what extent do (should) competencies vary as a function of the setting in which individuals are employed?

Ethical and Legal Issues
Who makes professional decisions: the school psychologist or administrators? Who defines what a[re] professional decisions (e.g., who determines classification of children? Who should decide what children to see, what diagnostic procedures to use, etc.)?

Professionalization of School Psychologists
Should school psychology be considered a unique professional discipline?

What are the problems of credentialing in school psychology?

How can school psychologists facilitate communication with each other, with other professionals, and with the general community?

Training Issues
How do training programs fail to meet the needs of school systems?

What should be new areas for training psychologists in the schools?

Accountability

To what extent are school psychologists accountable for the effectiveness of educational interventions?

To what extent are school psychologists responsible for the validity of their practices?

Note: The above issues and questions were selected from a more extensive list cited in J. Ysseldyke & R. A. Weinberg, "Editorial Comments: An Introduction," *School Psychology Review*, 1981, *10*, 118–119.

plished at Spring Hill provided the base for the next major APA–NASP joint project, the Olympia Conference.

The Olympia Conference on the Future of School Psychology. This conference was designed as a follow-up to Spring Hill; if Spring Hill had been designed to generate issues, than it was Olympia's role to develop action strategies based on these issues. While Spring Hill was a small gathering of leaders in school psychology, Olympia was intended to be more of a stratified random sample of practitioners, trainers, and students in school psychology, plus representatives from other professional organizations and federal agencies. Thus, 332 individuals from across the country attended the conference at the Olympia Conference Center in Wisconsin in the Fall of 1981.

The Olympia Conference was unique in several respects relative to previous national meetings of school psychologists. A major goal of the conference organizers was to get school psychologists individually and collectively to think about their future in the greater context of possible future worlds. Thus, the keynote speaker was a futurist who analyzed forces external to school psychology that were shaping the 1980s. Much of the conference was spent in small group activities whereby individuals were confronted with issues, most of which had been generated at the Spring Hill Symposium. The goal of these small group discussions was to utilize group process techniques (a Modified Delphi Process and Networking) deliberatively to consider high impact issues and appropriate actions. Desired outcomes of each group were plans for actions. The action plans generated by the many small groups were classified into three categories: legislative, practical, and professional. A detailed account of these action plans is provided by Meyers, Brown, and Coulter (1982).

The impact of the Olympia Conference may not be realized fully for sometime. Synthesis reports (e.g., Alpert, 1982; Hart, 1982; Trachtman, 1982), which were given at the close of the conference, were mixed with optimism and pessimism about the future. However, regardless of the future, school psychologists were once again reminded by Trachtman (1982) that the issue of the entry training level for the independent practice of school psychology had not been dealt with successfully at Olympia. Thus, while APA and NASP had demonstrated cooperation on a number of issues and on the organization of two major conferences, they still had not dealt with the issue which led to the creation of NASP.

With the description of the Olympia Conference completed, we have reviewed events over the course of 80 years that have influenced the development of school psychology. Our historical review has been selective. Although we have not intended to distort history, such a review seems to characterize the development of school psychology in a more orderly fashion than it actually occurred. As noted by Brown and Hanson (1979), school psychology may well have developed in very different ways throughout the United States. In fact, they report that in the Northeast, school psychology's roots were in clinical psychology, while in the Midwest and Far West school psychology had stronger developmental ties with education and counseling. Regardless of local or regional history, we hope the reader now has a better appreciation of school psychology's national heritage.

THE PROFESSION OF SCHOOL PSYCHOLOGY

In our review of events that have contributed to the development of school psychology, we briefly discussed aspects about the representational structure of the profession, noted that many individuals have been concerned about the role of psychologists in schools, and alluded to the fact that the relationship between special education and school psychology had become an important issue in the delivery of services to children and youth. In the remainder of this chapter, we will investigate these three issues in greater detail.

Legal and Representational Structure of the Profession

School psychology has existed traditionally as the result of statutes enacted within state departments of education that authorize certification of school psychologists (Brown, 1982). Thus, the legal basis for the practice of school psychology is the exclusive domain and responsibility of individual states. Without such a basis, the credentials of school psychologists would be questioned.

Most states clearly differentiate between the public and the private practice of school pyschology and have set up different mechanisms for identifying individuals who can practice in these two arenas. Therefore, since school psychology is practiced primarily in the public arena, its legal basis differs from clinical psychology, which is much more involved in the private practice arena. Clinical psychologists usually derive their authority to practice from state boards of psychological examiners.

The growth of school psychology can be traced directly to the rapid increase of the number of states enacting certification laws. In 1946, Horrocks reported that only seven states certified school psychologists. Approximately ten years later, Newland (cited in Cutts, 1955) reported that only 20 states and the District of Columbia had certification regulations governing school psychological personnel. By 1967, the number had increased to 38 (Traxler, 1967). The signing into law of P.L. 94-142 in 1975 appears to have been a final stimulant needed to get remaining states to establish certification procedures. Thus, by 1979, 49 states and the District of Columbia had standards and methods for certifying school psychologists (Brown & Horn, 1980).

Brown (1982) pointed out that trends in certification have been precursors to trends in licensure and to the expansion of university training programs. For example, during the 1970s, 11 states enacted private practice licensure procedures specially for school psychologists. Four states (i.e., California, Florida, Connecticut, and Illinois) even began licensing nondoctoral school psychologists for independent practice apart from psychology licensing boards (Bardon, 1982). Training programs have also increased in number, multiplying at a rate of approximately 10% per year and presently numbering well over 200 programs (Brown & Linstrom, 1978). Consequently, the number of students graduating from school psychology programs each year has been estimated to be 2200 nationally (Brown & Lindstrom, 1978).

As documented in our review of history, the national representational structure for school psychology has evolved over the past 35 years. Such a dual representation has resulted in the development of different philosophical approaches to training and practice. APA and the Division of School Psychology have influenced the practice of generic psychology through the development of *Standards for Providers of Psychological Services* (1977) and subsequently, *Specialty Guidelines for the Delivery of Services by School Psychologists* (1981). Together, these documents specify the basic training and supervisory levels for the practice of school psychology and provide a means of self-regulation to protect the public interest. The entry level for the provision of school psychological services according to these documents is after the sixth year of training. The title of ''professional school psychologist,'' however, is reserved for individuals possessing a doctorate and for those who complete sufficient training through 1985 to be grandparented into the title.

The leadership of NASP has also done a lot to promote the integrity of school psychology for they have produced a number of documents dealing with the training and practice of school psychologists (i.e., *Standards for Training Programs in School Pyschology*, 1978; *Standards for Field Placement Programs in School Psychology*, 1978; *Standards for the Provision of School Psychological Services*, 1978 [see Appendix A]; *Standards for the Credentialing of School Psychologists*, 1978). The NASP position on the educational entry level is that the sixth year or specialist degree is sufficient for use of the title school psychologist and the independent practice of school psychology in or out of a school setting. In addition, the NASP standards for entry into the practice of school psychology are competency based. The basic NASP model for generating the necessary array of competencies for practice is illustrated in Figures 1.1 and 1.2 and is divided into direct (Matrix D) and indirect (Matrix I) pupil service dimensions. Note in Figure 1.1 that the range in age of persons served is from infants through young adults and that a broad range of services can potentially be delivered to these persons. Figure 1.2, the Indirect Service Matrix, illustrates five roles or models of service and indicates that they are applicable across three levels of service: individuals, groups, and systems. Chapters 2 through 5 in this

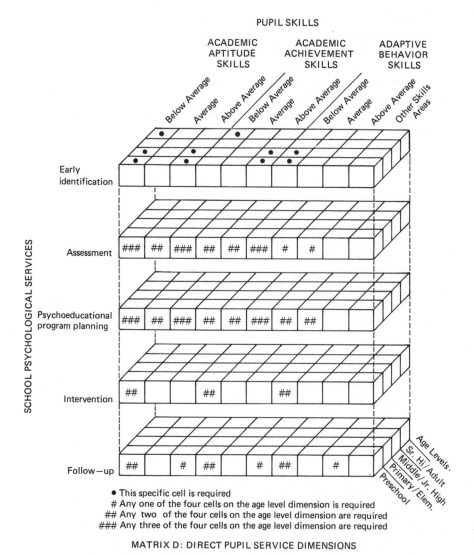

MATRIX D: DIRECT PUPIL SERVICE DIMENSIONS

Figure 1.1. Direct pupil services competencies for school psychologists. (From *Standards for Credentialing in School Psychology.* Reprinted by permission.)

text will elaborate further on many of the components of both indirect and direct service delivery matrices.

Accreditation of school pyschology training programs can occur through two groups at the national level: APA and the National Council for Accreditation of Teacher Education (NCATE) in conjunction with NASP. The Educational

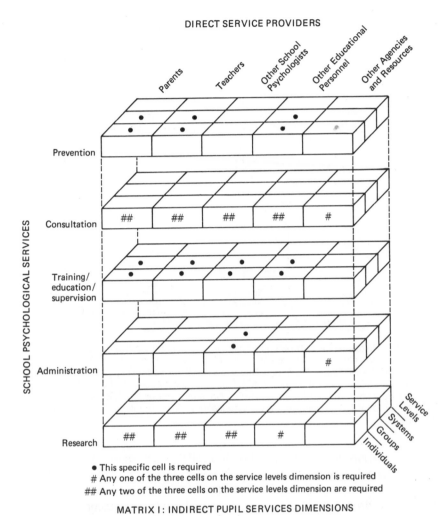

Figure 1.2. Indirect pupil services competencies for school psychologists. (From *Standards for Credentialing in School Psychology.* Reprinted by permission.)

Affairs Office of APA is responsible for accreditation of doctoral programs in school, as well as clinical, and counseling psychology. NCATE, usually in cooperation with NASP, accredits both doctoral and nondoctoral programs. In addition to the national accrediting bodies, most school psychology programs are also subject to approval by a state education agency (SEA) or deparment of public instruction. Brantley's (1977) schematization of the accreditation process helps to clarify the many relationships among accrediting agencies and training programs (see Figure 1.3).

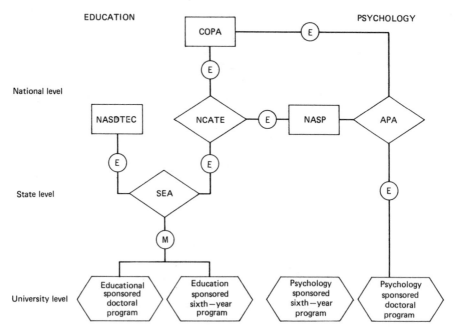

Figure 1.3. Relationships between accrediting agencies and training programs by level and area of sponsorship. (E = elective affiliations, M = mandatory affiliations, APA = American Psychological Association, NCATE = National Council for Accreditation of Teacher Education, SEA = state education agency, NASDTEC = National Association of State Directors of Teacher Education and Certification, NASP = National Association of School Psychologists, COPA = Council on Postsecondary Accreditation) (After Brantley, 1977. Reprinted by permission.)

As indicated in Figure 1.3, a dual or parallel process exists in the accreditation of school psychology training programs. However, APA, NASP, and NCATE explored ways in which they could collaborate in the accrediting process (Cardon & Brown, 1979). As a result, a trial joint accreditation process got underway in early 1982. Should a collaborative process be successful, substantial benefits may result for the entire field of school psychology. For example, school psychology would be perceived as a more unified force by psychological examining boards and state departments of education when credentialing procedures are developed in individual states.

Roles and Functions of School Psychologists

One of the most persistent concerns of school psychologists has been the identification of their role and function (Farling & Hoedt, 1971; Monroe, 1979). Evidence of school psychology's search for professional identity is reflected in portions of no fewer than six national conferences (i.e., Boulder Conference, 1950; Thayer Conference, 1954; Bethesda Conference, 1963; Vail Conference, 1973; Spring Hill Symposium, 1980; and Olympia Conference, 1981). Such a concern with role and function seems to stem from a strong need to retain an identity as a psychologist while working primarily in an educational setting (Sabatino, 1981).

Bardon (1972) aptly reflected the role confusion experienced by many school psychologists: "Is the school psychologist a task analyzer, behavior describer, diagnostic and management specialist, consultant to teachers, technologist of cognitive styles . . . modifer of the conditions of learning, test expert, program evaluator, behavior modifier, any of these, some of these, or all of these?" (p. 208) In the remainder of this section, we will explore five role models advocated for school psychologists and discuss factors influencing these models.

Numerous authors have written about the role issue in school psychology and it seems likely that every practitioner and trainer has at some point discussed (maybe even argued) their role. Thus, much more has been said about the role issue than can be discussed here, but a review of Gilmore's (1974) and Bardon's (1982) work should provide a good overview of this issue.

Gilmore (1974) believed that school psychology has been far more successful at defining what it is *not* than what it is. As a means of rectifying this negative approach, he developed a two-category system to characterize various role models of school psychology. The system's two categories were *operations* and *sources*. The operations category or "practices" refers to two dimensions: (a) the directness or indirectness of services provided; and (b) the degree to which a model is more service or science oriented. The sources category refers to the basis of a model according to each of three dimensions: (a) education or psychology as the parent discipline; (b) adopted from external sources or developed internally, indicating the origin and acceptance of information on which the model is premised; and (c) the relative emphasis on the theoretical as opposed to the applied practices inherent in the model. The combined use of these five dimensions within the broader two-category system provides a heuristic method for comparing various role models.

Five major role models for school psychologists have been recommended traditionally. They have been described as the clinical model (Bardon, 1965), the diagnostic–prescriptive or psychoeducational model (Valett, 1963), the educational programmer model (Reger, 1965), the systems-level problem solver model (Gray, 1963), and the preventive mental-health model (Bower, 1965). In the clinical model, Bardon envisioned school psychologists utilizing techniques developed in clinical psychology (i.e., assessment, counseling, etc.) to serve individual children. Valett's diagnostic–prescriptive model emphasized the remediation of academic problems with individual children. The educational programmer model developed by Reger also focused on learning problems of children, but emphasized a more behavioral orientation and extensive use of curricular materials to aide assessment and intervention. Both Gray's and Bower's models were oriented at a level greater than an individual child and involve consultative activities with educational personnel in order to effect change in a child. A comparative analysis of these five role models for school psychology using Gilmore's (1974) categories is illustrated in Figure 1.4.

According to Gilmore (1974), three aspects about the comparison of the five role models were significant. They were: (a) all models emphasize practice more than theory; (b) there is a substantial split between models adopted from other areas (i.e., clinical and preventive) and models developed within the field of school psychology (i.e., educational programmer, systems-level problem solver, and psychoeducational); and (c) the clinical model appears most identifiable, for it is ranked at the extremes on each dimension.

Recent trends have been to combine various roles. For example, Trachtman (1971) suggested an integration of roles by drawing heavily upon systems interventions (e.g., Gray, 1963) and individual interventions (e.g., Bardon, 1965, Valett, 1963). Abidin (1972) stressed consultation to change teachers' contingency systems and McDaniel and Ahr (1965) emphasized staff development via inservice both depending heavily upon the roles initially conceptualized by Gray (1963) and Bower (1965). Brantley and his associates (Brantley, Reilly, Beach, Cody, Fields, & Lee, 1974), plus Steinberg and Chandler (1976) have emphasized the increased role of school psychologists in community liaison and interagency planning.

| OPERATIONS | | SOURCE | | |
Direct	*Service*	*Education*	*Adopted*	*Theory*
Clinical	Clinical	Ed. programmer	Clinical	
Ed. programmer	Preventive	Systems level	Preventive	
Psychoeducational	Ed. programmer			
	Psychoeducational	Psychoeducational		
	Systems level			Psychoeducational
				Systems level
Systems level		Preventive	Ed. programmer	Ed. programmer
Preventive		Clinical	Systems level	Preventive
			Psychoeducational	Clinical
Indirect	*Science*	*Psychology*	*Developed*	*Practice*

Figure 1.4. Models ranked on five dimensions. (From Gilmore, 1974. Reprinted by permission.)

Factors Influencing Roles and Functions

Many factors in any given setting can influence the practice of psychology; thus, it is simplistic to talk about *the* role and *the* function of school psychologists. The assessment and testing functions, which are part of its historical origins, are probably the most common functions across individual practitioners; yet, there is no characteristic role for school psychologists. Bardon (1982) identified five major factors which he believed contributed to role diversity in the practice of school psychology. The five factors are: (a) level of functioning, (b) professional activity, (c) the immediate client, (d) level of educational program, and (e) the community served by schools. A brief examination of each of these factors is in order.

Level of Functioning. School psychology has moved through three gradations of service provision during the last 50 years (Bardon, 1982). Bardon and Bennett (1974) conceptualized these gradations as a continuum divided into three levels. Level 1 is psychometric service and primarily involves testing to identify and classify students who would qualify for special education. Level 2 services are still assessment oriented, but are broader than testing. Level 2 services are directed at students who qualify for special education, as well as students with other mild learning and behavior problems. Bardon describes the movement from Level 1 to Level 2 services as a movement from test score reporter and interpreter to that of psychoeducational clinician. He believes most school psychologists function at level 2. As a psychoeducational clinician, the psychologist is responsible for administering complete test batteries, observing students, interviewing significant adults (i.e., parents, teachers, etc.), and writing informative reports that summarize assessment findings. Advanced Level 2 service providers also have been involved in counseling and other forms of direct interventions with students and inservice training for teachers. Level 3 functioning is, of course, a further refinement of Level 2. It involves direct services to students such as assessment and intervention, plus systems-level actions which influence "school policies and procedures through supervision, education, and consultation with administrators, staff, and professionals in the community and in the development and evaluation of school programs and services" (Bardon, 1982, p. 9). Level 3 services can be conceptualized as an industrial/organizational model of school psychology, whereas Level 2 is seen as a clinical model.

According to Bardon (1982), one cannot simply move from Level 1 to Level 3; the process of movement is gradual and dependent on professional maturity and training. To move requires the intention to do so, with that intention related directly to school needs for the awareness of change.

Professional Activity. The basic professional activities of school psychologists can be categorized into five practice areas: assessment, direct intervention, consultation, education (inservice), and evaluation. As with level of functioning, Bardon (1982) believed these five practice areas were hierarchical in nature with respect to the frequency with which each is undertaken. Specifically, he believed most school psychological service providers were involved in assessment, many undertook direct interventions, and some were engaged in consultation and inservice education, while very few service providers were involved in program or systems-level evaluation.

Traditionally, assessment via standardized tests has been the primary professional activity of school psychologists. Many professionals, however, are beginning to reconceptualize assessment as *only* a portion of the problem-solving activities they can provide; they now see assessment as a component of consultation (Bergan, 1977; Elliott & Piersel, 1982; Gutkin & Curtis, 1982). As a result, consultation has become one of the major professional functions of school psychologists (Barbanel & Hoffenburg-Rutman, 1974; Cook & Patterson, 1977; Manley & Manley, 1978; Meachan & Peckham, 1978).

The Immediate Client. Comtois and Clark (1977) identified seven clients that school psychologists can potentially serve. They are: an individual student, a small group of students, a classroom of students, a teacher, a group of teachers, an administrator, or an entire educational system. We would add parents and families to this list.

Bardon (1982) observed that the order of potential clients, from individual student to entire educational system, suggested an increasing degree of power and influence on ever larger numbers of people. This analysis suggests that answering the frequently asked question "Who is the client" is dependent on answering other questions about a precipitating problem and a desired outcome. In sum, different clients will require different services and as services change so will one's perceived role.

Level of Educational Program Served. The developmental and educational levels of the person served influence the types of psychological services provided. Presently, the majority of school psychological services are focused on elementary school children. However, with the passage of P.L. 94-142 psychological services were extended downward to children of 3 years and upward to young adults of 21 years. Thus, there has been a surge of service and training concerning preschoolers (e.g., Paget & Bracken, 1983), followed by urgings to increase attention and services to secondary school students (e.g., Nagel & Medway, 1982). Further upward extension of school psychological services may also be at hand (Bardon, 1979; Sandoval & Love, 1977).

The pragmatics of providing psychological services to persons with significantly different developmental and educational levels are factors that must influence roles and functions of school psychologists. The cognitive complexity of students, the nature of instruction, the organization and management of schools, and social influences at different ages all interact to produce different individual needs. Hence, services that are effective will vary with the level of educational program served.

The Community Served by the Schools. The community in which a school is located greatly influences service delivery according to Bardon (1982). Socioeconomic status of the families in the community often effects level of expectations, parent involvement, and availability of resources. Another factor that seems to influence psychological services is the school setting. A rural setting usually places greater restrictions on time due to travel and lower staff intensity, while an urban setting frequently presents challenges of increased social and cultural diversity.

Based on Bardon's analysis of the roles and functions of school psychologists, there are at least three levels of functioning, five basic kinds of activities, with eight different clients, across three or more educational levels, in a variety of community settings. Thus, school psychology is a psychological specialty with multiple roles and functions—a complex profession that demands flexibility and clinical acumen.

The Interface Between Psychology and Special Education

The present-day relations between psychology and education are explicated by numerous areas of specialized human inquiry; however, school psychology and special education are the areas where applied as well as basic psychology and education truly interface. This interface is best exemplified by the services for the treatment of exceptional children (Elliott & Gutkin, in press).

The developmental histories of psychology, in particular school psychology and special education, are both rich and interrelated, sharing many persons and issues (Hewitt & Forness, 1974). A clear example of the common history of school psychology and special education was Witmer's laboratory clinic for children at the University of Pennsylvania. As documented earlier, Witmer's clinic served as a model for many public schools that later developed special classes for children with learning or behavior problems. Another example of common history that even pre-dated Witmer's clinic was the work of Binet and Simon with the French government, which led to the testing and classification of children for special classes. In fact, mental-abilities testing was probably the beginning of formal relations between school psychology and special education. Many other examples of psychology and special education's common history could be listed; however, an overriding concern is that the reader understands that the relationship between psychology and special education has been inextricably bound to society's perspectives on the treatment of exceptional children. These perspectives have changed radically over the past 50 year and are still evolving (Frampton & Gall, 1955), hence the relationship between special education and school psychology will continue to be a dynamic one.

Today the relationship between school psychology and special education is much more than the mental-abilities testing initiated by Binet and Simon. Psychological services for the educational benefit of children now include parent and teacher consultation, behavior management techniques, personalized instruction with specialized curriculum materials, modified classrooms, and direct therapy when necessary. Several writers have, in fact, commented that it is difficult to distinguish the development of school psychology from the delivery of programs and services to handicapped children and youth (Bennett, 1970; Elliott & Gutkin, in press; Sabatino, 1981). Indeed, the funds for school psychological services provided by state legislatures usually pass through a state education department. No wonder several authors have stated that the very existence of school psychology has been closely associated with the identification of handicapped children and youth for placement in special education programs (Catterall, 1972; Lambert, 1974; Sabatino, 1972).

Buktenica (1980) recently analyzed the nature of the relationship between special education and school psychology. He saw both disciplines working toward the same ends, but through separate efforts and believed that these disciplines currently "exist in a relatively cooperative, congenial, coterminous relationship of tension within the schools" (p. 228).

Buktenica used a three-level conceptual schema to further describe the interactions between school psychology and special education; the lowest amount of interaction was characteristic of the self-actional level, the next greatest amount of interaction occurred at the interactional level, and the most pervasive interaction occurred at the transactional level. At the self-actional level, people act under their own power. At the interactional level, one person is balanced against another person in a causal interconnection. Finally, at the transactional level, persons function in a mutually determined and interdependent relationship (Dewey & Bentley, 1949). Although these three levels of relating are not clearly discriminated, they seem to serve a useful analytic function in distinguishing the nature of relationships. Buktenica posited that most relationships between school psychologists and special educators currently occur at the self-actional level while some relations are at the interactional level. He characterized those at the interactional level as being similar to a "billiard ball" phenomenon, where each action resulted in an opposite and equal reaction. Very few relationships have been reportedly achieved at the transactional level. Currently, however, external forces are pressuring both disciplines toward a transactional working relation.

Other authors have also discussed the school psychology–special education relationship from slightly different perspectives than Buktenica. For example, Gallagher (1969) characterized the relationship as symbiotic since the psychologist is a necessary first step in any special education program. Lambert (1973) concluded that school psychologists' traditional sources of influence were the result of special education activities. Catterall (1972), following a similar logic, pointed out that over half of the finances for school psychology resulted from service relationships with special education. Miller and Dyer (1980) suggested that educational accountability and legal mandates have resulted in the further entwining of school psychology and special education. Finally, Sabatino (1981), encouraging a more extensive relationship between the disciplines, argued for "a realization on the part of school psychologists that they can greatly improve the quality of comprehensive special-education services through a team relationship with special educators" (p. 78).

Given the interface between school psychology and education, it is constructive to understand educators' perceptions of school psychologists. A number of researchers have investigated this issue by surveying school principals, teachers, and superintendents (Baker, 1965; Barclay, 1971; Dansinger, 1969; Giebink & Ringness, 1970; Gilmore & Chandy, 1973a, 1973b; Kahl & Fine, 1978; Kaplan, Clancy, & Chrin, 1977; Kirschner, 1971; Lesiak & Lounsbury, 1977; Medway, 1977; Perkins, 1964; Roberts, 1970; Roberts & Solomons, 1970; Schowengerdt, Fine, & Poggio, 1976; Styles, 1965). Miller and Dyer (1980) have done a comprehensive review of this research, plus the self-perception research of school psychologists (e.g., Keough, Kukic, Becker, McLoughlin, & Kukic, 1975). Therefore, we will only summarize these studies.

The overwhelming finding across superintendents, principals, and teachers in the research on educators' perceptions of school psychologists is that they do not have an accurate perception of the range of psychological services provided, nor of the time involved in the delivery of such services. As a result, Miller and Dyer (1980) concluded, "their [school psychologists] services are not as highly valued as they should be in some situations" (p. 416). This misperception of school psychological services by educators is a clear signal that better communication is needed in order to maximize professional cooperation and effective services for children and youth.

In sum, the profession of school psychology from the inception has been committed to help further the education and development of special children and youth. In order to accomplish this objective, school psychologists have found it necessary to work with educators. Thus, the relationship with special educators, although at times difficult, is a very important relationship for both the professions of school psychology and special education and for handicapped children.

CONCLUSION

In this first chapter, we have provided you with an overview of the profession of school psychology by focusing on historical developments, current roles and functions, and relations with special education. As a result, we hope you have gained the impression that school psychology is a unique profession. It has many responsibilities and many opportunities to contribute significantly to the further development of psychology, education, and the well being of human beings.

We intentionally did not provide you with a textbook definition of school psychology in this first chapter, although several such definitions exist (Bardon, 1982; Bardon & Bennett, 1974; Cutts, 1955; Symonds, 1942; Tindall, 1979; Valett, 1963; Walter, 1925). The reason for this omission is twofold: First, school psychology is not defined easily because of its diversity and continued development and second, our conceptualization of school psychology is predicated on a reciprocal determinism theory of human behavior within a service delivery system framework. The second reason, in particular, will be elaborated on throughout the remainder of the book. We believe that by reading this entire text you will arrive at a definition of school psychology—one that encompasses more than schools and yet is specific.

2

Service Delivery: Concepts and Models

Responsibility for the development of children and youth rests primarily with two social systems, families and schools. Even under optimal conditions, most children and youth will experience some problems in these two social systems, and consequently, both of the systems may experience stress. The kinds of problems children and youth experience are numerous and vary in significance; however, many of their problems are psychological in nature. Hence, there has been and will continue to be a need for human problem solving, as well as preventive mental health services within schools and families. Such services can be delivered effectively by psychologists who have been trained to work in educational settings.

Consultation, assessment, or intervention are classified frequently as psychological services for children, youth, and others who may be part of a problem (e.g., parents, teachers, etc.). These three types of services are actually part of a larger problem-solving process which can be used to conceptualize the delivery of psychological services to families and schools. Each of these three primary services and others will be discussed in detail in subsequent chapters. The present chapter will focus on the *process* of delivering psychological services in schools rather than on the *content* of those services.

To date, relatively little has been written specifically about the delivery of school psychological services even though it was a major topic at the Thayer Conference (Cutts, 1955). Instead of focusing on delivery systems, authors have examined the related areas of the roles of school psychologists (Bardon, 1965; Monroe, 1979; Reger, 1965; Valett, 1965) and the administrative organization of psychological services (Cutts, 1955; Elkin, 1963; Herron, Green, Guild, Smith, & Kantor, 1970; Rettke, 1971). These two areas are subcomponents of service delivery and respectively represent the *function* and *structure* of psychological service delivery. In keeping with the purpose of this chapter, however, we will examine primarily those works related to the structure of psychological services. The functional dimension will be covered in detail in the chapters on consultation, assessment, and intervention. Thus, in the present chapter, we will examine the *structure* of psychological services in schools and the *process* through which services are delivered to a client.

FUNDAMENTAL QUESTIONS OF SERVICE DELIVERY

Assuming that school psychologists have the knowledge and skills that can influence individuals' lives positively, four questions become important: What is a psychological problem? Who is the client? What are the major service goals of school psychologists? How are problems solved? Answers to these questions provide philosophical, theoretical, and pragmatic foundations for the development and delivery of school psychological services. Hersch (1968) asked similar questions as an effective means of analyzing the rising discontent in the field of community mental health. Such questions can also function as a useful heuristic for school psychology.

What Is a Psychological Problem?

Hundreds of books and articles have been written about the psychological problems of children and youth. Such sources have characterized individuals' problems as significant excesses or deficits (relative to an accepted standard) in any or all three of the following domains: cognitive, affective, and behavioral.

Several major taxonomic systems have been developed to classify children and adult psychopathologies. Probably the most widely used taxonomies include those developed by the American Psychiatric Association and embodied in the *Diagnostic and Statistical Manual-III* (DSM-III; 1980) and those proposed by the Group for the Advancement of Psychiatry (GAP, 1966). The two systems, however, have major shortcomings. First, they consist of narrative descriptions of disorders that are not defined operationally and have low reliability for specific diagnoses (Beitchman, Deilman, Landis, Benson, & Kemp, 1978; Tarter, Templer, & Hardy, 1975). Second, there is no evidence that the diagnostic categories in these systems differentiate among disturbed children in terms of important criteria such as prognosis or differential response to treatment (Edelbrock, 1979). Finally, neither of these systems offers school psychologists a classification system that is compatible with those outlined in state and federal special education mandates. These diagnostic systems also are based on a medical model approach to human problems, an approach that we believe is heuristically inadequate.

A brief discussion of four models of human behavior (i.e., the medical model, the behavioral model, the ecological model, and the reciprocal determinism model) may help provide a basis for defining a psychological problem. In general, models can provide a theoretical framework for understanding past behavior and predicting future behavior. Thus, models of human behavior have influenced how psychologists and educators view and interact with children, especially exceptional children.

The medical model in psychology emerged from psychoanalytic theory (Stuart, 1970). A central postulate of this model is that psychological disturbances are best understood and modified through the intensive study of intrapsychic life. The medical model assumes that (a) behavior that deviates in a negative direction from normative standards is a reflection of a personal disease (or disturbance, disorder, or dysfunction) and (b) behavior classified as deviant must be changed within the individual by a curative process (Reger, 1972). The first assumption implies that children who cannot be maintained or accommodated in a regular education program are suffering from an *internal* psychoeducational disorder. The second assumption also has practical implications that influence educational programs. Once children are classified as deviant or "diseased," the educational system must respond to cure them. Educational "cures" seem to come most frequently in the form of special classes that tend to isolate the "diseased" child from normal or healthy children.

The medical model of psychological and educational services for children who are experiencing learning and behavior problems has been seriously challenged on conceptual, empirical, and practical grounds (Reger, 1972; Szasz, 1960; Zubin, 1967). Szasz (1960) argued that many of the basic assumptions underlying the medical model were untenable. The assumption with which he took the greatest issue was that psychopathology was best conceptualized as "mental illness." He believed that psychotherapists dealt with problems in ordinary living rather than with mental illness. Therefore, psychological disturbance was better understood in the context of human value systems than in the context of mental symptoms. This conceptualization of psychological problems was influential precisely because it removed the locus of psychopathology from the human psyche and focused instead on the relationship between individuals and society.

Reger (1972) also questioned the utility of the medical model, particularly when used in special education.

> When a child is seen as a "patient" in school, when he is looked at as a carrier of a medical-model illness (or deviation, etc.) then the teacher and the school are relieved of much of the responsibility for the child. If he makes little or no progress, it

is because of him and his condition rather than the school teacher. (Reger, 1972, pp. 11–12)

Alternative models of human behavior, especially those which acknowledge the role other people and environmental factors have in shaping a child's behavior, are currently prominent in the eyes of many educators and psychologists. Chief among these are the behavioral and the ecological models. The major postulate of those espousing the behavioral model is that human behavior is primarily a function of environmental events (Skinner, 1953). The ecological model is built on a similar supposition, that is, human behavior results from a complex interaction between environmental factors and the individual characteristics of people (Barker, 1965, 1968; Hunt, 1967; Lewin, 1951; Reilly, 1974).

Both the behavioral and ecological models provide an alternative approach to understanding human behavior that is responsive to the criticisms directed at the medical model. For example, pathology is viewed as behavior that is deemed inappropriate (generally excessive or deficient) when compared to subjective norms and values, rather than as an "illness" in any absolute sense (Ullmann & Krasner, 1969). Advocates of both approaches reject a "mental illness" or intrapsychic causal explanation of psychopathology and instead are oriented toward the belief that human problems are primarily the result of interactions between people and their environments.

An ecologically-oriented model of behavior which also takes individuals' cognitions into consideration would be the most suitable model for analyzing the problems of all children, not just potentially abnormal children. Therefore, we believe the reciprocal determinism model (Bandura, 1974, 1977, 1978) of human behavior is the model of choice for school psychologists, as well as for other psychologists since they too interact with children and youth who experience a wide range of problems.

The reciprocal determinism model, deduced from social learning theory, conceptualizes human behavior as a continuous reciprocal interaction between an individual's thoughts, behaviors, and environmental factors. The term determinism is used by Bandura (1978) "to signify the production of effects by events, rather than in the doctrinal sense that actions are completely determined by a prior sequence of causes independent of the individual" (p. 345). Schematically (see Figure 2.1), Bandura represents reciprocal determinism as a triadic or three-way interaction among behavior (B), cognitions and other internal events that affect perceptions and actions (P), and external environment (E). Thus, the reciprocal determinism model extends the basic interactionist formula of behavioral and ecological models (i.e., $B = f(P,E)$ or behavior is a function of the interaction between person and environment factors) to include internal personal factors such as beliefs, values, and perceptions. The reciprocal interaction between and individual's personal factors (P) and behavior (B), although concep-

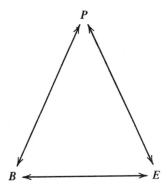

Figure 2.1. Schematic representation of Bandura's reciprocal determinism model of human behavior. (Adapted from Bandura, 1978. Reprinted by permission.)

tually simple, is the dimension that makes this model different and more heuristic than previous models of human behavior.

According to Bandura (1978),

[M]ost external influences affect behavior through intermediary cognitive processes. Cognitive factors partly determine which external events will be observed, how they will be perceived . . . and how the information they convey will be organized for future use. . . . By altering their immediate environment, and by arranging conditional incentives for themselves, people can exercise some influence over their own behavior. An act therefore includes among its determinants self-produced influences.

It is true that behavior is influenced by the environment, but the environment is partly of a person's own making. By their actions, people play a role in creating the social milieu and other circumstances that arise in their daily transactions. *Thus, from the social learning perspective, psychological functioning involves a continuous reciprocal interaction between behavioral, cognitive, and environmental influences.* (p. 345; emphasis added)

The reciprocal determinism model, although just beginning to stimulate empirical research (e.g., Sharpley, 1982), provides the most comprehensive system for understanding human behavior. Therefore, we have used it throughout this text to organize information about school psychological services.

Now that we have examined several major theoretical dimensions which underly conceptualizations of psychological problems, we are ready to define a psychological problem in general conceptual terms. From our perspective, a psychological problem is evidenced when an individual (child, teacher, parent) reports a significant discrepancy (excess or deficit) between a target person's current level of performance and a desired level of performance (Kaufman, 1971). A number of aspects of this definition require further elaboration. First, the person reporting the problem may or may not be the same person as the target person; regardless, the reporter in most cases would be considered a component of the problem. Second, the determination of whether a problem is characterized by a "significant discrepancy" is initially not questioned; however, once the current and the desired levels of performance are operationally defined, this "significant discrepancy" becomes a point of focus for discussion and possible treatment. This approach to the definition of psychological problems is predicated on the belief that such problems grow out of the unsuccessful or discrepant interactions between persons (e.g., child and peers, child and teacher, child and parent, etc.). Thus the target person and his or her interactions with the environment must be examined to understand and change the problem behavior.

Who is the Client?

An unresolved issue of the historic Thayer Conference was that "a school psychologist must often decide whether or not his first obligation is to an individual child or to the school as an organization" (Cutts, 1955, p. 87). Traditionally, clients for school psychologists have included: children and youth, both normal and abnormal; parents and/or entire families; and teachers and other significant educational personnel. The current emphasis on school psychological consultation research and evaluation services has served to increase this list of clients to include organizational units such as classrooms, schools, curriculum tracks within schools, and even entire school districts (e.g., see Snapp & Davidson, 1982). Thus potential clients for psychologists working in educational settings range from one child and a teacher and/or parent to an entire school district comprised of hundreds of children and educational personnel.

One's general conceptualization of who the school psychologist's clients are is influenced by several factors. Five major factors in determining potential clients are:

1. A psychologist's model of human behavior;
2. A psychologist's training or spectrum of competent services;
3. A psychologist's philosophy about preventive mental health;
4. Legal mandates; and,
5. Financial remuneration.

The extent to which these factors actually affect client selection and services may be influenced most by the work load or by the psychologist-to-student ratio within a given school district.

Psychologists subscribing to the medical model perspective of psychological problems will likely see pathological or disturbed children or youth as their main clients. Thus, in terms of a typical school environment, such psychologists would work primarily with the individual students referred to them for special education services (approximately 1 out of every 10 students). They may also interview parents and teachers, but are theoretically not likely to see them as part of the problem. Instead, the medical model psychologist would be concerned primarily with assessing and identifying the source or cause of a pathology within the client and with prescribing a treatment for the pathology. Such services have been characterized as tertiary prevention for they concentrate psychological services on children and youth having full-blown learning and/or personal-social problems (Caplan, 1964).

Psychological services for children and youth in need of special education services have been mandated by P.L. 94-142 and its subsequent state corollaries. As a result, there have been federal and state funds available for tertiary prevention (actually remedial) services. Consequently, psychologists subscribing to a medical model approach to children's problems have been directly reinforced for their test-and-place actions. This has led to some characterizations of school psychologists as "gatekeepers" for special education.

Psychologists subscribing to behavioral or ecological models of human problems have not always escaped the "gatekeeper" label for, in fact, they too are involved in the assessment and treatment of children referred for special education services. Such psychologists, however, tend to have a broader conception of who their clients are since they conceptualize human behavior primarily as a function of interactions between an organism and environmental events. Hence, a child or youth may be referred or singled-out as problematic, but behaviorally and ecologically oriented psychologists would also typically see individuals such as peers, teachers, or parents as part of any problem. Given a behavioral or ecological perspective, psychologists tend to work initially with their clients in the environment where a problem occurs and consequently resist the spontaneous test-and-place action. This service approach typically brings a psychologist into direct, as well as indirect, contact with many more people than a medical model service approach, and thus provides opportunities to analyze problem situations *with* "significant others" who in turn may function as primary change agents toward the solution of a problem.

Theoretically, a reciprocal determinism model of human behavior results in a broader conceptualization of the clients of school psychologists. Children and youth who are "at risk," as well as those who have significant problems would likely be the primary clients (approximately 3 out of every 10 children). In addition, the psychologist would also serve a variety of "normal" individuals who interact daily with one of the primary clients. Such an approach to school psychological services, therefore, can be characterized as achieving secondary and tertiary prevention (Caplan, 1964). Secondary preventions have high risk children or youth as their targets. Thus, secondary prevention services are directed toward early identification and intervention with individuals who may be having difficulties in one of the two major social systems, schools or families. The school psychological services that are particularly important to successful secondary prevention include: consultation with parents and teachers, inservice education about strategies for modifying children's learning and behavioral difficulties, and direct behavioral interventions. Some of these same services are also useful in promoting primary prevention, in other words, positive growth in psychologically healthy individuals.

To date, school psychologists have not been utilized significantly in the delivery of primary prevention services. Such services would increase the number of clients tremendously, for it could include essentially all "normal" and "abnormal" individuals in a school (i.e., 10 out of 10 students). Many have pointed out the potential benefits of primary prevention, believing that educational institutions are the optimal delivery systems; similarly, they have suggested school psychologists as primary service agents (Clarizio, 1979; Lemle, 1976; Ojemann, 1967; Platt & Spivack, 1976). In fact, a model primary prevention program for schools with psychologists as the primary service agents has been designed and tested by Allen and his associates (Allen, Chinsky, Larcen, Lochman, & Selinger, 1976).

A number of writers (e.g., Gutkin & Curtis, 1982; Meyers, Parsons, & Martin, 1979) believe that through school-based problem-solving consultation, psychologists are indirectly providing primary prevention services. This belief is premised on the assumption that knowledge and skills an individual gains through consultations with a psychologist about a particular problem are retained and generalized to other children before another problem surfaces. Some evidence to support this assumption has been presented by Ritter (1978), Jason and Ferone (1978), and Meyers (1975) and will be discussed in the chapter on consultation.

According to Trachtman (1981), the profession of school psychology has never defined its client satisfactorily. He believes a clear-cut resolution has been difficult for psychologists who "intuitively, are morally committed to children but, when they test reality, they are reminded that they are employed (and fired) by school systems" (Trachtman, 1981, p. 145). As a reaction to this client dilemma, Trachtman advocated that school psychologists adopt a parent-as-client philosophy. His rationale for this philosophy is based on the notion that schools serve parents; that is, parents at one time banded together and formed educational institutions to which they delegated the responsibility of educating their children. Quoting Trachtman,

> [T]he school, therefore, serves parents by educating children and, philosophically if not always in actuality, the responsibility must be carried out to the parents' satisfaction. Whereas the school-as-client reflects a pragmatic employer-employee relation, the child-as-client reflects a much more satisfying moral commitment for most of us, but the two definitions are frequently irreconcilable although the parent-as-client may offer a slightly more workable perspective. Here one can see parents as both ultimate employer and ultimately responsible for children's welfare. The working premise, therefore, is that our employer is the parents, collectively, and our client, the individual parent. (1981, p. 145)

In sum, our answer to the question of "Who is the client?" is "It depends!" This seemingly ambiguous response is based on the recognition that several factors can influence psychologists' conceptions of their target population. Some of the factors, such as one's model or theory of human behavior and training or spectrum of competent services, are controlled by the individual psychologist. Other factors, such as legal mandates, workload, financial remuneration, and educational philosophy, are more externally controlled. To the extent that psychologists influence these factors, they can determine who their clients will be. Handicapped children traditionally have been and will likely continue to be a high-needs population for school psychologists. However, with the recent increased interest in education for the gifted and preschool-age children, and the consistently increasing number of requests for inservice and consultation services, school psychologists' clients are increasing in number and variety. Finally, the parent-as-client philosophy espoused by Trachtman is an appealing general perspective for guiding the delivery of school psychological services.

What are the Major Service Goals of School Psychologists?

Regardless of one's conceptualization of who the client is, school psychology's *raison d' etre* is the delivery of psychological services to children and youth. As illustrated by the NASP masthead slogan, the general or overall goal for the profession is "serving the mental health and educational interests of all children and youth." This general service goal has been further operationalized by APA with the development of Specialty Guidelines for Delivery of School Psychological Services (see Appendix B).

In early 1980, the APA Council of Representatives adopted the "Guidelines for Delivery of Services by School Psychologists," along with similarly intended guidelines for practice by the other three (clinical, counseling, and organizational/industrial) recognized professional psychological specialities. Lambert (1981) believed that, with the support of APA boards and the committees of other school psychological organizations, the "guidelines will define practice and guide legislators, school administrators, and educational organizations to an understanding of appropriate school psychological services and their delivery to children, parents, and teachers" (p. 194).

For purposes of identifying the major service goals of school psychology, we will examine these guidelines. According to the Specialty Guidelines (American Psychological Association, 1982),

> *School Psychological Services* refers to one or more of the following services offered to clients involved in educational settings from pre-school through higher education for the protection and promotion of mental health and facilitation of learning:

a. Psychological and psychoeducational evaluation and assessment of the school functioning of children and youth through the use of screening procedures, psychological and educational tests (particularly individual psychological tests of intellectual functioning, cognitive development, affective behavior, and neuropsychological status), interviews, observation, and behavioral evaluations with explicit regard for the context and the setting in which the professional judgments based on assessment, diagnosis and evaluation will be used.

b. Interventions to facilitate the functioning of individuals or groups with concern for how schooling influences and is influenced by their cognitive, conative, affective, and social development. Such interventions may include, but are not limited to, recommending, planning, and evaluating special education services, psychoeducational therapy, counseling, affective educational programs, and training programs to improve coping skills.

c. Interventions to facilitate the educational services and child-care functions of school personnel, parents, and community agencies. Such interventions may include, but are not limited to, in-service school personnel education programs, parent-education programs, and parent counseling.

d. Consultation to and collaboration with school personnel and/or parents concerning specific school-related problems of pupils and students and the professional problems of staff. Such services may include, but are not limited to: assistance with the planning of educational programs from a psychological perspective; consultation to teachers and other school personnel to enhance their understanding of the needs of particular pupils; modification of classroom instructional programs to facilitate children's learning; . . . and the creation, collection, organization and provision of information from psychological research and theory to educate staff and parents.

e. Program development services to individual schools, to school administrative systems, and to community agencies in such areas as needs assessment and evaluation of regular and special education programs; . . . coordination, administration, and planning of specialized educational programs; the generation, collection, organization, and dissemination of information from psychological research and theory to educate staff and parents.

f. Supervision of school psychological services.

Certainly other more specific goals could be added to the list outlined in the Specialty Guidelines; however, items *a* through *f* capture the essence of most school psychologists' service goals. In sum, these goals illustrate the multifaceted nature of school psychology and the profession's belief that it has much to offer children, parents, educators, and educational systems.

How Are Problems Solved?

School psychologists' expertise typically is sought by parents or educators to help avoid a problem or to correct an ongoing problem. Hence, a common feature that characterizes most school psychological services is a problem-solving process. Specific principles and techniques of problem solving have been discussed by hundreds of authors [See Parnes, Noller, & Biondi, 1977 for an extensive list of works on problem solving]. Of specific interest to our conceptualization of problem solving is Osborn's (1963) work on basic principles of the problem-solving process, D'Zurilla and Goldfried's (1971) work relating the problem-solving process to psychotherapeutic processes, and Bergan's (1977) and Gutkin and Curtis' (1982) work in consultation. Within the school psychology literature, problem solving has been discussed most by researchers in the area of consultation (Bergan, 1977; Gutkin & Curtis, 1982; Meyers, Parsons, & Martin, 1979; Witt & Elliott, 1983) and thus, a comprehensive examination of it will be reserved for a later chapter. Briefly, however, we will overview basic stages of two problem-solving models because such models provide a process or "roadmap" for delivering most psychological services.

Bergan (1977) conceptualized a four-stage model of problem solving. His stages are referred to as (a) problem identification, (b) problem analysis, (c) plan implementation, and (d) problem evaluation. According to Bergan, when confronted with a problem, one should first work to get a clear, objective definition of the problem or problems. Once a problem has been identified and defined, the psychologist and the referral agent are ready to analyze factors that may be influencing the targeted problem. After a comprehensive problem analysis, some intervention (in the broad sense) designed to change the identified problem needs to be developed and implemented. Finally, after a suitable time period, the psychologist evaluates the intervention plan to determine the extent of problem resolution and plan effectiveness.

Another model of problem solving was conceptualized by Gutkin and Curtis (1982). Their model has seven stages and it too was designed specifically for use in consultation. As with Bergan's model, we have also found the Gutkin and Curtis model to provide a useful schema for guiding problem-solving activities. The seven stages are listed in Table 2.1.

Table 2.1   Problem-Solving Sequence

---

1. Define and clarify the problem.
2. Analyze the forces impinging on the problem.
3. Brainstorm alternative strategies.
4. Evaluate and choose among alternatives.
5. Specify consultee and consultant responsibilities.
6. Implement the chosen strategy.
7. Evaluate the effectiveness of the action and recycle if necessary.

Note: From "School-Based Consultation: Theory and Techniques" by T. B. Gutkin and M. J. Curtis. In C. R. Reynolds & T. B. Gutkin (Eds.), *The Handbook of School Psychology.* New York: John Wiley & Sons, 1982. Reprinted by permission.

A comparison of the two models of problem solving results in the conclusion that Gutkin and Curtis' model is essentially an elaboration of Bergan's model. The major difference is that Gutkin and Curtis are more explicit than Bergan concerning brainstorming and choosing alternative intervention strategies.

The utilization of a *process* for solving human problems enhances the probability that psychologists will be able to apply their knowledge and skills to a problem in an effective and efficient manner. Specific services or *content* such as psychoeducational assessment, direct observational interventions, teacher in-services, or consultation can be conceptualized, within a problem-solving process and hence be delivered systematically according to the stages in such a process. Perfunctory use of a problem-solving process may result in orderly and logical, yet ineffective services. Knowledgeable utilization of a problem-solving schema can provide a change agent with a method of analyzing a problem from an ecological perspective in order to determine what has been done, as well as what needs to be done procedurally.

ORGANIZATION AND DELIVERY OF SCHOOL PSYCHOLOGICAL SERVICES

Psychological services are only one of many services delivered *within* the complete social organization of a school. Consequently, the structure and administration of such services as they relate to the larger school organization and to specific psychological goals can have a significant impact on the effectiveness of service delivery.

In 1970, Herron and his associates stated, "There seems to be no universal plan for the organization of [school] psychological services. The current picture is one of disturbing diversity. There are highly organized services and there are very unorganized services" (1970, p. 211). Diversity is still an appropriate descriptor for school psychological services in the 1980s; however, we believe that these services are diversified less than in 1970 when Herron and his co-workers assessed the organizational status of school psychological services. Major factors acting to reduce the variance among psychological service systems have been the increase in special education legislation (e.g., P.L. 94-142, The Education for All Handicapped Children Act of 1975), the litigation concerning psychological testing and psychological treatment (e.g., *Larry P.,* 1979; Martin, 1978; *PASE,* 1980), and the continued development of service delivery standards by APA Division 16 and NASP.

All of the aforementioned factors have been significant forces in defining the legal and ethical boundaries of psychological practice in the schools. Within such boundaries, however, there is still wide latitude for organizing and delivering psychological services. Regardless of where psychological services are located administratively, a school psychological service unit is the "functional unit through which school psychological services are provided . . ." (APA, 1981). In fact, four organizational structures (Cutts, 1955), and at least five models of service (Gilmore, 1974), have been identified within which school psychologists commonly function. Thus, at this time, it is not possible to single out a best system of psychological service delivery; we will, however, review the conceptual dimensions fundamental to any service system.

Conceptual Dimensions of Service

School psychological services have been characterized as diverse or variable, yet when services are compared across school districts and other educational settings, they are probably more alike than different. When services vary significantly, we believe it is due primarily to the competence of psychologists and to the system or process of delivering services rather than the the content or types of services delivered. Three major conceptual dimensions along which services vary include: direct–indirect, centralized–decentralized, and proactive–reactive.

Direct–Indirect Services. Traditionally, psychological services have been conceptualized as direct services. In other words, a psychologist personally worked with an individual referred for services. This approach primarily characterizes the medical model of psychology. The types of services requiring direct contact between the psychologist and the referred individual include testing, counseling, and some forms of cognitive or behavioral treatments.

Indirect service delivery has begun to be used more frequently by psychologists, particularly those working in schools. Psychologists working in an indirect service model interact primarily with other professionals (e.g., teachers), paraprofessionals (e.g., teacher aides), and laypersons (e.g., parents) who in turn work directly with clients. Such a method of service delivery is characteristic of consultation. Other types of services that illustrate an indirect service approach include inservice training for educators, parent training, curriculum advisement, and some behavioral interventions. An illustration conceptualizing differences between direct and indirect service delivery models is displayed in Figure 2.2. This conceptualization was adapted from the consultation literature (Gutkin & Curtis, 1982), yet it also applies to school psychological services in general.

Monroe (1979) has used a direct–indirect service continuum concept as a means of characterizing five major roles or functions of school psychologists. The functions she identified were: counseling/therapy, psychoeducational assessment, consultative child study, inservice, and research. Although admittedly oversimplified, Monroe believed that counseling/therapy was the strongest example of direct service to children, while research represented the most extreme example of indirect service to children. Her schema for characterizing the rela-

DIRECT SERVICE DELIVERY MODEL

TEACHER ——referral——▶ PSYCHOLOGIST ——treatment——▶ CHILD

INDIRECT SERVICE DELIVERY MODEL

PSYCHOLOGIST ◀——referral—— TEACHER ——treatment——▶ CHILD
(consultant) ◀——consultation——▶ (consultee)

Figure 2.2. Direct and indirect service delivery models. (From Gutkin & Curtis, 1982. Reprinted by permission.)

tive relationships along the direct–indirect service continuum of the five primary functions of school psychologists is reproduced in Figure 2.3.

A common goal of both direct and indirect service models is to provide remedial services for problems. An additional important goal or objective of an indirect service model is to increase other professionals' or paraprofessionals' knowledge and intervention skills so that they can prevent or respond more effectively to similar problems in the future. Such an objective is consistent with

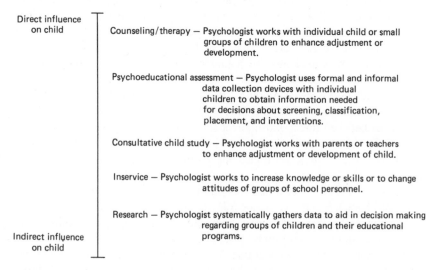

Direct influence on child

Counseling/therapy — Psychologist works with individual child or small groups of children to enhance adjustment or development.

Psychoeducational assessment — Psychologist uses formal and informal data collection devices with individual children to obtain information needed for decisions about screening, classification, placement, and interventions.

Consultative child study — Psychologist works with parents or teachers to enhance adjustment or development of child.

Inservice — Psychologist works to increase knowledge or skills or to change attitudes of groups of school personnel.

Research — Psychologist systematically gathers data to aid in decision making regarding groups of children and their educational programs.

Indirect influence on child

Figure 2.3. Influences of school psychological services on children. (From Monroe, 1979. Reprinted by permission.)

the suggestions of Albee (1968) and Miller (1969) who urged psychologists to "give psychology away" to non-psychologists as a means of promoting mental health. Theoretically, then, indirect service systems may have a greater capability for dealing with larger numbers of individuals than direct service systems because they utilize more persons in the treatment or remediation of problems.

Realistically, psychologists who wish to provide comprehensive services to children and youth will utilize both direct and indirect types of services. The sole use of either direct or indirect service techniques is probably indicative of an incomplete service model and should be avoided; both models are necessary because some cases demand the direct attention and skills of a psychologist, while others can be handled effectively by teachers, parents, or even peers. Thus, the task of psychologists is to be competent in a variety of services and to employ such services efficiently when they are needed.

Centralized–Decentralized Services. The organizational structure through which psychological services are administered and the physical location of the primary service providers are two major factors that influence the delivery of school psychological services. These two factors seem to have a strong effect on the actual, as well as the perceived, coordination and proximity of services. In general, we believe centralized organizations of psychological services are characterized as more coordinated, yet more distal to the majority of clientele. Decentralized organizations are characterized as less coordinated but more proximal to the majority of clientele. Thus, in theory, the organization and delivery of school psychological services can be meaningfully conceptualized along a centralized–decentralized continuum. This continuum is a summation of characteristics such as the degree of administrative coordination and the physical location of service providers.

Few writers or researchers, with the exception of Elkin (1963), have examined the centralized–decentralized dimensions of school psychological services. Therefore, one is left to theorize about the actual functionality of such a continuum until future investigators establish an empirical base. Theorizing and hypothesizing about the centralization or decentralization of school psychological services can, nevertheless, shed valuable light on the organization and utilization of such services.

Elkin (1963), in a chapter titled "Structuring School Psychological Services: Internal and Interdisciplinary Considerations" strongly advocated the centralization of such services. He argued as follows:

> The need for a well-integrated staff of well trained school psychologists functioning from a central office either via a pupil personnel section or an office of psychological services, under a Chief of Service is a practice which is essential to the efficient utilization of school psychologists administratively and professionally. Although the

trend has been increasingly toward centralization of psychological services, there are still school systems which maintain the atomistic mode of assignment. It would seem important to recognize that operating in this fashion is inadequate and wasteful. (p. 203)

Elkin believed the trend toward centralization of psychological services was based on the practical experiences of psychologists and educators and could be attributed to five categories of factors which he labeled: (a) benefits to children, (b) needs of the educational community, (c) confidentiality of communication, (d) supervisory requirements, and (e) utilization of professional staff.

Elkin believed there were three major, direct benefits of centralized services for children. First, he argued that continuity of contact and communication between any individual child and a given psychologist who had been involved previously with the child was desirable and highly probable within a centralized service mode. In fact, a psychologist could follow a child from school entry through high school graduation if need be. Such case flexibility may allow for quicker actions and less redundancies in services (e.g., developmental histories, parent interventions, etc.). A second benefit for children of centralized services results from the availability of organized and centralized record keeping systems. Such systems, according to Elkin, provide for more efficient storage and retrieval of critical information, as well as increased confidentiality of such information. A third benefit to children of centralized services may be the increased flexibility of staff utilization. Elkin elaborated upon this with an example in which psychologists could be assigned to high need schools temporarily to alleviate problems.

As to needs of the educational community, Elkin argued that group testing and evaluation programs could be administered best by a centralized psychology program. He also suggested that psychologists have valuable contributions to make to a variety of typical education committees.

Privacy and confidentiality were also part of Elkin's rationale for centralized psychological services. He believed that reports and other formal communications would be safer and that compliance with ethical codes concerning the confidential nature of many psychological contacts would be undoubtably easier within a central office removed from the schools.

The final component of Elkin's rationale for centralized services concerned issues of supervision of staff by a ''qualified'' chief of service and optimal staff utilization (or accountability). Many of the same examples used with the previous three features were also used as support for these final two components. In a centralized system of staffing there is the opportunity for peer review and consultation with colleagues, while in a decentralized system a psychologist is, by necessity, more independent and likely to receive less supervision.

In summary, Elkin identified several major strengths of a centralized model of school psychological services. Several of these identified strengths are not, however, idiosyncratic to a centralized model of psychological services. For example, confidentiality of communications and record keeping can probably be carried out with equal effectiveness in a decentralized service system. One must be aware that other factors such as psychologist:student ratio, number of schools within a district, perceived nature of psychologists (e.g., administrator- or teacher-like), and interest in preventive mental health will also influence decisions concerning the administrative structure of school psychological services.

To date, no writer has published a parallel article to Elkin's in support of a decentralized mode of psychological services; however, Phillips (1967, 1968, 1970) advocated a diagnostic-intervention class model that is clearly representative of a decentralized approach to delivering psychological services. It would seem that a decentralized service mode would have several appealing advantages. First, in a relatively decentralized system of psychological services, the service providers would be housed within the school or schools where they work, thereby increasing the number of contacts with potential consumers. Such an arrangement would seem to be particularly helpful in establishing consultation and preventive mental health activities. Specialized service units for particular populations of students (e.g., mentally handicapped, physically handicapped, delinquent, etc.) have also been an impetus for the decentralization of school psychological services. A final common reason experienced by both urban and rural school districts has been travel distance between a central office and the various schools desiring service. As a result, many psychologists have elected to increase their direct service hours by relocating to field offices in the various schools they serve.

In practice, we have observed a variety of service delivery systems that have a combination of centralized and decentralized features. In fact, the majority of psychological service models probably can be characterized at different points on the centralized–decentralized continuum with respect to various service features.

Proactive–Reactive Services. School psychologists' actions should be guided by *anticipated* or perceived mental health and educational problems. Reaction to an anticipated problem is proactive, while reaction to an *existing* problem is characterized as reactive. In general, most daily school psychological activities such as assessment, consultation, and intervention are in response to identified problems (and thus reactive). It is important to realize that these same activities can be used within a preventive framework as well. An analysis of psychological interventions that directly corresponds with the proactive-reactive continuum of services was explicated by Cowen (1977).

According to Cowen, a comprehensive system of mental health requires a three-level model of intervention. He refers to the first stage as primary prevention. Basically, primary prevention refers to lowering the rate of emotional, behavioral, and learning disorders in a given population and to building psychological health and resources in people. Healthy children are the main targets for primary prevention within schools, whereas secondary preventions have as their targets high risk children or youngsters whose problems are just beginning. Thus, secondary prevention usually involves the early identification of and intervention with children who are just beginning to have academic and/or behavior difficulties. The major objective of secondary prevention is to remedy problems before they become socially or emotionally incapacitating. The final level of prevention is referred to as tertiary. Tertiary prevention services are concentrated on children and youth having "full-blown" academic or behavior problems. The fundamental goal of this third type of intervention is to remediate or repair psychologically damaged individuals so they will be able to function productively.

Conceptually, when moving through the three levels of Cowen's prevention model, from primary prevention to secondary prevention to tertiary prevention, actions become more reactive and less proactive with regard to planning and delivering psychological services. To the chagrin of most school psychologists, a majority of services are delivered within the secondary and tertiary levels of prevention, with tertiary services taking the lion's share of the psychologist's time. In other words, most intervention efforts are for children and youth who are already experiencing difficulties.

A number of school and community psychologists have championed the call for preventive mental health services within schools (Allen, Chinsky, Larcen, Lochman, & Selinger, 1976; Clarizio, 1979a, 1979b). They argue correctly that the "school" has access to a large number of children over long periods of time during formative years; thus, there are many significant opportunities for educators to influence children's social and emotional development. School psychologists have the potential to become major contributors in the delivery of preventive mental health services if they can somehow reapportion their commitments to special education (i.e., secondary and tertiary prevention services) and assume a proactive service mindset.

A number of factors seem to stand in the way of the ready acceptance of proactive or preventive services for school children. The foremost problem is one of perception. Psychologists and educators seem generally to be overwhelmed by the complexities involved in designing and establishing preventive programs. Thus, a lack of know-how coupled with a relative paucity of prepackaged programs seem to be significant limiting factors. Other deterrents to prevention have been outlined by Clarizio (1979b). They include invasion-of-privacy and the difficulty of specifying and evaluating the goals of prevention.

A Taxonomy for the Delivery of Psychological Services

In the preceding section, three conceptual dimensions or continuums were discussed all of which we believe help characterize the major features of most school psychological delivery systems. A continuation of this conceptual discussion with respect to various psychological services (e.g., assessment, consultation, intervention, etc.) should provide the reader with a more integrated overview of the organization and delivery of school psychology services.

Catterall (1972) developed a taxonomy of prescriptive interventions. Briefly, his taxonomy included two interactive dimensions which he referred to as *directness of approach* and *focus of approach.* Directness of approach referred to a continuum of contact, direct or indirect, between a service provider and a client. Focus of approach referred to the primary target for change, the environment or an individual, and indicated whether the service provider was attempting change in the total environment or was trying to focus on an individual in a more personal way. We have found that Catterall's taxonomic system, with some modification of terminology, provides a useful conceptual schema for analyzing qualities of various school psychological services in addition to interventions. Schematically (see Figure 2.4), the interaction of the directness and focus dimensions results in four types of service: indirect environmental, direct environmental, indirect personal, and direct personal. When viewed from the reciprocal determinism perspective of human behavior, direct and indirect environmental services focus on the E of the PBE triad, while direct and indirect personal services focus on the P and B components of the model.

A more detailed discussion of interventions with respect to common behavior and adjustment problems will be provided in Chapter 5. Presently, however, we would like to use our modification of Catterall's intervention taxonomy to examine from a child-as-client perspective the directness and focus of five types of psychological services generally provided by school psychologists. These five types of psychological services are: assessment, consultation, intervention, research, and inservice education/training. A sixth type of service important to the practice of school psychology itself is supervision.

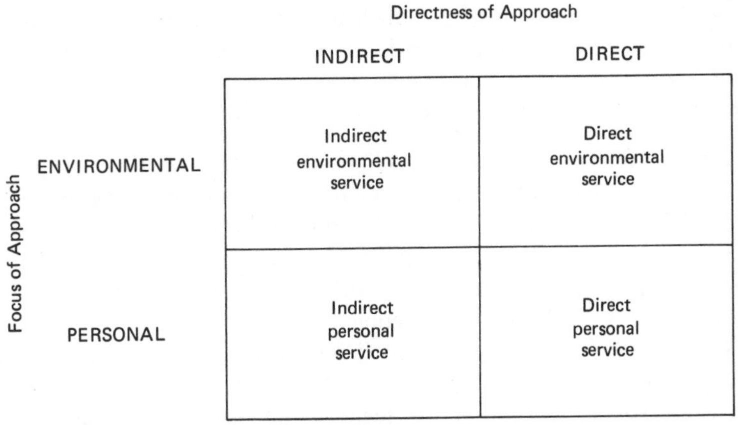

Directness of Approach

	INDIRECT	DIRECT
ENVIRONMENTAL	Indirect environmental service	Direct environmental service
PERSONAL	Indirect personal service	Direct personal service

Focus of Approach

Figure 2.4. Taxonomic dimensions of school psychological services.

Assessment. Assessment is a process that is characterized by the collection of information to aid in making several possible types of decisions about an individual. School psychologists use a variety of techniques to collect information about an individual and about his or her environment. Typical techniques include interviewing parents, teachers, or students; reviewing student records; testing with standardized instruments and informal inventories; and observing an individual's behavior in several situations. A detailed discussion of assessment and related measurement issues will occur in a later chapter. Presently, however, let's focus on classifying assessment activities into one or more of four basic types of service categories.

Traditional assessment practices are test-oriented, thus requiring a client to interact directly with a psychologist. The assessment activity of testing would therefore be considered a direct personal service. Parent or teacher interviews also can provide valuable information about a child–client. Such a technique does not directly involve the child, though significant persons who are frequently around him or her are involved. Hence, it can be considered an indirect environmental service. Both the review of a child's records and classroom observations of the child during the assessment process also would be considered indirect environmental services, for such services do not directly involve the child and are focused on other persons or objects within the child's daily environment.

Assessment services that are characterized as direct environmental or indirect personal are used relatively infrequently. An example of a direct environmental assessment service could involve diagnostic teaching in an area proven difficult as a result of a child's test performance. An example of an indirect personal assessment service could involve a child filling out a personality or careers inventory on his or her own and returning it to the psychologist for scoring and interpretation.

Assessment is truly a multifaceted process as it is possible to identify four categories of assessment services which involve a psychologist, a child, and significant others in the child's environment. Generally, in accordance with current school practice, most assessment services are direct personal or indirect environmental in nature.

Intervention. Interventions can be defined as strategic reactions by psychologists, educators, and/or parents to children's "inappropriate" behavior or "unsuccessful" learning. These strategic reactions take many forms according to Catterall (1972) and will be examined further in Chapter 5. However, a brief review and update of Catterall's work will provide a conceptual overview of various school psychological intervention services.

Traditionally, school psychologists' interventions with children involved talk or play therapies primarily and were intended as a means by which a child could gain insights into his or her feelings and behavior (Barbanel, 1982). Recently, most psychologists and educators have had a stronger affinity for behavioral therapies than "talk" therapies. A number of factors have contributed to such a large scale adoption of behavioral intervention techniques. Not only can they lead to enhanced clarity of communication, but they can also be more widely used in everyday classroom teaching and management.

As demonstrated by Catterall in 1972, interventions utilized by school psychologists could be classified in all four of the basic categories of service. With the addition of a few recent interventions such as self-monitoring (an indirect personal service) and biofeedback (a direct environmental service), Catterall's taxonomy would be up-to-date. From our experience as school psychology practitioners and trainers, we believe indirect environmental and direct environmental services are used most frequently. Although with the current research interest in self-monitoring and social skills training, we predict increased utilization of both indirect personal and direct personal services; further, when accomplished in concert with environmental intervention, services will epitomise the reciprocal determinism model of behavior and its changes.

Consultation. Consultation is defined frequently as a process of "collaborative problem-solving between a mental health specialist (the consultant) and one or more persons (the consultees) who are responsible for providing some form of psychological assistance to another (the client)" (Medway, 1979b, p. 276). A brief examination of the historical roots of consultation is necessary to understand fully consultation as a means for delivering school psychological services. To a large degree, consultation developed in response to dissatisfaction with traditional approaches to mental health services for both children and adults (Carter, 1975; Meyers, Parsons, & Martin, 1979). Primary among the targets of dissatisfaction was the medical model approach to psychology.

On a logistical and practical level, Albee (1968) argued that service delivery systems derived from the medical model had lead psychology into a serious shortage of personnel. Bower (1970) estimated approximately 10% of the children in public schools had some form of mental health problem. Albee's basic point was that as long as emotional stress and deviant behavior were viewed as "mental illness," we would require psychiatrists and doctoral psychologists to treat patients. He believed we could never produce the required number of "doctors" to meet the mental health needs of the nation. Albee's alternative approach involved consultation. Psychologists were encouraged to "give psychology away" by consulting with nonpsychologists to promote mental health.

Additional pressures specific to school psychology were also working to promote the development of a consultation service delivery model. Traditional school psychology was essentially an attempt to implement the medical model within a school setting (Herron, Green, Guild, Smith, & Kantor, 1970). Each step of the assessment-diagnosis-treatment sequence began to be questioned; similarly, referrals and time lags between referral and service kept increasing. As a result, many school psychologists began to think their time and knowledge could be used more efficaciously if they could devote time to consulting with school personnel as opposed to testing and placing children. By consulting with teachers, each of whom in turn worked directly with 20 or more children per year and hundreds over the course of a career, school psychologists believed they could serve far more students than through direct contact with individual children. According to Gutkin and Curtis (1982), the need for consultation services became even more evident with the onset of the mainstreaming movement and with the growing evidence of increasing work-related stress on teachers.

During the 1970s, there was a growing consensus among school psychologists that consultation ought to be one of the major, if not the major, service delivery model for the profession (Bardon & Bennett, 1974). As Meacham and Peckham (1978) reported after analyzing a national survey of school psychologists, "the consultation function is becoming more central and if the practitioners have their way, it will become primary" (p. 205).

Consultation practices and research will be discussed in detail in Chapter 3, but in order to classify them according to our four basic service categories, we must examine their core characteristics briefly. The major distinguishing characteristics of consultation are indirect service to children and a relationship between a consultant and consultee that is voluntary and collaborative in nature. Hence, from the perspective that a child is the client, consultation activities can best be classified as indirect environmental services because they are done around the client. In comparison to assessment and intervention services, consultation according to our classification system is a more focused or defined service. This does not imply that it is more important, effective, or efficient. In fact, such a classification is largely the result of consultation services conceptually preceding and subsuming many assessment and intervention services.

Research. Research is characterized as an empirical, fact-finding process which should inform individuals' decisions and actions. According to Phillips (1982),

> Research as the basis of action is effective to the extent that it makes the school psychologist (1) aware of the major variables relevant to a problem, (2) able to solve a problem . . . , and (3) capable of accomplishing these ends without reducing the present level of problem solving effectiveness of the school psychologist or others in the system. (pp. 24–25)

The domain of school psychology research is vast for it can be argued that all of the behavioral sciences serve as its appropriate research base. While such a view has legitimacy given the trend toward integration of school, family, and social services, the obstacles of encompassing such a large body of research are probably insurmountable. One way to scale down the research domain of school psychology is to let major service functions guide the development of research. Although still complex, a list of service functions such as that developed by

Hunter and Lambert (1974) and illustrated in Table 2.2, can serve as a research "menu" for school psychologists.

A more detailed discussion and investigation of school psychology research will be undertaken in Chapter 6. Presently, however, using our four categories of service, let's examine the nature of research relative to the delivery of psychological services for children.

Table 2.2   Role Functions Ascribed to the School Psychologist[a]

1. Serve all children in the schools.
2. Work frequently with groups, rather than individual children, parents, and teachers.
3. Act as advisor to total school program, including curriculum development.
4. Apply findings from child development, learning, social, and physiological psychology.
5. Handle staffing and guidance committees and work through multidisciplinary or team approaches.
6. Assist classroom teacher in educational programming and behavior management, especially in relation to effort to keep children in the regular classroom.
7. Deemphasize role in testing and classificatory diagnosis and emphasize diagnostic-intervention role.
8. Emphasize data-oriented problem solving and applied research.
9. Supervise lower-level school psychological services and related personnel.
10. Assume responsibility for increased services to culturally disadvantaged and other handicapped children.
11. Function as an expert in psychology and education.
12. Function as a consultant to teachers, administrators, and other school personnel.
13. Assume major role in preventive efforts in relation to drug abuse, dropouts, and disciplinary problems.
14. Provide expertise in process of decision making in scientific endeavors and in helping relationships.
15. Facilitate interaction of community resources and the school and coordinate all community psychological and service agencies with the school in referrals and follow-up.
16. Provide in-service education in child behavior and development and instructional and behavioral interventions.
17. Help administrative personnel establish and implement goals and behavioral objectives for instructional programs.
18. Deal adequately with ethical and value dilemmas encountered in assessing and modifying child, interpersonal, and organizational relationships.
19. Utilize effectively skills in social interaction and communication techniques.

Note: From "Reading and Evaluating Research in School Psychology" by B. N. Phillips. In *The Handbook of School Psychology* edited by C. R. Reynolds and T. B. Gutkin, New York, John Wiley & Sons, 1982. Reprinted by permission.

[a]Derived from Hunter and Lambert, 1974.

In general, the research activities of school psychologists are not made explicit to children, if children are involved directly at all. Therefore, most research happens around children and to children without their prior knowledge. [*Note:* If children are involved directly, they must be debriefed about the research according to APA's *Ethical Principles in the Conduct of Research with Human Participants* (APA, 1973)]. As a result, most school psychology research can be categorized as indirect environmental or direct environmental services.

Inservice Education. Inservice education can be defined as the presentation of desired information or skills by experts to authorities who directly or indirectly influence the academic or social–emotional development of children. Inservice training programs have been used traditionally to update educators' skills and to introduce innovation into education (McBride, 1982). According to Elliott and Witt (1981), school psychologists are potentially the best people in educational systems to develop and present inservice training programs. The primary reason for this is that school psychologists are generally conversant in a wide array of knowledge domains such as behavior management, assessment and evaluation, children's learning styles, instructional psychology, legal issues, and human development.

Inservice training can be conceptualized easily as a form of consultation, since in most cases an inservice trainer (consultant) works with trainees (consultees) to solve some identified problem related to the education of children (clients). Thus, when applying our four categories of service, we would characterize inservice education in essentially the same way we characterized consultation. That is, from a child-as-client perspective, inservice education is best described as an indirect environmental service. Recently, we have observed an increase in the popularity of psychological inservices specifically for the mental health of teachers and administrators. These inservices typically focus on problems of stress and burnout and training techniques for coping with such problems.

Supervision. Supervision is a service for psychologists which indirectly, but ultimately, affects the quality of services received by clients. Supervision has been characterized as a function of accountability, evaluation, and continuing professional development. Consequently, it is a central element in both the training and practice of school psychologists.

Quality and quantity of supervision for school psychology students and practitioners has been outlined in several of the NASP Standards and in the APA Specialty Guidelines, although some psychologists believe they are insufficiently defined (Murphy, 1981). The APA *Specialty Guidelines for the Delivery of Services by School Psychologists* (1981, Guideline 1, 1.2; see Appendix B) states:

Providers of school psychological services who do not meet the requirements for the professional school psychologist are supervised directly by a professional school psychologist who assumes professional responsibility and accountability for the services provided. The level and extent of supervision may vary from task to task. . . . (pp. 673–674)

This guideline has been interpreted to mean that a supervisor should be responsible for activities such as reviewing reports and test protocols as well as discussing intervention strategies and outcomes. At a minimum, it is required that each psychologist receive at least one hour per week of direct face-to-face supervision. Supervision of school psychology practica and internships is discussed in detail in the NASP *Standards for Field Placement Programs in School Psychology* (1978).

Since supervision is a service primarily for psychologists themselves, it does not fit well into a child-as-client perspective. However, using our four-category taxonomy of services, it seems that supervision is best characterized as an indirect environmental service whose aim is to assure quality services for children.

Alternative Organizational Forms for Administering School Psychological Services

Historically, administrators of progressive schools found it impractical to assign to regular teachers and supervisors all the functions implied in adequate psychological services (Hildreth, 1930). In large school systems, provisions for such services were made through the organization of bureaus of research, psychological clinics, or departments or child study and guidance. Similar bureaus were maintained by the leading state universities and by a number of state departments of education. The services of these latter bureaus were especially useful to smaller communities that were unable to support an independent bureau of their own. According to Hildreth (1930), the most complete description of early city school, state, and university bureaus are contained in reports by Chapman (1927), Martens (1924), and Deffenbaugh (1922).

Today, the organization and administration of psychological services within educational systems seems to assume at least four forms: a department of psychological services, a department of pupil personnel services, a department of special education, or an outside agency developed and operated by a state department of education or mental health. To our knowledge, detailed information has not been collected about differences in the actual services provided by psychologists from each of the four types of organizational forms. In fact, relative differences in the organizational forms may be more semantic than actual, with the possible exception of those services housed in an outside agency under the direction of a state department.

Cutts (1955), in her summarization of the Thayer Conference, described each of the four major organizational forms for school psychological services. Basically, her descriptions, although quite general, are still appropriate today. The major features she used to differentiate the four organizational forms were the personnel or staff background (training) and the functions of the department. For example, when describing a department of pupil personnel services she wrote, "a department often includes persons working in school psychology, school social work, school health services, guidance counseling, child accounting and attendance, home instruction, remedial teaching . . . , and special education for exceptional children of all types" (Cutts, 1955, pp. 78–79). A school psychology department, on the other hand, was comprised only of personnel trained as psychologists or psychometrists.

Regardless of the organizational form of a school psychological service unit, "a professional school psychologist is responsible for planning, directing, and reviewing the provision of school psychological services" (APA, 1981, p. 674). When the school psychological service unit "is composed of more than one person or is a component of a larger organization, a written statement of its objective and scope of services is developed, maintained, and reviewed" (APA, 1981, p. 675).

The organizational form assumed for the provision of school psychological services seems to be influenced by a variety of factors. Certainly, the number of psychologists on staff would be a major factor, along with the perceived importance of psychological services in the eyes of school administrators. Our experience suggests that the more staff members and the greater the perceived importance, the more likely the organizational form will be a separate department of school psychological services. The perceived recipients of psychological services may also affect the organizational placement of such services. For example, if all students are perceived as potential recipients of school psychological services, then the possibility of being organized as a separate department or of being embedded within a pupil personnel department seems conceptually more likely than the possibility of becoming part of a special education department. Interpersonal working relationships and professional turf issues may also influence the organizational form of services. As discussed in Chapter 1, the relationship between school psychologists and special educators is particularly complex and has become a focal issue for many professionals in both fields. Hence, the pairing of these two groups should be planned well to maximize cooperation and to minimize friction and duplication of services.

In discussing school psychological services, Herron and his associates (1970) emphasized the differential influence of an urban, suburban, or rural setting on the organization of such services. According to these writers, city schools have pressing social and family difficulties, with violence in and around schools also common. Thus, they believed family services were absolutely necessary, along with prevention programs, group therapy, and inservice training for teachers. Because of the complexity and significance of the problems encountered within urban schools, Herron et al. recommended a service structure where there was a director of pupil personnel to whom all service providers (e.g., psychologists, counselors, social workers, etc.) reported.

In a suburban school, psychological services were reported to be characterized by two types of organizational structures, both of which are more decentralized than in urban schools (Herron et al., 1970). One organizational approach used psychologists on a specialized basis for such things as handling of early admissions or readiness programs. In the other type of organization, psychologists were assigned to a single school where they did everything from prevention to placement. With both of these service approaches, psychologists appeared to be housed within a separate department of psychology rather than as a section of a pupil personnel department.

Herron and his associates (1970) characterized rural school psychological services as primarily a "one-person operation" where a psychologist usually functions under the direction of a state board of education or a county agency. In actuality, the rural psychologist is not usually a part of a particular department within a school district and consequently functions with a high degree of autonomy.

In conclusion, we believe it is important to reiterate that there is not a clear picture of just what the best organizational form may be for the administration of school psychological services. Regardless of the organizational form, school psychologists must be cognizant of the need for effective multidisciplinary functioning with other educational and mental health personnel. Good communication, collaborative problem solving, and mutual knowledge of and respect for other disciplines (e.g., speech pathology, counseling, special education, physical therapy, etc.) are critical factors in multidisciplinary services.

MODELS OF SCHOOL PSYCHOLOGICAL DELIVERY SYSTEMS

No single best model of school psychological services has been identified. A major reason for this is that service programs must be sensitive to the needs of consumers and aware of environmental constraints (e.g., organizational structure of services, financial ability to pay for staff and services, philosophy about the breadth and depth of services, and legal guidelines concerning services). Because the needs of consumers and the environmental constraints vary across school districts and states, school psychological service models also vary. Such variability of services does not, however, preclude an analysis and discussion of the typical processes by which school psychological services are delivered. In fact, a common core of consultation, assessment, and intervention procedures is identifiable in most states. This is due primarily to the implementation in the mid-70s of federal legislation such as P.L. 94-142 and its corollary state mandates; in many ways, they have functioned to standardize the process of providing services for handicapped children and youth.

Two delivery system models for school psychological services have been most prevalent in the literature. They are the diagnostic or assessment model (Catterall, 1972; Sabatino, 1972) and the consultation or problem-solving model (Bergan, 1977; Lambert, 1974; Meyers, Parsons, & Martin, 1979). In practice, a third, less discrete model exists, one which is a combination of the diagnostic and consultation models. The diagnostic model traditionally has been the favored model of service; however, many recent surveys of practitioners and trainers indicate that consultation is fast becoming the most preferred, or one of the most preferred, job functions of school psychologists (Gutkin & Curtis, 1982). Surveys of teachers, superintendents, and other school personnel indicate that consultation is a very important aspect of the services that psychologists bring to schools (Bardon, 1976; Cowen & Lorion, 1976; Fairchild, 1976; Gutkin, 1980). A detailed discussion of this shift from an assessment model toward a consultation model of service will be presented in Chapter 3. The present discussion will now focus on the development of a generic model of school psychological services that integrates components from both the assessment and the consultation models.

A Generic Model of School Psychological Service Delivery

The development of a generic model for the delivery of psychological services has much instructional value, but it is certainly subject to modification when implemented within any given school district because of numerous factors already discussed in this chapter. Our generic model of service delivery has been influenced by the work of researchers interested in human problem solving (Bergan, 1977; D'Zurilla & Goldfried, 1971; Osborn, 1963), by writers interested in the assessment process (Grimes & Reschly, 1980), and by legal and ethical guidelines established by legislative and professional bodies.

Our service delivery model is premised on six assumptions about work with potentially handicapped or troubled individuals. The six assumptions, with brief elaborative comments about each, are:

1. *Behavior and learning problems of children are functionally related to the setting in which they are manifested.* This assumption does not mean educational settings such as schools necessarily cause the psychoeducational problems children manifest in such settings; however, it does suggest the relationship may be primarily causal or that behavior is triggered by a factor(s) in the school environment. Thus, this as-

sumption indicates that it will often be necessary to evaluate an educational environment as well as a particular child.

2. *A primary goal of psychoeducational assessment is to determine what a child does and does not know, and how the child learns best so that successful interventions can be designed.* This assumption stems logically from the required end-product of assessment; in other words, in order to develop a valid individual education plan, *what* and *how* information about a learner is needed. Such a supposition is consistent with thorough consultative problem solving and with a skills-training approach to assessment.

3. *Techniques for individual diagnosis and intervention need to be supplemented with techniques for diagnosing and intervening in specific school settings and in the school as a social system.* The implication of this assumption is that it is not sufficient generally just to intervene at the level of an individual student's intrapsychic functioning. In order to enhance the probability of behavior change, it is also necessary to intervene on a broader level.

4. *The proximity in place and time of psychological services to the educational settings in which psychoeducational problems are manifested increases the effective utilization of these services.* This assumption is based on the premise that problem-solving communications among professionals working with a handicapped individual will be enhanced if they work in the same environment. The role of psychoeducational services should also be demystified the closer such services are to mainstream education.

5. *To enhance effective solutions to psychoeducational problems, psychological services should be directed toward the development and utilization of those resources indigenous to schools or educational settings.* This assumption signifies the essence of a consultation-oriented service system whereby consultants work indirectly with children through a consultee (i.e., teachers and parents), thus enhancing the consultee's ability to solve future problems. Additionally, this assumption illustrates the importance of designing interventions that realistically can be implemented in a classroom or other settings.

6. *Psychoeducational interventions for children require the ongoing attention of the person(s) who implemented them because over time a child's response to a particular intervention will change.* This final assumption has its base in behavioral psychology and serves to highlight the fact that psychoeducational service providers need periodically to follow-up on their suggested interventions with children. Such follow-ups allow for the refinement of a particular intervention and for general feedback concerning the effectiveness of one's previous actions.

The step-by-step sequence of our generic service model has been influenced strongly by a presentation given by Grimes and Reschly (1980). In fact, the procedural flow chart (See Figure 2.5) illustrating the core of our consultation-assessment-intervention service system has been adapted from a similar flow chart developed by Grimes and Reschly.

Step 1: Determine Appropriateness of Referral. A referral, whether formal or informal, is a signal to a psychologist that a student is perceived to be experiencing a problem. In other words, some significant adult(s) (usually a teacher or parent) believes the student's academic performance or behavior to be falling

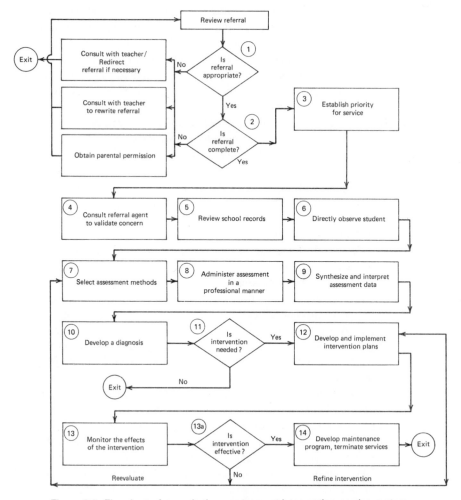

Figure 2.5. Flowchart of consultation-assessment-intervention service system.

short of some expected standard. The psychologist's task is to respond to the referral in order to determine whether it is "appropriate." What qualifies as an "inappropriate" referral will vary. Typically, some documentation of the perceived problem or concern, as well as an enumeration of previous teacher- or parent-directed interventions, is necessary before a psychologist should get involved. If the referral is deemed inappropriate and does not warrant a psychologist's direct or indirect involvement, then it should be directed to another service system.

Step 2: Review the Referral for Essential Components. If the referral is appropriate, the psychologist then determines whether the referral has all the essential components applicable to psychological services. This includes, but is not limited to, (a) a clear, behavioral statement of the problem and (b) the written permission of the student's parent or legal guardian in cases where the psychologist will be working directly with the student.

When the referral is incomplete, the psychologist should initiate the essential steps to secure the necessary information. This most likely will involve returning the referral to the referring agent so it can be revised. In the interim, consultation with teachers or parents, record reviews, and student observations could be initiated.

Step 3: Establish Service Priority. The demands for psychological services are usually numerous enough that some individual or group of individuals must decide who has priority in receiving those services. Some systems use a severity-of-problem scale, while others use the date of referral as a method for prioritizing recipients of services. Typically, the psychologist reviews referrals and his or her other time investments (e.g., research, inservice, etc.) with a principal or special education coordinator before prioritizing cases. When an appreciable delay between initial referral and expected date of service is anticipated, parents and teachers involved in the case should be notified of that delay.

Step 4: Consult with Referral Agent(s). The psychologist should meet at least once with the individual who referred a student in order to clarify and validate the student's difficulty before further interactions take place. This step is particularly necessary when there has been a significant delay between the referral date and the initiation of the psychologist's actual involvement. If the referral agent is not a parent, then the psychologist might also touch base with the student's parents or legal guardian to ensure optimal cooperation. If nothing more, this step provides for enhanced communication between psychologists, parents, teachers, and other persons central to the case.

Step 5: Review School Records. The psychologist, prior to an evaluation or intervention, should review and analyze a student's pertinent records. Information gleaned from such records can be classified under (a) sensory system (e.g., vision, hearing, etc.) integrity, (b) academic progress, (c) history of physical health, (d) history of emotional health, and (e) family or social history. A review of school records should be supplemented frequently by interviews with parents, school personnel, or other significant individuals.

Step 6: Direct Observation of a Student. It is imperative to observe a student within several different settings prior to initiating an intervention. However, we believe it is equally important to observe a student before initiating formal assessment activities. Whether one actually records specific behaviors or simply attempts to gain a better understanding of a student interacting within a particular setting, we believe such observations provide critical, basic information.

In situations where testing is likely to occur, it is often impossible to do an unobtrusive observation unless it takes place prior to working with the student directly. Thus, doing observations prior to meeting a student reduces the probability of reactivity and subsequently enhances the meaningfulness of an observation (Kazdin, 1979a, 1980a).

Step 7: Select Assessment Methods. Selection of assessment instruments and strategies should be based on the student's stated problem and on the psychologist's competencies. If a student requires an assessment beyond the competencies of a given psychologist, it is incumbent on that professional to get the service of another psychologist or other school personnel, or to assist the family in a referral to another agency.

Step 8: Administer Assessment in a Professional Manner. The psychologist should administer all tests and collect observations or ratings according to "recommended procedures." In other words, when administering and scoring standardized instruments, or when using non-standardized assessment methods, psychologists should adhere to the procedures outlined in test manuals and/or documented in the professional literature.

Step 9: Synthesize and Interpret Assessment Data. Once all the assessment data has been collected and quantified, the psychologist is responsible for analyzing and interpreting the results with respect to the stated problem(s). The communication of assessment findings usually takes the form of a written report and a verbal summary at a multidisciplinary staffing. Psychologists should be aware of their consumers' knowledge so as to write reports in an understandable and meaningful manner. Communication to all parties is facilitated by providing objective and concrete evidence to support interpretations (Shellenberger, 1982). Information and interpretations should be presented in a manner which takes into account measurement error and which recognizes the limitations of particular instruments. Finally, psychologists should not rely solely on their written reports or verbal summaries at staffings. if behavior change in a client is a desired outcome of the evaluation; follow-up contacts with or notes to the person(s) who will provide direct services are often necessary to ensure understanding and correct implementation of recommendations.

Step 10: Develop a Diagnosis. At the conclusion of the interpretation of assessment data, the psychologist is responsible for formulating a psychological-educational diagnosis. A psychological-educational diagnosis is often considered as only the identification of the dysfunctional behaviors and environmental conditions that warrant attention. In most states, guidelines for determining handicapping conditions (e.g., learning disabled, behaviorally impaired, educably mentally handicapped, etc.) have been developed by state departments of education or mental health and these guidelines in turn provide psychologists with assistance in deriving diagnoses. This is a very limited view of diagnosis; we believe it is important to go far beyond such a simplistic view and to include within the concept of diagnosis a thorough description of the problem, its antecedents, and its current milieu's, thus providing a diagnosis with ecological validity.

While it is acknowledged that multidisciplinary team members share information, it is the responsibility of a psychologist, as a team member, to formulate a professional opinion regarding a categorical diagnosis. A psychologist is also responsible for expressing a dissenting opinion in writing when a categorical diagnosis, placement decision, or other considerations are formulated with which the psychologist disagrees.

Step 11: Decide if Intervention Is Needed. Decisions about interventions, in most instances, follow a comprehensive consultation and/or assessment of a student. A psychologist formulates an individual opinion regarding the need for intervention, whether functioning as an assessment team member or individual consultant. In situations where a team is involved, other members should also have input about intervention plans. In situations where the psychologist is the primary or only person consulting with a teacher, parent, or other individual on a case, the decision-making responsibility about the need for intervention rests with the psychologist and that individual.

Step 12: Develop and Implement Intervention Plans. The psychologist, along with others (assessment team members or consultees), develops potential intervention plans for implementation in the least restrictive environment. These intervention plans should (a) correspond to the student's problem statement and diagnosis, (b) be practical, (c) contain behavioral objectives, and (d) be communicated in sufficient detail for implementation. If the student will be enrolled in special education, then the intervention plan would be included in an individual educational plan (IEP).

Step 13: Monitor the Effects of the Intervention. Psychologists are ethically responsible for following-up on interventions which they have helped to develop. Such periodic monitoring allows for corrections or adjustments in services, as well as providing a psychologist with valuable feedback about his or her diagnosis and intervention plans. According to P.L. 94-142 and most state special education guidelines, follow-up in the form of a psychological re-evaluation must occur at least every three years. Reviews of students' IEPs are to occur annually, and thus they provide another opportunity for psychologists to gain feedback and have input into the refinement of services. In most instances, however, we believe that three year re-evaluations and annual IEP reviews cause too long a delay in follow-up to be effective. Thus, we suggest that the monitoring of interventions should be on a weekly basis initially following implementation, and progress toward monthly contacts in order to stay in touch with a client's progress.

Step 14: Determine if Psychological Services Should Be Terminated. After an intervention has been in place for a ''reasonable'' period of time and improvement in a target student's behavior has been documented, the psychologist should formulate an opinion concerning the continuation of intervention services. A decision may be made to develop a generalization and maintenance plan; however, if generalization has occurred already, termination of services may be in order.

This 14-step model of school psychological services for referred students should not be viewed as a rigid process. Rather, it is an attempt to organize typical services in a logical, temporal order. In addition, readers should note that feedback or refinement loops are available at each major decision point, thus allowing for redefinition of a problem, further assessment of a student, or redesigning of an intervention. The various consultation, assessment, and intervention activities outlined within this model will be discussed in detail in later chapters.

SALIENT CHARACTERISTICS AND FEATURES OF SCHOOL PSYCHOLOGICAL SERVICE SYSTEMS

Recently published research on the profession of school psychology and concept papers concerning the interface among school psychological and other student services have provided numerous details about the function and structure of typical service systems. In this section, we have selected several salient characteristics and features of school psychological service systems for examination. These include: (a) functioning as part of a multidisciplinary team, (b) daily activities, (c) salary and work schedules, and (d) psychologist-to-student ratios.

Multidisciplinary Teams

Prior to 1975, school psychologists were the primary, if not the only, persons involved in the diagnosis and placement of handicapped students. With the advent of P.L. 94-142 and its state-level corollary mandates, the decision-making process for the assessment and placement of handicapped students became a team or group task. Specifically, Section 121a. 532(e) of P.L. 94-142 states, "The evaluation is made by a multidisciplinary team or group of persons, including at least one teacher, or other specialist, with knowledge in the area of suspected disability." Section 121a. 533(3) further requires each public agency to "insure that the placement decision is made by a group of persons, including persons knowledgeable about the child, the meaning of the evaluation data, and the placement opinions." Thus, educational decision-making teams comprised of teachers, parents, and support personnel (e.g., psychologists, counselors, speech pathologists, nurses, social workers, etc.) have been required to ensure such a mandate is carried out. These multidisciplinary teams have been referred to as child study teams, assessment teams, evaluation and placement committees, planning and placement committees, school appraisal teams, and admissions, review, and dismissal committees. The implicit rationale for a team approach to special education decision-making is based on the belief that a group decision provides safeguards against individual errors in judgement while enhancing adherence to due process requirements (Pfeiffer, 1980).

The team approach to assessment and decision-making has been used by mental health professionals for many years (Black, 1977). As a result, a number of writers advocated applying the team concept in the public schools (Buktenica, 1970; Falik, Grimm, Preston, & Konno, 1971; Hogensen, 1973). According to Pfeiffer (1981), "The key elements of a multidisciplinary team are a common purpose, cooperative problem solving by different professionals who possess unique skills and orientations, and a coordination of activities" (p. 330). Given these elements, multidisciplinary teams have been expected to provide a number of functional benefits beyond those provided by any single individual. These benefits include: greater accuracy in assessment, classification, and placement decisions; a forum for sharing differing views; provision for specialized consultative services to school personnel, parents, and community agencies; and, the resource for developing and evaluating individualized educational programs for exceptional students (Pfeiffer, 1981; Yoshida, 1980; Ysseldyke, Algozzine, & Thurlow, 1980).

The goals of multidisciplinary teams are embodied in P.L. 94-142 and its corollary state laws. According to Fenton, Yoshida, Maxwell, and Kaufman (1979) there are 11 goals which teams should accomplish for every student with special needs. These goals are to:

1. Determine the student's eligibility for special education.
2. Determine whether sufficient types of information about the student are available to the placement team before making decisions affecting the student's instructional program.
3. Evaluate the educational significance of such data.
4. Determine student placement.
5. Formulate appropriate year-long educational goals and objectives for the student.
6. Develop specific short term instructional objectives for the student.
7. Communicate with parents about changes in the student's educational program.
8. Plan information needed for future review of the student's program and progress.
9. Establish the specific date for placement team review.
10. Review the continued appropriateness of the student's educational program.
11. Review the student's educational progress.

Researchers (Pfeiffer, 1981; Yoshida, 1980) and practitioners have reported that many of the perceived benefits of multidisciplinary teams have not come to fruition consistently. No single factor can account for the apparent malfunctions of teams; rather, it is hypothesized that an array of intra- and inter-individual characteristics of team members, combined with the personal and procedural dynamics of a team, have resulted in these malfunctions. Serveral writers have criticized the team concept. Hefferin and Katz (1971) suggested that frequently teams generate ambiguous decisions, while Wallace (1976) argued that teams raise concerns over territoriality. Wing and Sarsley (1971) believed that teams increased role confusion.

To date, however, Pfeiffer (1980, 1981) is the only researcher who has attempted to analyze empirical results and to categorize the various problems commonly experienced in multidisciplinary teams. His analysis resulted in four categories of problems: (a) teams' unsystematic approach to collecting and analyzing diagnostic information, (b) the minimal involvement of parents and regular educators on teams, (c) teams' use of loosely construed decision making-planning processes, and (d) the lack of interdisciplinary collaboration and trust (Pfeiffer, 1981).

To date, no investigators have described, in full, a typical multidisciplinary meeting, although selected components of such meetings have been studied and described. For example, among the topics investigated are (a) team membership (Goldstein et al., 1980; Poland et al., 1979; Thurlow & Ysseldyke, 1979; (b) members' participation and satisfaction with meetings (Yoshida et al., 1978), and (c) length of meetings and team activities (Goldstein et al., 1980; Pfeiffer, 1981; Poland et al., 1979; Thurlow, 1980).

In an observational study of multidisciplinary teams working on students' IEPs, Goldstein et al. (1980) observed that the teams ranged from two to nine persons (resource teachers, parents, classroom teacher, student interns, evaluator, principal, counselor, speech therapist, and reading teacher) with 100% attendance by resource teachers and parents only. The remaining persons (which included school psychologists) attended these IEP-focused meetings less than 50% of the time. None of the meetings were attended by handicapped students.

Data collected by Yoshida and his associates (1978) in Connecticut indicated that persons involved in multidisciplinary team meetings most frequently were special education teachers, school administrators (principals), regular education teachers, and school counselors. The difference in team make-up observed between this study and the Goldstein et al. study appears to be due to the nature of the decisions being made. Specifically, in Yoshida's study, the team members were involved in a placement decision, while the teams Goldstein observed were developing IEPs (decisions concerning short- and long-term instructional objectives). An investigation by Poland et al. (1979) supports the hypothesis that team make-up does vary considerably with the decision to be made.

Yoshida et al. (1978) were the first to evaluate the team members' participation in meetings and their satisfaction with the meetings. They found that participation was related positively to satisfaction and that team members' roles were related positively to participation, but found little relationship between role and satisfaction. School psychologists, social workers, counselors, and administrators reported that they participated in decision-making more often than did regular or special education teachers. Regular teachers perceived themselves as low in participation and in satisfaction with the team decision-making process. According to Yoshida et al., the results showed "regular education teachers, who are pivotal persons in implementing the PT [PT = Planning Team] decisions, are low in participation and are generally not satisfied with the PT process" (1978b, p. 243). Probably the most important overall result of this study was that one's role was not found to relate to one's satisfaction.

Gilliam (1979) was interested in determining which roles were perceived as contributing most to the decisions reached by educational planning committees; therefore, he asked 130 participants at 27 meetings to rank in order the 15 roles most often represented on planning committees. He found that special education teachers, special education consultants, and psychologists, respectively, were thought to contribute the most to planning committees. Social workers, principals, and other administrators were ranked as the smallest actual contributors. Gilliam gave several alternative explanations for these results. First, persons in roles ranked high in importance seem to be in closer contact with children and their families, while persons in roles ranked lowest seem to be in closer contact with teachers. A second explanation offered by Gilliam was that "high importance roles are members who have hard data in terms of test scores, cumulative records, and diagnostic reports and are able to contribute information based on these data" (1979, p. 467). Both of these explanations appear to be true.

The most comprehensive data on the average length of team meetings was obtained by Poland et al. (1979) in their survey of 99 special education directors across 49 states. The directors reported meetings ranging in duration from 4 minutes to 16 hours; however, the average meeting was approximately 50 minutes. Pfeiffer (1981) reported a similar average meeting time for multidisciplinary teams in the northeast United States; 117 of the team members he surveyed reported spending approximately 30 minutes per meeting, while the remaining 30 members reported spending approximately 60 minutes per meeting. No team member selected more than one hour meeting time as typical.

Daily Activities

What do school psychologists do? This was the question Lacayo, Sherwood, and Morris (1981) asked 750 individuals from the 1978–79 NASP membership list. Each of the 750 randomly selected individuals received a one-page questionnaire listing 13 categories of activities. The categories were as follows: (a) psychological-educational assessment, (b) individual counseling, (c) group counseling, (d) consultation with parents, (e) consultation with teachers, (f) consultation with other school staff, (g) giving workshops or inservice training, (h) attending workshops or inservice training, (i) staff meeting or case conference, (j) reviewing referrals, writing case reports, or other office duties, (k) research or program evaluation, (l) driving from one educational facility to another, and (m) lunch, inactive, or personal time. Following the list of activities were half-hour time intervals from 7:30 A.M. to 6:00 P.M. Psychologists were asked to place a category code number or numbers within appropriate time intervals to indicate what they were doing on a given day.

Respondents to the survey represented a national distribution of psychologists working in public schools and totaled 335 individuals or 45% of the sample. Their responses, when summed and analyzed according to minutes spent per activity, resulted in rank ordering the activities as listed in Table 2.3.

The results indicated that psychoeducational assessment was the activity that consumed the largest portion of time. The next most time consuming activity involved reviewing referrals and writing case reports. Thus, reviewing referrals, assessment, and report writing accounted for approximately 40% of the sampled school psychologists' day. The second major block of time was allocated to consultation activities; 25% of the total was taken up by consultation with teach-

Table 2.3 Daily Activities of School Psychologists

Variable	M Minutes	SD	% of Time
Psychological/Educational Assessment	104	84	21%
Review/Write Up Cases	90	87	18%
Lunch/Personal Time	50	53	10%
Teacher Consultation	43	41	9%
Consultation with School Staff	43	47	9%
Staff or Case Meetings	38	53	8%
Parent Consultation	35	47	7%
Driving to Building Sites	29	42	6%
Individual Counseling	24	52	5%
Attending Workshops	10	47	2%
Giving Workshops	10	36	2%
Research/Program Evaluation	8	35	2%
Group Counseling	5	20	1%

Note: From N. Lacayo, G. Sherwood, & J. Morris, "Daily Activities of School Psychologists: A National Survey," *Psychology in the Schools*, 1981, *18*, 184–190. Reprinted by permission.

ers, parents, and school staff. Counseling activities involved 6% of the day, while attending or giving a workshop accounted for 4% of the day. Doing research and program evaluation occupied only 2% of the day.

Salary and Work Schedules

A national survey of school psychologists was completed in 1979 by Ramage. The purpose of the survey was to provide information for research and policy decisions in the field of school psychology. Questionnaires were sent in 1976 to members of NASP, APA Division 16, and to other school psychologists not identified by NASP or APA. The return rate of the questionnaires was 41% (2,743 out of 6,750). Amongst the plethora of information collected were data on school psychologists' salary schedules and on contract length.

In 1976, the majority of school psychologists working in schools reported earnings between $13,000 and $24,999, with the highest frequency between $16,000 and $21,999. The type of salary schedule under which school psychologists work varied. The most prevalent arrangement was for psychologists to be placed on a teacher-plus-an-increment schedule. Some psychologists, however, are on teacher's salary schedules while others are placed on administrator's salary schedules. A more recent salary survey conducted on the NASP membership (NASP, 1982) indicated that salaries of school psychologists (collapsed across all levels of training) ranged from $13,000 to +$40,000, with the greatest percentage of respondents earning between $22,000 and $24,000 for a school year (approximately 9½ months). The median salary of respondents also was within the $22,000 and $24,000 band.

With respect to length of contract, most of the school psychologists sampled in 1976 were working a 10-month contract. The length of contracts, however, ranged between 9 to 12 months. From our observations and experiences, it seems there is a general trend toward increasing the length of contracts toward 11 months. An impetus for such a trend has been the increased need for services to infants and preschoolers, both of which depend less on the traditional school year schedule.

Psychologists to Student Ratios

Ramage (1979), in her national survey of school psychologists, also investigated the ratio of psychologists-to-students in a school system. She found that the majority of school psychologists had a ratio between 1:2000 and 1:4000. Of the individuals who responded to the survey, 90% indicated they believed that the ratio ideally should be 1:2000 or less. Thus, on the basis of this opinion, there appears to be a shortage of school psychologists to perform appropriate functions.

For insights into the calculation of "appropriate" psychologist:student ratios, the reader is referred to an article by Valett (1965). He developed a formula for deriving the number of psychologists needed within a school system given basic information about assignments, case loads, financial support, and organization of services.

EVALUATION OF SCHOOL PSYCHOLOGICAL SERVICES

Evaluation of educational and psychological services became a major issue for psychologists during the late 1970s and early 1980s as attested to by the publication of the special issues of three major journals (See *Professional Psychology,* Vol. 8(4), 1977; *Journal of School Psychology,* Vol. 16(4), 1978; *School Psychology Review,* Vol. 9(3), 1980) and numerous other publications on the topic (e.g., Bennett, 1980; Maher, 1979; Sandoval & Lambert, 1977). The impetus for such an evaluation zeitgeist can be attributed to several forces. Internal to the profession of psychology are established standards of practice that emphasize the delivery of effective and efficient services (American Psychological Association, 1977; Pennington, 1977). In addition, such external forces as P.L. 94-142 and reductions in public school budgets have heightened public demand for the accountability of psychological services for school children with special needs (Koocher & Broskowski, 1977; Walker & Zinober, 1977).

School psychologists have been affected in two ways by the increased interest and demand for evaluation of services to children. First, they have been identified by several writers as the primary persons in schools qualified to do program evaluation (Kratochwill & Bergan, 1978, Maher, 1979, 1980; Payne, 1982). Second, the delivery of school psychological services and hence, school psychologists themselves, have been identified as also requiring and benefiting from evaluations (Bennett, 1980; Maher, 1979; Tomlinson, 1973, 1974). The focus of this section will be on the evaluation of school psychologists' performance and of school psychological service delivery systems. Of course, embedded within our discussion of the evaluation of individual school psychologists and their services will be important principles that apply equally to other types of program evaluations. Our discussion will begin with a review of techniques for evaluating individual psychologists and will progress to a review of guidelines for evaluating entire psychological service delivery systems.

Methods for Evaluating the Performance of Individual Psychologists

According to Bennett (1980), methods for evaluating the performance of school psychologists can be classified into three categories. His categories are (a) methods of direct evaluation, (b) methods of evaluation using the perception of others, and (c) methods of evaluation based on change in others.

Direct Evaluation. Methods of direct evaluation have dealt with either assessment of the psychologist's overall performance or with performance in a specific area. Clair and Kiraly (1971) believed that administrators were in the best positions to review objectively the performances of school psychologists. Thus, they advocated that administrators collect data relative to three functions of psychologists: diagnosis, intervention, and evaluation (individual assessment). Data of major importance included the number of pupil contacts, the time needed to complete psychological evaluations, and the number of in-service meetings conducted. In addition, they recommended that administrators review psychologists' personal logs, request ratings of psychologists from consumers, and establish an outside review panel of veteran school psychologists. A shortcoming of Clair and Kiraly's suggestions is that they do not provide information about interpreting the evaluation data.

Humes (1974) proposed an evaluation approach referred to as Planning, Programming, Budgeting Systems (PPBS). This approach specified objectives that were measurable steps toward general goals of service. Each performance objective (e.g., "providing consultative services to staff and administration regarding atypical children," p. 42) was to be measured in terms of efficiency and effectiveness. Efficiency of performance was based on the number of activities performed with respect to a specific objective. Effectiveness, according to the PPBS approach, is determined through direct observation of an individual psychologist. Humes, however, did not offer any guidelines for observing effectiveness.

Miller and Engin (1974) recommended the development of regional centers to which psychologists would report periodically for evaluation before qualifying for relicensing or recertification. At such a center, psychologists would be required to respond to a variety of simulated situations. For example, psychologists might be required to give an intelligence test to a child who appears on videotape and whose responses are computer-controlled. Another type of simulated task might require psychologists to respond to everyday problems contained in letters or memos. Miller and Engin suggested that all responses be documented and reviewed by an evaluation team on the basis of a set of competency-based objectives.

Research concerning the efficacy of the evaluation center approach to the direct evaluation of school psychologists has not been conducted; however, studies of the approach for assessing professionals in noneducational fields have been encouraging (Bennett, 1980). Possible disadvantages of the evaluation center model include time investment, cost, and the need to ensure test and task security.

The work of scholars interested in the direct evaluations of school psychologists' functioning in specific performance areas has been more successful than that of those evaluating overall performance. Two specific performance areas in which evaluation techniques have been developed are test administration and scoring, and consultative interviewing.

As part of an investigation of psychologists' scoring of intelligence test protocols, Miller and Chansky (1972) and Miller, Chansky, and Gredler (1970) derived a description of mechanical scoring errors made by examiners in scoring the Wechsler Intelligence Scale for Children; this description provides a possible framework for evaluating the specific skill of test scoring. Warren and Brown (1973) added to the further evaluation of specific testing skills by developing a checklist of errors to be used in evaluating the test administration skills of examiners.

The direct evaluation of consultation skills has been investigated by Bergan and his associates (Bergan, 1977; Bergan & Tombari, 1975; Kratochwill & Bergan, 1978) who have done seminal work in behavioral consultation. Through consultation research, they have established that three factors are especially critical in determining consultative outcomes. These factors are service efficiency, skill in applying psychological principles, and interviewing ability. Measures of service efficiency included the average time from referral to initial interview and the psychologist's case load. Skill in application of psychological principles was measured in terms of flexibility and included principles such as modeling; prompting; establishing, altering, or removing a discriminative stimulus; and extinction. Interviewing skill was determined by analysis of tape recordings made during a series of consultation sessions. Evaluators of school psychologists could use much of the work of Bergan and his colleagues to assess practitioners' consultations.

Evaluation Using Perceptions of Others. Conti and Bardon (1974) proposed that consumers of school psychological services (i.e., teachers, parents, students, etc.) should provide the primary data upon which to base evaluations of individual psychologists. Fairchild (1974, 1975) also believed consumer perceptions were useful in evaluating school psychologists. Specifically, he suggested eliciting feedback from school personnel as to the effectiveness of services, distributing follow-up questionnaires to teachers and parents, and contacting parents by telephone in order to gain information. No method was presented, however, for synthesizing all this varied information into a meaningful statement about an individual's performance.

Lambert and her associates (Lambert, Sandoval, & Corder, 1975; Sandoval & Lambert, 1977) believe that teachers are the best consumer information sources for school psychological services. Therefore, they have developed a variety of questionnaires to gather information. One method assesses teacher perceptions through vignettes outlining the case history of a child, accompanied by a list of school personnel whom they are requested to rate according to helpfulness in solving the child's problem. The assumption underlying this method is that teachers will continue to request assistance from psychologists who have helped them in the past. In another type of questionnaire, teachers are presented a list of possible psychological services and asked to identify those received and those not received during a specified period. Specific examples of services are provided (e.g., "helped me to plan ways to involve the child's parents in his educational program"); consequently, qualitative information about services is more apparent. A third instrument utilized by Lambert and her colleagues is referred to as the "psychologist's activities inventory." This instrument is a 40-item checklist that requires teachers to indicate the extent to which a particular activity characterizes the work of a psychologist and indicates whether the teacher desires more or less of that activity.

Lambert and her associates also proposed using measures such as teacher attendance on days the psychologist is scheduled to be in the school or counting the number of people who eat lunch with the psychologist. In addition, they believed that an examination of the number and types of referrals from teachers, and of the requests for assistance by parents and school administrators would facilitate determining whether consumers viewed a psychologist as helpful in a variety of situations.

Several researchers have questioned the use of teacher judgments as a means of evaluating school psychologists' performance (Gerken & Landau, 1979; Medway, 1977; Szmuk, Docherty, & Ringness, 1979). Collectively, these researchers have reported frequent disagreement between teachers' and school psychologists' perceptions as to psychologist effectiveness, activities performed, and amount of time spent in various activities. In contrast, Hughes (1979) found that school psychologists and their supervisors agreed in their perceptions of school psychologists' performance.

In conclusion, the data suggest that teacher judgments of school psychologists' performance are not consistent with those of school psychologists or other supervisory personnel. Schowengerdt, Fine, and Poggio (1976) believed the discrepancy between teachers' and psychologists' evaluative judgments were affected more by personality characteristics of the psychologist than by the psychologist's ability to resolve a referral problem. Thus, presently, there are no validated instruments utilizing the perceptions of others for the evaluation of school psychologists.

Evaluations Based on Changes in Others. Tomlinson (1973, 1974) has been the primary proponent of an evaluation method whereby the effectiveness of a psychologist is assessed against the behavior of a mediator (i.e., teacher or parent, in most cases) and the behavior of a target child. According to Tomlinson's approach, a set of target behaviors for each referred case is specified and a behavioral description of each target behavior, measured in terms of current functioning level, is developed by the psychologist. Following the completion of a case, a follow-up interview with the mediator(s) is done to determine both whether the psychologist's recommendations were implemented and what changes occurred in the target behavior. After conferring with the mediator(s), a psychologist rates the direction and degree of behavior change exhibited by the target child.

Tomlinson employed this method of evaluation with a metropolitan staff of school psychologists and found it to be an effective technique. He is aware, however, that the method can be criticized since it depends upon teachers' reports of behavior change and psychologists' ratings of effectiveness.

In conclusion, there are presently no validated instruments or techniques for evaluating school psychologists through change in clients' behavior. The general premise of proponents of this type of evaluation method is questionable since it fails to account for numerous behavior change variables other than those manipulated by a psychologist.

As can be discerned from our examination of evaluation techniques, the persons responsible for the evaluation of an individual school psychologist's performance are working in an area devoid of empirically validated instruments. Bennett (1980), however, has developed a rather extensive list of recommendations which should, if followed, improve the quality of any evaluation. In general, Bennett subscribes to a multivariate model of evaluation in which the functions to be assessed vary according to the way in which a psychologist's role has

Table 2.4   Bennett's Recommendations for Evaluation of School Psychologists[a]

1. Specify the purpose for evaluation.
2. Specify the role(s) and function(s) of the psychologist to be assessed.
3. Specify the duties performed by the psychologist in the particular role(s) and function(s) served.
4. Specify the function(s) most central to the role(s) served. Then specify the duties most central to the function(s) performed.
5. Determine whether processes and/or products associated with specific duties should be evaluated.
6. Choose instruments for evaluating the processes and products associated with those specific duties judged most central to the role.
7. Make attempts to check the reliability of your assessments with another evaluator.
8. Evalute each specific duty using as many instances of the process or product as is practical.
9. Evaluate each specific duty, trying to gather as representative a sample of process or product as possible.
10. Synthesize the data gathered.
11. Interpret the synthesized data.
12. Make a determination as to the validity of the assessment.
13. Give the psychologist feedback as soon as possible regarding the results of evaluation.
14. Formally report evaluation results.
15. Use the data gained from assessment for the purpose specified at the beginning of the evaluation process.

[a]Adapted from Bennett (1980).

been defined. An outline of Bennett's evaluation recommendations appears in Table 2.4. The reader is referred to the original article for a detailed discussion of each recommendation.

Methods for Evaluation of School Psychology Delivery Systems

The evaluation of an entire psychological service delivery system would seem to be a tremendous undertaking in a school district employing more than four or five psychologists. A comprehensive evaluation certainly would involve several levels of assessment, starting with the performances of individuals within a given service unit and moving to an analysis of interactions among the groups of service providers within an entire school district. Maher (1978, 1979, 1980), who perhaps has written the most on the evaluation of school psychology delivery systems, developed and researched a set of evaluation guidelines which provide for just such a comprehensive evaluation.

In order to comprehend Maher's guidelines fully, a reader needs to understand his conception and description of service delivery. According to Maher (1979), a school psychology service delivery system can be thought of as an open social system possessing a definable structure and functioning in a particular manner. Specifically, Maher (1979) states:

> In terms of *structure,* a System has boundaries that filter the kind and rate of interactions the System has with its external environment (e.g., pupils, teachers, instructional systems). System *function* is characterized by (a) *input* in terms of psychologists, clients, materials, and constraints; (b) *throughput,* which involves the delivery of assessment, intervention, evaluation, and consultation services; (c) *output,* consisting of products delivered such as the amount of services rendered to various client types; (d) *outcome,* which denotes change in client behavior, motivation, or attitude; and (e) *feedback,* whereby information is received by the System for modification of its functioning. (p. 204)

Using the characteristics of a system's structure and functions as an organizer, Maher outlined and operationalized the eight evaluation guidelines which follow.

System Structure. Prior to assessing any service system, an evaluator needs to have an understanding of the various services provided by the system and of the purposes such services fulfill. Thus, Maher's first guideline is: *The system is defined by a conceptual framework.* In applying this guideline, it was suggested that systems have a procedure manual detailing service policies and practices. Such a manual facilitates communications with consumers as well as evaluators. The flowchart of consultation-assessment-intervention services discussed and illustrated (see Figure 2.3) earlier in this chapter could also provide the type of conceptual framework Maher advocates.

System Input. Standards of professional practice and special education legislation require that handicapped students be identified and their psychological needs be assessed in a manner that is technically adequate. Therefore, it is desirable for a service system to have specified procedures for identification and assessment purposes. Consequently, Maher's second evaluation guideline is: *The System has procedures for the identification and assessment of clients.*

Once students are identified, assessed, and determined to need help, individual intervention programs must be designed to address their needs. The various intervention programs offered should be monitored and modified when necessary to ensure appropriate services. It follows that Maher's third evaluation guideline is: *The System maintains a compendium of current school psychology services and programs which are provided to its clients.*

In some cases, students referred for school psychological services have contact with other service systems, many of which are internal to the school district but beyond the System's boundaries (e.g., guidance and counseling department, school health department). Some contacts may also be external to the school district, such as a community mental health center or hospital. In order to eliminate redundancy of service delivery efforts among service providers, it would be helpful to explicate procedures for increasing intersystem services coordination. Hence, Maher's fourth evaluation recommendation is: *The System has procedures for identification of services and programs outside its boundaries which impact on mutual clients.*

System Throughput. A major goal implicit in all psychological services is the improvement of human functioning. Thus, students identified as clients of the System should be provided "appropriate" service programs. According to Maher, appropriate programs are those which have a design based on technically adequate assessment information and which are linked to goals with specific evaluative criteria (goal indicators). A fifth evaluative guideline follows from this and is stated: *The System has provisions for ensuring a planned sequence of appropriate goal-oriented programs for its clients.*

System Output and Outcome. In order to continue to provide "appropriate" psychological services, the impact of such services on client functioning in the behavioral, emotional, and social domains needs to be reviewed on a regular basis. Such a review should involve the use of two kinds of evaluation methods: process evaluation and outcome evaluation (Maher, 1979).

Process evaluation focuses on System output. The intent is to assess the extent to which programs and services are operating according to predefined plans or criteria (Scriven, 1974). Information critical to a process evaluation of a school psychological delivery system would include variables such as (a) frequency of services rendered relative to services that were planned, (b) quality of services rendered, and (c) positive and negative side effects related to service delivery. Outcome evaluation focuses on System outcome. In other words, outcome evaluation provides information on the degree to which clients are progressing toward program goals. Goal attainment scaling techniques are particularly useful in documenting client progress (Kiresuk & Sherman, 1968).

Based on the need for frequent review of services, Maher recommended a sixth evaluation guideline: *The System has a review process to ascertain that services and programs are being provided and that client progress is occurring as expected.*

System Feedback. The needs of clients change over time; therefore, school psychological services must be flexible and adapt to address clients' needs. Flexibility of services is enhanced through the maintenance of information about client variables (e.g., needs, goals, and degree of goal attainment) and system variables (e.g., amount of service time provided, frequency of services delivered, and costs of services). Such an information bank aids decision-making and provides valuable evaluative data. Hence, it is desirable for a service delivery system to develop an organized store of information about its clients and services. It logically follows that Maher's seventh evaluation guideline is: *The System possesses evaluation capability.*

A school psychology service system, to remain an open social system, must maintain permeable boundaries in relation to other service systems both within and outside the school district. Maher believes regular self-evaluations enhance the probability of the system remaining open. Therefore, he recommended as the eighth evaluation guideline that: *The System has a procedure for evaluation of itself.* According to Maher, such a self-evaluation involves three tasks: (a) determining the extent to which evaluative information used by the System is valid, reliable, representative, and is managed in a confidential manner; (b) assessing the extent to which the System engages in research and development activities to test and validate alternative programmatic strategies; and (c) obtaining an understanding of the strengths and weaknesses of the System as perceived by its clients and by System staff.

CONCLUSION

This discussion of the evaluation of psychologists and their services completes our examination of school psychological service delivery systems. Just as at the conclusion of a good evaluation, we hope you have gained valuable insights into the structure and function of school psychological services and are now armed with knowledge and skills which will enable you to refine the services you provide to children, parents, and teachers in the future.

Chapters 3, 4, and 5 focus on three central services of school psychologists: consultation, assessment, and intervention. Based on the present chapter, readers should have an appreciation of the interdependencies among these three types of service. Consequently, we chose to order the chapters in a way that reflects the typical sequence in which consultation, assessment, and intervention take place. Be prepared for detailed discussions of these three major service functions.

3

Psychological Consultation: Indirect Service Delivery[1]

Consultation is viewed as a significant component of all school psychological service delivery systems and has become one of the major professional functions for school psychologists. Despite this substantive interest in consultation, however, there is still much confusion among school psychologists as to what constitutes consultation, per se. Part of the problem is that the term "consultation" is used in so many contexts and in reference to so many different types of service relationships that the word has almost become devoid of meaning (Gallessich, 1973; Gibbins, 1978; Reschly, 1976). Barry (1970) observes, "Today almost everyone is a consultant. Every program has consultants. Sometimes it seems as if there are more consultants than consultees!" (p. 362). As noted in Chapter 2, there is no single definition of consultation with universal support. We favor Medway's (1979b) approach, which defines consultation as a process of "collaborative problem-solving between a mental health specialist (the consultant) and one or more persons (the consultees) who are responsible for providing some form of psychological assistance to another (the client)" (p. 276).

CORE CHARACTERISTICS OF SCHOOL BASED CONSULTATION MODELS

Although there are numerous specific approaches to consultation that differ along a variety of dimensions, there exists a central core of elements that are common

[1]Sections of this chapter were adapted from Gutkin and Curtis (1982).

to almost all consultation models. These elements, which serve to define the interactive process between the consultant and the consultee, are presented below.

Indirect Service Delivery

The single most definitive aspect of consultation is the indirect service delivery concept. In the more traditional system of direct service delivery, the psychologist's primary contact is with a client (or patient) who receives services directly from the psychologist. Psychotherapy and counseling are common exemplars of direct services. Psychologists working from an indirect service delivery model, however, primarily interact with other professionals (consultees) who work directly with clients, rather than with the clients themselves. In school-based consultation, the consultant is typically a school psychologist, the consultee is typically a teacher, and the client is typically a student. Of course, other alignments are also possible, such as when principals, teacher aides, or parents serve as consultees. Regardless of the specific case, however, when functioning as a consultant, the psychologist provides indirect services to clients by working with consultees who have direct contact with clients. These relationships were illustrated in Figure 2.2 and are repeated in Figure 3.1.

Focus of Consultation

School-based consultation focuses on professional problems. Personal, nonprofessional data are discussed only as they relate to presenting work-related

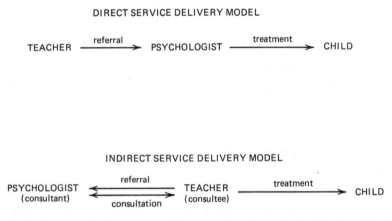

Figure 3.1. Direct and indirect service delivery models. (From Gutkin & Curtis, 1982. Reprinted by permission.)

issues (Caplan, 1970). In this sense, consultation is clearly distinct from psychotherapy. Within these confines, problems relating to both prevention and remediation are appropriate foci for consultation.

Goals of Consultation

Every consultation model has a dual set of goals. One goal is to provide remedial services for presenting problems; another goal is to improve consultees' functioning so they can prevent and/or respond more effectively to similar problems in the future. The degree of emphasis placed on each of these goals varies across consultation models, but both goals should always be present in the consultant's mind as he or she works with consultees.

Consultant—Consultee Relationship

In consultation, the consultant's ability to deliver a service to the client is dependent upon the behaviors of the consultee. As such, the establishment of an open, trusting relationship between the consultant and the consultee is of paramount importance (Dinkmeyer & Carlson, 1973; Martin, 1978; Williams, 1972). As Russ (1978) points out:

> First, the fact that the consultant accepts, respects, and sees the consultee as a significant person aids in helping the consultee to see his/her own potential as an effective person. The expectation that change is possible, a message the consultant is continually giving, is often a first step in fostering change. Second, within the context of a "safe" relationship, consultees will be more able to take risks, both in thought and action. Third, a trusting relationship is more facilitative for expressing feelings and exploring attitudes. Fourth, modeling of the consultant's problem-solving behavior is more likely to occur if the consultant is respected and becomes a significant person to the consultee. (p. 149)

Rapport between the consultant and the consultee is thus seen as a prerequisite to effective consultation.

Coordinate Status. Among the most important aspects of the consultation relationship is the coordinate status of the consultant and the consultee (Caplan, 1970). It is believed that hierarchical power relationships might restrict the free flow of communication and the development of rapport (Alpert, 1977; Kramer & Nagel, 1980; Kurpuis, 1978; Pryzwansky, 1974; Tageson & Corazzini, 1974). The consultee is thus viewed as an equal rather than as a subordinate to the consultant and therefore has equal authority in the decision-making process.

Both the consultant and the consultee are considered to be professionals. The psychologist is viewed as an expert in the area of human behavior while the teacher is viewed as an expert in the area of education and the workings of the classroom. By collaboratively combining these areas of expertise, the consultant and consultee can create a rich mix of ideas from which creative responses to presenting problems are likely to arise (Sandoval, 1977). In support of these assumptions, Wenger (1979) reported increased consultee satisfaction with collaborative as opposed to non-collaborative consultation contacts.

Involvement of the Consultee in the Consultation Process. The active involvement of the consultee in the consultation process is seen as a crucial element in successful consultation (Carter, 1975; Dinkmeyer & Dinkmeyer, 1976; Feldman, 1979; Sandoval, Lambert & Davis, 1977; Zins & Curtis, 1981). For one thing, it is believed that "the consultant can seldom learn enough about the classroom, teacher(s), or the various human ecological systems operating to 'really' know what a better course of action would be in order to improve a particular environment" (Pyle, 1977, p. 193). Furthermore, failure to involve the consultee in the consultation process might result in the consultee's failure to "own" resulting treatment plans and may thus decrease the probability that the consultee will properly carry out the interventions to which they have agreed (Curtis & Anderson, 1976). Reinking, Livesay, and Kohl (1978) have provided some empirical support for this latter assumption by demonstrating that a consultee's implementation of programs generated as a result of consultation is directly related to the degree of consultee involvement in the problem-solving process. Similarly, Colligan and McColgan (1980) reported that satisfaction with consultative services increased as a function of consultee involvement in all stages of the consultation process.

Consultants are responsible for helping consultees become active in the consultation process. Some have argued that this is an uphill struggle because: (a) consultees often want psychologists to provide them with quick solutions, easy answers, and confirmations of their own perceptions rather than to engage them in mutual problem solving (Berkowitz, 1975; Lambert, 1976; Lambert, Yandell, & Sandoval, 1975; Sandoval, Lambert & Davis, 1977), and (b) most teachers are ill prepared to assume their responsibilities as consultees because they have received little, if any, training for this function (Bardon, 1977). Studies addressing this issue have produced mixed results. Gutkin and Curtis (1982) provide an extensive list of studies showing that teachers and other school personnel feel quite positively about consultative approaches, often preferring them over the more traditional service delivery models in which they typically have a more passive role. After surveying active teachers, Foster and O'Leary (1977) concluded, "a majority of teachers favor normal class placement for the conduct problem child. Special classes are generally disliked and seen as less desirable

than many other ways of handling behavior problems . . . services or consultation in the regular classroom received the highest teacher ratings'' (p. 109). Ford
and Migles (1979), however, reported that teachers generally preferred school
psychologist activities "which did not require the school psychologist to intrude
on teacher's perogatives" although "teachers . . . using 'open education' methods were significantly more likely to value more indirect, preventive, and collaborative school psychology services than their colleagues'' (p. 372).

Medway (1979a) and Vernberg and Medway (1981) found that teachers
more frequently believe student problems to be the result of home and/or child
factors rather than variables relating to the teaching environment. It is quite
possible that attitudes such as these leave teachers feeling impotent and thus
resistant to being involved actively in consultative problem solving. Gutkin and
Ajchenbaum (in press) and Clark and Gutkin (1982), in fact, found that teacher
preferences for consultation services were related positively to the degree of
control they felt they had over presenting problems.

Experience tells us that there is a considerable range of variability among
consultees regarding the degree to which they desire to be involved in the
consultation process. As such, school psychologists will have an easier time
getting some consultees actively involved than others. Whatever the degree of
difficulty, however, consultee participation along with the consultant is an
important goal towards which the consultant should strive.

Consultee's Right to Reject Consultant's Suggestions. An explicit aspect of
the consultation process is the consultee's right to reject any suggestion made by
the consultant (Alpert, 1976; Beisser & Green, 1972; Caplan, 1970; Fisher,
1974; Meyers, 1973). Although Bowers (1971) humorously suggested a variety
of ways in which psychologists can intimidate others, the fact of the matter is that
school psychologists do not have the administrative power to force consultees to
take steps against their own will (Sandoval, Lambert, & Davis, 1977; Martin,
1978). As has been noted:

> Once the door to the classroom is closed, there is little that any of the educational
> specialists can do to insure the occurrence of any event that the teacher does not want
> to occur. . . . We must recognize that if a teacher decides that a remedial program is
> inappropriate, it is highly likely that the plan will never be implemented. This would
> be true regardless of the actual quality of the particular program. (Gutkin & Curtis,
> 1981, pp. 220–221)

Attempting to force a consultee to accept a consultant's suggestions typically results in a situation where either the consultee refuses to act on the
recommendations, or the recommendations are carried out by the consultee in
such a way as to ensure their failure. The development of a power struggle
between the consultant and the consultee would also seriously damage rapport

and thus lower the probability of success in subsequent consultation intended to arrive at new, more effective interventions (Dorr, 1977).

The consultee's right to reject consultant suggestions, however, should not lead the consultant prematurely to abandon ideas that he or she thinks are viable even though they are not to the consultee's liking (Abidin, 1972). Consultants should, of course, consider consultees' reasons for rejecting ideas and determine if these objections have merit. Beyond this, however, consultants should use all their persuasive powers, short of creating a win-lose power struggle, to help consultees see the validity of the strategies that they are proposing. If this fails, consultants may often be better off to go along with the consultees' ideas, although extreme circumstances may call for the use of confrontation techniques. If a consultee's alternative solutions prove effective, then the presenting problem is solved and the consultation is deemed a success. If, on the other hand, the consultee's ideas do not produce the desired results, the consultee may well be ready to reconsider the consultant's original suggestions, provided that the rapport between the consultant and the consultee has remained strong.

One final point needs to be considered in relationship to the consultee's right to reject the consultant's suggestions. Regardless of the consultee's opinion, the consultant should not negotiate points of fact. For example, if a consultee insists that a child with a given IQ is retarded despite evidence of adequate adaptive behavior, the consultant is compelled to point out that the IQ may actually be markedly higher when one takes into account the test's standard error of measurement and that the diagnosis of retardation requires concomitant subnormal functioning in the sphere of adaptive behavior. From the perspective of consultation theory, the objective would be to point out these facts to the consultee without endangering rapport and the consultee's coordinate status.

Voluntary Nature of Consultation. As might be surmised from the concepts previously presented, the consultation relationship should be one which is voluntary (Alpert, 1976; Fisher, 1974). Trying to force a teacher to serve as an effective consultee is very difficult (Gaupp, 1966). Hinkle, Silverstein, and Walton (1977) report retrospective data indicating that consultees' failure to adopt recommendations occurs most often when principals request teachers to obtain consultation when the teachers themselves do not want consultative assistance.

Ideally, consultation should be initiated by the consultee, who is seeking assistance with a particular problem (Dinkmeyer & Carlson, 1973). Consultee initiation reflects at least two factors that are important for effective consultation. First, the consultee recognizes that a problem exists. Such is not always the case when consultation is initiated by persons other than the consultee. Second, the fact that the consultee has initiated contact suggests he or she may be motivated to do something about the problem (Curtis & Anderson, 1976a). As Lambert (1974) pointed out, however, the reality of school consultation frequently involves initial contacts made by the consultant, sometimes at the request of the principal. The bottom line, nevertheless, is not who initiates the relationship but rather whether the continuation of the relationship is voluntary. Therefore, it may be appropriate for a consultant to approach a teacher as long as the final decision to continue or terminate the relationship resides with the consultee.

Obviously, there will be times when involuntary relationships with teachers will be mandated (Lambert 1974; Sandoval, 1977). Psychologists are frequently assigned by central adminstration staff, IEP teams, principals, and/or parents to work with teachers who do not want their assistance. Especially subtle and problematic are those instances in which a teacher is ordered to work with a psychologist but, for the purposes of saving face for the teacher, the psychologist is never overtly informed of the mandatory nature of the interaction. In such cases, consultation may prove to be ineffective.

Confidentiality. An essential element of the consultation process is the confidentiality of information shared between the consultant and the consultee (Caplan, 1970; Curtis & Anderson, 1976; Sandoval, Lambert, & Davis, 1977). The consultee's awareness that whatever is shared with the consultant will go no further than the consultant, creates a mind set for the consultee which facilitates the open, honest communication necessary for effective consultation. Consultees are unlikely to discuss their professional shortcomings or other sensitive matters if they feel this information will be made available to either superiors, subordinates, or peers. Indirect empirical support for this position comes from an analogue study which reported client self-disclosure during a clinical interview fluctuated as a function of varying levels of confidentiality (Woods & McNamara, 1980). At all points during a consultation, there should be agreement between the consultant and the consultee as to which aspects of their relationship are public and which are confidential. This confidentiality, of course, has no legal status unless the consultation occurs in a state with laws which deem communication with a psychologist to be privileged information.

Confidentiality can be a sensitive issue. For example, many principals will claim that because they are legally and administratively responsible for everything that transpires in their schools, they have a legitimate need to know the content of consultant–consultee interactions. While this need seems to be justifiable, it is usually the case that what the principal really needs to know is not the content of the communication as much as the products and decisions resulting from the consultation. There should be no problem in informing a principal of the latter (e.g., Johnny is going to be given stars as a reward for completing his math assignments) as long as the former (e.g., Mrs. Smith feels that her teaching skills in the area of third grade mathematics are below par) remains confidential (Alpert, 1976). A similar line of logic can be applied to sharing information with parents and groups such as IEP teams.

Consultant Process vs. Content Expertise

The distinction between process and content is particularly critical for conceptualizing consultation interactions. Content can best be understood as the informational components that are discussed during a consultation. Process, on the other hand, relates to the manner in which this information gets used. For example, the content elements of a typical case could include things such as a list of the referred child's problems, facts about his or her home situation, test scores, a description of effective interventions, etc. Process issues for this same case would include, among other things, the nature of the relationship between the consultant and consultee (e.g., coordinate vs. hierarchical status), clarity of verbal communication, degree of consultee involvement in problem-solving efforts, whether the generation of possible solutions for the presenting problem is withheld until the problem has been adequately defined, etc.

First and foremost, school psychologists serving as consultants must be process experts, even if they have little content expertise (Raffianiello, 1981). Schein (1969), Williams (1972), and Broskowski (1973) point out that consultants can be effective even if they are consulting in areas about which they have little content expertise, as long as they understand the process of problem solving and are able to steer the consultation interaction in directions which are consonant with this process. We disagree somewhat with this position because content expertise is critical for a school psychologist's credibility with teachers and other educational personnel; we do agree, however, that the major responsibility of the consultant during consultation is to maintain and direct the problem-solving process. It is not the consultant's responsibility to have all of the facts and all of the answers regarding the problems raised (Schein, 1978; Williams, 1972). The contribution of content expertise during consultation is the responsibility of *both* the consultant and the consultee. It is, however, the consultant's responsibility to be expert in the interpersonal processes by which problems come to be solved (Hollister & Miller, 1977) and to help the consultee learn to use these processes more effectively (Russ, 1978). In support of these assumptions, Wilcox (1980) found that consultees' attitudes towards a consultant and the consultation process were significantly related to consultants' process control in group consultation settings (*r*s were .88 and .83, respectively).

MAJOR APPROACHES TO SCHOOL-BASED CONSULTATION

What follows is a presentation of three major models of school-based consultation, that is, ecological, mental health, and organizational consultation. These models all have the core characteristics of school-based consultation, but differ in regard to: a) the psychological theories upon which they are premised, and b) the assessment and intervention practices upon which they depend most heavily.

Ecological Consultation

Terminology Issues. Prior to discussing the ecological consultation model in some detail, a brief word regarding terminology is in order. Many readers may recognize the concepts discussed in this section as points typically associated with consultation models carrying other names, for example, "problem-solving" (Gutkin & Curtis, 1982) and "behavioral" (Bergan, 1977) consultation. The title "ecological" consultation, however, is used in this text for a variety of reasons. While the name "problem-solving" consultation provides an accurate descriptor of the processes occurring within that approach (D'Zurilla & Goldfried, 1971; Osborn, 1963), it fails to distinguish this particular consultation model from others. The confusion results from the fact that *all* consultation models are designed to solve problems, even though the process of each is somewhat different. To single out a particular method as "problem-solving" consultation incorrectly implies that other consultation approaches are less likely to generate solutions to presenting problems.

Although the term "behavioral" consultation currently enjoys considerable popularity, it is also a less than optimal descriptor. As several authors have noted (e.g., Gallessich & Davis, 1981; Keller, 1981), the practice of this technique is based on a range of psychological theories and research that is broader than this title implies. The school psychologist employing "behavioral" consultation is not, in fact, limited to a behaviorist paradigm, although many school personnel upon hearing this term automatically (albeit, incorrectly) envision a rigid application of behavior modification approaches.

The title "ecological" consultation is preferred because it describes most accurately the complex theory base within which lies much of what has previously been referred to as "problem-solving" and "behavioral" consultation. Several recent works, in fact, have focused on the underlying points of commonality between behavioral and ecological psychology (Petrie, Brown, Piersel, Frinfrock, Schelble, LeBlanc, & Kratochwill, 1980; Rogers-Warren & Warren, 1977).

Underlying Psychological Theory. The assessment and intervention information generated during ecological consultation primarily reflects the theory and research of ecological and behavioral theories of psychology. Of particular import has been Bandura's (1978) notion of reciprocal determinism. Client behavior (B), the personological characteristics of the client (P), and the environment within which the client functions (E) are viewed as inextricably interrelated. Modification within any of these three dimensions is thought to have an impact on each of the others. Planned changes in any or all of these three spheres can be brought about by manipulating variables associated with any or all of them. The client's behavior, personology, and environment form an ecosystem within which each is mutually and reciprocally influenced by the others (see Figure 2.1 or 3.2).

Within this framework, presenting problems are conceptualized as resulting from an inappropriate fit between *B, P,* and *E* rather than as the result of any one of these three dimensions in isolation from the others. The traditional, medical model, "blame the victim"mindset is thus viewed as inappropriately simplistic due to its near exclusive focus on P variables. From an ecological perspective, psychological and educational problems can be understood and resolved only by addressing the complex and reciprocal interactions between *B, P,* and *E* variables. It is assumed that psychologists can not design adequate interventions and treatment plans for children unless they understand and influence the environmental context within which behavioral and personological problems arise. Although built on a broader base of psychological theory, this conceptualization of school psychological services is not unlike the psychosituational and systems analysis models espoused earlier by Bersoff (1973) and Minor (1972), respectively.

Assessment and Intervention. When using ecological consultation, the collection of assessment data and the generation of intervention strategies are structured around the work of Osborn (1963), who set forth most of the basic principles of problem solving, and the works of D'Zurilla and Goldfried (1971), Heppner (1978), and Carkhuff (1973), who related this problem-solving process to the delivery of psychological services for individual clients. Table 3.1 presents one version of this problem-solving sequence which may be particularly useful for school-based consultants. Although many variations of this material have been presented in school psychology literature (e.g., Bergan, 1977; Brown & Kelly, 1976; Hollister & Miller, 1977; Schmuck, Runkel, Arends, & Arends, 1977), differences among them have been largely limited to terminology rather than substance. The reader can best observe this by comparing the steps presented in Table 3.1 (also presented in Table 2.1) with those recommended, for

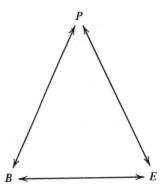

Figure 3.2. Adapted from Bandura, 1978. Reprinted by permission.

Table 3.1   Problem-solving Sequence

1. Define and clarify the problem.
2. Assess and diagnose the problem.
3. Brainstorm interventions.
4. Evaluate and choose among alternatives.
5. Specify consultee and consultant responsibilities.
6. Implement the chosen strategy.
7. Evaluate the effectiveness of the action and recycle if necessary.

Note: Adapted from T. B. Gutkin & M. J. Curtis, "School-Based Consultation: Theory and Techniques." In C. R. Reynolds & T. B. Gutkin (Eds.), *The Handbook of School Psychology.* New York: John Wiley & Sons, 1982. Reprinted by permission.

example, by Bergan (1977), that is, problem identification, problem analysis, plan implementation, and plan evaluation.

Although presented as a specific sequence of events, actual problem solving rarely proceeds in the exact lockstep order which is depicted in Table 3.1. Movement back and forth between steps is quite frequent because: (a) the verbal interaction between consultant and consultee cannot be controlled to the point where their communications follow the theoretical sequence in a precise fashion, and (b) information arising at any particular step may suggest a need to reinterpret material from a prior step. The ordering of steps presented in Table 3.1 should be viewed by the reader as a set of flexible guidelines to be adhered to when the situation permits, rather than as a rigid sequence of events.

Step 1: Define and Clarify the Problem. Most authors agree that defining and clarifying the presenting problem is a critical first step in the problem-solving process (Curtis & Anderson, 1976; Hollister & Miller, 1977; Meyers, Parsons, & Martin, 1979). The *manner* in which a problem is defined sets important parameters for the remainder of the consultation interaction (Deno, 1975). Tombari and Bergan (1978), for example, found the use of behavioral rather than medical model problem definitions and verbal cues positively affected consultee expectations for problem resolution. In another study of consultation outcomes, Bergan and Tombari (1976) reported that "Once consultative problem solving . . . was carried through problem identification, problem solution almost invariabley resulted" (p. 12).

Although the problem definition stage appears on the surface to be quite simple, it is, in fact, one of the most difficult tasks facing the consultant. Inexperienced consultants tend to rush through this stage in an attempt to reach the solution generation phase of the process. Curtis and Watson (1980) have

provided data which indicate that low skill consultants may inadvertantly reinforce consultee's tendencies to move too rapidly through problem definition and
into the evaluation of problem solutions. Under these conditions, the ensuing
analysis of the problem and the brainstorming of alternatives will be less than
satisfactory because of the consultant's and consultee's failure to invest more
effort and time in the problem definition stage. The same study, however,
demonstrated that working with highly skilled consultants resulted in improved
problem definition skills for consultees.

A useful problem definition is one that is stated in concrete, behavioral
terms (Witt & Elliott, 1983). If at all possible, the identified behavior should be
one which is both observable and amenable to quantification. Unfortunately,
Lambert's (1976) study of elementary school teachers led her to conclude that
teachers experience considerable difficulty when trying to specify pupil problems
in this manner. She found that teachers tended to report student problems with
general and vague statements (e.g., the child is poorly motivated, the student has
low ability) rather than in terms that have clear implications for ''operational
changes in classroom practice'' (p. 516).

Typically, presenting cases will have more than one identifiable problem.
Experience tells us that children most often evidence multiple rather than singular difficulties. Social-adjustment problems, for example, often occur concomi-
tantly with academic and family dysfunction. Low achievers frequently experience emotional as well as academic difficulties. In order to develop an effective
problem definition under these circumstances, the consultant should help the
consultee divide the problem into its component parts, prioritize these component parts, and then work toward a behavioral definition for the most important
component that has been identified. This procedure helps the consultee reduce
the complexity of a problem so that he or she can avoid being overwhelmed.

Before leaving the problem definition phase, the consultant should engage
the consultee in an examination of goals for the client (Curtis & Anderson, 1976;
Witt & Elliott, 1983). Even after consensus has been reached on problem definition, the consultant and consultee may not agree on goals (Smith, 1981). In such
cases, a constructive airing of differences will be important. It is also critical that
the consultee's expectations for client improvement be realistic. Lack of attention to this task may result in consultee and consultant perceptions of failure even
when an effective intervention has been implemented. If, for example, a child
engages in less than two social interactions with peers per day and a teacher's
goal is to design an intervention which will make the child one of the class' most
popular students, the consultant would be remiss if he or she failed to help the
consultee explore whether such a goal was realistic. Proceeding with the problem-solving process without the identification of a more realistic goal would
almost certainly doom the entire process to failure.

Step 2: Assess and Diagnose the Problem. The major task at this stage is to assess and diagnose the presenting problem and the ecological context within which it is occurring. The consultant, in effect, helps the consultee conduct a force field analysis (Lewin, 1951) of the current situation. Data relating to behavioral, personological, and environmental variables should be explored in depth at this point. What factors contribute to the problem or impede its resolution? How do these factors interrelate with each other and cause or support the continuation of the problem? Of equal relevance, but often overlooked by consultees, what factors may facilitate the problem's resolution? Although some consultees may protest to the contrary, no situation is entirely bleak. No child is entirely without strengths that can be built on. No school system is entirely without the kinds of support that contribute to the establishment of effective programs. The consultant must help the consultee discover the range of available resources in order to help construct an effective intervention (Hollister & Miller, 1977).

Data gathering procedures yielding information pertaining to B, P, and E are all relevant and potentially important. The best data sources, however, will be those which provide information regarding the reciprocal interactions among B, P, and E rather than those which shed light on B, P, and E in isolation from each other. Teacher interview and classroom observation are thus the primary sources of assessment data for school psychologists using the ecological model of consultation. Both of these approaches provide an opportunity to assess the manner in which the child's behavior, personality, and environment interact and mutually influence each other. For cases in which the presenting problem is more home than school based, parent interview and home observation would be logical substitutes.

Although teacher interviews will usually be a good source of accurate data, consultants should not take this for granted in any given instance. There is, for example, research evidence to indicate that teachers are not always accurate observers of their own behavior or that of the children in their classrooms (Hook & Rosenshine, 1959). This should come as no surprise given the fact that they are extraordinarily busy. Jackson (1968) reports that teachers engage in as many as 1,000 interpersonal interactions each day and are relatively untrained in observational techniques. One of the consultant's goals, of course, would be to improve the consultee's observational skills when they are inadequate. We note, however, that because teacher interview data reflect the consultee's subjective perceptions of the problem and because the teacher is a major part of the ecological system within which the problem exists, teacher interviews should always be looked upon as significant even when the resulting information does not provide an accurate picture of reality. In such instances, the consultant would need to collect data from additional sources to determine the objective facts of the situation. The consultant's ability to see the problem through the consultee's eyes is, however, always an important ingredient in successful consultation. Conducting a skillful interview with the consultee should always be of great value to the consultant in this regard.

Depending on the specifics of the situation, interview and observation may not provide enough data for the consultant and the consultee to generate effective interventions. In these instances, interview and observation data will have to be supplemented with information from other sources. Norm and criterion referenced tests, behavior assessment, sociometrics, work samples, child interviews, medical history, etc. may each provide additional useful information.

Although many ecological consultants have tended to shy away from using normative test data, we believe it is important to avoid "throwing out the baby with the bath water." Norm referenced tests are not the assessment source of first choice because they generally emphasize P data in isolation from the relevant B and E elements; they do, however, supply information that has a legitimate place within the reciprocal determinism paradigm. Probably the greatest problem with normative test scores is the way in which they are misused. After being exposed to WISC-R, TAT, Bender, etc. types of information, there seems to be a tendancy among both consultants and consultees inadvertantly to drift away from an ecological mindset (i.e., the problem lies in the inappropriate fit between B, P, and E) and towards a medical model perspective (i.e., the child is "sick"). Although consultants can overcome this problem for themselves by exercising some mental discipline, it is often more difficult to control the consultee's reactions to these types of data because they may serve to reinforce the consultee's preconceived medical model image of a child's problem. Deno (1975) presents a case study and Bergan, Byrnes, and Kratochwill (1979) report empirical evidence supporting this theory. School psychologists should thus be cognizant of the potential problems involved in placing too much emphasis on norm referenced test scores during a consultation interaction. They must, however, remain receptive to the appropriate use of these data when relevant to the case in question.

The ecological orientation to consultative services also underscores the enormous complexity of diagnosis. Because presenting problems are viewed as an inappropriate fit between B, P, and E variables, comprehensive diagnoses have to take account of each of these dimensions as they interact and mutually influence each other. Current diagnostic systems, such as those provided by PL 94-142, DSM III, GAP, etc., are almost exclusively oriented towards identifying pathologies existing within the client (P variables) and are thus conceptually inadequate for the task at hand. In point of fact, there is at this time no adequate formal classification nosology that is capable of deriving reliable and valid diagnoses accounting for the interaction among B, P, and E variables.

Step 3: Brainstorm Interventions. At this point in the process, the consultee and the consultant should have a clear understanding of the problem definition and of the ecological context within which the problem occurs. They are now prepared to begin enumerating potential solutions.

Whenever possible, four rules of brainstorming should be followed. First, produce as many ideas as possible. It is presumed that the more solutions the consultant and consultee are able to produce, the more likely they are to design an ideal or high quality solution. For example, empirical research has demonstrated that ideas generated during the latter portions of brainstorming are more creative than thoughts that are produced early on (Parnes & Meadow, 1959). Second, free-wheeling is encouraged. The consultant and consultee should let their imaginations run loose. D'Zurilla and Golfried (1971) caution participants, however, they should engage in "limited-criteria thinking" rather than "free association." The consultant and consultee should limit their responses "so that they are clearly relevant to dealing with such-and-such a problem or situation" (p. 115). Total suspension of judgment is thus seen as inappropriate. Third, at this point in the process, criticism of ideas is ruled out. Both the consultant and the consultee should refrain from evaluating the quality of the ideas generated because this would serve to reduce the number of ideas that might otherwise be produced. Fourth, combine and modify the ideas generated earlier. The consultant and consultee may find revision and synthesis of individual ideas will result in a new strategy that is superior to the originals. D'Zurilla and Goldried (1971) and Heppner (1978) discuss a considerable body of research that addresses the efficacy of this four-step brainstorming process.

As might be expected from an ecological approach to consultation services, the range of interventions logically consistent with this paradigm are enormous. The consultant and consultee are free to choose from either the *B, P,* or *E* spheres, or some combination of these dimensions, in order to bring about improvement in presenting problems. Specific choices will, of course, depend on the particulars of each presenting case, although some general rules can be pointed out.

Most often, the consultant and consultee will opt for extra-personal strategies (Meyers, 1973) drawn from the *B* and *E* spheres because they are usually easy to implement, compatible with the workings of classrooms and schools, fast acting, and relatively inexpensive. Behavior modification and modeling (O'Leary & O'Leary, 1977; Sulzer-Azaroff & Mayer, 1977) are among the most frequently utilized interventions of this kind. Special class placement, curricula modifications, and family/home interventions, among many other possibilities, also fall into this group.

At times, however, the most logical solution will be to invoke some form of direct therapy for the client which is designed to alter personological traits, that is, a *P* intervention. For example, with recent assertions of a causal connection between locus of control and school achievement (Bar-Tal & Bar-Zoher, 1977), a consultant and consultee might reasonably choose to rely on counseling interventions as did Felton and Biggs (1972, 1973), and Majumder, Greever, Holt, and Friedland (1973) to increase an underachieving student's internality. In this instance, a counseling intervention may prove to be more efficient than trying to initiate a host of environmental and behavioral strategies in a large number of different academic classrooms with a large number of different teachers. Some of the most interesting *P* interventions have been of a proactive, preventive nature, such as those reported by Spivack, Platt, and Shure (1976), who developed therapy groups to improve the social problem-solving and coping skills of young children.

Step 4: Evaluate and Choose Among Alternatives. After completing the brainstorming stage, the consultant and consultee must choose an alternative(s). Both D'Zurilla and Goldfried (1971) and Heppner (1978) cite research which indicates that individuals are often unable to recognize the best solution for a problem among a list of alternatives. The consultant should strive to ensure the choice of strategies to be used in response to the presenting problem is not made hastily; further, the consultant should help the consultee review each alternative from a variety of perspectives. The final choice of intervention techniques, however, *rests with the consultee,* who must, after all, carry out the treatment plan.

When reviewing the list of alternatives, the consultant and consultee should consider the ecological impact of each. That is, they must remember that classrooms are ecological systems. As such, changes in any one aspect of the system will result in changes in other aspects of the system as well (Petrie, Brown, Piersel, Frinfrock, Schelble, LeBlanc, & Kratochwill, 1980). For example, if a teacher chooses to dramatically increase his or her level of attention to a particular child during reading lessons, will he or she have to decrease attention to other children by a corresponding amount? If so, what impact will this decreased attention have on the class as a whole or on the other children who also require a great deal of attention during reading? Do the potential gains from this intervention outweigh the potential losses? Sarason (1971) provides a helpful discussion of how failure to view change from an ecological perspective often results in unintended outcomes which directly undercut the most significant effects of planned change. One technique which we have found to be effective in predicting the ecological effects of a proposed intervention is to return to the forces discussed in Step 2 of the problem-solving process and to consider the impact of the proposed intervention on each of these forces.

Step 5: Specify Consultee and Consultant Responsibilities. This is a crucial step and one that is often overlooked. Unless the issues inherent in this step are openly discussed, the planned intervention may "fall between the cracks" and, to everyone's frustration, little will be accomplished. It is always a good idea to specify the "who," "when," "where," and "how" types of issues after the consultant and consultee agree on a course of action. For example, in a case where a consultee has chosen to establish a token economy for a first-grade class, who will be responsible for obtaining the gold stars or other materials that will be needed for contingent reinforcement of children in the class? When will the intervention be started? Where will it be conducted (e.g., homeroom, reading class, lunchroom)? How will the consultee keep track of how many gold stars and points each child has? How often will back-up reinforcers be distributed? Attention to these seemingly minor details can easily make the difference between an effective program and an ineffective one. There are altogether too many cases where lack of attention to details has resulted in the failure of what otherwise might have been a highly effective intervention.

Step 6: Implement the Chosen Strategy. A consultant should never assume that a verbal agreement to implement a particular treatment program necessarily means that the program will be carried out. If the consultant has done a good job of involving the consultee in the design and selection of the proposed intervention, then there should be relatively few instances of failure to enact a plan due to consultee resistance. There are, however, many legitimate problems that consultees encounter, and these problems may well reduce their motivation to carry through with a planned intervention. For example, a consultee may have tried the plan for a few days and become disappointed with the results. Alternatively, the consultee may have found the treatment to be more time consuming than was originally anticipated. Sometimes consultees will not realize they are lacking the essential technical skills until they actually attempt to implement a program. In the harried worlds of many school-based personnel, it is not unusual for some unexpected (e.g., a child breaks a leg during recess on the playground) or expected (e.g., parent-teacher conferences) events to distract temporarily a consultee's attention from the intervention plans agreed upon with the consultant. All of these issues, and many others, can and should be addressed via additional consultative contacts. Thus, there is a clear need for systematic follow-up in order to prevent these types of problems from derailing a potentially effective intervention.

Step 7: Evaluate the Effectiveness of the Action and Recycle If Necessary. Short term follow-up of assessment hypotheses and of treatment implementation is a crucial element of effective consultation. The consultant's role at this stage is to work with the consultee to evaluate the effectiveness of the actions taken as a result of the consultation process (Meyers, Parsons, & Martin, 1979). In those instances where intervention has either been unsuccessful or less than adequately effective, the consultant should encourage the consultee to join him or her in returning to an appropriate earlier point in the problem-solving process. Even when treatment has produced satisfactory results, the consultant should continue to check in with the consultee because the ecology of the presenting situation will evolve with time and thus the effectiveness of the planned intervention may not remain stable.

Mental Health Consultation

Terminology Issues. As with the ecological approach, a brief discussion of terminology is necessary prior to presenting the mental health consultation model. Specifically, there is some confusion in the literature as to what constitutes mental health consultation. Many writers (e.g., Lachenmeyer, 1980; Meyers, Parsons, & Martin, 1979) use the term in a generic sense to refer to all types of consultation concerning mental health issues. This more general definition would include both ecological and organizational systems of consultation. For this text, however, we will use a more restricted definition of the term in order to facilitate an examination of the similarities and differences between the various consultation models. As such, the subsequent discussion of mental health consultation refers specifically to the concepts originally developed by Gerald Caplan (1964, 1970).

Underlying Psychological Theory. Depending upon the particular aspect of the mental health consultation model that is under examination, different bodies of psychological theory and research come to the fore. Although Caplan presents four different types of mental health consultation (i.e., client-centered case consultation, consultee-centered case consultation, program-centered administrative consultation, and consultee-centered administrative consultation), the centerpiece and unique contribution of his work has clearly been consultee-centered case consultation (*CCCC*). Within this area, the activities of the consultant are primarily directed by psychodynamic personality theories and research, although environmental issues are implicitly recognized (Meyers, 1981). This focus results from the manner in which presenting problems are conceptualized in CCCC. Unlike ecological consultation, where the consultant's attention is focused on the *B, P,* and *E* elements of the *client's* problem, the *CCCC* approach focuses attention on the *consultee* and his or her inability to cope with a particular case. For example, using ecological consultation methodologies, a consultant might work with a consultee to determine why a particular child is continously hostile to his or her teacher and peers. The outcome of such a consultation would typically be a series of planned interventions which are designed to reduce the occurrence of the child's problem behavior(s). With *CCCC,* however, the consultant's main concern is not with the causes of the child's behavior problems and potential solutions for it, but rather with determining why the consultee can not handle this specific problem more effectively on his or her own, as well as with implementing strategies to improve the consultee's professional functioning. Within this framework, psychodynamic, intrapsychic theories of human behavior play a major role as the consultant works to assess the consultee's problems and to make appropriate interventions.

Assessment and Intervention. Caplan (1970) discusses four major reasons why a consultee might be in need of *CCCC*. Specifically, the consultee may be experiencing a lack of knowledge, skill, self-confidence, or objectivity.

Lack of Knowledge. A consultee's inability to deal effectively with a presenting problem may stem from his or her lack of knowledge or understanding of a particular body of information. A teacher's ignorance of operant theory, for example, may prevent the teacher from understanding why a student persists in disrupting the class despite teacher reprimands and requests for order. The consultant's primary responsibility in circumstances such as this is to help the consultee acquire whatever information is necessary for him or her to cope more successfully with the presenting problem. Sometimes this knowledge may be within the consultant's areas of expertise, in which case he or she can directly provide the necessary information. In other instances, the consultant's function will be to help locate other persons or resources that can assist the consultee.

Lack of Skill. Often a consultee may have a cognitive grasp of relevant theory and research but yet lack the skills to effectively implement this knowledge. If the skill deficit is one in which the consultant has obtained mastery, options such as modeling, behavior rehearsal, and inservice are each viable intervention options. In other instances, the consultant should help the consultee to find other qualified professionals who can provide similar services.

Lack of Self-Confidence. In those instances in which *CCCC* is needed because of problems in self-confidence, the consultant's support of the consultee becomes crucial. Active listening skills are particularly important for the consultant. Often, inexperienced consultants fail to perceive the significance of helping consultees deal with a lack of self-confidence because these interactions typically lack a clear focus on a child-related problem. Quite to the contrary, however, the consultee's faith in the quality of their own professional ideas and inclinations is a critical ingredient for successful teaching. Time spent uplifting a consultee's self-confidence is well expended even if specific client-related problems are not directly resolved. This is particularly common in school settings, where teaching is often a "lonely profession" (Sarason, Levine, Goldenberg, Cherlin, & Bennett, 1966), and supportive comments from colleagues and administrators are often too few and far between.

Lack of Objectivity. Consultees suffer from a lack of objectivity when they become emotionally involved in a case and lose their normal professional distance. Caplan considers lack of objectivity to be the most frequent cause of consultee difficulties leading to *CCCC*. He states, "In a well-organized institution or agency in which there is an effective personnel system, good administrative control and a well-developed supervisory network, most cases that present themselves for consultee-centered case consultation fall into this fourth category" (1970, p. 131). Many would disagree with this hypothesis in regard to school systems, however, because the existence of an "effective personnel system, good administrative control and well-developed supervisory network" is often a questionable reality. Preliminary research findings (Gutkin, 1981), in fact, indicate that consultee lack of knowledge, skill, and self-confidence are more pervasive problems among school personnel than is the lack of objectivity. All are in agreement, however, that consultee lack of objectivity is a real problem and one with which school psychologists should be prepared to cope.

Consistent with the psychodynamic theories upon which *CCCC* is based, Caplan (1970) delineates five causes for lack of objectivity: (a) direct personal involvement of the consultee with the client, (b) simple identification of the consultee with the client, (c) transference of consultee experiences and psychic difficulties onto the client's case, (d) characterological distortions of perception and behavior on the part of the consultee in regards to the client, and (e) theme interference. Unless there are indications to the contrary, Caplan assumes the consultee is suffering from theme interference. In this condition, the consultee irrationally associates his or her own unresolved, personal psychological problems with current work difficulties. The result is an increasing level of consultee emotionality and a corresponding decrease in the consultee's ability to utilize his or her own professional skills.

A theme has two major components, an "initial category" and an "inevitable outcome." The former describes a situation or set of events that is psychologically charged for the consultee, while the latter characterizes an unpleasant outcome which the consultee believes will *inevitably* result whenever the former is present. A theme becomes activated when the consultee fits some aspect of a current case into the "initial category" and comes to feel that he or she is powerless to prevent the "inevitable outcome" from befalling the client.

A concrete example will help to illustrate the theme interference construct. Ms. Smith is a fourth-grade teacher with the following theme: "All children who are not sufficiently disciplined by their parents (the initial category) will grow up without self-control and thus lead unhappy lives as adults (the inevitable outcome)." Robert is a child in her class who is failing multiple subjects and one who Ms. Smith believes is not receiving adequate parental discipline. Because Ms. Smith perceives Robert to fit the "initial category," she assumes that he will suffer the "inevitable outcome." Ms. Smith becomes distraught, loses her professional objectivity, and is unable to handle Robert's academic problems. She approaches the psychologist fearing that Robert is headed for serious difficulty. In fact, however, Robert's problems are no worse than those of several other children in the class, all of whom Ms. Smith is competently teaching without the aid of outside assistance. The real problem in this case is the intrusion of Ms. Smith's theme rather than Robert's academic performance. She could cope with the latter were it not for the former.

Although the themes described by Caplan in his writings are often highly psychodynamic in nature, there is nothing inherent in the theme interference construct that limits it to being the result of significant consultee pathology. We believe that themes occur across a broad severity continuum, ranging from those that might result from diagnosable psychological disturbances in the consultee [e.g., All people who masturbate excessively damage their nervous systems and blunt their intelligence, (Caplan, 1970, p. 146)] to those that could be caused by common occupational biases (e.g., All children from single parent families and homes with working mothers develop an excessively intense need for adult attention and thus do poorly in school).

To assess the presence and characteristics of a theme, the consultant looks for affective and cognitive responses by the consultee that are symptomatic of a lack of objectivity. In the affective domain, the consultant looks for a variety of verbal (e.g., choice of emotionally charged words, voice tone) and nonverbal (e.g., facial expressions, muscle tension) signs that indicate increased emotionality and anxiety as the consultative interview draws closer to the theme, and decreasing signs of upset as the discussion moves away from this same topic. Regarding the consultee's cognitive behavior, the primary symptom to watch for is a stereotyping of people and events related to the client's situation. For example the client or a closely related person is described by the consultee in a manner which is exaggerated, cliched, oversimplified, and substantially out of step with objective reality.

Caplan (1970) has proposed several techniques for helping to reduce theme interference in a consultee. One strategy is to "unlink" the presenting problem from the theme by convincing the consultee that the client does not fit the "Initial Category." For example, if the theme is "All children who are brought up in nonreligious families grow up to be socially maladjusted adults," the consultant could attempt to show the consultee that in the current case the client is not being subject to an unusual lack of religious training. If successful with this intervention, the consultee will "unlink" this client from the theme and will return to his or her normal professional efficiency.

Although "unlinking" may resolve the presenting problem, Caplan (1970) argues against using this tactic because it leaves the consultee's theme intact. Instead, Caplan proposes four techniques to reduce theme interference, all of which are intended to weaken a consultee's theme and thus enable the consultee to cope effectively with the presenting problem and future problems of a similar nature. Caplan states,

The goal of the consultant's intervention is to invalidate the obligatory link between the two categories that express the theme. The consultant accepts and supports the displacement of the theme onto the client's case and the definition of this case as a test case by concurring with the Initial Category in all its details that are personally meaningful to the consultee. The consultant engages the consultee in a joint examination of the link between the Initial Category and the Outcome Category and helps the consultee realize that this outcome is not inevitable . . . if we can demonstrate that on even one occasion in an authentic test case that meets all the consultee's unconscious requirements the connection between the categories does not hold, we will dissipate or weaken the theme. (1970, pp. 166–167)

The first of these strategies is called "verbal focus on the client." In this approach, the consultant verbally examines the presenting problem with the consultee. "The consultant demonstrates that although the Inevitable Outcome is one logical possibility, there are other possibilities too; and that the evidence indicates that one or more of these is more probable than the doom that the consultee envisages" (Caplan, 1970, p. 167).

The second approach is called "verbal focus on an alternate object—the parable." When the presence of a highly sensitive theme makes discussion of the client's problem emotionally upsetting to the consultee, Caplan (1970) recommends the consultant direct discussion away from the client's situation and onto a case which is superficially as different as possible from the presenting case but which retains the essential elements of the theme. Caplan hypothesizes that use of a parable allows the consultant to weaken the theme while preventing the consultee's unconscious conflicts from becoming conscious.

Caplan's (1970) third tactic for reducing theme interference is termed "nonverbal focus on the case." The essence of this technique is for the consultant to remain calm and relaxed, thus nonverbally signaling the consultee that the expected Inevitable Outcome and the negative consequences associated with it are rather unlikely. Caplan hypothesizes that this approach will work only if the consultee perceives the consultant to have fully grasped the seriousness of the "Inevitable Outcome." Without this element, the consultee will dismiss the consultant's calm demeanor as a reflection of either indifference or lack of insight.

The fourth and final approach to reducing theme interference is "nonverbal focus on the consultation relationship." Caplan hypothesizes that consultees will often express themes in the way they relate to the consultant. In *The Theory and Practice of Mental Health Consultation,* Caplan (1970) describes a case with the following theme: "A weak and helpless woman who builds a link with a big powerful man and becomes dependent upon him will inevitably be exploited and belittled by him" (p. 180). Caplan notes that the consultee was acting out this theme in her relationship with the consultant by being unnecessarily deferential to him and by anticipating the consultant's belittling of her. The consultant dealt with this by taking on the role of a powerful male figure but then coupling this activity with a recognition of the consultee's professional expertise, power, and authority. The consultant thus helped the consultee weaken the presenting theme by manipulating his relationship with the consultee so as to invalidate the link between the Intial Category and the Inevitable Outcome.

Although the work of Gerald Caplan has been a milestone in the history and development of consultation theory, some argue that his approaches to the reduction of theme interference are too psychodynamic and without empirical support at this point in time (e.g., Meyers, Parsons, & Martin, 1979). We accept Caplan's assumptions that consultee effectiveness can be seriously impeded by the loss of professional objectivity, but seriously question his psychoanalytic line of logic put forth to account for this phenomenon. Alternative, situationally-based explanations can adequately account for most consultee behaviors, including the loss of professional objectivity. Meyers, Friedman, and Gaughan (1975), for example, present exploratory evidence which supports the use of direct confrontation techniques during *CCCC,* a technique frowned upon by Caplan for fear of elevating subsconscious conflicts to the fore. We are in substantial agreement with Meyers, Parsons, and Martin (1979) when they concluded:

> More readily implemented and effective techniques might become apparent if the teacher's lack of objectivity were defined in more objective and behavioral terms. The resulting consultation techniques should be related directly to the problem definitions, and they should be more straightforward and more readily understood by both consultant and consultee. This approach is more consistent with the idea that environmental factors influence behavior. Although consultants advocate this principle when helping teachers to understand the environmental factors that can influence students' problems, this principle seems to be ignored in Caplan's ego-based conception of teacher problems. It needs to be made clear that the teacher's lack of objectivity can be helped, not only through intrapersonal clinical techniques and insight, but also through modifying the teacher's school environment. (p. 135)

Organizational Consultation

Underlying Psychological Theory. Unlike ecological and mental health (*CCCC*) consultation, organizational consultation (often referred to in the literature as organization development) focuses on issues relating to groups, organizations, and systems rather than individuals. Organizational consultants thus rely primarily on theories and concepts emanating from social and organizational psychology.

> An underlying assumption is that schools consist of behavioral and programmatic regularities that do not depend for their existence on particular personalities. . . . Many mental health and learning difficulties arise because of the student's participa-

tion in an unhealthy educational system . . . acting on that educational system as a target for improvement offers a promising, indirect strategy for ameliorating the mental health and academic learning problems of individual students. (Schmuck, 1982, p. 830, 833)

Much of what the children and staff of a school accomplish (or fail to accomplish) is theorized to result directly and indirectly from the nature of that school and from its subsystems as integrated, holistic entities. Sarason (1971) referred to these phenomena as the "culture" of a school and argued that the success of those wishing to bring about change in school settings has been seriously hampered by a failure to view change from an organizational perspective. School psychologists and other school specialists have limited their own impact by relying too extensively on

a psychology of the individual; that is, we learn, formally or informally, to think and act in terms of what goes on inside the heads of individuals. In the process it becomes increasingly difficult to become aware that individuals operate in various social settings that have a structure not comprehensible by our existing theories of individual personality. In fact, in many situations it is likely that one can predict an individual's behavior far better on the basis of knowledge of the social structure and his position in it than one can on the basis of his personal dynamics. (Sarason, 1971, p. 12)

Assessment and Intervention. An abundance of school problems may profitably be addressed from an organizational perspective. For example, we know from both experience and research (Elliott & Gutkin, in press) that special education programs are often ineffective in a variety of ways. Rather than trying to cope with this situation on a case by case basis, an organizational consultant would take a broader perspective and examine the system by which special education children are identified, referred, diagnosed, and treated. Among many other possibilities, this broader approach may lead to an intensive analysis of, and intervention with, a school district's multidisciplinary/IEP teams. Parenthetically, research leads one to conclude that a large percentage of multidisciplinary/IEP teams function ineffectually (Fenton, Yoshida, Maxwell, & Kaufman, 1979; Pfeiffer, 1981; Yoshida, Fenton, Maxwell, & Kaufman, 1978).

Another common contemporary problem is teacher burnout. As in the previous example, an organizational consultant would approach this issue from a systems perspective. Rather than focusing on individual teachers and their personality strengths and weaknesses, or on the teacher's individual students and their strengths and weaknesses, an attempt would be made to assess the situation at a more macro-level. The problem may lie with inadequate interpersonal and professional support systems for the teaching staff. In cases such as this, the development of a more open school atmosphere, in which teachers are encouraged to seek out their colleagues under non-stressful circumstances, may help a great deal. The interested reader is referred to pages 83–86 of Meyers, Parsons, and Martin (1979) where a case just such as this is discussed.

Yet another situation requiring organizational consultation could arise in a school in which massive numbers of children are experiencing academic difficulties. For the sake of discussion, let us presume that 80% of the students in school are substantially below grade level in reading. Under such a set of circumstances, it would appear to be an act of futility to cope with this situation on a child-by-child or teacher-by-teacher basis. The rational way to proceed would be to examine the school's reading program and redesign it as appropriate.

When working on any of the above or related problems, organizational consultants focus their attention on a long list of group, organizational, and systems phenomena. Although exhaustive discussion of these parameters is beyond the scope of this chapter, a few of the most central targets of assessment and intervention can be highlighted. Chapters by Schmuck, Snapp and Davidson, and Lundquist in *The Handbook of School Psychology* (Reynolds & Gutkin, 1982) provide more detailed discussions of these and closely related issues.

Traditionally, organizational analyses and interventions have focused on the formal structure of a system. What are the hierarchical relationships? Who has authority over whom? Where is everyone's place on the organizational chart? While these issues of formal organizational structure are still considered to be important, they are now viewed as only one part of a larger picture. Much (if not most) of the behavior that occurs within an organizational context is thought to be influenced by the organization's informal structure. Spontaneous, unplanned communication networks, status differences, territorial disputes, etc. all have an impact on the effectiveness with which an organization functions. Each of these aspects of formal and informal structure may be important points on which to focus during an organizational consultation effort.

Schmuck, Runkel, Arends, and Arends (1977) and Schein (1969) provide detailed discussions of other dimensions of organizational functioning that must be considered by the consultant. For example, they discuss communication processes among organization members as a key element. Do people communicate clearly with each other or do vital misunderstandings arise when the messages of particular individuals and subgroups are misinterpreted by other individuals and subgroups? Many educational specialists and teachers seem to expect clear communication to occur as a simple function of the good intentions of all concerned. Unfortunately, the ability to express oneself accurately and understand what is being said by others is a skill which many competent professionals do not possess unless they receive specific training in that area. In addition to the books by Schmuck et al. (1977), and Schein (1969), the reader is referred to discussions on the technology of communication by Gutkin and Curtis (1982) and Bergan (1977).

Many of the most important group and organizational events that occur in schools take place within the context of formal meetings. The quality of these meetings often determines the efficacy of educational programs carried out for children. Among the elements that an organizational consultant monitors are: (a) group leader behavior: it is assumed that democratic and shared leadership styles are superior to authoritarian or laissez-faire approaches; (b) goal and agenda setting: goals and agendas for meetings should be clearly established either prior to meetings or as one of the first actions taken by the group; (c) member participation: encouraging a broad range of persons to participate actively in meetings is almost always better than having a small handful of overly vocal members and a majority of passive persons; (d) group problem-solving style: problems should typically be dealt with systematically (i.e., define the problem, assess and diagnose the problem, brainstorm solutions, etc.) rather than haphazardly (e.g., solutions are suggested before sufficient attention has been paid to problem definition and analysis); and (e) conflict resolution: it is assumed that conflicts often arise during meetings and these are best handled overtly and constructively rather than pretending they do not exist.

Group norms are another important area to examine during organizational consultation. How does the school staff view the school, their jobs, and the roles of others? How are school personnel expected to act under various circumstances? Is it possible to ask for help with a professional problem and still be viewed as competent by one's colleagues? Do the teachers and administrators see each other as adversaries or partners? The answers to these and many other similar questions provide important diagnostic data for the organizational consultant as he or she strives to assess a problem situation and design an appropriate intervention.

The assessment and diagnostic tools used to answer all the above and many other related questions during organizational consultation do not differ sharply from those used for ecological and mental health consultation. The most significant difference, of course, is that these tools are applied to organizational issues rather than to the problems of individual students and staff.

As in ecological and mental health consultation, interviews and observation are the two primary assessment approaches for organizational consultants. By conducting interviews with key organizational members and a representative sample of other persons, the consultant can amass a large quantity of data regarding everyone's perceptions of how a school functions, and its strengths, weaknesses, and critical issues. As was discussed regarding both ecological and mental health consultation, these consultee perceptions are of critical importance even if they are partially (or even completely) inaccurate. To be successful, the consultant will need to know not only what "really" occurs in the school, but also what everyone thinks is occurring. This latter, subjective reality is considered to be just as significant as the former, objective reality. Consultee interviews serve as a major source of data regarding subjective perceptions and, to a lesser extent, also supply the consultant with objective information about organizational functioning.

To check the veracity of consultee perceptions, it is important for the consultant to observe directly as much of the organization's functioning as possible. The consultant should be aware, however, that his or her observations may also be somewhat biased, although the itinerant nature of most school psychologists' jobs allows them to be more detached and thus more objective than members of the consultee organization. Large discrepancies between the consultant's observations and the consultees' perceptions may provide important clues regarding consultees' hidden agendas and goals. When consultant observations and consultee perceptions are congruent, the consultant may feel an increased sense of confidence that he or she has gotten a good picture of the "reality" of how that organization operates.

As in other forms of consultation, psychometric instruments often provide an important supplement to the data collected via interview and observation. Often these tests reveal new data because they are anonymous in nature and the consultees are thus less reticent to share particularly sensitive opinions than when they are in an interview situation. Most of these tests are tailor-made by the consultant for the particular problem with which he or she is working. As such they typically lack adequate prior study to determine their reliability and validity and should thus be used exclusively for the purpose of generating tentative hypotheses rather than as accurate indications of reality. There are a few standardized instruments which address organizational phenomena, such as the Organizational Climate Description Questionnaire (OCDQ) (Halpin & Croft, 1963) and the Leader Behavior Description Questionnaire (LBDQ) (Halpin, 1966), but typically tests such as these have also not undergone the psychometric scrutiny that we have come to expect from measures of individual abilities.

Once data are gathered and a diagnosis of the problem is made, a wide array of interventions are available to the organizational consultant. Again, the reader is referred to Schmuck et al. (1977) for a more detailed discussion than is possible in this chapter.

One dimension for the consultant to consider is whether to carry out an intervention in a retreat or a work situation. Retreats have the advantage of creating a more flexible mind-set among the consultees because they are in a relaxed atmosphere away from the sights, sounds, and pressures of the office. The primary disadvantage of retreats is that new behaviors learned under these special circumstances may not generalize back to the work setting. As a result, it is important to follow-up on retreats with additional on-site training and consultation. If the consultant limits the intervention to the work site, he or she will not have to contend as much with problems of generalization; on the other hand, the consultees may be less willing to try out new behaviors and organizational patterns.

A related issue for the consultant to consider is whether to focus the intervention on simulations and group games or on actual work problems. As with retreats, simulations and games are often less threatening to consultees than real work problems and therefore may lead to an increased willingness to experiment with new ideas and behaviors. Again, however, the consultant must be concerned with the issue of generalization. Specifically, will new organizational behaviors learned on simulated problems generalize to actual work difficulties? If the consultant limits his or her intervention to real job related issues, he or she is likely to experience less difficulty with generalization but more difficulty in generating new consultee behaviors and organizational growth.

For the sake of illustration, a few organizational consultation interventions will be described in brief. The Lake St. Clair Incident (Canfield & Starr, 1978) is a good example of a game type of intervention that would most often be used in a retreat setting. The point of this game is both to demonstrate how problem-solving processes effect decision-making and to sensitize participants to their behaviors and tendencies in group situations. The game is played as follows. Participants are to imagine they are alone in a boat on Lake St. Clair, a large and cold body of water, when their ship suddenly starts to sink. They have access to 15 items on their boat, including such things as life jackets, a canoe paddle, flash lights, etc., and only a few minutes in which to decide what to take with them before the boat goes under. The task is to rank-order the 15 items, indicating which they would take first, second, third, and so on. The consultant has access to the "correct answer" as determined by the U.S. Coast Guard. A simple computational technique is provided for determining the quality of consultee responses by comparing them with the Coast Guard's recommendations. Norms are also provided. The consultees' task of rank ordering the 15 items is carried out under three different sets of conditions: (a) individual problem solving, in which each participant must work entirely on his or her own, (b) consultative problem solving, in which each person is free to consult with others for information and opinion but must rank-order the 15 items by themselves, and (c) consensus problem solving, in which each person is assigned to a group with the stipulation that each group must rank-order the items based on a group consensus.

Taking part in the Lake St. Clair exercise vividly points out to consultees how the nature and quality of their decisions fluctuate as a function of the problem-solving method which they use. The degree to which they utilize the knowledge of others in the consultative problem-solving condition and their style of interaction with other group members in the consensus problem-solving condition provide good clinical data for subsequent discussions and analyses of individual and group problem-solving styles. When used in conjunction with other training and consultative techniques, exercises such as the Lake St. Clair Incident should help organization members to be more sensitive to, and to modify, dysfunctional problem solving and group processes occurring at their school.

As a follow-up to the Lake St. Clair Incident exercise, a consultant might continue to work with organization members at the work site, using actual team meetings as a stimulus element. Many options present themselves. For example, the consultant might videotape a meeting and have the team analyze and critique their own behavior. Another option would be to set aside time at the end of each meeting for team members to discuss the strengths and weaknesses of the meeting. If the consultant wishes to make this feedback even more immediate, he or she could stop the meeting at points of interest and have the team members discuss the group and problem-solving processes that have occurred up to that point.

Survey feedback is another often used intervention technique. As discussed previously, the organizational consultant may want to supplement his or her interview and observation data by using various types of anonymous questionnaires. If the data gathered from these questionnaires are fed back to the members of the organization, they provide an excellent basis for discussion and problem solving. Again, the reader is reminded that these questionnaires are often psychometrically crude and, as such, the results of a survey should be presented as points for discussion rather than as accurate reflections of reality. If used properly, survey feedback can be an effective component of an organizational consultation intervention.

Although not always viewed as such, inservice is a form of organizational consultation. By working with small and large groups of school and mental health professionals, inservice activities provide school psychologists with excellent opportunities to intervene in educational organizations on a systematic basis. An inservice program on problem solving, for example, could dramatically alter a school's organizational norms regarding referral processes, faculty meetings, multidisciplinary team meetings, parent conferences, etc. In our experience, inservice presentations are most effective when they are followed by contacts with members of the audience to assist them in translating the ideas learned at the inservice into behaviors in the natural environment. This is facilitated by including time for behavioral rehearsal of newly obtained skills as an integral part of the inservice itself. Detailed discussions of both the conceptual and "nuts and bolts" elements of inservice can be found in McBride (1982) and Elliott and Witt (1981).

FACTORS AFFECTING IMPLEMENTATION OF CONSULTATION SERVICES

Entry

Most schools take a period of time to become acclimated to consultation services. Teachers and other school personnel who have become accustomed to psychological services that are premised on medical model assumptions often require a chance to grow accustomed to this different approach.

At its most basic level, successful consultation requires the establishment of a trusting relationship between the consultant and the consultee. As with all interpersonal and interprofessional relationships, this will require time and should not be rushed. Teachers may also feel initially uncomfortable and insecure when asked to collaborate with a consultant on solving a problem if their prior experiences with psychologists have primarily been limited to making referrals and passively waiting for a diagnosis and a list of recommendations. Those teachers who are used to having the psychologist remove a child from their room for testing may likewise be threatened and confused when a consultant spends a good deal of time observing the teacher's class and the behavior of a referred child in that class. Additionally, naive consultees may have problem-solving tendencies that run counter to the consultant's approaches. As discussed earlier, for example, Lambert (1976) found that most teachers describe student problems in a vague, general manner rather than in concrete, specific, behavioral terms. Similarly, the ''natural instincts'' of untrained problem solvers run counter to the rules of brainstorming, in which judgments regarding the quality of ideas are supposed to be withheld until a long list of possible solutions has been generated.

Each of these and numerous other factors combine to create what has been termed an ''entry period'' for the consultant. ''Entry into the consultee systems is a keystone to the consultation process. The way in which entry is handled sets the emotional climate for what is to follow . . .'' (Schroeder & Miller, 1981 p. 159). During this time, the consultant should try to educate the potential consultees regarding consultation services, strive to establish his or her professional credibility as a psychologist, and work to create a positive rapport with members of the school staff and community. Until these tasks are accomplished, the consultant will, in all likelihood, be underutilized. In some instances, unfortunately, these necessary elements never fall into place and successful consultation thus becomes extremely difficult and unlikely.

How long it takes to gain ''entry'' into a school will vary, of course, with the nature of the specific school, its needs, and the skills and personality of the consultant. Lambert (1974) estimated that entry often requires six months. We have found that in many instances this may be an underestimate.

Clearly, functioning as a consultant in a school setting is considerably more complex than simply announcing the availability of these services. Patience and sensitivity are prerequisite virtues for success. Sarason, et al. (1966), have provided a most insightful and useful discussion of the entry period and how to cope with it. They emphasize a proactive approach in which consultants introduce themselves to all potential consultees, explaining the nature of consultation services *before* any cases are referred to them. Negotiation of an explicit contract with the school principal in order to determine the consultant's role prior to the delivery of any actual services is also believed to facilitate entry. Lambert (1974) detailed the need to establish trust and rapport with consultees as a prerequisite to successful entry into a school as a consultant.

Resistance

As in psychotherapy, resistance to consultation is not unusual (Abeles, 1979; Wolman, 1965). Often, consultee resistance is caused by an incomplete entry process (i.e., the consultee has never come to trust the consultant and/or does not fully understand his or her role in the consultation process) or inappropriate consultant behavior. Resistance may occur, however, even when neither of these situations is present.

One factor believed to foster resistance is the time demands made on consultees during the consultation process. Although there appears to be considerable variation among consultants (Abidin, 1977), consultation requires a considerable amount of consultee time. Unfortunately, increased consultant skills do not reduce the time required. Curtis and Watson (1980) reported that sessions with highly skilled consultants involved approximately twice as much time as those with lesser skilled consultants. Unfortunately, time is in short supply for most teachers who typically have more academic, behavioral, administrative, and parental concerns to deal with at any given moment than they can effectively handle (Sarason, 1971). This problem is eased in some schools by the presence of free periods, ancillary personnel who take classes for specialty instruction (e.g., music, art, library teachers) and teacher aides (Tobiessen & Shai, 1971). However, even under these circumstances, consultants often will not be able to have adequate access to a great number of consultees. In this sense, consultation services are currently somewhat incompatible with the daily realities of many teachers.

On the other side of this coin, however, the use of consultative rather than testing services seems to reduce the time lag between referral and the implementation of treatments (Fairchild, 1976; Tobiessen & Shai, 1971). Any such reduction in time is beneficial given the huge case backlogs, sometimes resulting in a two-year time delay in service delivery in large urban districts (Block, personal communication, 1975), and the serious manpower shortages in psychology (Albee, 1968; Cowen & Gesten, 1978; Sarason, 1976).

Another factor thought to promote resistance to consultation is the subtle yet perceptible implication that the consultee may be part of the presenting problem. Under the more traditional, medical model approach to child dysfunction, the problem was conceptualized as residing within the child; a "blame the victim" mentality predominated. Under ecological, mental health, and organizational consultation systems, it is assumed that a child's classroom difficulties are the result of a complex interaction of the following factors: the child's characteristics; the approaches taken by teachers, parents, and others; the nature of the child's academic environment; and the organizational characteristics of the school. Blame is not so easily and exclusively assigned to the referred student. In fact, each adult involved with the child is subject to having his or her behavior scrutinized. In reality, the consultant is concerned primarily with remedying the referral problem and is not interested in assigning blame to anyone. Despite these good intentions, however, consultees may come to feel that they are being blamed for the child's problem, especially in those cases in which suggested solutions to the child's problem involve modifying the consultee's behavior. After having experienced this, the consultee may resist taking part in future consultations. Some might argue that this turn of events is a reflection of a poorly trained consultant. We contend that while an unskilled consultant would certainly exacerbate this situation, even the most sophisticated consultants will not be able entirely to avoid this phenomena with all of their cases.

A most problematic situation for a consultant occurs when a consultee has a purposeful hidden agenda. For example, a teacher asks to consult with the psychologist concerning a student who was diagnosed previously as emotionally disturbed and who is currently being mainstreamed. The teacher is *overtly* asking for assistance in working with this child but is *covertly* trying to undermine the consultation process and strengthen his or her argument with the principal that emotionally disturbed children cannot be handled effectively in regular education classes. Although consultee behavior will vary in this situation, the consultant should become sensitive to the possible presence of hidden agendas if the consultee resists working towards a concrete, behavioral problem definition or insists upon unrealistic goals for the client. If the situation is extreme and other techniques fail, the consultant may have to confront the consultee in an attempt to make overt the consultee's covert agenda. Parenthetically, the alert reader may recognize that these same symptoms could also indicate theme interference, thus requiring an entirely different intervention.

There are, of course, many other possible causes of consultee resistance. For example, Piersel and Gutkin (1983) theorized that resistance occurs whenever consultees perceive consultation as leading to punishment or inadequate reinforcement.

Funding

School psychologists wishing to utilize large percentages of their time in consultative activities often find themselves swimming upstream against PL 94-142 and analogous state legislation (Gutkin & Tieger, 1979; Mowder, 1979). While consultative services are permitted by PL 94-142 and are consistent with the intended spirit of the law (Alpert & Trachtman, 1978; Gibbins, 1978), they typically cannot compete with the financial payoffs produced for school districts by psychoeducational assessment, diagnosis, and placement (see Gutkin & Tieger, 1979, for an extensive analysis of this problem). Among the most complex issues is the difficulty school psychologists have in documenting the cost effectiveness of prevention, even though credible economic arguments can be made to support such activities (Harper & Balch, 1975).

Consultee, Consultant, and School Organizational Characteristics

Whether consultation services are implemented appropriately may depend partly on selected characteristics of the consultee. Recent evidence suggests a positive relationship between the degree of control that consultees perceive they have over presenting problems and their stated preference for consultative services (Clark & Gutkin, 1982; Gutkin & Ajchenbaum, in press). Other consultee dimensions have also yielded interesting though often inconsistent results. Goldman and Cowan (1976), for example, reported a varying relationship between consultee locus of control and use of consultation services, depending on the particular locus of control measure that was employed. Alpert, Ballantyne, and Griffiths (1981) found no relationship between the locus of control of consultees involved in successful versus unsuccessful consultations, although they did find the former group to be higher in authoritarianism and dogmatism than the latter group. Conflicting evidence also exists regarding the relationship between the number of years of consultee teaching experience and consultee preferences for consultative services (Baker, 1965; Gilmore & Chandy, 1973; Iscoe, Pierce-Jones, McGhearty, & Friedman, 1967). A recent study by Gutkin and Bossard (in press), however, indicates that years of experience in a particular school may be positively related to preferences for consultation services, while total years of experience may be negatively correlated.

Although there is little research specifically addressing the issue, it is assumed that the quality of consultative services is dependent to a large degree on the skill level and motivation of the consultee. By definition, psychologists indirectly deliver consultative services to children through a consultee. While the consultative process is designed to improve consultee skills, it is unlikely that consultation could be properly implemented when either consultee motivation (Curtis & Anderson, 1977) or skills are below some minimum criteria. Unfortunately, it is impossible at this time either to define these criteria or to determine how many school personnel would not meet them. It is clear, however, that some number of educational professionals (hopefully a relatively small percentage) will be inadequate as consultees and will thus seriously jeopardize the success of consultation interactions with them. Some have argued that consultation is an effective technique for making competent persons even more competent but is resisted by consultees with lesser skills who may need help the most (Gallessich,

1974). Furthermore, there is now some evidence that suggests that consultants themselves tend to prefer working with consultees who are more responsive to consultative interactions and less in need of a consultant's assistance (Alpert, Ludwig, & Weiner, 1979; Alpert, Weiner, & Ludwig, 1979). In other words, those consultees who are most in need of assistance may be less likely to receive it, at least to the extent to which such assistance would be influenced by the preferences of the consultant.

As might be expected, the implementation of consultation services is partly a function of consultant characteristics. Consultant skill, for example, has been shown to be positively related to consultees' use of consultation services (Bossard & Gutkin, 1983), consultees' stated willingness to work with consultants (Curtis & Zins, 1981), consultees' satisfaction with consultation services (Schowengerdt, Fine, & Poggio, 1976), and the quality of consultation outcomes (Bergan & Tombari, 1976; Curtis & Watson, 1980). Contrary to these findings, Gutkin and Bossard (in press) found no relationship between consultant skill and consultees' attitudinal preferences for consultation services. Regarding other dimensions of consultant characteristics, Alpert, Ballantyne, and Griffiths (1981) reported no differences between high and low success consultants on educational values, need for assistance, locus of control, authoritarianism, dogmatism, and conservatism.

Perhaps the most basic consultant variable regarding the implementation of consultation services is whether the psychologist has received any formal consultation training. Although experience should not be discounted, we believe that on-the-job training is a poor substitute for graduate coursework and supervised practica. Unfortunately, most school psychologists who are currently practicing have little, if any, formal training in consultation. Only 46% of the school psychology programs surveyed by Bardon and Wenger (1974, 1976) reported an emphasis on consultation training. The current situation is essentially unchanged. In a more recent survey, Meyers, Wurtz, and Flanagan (1981) reported that only 40% of surveyed programs offered course work designed solely for training in school consultation, although 75% offered some form of experiential component. It would appear to be self-evident that increased use of psychological consultation services in school settings can only be brought about if larger proportions of practicing school psychologists receive intensive training as consultants. If the profession would like to move in this direction, as every recent survey indicates it does, it behooves us to create a more effective and intensive system of inservice training than currently exists for our colleagues.

Consonant with the assumptions underlying organizational consultation, several studies have shown a relationship between the implementation of consultation services and various organizational characteristics, even though the findings in these studies have not been completely consistent. Kuehnel (1975), for example, reported a positive correlation between schools' attitudes towards mental health consultation services and the openness of their organizational climate. Indirect support for this outcome was provided by Ford and Migles (1979) who discovered that teachers in open classrooms expressed a more positive attitude towards consultation services than those in more traditional class environments. While Bossard and Gutkin (1983) and Gutkin and Bossard (in press) found no relationship between either consultee attitudes toward, or use of, consultation services, and organizational climate, both studies reported significant correlations with various principal leadership behaviors. These latter findings are indirectly supported by Williams, Wall, Martin, and Berchin (1974), who found that a school faculty's ability to adopt and utilize innovations was related to principal leadership style.

RESEARCH FINDINGS

We conclude this chapter with a brief overview of research relating to the efficacy of consultation approaches. Recent reviews of this body of literature by Medway (1979b), Mannino and Shore (1975), and Fullan, Miles, and Taylor (1980) all concluded that consultation interventions appear to be effective much of the time in remediating the problems of clients, consultees and organizations. The first two papers reported that at least partial success was achieved in approximately 75% of the published research studies regarding ecological (referred to by these authors as behavioral consultation), mental health, and organizational consultation, while the latter investigation found a 50% success rate in organization development interventions in school settings.

Despite these reasonably high success rates, however, Medway (1979b), Mannino and Shore (1975), and Fullan, Miles, and Taylor (1980) all pointed out that the consultation literature suffers from several research design deficiencies which have the effect of reducing our confidence in their findings. For example, much of the consultation literature is based on self-report rather than on data resulting from direct observation. These studies are thus founded to some extent on subjective consultant and consultee perceptions rather than on objective behavioral changes in either the consultee or the client. Many of these investigations fail to utilize an adequate control group. There is often little or no operational definition regarding the specific nature of consultants' behavior as they work with their consultees, thus making replication extremely difficult and limiting our ability to distinguish between the essential and irrelevant elements in consultation processes. Too many of the consultation studies also suffer from a lack of long term follow-up of short term findings. Possible solutions for these and other related research design problems include the use of small N or time series designs (Bergan, 1977; Kratochwill & Bergan, 1978; Meyers, Pitt,

Gaughan, & Freidman, 1978; Parsons, 1977), simulations (Flaherty, 1979; Rieke & Curtis, 1981), and techniques of organizational analysis (Maher, 1980; Schmuck & Miles, 1971; Schumck et al., 1977).

Thus, much like any area of research endeavor that focuses on complex psychological interventions occurring in natural, poorly controlled settings, the knowledge accumlated regarding school consultation is clearly not without its methodological flaws. We note, however, that despite research design problems, it would be unreasonable to ignore the growing body of research and the clear indications that consultation techniques do appear to be successful in a high percentage of instances. While we eagerly await more effective research designs and a more precise foundation of data, the positive conclusions of Medway (1979b), Mannino and Shore (1975), and Fullan, Miles, and Taylor (1980) represent the most reasonable interpretation of research findings at this point in time.

A number of investigations have been conducted to shed light on the efficacy of consultation as a preventive technique. The results of these studies have generally been quite positive. Representative of these findings are the following: (a) teachers believe their professional skills to have improved as a result of being exposed to consultation services (Gutkin, 1980; Hinkle et al., 1977; Zins, 1981); (b) teachers in schools having consultants find problems to be less serious than teachers in matched schools without consultants who were presented with an identical list of child problems (Gutkin, Singer, & Brown, 1980); (c) referral rates drop dramatically after 4–5 years of exposure to consultation services (Ritter, 1978); (d) client gains following consultation services may generalize to other children in the same class as a result of increased teacher effectiveness (Jason & Ferone, 1978; Meyers, 1975); (e) teachers who work with effective consultants demonstrate significant improvements in their perceptions and understanding of childrens' problems (Curtis & Watson, 1980); (f) underachieving children whose teachers and parents received consultation type services during their fourth, fifth, and sixth grades achieved significantly better on several academic measures at the time of high school graduation than a control group of underachievers (Jackson, Cleveland, & Merenda, 1975); (g) psychological consultation, early screening, and the use of paraprofessionals can be combined to effect secondary prevention in school settings (Cowen, Trost, Lorion, Dorr, Izzo, & Isaacson, 1975); and (h) a range of behavioral difficulties can be prevented by consulting with teachers and parents regarding interpersonal problem-solving skills for children (Spivack, Platt, & Shure, 1976). Although these and other related studies are still too few in number to be conclusive, they are nonetheless encouraging. Additional research is needed to determine further whether prevention can be achieved effectively and efficiently through the use of consultative approaches.

Determining the relative efficacy of ecological (referred to by several authors as behavioral consultation) versus mental health versus organizational consultation has also received some research attention. Each can be viewed as a variation on a theme, the theme being the core characteristics delineated earlier in this chapter. The question of which of these variations is most effective, and under what circumstances is one approach more helpful than another, is an issue deserving serious attention. Unfortunately, there is too little research evidence available at this time to answer conclusively any of these questions. Although both Jason and Ferone (1978) and Medway and Forman (1980) found some support for behavioral as opposed to mental health consultation, both sets of authors noted that their results were quite mixed on a number of variables and that generalizability of their findings was an area of concern. In a similar investigation, Jason, Ferone, and Anderegg (1979) concluded that, "None of the interventions demonstrated consistently positive results on all outcome criterion measures. Rather, complex interrelationships emerged, with several consultation approaches yielding positive findings on certain indices and negative results on others" (p. 112). The solution to this intricate puzzle awaits future empirical investigation.

Finally, we turn to research focusing on the opinions of those who provide and consume psychological consultation services in school settings. In this area at least, the results of virtually every investigation have been very similar. Whether making inquiry of school psychologists, teachers, principals or superintendents, consultation services are viewed as one of the most important of all the school psychologist's functions. A considerable number of surveys reveal a desire on the part of many school personnel for an increased emphasis on consultation (see Gutkin & Curtis, 1982, for an extensive reference list). Indicative of this trend are the findings reported by Meacham and Peckham (1978) in a national survey of school psychologists which found consultation to be the highest preference activity among practitioners.

4

Psychological Assessment of Persons, Behaviors, and Environments

School psychology as a profession developed primarily as a result of school systems' needs to provide a more precise and reliable means of classifying and identifying children for special education programs. Originally, psychological testing was the primary role of school psychologists and it remains a major component of their current functioning. Though the role of the school psychologist is changing gradually, many still consider high level testing and assessment skills to "run like a gold core" through school psychology (Page, 1982) and research on testing and assessment tends to dominate the school psychology research literature (Clark & Reynolds, 1981; Reynolds & Clark, in press). Measurement, testing, and assessment are complex as well as controversial topics but are central to the training of the school psychologist.

Of the three components comprising the reciprocal determinism paradigm—that is, person, behavior, and environment—the majority of school psychological assessments have focused on the internal characteristics of individual children. This phenomenon reflects the medical model orientation of traditional school psychology and special education. With the growth of more ecological approaches to services, however, the preponderant emphasis on assessing person variables becomes more and more inappropriate. Contemporary school psychologists must develop refined skills for the assessment of behaviors and environments as well. The use of a reciprocal determinism model does not diminish the importance of assessing the internal traits of individual children; rather, it highlights the fact that assessment of these traits exclusively is insufficient. Comprehensive assessments should include detailed considerations of person, behavior, *and,* environmental dimensions.

In this chapter, we discuss assessment within a broad ecological framework, consistent with the reciprocal determinism model. Issues and techniques relevant to the assessment of persons and behaviors are intermixed because all are pertinent to assessments conducted by School Psychologists and are often difficult to separate from each other. The section on the assessment of environments helps to underscore the importance of activities in this category. We begin with a discussion of the assessment *process,* that is, factors describing how assessments should be carried out regardless of whether they focus on person, behavior, or environment variables.

THE ASSESSMENT PROCESS

To understand the value and purposes of assessment, it is necessary to view assessment as a process. Often school psychologists fail to derive maximum benefit from their assessment activities because they limit their focus to the instruments and devices employed while failing to conceptualize the interrelation of these particulars and the many diverse aspects of their roles. As with consultation and intervention functions, a process perspective provides a vehicle for integrating seemingly discrete assessment activities and facilitates the use of meaningful service delivery models.

Relationship of Assessment and Testing

Assessment and testing are not synonomous. Assessment is a *comprehensive process* of deriving meaning from data, achieving a broad but detailed description and understanding of individuals, behaviors, environments, and the reciprocal interactions among each of these elements. Properly carried out, assessment is a dynamic synthesis and evaluation of multiple sources of data believed to be relevant to the status of the individuals, behaviors, and environments being examined. Assessment is open-ended in the sense that new information can quickly alter one's perception of the problem.

Testing is a subset of assessment. The administration of tests is one particular method, among many others, for obtaining data (e.g. observations, interviews, questionnaires, etc). Psychologists who equate assessment with standardized testing necessarily limit the scope and breadth of the data available for problem solving. Clearly, testing is a crucial component of the assessment process, one which often results in the development of critical insights necessary for decision making and planning. By itself, however, testing is usually insufficient and must be supplemented by other sources of information.

Relationship of Assessment to Consultation and Intervention

Assessment, consultation, and intervention processes are, and should be, closely intertwined. As described in the consultation chapter (Chapter 3), assessment is an integral component of ecological, mental health, and organizational systems of consultation. At some point in each of these approaches, the psychologist directly (by him or herself) or indirectly (through a teacher, parent, etc.) must gather data for use in the problem-solving process. Although the types of information collected in an ecological versus mental health or organizational consultation approach might differ dramatically, each system requires the accumulation of data to be effective. Put another way, problem solving cannot be carried out successfully in a vacuum of information. Assessment processes are thus an integral aspect of all consultation models.

The design of school psychological interventions are also tied closely to the assessment process. Assessment provides the data and hypotheses upon which effective treatments are built. Generating programs and plans to resolve problem situations without adequate assessment data is both self-defeating and extraordinarily inefficient. This does not mean that formal testing is required for every presenting problem. It is the psychologist's responsibility to determine what information is needed and how to go about obtaining it. By whatever means are most appropriate, the collection of data and the generation of hypotheses that result from the assessment process are essential ingredients in developing effective interventions.

Multiple Sources of Data

In the assessment process it is necessary to entertain and evaluate data (i.e., information) from a variety of sources regarding multiple factors if assessment is to be regarded as ecologically valid. The situation at hand will dictate the relevance and appropriate weighting of each piece of information, but in most instances comprehensive evaluations should include an assessment of person, behavior, and environment variables. Each of these factors takes on more or less importance for individual children. More specialized types of knowledge may be required for any given case. For example, in certain genetically based disorders of learning, a thorough history of all immediate family members may be necessary prior to achieving a good understanding of the nature of a child's difficulty.

Elliott and Piersel (1982) have proposed a funnel analogy to conceptualize the assessment process (Figure 4.1). Assessment is viewed as a process which progresses from a global, nonspecific view of the problem to a narrower, well defined perspective. Within the funnel, assessment techniques are arranged in order based upon the degree to which instructionally specific versus diagnostic information is provided. Thus, assessment becomes increasingly focused as one moves from screening decisions through diagnostic decisions to educational

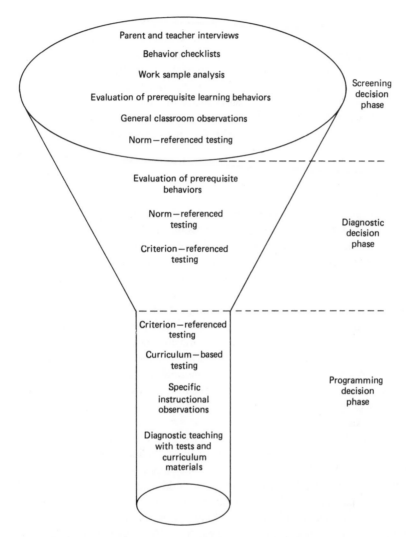

Figure 4.1. The assessment funnel. (Reproduced from Elliott & Piersel, 1982, with permission.)

programming decisions. In other words, the process serves to determine whether a child has a problem, what the problem is, and finally what can be done about it.

Assessment as Hypothesis Testing

Psychoeducational, behavioral, and environmental assessment are far from exact sciences, just as are the clinical assessment procedures of medicine and related specialties. When used in diagnosis, assessment allows one to narrow the number of hypotheses under serious consideration and to reduce the number of viable strategies from which to choose. There are no guarantees that the first strategy adopted or the first program designed will be the most effective (or be effective at all, for that matter). Kaufman (1979) has described the attitude of the psychologist involved in assessment to be properly that of a "detective" who, with a comprehensive knowledge of psychological theories, generates hypotheses by evaluating, synthesizing, and integrating data gleaned from the assessment process.

Decision Making

School psychologists are confronted with a variety of complex decisions at the conclusion of an assessment. Such decisions can be categorized as screening, classification, intervention-planning, placement, and program evaluation. Typically, these decisions require knowledge about students' strengths and weaknesses, educational resources (e.g., materials, programs, and personnel), environmental factors (e.g., parents' interest, student-teacher ratio, physical structure of a classroom, etc.), and classification or diagnostic systems.

Decisions concerning the classification and placement of individuals are perhaps the most difficult. Psychologists and educators, as well as the lay public, have been concerned about error in diagnoses and the possible negative effects of labeling individuals as handicapped or abnormal (Hobbs, 1975). Such concern is necessary; however, we believe the probability of making an informed decision is enhanced greatly by following a comprehensive process of evaluation.

Experienced psychologists recognize the inexactness of current classification methods, but they understand that labels such as learning disabled (LD) or behaviorally impaired (BI) serve primarily as "admission tickets" for needed services. The key decisions are those of programming or intervention planning, rather than classification. Knowing that a child qualifies as LD is not scientific enough. Knowing a child's academic and behavioral strengths and weaknesses and how these can be influenced is what must be communicated as a result of an assessment. Thus, regardless of the diagnosis, assessment information must lead to intervention.

Follow-up Evaluation

Crucial to the assessment process, and far too frequently neglected or overlooked, is the follow-up evaluation that should occur after more formal diagnostic assessments have been made and habilitative recommendations implemented. There are no absolutes in psychological and educational testing; that is, there is no profile of assessment results that has been inexorably linked with a single method of remediation or intervention that will always be successful. The follow-up component of the assessment process is crucial for the fine tuning of existing intervention procedures and in many cases more massive overhauling of treatment plans.

SOME ESSENTIALS OF MEASUREMENT

Measurement is a set of rules for assigning numbers to objects or entities. A psychological measurement device (typically a test) provides a set of rules (the test questions, directions for administration, scoring criteria, etc.) for assigning numbers to an individual; these numbers are believed to be representative of a psychological trait, attribute, or behavior of the individual or of a characteristic of the environmental setting. Psychological tests are the nonexclusive tools of assessment.

It is also important to understand that all tests are psychometric in nature, regardless of the school of psychology from which they hail, be it behavioral, psychodynamic, gestalt, or other. The psychometric characteristics of a test should have a substantial impact on the choice, use, and interpretation of tests. Clinical judgment must be based in real data and predicated on theories of human behavior. Interpretation of psychological tests requires more than a technician with good common sense and keen intuition; these are all merely prerequisite skills to intelligent test use. At a minimum, school psychologists must have a complete understanding of the following concepts:

1. Scales of measurement (i.e., nominal, ordinal, interval, and ratio scales).
2. Norms and reference groups.
3. Units of measurement (i.e., raw versus standard scores and measures of dispersion such as the standard deviation).
4. Test reliability and its relationship to measurement error.
5. Test validity.
6. Basic univariate and multivariate statistics.

Scales of Measurement

Many pieces of information are necessary before one can attach the proper meaning to a test score. One of the most basic requisites is knowledge of what scale of measurement has been employed. Different scales of measurement have quite different properties and convey different levels of information. The four basic scales of measurement include nominal, ordinal, interval, and ratio scales. As one moves from nominal scales toward ratio scales, increasingly sophisticated levels of measurement are possible. Frequently, problems are caused by not knowing what scale is being employed, most notably in attempting to interpret ordinal data (e.g., grade equivalents) as interval data.

A nominal scale of measurement is an exclusively *qualitative* system of categorizing people (or objects, traits, or other variables) or observations about people into classes or sets. Diagnostic categories such as attention deficit disorder, learning disabled, or anxiety neurosis represent nominal scaling categories. Sex is another example of a nominal scale. Nominal scales provide so little quantitative information about the members of the categories that some writers prefer to exclude nominal scales from the general rubric of measurement (e.g., Hays, 1973), as we are unsure of the quantitative relationship among nominal categories.

Ordinal scales provide rudimentary quantitative information regarding an observation. Ordinal scales allow one to rank objects or people according to the amount of a particular attribute they display. However, they do not tell how far apart each observation is from the next one.

Interval scales afford far more information about observations and can be mathematically manipulated with greater confidence and precision than nominal or ordinal scales. In order to have an interval scale of measurement, it is necessary to know not only the information provided by an ordinal scale, but also how far apart each person is concerning the attribute in question. The distinguishing feature of an interval scale, then, is knowledge of the distance between objects in terms of some quantity of an attribute. Most of the measurement scales used in psychology fall under the rubric of interval scales. However, the interval scale has no true zero point, where zero designates total absence of an attribute. If one were to earn an IQ of zero on an intelligence test, this would not indicate the *absence* of intelligence, for without intelligence no human could remain alive.

Ratio scales possess the attributes of other scales but also have a true zero point. With a ratio scale, zero indicates the complete absence of the attribute under consideration. With an interval scale, as on intelligence tests, it would be incorrect to state that a person with a score of 100 is twice as intelligent as a person with a score of 50. A ratio scale would make such comparisons appropriate. Fortunately, it is not necessary to have ratio scales to attack the vast majority of problems of assessment in psychology. Those wishing to explore this topic will find a more mathematical presentation of scales of measurement in Hays (1973).

Norms and Reference Groups

To understand more fully an individual's performance on a test, it is necessary, except in the case of certain very specific types of tests (and usually even then only under special circumstances, e.g., see later discussions of criterion-referenced and behavioral assessment), to evaluate an individual's performance relative to that of some selected group of individuals. To know that an individual answers 60 out of 100 questions correctly on a history test and 75 out of 100 questions correctly on a biology test conveys very little information. On which test did this individual earn the better score? Without knowledge of how a relevant group of persons would perform on these tests, the question of which score is better cannot be answered.

The area of norms is one that frequently causes some confusion and we will thus discuss this topic further. When developing norms for test interpretation, many factors must be considered. Ebel (1972) and Angoff (1971) have discussed a number of the necessary conditions for the appropriate development and use of normative reference group data. The following are taken principally from these two sources, especially the latter, with some elaboration by the present authors. Some of these conditions place requirements on the test being normed, some on the psychological trait being measured, and others on the test user. All affect test score interpretation.

1. The psychological trait being assessed must be amenable at least to ordinal scaling. If a nominal scale was employed, only the presence or absence of the trait would be of interest and relative amounts of the trait could not be determined; norms, under this unusual condition, would be superfluous if not distracting or misleading.

2. The content of the test must provde an adequate operational definition of the trait under consideration. With a proper operational definition, other tests can be constructed to measure the same trait and should yield comparable scores for individuals taking both tests.

3. The test should assess the same psychological construct throughout the entire range of performance.

4. The normative reference group should consist of a large random sample that is representative of the population for whom the test is to be administered later.

5. The sample of examinees from the population should ". . . have been tested under standard conditions, and . . . take the test as seriously, but no more so, than other students to be tested later for whom the norms are needed" (Ebel, 1972, p. 488).

6. The population sampled to provide normative data must be appropriate to the test and *to the purpose for which the test is to be employed*. The latter point is often misinterpreted, especially with regard to the evaluation of exceptional children, and many adequately normed psychological tests are maligned inappropriately for failure to include significant numbers of handicapped children in their normative sample. The major intelligence scales designed for use with children (i.e., the various Wechsler scales and the McCarthy Scales of Children's Abilities) have

been normed on stratified random samples of children representative of children in the United States at large. With this as the reference group, scores from these scales may be interpreted correctly as providing an indication of a child's current intellectual standing with regard to other children in the United States. Some authors (e.g., Salvia & Ysseldyke, 1981) criticize tests such as the McCarthy Scales as inappropriate for measuring the intellectual level of various categories of exceptional children because large numbers of these children were not included in the test's standardization sample. Whether this is a valid criticism depends on the purpose to which the test is applied. If the knowledge of an emotionally disturbed child's level of intellectual functioning, relative to his or her age mates in the United States, is desired, comparing the child's performance on an IQ test to that of other emotionally disturbed children would be inappropriate. However, if we were interested in learning how the child compared intellectually to other emotionally disturbed children, then a reference group of emotionally disturbed children would be appropriate. (However, the latter information is not frequently sought nor has it been shown to be more useful in developing apppropriate intervention strategies.)

Salvia and Ysseldyke (1981) would likely agree with the basic premise of the preceding argument, although they contend that it would be inappropriate to base predictions of future intellectual or academic performances on test scores for an exceptional child when these scores have been derived through comparison with the larger, normal population's performance. To make predictions, they would first require that the reference group from which scores are derived be a group of similar sociocultural background, experience, and handicapping condition. While this may be an appropriate, if not noble, hypothesis for research study, implementation of practice (assuming that the hypothesis is correct) must await empirical verification, especially since it runs counter to traditional practice. Indeed, it is our major thesis that all interpretations of test scores should be guided principally by empirical evidence. Once norms have been established for a specific reference group, the generalizability of the norms becomes a matter for actuarial research; just as norms based on one group may be inappropriate for use with another group, the norms may also be appropriate and a priori acceptance of either hypothesis would be incorrect (Reynolds & Brown, in press). Current evidence demonstrates rather clearly that test scores predict most accurately (and equally well for a variety of subgroups) when based on a large, representative random sample of the population, rather than on highly specific subgroups within a population (e.g., Hunter, Schmidt, & Rauschenberger, in press; Jensen, 1980; Reynolds, 1982b). Exceptions will be found, however. The System of Multicultural Pluralistic Assessment (SOMPA; Mercer & Lewis, 1979) was normed on a very large sample of children from California. Despite the size and representative nature of this sample for children in California, these norms have not withstood empirical evaluation for children in other states such as Arizona, Texas, and Florida.

7. Normative data should be provided for as many different groups as it may be useful for an individual to be compared. While this may at first glance seem contradictory to the foregoing conclusions, there are instances when it is useful to know how a child compares to members of other specific subgroups and, whenever possible, such data should be made available. The larger the number of good reference groups available for evaluating a child's performance on a test, the more useful the test may become.

Once the reference group has been obtained and tested, tables of standardized or scaled scores are developed. These tables are based on the responses of the standardization sample and are frequently referred to as norms tables. There are many types of scaled scores or other units of measurement that may be reported in the "norms tables," and just which unit of measurement has been chosen greatly influences score interpretation.

Units of Measurement

Raw scores, determined by summing the number of correct responses to a series of test items, are quite tedious to manipulate and to interpret properly. Raw scores are typically transformed to another unit of measurement, scaled scores being preferred but other units such as age and grade equivalents being equally common. Converting raw scores into scaled scores involves creating scores with a predetermined mean and standard deviation that remain constant across some preselected variable such as age.

The mean score on a test is simply the average score. The standard deviation (SD) is a measure of the dispersion of scores about the mean. If a test has a mean of 100 and an individual earns a score of 110 on the test, we still have very little information except that the individual did not perform at a level below average. Once the standard deviation is known (if the distribution of scores approaches normality), it can be determined how far from the mean the score of 110 falls. A score of 110 takes on far different meaning depending upon whether the SD of the scores is 5, 15, or 30.

Once the mean and the standard deviation of test scores are known, the individual's standing relative to others on the attribute in question can be determined. The normal distribution or normal curve (or sometimes called bell curve because of its shape) is most helpful in making these interpretations. Figure 4.2 displays the normal curve and shows its relationship to various standard score systems.

Standard scores such as those shown in Figure 4.2 (z-scores, T-scores, etc.) are developed for ease of interpretation and are typically linear transformations of raw scores to a desired scale with a predetermined mean and SD. Most tests designed for use with children, along with some adult tests, standardize scores within age groups so that a scaled score at one age has the same meaning at all other ages. Thus, a 10-year-old who earns a scaled score of 105 on a particular test has the same percentile rank within his or her age group that a 12-year-old with the same score has in his or her age group. That is, the score of 105 will fall at the same point on the normal curve in each case.

Not all scores have this property. Grade equivalents are one popular type of score that is abused frequently because it is assumed to have scaled score proper-

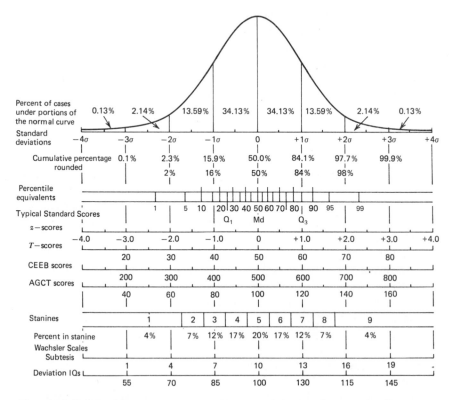

Figure 4.2. Relationships between the normal curve, relative standing expressed in percentiles, and various systems of derived scores. (From Test Service Bulletin No. 50, courtesy of The Psychological Corporation.)

ties when in fact these scores represent only an ordinal level measurement. Grade equivalents ignore the dispersion of scores about the mean even though the dispersion changes markedly from grade to grade. Under no circumstances do grade equivalents qualify as standard scores.

Table 4.1 illustrates the problems of attempting to use grade equivalents in evaluating a child's academic standing relative to his or her peers. Frequently in research as well as in clinical practice, children of normal intellectual capacity are diagnosed as learning disabled through the use of grade equivalents when they perform "two years below grade level for age" (or some variant of this such as 1.5 years below) on a test of academic attainment. The use of this criterion for the diagnosis of learning disabilities or other academic disorders is clearly inappropriate (Reynolds, 1981c). As seen in Table 4.1, a child with a grade equivalent score in reading two years below the appropriate grade placement for his or her age, may or may not have a reading problem. At some ages, this is well within the average range while at others a severe reading problem may be indicated.

Grade equivalents have a tendency to become standards of performance as well, which they clearly are not. Contrary to popular belief, grade equivalent scores on a test do not indicate the grade level of reading text a child should be using. Grade equivalent scores simply do not have a one-to-one correspondence with reading series placement or the various formulas for determining readability levels.

Grade equivalents are also inappropriate for use in any sort of discrepancy analysis of an individual's test performance and for use in many statistical procedures for the following reasons among others (Reynolds, 1981c).

1. The growth curve between age and achievement in basic academic subjects flattens out at upper grade levels. This can also be observed in Table 4.1 where it is seen that there is very little change in standard score values corresponding to two years below grade level for age after about grades 7 or 8.

2. Grade equivalents involve an excess of extrapolation. However, since tests are not administered during every month of the school year, scores between the testing intervals (often a full year) must be interpolated on the assumption of constant growth rates. To interpolate between frequently extrapolated values, based on an assumption of constant growth rates, is a somewhat ludicrous activity.

3. Different academic subjects are acquired at different rates and the variation in performance varies across content areas so that "two years below grade level for age" may be a much more serious deficiency in math, for example, than in reading comprehension.

4. Grade equivalents exaggerate small differences in performance between individuals and for a single individual across tests.

Standard scores are far superior; their principal advantage with children lies

Table 4.1 Standard Scores and Percentile Ranks Corresponding to Performance "Two Years Below Grade Level for Age" on Four Major Reading Tests

Grade Placement	Two Years Below Placement	Wide Range Achievement Test		Peabody Individual Test[a]		Woodcock Reading Mastery Test[b]		Stanford Diagnostic Reading Test[b]	
		SS[c]	%R[d]	SS	%R	SS	%R	SS	%R
1.5	Pk.5	65	1	—		—		—	
2.5	K.5	72	3	—		—		64	1
3.5	1.5	69	2	—		64	1	64	1
4.5	2.5	73	4	75	5	77	6	77	6
5.5	3.5	84	14	85	16	85	16	91	27
6.5	4.5	88	21	88	21	91	27	92	30
7.5	5.5	86	18	89	23	94	34	93	32
8.5	6.5	87	19	91	27	94	34	95	37
9.5	7.5	90	25	93	32	96	39	95	37
10.5	8.5	85	16	93	32	95	37	95	37
11.5	9.5	85	16	93	32	95	37	92	30
12.5	10.5	85	16	95	37	95	37	92	30

[a]Reading comprehension subtest only.
[b]Total test.
[c]All standard scores in this table have been converted for ease of comparison to a common scale having a mean of 100 and a standard deviation of 15.
[d]Percentile rank.
Source: From Reynolds (1981c).

in the comparability of score interpretation across age. By "standard scores," we refer, of course, to scores scaled to a constant mean and SD such as the Wechsler Deviation IQ and not to ratio IQ types of scales employed by the early Binet and the Slosson Intelligence Test which give the false appearance of being scaled scores. Ratio IQs or other types of quotients have many of the same problems as grade equivalents and should be avoided for many of these same reasons.

Standard scores are more accurate and more precise. Interpolation of scores to arrive at an exact score point is typically not necessary, whereas the opposite is true of grade equivalents. Extrapolation is also typically not necessary for scores within three standard deviations of the mean, which account for more than 99% of all scores encountered.

Scaled scores can be set to any desired mean and standard deviation with the fancy of the test author frequently the principal determinant. Fortunately, a few scales can account for the vast majority of standardized tests. Table 4.2 shows the relationship between various scaled score systems. If reference groups and reliability coefficients are comparable, Table 4.2 can also be used to equate scores across tests to aid in the comparison of a child's performance on tests of different attributes.

Test Reliability and Measurement Error

When evaluating test scores, it is also necessary to know just how accurately the score reflects the individual's standing on the trait in question. Typically, tests do not assess every possible relevant behavior. Rather, a domain of possible questions or test items is defined and a sampling of the domain is conducted to formulate a test with an estimable amount of sampling error. Psychological and educational tests are thus destined to be less than perfectly accurate. Certainly, psychological tests contain errors produced from a variety of other sources as well, most of which are situational. Error due to domain sampling is the largest contributor to the degree of error in a test score, however (Nunnally, 1978). It is fortunate that this type of error is also the easiest and most accurately estimated and is typically reported in test manuals as a reliability coefficient, the most useful being Cronbach's (1951) alpha reliability estimate. Reliability conveys information on the relative accuracy of test scores and is second only to validity in importance when evaluating tests and testing data.

Test Validity

Reliability refers to the degree of accuracy of a test score (i.e., the degree to which the true score is reflected in the obtained score). Validity refers to what the test measures and not specifically how well the test measures a particular trait,

Table 4.2 Conversion of Standard Scores Based on Several Scales to a Commonly Expressed Metric

Scales

$\bar{X} = 0$ $SD = 1$	$\bar{X} = 10$ $SD = 3$	$\bar{X} = 36$ $SD = 6$	$\bar{X} = 50$ $SD = 10$	$\bar{X} = 50$ $SD = 15$	$\bar{X} = 100$ $SD = 15$	$\bar{X} = 100$ $SD = 16$	$\bar{X} = 100$ $SD = 20$	$\bar{X} = 500$ $SD = 100$	*Percentile Rank*
2.6	18	52	76	89	139	142	152	760	99
2.4	17	51	74	86	136	138	148	740	99
2.2	17	49	72	83	133	135	144	720	99
2.0	16	48	70	80	130	132	140	700	98
1.8	15	47	68	77	127	129	136	680	96
1.6	15	46	66	74	124	126	132	660	95
1.4	14	44	64	71	121	122	128	640	92
1.2	14	43	62	68	118	119	124	620	88
1.0	13	42	60	65	115	116	120	600	84
.8	12	41	58	62	112	113	116	580	79
.6	12	40	56	59	109	110	112	560	73

Score Points									
.4	11	38	54	56	106	106	108	540	66
.2	11	37	52	53	103	103	104	520	56
0.0	10	36	50	50	100	100	100	500	50
-.2	9	35	48	47	97	97	96	480	42
-.4	9	34	46	44	94	94	92	460	34
-.6	8	33	44	41	91	90	88	440	27
-.8	8	31	42	38	88	87	84	420	21
-1.0	7	30	40	35	85	84	80	400	16
-1.2	6	29	38	32	82	81	76	380	12
-1.4	6	28	36	29	79	78	72	360	8
-1.6	5	26	34	26	76	74	68	340	5
-1.8	5	25	32	23	73	71	64	320	4
-2.0	4	24	30	20	70	68	60	300	2
-2.2	3	23	28	17	67	65	56	280	1
-2.4	3	21	26	14	64	62	52	260	1
-2.6	2	20	24	11	61	58	48	240	1

Source: From Reynolds (1981c).

129

though this is certainly a consideration when evaluating validity. Validity, as with reliability, is not a dichotomous characteristic of tests but exists on a continuum. The question of validity is whether the test measures what it is purported to measure. For a test such as the Wechsler Intelligence Scale for Children—Revised (WISC-R) (Wechsler, 1974) to be considered valid, it must be demonstrated to measure intelligence. The validation process is not a static one; validation is more than the corroboration of a particular meaning of a test score; it is a *process* for developing better and sounder interpretations of observations that are expressed as scores on a psychological test (Cronbach, 1971).

Quite a bit of nomenclature has been applied to test validity with Messick (1980) recently listing some 17 "different" types of validity that are referred to in the technical literature. Traditionally, validity has been broken into three major categories, termed content, construct, and predictive or criterion-related validity. These are the three types of validity distinguished and discussed in the joint *Standards for Educational and Psychological Tests* (American Psychological Association, 1974, now under revision). Content validity is most clearly related to the internal properties of a test, while construct validity cuts across both of the broader categories and criterion-related validity is definitely a question of external validity.

The content validity of a test is determined by how well the test items sample the set of behaviors about which inferences are to be drawn on the basis of the test scores. Criterion-related validity refers to comparisons of test scores with performance levels on accepted criteria of the construct in question or to the level of prediction of performance at some specified future time on an accepted criterion that provides a direct measure of the trait to be measured by the test. Criterion-related and predictive validity are determined by the degree of correspondence between the test score and the individual's performance on the criterion. If the correlation between these two variables is high, no further evidence may be considered necessary (Nunnally, 1978).

Construct validity of psychological tests is one of the most complex issues facing the psychometrician and permeates all aspects of test development and test use. For the most part, psychology deals with intangible constructs. Intelligence is one of the most intensely studied constructs in the field of psychology, yet it cannot be directly observed or evaluated. Intelligence can only be inferred from the observation and quantification of what has been agreed upon as "intelligent" behavior. Personality variables such as dependence, anxiety, need achievement, and so on, cannot be observed directly; their existence must be inferred. Construct validity involves considerable inference on the part of the test developer and the researcher; construct validity is evaluated by investigating just what psychological properties a test measures.

Prior to being used for other than research purposes, a test must be clearly shown to demonstrate an acceptable level of validity. For use with various categories of exceptional children, validation with normally functioning individuals should be considered insufficient. A test's validity needs to be demonstrated for each category of exceptional children with whom it is used. This can be a long and laborious process but is nevertheless a necessary one. There are many subtle characteristics of various classes of exceptional children that may cause an otherwise appropriate test to lack validity with special groups (e.g., Newland, 1980).

As has been noted by Cronbach (1971) and others, the term "test validation" can cause some confusion. In thinking about and evaluating validity, it must always be kept in mind that one does not ever actually validate a test but only the interpretation that is given to the score on that test. Any single test may have many applications and even a test with originally a singular purpose may prove promising for other applications. Each application of a test or interpretation of a test score must undergo validation. Whenever hearing or reading that a test has been validated, it is necessary to know for what purpose it has been validated, that is, what interpretations of scores from the instrument in question have been shown empirically to be justifiable and accurate.

ASSESSMENT METHODOLOGIES

A variety of assessment methods are available for the evaluation of children. Some of these methods grew directly from specific schools of psychological thought such as the psychoanalytic view of Freud (projective assessment techniques) or the behavioral views of Watson and Skinner (behavioral assessment). Other methods have grown out of controversies within and between existing academic disciplines, such as personality theory and social psychology. New and refined methods have come about with new developments in medicine and related fields, while other new testing methods stem from advances in the theory and technology of the science of psychological measurement. Still other new techniques stem, unfortunately, from pure psychological and educational faddism with little basis in psychological theory and little if any empirical basis. Any attempts to group tests by characteristics such as norm-referenced versus criterion-referenced, traditional versus behavioral, maximum versus typical performance, and so on, have some shortcomings but these groupings can nevertheless prove useful as didactic distinctions.

As will be seen in the pages that follow, the lines of demarcation between assessment methods and models are not as clear as many contend. In many cases, the greatest distinctions lie in the philosophical orientation and intent of the user. As one prominent example (though conflicting claims appear), many "behavioral" assessment techniques are as bound by norms and other traditional psychometric concepts as are traditional intelligence tests. Even trait measures of personality end up being labelled by some as behavioral assessment devices (e.g., Barrios, Hartmann, & Shigetomi, 1981). The division of models and methods of assessment which follows is based in some part on convenience and clarity of discussion, but also with an eye toward maintaining the most important conceptual distinctions between these assessment methods.

Approaches to Assessment

Before taking up specific assessment models and methods, we must first establish a theoretical foundation for the collection and interpretation of assessment data. The field of assessment, like all substantive areas in psychology, is replete with a wide array of theoretical viewpoints. Given the limitations of space, we will not describe each of these viewpoints in detail. Instead, what follows are separate discussions of two areas within assessment where practice is most likely to be influenced by the philosophical, technical, or theoretical orientation of individual psychologists. In the first section, we draw the distinction between traditional norm-referenced assessment and behavioral assessment. Following that, we describe the clinical versus actuarial continuum on which assessment data can be interpreted.

Distinction Between Traditional Norm–Referenced Assessment and Behavioral Assessment. The two major models of assessment employed in school psychology today are behavioral assessment and what is referred to as traditional or norm-referenced assessment. These models are seen by extremists as antagonistic, incompatible techniques of assessment. We, on the other hand, see these two models as distinct yet complementary methods of assessment. Since these are the two major models of assessment in school psychology, we will examine them in order to understand the methodological and conceptual distinctions between them before addressing the various models and methods of assessment in a singular fashion.

The primary distinctions between traditional and behavioral approaches to assessment stem from differing conceptions of the causes of behavior. Although both models seek understanding of the individual with the goal of developing helpful interventions, these models look to different places to achieve this understanding. This difference is a direct result of the schools of psychological thought from which each developed (Nelson & Hayes, 1980).

Traditional assessment methods have their roots in trait theories of behavior and in psychodynamic thought. When seeking to understand, explain, and modify behavior, traditional assessment methods look for causes residing primarily *within* the individual. Behavioral assessment methods, taken to the other extreme, have their roots in the behavioral revolution of Watson, Skinner, Pavlov, and related theorists. Behavioral assessment focuses on an individual's *environment* for the determinants of behavior. Only among staunch traditionalists has this distinction held entirely. Most modern behaviorists (e.g., Bowers, 1973; Mischel, 1968) have adopted an interactionist position and view, that is, behavior as a function of *both* environmental and organismic or personological variables. Bandura's reciprocal determinism model of human behavior epitomizes this interactionist position. People do not behave in vacuums but neither does the environment totally direct behavior independent of an active central nervous system within the individual.

Traditional and behavioral assessments are thus distinct yet complementary models. Collectively, the models provide a means of assessing many important human characteristics. Perhaps the most important distinction between these two models of assessment is the level of inference required in interpreting human responses. Behavioral assessment is a low inference model because its adherents observe and record behavior and do not attempt to infer intangible constructs (e.g., anxiety) that underly behavior. Traditional assessment approaches may be characterized as high inference techniques since they are typically employed to allow one to make inferences about the cognitive processes underlying behavior. Goldfried and Kent (1972) nicely illustrated this difference in level of inferences for assessment and prediction decisions in both the behavioral and traditional models (see Figure 4.3).

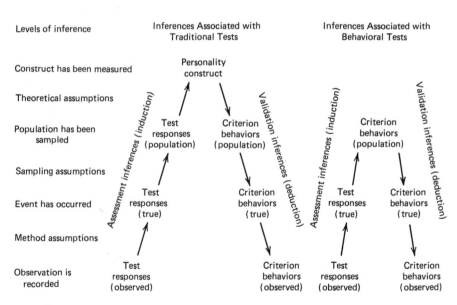

Figure 4.3. Levels of inference in traditional and behavioral tests. (Reproduced from Goldfried & Kent, 1972, copyright American Psychological Association, with permission of authors and publisher.)

The low level of inference and avoidance of covert constructs has been stressed as a major strength of behavioral methods; however, it can at the same time be a weakness. As Nathan (1981) has so clearly pointed out, the ability to infer the nature of underlying cognitive processes can lead to the development of better treatment methods for some disorders. For other disorders, high levels of inference are neither necessary nor desirable; they can also create more confusion than consolidation in arriving at a treatment plan. In those instances, behavioral assessment is readily seen as more appropriate. Thus we see again, and even in the midst of the most major of distinctions between these seemingly antithetical techniques, their true complementarity.

The actual methods through which traditional and behavioral assessments take place typically have differed. Behavioral assessment relies predominantly on direct observation and on the recording of specific behaviors, preferring the natural environment as the site of the assessment. Traditional assessment methods have relied on more indirect methods such as self-report, structured interviews, and performance on those standardized tasks believed to represent covert skills or processes, with testing sometimes occurring in the natural environment but more often in a secluded, artificial setting with only the psychologist and the client present. As will be seen later, this distinction is beginning to blur as books on behavioral assessment describe traditional norm-referenced personality tests as coming under the rubric of behavioral methods.

As alluded to above, another area of differentiation relates to the scope or breadth of the assessment. Behavioral methods focus on specific behaviors as they are presented in multiple settings. Traditional assessment methods have focused on more global traits, evaluated in a single setting with the belief that such measurements are generalizable across settings.

Writers have cited numerous other distinctions between these models of assessment such as the timing of the assessment (i.e., in the behavioral model, assessment is ongoing and in the traditional model it typically occurs in only one session), the role of actual behavior (i.e., in the behavioral model, behavior is a sample of a larger repertoire and in the traditional model it is an indication of an underlying trait), and the role of the history in the assessment (i.e., ignored for the most part in the behavioral model but seen as a crucial determinant of current behavior in the traditional model). Hartmann, Roper, and Bradford (1979) compiled the various ways in which writers have contrasted behavioral and traditional approaches to assessment. Their orderly compilation provides a useful summary for this section (see Table 4.3).

Clinical versus Actuarial Interpretation of Test Scores. Assessment strategies can be viewed on a continuum from purely clinical to rigidly actuarial. Neither extreme appears to be best for application to individual assessment techniques.

Table 4.3   Differences Between Behavioral and Traditional Approaches to Assessment

Assumptions	Behavioral	Traditional
1. Conception of personality	Personality constructs mainly employed to summarize specific behavior patterns, if at all	Personality as a reflection of enduring underlying states or traits
2. Causes of behavior	Maintaining conditions sought in current environment	Intrapsychic or within the individual
Implications		
1. Role of behavior	Important as a sample of person's repertoire in specific situation	Behavior assumes importance only insofar as it indexes underlying causes
2. Role of history	Relatively unimportant, except, for example, to provide a retrospective baseline	Crucial in that present conditions seen as a product of the past
3. Consistency of behavior	Behavior thought to be specific to the situation	Behavior expected to be consistent across times and settings
Uses of data	To describe target behaviors and maintaining conditions	To describe personality functioning and etiology
	To select the appropriate treatment	To diagnose or classify
	To evaluate and revise treatment	To make prognosis; to predict
Other characteristics		
1. Level of inferences	Low	Medium to high
2. Comparisons	More emphasis on intraindividual or idiographic	More emphasis on interindividual or nomothetic
3. Methods of assessment	More emphasis on direct methods (e.g., observations of behavior in natural environment)	More emphasis on indirect methods (e.g., interviews and self-report)
4. Timing of assessment	More ongoing; prior, during, and after treatment	Pre- and perhaps post-treatment, or strictly to diagnose

(*continued*)

135

Table 4.3   *(Continued)*

5. Scope of assessment	Specific measures and of more variables (e.g., of target behaviors in various situations, of side effects, context, strengths as well as deficiencies)*	More global measures (e.g., of cure, or improvement) but only of the individual

Source: D. P. Hartmann, B. L. Roper, & Bradford, D. C., "Source Relationships Between Behavioral and Traditional Assessment," *Journal of Behavioral Assessment,* 1979, *1,* 3–21. Reproduced by permission of the author and publisher.

By purely clinical interpretation, we refer to subjective analyses of test performance that stem almost entirely from theories of behavior without empirical guidance, analyses based in large part on ancedotal evidence and personal experience, and frequently unique from clinician to clinician. Rigid actuarialism, on the other hand, seeks to remove the psychologist completely from the process once the test scores have been obtained. At its extreme, actuarialism would place all scores into a complex mathematical equation or computerized decision tree that would yield all the diagnostic and treatment information. Actuarial systems have a number of advantages over clinical procedures, the most notable being their extreme reliability. Actuarial systems cannot, however, evaluate all pertinent variables. The programming and input problems at this point appear insurmountable.

Actuarially assisted clinical judgment seems to offer the best model for test use and interpretation. This requires a well-informed technician who is trained to think in analytic and synthetic modes, who has a problem-solving orientation, and who is able to call upon knowledge of statistics, psychometrics, and such basic psychological sciences as differential psychology, developmental psychology, learning theory, and social psychology. This theme will be repeated throughout this chapter because of its fundamental importance to using assessment in such a way as to benefit children. Unquestionably, uninformed or careless psychological testing and assessment can be harmful to the children it is intended to serve. Careful thought and analysis, on the other hand, guided by empirical research related to testing (the actuarial data), coupled with a healthy respect for the influence of a test's psychometric properties on its interpretation and mastery of the basic sciences of psychology and education, should produce the best possible results. Above all, in the use of psychological tests, there is no substitute for the human thinking and reasoning process. At the same time, such thinking must be guided by empirical study.

Foci of Assessment

Assessment of Persons and Behaviors. At the beginning of this chapter, we suggested that a comprehensive assessment should obtain information about all aspects of the reciprocal determinism triad (i.e., person, behavior, environment). In this section, we address assessment models and methodologies that are appropriate for either *persons* or *behaviors*. These two elements are combined here because some assessment methods may be appropriate for either internal person variables or for observable behaviors, depending upon the level of inference utilized. Without question, most assessment technology has been developed for the purpose of assessing children's behaviors and attributes. Far less attention has been foused on assessment of the environment; this topic will be discussed in the following section. In this section, we will discuss four major approaches to the assessment variables in the person or behavior categories: traditional norm-referenced assessment, criterion-referenced assessment, projective assessment, and behavioral assessment.

Traditional Norm-referenced Assessment. Intelligence, achievement, and special abilities. These assessment techniques have been grouped together primarily due to their similarity of content and, in some cases, their similarity of purpose. There are, however, some basic distinctions between these measures. Intelligence tests tend to be broad in terms of content, with items that sample a variety of behaviors that are considered to be intellectual in nature. Intelligence tests are used to evaluate the current intellectual status of the individual, but also to predict future behavior on intellectually demanding tasks and to help achieve a better understanding of past behavior and performance in an intellectual setting. Achievement tests have a more narrowly defined content, sampled from a specific subject matter domain that typically has been the focus of purposeful study and learning by the population for whom the test is intended. Intelligence tests, by contrast, are oriented more toward testing intellectual processes and contain items that are more related to incidental learning and not items as likely to have been specifically studied as are achievement test items. Tests of special abilities, such as mechanical aptitude and auditory perception, are as narrow in scope as achievement tests though they focus on process rather than on content. The same test question may appear on an intelligence, achievement, or special-ability test, however, and closely related questions frequently do. Tests of intelligence and special abilities also focus more on the application of prior acquired knowledge, whereas achievement tests focus on testing just what knowledge has recently been acquired. The focus should not be on single items; it is the collection of items and the use and evaluation of the individual's score on the test that are the differentiating factors.

    Intelligence tests are some of the oldest devices in the psychometric arsenal and are likely the most frequently used tests especially for children being evaluated for mental retardation, learning disabilities, and intellectual giftedness. Until rather recently, mental retardation was defined almost exlusively on the basis of intelligence test performance and intellectual giftedness. Indeed, in many school districts throughout the country, this is still the case. Since the translation and modification of Alfred Binet's intelligence test for French schoolchildren was introduced in the United States by Lewis Terman (of Stanford University, hence the Stanford–Binet Intelligence Scale), a substantial proliferation of such tests has occurred. Many of these tests measure very limited aspects of intelligence (e.g., Peabody Picture Vocabulary Test, Columbia Mental Maturity Scale, Ammons and Ammons Quick Test) while others give a much broader view of a person's intellectual skills, measuring general intelligence as well as more specific cognitive skills (e.g., the various Wechsler scales). Unfortunately, while intelligence is a hypothetical psychological construct, most intelligence tests were developed from a primarily empirical basis, with little if any attention given to theories of the human intellect. Empiricism is of major importance in all aspects of psychology, especially psychological testing, but is insufficient in itself. It is important to have a good theory underlying the assessment of any theoretical construct such as intelligence.

The intelligence tests in use today are for the most part individually administered. For a long time, group intelligence tests were used throughout the public schools and in the military. Group tests of intelligence are used quite sparingly today because of their many past abuses and the limited amount of information they offer about the individual. Very little educationally relevant information can be gleaned from a group intelligence test that cannot be better obtained from group achievement tests. Individual intelligence tests are far more expensive to use, but offer considerably more and better information. Much of the additional information, however, comes from having a highly trained observer (the psychologist) interacting with the person for more than an hour in a structured setting, with a variety of tasks of varying levels of difficulty.

The most widely used individually administered intelligence scales with children today are the Wechsler scales, the McCarthy Scales of Children's Abilities, and the Stanford–Binet Intelligence Scale (Form L–M). Though the oldest and best known of intelligence tests, the Binet has lost much of its popularity in recent years. The Stanford–Binet offers only a single summary score of an individual's performance; furthermore, the test has been modified only slightly in more than 40 years and does not lend itself to ipsative interpretation (i.e., evaluating intraindividual differences in various mental abilities). The most recent norming of the Stanford–Binet (1972) also leaves much to be desired; very little is known or has been made public about this sample. The Stanford–Binet has long been known to be a poor measure of intelligence for adults because of its limited ceiling and rather narrow sampling of abilities at upper ages. Until recently, the Stanford–Binet had maintained its popularity in the assessment of young children from about 2½ to 6½ years. With the introduction of the McCarthy Scales in 1972 and its increasing acceptance by users in the field, use of the Stanford–Binet, even at these younger age levels, has declined significantly. The Stanford–Binet has problems in addition to its antiquated nature and the lack of precise information regarding the 1972 normative sample. There is a tendency toward racial and sexual stereotyping of behavior in the test items, and the use of Mental Age scores yielded by the scale are misleading (Shorr, McClelland, & Robinson, 1977). Although a revision of the Stanford–Binet is underway, it does not appear that it will be available in the next 5 years. Thus, for now, it is perhaps best to relegate this venerable scale to the history of psychological assessment. As Friedes (1972) has kindly offered, *Requiescat in pace.*

The McCarthy Scales (McCarthy, 1972) was designed as a measure of intellectual skill for children between the ages of 2½ and 8½ years. It consists of 18 subtests divided into 5 subscales: Verbal, Perceptual–Performance, Quantitative, Memory, and Motor. All but the gross motor tasks are collapsed into a global intelligence scale called the General Cognitive Scale. Dorothea McCarthy was a developmental psycholinguist who worked with children for many years and the McCarthy Scales reflect her clinical acumen and extensive experience with this age group, in addition to the considerable psychometric sophistication provided by Alan Kaufman (then project director for development of the McCarthy Scales) and his staff at The Psychological Corporation. Kaufman, and his wife Nadeen, have provided an excellent, in depth volume on the use and interpretation of the McCarthy Scales (Kaufman & Kaufman, 1977) that should be consulted by all users of the test. A more recent review of research on the McCarthy Scales is also available (Kaufman, 1982). The McCarthy Scales is a comprehensive measure of intelligence for the young child, expressly designed with the young child in mind, and is making significant contributions to our understanding of cognitive functioning in this age group.

The Wechsler scales, referring to the Wechsler Adult Intelligence Scale-Revised (WAIS-R, Wechsler, 1981), Wechsler Intelligence Scale for Children-Revised (WISC-R, Wechsler, 1974), and the Wechsler Preschool and Primary Scale of Intelligence (WPPSI; Wechsler, 1967), have enjoyed immense popularity with psychologists since their inception (the original WISC in 1949, and the WAIS in 1955). The WISC-R and WAIS-R are by far the instruments of choice for most psychologists in evaluating the intellectual functioning of school aged children and adults, respectively. The WPPSI, designed only for use with children between the ages of 4 and 6½ years, has not attained the same popularity of use as the WISC-R and WAIS-R, even though it is a comparable tool from a purely psychometric perspective. The WPPSI is a downward extension of the 1949 WISC, which was itself a downward extension of the earliest of the adult Wechsler Scales (The Wechsler–Bellevue; Wechsler was chief psychologist at Bellevue Hospital, thus the name Wechsler-Bellevue for his early work in developing an intelligence test). The WPPSI is thus not as directly relevant to a child's normal activities as scales designed specifically for this younger group. The WPPSI is also somewhat long for the young child; without frequent changes in activities, the preschooler's attention rapidly wanes. The WPPSI is nevertheless used with some frequency with this age group and can provide considerable information in the quest to understand the intellectual functioning of the young child.

For the school aged child between the ages of 6 and 16½ years, the WISC-R is by far the instrument of choice in the assessment of intellectual functioning. It provides a relatively broad sampling of cognitive skills, calling upon a variety of verbal and nonverbal skills, and involving several levels of abstraction. The test is quite reliable and has accumulated a hulking mass of empirical investigation over the past 30 years. The WISC-R, like other Wechsler scales, is divided into a Verbal Scale, a Performance (or nonverbal) Scale, and a summary Full Scale. The Verbal and Performance Scales are each composed of 5 subtests, with an alternate available in case an error is made or additional information is needed. The WISC-R has proved to be quite valuable in evaluating the intellectual functioning of school aged children, in understanding their current performance, and in suggesting alternatives for intervention.

Intelligence testing, while it can be very useful with exceptional children, is also a controversial activity, especially with regard to the diagnosis of mild mental retardation among minority cultures in the United States. Used with care and compassion, as a tool toward understanding, such tests can prove invaluable. Used recklessly and rigidly, they have the potential to cause irreparable harm. Extensive technical training is required to master the administration of an individual intelligence test (or any individual test for that matter). Even greater sensitivity and training are required to interpret properly these powerful and controversial devices. Extensive knowledge of statistics, measurement theory, and the existing research literature concerning testing is a most basic prerequisite to using intelligence tests. To use them well requires mastery of the broader field of psychology, especially differential psychology, the most basic of the psychological sciences that focuses on the psychological study and analysis of human individual differences and the theories of early cognitive development.

Achievement tests of various types are used throughout the public schools with regular classroom children as well as with exceptional children. Most achievement tests are group tests administered with some regularity to all students in a school or system. Some of the more prominent group tests include the Iowa Test of Basic Skills, the Metropolitan Achievement Test, the Stanford Achievement Test, and the California Achievement Test. These batteries of achievement tests typically do not report an overall index of achievement but rather report separately on achievement in such academic areas as English grammar and punctuation, spelling, map reading, mathematical calculations, reading comprehension, social studies, and general science. The tests change every few grade levels to accomodate changes in curriculum emphases. Group achievement tests provide schools with information concerning how their children are achieving in these various subject areas relative to other school systems throughout the country and relative to other schools in the same district. They also provide information about the progress of individual children and can serve as good screening measures in attempting to identify children at the upper and lower ends of the achievement continuum. Group administered achievement tests do not help much in achieving a good understanding of the academic performance of these individuals; that is, they do not provide sufficiently detailed or sensitive information on which to base major decisions. When decision making is called for or an in-depth understanding of a child's academic needs is required, individual testing is needed.

There is a growing number of individually administered achievement tests. Some are broad measures of academic attainment that attempt to assess many areas of academic skill. For example, the Peabody Individual Achievement Test (PIAT) provides scores in the areas of Mathematics, Spelling, Reading Recognition, Reading Comprehension, and General Information. Although the PIAT is used frequently for differential diagnosis of academic disorders, this use is probably inappropriate due to the large general achievement factor inherent in such a scale and the relatively low reliability of the individual subtests of the PIAT (Reynolds, 1979a).

Typically, one administers an individual test of achievement to obtain an in depth understanding of a child's academic skill in a single area of achievement. In this regard, the Woodcock Reading Mastery Tests (WRMT; Woodcock, 1973) are a more typical entry. The WRMT provides 5 reading scores for subtests entitled Word Attack Skills, Word Recognition, Word Comprehension, Passage Comprehension, and Letter Recognition. An overall summary score of the child's reading ability is also provided. By observing how a child with a reading difficulty responds to such different skill areas, considerably greater insight is possible than with a general measure of reading achievement. Tests which are conceptually similar to the WRMT are available for math, spelling, and writing skills as well. Many such tests are reviewed and discussed at some length in Buros' *Mental Measurement Yearbooks*.

Tests of special abilities are specialized methods for assessing thin slices of the spectrum of abilities for any single individual. These measures can be quite helpful in further narrowing the field of hypotheses about an individual's learning or behavior difficulties, especially when used in conjunction with intelligence, achievement, and personality measures. The number of special abilities that can be assessed is quite large. Some examples of these abilities include visual–motor integration skill, auditory perception, visual closure, figure–ground distinction, oral expression, tactile form recognition, and psychomotor speed. While these measures can be useful, depending upon the questions to be answered, one must be particularly careful in choosing an appropriate, valid, and reliable measure of a special ability. The use and demand for these tests are significantly less than that for the more popular individual intelligence and achievement tests. This in turn places some economic constraints on development and standardization procedures. Test development and standardization is a very costly enterprise when properly conducted, and one should always be on the lookout for the "quick and dirty" entry into the ability-testing market. There are some very good tests of special abilities available; however, special caution is also needed. One should also be aware of the fact that simply because an ability is named in the test title is no guarantee that the test in question is indeed a measure of that particular ability. As with any other test, just what is actually being measured by any collection of test items is a matter for empirical investigation.

To summarize, norm-referenced tests of intelligence, achievement, and special abilities all provide potentially important information in the assessment process, yet each supplies only a piece of the needed data. Equally important are observations of how the child behaves during testing and in other settings, and performance on other measures.

Norm-referenced, objective personality measures. Whereas tests of aptitude and achievement can be described as maximum performance measures, tests of personality can be described as typical performance measures. When taking a personality test, one is normally asked to respond according to one's typical actions and attitudes and not in a manner that would present the "best" possible performance (i.e., most socially desirable). The "faking" or deliberate distortion of responses is certainly possible, to a greater extent on some scales than others (e.g., Jean & Reynolds, 1982), and is a more significant problem with personality scales than with cognitive scales. Papers have even been published providing details on how to distort responses on personality tests in the desired direction (e.g., Whyte, 1967). While there is no direct solution to this problem, many personality measures have built in "Lie" or social desirability scales to help detect the deliberate faking that tends to make one look as good as possible. The use and interpretation made of scores from objective personality scales also have implications for this problem. Properly assessed and evaluated from an empirical basis, response to the personality scale is treated as the behavior of immediate interest and the actual content conveyed by the item becomes nearly irrelevant. For one example, there is an item on the Revised-Children's Manifest Anxiety Scale (RCMAS; Reynolds & Richmond, 1978), a test designed to measure chronic anxiety levels in children, that states "My hands feel sweaty." Whether the child's hands actually do feel sweaty is irrelevant. The salient question is whether children who respond "True" to this question are in reality more anxious than children who respond "False" to such a query. Children who respond more often in the keyed direction on the RCMAS display greater general anxiety and exhibit more observed behavior problems than do children who respond in the opposite manner. While face validity of a personality or other test is a desirable quality, it is not always a necessary one. It is the actuarial implications of the response that hold the greatest interest for the practitioner who is assessing a child. Personality scales are frequently called on to provide data when assessing children who have been referred due to behavior problems (Ysseldyke, Algozzine, Regan, & McGue, 1981), though they can also be useful in evaluating academic disorders and helping design appropriate therapeutic and curricular programs for such children (Anderson, 1981).

Due to their emphasis on inner psychological constructs that are difficult to infer, personality scales pose special problems of development and validation. A reasonable treatment of these issues can be found in most basic psychological measurement texts (e.g., Anastasi, 1976; Cronbach, 1970). The state of the art in objective personality testing indicates that the majority of these scales are appropriate only for research or for purely clinical purposes, even though the area of personality testing is the most rapidly proliferating of all areas of commercially published psychological tests (Reynolds & Elliott, 1983). Several examples of the personality scales that are being used currently in the evaluation of children's personalities follow.

Anxiety has been shown to be related to a number of behavioral and cognitive disturbances. There are a number of scales available for the measurement of children's anxiety levels; two of the most widely used and researched scales are the RCMAS (Reynolds & Richmond, 1978) and the State-Trait Anxiety Inventory for Children (STAIC; Spielberger, 1973). The RCMAS contains 28 anxiety and 9 Lie (or social desirability) scale items. It is primarily a measure of generalized trait anxiety (A_g) but it can be broken into 3 subscales of anxiety which have been designated *Physiological Anxiety, Worry and Oversensitivity,* and *Concentration Anxiety.* These names correspond to the content of the items defining these factors. The STAIC consists of two 20 item scales, one designed to measure state anxiety, a transient mental climate, and the other trait anxiety, essentially the same factor measured by the general score of the RCMAS (Reynolds, 1980).

While brief scales such as these are helpful in evaluating and assessing children's mental status, a number of broader, and hence much longer, personality scales for children have been developed over the years to measure multiple personality traits. The Personality Inventory for Children (PIC) by Wirt, Lachar, Kleindinst, and Seat (1977; also see Lachar & Gdowski, 1979) has gained rather quick acceptance in this field given its recent publication. The PIC has been under development since the 1950's, however, and has been used in numerous dissertations at the University of Minnesota over the last several decades. The PIC has 12 content scales designated as Achievement, Intellectual Screening,

Development, Somatic Concern, Depression, Family Relations, Delinquency, Withdrawal, Anxiety, Psychosis, Hyperactivity, and Social Skills. The PIC was unquestionably designed to mimic the Minnesota Multiphasic Personality Inventory (MMPI) as much as possible, but differs from this widely used adult scale in two important ways (Achenbach, 1981). First, information is taken on the scale as reported by the mother or some significant other person in the mother's absence rather than having the child complete the scale. Second, the items were not developed through the use of pre-existing criterion groups. As should be obvious, it is primarily the mother's personality as it interacts with the child's behavior that is being assessed. Evaluation of the usefulness of the PIC will rest on actuarial studies of its utility in predicting children's actual behavior and on its ability to allow accurate grouping and classification of child behavior problems. The PIC can provide a good point of demarcation in family therapy and in counseling parents since it yields information on the interaction described above. A computerized scoring and interpretive service has been developed by the publisher, much like computerized MMPI services, but it tends only to cluster and print in paragraph form items checked by the respondent.

Other scales designed as broad measures of the child's personality which are also completed by the child include such tests as the California Test of Personality, the Children's Personality Questionnaire, and the Early School Personality Questionnaire. The *Mental Measurements Yearbooks* prepared by the Buros Institute of Mental Measurement are a good source of information about the substantial (and growing number) of personality scales for children.

Neuropsychological assessment. Perhaps the most rapidly growing and controversial area of interest in the evaluation of children has been that of neuropsychological assessment. Attesting to the interest in this topic, neuropsychological testing has been the subject of many recent books (e.g., Hynd & Obrzut, 1981), new journals (e.g., *Clinical Neuropsychology*), special issues of journals (e.g., Hynd, 1981), and even a debate at the annual meeting of the American Psychological Association in 1981.

Much of the controversy stems from three factors: (1) a simplistic view of neuropsychological assessment as merely a set of tests, (2) rejection by many of a nomothetic approach to the amelioration of childhood disorders, and (3) a naive belief that neuropsychological techniques always result in a vague and useless designation of a child as having minimal brain damage or minimal brain dysfunction (MBD). Far from being a set of techniques, the major contribution of neuropsychology to the assessment process is the provision of a strong paradigm from which to view assessment data (Reynolds, 1981a). Without a strong theoretical guide to test score interpretation, one quickly comes to rely on past experience, illusionary relationships, or trial and error procedures when a child with unique test performance is encountered. As with most areas of psychology, there are competing neuropsychological models of cognitive functioning, any one of which may be most appropriate for a given child. Considerable knowledge of neuropsychological theory is thus required to evaluate properly the results of neuropsychological testing.

For the past three decades, clinical testing in neuropsychology has been dominated by the Halstead–Reitan Neuropsychological Battery (HRNTB), although the Luria–Nebraska Neuropsychological Battery is now also being used widely. The HRNTB consists of a large battery of tests and requires a full day to administer. There is little that is psychologically or psychometrically unique about any of these tests; indeed, they are all more or less similar to other tests that psychologists have been using for the past 50 years. The HRNTB typically includes a traditional intelligence test, such as one of the Wechsler Scales or the Henmon–Nelson Test of Mental Ability. The HRNTB is unique in the particular collection of tests involved and the method of evaluating and interpreting performance. While supported by actuarial studies, HRNTB performance is evaluated in light of existing neuropsychological theories of cognitive functioning, giving the Battery considerable explanatory and predictive power.

Current neuropsychological models of cognitive functioning have been discussed extensively and debated as of late (e.g., Das, Kirby, & Jarman, 1979; Reynolds, 1981b) and the design of educational strategies based on neuropsychological test results presented in some detail (e.g., Hartlage & Reynolds, 1981). Neuropsychological testing techniques have been demonstrated to be useful in planning instructional programs for children with learning disorders (Hynd & Obrzut, 1981; Reynolds, 1981a), and they can be very helpful in the evaluation of exceptional children. With more serious disorders, such as when there are clear implications of central nervous system involvement, neuropsychological assessment should be considered a nearly routine procedure. Neuropsychological approaches can be most helpful in defining areas of cognitive–neuropsychological integrity and not just in evaluating deficits in neurological function. Neuropsychological techniques can also make an important contribution by ruling out specific neurological problems and pointing toward environmental determinants of behavior. The well-trained neuropsychologist is aware that the brain does not operate in a vacuum but is an integral part of the ecosystem of the child. As with other methods of assessment, it must be pointed out that used wisely and skillfully, neuropsychological assessment has much to offer the assessment process; poorly or carelessly implemented, it can create seriously false impressions, lessen expectations, and promulgate a disastrous state of affairs for the child it is designed to serve.

Adaptive behavior assessment. The assessment of adaptive behavior is more a content area for assessment than it is a model or a new method of testing. As a content area, it has been with psychology for some time under such rubrics as social maturity and social intelligence. It is briefly presented here as an important area of assessment because of renewed interest and vitality in the area. This interest is primarily a function of changing emphasis in definitions of mental retardation and legal mandates, such as provided by PL 94-142 (see Chapter 6), so that it includes the assessment of adaptive behavior when evaluating potentially handicapped children. Though the area of mental retardation has been the primary focus of adaptive behavior assessment, it may have even greater value in assisting placement decisions for emotionally disturbed or behaviorally disordered individuals.

The American Association on Mental Deficiency (AAMD) is the primary professional organization that has been responsible for evaluating and defining the field of mental retardation. Legal designations of mental retardation have typically followed very closely the terminology and operational definitions of this disorder as promulgated by the AAMD. The 1961 AAMD diagnostic and classification system of mental retardation recognized two primary aspects of functioning that must be significantly below average before a diagnosis of mental retardation is warranted: intelligence and adaptive behavior. Revisions of the AAMD system in 1973 and again in 1977 have added increasing emphasis to the role of adaptive behavior in the appraisal of mental retardation. The AAMD also commissioned the development and publication of scales for the measurement of adaptive behavior. The AAMD now publishes separate versions of its scale for use in institutionalized and in public school settings. Conceptually, intelligence and adaptive behavior are considered to be equal partners as indications of mental retardation. In practice, however, this is seldom the case because intelligence and achievement measures are weighted more heavily. This is likely due largely to major conceptual and technical issues surrounding the measurement of adaptive behavior.

Most attempts to measure adaptive behavior require a third party informant such as a teacher, parent, or other care-giver. The informant is questioned regarding an individual's behavior at home, in the community, and possibly in school and other settings. Questions often pertain to a child's ability to choose foods properly and feed him or herself, getting dressed in the morning, skill with buttons, zippers, and snaps, bathing, finding one's way in the neighborhood or community, answering the telephone and taking messages, running simple errands, playing age appropriate games with other children, and managing time, money, and other personal resources, among other behaviors. Whenever a third party informant is used, the validity of the responses is always an issue. Seldom is a single individual knowledgeable concerning all aspects of another person's adaptive behavior. On the AAMD Adaptive Behavior Scale, Public School Version, teachers are advised to make their best guess for areas of adaptive behavior about which they have insufficient information.

Scales are now being published that allow the direct assessment of a child's adaptive behavior. While these techniques are new and not well researched, they appear promising in that they remove one more level of inference from the assessment process. Direct assessment of the child's adaptive behavior certainly seems preferable but is a difficult task. The method of assessment of adaptive behavior (i.e., direct by having the child perform standardized adaptive tasks vs. indirect by questioning a third party informant) also interacts with our conceptualizaton of the meaning of adaptive behavior. The method of measurement can affect our conceptualization of a concept just as it certainly has major impact on our operationalization of the concept.

Defining and conceptualizing adaptive behavior have not proven easy, consensual tasks. Are intelligence and adaptive behavior correlated or are they totally independent constructs of human behavior? The answer to this question has considerable impact on the development and the use of measures of adaptive behavior. It is possible to develop measures based on either set of assumptions or any combination of these assumptions. To make adaptive behavior measures independent of intelligence seems artificial as it requires the elimination of any item from the scale that would show a positive correlation with traditional tests of intelligence such as the WISC-R. The domain of behavior to be sampled is critically dependent on our conceptualization of adaptive behavior. Items that measure such seemingly adaptive skills as making change and keeping checkbook records may be eliminated from consideration under such a restrictive position and the content validity of adaptive behavior measures would be severely compromised. Consensual definition of adaptive behavior has not yet been achieved, and psychologists should be careful to understand the assumptions underlying the measures of adaptive behavior chosen for use.

Though acknowledged for some time, adaptive behavior and its assessment have only recently come under intense study. It appears to be an important area for assessment conceptually as well as being mandated under certain circumstances by federal and state statutes. What of the methods and the meaning of adaptive behavior assessment? What are their implications for placement and for developing intervention programs? These questions are amazingly complex and best dealt with in the context of training in individual assessment techniques. It is important to realize, however, that answers to these questions are going to be unsatisfactory for some time. We simply do not know enough about this domain of assessment yet. We are being forced to employ measures of adaptive behavior in the evaluation of children without being fully prepared to do so. We must exercise special care in interpreting this information, recognizing that conceptualizations of adaptive behavior are continuing to be shaped and also that what we believe is best today may change radically over a relatively short period of time.

Criterion-referenced Measurement. In contrast to norm-referenced assessment, which compares or "references" a person's performance to others who take the test, the application of criterion-referenced assessment is frequently to determine which individuals have reached some preestablished level of achievement. For example, many schools have established competency evaluations for determining whether a high school student should be allowed to graduate. In most instances, these tests are criterion-referenced because a student must achieve at established levels in various subject areas in order to be considered eligible for graduation. It really doesn't matter how much better than the criterion or how much worse a student performs. It is simply a pass/fail situation in which the student either does or does not display the skill.

Criterion-referenced assessment can be illustrated further by referring to differences in the methods used by some graduate and professional schools to evaluate students. A medical school, for example, may be concerned that everyone achieve surgery skills at some established criterion level (e.g., the patient recovers in a minimal amount of time and there are no complications). However, some schools use a norm-referenced approach in which they admit more students than they expect to graduate and then "weed out" the weaker students by administering difficult tests and passing only those individuals with the top scores. Though used often in these ways, criterion-referenced tests do not take their name from the use of a mastery level cut-off or "criterion." This name is taken to reflect the direct linkage between the test items and a specific set of objectives.

The primary usefulness of criterion-referenced assessment is in identifying the specific skills a child does or does not have. For example, following administration of a criterion-referenced reading test, a psychologist would know the specific reading tasks and skills that the child can and can not perform. Since most skills have been studied extensively and have been broken down into a series of steps (i.e., hierarchies), the test results could be used to determine the next most logical skill to teach the child. Thus, unlike norm-referenced assessment, there are direct implications for teaching without the need for large inferential leaps.

A related advantage is the ability to use criterion-referenced tests in formative evaluation. Formative evaluation consists of assessing a child regularly, usually daily, when skills are being learned. By doing this, it is possible to note student progress, to determine if instruction is effective, and to aid in planning the next skill to be taught. Since the focus is on *skills* rather than on a construct such as intelligence, knowing what to teach and how to measure it are simplified.

The primary problem with this form of assessment is establishing a suitable criterion. If a test were needed to determine whether students had mastered high school mathematics, for example, exactly which skills should be included in the test? Some individuals may feel that geometry is an essential skill that must be included, while others may disagree and want no geometric concepts on the test. After it is decided to include a particular skill, another problem is to decide the level at which the skill must be performed in order for the student to pass. Should a student pass the test if 90% of the questions are answered correctly or only if 100% are correct? These decisions must be thought out carefully because setting inappropriate criteria may cause a student to struggle unnecessarily with a concept on which the standard has been set at too high a level or pass a student on to a higher level of challenge when they have failed to master easier levels of subject matter because the criteria was set at too low a level.

An assumption made by advocates of criterion-referenced testing is that a child who fails to master a concept does so because of lack of exposure to the material. It is further assumed that additional instruction related to the concept will allow a child to pass the test when it is administered a second or third time. These assumptions may be inaccurate for some youngsters in special education. Additional instruction of the wrong type may not benefit some children and may result in a child repeatedly failing the tests.

A potentially troublesome aspect of this form of assessment is that the skills assessed by the test will become goals for instruction rather than selected samples of what the child should know. Teachers may narrow the focus of their instruction and simply teach in accordance with what is measured on the test. Becoming chained to a test in this manner can result in a loss of the richness and variety that characterize good instruction.

Projective Assessment. The projective assessment of personality has a long, rich, but very controversial history in the evaluation of clinical disorders and the description of normal personality. This controversy stems largely from the subjective nature of the tests used and from the lack of good evidence of predictive validity coupled with sometimes fierce testimonial and anecdotal evidence of their utility in individual cases by devoted clinicians.

The subjectiveness of projective testing is an inherent characteristic of the technique that often results in disagreement concerning the scoring and interpretation of an individual's responses to the test materials. That is, for any given response by any given individual, members of a group of competent professionals would be likely to give differing interpretations regarding the meaning and significance of the response.

Projective testing requires that an individual be presented with an ambiguous stimulus, such as an ink blot or an incomplete sentence, and asked to respond with the first thought or series of thoughts that come to mind or to tell a story about the stimulus. Typically, no restrictions are placed on the individual's response options. He or she may choose to respond with anything so desired. In contrast, on an objective scale, a respondent must select from among the response options provided by the test.

The basic assumption underlying projective testing is taken from Freud (Exner, 1976). The assumption is that when responding to an ambiguous stimulus, individuals are influenced by their needs, interests, and psychological organization and tend to respond in ways that reveal, to the trained observer, their motivations and true emotions, with far less interference from the conscious control of the ego. Other psychodynamic theories are applied to the evaluation of test responses, however, and herein too lie problems of subjectivity. Depending upon the theoretical orientation of the psychologist administering the test, very different interpretations may emerge. Despite the controversy surrounding these tests, they remain very popular; as reported in 1971, 5 of the 10 most frequently used tests in psychology were projective techniques (Lubin, Wallis, & Paine, 1971).

Evidence of criterion-related and predictive validity have proven especially tricky for advocates of projective testing. While it is apparent that techniques such as the Rorschach Inkblot Test are not amenable to study and validation through the application of traditional statistical and psychometric methods, many clinical researchers have made such attempts with less than heartening results. None of the so-called objective scoring systems for projective devices has really proved to be valuable in the prediction of behavior, nor has the use of normative standards been fruitful with these techniques. This should not be considered so surprising, however; it is indeed the nearly completely idiographic nature of projective techniques that can make them useful in the evaluation of a specific child. These techniques allow for any possible response to occur, without restriction, and can be rather revealing of many of a child's *current* reasons for behaving in a specific manner. When used as part of an assessment, as defined in this chapter, projective techniques can be quite valuable. On the other hand, when applied rigidly and without proper knowledge and consideration of the child's ecology, they can, as with most tests, be detrimental to our understanding of the child. For a more extensive review of the debates over projective testing, the reader is referred to Exner (1976), Jackson and Messick (1967, part 6), and O'Leary and Johnson (1979).

Projective methods can be divided roughly into three categories according to the type of stimulus presented and the method of response called for by the examiner. The first category calls for an oral response and interpretation of ambiguous visual stimuli by the child. Tests in this category include such well known techniques as the Rorschach and the Thematic Apperception Test (TAT) and its several variants. The second category includes completion methods, whereby the child is asked to finish a sentence when given an ambiguous stem or to complete a story begun by the examiner. This includes such techniques as the Despert Fables and any of a number of sentence completion tests. The third category includes projective art, primarily including drawing techniques, though sculpture and related art forms have been used. In these tasks, the child is provided with the necessary materials to complete an artwork (or simple drawing) and is given instructions for a topic, some more specific than others. Techniques such as the Kinetic-Family-Drawing, the Draw-A-Person, and the Bender–Gestalt Test fall in this category. The use of these methods with children has been described by Koppitz (1982) and several of the examples are described further below.

The set of 10 inkblots known as the "Rorschach" is perhaps the most famous of all psychological tests throughout the world. First published by Hermann Rorschach in 1921, perhaps prompted by work originated by Binet in the use of inkblots to test imagination in children, the popularization and further development of the inkblot technique for the projective study of personality occurred in the United States following Rorschach's untimely death in 1922 at the age of only 38 (Exner, 1976). The use of the term Rorschach now refers only to the set of 10 plates published by Rorschach himself. A variety of schools of interpretation and scoring of the Rorschach developed in the United States. Exner (1976) notes at least 5 major schools and it appears that the specific method of Rorschach interpretation employed is based largely on the school to which one's mentor may trace his or her Rorschachian roots. Rather heated exchanges between these various devotees have taken place over the last 50 years.

The Rorschach takes nearly an hour to administer properly and requires extensive training and more supervised experience than most tests for accurate interpretation. A child views the ink blots, each in turn, and reports what each blot (or parts of each blot) resembles. Responses are recorded verbatim and analyzed according to three very broad categories: the location of the area of the blot used by the child, the specific features of the blot that caused the child to interpret the blot in the specified manner, and the actual content of the response. A number of other factors may also be scored, such as the popularity or unusual nature of the response (i.e., how often the response is given by others) and the degree of organization imposed on the blot by the child. Interpretation of the Rorschach to achieve an understanding of the individual is a complex process that requires someone of considerable expertise both with people as well as with the method. Very elaborate computer-attempted Rorschach interpretations have not been successful (Exner, 1976).

The TAT is a projective story-telling technique wherein the subject is presented with an ambiguous picture and is asked to relate a story typically containing elements describing what is happening in the picture, what happened just before the picture, what is going to happen next, and an explanation or description of how the people in the story feel. Binet had also been a pioneer in the use of pictures to measure ideation, but the technique was not adequately formalized or popularized until the publication of the TAT by Murray in the 1930s. There has developed an even greater diversification of scoring systems for the TAT than for the Rorschach. A form of the TAT using animal figures has been developed for use with children (the CAT) as well as a children's set with human figures (CAT-H) in much the same poses as the animal form. Subsequently, noting that children may respond more to manipulative material, a puzzle form of the CAT was developed. Stories derived from the TAT and its derivatives reflect a variety of need states in the child but can be difficult to score accurately. Frequently with children, examiners are aided in understanding the individual child most by examining recurrent themes and symbolic figures in a child's stories.

Incomplete sentence methods have been quite popular, especially in the evaluation of children and adolescents. Although specific forms are available (e.g., Rotter Incomplete Sentences Blank) with elaborate scoring systems, part of their popularity with children lies in being able to develop or modify incomplete sentence stems for the specific child and his or her referral problem in order to gain maximum utility. Traditional work in validation has proven most promising with these of all the projective methods. Indeed, children can be surprisingly candid and informative in their responses to the direct nature of this method.

Projective drawing techniques, such as the Draw-A-Person (DAP), are another area of great controversy. Frequently with children, drawing tests double as measures of cognitive skill, due to the clear developmental sequence of children's drawings. IQ and emotional status are thus hopelessly confounded in such methods, along with age and sex, all producing a complex interaction with the child's visual-motor integration skills. The hypothesis underlying the use of projective drawings is similar to other projective techniques; the unique contribution of projective drawings lies in their nonverbal nature. They require a minimal mastery of language because the child need not verbalize any reponse, although some questioning typically occurs to clarify aspects of the drawing. Following the DAP, the Kinetic-Family-Drawing (KFD), wherein a child is asked to produce a picture of all the members of his or her family all doing something, is probably the most popular human figure drawing technique with children. In spite of their confounding of age, sex, IQ, and visual-motor skill, the projective drawing techniques appear to be able to contribute to understanding a child's current status, but they do not stand up well against traditional psychometric standards.

Behavioral Assessment. The rapid growth of the fields of behavior therapy and applied behavior analysis has lead to the need for an assessment methodology that is consistent with the theoretical and practical requirements of these appraoches to the modification of human behavior. Thus the field of behavioral assessment has developed and grown at an intense pace. Book-length treatments of the topic have now become commonplace (e.g., Haynes & Wilson, 1979; Hersen & Bellack, 1976; Marsh & Terdal, 1981) and entire journals are now devoted to research regarding behavioral assessment (e.g., *Behavioral Assessment*).

Goals, uses, and models. Thè goal of behavioral assessment is to identify meaningful response units and their controlling variables for the purposes of understanding and altering behavior (Nelson & Hayes, 1980). Within educational and clinical settings, behavioral assessment is used primarily to determine the features of an individual and his or her environment that maintain behavior. Several unique features of behavioral assessment make it very useful in the treatment of learning and behavior problems. First, behavioral assessment is individualized: it is specific and tailored to an individual's problem. Second, it is by design linked closely to any treatment plan implemented. Third, behavioral assessment is continuous in nature for it is utilized not only in problem identification but in the monitoring and final evaluation of a given problem as well.

According to Kratochwill (1982), several models of behavioral assessment have evolved through the development of behavior therapy (e.g., S-R model, A-B-C model, S-O-R-K-C model). The basic S-R or stimulus-response model developed by Skinner (1953) has provided the basis for the majority of models; however, the most commonly used model of behavioral assessment is probably the S-O-R-K-C (S=stimulus, O=organism, R=response, K=contingency, C=consequence) scheme developed by Kanfer and associates (Kanfer & Phillips, 1970; Kanfer & Saslow, 1969). This scheme has seven major components:

1. *Initial analysis:* An analysis of the problem situation, in which the various behaviors that brought the client to treatment are specified.
2. *Problem situation classification:* A clarification of the problem situation, in which various environmental variables (e.g., stimuli and responses) are specified.
3. *Motivational analysis:* An analysis in which reinforcing and punishing stimuli are identified.
4. *Developmental analysis:* An analysis in which biological, sociological, and behavioral changes of potential relevance to the treatment are identified.
5. *Self-Control analysis:* An analysis in which the situations and behaviors that the client can control are identified.
6. *Social situations analysis:* An analysis of situations in which the interpersonal relationships of individuals in the client's environment and their various aversive or reinforcing qualities are specified.
7. *Socio-cultural physical environment analysis:* An analysis in which normative standards of behavior and the client's opportunities for support are evaluated.

Ciminero and Drabman (1977) analyzed the S-O-R-K-C model and identified several positive features. For example, they believed that the model was comprehensive, attending to components frequently ignored in other models (e.g., biological, socio-cultural, reinforcement history, developmental factors).

In addition, they perceived the model as balanced in terms of assessing both positive and negative behaviors.

Conceptual framework. Given the rapid growth and diversity of models of behavioral assessment, we found that Cone's (1977, 1978) Behavioral Assessment Grid (BAG) provides a useful organization of three important aspects of the behavior assessment process: contents assessed, methods of assessment, and types of generalizability established. The depiction of the Behavioral Assessment Grid in Figure 4.4 illustrates the relationships among contents, methods, and universes of generalization.

The contents of a behavioral assessment have commonly been conceptualized into three domains: motor, physiological, and cognitive. Motor content is clearly the easiest to observe and consequently has been the most frequently assessed domain. Walking, hitting, and talking are examples of motor activities. Physiological contents include activities of muscles and glands autonomically innervated, as well as tonic muscle responses. Heart rate, muscle tension, and galvanic skin response are examples of physiological activities that can be measured accurately. Cognitive contents recently have become a major aspect of behavioral assessment and treatment. According to Kratochwill (1982), cognitive contents must be defined in the context of the particular referents used. For example, while verbal behavior can be classified as motoric content when one is referring to the act of speech, the referents may be motoric, cognitive, or physiological. When verbal behavior refers to private events such as feelings or thoughts, the referents are cognitive.

At least eight methods of behavioral assessment have been identified. As indicated in Figure 4.4, these eight methods can be categorized along direct and

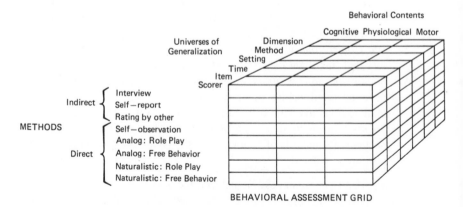

BEHAVIORAL ASSESSMENT GRID

Figure 4.4. The Behavioral Assessment Grid (BAG). (Reproduced from Cone, 1978, copyright Association for the Advancement of Behavior Therapy, with permission of author and publisher.)

indirect dimensions. Interviews, self-reports, and ratings by others are categorized as indirect because they are either retrospective in nature or a verbal representation of more clinically relevant activities which happened at another time and in another place. The direct methods of behavioral assessment [i.e., (a) self-observation, (b) analog: role play, (c) analog: free play, (d) naturalistic: role play, and (e) naturalistic: free play] vary according to *who* does an observation and the *conditions* under which it occurs, yet all of them have observational recording and analysis of behavior content as a central function. A detailed examination of each of these methods is available in Kratochwill's (1982) review of advances in behavioral assessment. In the next section, however, we will examine several critical dimensions of behavioral observation since it represents the methodological core of behavioral assessment.

Generalization of assessment data is an important concern with any type of assessment method. However, given the specificity (with regard to target behaviors and environmental variables) involved in a behavioral assessment, the issue of the generalizability of one's data has maintained a critical role in discussions of reliability and validity (Kazdin, 1979). According to The BAG conceptualization, the various behavioral measures should be concerned about generalization across six major universes: scorer, item, time, settings, method, and dimension. Hence, psychologists employing behavioral assessment methods should plan ways to demonstrate the generalization of their findings. This usually involves, at a minimum, multiple observations of the target behavior(s) across time and places by at least two observers or raters. Ideally, multiple methods of assessment [e.g., (a) interview, (b) analog: free play, (c) naturalistic: free play] would also be used to determine generalization of methods.

Behavior observation: techniques and issues. The direct observation of motoric behaviors has been and probably will continue to be the most widely used method x content function of behavioral assessment. Consequently, applied and research psychologists interested in conducting behavioral assessments must possess a variety of observational skills.

Numerous sources discuss and explain techniques and issues in the observation of behavior (e.g., Sulzer-Azaroff & Mayer, 1977). Allessi (1980), however, authored an article that we found to be particularly comprehensive and oriented toward school psychologists. Thus, we will utilize many of his thoughts to review briefly observational techniques in educational settings. According to Allessi (1980), there are five basic approaches to observing and recording behavior. These include interval recording, time sample recording, event recording, duration recording, and latency recording.

Interval recording techniques result in a measure of the number of intervals or time blocks (usually 15- or 30-second units for a period of 20 to 30 minutes) within which a target behavior is observed to occur. Interval recording is the easiest observational technique to use. The observer simply watches for the target behavior and records its presence if it occurs at any time, regardless of duration, during the specified time unit. Interval recording is considered appropriate for observing behaviors which occur at a moderate but steady rate.

Time sample recording results in a measure of the number of times the behavior was observed to occur at pre-specified sampling points in time. For example, an observer looks for the target behavior at the end of every 15-second interval. If at that very second the target behavior is present, it would be recorded affirmative; otherwise, the behavior would be considered absent. This technique has its advantages and disadvantages. The advantage is that you can do other things between observations, such as observe several other pupils. The disadvantage of time sampling is that you get a much smaller sample of observation time relative to interval recording. Like interval recording, time sampling is useful to observe behaviors that occur at a moderate but steady rate.

Event recording requires an observer to note the precise number of occurrences of a target behavior during a given time frame. The observer must be able to discern exactly when a behavior stops and starts in order to get an accurate frequency count. Consequently, a clear, operationalized definition of the target behavior is essential to reliable event recording. Alessi recommends event recording for behaviors that occur very often, very seldom, or very briefly. It is also a useful method for recording behaviors that result in a permanent product.

Duration recording is an observational technique designed to measure the precise length of time a target behavior lasts or persists. Like event recording, an observer must have a well operationalized definition of the target behavior so that he or she can determine when it starts and stops. Duration recording generally is used less frequently than any of the three previously mentioned observational techniques; however, when duration of a target behavior is the critical issue, it is the method of choice. For example, if a teacher is interested in reducing the time that it takes a student to complete independent seat work, then periodic measures of duration of time engaged in independent seat work will provide an empirical record by which to assess the student's progress.

Latency recording results in the masurement of the precise length of time between a specified event and the onset or completion of a target behavior. For example, if the target behavior was lining-up for lunch without talking and the specified event which triggered this target behavior was a bell, then the time elapsing between the sounding of the bell and students standing quietly in a line would be recorded as the latency measure. Latency recording is subject to some of the same difficulties that duration and event recording experience with regard to target behavior definition and the assessment of when the behavior starts and stops. Consequently, latency recording should be used sparingly and primarily with problems of compliance.

Regardless of the recording technique used, there are a number of practical and research issues that help determine the reliability and validity of a behavioral assessment. Two salient issues with which school psychologists should concern themselves are (a) reactivity of the individuals being observed and (b) interpretation of observational data.

Reactivity is a source of error associated with most assessment instruments, but is particularly relevant to behavioral observation. Reactivity occurs when "the assessment procedure results in the modification of the behavior of subjects being assessed" (Haynes & Horn, 1982). In behavioral observation, reactive effects occur when the process of observing an individual or group alters, either permanently or temporarily, their behavior. Consequently, generalizability or external validity of the data derived from the observations cannot be assumed (Baum, Forehand, & Zegiob, 1979).

Researchers have indicated that behavioral observation is not always associated with reactivity, yet under some conditions it does occur and results in methodologically and clinically significant effects (Johnson & Bolstad, 1975; Kent, O'Leary, Dietz, & Dirament, 1979). The reactive effects associated with behavioral observation have not been consistent. Some researchers have reported increases in target behavior, some have found decreases in behavior rates, while still other researchers have reported differential effects on behavior rates for different behaviors of the same subject (Kazdin, 1982; Zegiob & Forehand, 1978).

In their review of research on reactivity, Haynes and Horn (1982) synthesized a list of recommendations for minimizing or controlling the reactive effects due to behavioral observation. The strategies they listed include: (a) use of participant observers, (b) use of covert observation, (c) use of audio and video recorders, (d) minimization of subject–observer interaction and other discriminative properties of observers, and (e) use of a number of observers or observation procedures so that differential effects cancel out.

A potential shortcoming of observational data is that an individual's performance is difficult to interpret or to place in the large context of his or her peers because of a lack of normative data. Normative samples, which have been obtained for many psychological tests and inventories in order to provide a relative basis for interpreting individuals' performances, have not been established for many behavioral observation methods. Therefore, unless an individual's performance is so extreme that a target behavior is performed excessively or virtually not at all, it is difficult to determine the individual's relative standing among peers. Many behavioral assessments and interventions are concerned primarily with extreme behavior, so normative data are not always necessary. Yet several behavioral therapists have called for the establishment of normative data (Hartmann, Roper, & Bradford, 1979; Kazdin, 1981). Such normative data could serve as a basis for identifying individuals whose behaviors warrant treatment and also provide a means for evaluating the treatment effects for a given behavior.

As a remedy for the lack of normative data, Allessi (1980) recommended an observational comparison approach whereby an observer collects data simultaneously on the referred individual and on a "normal" individual in the same setting. "The 'referred pupil/comparison pupil' (cf. Walker & Hops, 1976; Lindsey, 1971) strategy gives the psychologist a local norm with which to compare data collected on the referred pupil [and] the behavior of another pupil of the same sex in the same situation but who has not been identified as experiencing behavior adjustment difficulties" (Allessi, 1980, p. 31). In addition, the observer can also take brief samples of behavior from the entire class to provide a greater contextual comparison for the referred individual. In sum, the development of local or micro norms presently provides the best means for normative interpretation of behavioral observation data.

Phases of behavior assessment. Kratochwill (1982) synthesized the conceptual work of several authors concerning stages or phases of behavioral assessment and also used the terminology of behavioral consultation to arrive at a six phase process model of behavioral assessment. The six phases are: problem identification, problem analysis, plan implementation, plan evaluation, generalization, and follow-up. Given your acquaintance with problem-solving consultation as a result of previous discussion in both Chapters 2 and 3, you should have little difficulty understanding the process model of behavioral assessment. A brief overview of each stage or phase is discussed in the following paragraphs.

Phase 1. *Problem Identification* focuses on the definition of the specific target behavior. Assessment in this phase generally involves measures such as interviews or behavior rating scales which help to define the scope and nature of the target problem

Phase 2. *Problem Analysis* focuses primarily on the defined target behavior and the environmental events that surround it. Direct assessment methods such as self-monitoring, analog assessment, and direct observation are helpful in establishing a baseline level of the target behavior.

Phase 3. *Plan Implementation* is primarily concerned with the use of previous assessment data to design a treatment or intervention that will lead to change in the target behavior. During this phase, assessment methods are used primarily to monitor the treatment to determine whether it is functioning as intended. Therefore, the direct assessment methods used in the previous phase are usually repeated throughout this phase.

Phase 4. *Plan Evaluation* focuses on the monitoring of the "final" treatment that was implemented. The goal of this phase is too assess the overall effectiveness of the treatment. Thus, both direct and indirect behavior methods are usually employed.

Phase 5. *Generalization* focuses on the extent to which the "treated" behavior transfers across situations and individuals. Thus, an

Phase 6. assessment of the "treated" behavior, preferrably via direct observation, should be completed in various naturalistic settings to determine generalization.

Phase 6. *Follow-Up* concerns the "long-term" re-evaluation of the stability of the treatment on the target behavior. Direct observations are desired; however, brief indirect measures such as self-reports can be helpful. This phase should provide valuable feedback data to the psychologist which in turn may be helpful in the design of future treatments.

From this brief discussion of the behavioral assessment process it should be evident that behavioral assessment is an ongoing method of gathering information about the status of an individual's functioning. Such a process serves to link assessment and intervention while functioning within a problem-solving consultation framework. In sum, the phases of behavioral assessment as conceptualized by Kratochwill (1982) clearly differ from those of traditional assessment.

Perspectives on behavioral assessment. Although behavioral assessment is developmentally in its infancy compared to traditional norm-reference assessment methods, unquestionably it plays a valuable role in the assessment and treatment of individuals in educational settings. Yet, both traditional and behavioral methodologies must be viewed as complementary assessment methods. In fact, researchers' examinations of the assessment practices of behavior therapists and behaviorally-oriented school psychologists indicate that traditional assessment practices are still used extensively (Anderson, Cancelli, & Kratochwill, 1979; Wade, Baker, Morton, & Baker, 1978).

Over the past several years, Nelson and her associates (e.g., Nelson & Hayes, 1980; Nelson & Bowles, 1975) have argued for the best of both worlds; in other words, they have advocated the integration of traditional normative assessment (as in the IQ test) with direct observational assessment methods. This approach is intended to provide cognitive and behavioral data, plus an opportunity to begin to establish behavior norms in a testing situation that is highly standardized. We believe this is a positive step and should enhance the future of behavioral assessment.

Assessment of Environments

Rationale for Environmental Assessment. By conceptualizing school psychologists' assessment roles within a reciprocal determinism paradigm, it becomes immediately and undeniably evident that assessment of environments is an activity of major importance. To understand the human condition and to reach accurate diagnostic/prognostic conclusions, one must comprehend the nature of the environments within which clients function. At this point there can be no doubt that environmental factors have a profound direct and indirect impact on the behavior and personological characteristics of children. The research literature in educational psychology is replete with data highlighting the significant impact of environmental variables in school and other educational settings. Among many other journals of major interest, readers are referred to the *American Educational Research Journal* and the *Review of Educational Research,* both of which are journals of the American Educational Research Association (AERA), and the *Journal of Educational Psychology,* an APA journal, to sample this extensive body of information.

Operant psychology is clearly the most thoroughly investigated of all the theoretical perspectives postulating a major role for environmental factors; however, empirical support for the impact of environment comes from a multitude of other sources as well. The following is a representative, albeit minor, sampling of this literature.

1. Following an extensive literature review, Centra and Potter (1980) concluded that student learning outcomes are influenced by school district conditions, within-school conditions, teacher characteristics, teacher behavior, student behavior, and student characteristics. Figure 4.5 presents their model of causal and correlational relationships and enumerates the variables they examined.

2. A review of research regarding the effects of open education led Giaconia and Hedges (1982) to conclude, "Open education programs *can* produce greater self-concept, creativity, and positive attitude toward school" (p. 600).

3. Research reviews conducted by Leithwood and Montgomery (1982) and Anderson (1982), respectively, detail the influence of principals' behavior and school organizational climate on a wide variety of educational phenomena.

4. A meta-analysis of teacher questioning behavior led Redfield and Rousseau (1981) to the conclusion that using higher cognitive questions (i.e., questions requiring students to manipulate information) results in greater achievement than the use of lower cognitive questions (i.e., questions focusing on the recall of factual information).

5. Johnson, Skon, and Johnson (1980) produced data indicating that the cooperative, competitive, or individualistic nature of student groups has a significant impact on student achievement for high, medium, and low ability first graders working on categorization and retrieval, spatial-reasoning, and verbal problem-solving tasks.

6. A meta-analysis of research on class size revealed "a substantial relationship between class size and teacher and pupil attitudes as well as instruction. Favorable teacher effects (workload, morale, attitudes toward students) are associated with smaller classes as are favorable effects on students (self-concept, interest in school, participation). Smaller classes are associated with greater attempts to individualize instruction and better classroom climate" (Smith & Glass, 1980, p. 419).

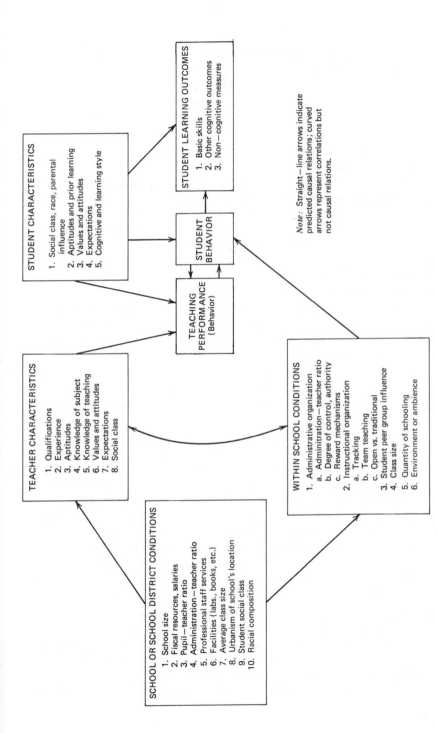

Figure 4.5. Structural model of school and teacher variables influencing student learning outcomes (Reproduced by permission from Centra & Potter, 1980.)

7. After a review of research pertaining to the impact of physical variables in the classroom, Weinstein (1979) concluded that student achievement and nonachievement behaviors/attitudes could be affected by environmental variables such as seating location and crowding, respectively. She went on to state, "Relatively minor design modifications introduced into already functioning classrooms have been shown to produce changes in students' spatial behavior, increased interaction with materials, decreased interruptions, and more substantive questioning" (pp. 598–599).

8. A meta-analysis conducted by Luiten, Ames, and Ackerson (1980) indicated that the use of advance organizers may enhance student learning and retention across a wide range of content areas, grade levels, and ability groups.

9. A study by Beckerman and Good (1981) indicated that both high and low aptitude students in classrooms where more than a third of the students were classified as high aptitude and less than a third were classified as low aptitude attained higher levels of achievement in mathematics than comparable students in classrooms in which this situation was reversed.

10. Leinhardt, Zigmond, and Cooley (1981) presented data indicating that, for learning disabled children, the total time spent in reading was significantly related to a variety of teacher instructional behaviors, teacher affective behaviors, and instructional pacing.

11. After reviewing research studies covering nearly 15,000 students, Lysakowski and Walberg (1982) reported that instructional cues, student participation, and receipt of corrective feedback all had a robust and positive impact on student achievement.

Above and beyond theoretical and research foundations, detailed assessment of educational environments can be thoroughly justified simply on the basis of practicality. In point of fact, the overwhelming majority of school psychologists' recommendations and interventions primarily involve manipulation of the environment. Whether suggesting special class placement, a behavior modification program, curricula revisions, creation of a peer tutoring program, parent training, or an organizational development project, the psychologist is making planful changes in the environment so that he or she may effect meaningful improvements in behavior and personological characteristics of children. Phillips (1982) proposed five categories of school psychological interventions based on his review of theory, research, and practice: (a) ecological and organizational interventions, (b) instructional and curricular interventions, (c) individual and group therapy interventions, (d) social and observational interventions, and (e) behavioral interventions. With the exception of the individual and group therapy category, all the others rely primarily on environmental modifications. It is interesting to note, however, that even in the therapy category, many of the actions taken or recommended by school psychologists are environmentally based (see Chapter 23, "Other Therapies for Children—Some Brief Looks," in Reynolds and Gutkin, 1982). Given these facts, it would seem axiomatic to scrutinize carefully the environment as a major component of school psychological assessments.

Obstacles to Environmental Assessment. Unfortunately, we find that environmental assessment typically receives a low priority among practicing school psychologists. We can hypothesize a number of reasons to account for this phenomenon. First, most school psychologists were trained under a medical model orientation and thus focus primarily on the characteristics and disabilities of referred children, relegating the influence of environment to a level of secondary or tertiary importance. This trend is reinforced by most texts addressing assessment which typically devote little or no space to the evaluation of environment. Happily, there are a few notable exceptions to this trend. Among books on general assessment techniques, Helton, Workman, and Matuszek (1982) and Elliott and Witt (1981) discuss environmental assessment in some detail. Books focusing exclusively on this issue include those by Moos (1979), Smith, Neiwsorth, and Greer (1978), Fox, Schumck, Egmond, Ritvo, and Jung (1973), and Fox, Luszki, and Schmuck (1966).

Second, environmental assessment may be resisted by principals, teachers, parents, etc. because it raises the possibility in their eyes that they may be blamed for a child's difficulties. Just as examination of a child leads to statements of his or her weaknesses, educators and parents may fear that assessment of their school, classroom, home, etc. will result in findings of deficiencies for which they may be held accountable. Of course, no form of assessment should focus excessively on weaknesses as opposed to strengths, and the purpose of assessment is to diagnose and remediate complex problems rather than to assign blame. The subjective perceptions of the adults who populate the world of referred children, however, may lead them to feel threatened by environmental assessments and cause them to discourage its use.

Third, the implementation of environmental assessment techniques has been seriously hampered by the lack of accepted and comprehensive theories. Perhaps the most sophisticated theoretical work in this area has been done by Barker and his associates (1968, 1978), but even here a great deal of necessary conceptualization remains to be done. Without a well-articulated theory, persons attempting to design assessment tools to measure environmental factors are left without a clear direction in which to proceed. An analogous situation would exist if behavior modifiers were forced to collect behavioral data without operant, social learning, or cognitive–behavioral theory to help them discriminate relevant and irrelevant pieces of information. Although the situation appears to be improving, most instruments that have been designed to measure environmental phenomena are the results of pragmatic, situational needs of particular practitioners rather than a priori theoretical formulations. Without additional theoretical advances in environmental psychology, the development of a technology of environmental assessment will be seriously hampered.

Finally, school psychologists have tended to direct environmental assessment into the area of program evaluation rather than utilizing it primarily for the benefit of individual students. Within this realm, a good deal has been accomplished, addressing both the political processes and the technical content of environmental assessments. The reader is referred to the special issue of *Journal of School Psychology* devoted to program evaluation (Hoover, Maher, & Phillips, 1978) and Payne's (1982) chapter on the same topic in *The Handbook of School Psychology*. Without in any way denigrating the importance of program evaluation, it does seem to have captured the imagination of many school psychologists interested in examining environmental phenomena and thus taken too much of the field's creative energies away from refining the theory and practice of environmental assessment. We believe that with sufficient thought, many of the advances accomplished in the area of program evaluation could be put to use for assessing the environments of individual children.

Techniques of Environmental Assessment. The following is a selected review of a variety of environmental assessment techniques and instruments. Although space limitations prohibit a thorough discussion of any particular approach, we hope that from this presentation the reader can get a picture of the breadth of available methodologies and some of their uses, strengths, and weaknesses. As a group, many of these techniques are relatively weak from a psychometric perspective. That is, data on norms, reliability, and validity are often quite limited. Users of these methods, therefore, must be careful not to overinterpret the data they derive. The reader is referred to books such as those by Ciminero, Calhoun, and Adams (1977) and Haynes and Wilson (1979) for a thorough discussion of methodologies commonly used for the assessment of environments (e.g., direct observation, self-report inventories, interviews, analog measures) and to journals such as *Behavioral Assessment*.

Teacher–Student Interactions. Given the reciprocal determinism paradigm, it is easy to see that assessment of teacher-student interactions may prove to be critical in a wide variety of situations. There are a considerable number of instruments available for this purpose. The following are a few of the most widely used. A large number of additional instruments are described in Mirrors for Behavior III (Simon & Boyer, 1974).

1. Flanders System of Interaction Analysis (Flanders, 1966). According to Simon and Boyer (1974), the Flanders System of Interaction Analysis is "the most widely known and used classroom observation system" (p. 92). The instrument includes ten categories of responses covering both teacher and student behaviors. Teacher behaviors include: (a) accepting feelings, (b) praising or encouraging, (c) accepting or using ideas of student, (d) asking questions, (e) lecturing, (f) giving directions, and (g) criticizing or justifying authority. Student behaviors include: (a) student talk—response to the teacher, (b) student talk—initiated by student, and (c) silence or confusion. In his book on this system, Flanders (1970) goes into enormous detail on how to use the data that are generated and the research relating his method to teacher effectiveness.

2. Ecological Assessment of Child Problem Behavior (Wahler, House, & Stambaugh, 1976). This system includes two major sets of category codes, that is, six stimulus codes and eighteen behavior codes. The stimulus codes "are intended to provide a sample of those classes of adult and peer social stimuli that commonly appear in temporal association with any child's desirable and deviant behavior" (p. 6). The stimulus codes are: (a) instruction, non-aversive, (b) instruction, aversive, (c) social attention adult, non-aversive, (d) social attention adult, aversive, (e) social attention child, non-aversive, and (f) social attention child, aversive. The behavior codes "provide a comprehensive sampling of five general classes of desirable and deviant child behavior. The reader should keep in mind that none of the classes and their included category codes can be given a priori listings as desirable or deviant" (p. 13). The five classes of behavior and their associated behavior codes are as follows: (a) compliance-opposition, including compliance, opposition, aversive opposition, and complaints, (b) work, including sustained school work, sustained work, and sustained attending, (c) social, including social approach adult, social approach child, mand adult, mand child, social interaction adult, and social interaction child, (d) play, including sustained toy play, (e) autistic, including self-stimulation, object play, sustained non-interaction, and self-talk. Reliability and validity data are inadequate in scope, the former being limited to interobserver agreement for six subjects observed in their school and home settings, and the latter consisting entirely of comparisons with information gathered through interviews.

3. Teacher-Pupil Interaction Scale (Goodwin & Coates, 1977). The Teacher-Pupil Interaction Scale (TPIS) was designed specifically for psychologists and other persons working with teachers and other adults within a behavioral consultation framework. Among the attractive elements of the system are the simultaneous recordings of both teacher and student behaviors with a single mark and the fact that both target and other pupils are observed, thus providing a basis for within class comparisons of teacher-child interactions. Teacher behavior categories include: (a) instructing, (b) rewarding, (c) non-attending or neutral, and (d) disapproving. Pupil behavior categories include: (a) on-task, (b) scanning behavior, (c) social contact, and (d) disruptive behavior. A procedure is presented by the authors to train observers to attain agreement coefficients of .80 or better using formulae provided by Scott (1955). Validity data are scanty.

Teacher-Child Dyadic Interaction (Brophy & Good, 1969). The Teacher-Child Dyadic Interaction scale provides information reflecting the quality of verbal exchanges between a teacher and a student in response to the teacher's questioning behaviors. The data coding system reveals the types of questions asked by the teacher, the accuracy of responses given by the student, and the nature of the teacher's reactions to the student's answers. The general classes of activities assessed and specific data codes are as follows: (a) response opportunities, including discipline questions, direct questions, open questions, and call outs, (b) level of question, including process questions, product questions, choice questions, and self-reference questions, (c) child's answer, including correct answers, part-correct answers, incorrect answers, and no response, and (d) teacher's feedback reaction, including praise, affirmation of correct answers, no feedback reaction, negation of incorrect answers, criticism, process feedback, gives answer, asks other, call out, repeats question, rephrase or clue, and new question. After considering the available reliability and validity data, Helton, Workman, and Matuszek concluded, "We are satisfied with the technical adequacy of the system for both research purposes and for use in conditions analysis with individual children" (p. 297).

Assessment of Peer Relationships. Assessments of peer relationships in schools and other education settings may provide school psychologists with important pieces of information, helping them to understand the ecology of a child's situation. Sociometric measurement has been the most common technique used for this purpose. Although there are many alternative ways to conduct a sociometric examination, the core elements of the technique can be explained rather quickly.

As detailed in the classic book by Gronlund (1959) on sociometry, the technique basically consists of asking persons to rate other persons in a group in reference to a criterion. This criterion may vary along several dimensions. For example, the difference between general and a specific criterion would be reflected by instructions to rank order fellow classmates according to whom the respondent likes best versus with whom he or she would most like to do homework. Sociometric questions may also vary according to whether the rating is being done in regard to an actual or a hypothetical situation. "List three children you would most like to work with in reading group" would be an example of the former, while "Choose three children you would most like as your brother or sister" illustrates the latter. Sociometric questions can also be posed in positive or negative terms. For instance, a teacher could ask his or her students to indicate which students they would most like or least like to be class president. Another variation is asking persons to list a limited number of group members according to a criterion (e.g., Name three classmates whom you would like to sit next to you) versus asking each person to rate every other person in the group (e.g., Rank order all of your classmates according to whom you would most like to sit next to you). Recent evidence (Morrison, 1981) indicated that the ways in which the sociometric questions are structured along these types of dimensions can influence the results of the assessment.

The data collected through sociometry can be displayed in a variety of formats. The use of a sociometric matrix (see Figure 4.6) and sociogram (see Figure 4.7) are the most common. The Sociogram, in particular, usually allows for an easy visual determination of a child's status in a group regarding the criteria used for the sociometric question. An examination of the sociogram in Figure 4.7, for example, reveals that MB is a "star," that is, he or she received a high number of choices, while PA is an "isolate," that is, he or she received

	Chosen	John	Mary	Jim	Susie	Ralph	George	Paul
Chooser								
John			1		2			
Mary				2	1			3
Jim					2	3	1	
Susie			2	3		1		
Ralph				3	2		1	
George			3	2				1
Paul					2	3	1	
Chosen as								
1st choice		0	1	0	1	1	3	1
2nd choice		0	1	2	4	0	0	0
3rd choice		0	1	2	0	3	0	1
Total		0	3	4	4	4	3	2

Figure 4.6. A sample sociometric matrix. (Reproduced by permission from Helton, Workman, & Matuszek, 1982.)

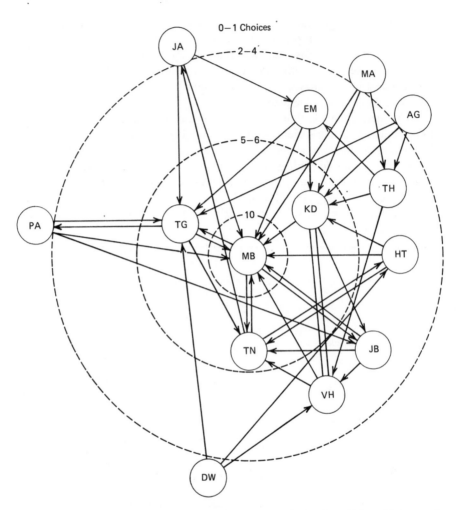

Figure 4.7. A sample sociogram. (Reproduced by permission from Helton, Workman, & Matuszek, 1982.)

only one choice. The sociogram also highlights the structural pattern of social groups or cliques by indicating mutual choices among group members, e.g., TN with HT and MB.

In summary, sociometric techniques appear to be an easy, quick, and inexpensive method for assessing peer relationships in a group setting. Although continuing research is necessary, Gronlund (1959) reported that sociometric results generally have high internal consistency and test-retest reliabilities. Regarding validity, he states, "studies have shown that sociometric results are significantly related to the actual behavior of pupils, to teachers' judgments of pupils' social acceptance, to adults' ratings of pupils' social adjustment, to the reputations pupils hold among their peers, to specific problems of social adjustment, and, within limits, to problems of personal adjustment'' (p. 183). When assessing peer relationships, sociometric data can typically be enhanced further by direct observations of group events and interviews with group members.

Assessment of Classroom Climate. A substantial number of measurement devices have been constructed for the purposes of assessing classroom climate. As in the previous sections, our discussion is necessarily limited by space considerations. Interested readers are referred to Anderson (1982) for both greater depth and breadth regarding this topic.

The *Classroom Environment Scale* (CES) (Trickett & Moos, 1973) is one of the many scales designed to assess classroom climate. Its relatively unique feature is that it was designed specifically to measure the psychosocial environment of junior and senior high school classes rather than those at the elementary school level. The instrument's theoretical rationale, development, and technical properties are discussed extensively by Moos (1979). The CES measures three domains of classroom environment: (a) relationship dimensions, including student involvement, student affiliation, and teacher support, (b) personal growth or goal orientation dimensions, including task orientation and competition, and (c) system maintenance and change dimensions, including order and organization, rule clarity, teacher control, and innovation. Data collected with this instrument from 200 classes and subsequently analyzed using multivariate cluster analysis techniques yielded six classroom profiles. They are labeled: innovation oriented, structured relationship oriented, supportive task oriented, supportive competition oriented, unstructured competition oriented, and control oriented.

> The cluster solution makes good conceptual and empirical sense. The first two groups of classes emphasize involvement and student-student and teacher-student relationships. One of these groups is relatively unstructured and stresses openness and change, whereas the other is relatively structured because of the considerable focus on clarity and organization. The second two groups emphasize different aspects of classroom goal orientation within a generally cohesive framework focused primarily on teacher support. The last two groups are similar in that they both lack emphasis on the relationship areas. One of the clusters stresses goal orientation (primarily competition), but does so within a framework lacking both cohesion and structure. The final cluster, control oriented, primarily emphasizes stability and organization. (Moos, 1979, pp. 156–157)

Information such as this for individual classrooms will often prove to be an important part of the ecology of presenting problems and may give the psychologist important leads in determining optimal class placements for referred students.

Assessment of Family Interactions. There can be little question that patterns of family interaction are a major force in the development and behavior of children. The increasing interest of school psychologists in family phenomena is reflected by two recent issues of *School Psychology Review* devoted to that topic (Guidubaldi, 1980; Shellenberger, 1981) and a chapter in *The Handbook of School Psychology* on family therapy (Petrie & Piersel, 1982). Extensive discussion regarding the assessment of families can be found in several books (e.g., Conger, 1981; Haynes & Wilson, 1979; Reid, 1978). As with the assessment of other environmental factors, family interactions can be examined with a variety of methodologies, including questionnaires [e.g., Family Environment Scale (Moos, Insel, & Humphrey, 1974)], direct observation [e.g., Family Interaction Scales (Riskin, 1964), Behavioral Observation Scoring System (Burgess & Conger, 1978)], interviews [see Helton, Workman, & Matuszek (1982) for a brief discussion on this topic] and analogue techniques [see Haynes & Wilson (1979) for a detailed discussion of this literature].

For the purposes of this discussion, the theoretical framework for family assessment provided by Conger (1981) may be more relevant than an analysis of any individual instrument or methodology. As shown in Table 4.4, a comprehensive assessment of familial patterns should include an examination of individual family members, the family as an ecological system, and the interface between a family and the larger community within which it exists. Clearly, this is a large undertaking for a school psychologist, or even an entire multidisciplinary team. Given the central role that families typically play in the quality of childrens' lives, however, we believe that inclusion of family data is an essential element of most psychological assessments.

Assessing Organizational Phenomena. The organizational characteristics of educational settings have a broad and significant impact on all persons who function within them and on the effectiveness and efficiency with which goals are attained. Gibson and Likert (1978), for instance, report a number of studies indicating that schools with democratic rather than authoritarian administrative styles have better achievement, higher morale among children and teachers, better communication, and fewer labor problems. A wide variety of research and review articles in a special issue of *Teachers College Record,* entitled "Making Change Happen" (Jennings, 1976), supports the hypothesis that organizational variables often have a powerful impact on the success and failure of innovative classroom practices. Books such as those by Carver and Sergiovanni (1969) and Owens and Steinhoff (1976) further document the diverse and complex theoretical and empirical relationships between organizational phenomena and meaningful educational outcomes.

An almost limitless number of informal techniques are available for assessing educational organizations [see Schmuck, Runkel, Arends, & Arends (1977)

Table 4.4   An Ecological–Systems Approach to Assessing Family Relationships

Level of Analysis	Illustrative Measures
1. The individual family member	a. Social background (parents)
	b. Experiences in family of origin (parents)
	c. Mood: depression, beliefs, anxiety, self-thoughts
	d. Intellectual functioning
	e. Excessive, deficient, or inappropriate behavioral characteristics
2. The family system	a. Structure
	(1) number of adults;
	(2) number of children;
	(3) ages of parents and children;
	(4) living conditions
	b. Perceptions or attributions by family members of one another
	c. Patterns of interaction:
	(1) reciprocity—mutual reinforcement or mutual punishment;
	(2) equity;
	(3) coercion;
	(4) competition;
	(5) cooperation
3. The community	a. Social position:
	(1) economic status;
	(2) educational success;
	(3) geographic location;
	(4) desirability of employment
	b. Contacts with social agencies:
	(1) voluntary as desired;
	(2) coercive—economically necessary or instigated by others
	c. Social relationships:
	(1) friendship networks;
	(2) extended family

Source: Reproduced from Conger, 1981, with permission.

and Lundquist (1982) for hundreds of ideas and suggestions]. The following are a few of the many areas that are addressed: (a) formal and informal power hierarchies, (b) conflict management, (c) group norms, (d) communication patterns, (e) problem–solving styles, and (f) decision–making strategies.

Among the more frequently conducted areas of formal assessment have been leadership behavior and organizational climate. The *Leader Behavior Description Questionnaire* (LBDQ) (Halpin, 1966) provides a measure of leader consideration, that is, "behavior indicative of friendship, mutual trust, respect and warmth in the relationship between the leader and the members of his staff" (Owens, 1970, p. 124), and leader initiating structure, i.e., "the leader's behavior in delineating the relationship between himself and the members of his workgroup, and in endeavoring to establish well-defined patterns of organization, channels of communication, and methods of procedure" (Owens, 1970, p. 124). The *Organizational Climate Description Questionnaire* (OCDQ) (Halpin & Croft, 1963) measures both teacher and principal behaviors which can be combined into eight subscales and compared against six school climate profiles, that is, open climate, autonomous climate, controlled climate, familiar climate, paternal climate, and closed climate [the reader is referred to Owens (1970) for a detailed description of each of these profiles].

One of the most frequently used tools for organizational assessment has been survey guided development (also called survey feedback). This technique has three principal steps. First, surveys uniquely designed for the organization under study are anonymously completed by organization members. Second, these data are summarized in meaningful ways that continue to protect respondents' anonymity, for example, by grade level. Finally, the summarized information is fed back to staff members to assess its accuracy, and to evoke discussion and subsequent intervention. One of the most interesting aspects of survey guided development is the fact that it is simultaneously both an assessment device and an intervention technique. In this latter capacity, Fullan, Miles, and Taylor (1980) report from their literature review that it is among the most effective organization development strategies. A detailed discussion of the theory and pragmatics of survey guided development is provided by Hausser, Pecorella, and Wissler (1977).

ISSUES AND CURRENT TRENDS IN PSYCHOLOGICAL ASSESSMENT

Psychology and education are prone to the influence of fads and to political pressure. For these reasons, as well as others, psychologists must view "advances" or "new" techniques in assessment with a healthy dose of scientific and professional skepticism. The rapid and immense impact of PL 94-142 and its heavy demands for assessment and documentation prompted a flurry of tests being published with poor norms and little if any research base, all of which promised to provide the necessary answers to the problems being experienced by handicapped children. Many of these tests are colorfully and attractively packaged, and very well marketed, and have titles that promise much more than they can deliver. They are, for the most part, a repackaging of old materials (and sometimes stale ideas) or the publication of someone's informal testing techniques accompanied by normative data. The unwary can quickly be led astray by such materials and by the promise of new techniques that will yield great insights.

Rather than a repackaging of old ideas, renorming and updating of old instruments or the development of new tests around old, tiring themes and concepts, rather than from the advent of new statistical modeling of test scores, new directions and advances in psychological assessment must come from advances in basic psychological theorizing. All work in psychology, regardless of how applied it may seem, should be guided by psychological theory and empirical findings relating to psychological theory, as each guides the other in a reciprocal relationship. Data shape theories and theories shape the type of data being generated. As new theories are developed and existing theories honed and otherwise modified, new tests will be developed and new paradigms for viewing test data will occur; these will represent the greatest new directions in assessment.

Because school psychology is evolving so rapidly and is influenced by so many different issues and developments, space does not permit a complete or thorough discussion of all of them. In this section, we have chosen to highlight the issues of early screening and test bias because of their overwhelming importance to current practice. We conclude with a brief sampling of research pertaining to the latest developments in psychological assessment.

Early Screening: Concepts and Issues

It is generally not economically feasible or physically likely that a comprehensive evaluation of every child be periodically undertaken. Yet it is generally accepted that the earlier a problem is detected, the greater the likelihood that it can be corrected or at least held to its minimum impact. For these reasons, the development and application of effective screening procedures has attracted considerable interest. The direct goal of screening is to identify children who have or are most likely to develop learning, behavior, or other problems that interfere with appropriate social, emotional, and cognitive development. Screening tests are designed to be administered to large numbers of children and are typically quick and easy to administer. At school age levels, most screening tests are group administered.

Screening is conducted on a probability basis and reduces the cost of identifying exceptional children by specifying those children most likely to have problems. However, a screening test is not a criterion measure and no matter how badly a child performs on a screening test, it does not necessarily mean that the child is handicapped. Instead, test results indicating that a child may be handicapped can serve as the basis of referral for a comprehensive psychological assessment. Properly employed, screening tests have a built-in pathological bias; that is, the screening test should identify more children as potentially handicapped than would be expected on the basis of prevalence estimates. Whenever a screening test is "in doubt" regarding a child's performance, the child should be declared at risk and referred for an individual evaluation. The purpose of the individual evaluation is to determine (a) that the child was incorrectly identified and is not handicapped or in need of special services, or (b) to confirm and more accurately appraise the specific problem(s) the child is experiencing and to provide appropriate classification and delineation of a suitable intervention program.

Many screening procedures provide rather limited, restrictive samples of behavior and are of limited utility in diagnostic decision making and instructional planning. Screening tests are usually less accurate measures of skills, and since they are expressly designed to detect areas of deficiency or handicap, they do not typically allow for the identification of a child's strengths. The results of a screening test, while useful in the context of the assessment process, cannot substitute for a comprehensive individual assessment and cannot be allowed to override the outcome of an individual evaluation. Even though many screening tests are individually administered, individual administration per se does not elevate the status of the test.

Depending on the age at which screening is being conducted, and whether one is looking for a specific problem or more generalized difficulties, the nature of the screening test will change dramatically. Screening for developmental disabilities generally begins at birth, when a child's Apgar score is determined. The Apgar determines a grossly defined level of general physiological well-being in the newborn by assessing such general characteristics as color, muscle tonus, and some reflexes. Children with very low Apgar scores at birth generally will continue to have problems, but a moderate or high score tends not to be predictive. Certain other specific medical screening tests are conducted at this time to detect such disorders as galactosemia and phenylketonuria which may result in severe handicapping conditions if not detected early. Tests for Down's syndrome and a host of other genetic disturbances may also be required if suspicions of abnormality arise or are in the family history. In many cases, the evaluation of genetic abnormalities occurs prior to birth.

Once the child is a few days old, more meaningful psychological assessment becomes possible. The Neonatal Behavioral Assessment Scales (NBAS) are becoming popular in the evaluation of the infant's response to the environment and interaction with adults. Recent work on the NBAS suggests that it may be useful in identifying children who, without intervention, will exhibit a myriad of behavioral problems later in life. Although not specifically a screening technique, the Bayley Scales of Infant Development are also quite useful in evaluating the current mental and psychomotor development of infants up to 36 months, aiding primarily in the detection of less obvious delays in the development of cognitive and motor skills.

As children become older, screening on the basis of cognitive skill becomes more important and more feasible in the detection of potential psychological or educational handicaps. Screening for specific disturbances continues, however, and virtually every child in the United States undergoes screening for sensory defects early in life. At the preschool level, most screening tests must be individually administered, due to the nature of young children (behaviorally labile, distractible, and unaccustomed to the disciplined nature of group testing). A host of such tests are available, yet it seems that the most efficacious approach is to employ short forms of the major individually administered scales for this age group (Reynolds & Clark, 1983). These short forms (such as those derived from the McCarthy Scales) are typically at least as reliable as other brief tests, have more validity information available, are almost without exception better normed and more well-standardized than other tests for the preschooler, and take no more time to administer. However, more highly trained personnel are usually required. Short forms of the major scales have an added advantage in that, if a child is recognized to be at risk on the screening measure, the remainder of the scale can be administered without a duplication of effort.

As children begin kindergarten, group tests become more prevalent as screening techniques. Although called group tests, a teacher and an aide are typically necessary for testing groups of kindergarten children ranging in size from 4 to 10. Larger groups can quickly become unmanageable at this age. Kindergarten screening tests focus heavily on visual–motor skill and such pre-academic skills as color naming, letter naming, and determining similarities and differences between objects or pictures. Some, such as the Boehm Test of Basic Concepts, directly assess the child's knowledge of basic language concepts or other narrowly defined skills.

Once reaching school age, nearly all screening occurs as a function of group administered standardized tests. At one time, group intelligence tests were widely used for group screening. However, these tests were subject to such abuse and ill-informed interpretation that they have all but been banned in most public school systems. Screening tests now used in the schools focus largely on academic skill development, particularly in the areas of reading and arithmetic. Some screening occurs for emotional and behavioral problems through the use of brief personality scales or teacher-completed problem behavior checklists but this practice is not widespread. For school age children, much screening occurs through informal evaluation of academic performance and behavior by the child's teacher, who, on noticing aberrant performance, typically initiates referral for an individual evaluation.

A number of objections to the formal screening of children have been raised, especially at the preschool level. One major objection to the early identification of handicapped children is the assumed negative impact of attaching a formal, codified label to a child at such an early age. Even without the application of a formal, codified label by a professional diagnostician, teachers, parents, and peers engage in a constant form of informal labelling that is almost certainly more harmful than the administrative labelling by a recognized professional. Indeed, research shows that young children with certain types of learning problems are likely to be perceived as emotionally disturbed by school personnel rather than being seen as slow learners or as having a specific learning problem. Contrary to the popular press view, the issue of whether formal labels have any net detrimental effects on children is still under debate in the scholarly literature and is far from being settled. Other writers have objected to the early screening and identification of handicapped children on the basis of potential deleterious effects on the mother-child attachment relationship and the parents' feelings of responsibility in child-rearing. Still others object to the identification and diagnosis of disorders that we do not yet know how to treat. These criticisms and others have been reviewed by Reynolds (1979b) and do not seem to hold as cogent arguments against early screening and identification of handicapping conditions. Properly carried out and followed through, screening is one of the most important aspects of the assessment process.

The Problem of Cultural Bias in Psychological Assessment

The issue of potential cultural bias in educational and psychological tests has been with psychology since at least the 1920's. However, the past two decades, with their insurgence of support and concern for individual liberties, civil rights, and social justice, have seen the issues involved in test bias become a substantial focus of concern by psychologists, educators, and the lay public alike. Lawmakers and the courts have also begun to evidence increasing concern as witnessed by the passage of the so-called truth-in-testing legislation in New York State and the contemplation of similar bills at the Federal level. Two major federal district courts of equivalent rank have recently handed down opposite legal decisions regarding whether tests are biased against black children (*Larry P.*, 1979; PASE, 1980).

Much of the furor over bias in testing, as well as the court cases, has centered around the use of intelligence tests to evaluate minority children suspected of mental retardation. Even though definitions and conceptualizations of mental retardation have been modified over the last decade to add emphasis to a child's adapative behavior (ability to function independently within his or her own culture and within the larger society) and social maturity, level of intellectual functioning remains an important consideration in the diagnosis of mental retardation. Since black children as a group earn a lower mean score on intelligence tests (e.g., Reynolds & Gutkin, 1981), a significantly larger proportion of black than white children are diagnosed as mildly mentally retarded. While the true cause of the mean difference in performance of blacks and whites in intelligence tests is not yet known, one proposed explanation (among many) is that the tests are faulty. This explanation has become known as the cultural test bias hypothesis. Briefly, it contends that minority children do not earn lower socres on intelligence tests due to less ability but rather due to an inherent cultural bias of the tests that causes the tests to be artificially more difficult for minority children. These biases are generally thought to stem from the white middle-class orientation of test authors and publishers and from the lack of relevant experience for taking such tests among blacks and other minority children. While psychologists have been aware of the potential for such problems since the early days of testing (Reynolds & Brown, in press), most significant research on bias in testing is relatively recent.

The Association of Black Psychologists' early efforts to raise the consciousness of the psychological community were successful in spurring much empirical research on the various issues involved and also resulted in the appointment of an American Psychological Association committee to study the issues (Cleary, Humphreys, Kendrick, & Wesman, 1975). At its 1969 annual meeting, the Association of Black Psychologists adopted the following official policy statement on educational and psychological testing:

> The Association of Black Psychologists fully supports those parents who have chosen to defend their rights by refusing to allow their children and themselves to be subjected to achievement, intelligence, aptitude and performance tests which have been and are being used to A. Label black people as uneducable. B. Place black children in "special" classes and schools. C. Perpetuate inferior education of blacks. D. Assign black children to educational tracts. E. Deny black children higher educational opportunities. F. Destroy positive growth and development of black people.

Many potentially legitimate objections to the use of educational and psychological tests with minorities have been raised by black and other minority psychologists. Too frequently the objections of these groups are viewed as fact without a review of any empirical evidence (e.g., CEC, 1978; Chambers, Barron, & Sprecher, 1980; Hilliard, 1979). The problems most often cited in the use of tests with minorities typically fall into the following categories (Reynolds, 1982b).

1. Inappropriate Content. Black or other minority children have not been exposed to the material involved in the test questions or other stimulus materials. The tests are geared primarily toward white middle class homes and values.

2. Inappropriate Standardization Samples. Ethnic minorities are underrepresented in the collection of normative reference group data. Williams (Wright & Isenstein, 1977) has criticized the WISC-R standardization sample for including blacks only in proportion to the United States total population. Out of 2200 children in the WISC-R standardization sample, 330 were minority. Williams contends that such small actual representation has no impact on the test. In earlier years, it was not unusual for the standardization samples of even the most major tests to be all white (e.g., the 1949 WISC).

3. Examiner and Language Bias. Since most psychologists are white and primarily speak only standard English, they intimidate black and other ethnic minorities. They are also unable to communicate accurately with minority children. Lower test scores for minorities are said largely to reflect this intimidation and difficulty in the communication process rather than lowered ability levels.

4. Inequitable Social Consequences. As a result of bias in educational and psychological tests, minority group members, who are already at a disadvantage in the educational and vocational markets because of past discrimination, are disproportionately relegated to dead end educational tracks and thought unable to learn. Labelling effects also fall under this category.

5. Measurement of Different Constructs. This position asserts that the tests are measuring significantly different attributes when used with children from other than the white middle class culture. Mercer (1979), for example, contends that when IQ tests are used with minorities, they are measuring only the degree of Anglocentrism of the home.

6. Differential Predictive Validity. While tests may accurately predict a variety of outcomes for white middle class children, they fail to predict at an acceptable level any relevant criteria for minority group members. Corollary to this objection is a variety of competing positions regarding the selection of an appropriate, common criterion against which to validate tests across cultural groupings. Scholastic or academic attainment levels are considered by a number of black psychologists to be biased as criteria.

Contrary to the position of a decade ago, a considerable body of research now exists in each of the above areas of potential bias in assessment. To the extent that the cultural test bias hypothesis is a scientific question, as it must be to receive rational consideration, it must be evaluated by means of a thorough consideration of carefully conceived research. As with other scientific questions, one must be guided by the data. Recently the evidence regarding the cultural test bias hypothesis has been reviewed extensively (Jensen, 1980; Reynolds, 1981d,

1982b) and debated (Reynolds & Brown, in press). Empirical research into the question of bias has failed to substantiate the existence of cultural bias in well constructed, well standardized educational and psychological tests when used with native born American ethnic minorities. The internal psychometric characteristics of intelligence and other aptitude tests behave in essentially the same manner across ethnic groupings, and the tests predict later and concurrent academic performance equivalently for all groups. While most of this research has focused on adults and school age children, recent studies have also dealt with preschool tests. Across the age span, with a variety of tests and criteria, the results have been quite consistent. Whatever intelligence tests are measuring for white middle class children, be it scholastic aptitude, learning potential, or intelligence, they are most likely measuring the same construct when used with native born ethnic minorities.

Other areas of bias remain to be investigated extensively. The potential for bias in personality scales is surely greater than that for cognitive scales, yet this area has been meagerly researched compared to the cognitive arena. Several interesting studies of bias in the evaluation of personality and behavior disorders have recently appeared and these illustrate well some of the problems, as well as the importance, of this area of study. Lewis, Balla, and Shanok (1979) reported that black adolescents who were seen in community mental health centers and who displayed behaviors symptomatic of schizophrenia, psychoneurosis, paranoia, and other disorders were frequently considered to be merely displaying normal "cultural aberrations" appropriate to coping with the antagonistic white culture. White adolescents exhibiting similar behaviors, on the other hand, were given psychiatric diagnoses and referred to residential treatment facilities. Lewis et al. contend that the failure to diagnose mental problems in the black population results in an inappropriate, discriminatory denial of services. Another study (Lewis, Shanok, Cohen, Kligfeld, & Frisone, 1980) found that, among court ordered referrals, many seriously emotionally disturbed and highly aggressive black adolescents are being sent to correctional facilities while equally disturbed white adolescents are assigned to residential treatment facilities. Such differences in test interpretation can be attributed directly to critics of testing who contend that behaviors unacceptable in society-at-large are not only acceptable in the black culture but adaptive and in some cases necessary. Through such criticisms, psychologists are led to believe that aggression and violence are not pathological among certain groups and are led to interpret behavioral and personality scales differently. Just as with intelligence tests, personality scale interpretations should not be modified on the basis of unsubstantiated opinion.

There is thus far relatively little study of the issue of bias in the evaluation of behavior and personality and, again, conflicting opinions abound. While some minority spokespersons (e.g., R. L. Williams) claim that entirely distinct tests are needed to assess the black personality, Lewis and her colleagues believe it is

discriminatory to interpret these tests and the behaviors they represent any differently for black children. The research that has been done in this area has been
reviewed by Reynolds (1981d) and has focused on objective personality measures. Reynolds reports that thus far, research results with personality scales
parallel findings with cognitive measures but also states "work with regard to
bias in personality assessment must be considered preliminary at present. Much
needs to be done. Though the results thus far are promising with the cross-group
validity [of these scales] . . . and tends to support the position of Lewis and her
colleagues, many other scales need to be examined and work . . . expanded and
replicated with other samples. In the meantime, however, we must be guided by
the existing data" (Reynolds, 1981d, p. 27).

The issues regarding cultural bias in psychological and educational assessment are complex and not given to simple resolution. The strong emotions
spirited forth from otherwise competent, objective professionals is a further
indication of the level of complexity involved in the issues of bias. The controversy over bias will likely remain with psychology and education for at least as
long as the nature/nurture controversy, even in the face of a convincing body of
evidence failing to support the cultural test bias hypotheses. Bias in intelligence
testing will remain in the spotlight for some time to come as well, especially now
that the Larry P. (1979) and PASE (1980) decisions have been appealed, and
especially given their propensity to elicit emotional, polemic arguments.

The empirical evidence regarding test bias does not support the contentions
of minority spokespersons. Scattered, inconsistent evidence for bias exists, yet
only for bias in support of disadvantaged ethnic minorities. The few findings of
bias do suggest several guidelines to follow in order to ensure nonbiased assessment: (a) assessment should be conducted with the most reliable instrumentation
available, and (b) multiple abilities should be assessed. In other words, psychologists need to view multiple sources of accurately derived data prior to making
decisions concerning children. Hopefully, this is not too far afield from what has
actually been occurring in the practice of psychological assessment, though one
continues to hear isolated stories of grossly incompetent placement decisions.
This is not to say that psychologists should be blind to a child's environmental
background. Information concerning the home, community, and school environment must all be evaluated in the individualized decision-making process. Some
would deny services to minority children, claiming that they are not handicapped
but only artificially appear so on culturally biased tests. However, the psychologist cannot ignore data demonstrating that low IQ ethnic, disadvantaged children are just as likely to fail academically as are white, middle-class low IQ
children, provided that their environmental circumstances remain constant.

Indeed, recall that it is the purpose of the assessment process to beat the
prediction, to provide insight into hypotheses for environmental interventions
that prevent the predicted failure. Low IQ minority children have the same

entitlements to remedial, compensatory, and preventive programs as the white middle class low IQ child, and ethnic minorities should not be denied services on unfounded assumptions that the test caused the low score rather than a deficiency or dysfunction on the part of the child or the child's environment. These issues and the empirical research to date with children are reviewed in detail in Reynolds (1981d, 1982b) and Reynolds and Brown (in press).

Emerging Directions in Assessment Research and Practice

In this final section of the chapter we summarize briefly several new developments that are most likely to have a profound impact on the future of assessment in school psychology.

One area of new direction in assessment stems from the earliest work in psychological testing. Galton was interested in reaction time and measures of sensory skill as measures of mental capacity. When these measures did not turn out to be directly related to more observable criteria of intelligence, such seeming simplistic notions of measurement were abandoned by the psychometric community. Recently, Jensen (1979, 1980b) has rekindled interest in this area through a thorough analysis of past efforts and a new approach to the measurement and interpretation of reaction time data. By evaluating information that had previously been considered a nuisance or a byproduct of such studies (primarily intraindividual variation in response times to a constant level of stimulus complexity), Jensen has developed multiple regression models of the relationship between reaction time and the traditional measures of intelligence (e.g., WISC-R) that produce correlations nearly as large as the correlations between intelligence tests. Through such work, Jensen and his student Vernon (1981) are significantly enhancing our understanding of the nature of intelligence and of the interpretations that can be given to traditional measures of intelligence. As these methods become more refined and as the theory underlying these relationships becomes more sophisticated, major new techniques for the practical assessment of children's intellectual power may result.

Research by Eysenck (1980) and his colleagues on the physiological basis of intelligence also has considerable promise to deliver ultimately new methods for the evaluation of intelligence. In work evaluating intraindividual variation in the electrophysiological response of the brain to repeated stimulation with the same stimulus, Eysenck reports substantial correlations with psychometric measures of intelligence. Although at first seemingly unrelated, Eysenck's and Jensen's work appear to have highly similar theoretical underpinnings and are leading us, perhaps, to a new conceptualization of the nature of intelligence and of the human information processes. Such advances in theory must precede any new techniques and methods in psychometric assessment.

The Kaufman Assessment Battery for Children (K-ABC; Kaufman & Kaufman, 1983) is a good example of a new direction in psychological assessment. The K-ABC is based primarily on Luria's theory of the neuropsychological functioning of the brain as modified and researched over the last three to four decades. While the K-ABC has some interesting and innovative features in the various tasks that the child is required to perform, there are still only a few truly "new" or totally unique tasks that have not been used by other tests or at least in the experimental psychology literature. Yet the K-ABC represents a significant advance as well as a new direction in assessment because of the paradigm it offers for interpreting the data it provides about a given child. K-ABC data, cast into a sound neuropsychological paradigm, have far more practical and heuristic value than traditional views of a child's performance on such tasks. The K-ABC was a long time coming. Psychological tests soundly based in psychological theory (with the exception of the personality field) are unfortunately the exception rather than the rule, but will perhaps be on the increase following the impetus of the K-ABC.

Bergan (1981) has recently proposed a new model of assessment that he has deemed path-referenced assessment. Based in large part on structural modeling of behavior and learning hierarchy theories of the acquisition of new material, Bergan's methods have many implications for the development of specific instructional programs as a direct outcome of the assessment process. The future will almost certainly see a significant amount of time devoted to the research and development of path-referenced techniques. These methods require far more extensive developmental work than traditional testing methods and are more dependent upon strong, successful theories. Bergan's model is exciting nevertheless, but application is not imminent. Much developmental work is needed. If Bergan's speculations for this method are upheld, it could signal a quantum leap in the applicability of assessment to stubborn educational problems.

The blind empiricism of behavioral observation scales and behavior checklists was perhaps necessary in the early stages of development of behavioral assessment. Now, however, it is showing signs of yielding to the development of instruments based on carefully defined and empirically articulated dimensions of children's behavior. This effort, when in full swing, will be a welcome advance in our understanding of behavioral disorders of children, will allow us to assess these problems in a much more refined manner, and ultimately will lead to better treatment plans—the ultimate goal of the assessment process.

The development of individual educational programs for handicapped children and youth, called for by PL 94-142, presents a major challenge to psychologists who work in educational settings. Many psychologists have recognized the shortcomings of standardized tests when it comes time to make individualized educational recommendations because such tests often do not correspond or overlap well with a student's curriculum (Jenkins & Pany, 1978; Leinhardt & Seewald, 1981). According to Ysseldyke's (1978) research, "Teachers want to know specifically what to do for and with children, both behaviorally and academically'' (p. 374). Traditional norm-referenced assessment and behavioral assessment methods have not adequately addressed this problem. Consequently, many professional psychologists have taken a more informal or direct approach to assessment, adding techniques such as task analysis, diagnostic teaching, and curriculum-based testing to their assessment repertoire (Elliott & Piersel, 1982; Smith, 1980; Tidwell, 1980). Several psychologists and special educators have even elaborated similar approaches to assessment in which children's learning and behavior skills are evaluated primarily via curriculum materials and behavioral observations (Eaves & McLaughlin, 1977; Kratochwill & Severson, 1977; Ysseldyke, 1979). Kratochwill and Severson (1977) developed an approach called Process Assessment, while Ysseldyke (1979) referred to his method as Differentiated Assessment. Perhaps the most integrated and comprehensive approach involving informal or nonstandardized techniques is the Systems Approach to Assessment outlined by Eaves and McLaughlin (1977). The major goal of all these systems of informal assessment is to determine *what* a child does and does not know or do, and *how* the child learns best, in order that successful educational interventions can be designed.

Much work remains to be done if the process of informal assessment is to flourish. By design, informal assessment is experimental in nature. In other words, the psychologist must behave as a researcher and try to unravel and understand the interaction among child, task, and environmental variables within a given educational setting. Such a role requires a command of traditional and behavioral assessment methods, plus advanced knowledge in areas of developmental and learning psychology, curriculum design, and instructional methods. Such requirements thus limit the number of individuals capable of doing a comprehensive informal assessment.

Any discussion of the future would be incomplete without mention of the effects which the computer is sure to have. Currently, computerized applications of psychological assessment are proliferating at a fast pace. However, these applications have only begun to scratch the surface of the possibilities for which the computer is appropriate. The most common of the present applications is to modify paper-and-pencil tests such that they can be administered via a microcomputer. Such simplistic applications are useful in that they reduce the amount of time required for administration, scoring, interpretation, and report writing. However, more exciting and unique applications are on the horizon because the computer has the capacity to *interact* with an examinee. Programs are being developed in which problem-solving skills will be assessed such that each problem presented is relatively unique and functions to test the limits of the particular child at the terminal. The memory capacities, video possibilites, and speed of the current generation of microcomputers are already having a marked impact. One wonders what the next ten years will bring.

In summary, it is from basic psychological research into the nature of human information processing and behavior that advances in psychological assessment must come. While some of these advances will be technological ones, the more fruitful area for movement is in the development of new paradigms of test interpretations, such as are being attempted by Bergan and the Kaufmans. With each advance, with each "new" test that appears, we must proceed with caution and guard against jumping on an insufficiently researched bandwagon. Fruitful techniques may be lost if implemented too soon to be fully understood and appreciated; children may also be harmed by the careless or impulsive use of assessment materials that are poorly designed (but attractively packaged) or lack the necessary theoretical and empirical grounding. When evaluating new psychological assessment methods, surely *caveat emptor* must serve to temper our enthusiasm and our anxiousness as we attempt to provide helpful information about children in the design of successful intervention programs.

5

Psychological Interventions: Direct Service Delivery

The successful treatment and prevention of children's learning and adjustment problems represents the ultimate goal of any psychological intervention. What can be done to help children with various problems? Proposals for answering this question abound, each with its own adherents. Some psychologists choose to treat a child on a one-to-one basis, while others stress the necessity of treatment in a group. Many psychologists work directly with the child, while others provide only consultative services. The focus of many treatments is to reduce a child's internal conflict, while numerous alternative treatments emphasize the importance of behavioral change as the primary criterion for judging the success of treatment.

Given the diversity of competing philosophies, it is important to have a basis for selecting an appropriate intervention for a particular child. This chapter will provide a conceptual rationale for the selection and application of various treatment approaches. In addition, specific treatment methodologies will be discussed and evaluated.

THE LINK BETWEEN INTERVENTION, ASSESSMENT, AND CONSULTATION

Conceptually, it makes sense that this chapter should follow the consultation and assessment chapters; similarly, this order parallels what should happen in practice (the reader is referred to the generic model for school psychological service delivery in Chapter 2). The proper application of appropriate assessment and consultation skills is a prerequisite to designing successful intervention strategies. Even the best intervention strategy is doomed if it is applied to an improperly defined target behavior or presented in an unacceptable manner.

For example, a teacher who is concerned about a child's daydreaming behavior would use markedly different intervention strategies depending upon whether assessment had indicated that the child *could not* or *would not* complete assigned school work. If the child lacks the skills to complete assignments, perhaps he or she daydreams out of frustration. Such a child may require an individualized skill development program that is more in line with his or her ability. Another child who simply does not *want* to work on the assignments and *prefers* to daydream may require a motivational program to increase the rate of assignment completion.

Attention to consultative variables can also contribute to the success or failure of an intervention. In the previous example, calling the motivational system a "behavior modification" program versus a "responsibility" program may influence a teacher's decision to use it (Kazdin & Cole, 1981). Further, within the consultation literature there is evidence to suggest that allowing a teacher to be involved in the development of the intervention increases the probability that she or he will actually use that intervention (Reinking, Livesay, & Kohl, 1978). Thus, the use of treatment strategies is inextricably intertwined with ongoing consultative and assessment activities.

Prevalence of Problems

What proportion of children manifest learning and adjustment problems significant enough to warrant intervention? What types of problems do these children exhibit? Although a significant amount of data has accumulated in response to these questions, the answers remain relatively unclear. The reason for this is the lack of precision in defining and differentiating various problems. For example, one study may refer to "nervous behavior" while another may term the same cluster of behaviors "impatient" or "unreflective." Widespread discrepancies in prevalence rates exist even within relatively well defined categories such as school phobia and hyperactivity (Achenbach, 1974).

Despite these difficulties with definitional specificity, however, it is possible to draw some general conclusions about the types of problems most frequently encounted in educational settings. Christenson, Algozzine, and Ysseldyke (1981) reported that 92% of referred students are eventually evaluated, and 73% of the referred students are placed in special education programs. Generally, academic difficulties are listed as the most prevalent category of problems, followed closely by adjustment problems (Lambert, 1976; Nicholson,

1971). Physical disabilities represent a third category but comprise only about 1% of the total referrals (Nicholson, 1971). The most common types of learning problems include (in order of decreasing frequency): verbal skill deficits, poor work habits, cognitive ability deficits, and quantitative skill deficits (Lambert, 1976).

Estimates of the percentage of children with various behavior and adjustment problems are generally in the range of 20 to 25% (Achenbach, 1974). The percentage of students with various types of conduct and personality problems (from Stone, 1981) are displayed in Table 5.1. People who work directly with children (i.e., teachers and school psychologists) generally indicate higher levels of adjustment problems than individuals with no direct interaction (i.e., statisticians in government agencies) with children (Balow, 1979).

Definition of a Problem

For our purposes here, a problem is defined as a significant discrepancy between observed behavior and expected behavior. This definition is intended to be somewhat vague so that it can be applied to a variety of situations and types of problems. What is a "significant discrepancy?" How is "expected behavior" defined and by whom? The answers to these questions are important because they influence the type and intensity of the interventions applied to children. One person may tolerate a greater discrepancy from expectations than another. Individuals who work with children obviously differ in terms of the level of their expectations. At the center of this issue are three factors influencing whether a child will be classified as a problem: (a) the extent to which the child deviates from environmental norms, (b) the extent to which the child deviates from developmental norms, and (c) the referral agent's tolerance level.

Environmental Norms. All social settings have expectations for behavior which are either implicit or explicit. A major determiner of these expectations is the past behavior of individuals in that setting. Although a wide range of behaviors may occur in any one setting, there usually exists some conception of what is "normal" behavior for that setting. Individuals will be considered a problem to the extent that their behavior deviates from the norm for that environment. The same behaviors considered normal and expected in one environment may be considered abnormal in another environment. Further, environmental norms may change over time such that behaviors once considered abnormal in a particular environment may, at a later time, be considered within normal limits.

Some concrete examples will illustrate these points. A behavior such as heterosexual petting on school grounds is one which appears to be more commonplace today than ten years ago. Children who move from one city to another are likely to be exposed to marked differences in environmental expectations. For example, a fourth grade child who is reading at a third grade level may be

Table 5.1 Percent of Children Classified by Teachers on Each Conduct Problem According to Degree of Severity

| | Percent Checked | | | | | | | |
Item	Not a Problem		Mild		Moderate		Severe	
	Boys	Girls	Boys	Girls	Boys	Girls	Boys	Girls
Restlessness; inability to sit still (squirms, fidgets)	47	70	27	19	17	8	9[a]	3
Distractibility; easily distracted	51	70	25	18	16	9	8	3
Disruptiveness; tendency to annoy and bother others	52	77	25	15	15	6	9	3
Inattentiveness; shortness of attention span	55	72	23	17	14	7	8	3
Attention-seeking; "show-off" behavior	58	82	22	12	13	4	7	2
Boisterousness; rowdiness	68	89	18	7	9	3	5	1
Disobedience; difficulty in disciplinary control	68	88	18	8	10	3	5	1
Fighting	69	90	16	6	10	3	4	1
Hyperactivity (running about, jumping up and down)	71	88	16	8	8	3	5	2
Uncooperativeness in group situations	74	88	15	8	7	3	4	1
Irritability; hot-tempered; easily aroused to anger	75	89	14	7	7	3	4	1
Impertinence; sauciness	77	87	14	9	6	3	3	1
Negativism; tendency to do the opposite of what is requested	80	91	12	6	5	2	3	1
Destructiveness in regard to his own and/or others' property	85	95	9	4	4	1	2	1

Behavior								
Temper tantrums	86	93	8	4	4	2	2	1
Profane language; swearing, cursing	86	96	9	3	4	1	2	1
Jealousy over attention paid to other children	87	86	9	10	3	3	1	1
Truancy (absent without parent's knowledge; "play hooky")	97	99	2	1	1	1	1	1
Self-consciousness, easily embarrassed	58	57	30	32	9	9	2[b]	2
Lack of self-confidence	59	61	28	28	9	9	4	2
Easily flustered and confused	65	71	23	21	8	6	4	3
Shyness; bashfulness	67	59	24	30	7	9	2	2
Feelings of inferiority	69	71	22	21	7	6	3	2
Hypersensitivity; feelings easily hurt	73	71	19	20	6	6	3	2
Preoccupation; "in a world of his own"	76	83	15	11	6	4	3	1
Sluggishness; lethargy	82	88	12	9	5	3	2	1
Anxiety; chronic general fearfulness	84	85	11	12	3	3	1	1
Social withdrawal; preference for solitary activities	85	86	10	10	3	3	1	1
Doesn't know how to have fun; behaves like a little adult	85	82	11	13	3	3	1	1
Reticence; secretiveness	88	88	9	9	3	2	2	1
Aloofness; social reserve	88	86	10	11	2	2	2	1
Drowsiness	89	92	8	6	3	3	2	1
Depression; chronic sadness	92	89	5	7	2	2	3	1
Complaints of aches and pains	92	89	5	7	2	3	3	1
Proneness to illness and/or accidents	92	91	5	5	2	2	2	1
Absence from school for trivial reasons	93	93	4	4	2	2	2	1

[a]Failure of any row to total 100% is due to rounding.
Source: From Stone (1981) with permission of author and publisher.

about average in one school district but may require remedial reading programs in another district where the overall reading level is higher.

Deviations from environmental norms are taken seriously in most educational settings. Part of the reason for this approach is that it is easier to manage a group of children with similar types of behavior than children who behave in different ways. "Teachers foist a large number of rigid rules and regulations upon students so as to make their behavior far less varied, more uniform, and more predictable" (Mehrabian, 1976, p. 156). Although this convenience component should be one aspect of classroom management, if followed to its logical extreme, strict adherence to environmental norms would be achieved only if everyone behaved in exactly the same manner. This is analogous to equating appropriate behavior with *conforming* behavior. Consequently, environmental norms should be applied only in combination with other factors when deciding whether a behavior is problematic enough to require intervention. Considering the contributions made to society by such nonconformists as artists and inventors, it becomes obvious that compliance with environmental norms as a behavioral goal for classrooms or as a complete definition of adjustment is inadequate and incomplete.

Developmental Norms. A psychologist is confronted by a mother who is worried about her son. It seems he has been kissing her on the lips for 10 to 15 second periods and she is concerned that there may be sexual overtones to the kisses. Another psychologist is asked to testify in court on behalf of a boy who has been caught exposing himself to a 3-year-old neighbor. The first question the reader may have about these cases is "How old were the boys involved in these two cases?" The answer to this question is important because whether or not either case represented "abnormal" behavior is a function of age. In the first case, if the boy were under four years of age, any psychologist knowledgeable of child development would assure the mother that most boys in that age group love their mothers; seemingly passionate kisses are not uncommon. In the case of the boy exposing himself to a 3-year-old, age is also a critical variable in labeling the act deviant. This may be surprising to many people in a community who would consider indecent exposure, in any context, to be deviant.

Reference to developmental norms reveals surprisingly high frequencies of "abnormal" behaviors in "normal" children (Thomas, Chess, & Birch, 1968). Longitudinal studies of normal children such as the one presented in Table 5.2 illustrate that many behaviors which might be labeled by society as abnormal are relatively normal from a developmental perspective.

How does one determine when a behavior merits intervention from a developmental perspective? This task is made difficult because:

The expanding knowledge of children indicates that "abnormal" behavior among normal children is plentiful. We now recognize that no child is completely free from

Table 5.2   Percentages of "Normal" Children Who Have "Abnormal" Problems

	Age in Years									
	1¾		5		8		11		14	
Problem	Boys	Girls	Boys	Girls	Boys	Girls	Boys	Girls	Boys	Girls
1. Disturbing dreams	16	13	20	29	22	23	26	42	6	4
2. Nocturnal enuresis	75	73	8	10	12	14	15	10	11	0
3. Insufficient appetite	7	10	23	31	16	21	7	13	0	0
4. Masturbation	9	8	8	6	6	2	4	0	0	0
5. Nail-biting	5	3	8	17	16	23	30	40	33	22
6. Thumbsucking	21	33	5	19	3	12	4	3	0	0
7. Excessive activity	29	17	46	35	38	16	30	16	11	0
8. Speech problems	30	17	18	8	6	12	7	5	0	4
9. Lying	0	0	49	42	41	19	11	0	6	0
10. Stealing	7	3	10	4	9	5	0	0	0	0

[a]Percentages are of children in a longitudinal study whose mothers reported that the specific behavior was present in a degree judged by the investigators to represent "problem behavior."
Note: Adapted from Macfarlane, Allen, and Honzik (1954, pp. 66–69). Originally published by the University of California Press; reprinted by permission of the Regents of the University of California.

emotional difficulties. The prevalence of problems is, in fact, so widespread that some psychologists doubt that these deviations should be regarded as abnormal. (Clarizio & McCoy, 1976, p. 4)

Those children who are cause for concern should display two characteristics: (a) their behavior should be relatively deviant for their developmental age despite an environment supportive of adaptive behavior and (b) the maladaptive behavior should be maintained consistently. Thus temporary deviations from age-appropriate behavior should be *expected*.

Tolerance Level of Referral Agent. A third major determiner of whether a child will be considered a candidate for intervention is the referral agent's (e.g., teacher, parent) tolerance for the behaviors exhibited by the child. Information from several sources suggests that this may be the most important variable influencing whether or not a child will be referred for treatment (McDowell, Adamson, & Wood, 1982; Rich, 1982).

One source of such evidence is the extremely large number of children whom teachers are willing to call behavior problems. For example, Rubin and Balow (1978) conducted a longitudinal study of 1,500 students in elementary school with the following results:

> Among subjects who received six teacher ratings, 60% (68% of the boys and 51% of the girls) were considered a behavior problem by at least one teacher. Thus, it becomes apparent that behavior that at least one teacher is willng to classify as a problem is the norm rather than the exception for elementary school children. (p. 109)

These data suggest that a *majority* of children are identified as having problems. It is illogical to label all of these children as problems when 60% of an unselected population is so classified. The operative issue is that many teachers expect conformity. Rhodes (1977) has termed such expectations an "illusion of normality." In many cases it is these expectations and the teachers' tolerance for violations of these expectations that require alteration. As Ross (1974) asserts:

> Could it be that elementary schools are so structured and teacher behavior so programmed that the "normal," to be expected behavior of children is to emit responses the teacher identifies as restlessness and distractability? If this is the case, the modifications called for are situational–environmental and should not have their focus on changing the behavior of the children so that they "adjust" to what may be an intolerable situation. (p. 24)

Interestingly, teachers often attribute the blame for children's behavior to sources beyond their control. The National Education Association (1979) surveyed teachers to determine their perceptions of why children did poorly in school. The results indicated that 81% of the teachers attributed the blame to problems in the child's home, 14% blamed the children, 4% blamed the manner in which schools were organized, and only 1% blamed inadequate instruction.

It is easy to blame the teacher for having expectations of conformity and for a low tolerance level. However, teachers are often the victims as much as they are the problem. The alarmingly high referral rates and other problems may stem from an intolerable situation in which the teacher is placed. For example, teachers are frequently required to teach a classroom of 30 behaviorally diverse students. An administrative hierarchy often dictates what they teach and when they teach it. Merit raises and approval of colleagues may be a function of the degree to which they control their students. "If a teacher is devalued because he or she cannot control a disruptive student, is it little wonder that the teacher prefers that the student be assigned elsewhere?" (Rich, 1982, p. 69). This kind of problem is likely to lead to a request for interventions but it is not likely to be resolved by them. Instead, once an individual problem is resolved satisfactorily, the teacher is likely to have another problem waiting in the wings. As Witt and Elliott (1982) have indicated, there is no "last" referral: Once the most severe problem is eliminated, the next most severe becomes the target of concern. Kornblau and Keogh (1980) aptly summarized this issue by indicating that "it is not realistic to expect teachers to work equally effectively with all pupils; but it is realistic to expect teachers to be sensitive to their own perceptions of their pupils" (p. 99).

SOME ASSUMPTIONS ABOUT SCHOOL PSYCHOLOGISTS AS INTERVENTION SPECIALISTS

In this section we will examine some of the assumptions, concerns, and constraints under which school psychologists operate. Although school psychologists may work in a variety of educational settings, these assumptions apply most readily to those who work in the public schools.

Proactive versus Reactive Services

In Chapter 2, we defined an intervention as a "strategic reaction by psychologists, educators, and/or parents to children's inappropriate behavior or unsuccessful learning." From this definition it is obvious that most school psychologists implement interventions as *reactions* to problems. This is a result of professional training, the preferences and expectations of school psychologists, and perhaps, an overriding concern for individual children. In addition, most educational systems are reactive in nature. For example, most special education programs operate only after problems have been identified, usually problems with the *child*. The child is presumed to have the problem, not the teacher, not the curriculum, not the classroom environment.

Reactive forms of service delivery do not represent the desired state of affairs for most psychologists, but they do represent reality (Miller, Witt, & Finley, in press). Most interventions that are devised or implemented by school psychologists will be in reaction to an already existing problem. Our experience has been that it is the rare school psychologist who engages to any significant degree in proactive or preventive interventions. This situation is unfortunate because school psychologists are in a position to observe the occurrence of the types of referrals that occur repeatedly and may be in a position to correct the problem at the source. If the same type of referral is observed 20 times in one semester, it is more efficient to react to each individual referral or to intervene at a common source of each referral? If repeated academic failure of Hispanic students is observed for a given school, are school psychological services more prudently directed at the individual case level or toward finding the source of the problem?

Business operations provide a useful parallel and contrast to the operation of educational institutions. Imagine, for example, a corporation whose product line included the manufacture of threaded nuts and bolts to a given specification. Imagine further that the management of this corporation discovered regular deficiencies in the diameter and density of their products. Their conclusion would likely be that some aspect of their system was functioning inadequately and was in need of correction. Perhaps an effort would be made to correct each of the deficient products, a time-consuming and costly process. It is safe to assume, however, that a change in the machinery that caused the problem would be the more likely remedy.

In contrast with business, schools tend to focus on peripheral reactive solutions. For example, schools tend to send Teacher A's "discipline" problems to the school principal repeatedly, despite the fact that, year in and year out, Teacher A always refers proportionately more students for disciplinary action than any other teacher. Perhaps it is easier from an administrative perspective to treat the symptoms than the source in cases such as these. As a result, school psychologists most frequently react to failures rather than seeking to implement proactive solutions. The cycle becomes self-perpetuating.

Direct Versus Indirect Services

Direct interventions include those in which the psychologist is in direct contact with the child. Examples in this category include counseling and play therapy. Indirect interventions are those carried out with the child by a third party such as a parent or teacher. These are referred to as indirect interventions because the psychologist may devise or suggest the intervention but does not carry it out directly with the child.

Although school psychologists will be called on to be involved in both direct and indirect intervention strategies for individual cases, indirect interventions are probably the more common (see Chapter 3). This is the case for two reasons. First, because of the sheer numbers of students, staff, decisions, and problems encountered by the typical school psychologist, it is impossible to meet with many students on an individual basis. Indirect service delivery represents a much more efficient use of time. Second, significant support for indirect interventions comes from behavioral and ecological theory itself. Within these theoretical frameworks, behavioral change is assumed to occur more quickly and to generalize more readily if it is conducted in the natural environment rather than in the psychologist's office (Kanfer & Goldstein, 1980). Teachers, for example, who are with a child six hours per day can correct and prevent problems on an ongoing basis. A psychologist, on the other hand, who is able to see a child only one or two hours per week may have less of an impact. Further, once a teacher learns new interventions, these techniques can be applied to other children with whom the teacher has contact.

Specific Versus Global Interventions

Specific interventions are those designed to meet a specialized need of an individual child. Examples of interventions in this category include a program for remediating "*b*" and "*d*" reversals or an intervention designed to decrease verbal tics in a child with Tourette's syndrome. In contrast, interventions at the global end of the continuum are those which are designed to meet the more general needs of children. The most common example of a global intervention is placement in a special class.

Are school psychologists more involved with global or specific interventions? Although no data are available, our experience has been that most school psychologists will be involved primarily with global interventions. In all likelihood, if a school psychologist offered one global recommendation, such as placement in a classroom for emotionally disturbed children, and five specific recommendations at the same staffing, the global recommendation would be the most likely one to be followed. This assumption may result from that fact that school psychologists have been cast into the role of special education's "gate-keeper" (Ysseldyke, 1978) and are viewed as making placement decisions. Alternatively, it may be that the recommendations offered by school psychologists in the past have not been that helpful to teachers and other direct service personnel (Howell, Kaplan, & O'Connell, 1979).

APPROACHES TO TREATMENT

A vast body of theoretical, conceptual, and practical literature related to the interventions used in educational settings has developed over the years. In order to present relevant aspects of this literature in an organized fashion, we will categorize various treatment approaches according to their theoretical origins. The three theoretical orientations selected include: (a) the medical model, (b) the behavioral model, and (c) the ecological model. The first two models were included because the vast majority of educational programs are variations of one of these two models (McDowell, Adamson, & Wood, 1982). The ecological model, while not used as widely, possesses some positive aspects of the other two theoretical orientations, and in many ways, is more comprehensive than either.

Medical Model

The hallmark of the medical model is a primary, but not an exclusive, focus on *intra*child variables. According to Rezmierski, Knoblock, and Bloom (1982), many terms are subsumed under psychoeducational rubric including: "psychoanalytic treatment, psychotheraputic education, psychoeducational programming, psychodynamic education and even educational programs with a psychological emphasis" (p. 48). To some degree, the diverse array of treatment approaches within this model are all decendents of a psychodynamic or a medical model approach to behavior. Interventions in this category share three assumptions. First, an appropriate treatment can not be selected without a thorough diagnosis of the underlying problem. Second, the behavioral manifestations of a problem stem from an underlying cause. Third, children with similar diagnoses may receive similar treatments.

The conceptual underpinnings of the medical model have had a significant impact on the manner in which current educational problems are operationalized and, in fact, underlie the present system of categorical special education in most states today (Macht, 1980). A complete treatment of the medical model is beyond the scope of this book, but the interested reader is referred to Rezmierski, Knoblock, and Bloom (1982), Rich, Beck, and Coleman (1982) or Dembinski, Schultz, and Walton (1982) for recent reviews of research in this area. What follows are descriptions and evaluations of the most common interventions which derive from the medical model.

Special Classes. Perhaps the most pervasive influence of the medical model can be seen in the development and proliferation of special classes designed to meet the behavioral and academic needs of children with various handicapping conditions. Since this model assumes that ''Something is wrong with the student, preventing him (sic) from succeeding'' (Howell, Kaplan, & O'Connell, 1979, p. 49), a logical course of action is first to determine a diagnosis for the child and then place him or her in a classroom designed to treat children with similar problems. Although most modern special education classrooms treat symptoms rather than causes, the remaining influences of the medical model are quite apparent in the structure and function of these classrooms.

It is important to distinguish the historical influences of the medical model from its current emphasis. Historically, this model has assumed that intrachild variables such as emotional disturbance, mental retardation, and learning disabilities were primarily responsible for children's learning and adjustment problems (Macht, 1980). Since the problem was assumed to be intrachild, the treatment was also focused on the child. Special classes represented an attempt to expose the child to an intensive therapeutic environment which attempted to get at the root of the child's problem. Segregating children with similar problems made it possible to apply similar types of interventions. Play therapy or psychoanalysis were typical interventions for emotional problems from this genre. In the area of learning difficulties, adherents to this model also ''place the locus of the problem within the child and assume that the dysfunction itself is unremediable and must be bypassed or, at best, be compensated for'' (Quay, 1973, p. 166).

The diagnosis and placement of children in special classes remains a part of the current educational system, but the activities and philosophies of individual classrooms usually do not adhere to a strict medical model. Contributing to this shift in emphasis has been research indicating: (a) that children with the same diagnosis (e.g., learning disability) may need to be taught with different methods; (b) treatment of intrachild problems has proven less successful than treatment of observable behaviors and skills; (c) environmental factors play an extremely important role in influencing whether a child will exhibit a problem; and (d) educational labels such as LD and EMR are educationally irrelevant (Howell, Kaplan, & O'Connell, 1979); that is, they provide teachers with little or no information on which to base instruction and treatment.

Although special classes have changed markedly in the last several years, two major problems still exist. First and foremost, there is little or no evidence available to document that placement of the majority of mildly handicapped children in special classes results in more favorable outcomes than continued placement in the regular classroom (Carlberg & Kavale, 1979). A meta-analysis of 50 studies by Carlberg and Kavale (1979) concerning the efficacy of special classes arrived at the following conclusions:

> The results of the existing research when integrated statistically demonstrated that special class placement is an inferior alternative to regular class placement in benefitting children removed from the educational mainstream. No great differences among the classes of outcome measures were identified. Thus, regardless of whether achievement, personality/social, or other dependent variables were chosen for investigation, no differential placement effect emerged across studies. (p. 304)

The reader is referred to Elliott and Gutkin (in press) for a more comprehensive review of the efficacy of special classes.

Another problem with special classes is that children must be labeled in order to receive services. Some authorities have questioned whether the negative effects of labeling outweigh the positive effects, if any, of special class placement (Critchley, 1979). The most comprehensive study of the effects of labeling was conducted by Nicholas Hobbs (1975) who directed the Project on Classification of Exceptional Children. This study yielded a three-volume compendium which drew the following conclusions about the effects of labeling:

> (a) labels are applied imprecisely; (b) labeled children are stigmatized; (c) labels yield too little information for planning; (d) the classification of children with multiple problems in terms of a dominant set of attributes leads to the neglect of other conditions; (e) classification tends to be deviance oriented; (f) classification systems are insensitive to the rapid changes that take place in children; (g) classification of children can result in the disregard of important etiological factors.

Although other studies have failed to detect any negative influence of labels (Macmillan, Jones, & Aloia, 1974), the debate has resulted in a questioning of the categorical placement system.

In summary, special classes continue to remain a widely used intervention option for both academic and adjustment problems. Without question, there will continue to be a need for such classes, especially for severely handicapped children. However, their usefulness for mildly handicapped individuals is in question.

Diagnostic-Prescriptive Teaching. The underlying basis for diagnostic–prescriptive teaching rests on the notion of aptitude × treatment interactions (ATIs). ATIs have a long history in psychological and educational research and are based upon the seemingly simple premise that children respond to instruction in different ways. The goal of using an ATI is to determine a child's strengths and weaknesses and then to teach accordingly. A common example is for children who are auditory, as opposed to visual, learners to be instructed using an auditory approach to reading instruction such as phonics.

Although the use of ATIs has enormous intuitive appeal, research efforts, even in the laboratory, have not established empirical support for using them as a basis for intervening with children (Cronbach & Snow, 1977; Fry & Lagomarsino, 1982; Hessler & Sosnowsky, 1979; Miller, 1981; Ysseldyke & Mirkin, 1982). Two primary problems have been identified in the failure of the ATI methodology. First, the reliability of the tests used to assess aptitude frequently have been insufficient to conduct the precision measurements required in order to establish individual strengths and weaknesses (Ysseldyke & Mirkin, 1982). A second problem with ATIs has been the preoccupation with identifying only a *single* learner attribute (Howell, Kaplan, & O'Connell, 1979). For example, auditory versus visual learning ability is singled out as *the* critical variable on which to base instruction. Such an instructional program may ignore other equally relevant aspects of how instruction should occur and what it should contain. Howell, Kaplan, and O'Connell (1979) suggest that instruction should go beyond focusing on single learner attributes:

> Some children learn best in the presence of other children rather than in isolation or with one-to-one instruction from the teacher. Others learn best with one-to-one instruction from an older peer rather than an adult. Some children are turned on by printed material, for example, workbooks or picture books, while others are turned on by machines. Some children learn best visually while others require material to be presented in an auditory fashion. Mode of response can be as important as the mode of presentation. While some youngsters enjoy a verbal exchange, others prefer to write or mark their answers. (p. 105)

The point is that instead of just focusing on auditory versus visual, for example, school psychologists might help teachers expand the range of variables which they should consider in developing treatment programs. More often than not, and likely *the* most serious problem in ATI research and practice, children are diagnosed as handicapped primarily on the basis of some single attribute and then *grouped* into special classes, all to receive basically the same instruction. Thus, the concept of ATI has not been operationalized at the individual level that would be necessary for it to work, if it does work. Despite the problems with ATI-based instructional programs, they remain in widespread use (Arter & Jenkins, 1977). Apparently their intuitive appeal has influenced many special educators interested in the cookbook approach to instruction.

Play Therapy. Depending upon the orientation of the therapist, play therapy may be considered an intervention based on the medical model because of its focus on uncovering and resolving internal states of conflict as a means to behavior change. Play therapy typically involves the interaction of a child and a therapist in a room equipped with a variety of play materials. The specific material may vary with the therapist's orientation, but it often includes puppets or dolls, drawing materials, balls, and playdough or modeling clay. Older children often prefer checkers and dominoes. Although psychologists may differ in theoretical orientation and in the specific procedures utilized, they share the basic assumption that children express aspects of their personality development through play (Moustakos, 1953).

Opinions vary concerning the role of play in the therapeutic process. Some feel the therapeutic effects of play itself are secondary both to the value of the relationship between the child and the therapist and to the insight that play provides the therapist about the nature of the child's problems (Axline, 1978; Winnicott, 1971). Others, while not denying the importance of relationship factors and of the development of insight, argue that play itself has decided cathartic value for the child (Barbanel, 1982).

Systematic evaluations of play therapy are lacking. The research available is typically flawed methodologically or is of the case study variety (Achenbach, 1974). Thus, results must be interpreted cautiously. In general, the available literature has suggested that play therapy is useful for improving social relationships, both with peers and adults (Moulin, 1970; Thombs & Muro, 1973). However, when compared with other forms of therapy, especially behavior therapy, play therapy has consistently been judged inferior (Clement & Milne, 1967; Ney, Palvesky, & Markley, 1971). The positive effects observed when play therapy is used alone may result from the additional adult attention directed toward individuals involved in play therapy. Factors such as these have typically not been controlled in research studies. We conclude this discussion of play therapy with the following summary: "Playgroup procedures are based much more on opinion than in data. Not only is the traditional model . . . questionably effective, but nothing is known about *why* it is effective when it is." (Claiborn & Strong, 1982, p. 546)

Counseling. From a variety of theoretical perspectives, individual and small group counseling continue to enjoy widespread use by school psychologists. A recent study of the interventions preferred by teachers indicated that this mode of treatment was one of the most preferred for children with immature or un-manageable behavior (Algozzine, Ysseldyke, Christenson, & Thurlow, 1982). Although counseling is an accepted form of treatment within a variety of the-oretical orientations, it is discussed here under the rubric of psychoeducational theory because of its focus, in the context of reciprocal determinism, on person rather than environmental or behavioral variables.

Counseling focuses on current and future adjustment problems of relatively normal students. Although school psychologists approach counseling from a variety of theoretical orientations, the trend has been to use short-term therapies that fit the immediate goals of the school rather than more time-consuming therapies such as psychoanalysis, which are impractical and incompatible with the goals of most schools (Bardon & Bennett, 1974). The goal of counseling is to understand and resolve the immediate problem or problems that precipitated counseling. Neither the utilization of historical information nor the interpretation of personality dynamics is given much emphasis. There is more of a focus on the clarification of the current situation and on the individual's alternative courses of action.

Psychologists who utilize counseling as a theraputic intervention in the schools should be aware of several potential difficulties associated with its use (Bardon & Bennett, 1974). First, counseling is a form of direct intervention and as such represents a tremendous time commitment to an individual child. Given the large numbers of children with whom school psychologists are expected to work, it is often impractical to commit one or two hours per week to an indi-vidual child, especially if other community resources can be made available. This is not to say that school psychologists should not conduct counseling with chil-dren for whom no other treatment is appropriate. Instead, we suggest that the needs of individual children must be balanced with the needs of the entire school.

A second potential problem is that counseling services are not explicitly required by law. Because of this, many administrators will not include them as part of the job description of school psychologists in particular districts. The intent of such mandates appears to be directed more toward meeting the mini-mum requirements of the law than meeting the needs of school children.

A final problem with counseling relates to the lack of empirical support for the use of counseling interventions. Specifically, research has suggested that traditional forms of counseling are less effective than other interventions, such as teacher consultation or behavior management, in producing *behavior change* (Alper & Kranzler, 1970; Lauver, 1974; Marlowe, Madsen, Bowen, Reardon, & Logue, 1978; Palmo & Kuzniar, 1972; Randolf & Hardage, 1973). Research on the efficacy of counseling yields much more positive results when behavior change is not the primary dependent variable. For example, changes in decisive-ness (Schweisheimer & Walberg, 1976), self-acceptance (English & Higgens,

1971), perceptions of self-efficacy (Tyler & Gatz, 1975), and other subjectively measured variables are reported regularly.

Regardless of the limitations that impact the use of counseling, many school psychologists will continue to use it as a therapeutic intervention. The reasons for this continued use include the effectiveness, or perceived effectiveness, of counseling for certain problems and the personal preferences of individual school psychologists. Perhaps a more subtle factor in the continued use of counseling is the mystique surrounding its use. This mystique reflects a lack of understanding concerning counseling on the part of administrators, teachers, and parents and often translates into requests for counseling. This point has been summarized by Bardon and Bennett (1974):

> Teachers and administrators usually seek any service that may help a pupil who is having or causing problems. Sometimes they expect the psychologist to produce through counseling a complete and immediate change in the way the pupil functions. Counseling is interpreted as a special secret way to get children to change. Such faith in the magic of the techniques is, unfortunately, misplaced . . . 'Joe is so miserable, he wants so badly to have friends. But he teases others, bothers them, and just does everything that turns others off. Couldn't you just talk to him?' For a school psychologist to give Joe a lecture on how to win friends and influence people is no more likely to be effective than for his parents, teacher, or principal to lecture him. (pp. 97–98)

Behavioral Model

Any review of the intervention practices conducted in educational settings would be incomplete without mention of the treatment strategies derived from the behavioral model. Its widespread use in a variety of settings, the proliferation of journals devoted exclusively to behavioral methods (e.g., *Journal of Applied Behavior Analysis, Behavior Therapy*), and even the large number of negative reactions to behavioral methodologies all attest to the growth and influence of this model (Kazdin, 1978a).

Part of the appeal of the behavioral approach is its apparent simplicity. We say *apparent* simplicity because many of the "failures" in the application of behavioral principles have resulted from the improper application of intervention techniques. For example, a teacher who decides to implement an extinction program for a particular inappropriate response may simply ignore the behavior when it occurs. However, it is not that simple for some teachers to ignore inappropriate behavior. Thus, the teacher may inadvertently reprimand children who misbehave every so often. If the reprimand functions as a reinforcer, as it often does, then the teacher has placed the child on a variable ratio reinforcement schedule and high rates of the unwanted behavior may occur. This is but one example of the complexity of implementing "simple" behavioral interventions. The problems, of course, are magnified when working with highly complex skills and/or programs such as those for the development of language or social skills in severely retarded children.

The behavioral model is premised on the notion that behavior is strengthened or weakened by its antecedents and its consequences (Kazdin, 1982b). Most frequently, this premise is translated into treatment strategies that reinforce desired behavior in an attempt to strengthen it. Punishment techniques are used occasionally to consequate inappropriate behavior. The focus of treatment is usually on individual behaviors as targets for change. Typically, the behavior change can take one of three forms: (a) the increase of the appropriate behaviors that the child has failed to learn, (b) the decrease of the inappropriate behaviors that are detrimental to adaptive functioning, and (c) the alteration of responses that are elicited by too many or inappropriate stimuli (Ross, 1974).

The behavioral model has several requirements central to its successful application. First, the focus of an intervention is on behavior itself rather than on some hypothetical, underlying, intrapsychic process which is not open to scientific scrutiny. This philosophy is in stark contrast to that of the psychoeducational model whose primary focus is on intrachild factors. Second, everyone in the child's environment, whether intentionally or inadvertently, whether willing or unwilling, is an intervention agent (Suran & Rizzo, 1979). The more individuals who are involved in the treatment program, the greater the likelihood for success. Assessment must be ongoing and must provide formative information. The necessity of collecting data concerning changes in the target behavior is central to evaluating and modifying treatment.

Next, we will provide a sample of intervention techniques derived from the behavioral model. The interventions selected for presentation were chosen because, in our experience, they represent some of the most widely adopted and/or researched. For a more comprehensive treatment of behavioral interventions, the reader is referred to Kazdin (1982b) and Ollendick and Cerny (1981).

Token Reinforcement. In its most general form, token reinforcement consists of providing secondary reinforcers such as points, play money, or other tokens contingent on the satisfactory performance of specified target behaviors. The secondary reinforcers can then be exchanged for other activities or tangibles. Token reinforcement systems range from very elaborate programs with social level systems and fully stocked "stores" to simple systems where a teacher places checkmarks at the top of a child's worksheet. Extensive reviews of token systems are available elsewhere (Kazdin & Bootzin, 1972; Kazdin, 1982a).

An often cited study by Ayllon and Roberts (1974) will illustrate the use of token reinforcement. This study is interesting because it shows that discipline problems were eliminated *without* contingencies on nondisruptive behavior. Instead, contingencies were applied to academic performance only. Specifically, fifth-grade students could earn points for the accurate completion of assigned class work. The requirements for earning points and the cost of back-up reinforcers were posted throughout the classroom (see Table 5.3). Each day children were given a small card indicating the number of points earned the previous day and listing the ways in which the points could be "spent." On presentation of the card, the teacher would allow the child to engage in a desired activity. Results indicated that not only did accuracy and assignment completion increase, but also that inappropriate behavior decreased even though no contingencies were attached directly to those behaviors. The authors suggested a preference for "teaching them better so they may sit still" instead of the more traditional "making them sit still so they will learn."

In some instances it may be necessary to use token systems to decrease undesirable behaviors rather than to increase desirable responses. Witt and Elliott (1982) described an intervention for accomplishing this goal: the Response Cost Lottery. The system required a teacher to place four small slips of colored paper on students' desks. Students were told that a slip of paper would be removed

Table 5.3 Requirements for Earning Points and Back-up Reinforcers for Ayllon and Roberts' (1974) Token Economy.

Points Earning Criteria for Fifth-Grade Reading Class

1. 80% correct on workbook assignments = 2 points
2. 100% correct on workbook assignments = 5 points

Back-up Reinforcers	
Daily	
1. Access to game room (per 15 minutes)	2 points
2. Extra recess time (10 minutes)	2 points
3. Buy a ditto master	2 points
4. Have ditto copies run off (per copy)	1 point
5. Review grades in teacher's book	5 points
6. Reduce detention (per 10 minutes)	10 points
7. Change cafeteria table	15 points
8. Have the lowest test grade removed	20 points
9. Become an assistant teacher	Auction
Weekly	
1. See a movie	6 points
2. Have a good work letter sent to parents	15 points
3. Become the classroom helper for one week	Auction
4. Become the ball captain for one week	Auction
5. Do bulletin board (will remain up for three weeks)	Auction

Source: From Ayllon and Roberts (1974). Reprinted with permission of authors and publisher.

each time the teacher witnessed an incident of misbehavior. Slips which remained at the end of the session could be placed in a box for a lottery at the end of the week. Of course, the better each student's behavior, the greater the chances of winning the lottery. The winners received extra privileges or special use of materials that were already in the classroom. The results indicated marked increases in appropriate behavior during periods when the Response Cost Lottery was in effect.

The two token systems just discussed placed contingencies on each student. An alternative is to implement group contengencies in which each member of a group must perform in a satisfactory manner in order for any member of the group to receive reinforcement. Perhaps the most widely known group contingency is the Good Behavior Game and its variations (Harris & Sherman, 1973). Barrish, Sanders, and Wolf (1969) described the original version of the Good Behavior Game in which students were first divided into teams (i.e., by rows or according to sex). Following that, classroom rules were stated explicitly to the students. Once the game began, rule infractions by a team member resulted in a mark on the blackboard against the team. All teams could "win" the game by keeping the number of marks below a specified level. Winning teams received extra privileges. This, as well as other versions of the Good Behavior Game, have all produced dramatic improvements in student behavior. Two advantages are associated with the use of group contengencies such as the Good Behavior Game. First, group contengencies are more convenient because consequences are more easily delivered to a group than to an individual. Second, the peer group actively supports and imitates appropriate behavior. All behavior must be monitored closely, however, because peers have been reported to make threatening statements and gestures to individuals who behave inappropriately (Harris & Sherman, 1973).

The effectiveness of various token reinforcement systems makes them a viable intervention. However, several possible disadvantages are also apparent. First, research suggests that a number of individuals fail to respond to token systems (Ayllon & Azrin, 1968). For example, some children in the Good Behavior Game are *reinforced* by having marks placed on the blackboard, despite condemnation by peers. Although variations in back-up reinforcers generally increase the rate of compliance with a system, noncompliance must always be monitored. A second problem is the maintenance of treatment following a "honeymoon" period. That is, many interventions are effective only for short time periods because of novelty or because it may take students a while to learn to circumvent a particular system. Following a brief honeymoon period, treatment gains may disappear. Although treatment gains are unlikely to diminish if reinforcers are selected appropriately, it is not always possible to obtain suitable reinforcers given the contraints under which many educational settings operate (Witt & Elliott, 1982).

A third potentially adverse effect associated with the use of token reinforcement systems centers around the overjustification hypothesis which suggests that "a person's intrinsic interest in an activity may be undermined by inducing him to engage in that activity as an explicit means to some extrinsic goal" (Lepper, Greene, & Nisbett, 1973). This is best illustrated by an example of unknown origin.

> The story goes that an old man was troubled by a group of young boys who would come by his house everyday after school. Each day the boys would shout insults and obscenities at the old man in the house. One day the old man greeted the boys cheerfully as they were coming past his house and told them how much he enjoyed their "performance" each day. That day, he offered to pay them each a nickle if they would really give a good show and shout the insults real loud and forcefully. Of course, the boys agreed readily and gave a truly good performance. The next day, the old man greeted the boys, but this time he told them he could only pay three cents. The boys were a little disgruntled but agreed to continue their antics. The following day, the old man told the boys that he could not afford to pay them anything that day, but he asked them to go ahead and do the shouting anyway. The boys were offended, saying "We won't work for nothing," and refused to do any "work" that day or any day thereafter.

A similar situation can occur with the use of extrinsic reinforcement. Children who are reinforced for a task may refuse to perform that task once reinforcment is removed. The use of fading and intermittent reinforcement procedures may decrease the likelihood of an overjustification effect; however, the willy-nilly application and withdrawal of token reinforcement programs may do more harm than good.

Home-Based Reinforcement. Home-based reinforcement programs, designed to modify classroom behaviors, are well established interventions that have proven useful for controlling a wide variety of student behaviors across a wide array of situations (Atkeson & Forehand, 1979). Typically, a teacher and a student's parents agree to work together to establish some common goals for the child's performance at school. The teacher reports, by means of a note to the parents, the degree to which a child has performed appropriately at school. Parents subsequently institute contingencies in the home, depending upon the student's performance described in the note. Sending home a note usually requires considerably less effort than is needed for even simple token economies or other interventions based solely in the classroom. Additionally, the type and quality of reinforcers available in the classroom pale by comparison with those available to parents.

Home-based systems have been used successfully to decrease disruptive classroom behaviors (Ayllon, Garber, & Pisor, 1975), to increase appropriate academic behaviors (Saudargas, Madsen, & Scott, 1977), and to effect positive changes in some combination of academic and disruptive behaviors (Witt, Hannafin, & Martens, in press). Students on whom home-based programs have been applied successfully include those from both regular and special classes (Bailey, Wolf, & Phillips, 1970), those with academic skill deficits (Ayllon et al., 1975; Shumaker et al., 1977) and those with severe emotional problems (Coleman, 1973).

Illustrative of home-based reinforcement, Witt et al., (in press) utilized an "assignment-home" rather than a note-home system to improve the academic performance and appropriate behavior of three fourth-grade students. The program was initiated by a meeting with the teacher, the child's parents, and a school psychologist. At the conference, the parents' cooperation was elicited and they were told that each day their child should bring home a workbook assignment with the percentage of correct responses indicated. The parents were asked to provide praise, privileges, and encouragement for both the items completed correctly on the daily assignment *and* for improvement over time. The parents were given information on how to praise their children and how to select privileges. The use of the actual assignment as the "note home" was a unique feature of the study and it had the advantages of providing more detailed feedback about their child's performance as well as a means to providing instruction at home. The results of the study are displayed in Figure 5.1. As can be seen, academic performance increased and was associated with simultaneous decreases in inappropriate behaviors. The latter changes occurred despite no direct contingencies upon inappropriate behavior.

Many of the same cautions which apply to other token reinforcement systems also apply to home-based reinforcement. Thus, generalization and maintenance of treatment effects and problems related to overjustification must be dealt with. Additional problems are related specifically to the use of parents. It is often difficult to get parents to participate because of a lack of time or interest. Parents are also apt to change the contingencies unsystematically. They suddenly may add the requirement that the child clean his or her room, for example, in order for reinforcement to be delivered. Such changes can lessen or eliminate the effectiveness of home-based programs.

A major advantage of home-based systems is the opportunity to include parents as part of the solution rather than as part of the problem. Research has suggested that parents often feel blamed by the school for their child's problem (Witt, Miller, McIntyre, & Smith, in press). This feeling is worsened because the school may treat parents as "partially incompetent junior partners who are to be convinced of the righteousness of education" (McCafee & Vergason, 1979, p. 7). Thus, the goodwill which parents may feel about being included as equal partners in a home-based system may be as important as the effects of the treatment program itself. From a legal and ethical perspective, home-based reinforcement eliminates many problems because neither disciplinary procedures nor

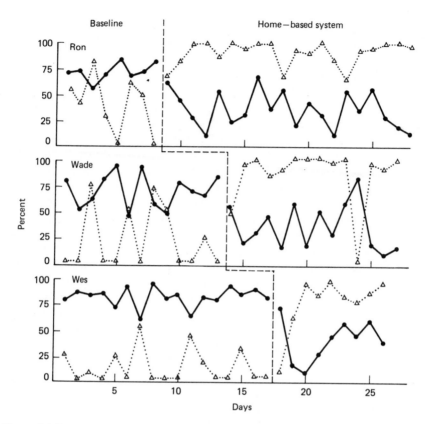

Figure 5.1. Percent of correct responses (triangular data points) and percent of inappropriate behavior (circular data points) for each day of experiment across three students in Witt et al. (in press) home-based reinforcement study.

positive reinforcers have to be used at school (Atkeson & Forehand, 1979). Finally, the procedures are attractive because they can be implemented with minimal time and resource commitments on the part of the school.

Cognitive Behavior Modification. The final class of interventions based upon the behavioral model is referred to as cognitive behavior modification. With the emphasis of the behavioral model on *observable* responses, the use of "cognitive" in the title may seem like a contradiction in terms. It requires some adjustment in one's thinking to label inner speech, which is a primary datum of cognitive behavior modification, as behavior. However, the vast majority of psychologists, behavioral and otherwise, are now in agreement with Bellack and Hersen (1977) who stated: "More and more, it has become apparent that a black box S–R (stimulus–response) model, in which the individual is viewed as a passive responder to the environment, is not adequate to explain substantial portions of behavior'' (p. 96). The proliferation of research in the area of cognitive behavior modification has given rise to methodologies for treating a wide array of children's problems including those which were not accessible through traditional behavioral methods.

The theoretical underpinnings of cognitive behavior modification can be traced to a variety of sources; however, the work of Luria (1961) is central. Luria has proposed a three-stage theoretical model for the manner in which a child's thoughts come to regulate behavior. Initially, a child's behavior is not self-regulated; instead, it is directed by the speech of the adults around the child. In the second stage, a child develops some ability for self-regulation, but self-verbalizations function more as stimuli for behavior rather than as true semantic regulators. In Luria's final stage, the child's self verbalizations truly serve a self-regulatory function (Michenbaum & Burland, 1979).

Although many different applications of cognitive behavior modification exist, most share some common components (Michenbaum & Burland, 1979). Typically, the goal is to teach children to mediate their own behavior through the use of self-talk. In one program (Michenbaum & Goodman, 1971), the first step in accomplishing this goal is for an adult model to perform a task while talking aloud. The object is to verbalize statements and questions germane to correct task completion. These include questions about the task itself, about how to approach the task for correct performance, and about self-correction and self-reinforcement for good work (Finch & Spirito, 1981). The process can be illustrated by reference to the methodology used by Michenbaum and Goodman (1971) who trained impulsive children to copy geometric figures:

> Okay, what is it I have to do? You want me to copy the picture with the different lines. I have to go slowly and carefully. Okay, draw the line down, down, good; and then to the right, that's it; now down some more and to the left. Good, I'm doing fine so far. Remember, go slowly. Now back up again. Just erase the line carefully. Good. Even if I make an error I can go on slowly and carefully, I have to go down now. Finished. I did it! (p. 117).

In the second step, the child performs the same task while being instructed and guided by an adult. In the third step, the child whispers instructions to him or herself, and in the final step, the child guides performance using inaudible speech.

A major tenet of cognitive behavior modification is that self-verbalizations will translate into improvements in overt behavior. This tenet has been supported by studies concerned with aggressive behavior (Robin, Schneider, & Dolnick, 1976), hyperactivity (Goodwin & Mahoney, 1975), and appropriate classroom behavior (Burgental, Whalen, & Henker, 1977).

From the perspective of a school psychologist, a major disadvantage of cognitive behavior modification is that, as a direct intervention, it may be too time-consuming. This disadvantage is partially offset by the fact that most cognitive behavior modification strategies require a relatively short time commitment compared to other types of direct intervention. In addition, these techniques may represent the method of choice for addressing certain problems such as anxiety or low self-concept.

Ecological Model

In Chapter 2, we introduced Bandura's (1978) ecologically oriented model of behavior called reciprocal determinism. Here, we will apply that model to the use of interventions in educational settings. Bandura's, as well as other ecological models, represents an approach to the study of relations between person (i.e., internal cognitive), behavioral, and environmental systems. The central feature of ecological definitions is the reciprocal relationship between systems. Thus, while the behavioral models, for example, are concerned with the effects of the environment on cognitions and behavior, the ecological model is equally concerned with the reciprocal effects of cognitions and behavior upon the environment. This is not to say that interventions derived from other theoretical models would not also be used within an ecological framework, but their impact would be evaluated in the broader context of their long-term and widespread treatment impact. As Hobbs (1975) explains, "the objective is not merely to change the child but to make the total system work" (p. 114).

The ecological model is not so much a way of categorizing interventions subsumed under it as it is an approach or a framework for assessment and intervention. The model assumes that each child is unique and that no one technique or strategy will be appropriate across all children, behaviors, or environmental systems. The interventions utilized with this model are not different from those used with most other models of human behavior. The differences can be seen in the ways the intervention is used, the effects it is presumed to have, and the methods used to monitor such effects.

Specific intervention strategies will not be discussed in this section since techniques from the medical and behavioral models are generally used within the ecological model. Instead, we will elaborate on the assumptions of the ecological approach and discuss two aspects of the ecological model which have direct implications for the involvement of school psychologists: behavioral covariation and good teaching.

Assumption 1: Interventions Should Focus on the Entire Ecological System. Instead of focusing entirely on the child, proponents of the ecological model emphasize the need to consider the child as part of a classroom, a peer group, a family, a community, and a physical environment. Interventions must take into account how the ecological system will support a child's altered behavior. For example, attendance in school past the eighth grade, and thus not earning income for the family, is an activity which is not typically supported by members of the Yaqui Indian community of central Arizona. Interventions directed at truancy will probably be doomed to failure if this culturally-based expectancy is not incorporated into treatment. Thus, interventions incorporating some combination of work and study may be more likely to succeed.

Another implication of this assumption is that interventions should occur at various levels (i.e., school, community, physical environment) in a child's ecological system. Thus, a program for children with behavior disorders which *only* takes the child out of a classroom and "fixes" him or her for return to the classroom is inadequate. Instead, the assumption is made that other aspects of the system, in addition to the child, are discordant and are in need of attention. Directing interventions only at the child is analogous to the farmer blaming only the seed for a crop failure when improper tillage methods and climate may be more responsible.

Assumption 2: Interventions in a Behavioral Ecology May Have Complex and Unanticipated Consequences. One implication of an ecological approach is that relatively "simple" interventions may have effects on systems far beyond those requiring attention. For example, Willems (1974) offered the story of the bearded tit which illustrates that even the most benign interventions may backfire.

> An ornithologist with a European zoo wished to add a bird called the bearded tit to the zoo's collection. Armed with all the relevant information he could find about the tit, the ornithologist went to great pains to build the right setting. Introducing a male and female to the setting, he noted that, by all behavioral criteria, the birds functioned very well. Unfortunately, soon after the birds hatched babies, they shoved the babies out of the nest, onto the ground, where they died. This cycle, beginning with mating and ending with the babies dead on the ground, repeated itself many times.

> The ornithologist tried many modifications of the settings, but none forestalled the infanticide. After many hours of direct observation of tits in the wild, the ornithologist noted three patterns of behavior that had missed everyone's attention. First, throughout most of the daylight hours in the wild, the parent tits were very active finding and bringing food for the infants. Second, the infants with whose food demands the parents could hardly keep pace, spent the hours with their mouths open, apparently crying for food. The third pattern was that any inanimate object, whether eggshell, leaf, or beetle shell, was quickly shoved out of the nest by the parents. With these observations in mind, the ornithologist went back to observe his captive tits, and found that during the short time a new brood of infants lived, the parents spent only brief periods feeding them by racing between nest and the food supply, which the ornithologist had provided in abundance. After a short period of such feeding, the infants, apparently satiated, fell asleep. The first time the infants slept for any length of time during the daylight hours, the parents shoved them (two

inanimate objects, after all) out of the nest. When he made the food supply less abundant and less accessible, and thereby made the parents work much harder to find food, the ornithologist found that the infants spent more time awake, demanding food, and that the tits then produced many families and cared for them to maturity. (pp. 152–153)

Thus, even though the ornithologist felt he was helping, and the short-term data supported him, his providing ready access to food was having an overall deterimental effect. The example is a good one because it represents the complex interdependencies and interrelationships which occur in the natural environment. It also illustrates the very serious consequences which can result from even the most benign interventions.

Examples such as this one from the biological sphere probably do not surprise anyone at this point; increasingly, we are made aware of the consequences of disturbing the ecology of any member of a food chain or even of using aerosol cans whose deleterious effects on the ozone layer are now common knowledge. Common sense and federal law now prevent us from large scale intrusions into our environment. However, according to Willems (1974), we have been "childishly irresponsible" in the way in which we have introduced interventions into a behavioral ecology.

The effects of disturbing the behavioral ecology of a child can be quite pronounced. For example, Forehand, Breiner, McMahon, and Davies (in press) monitored the effects of a parent training program to improve the home behavior of oppositional children. Although the program was effective in reducing oppositional behavior at home, its implementation corresponded with marked *increases* in inappropriate behavior at school. These changes occurred despite no alteration in school routine. In fact, in a multiple regression analysis, with behavior at school as the criterion, a combination of therapeutic change scores and pretreatment level of inappropriate school behavior accounted for 70% of the variance! The study is illustrative of the interdependent nature of responses within a child's repertoire because decreases in inappropriate behavior at home were associated *several hours later* with increases in inappropriate behaviors at school. Fortunately, Forehand et al., monitored behavior at school even though school behavior was not the primary focus of the investigation. Many investigators and practitioners do not monitor untreated behaviors and are surprised when events such as this happen "mysteriously." However, as Hardin (1969) points out, "we can never do merely one thing." Adherence to the ecological model forces us to *assume* that intervention "side effects" will occur; such adherence also mandates that we be alert to and monitor such effects.

Assumption 3: Interventions Should Disrupt the Child's Natural Ecological System as Little as Possible. Stated another way, this assumption tells us to utilize those interventions that are the most practical but least disruptive to normal patterns of living (Hobbs, 1975). Thus, the trends toward normalization of the handicapped and placement of children in the least restrictive environment are consistent with an ecological model. Illustrative of this least disruption principle, Project Re-ED (Re-Education of Emotionally Disturbed Children) exemplifies how even the residential treatment of severely emotionally disturbed children can be accomplished within an ecological framework (Hobbs, 1975). According, to Hobbs, the goals of Project Re-Ed were to remove a child the least possible distance in *space* and *time* from the people with whom he or she must learn to live. With regard to *space,* this meant that Project Re-Ed schools were located in the child's own community so that family members could visit frequently and so that the child could go home for weekends. Children also visited their regular schools frequently so as to maintain contacts with friends and a sense of identity with the school. With regard to *time,* Project Re-ED attempted to treat the children as quickly as possible and then return them to their natural environment. Disrupting a child's ecological system as little as possible is consistent with the overall goal of the model: restoring the entire system to a productive equilibrium.

Assumption 4: Ecological Interventions Are Eclectic. Virtually every intervention can be viewed as an ecological intervention. Further, the ecological model can be used by a variety of disciplines; its use requires "someone who can move freely among and communicate with diverse disciplines in the performance of a liaison function—linking up all the individuals concerned about the child and coordinating the planning and programming. . . ." (Hobbs, 1975, pp. 129–131).

Since each child is unique, intervention systems and interventionists may vary from case to case. In a particular case, it may be best to place the child on medication, to engage the parents in family therapy, or to find a job for an unemployed father. According to Swap, Prieto, and Harth (1982), the fact that interventions are eclectic and that they are applied in unique ways to individual cases represents both the power and the limitations of the model. On the one hand, our ability to generalize the results of an intervention to other settings is limited, but on the other hand, we have the freedom to utilize and assess interventions in unique and creative ways.

Two Implications of an Ecological Model. We conclude this discussion of the ecological model with a brief review of two areas of research which have implications for psychologists who design interventions in educational settings. The first area to be discussed, behavioral covariation, is a method of utilizing the relationship between behaviors within the repertoires of individual children. The second area relates to what might be the best intervention of all: good teaching.

In the previous sections, we have alluded to intervention "side effects" as the potentially problematic consequences of disturbing a behavioral ecology. However, as Willems (1974) asserts: "When we think in terms of environment–behavior *systems,* we can see that there is a fundamental misconception embedded in the popular term 'side effects.' . . . . What we so glibly call side effects no more deserve the adjective 'side' than does the 'principal' effect—they are all aspects of the interdependencies that we need so badly to understand'' (Willems, 1974, p. 155). Thus, while the term ''side effects'' may imply accidental or unintentioned effects, research is beginning to accumulate which suggests that these effects occur in a very systematic manner—so systematic, in fact, that they can be utilized and manipulated to great advantage.

Research concerning the relationship between academic accuracy and on-task behavior will illustrate the use of behavioral covariation. These two behaviors typically co-vary in a positive direction (Ayllon & Roberts, 1974; Witt et al., in press). That is, when one behavior increases in frequency, so does the other. Attempts to manipulate the relationship between these two variables have indicated that interventions designed to increase on-task behavior did not result in concomitant increases in academic accuracy. Interventions that increased academic accuracy were however associated with improved on-task behavior (Ayllon & Roberts, 1974; Witt et al., in press). A specific implication of this research is to demonstrate the futility of the numerous attempts by teachers and researchers to increase on-task behavior so that children will improve in their school work. A broader implication is the suggestion that it may be possible to change one behavior by intervening in another. For example, it may be very costly, time consuming, inefficient, and undesirable to intervene in a deviant behavior such as inappropriate talking in the classroom. However, it may be possible to intervene indirectly on these deviant actions by modifying other correlated behaviors. In addition, interventions aimed at replacing inappropriate or maintaining appropriate behavior may be optimally effective if they are developed in accordance with the interrelationships among behaviors in an individual's repertoire. Although our understanding of behavioral covariation is still developing, the possibility of utilizing indirect behavioral interventions by manipulation of response–response relationships offers unique and creative intervention options.

Another creative and unique opportunity for school psychologists to apply their skills is in the improvement of teaching. Without any question whatsoever, the best classroom intervention available is classroom teaching conducted by teachers who maintain good classroom organization and who are able to relate on a personal level with students. Misbehavior simply does not occur with high frequency in such classrooms. One only needs to think back to elementary school to the teacher, and everybody has had one like this, who was able to quell talking in mid-sentence by just looking at a student in a certain way. No fancy interventions were needed, just that look. Good teaching, while it could apply to any of the models, is most appropriately discussed under the ecological rubric because much of the research describing good teaching stems from an ecological orientation. Although most school psychologists will not be involved in teaching, knowledge of the literature relating to good teaching provides an effective means for contributing to the improvement of teaching in regular and special education classrooms.

The cornerstone research in the area of classroom management was conducted by Kounin (1970) who videotaped 49 classrooms in order to determine teacher behaviors related to two student variables: work involvement and freedom from deviancy. Using the teacher variables presented in Table 5.4, Kounin was able to predict, with great accuracy, the degree to which students in a classroom behaved and completed assignments. Thus, the extent to which a teacher is able to demonstrate that he or she "knows all" and "sees all" (with-it-ness) is an important classroom management technique. When teachers are engaged in group discussion or lecturing, the best predictors of student involvement include: with-it-ness, smoothness, and momentum. During seat work, the best predictor of work involvement was seatwork variety. Kounin has operationally defined each of the teacher behaviors in Table 5.4 to the point that they could be translated easily into goals for inservice programs. Since Kounin's results are correlational, they must be interpreted cautiously. It may be that teachers who displayed "with-it" behavior had easier students to manage.

Some related research has focused on techniques for beginning the school year, a most important time period to establish a good classroom regimen (Emmer & Evertson, 1982). This research suggested that effective teachers spent a considerable amount of time during the first weeks of school teaching children to behave. "They had carefully thought out procedures for getting assistance, for turning in work, and standards for conduct during seatwork, group work or whole class activities" (Emmer & Evertson, 1982, p. 9). Contrary to the old

Table 5.4   Explanations for Each of Kounin's Teacher Behaviors

Teacher Behavior	*Meaning*
1. With-it-ness	Teacher behavior which communicates to students that the teacher "knows all and sees all"
2. Overlapping	Reflects extent to which teacher can juggle several activities simultaneously
3. Smoothness	Ability to move smoothly through a lesson without getting sidetracked by minor disturbances or interrupting
4. Momentum	Avoiding activities which slow down a lesson such as telling an unrelated anecdote
5. Group Alerting	Keeping students alert when they are not reciting by asking questions unexpectedly or creating suspense
6. Seatwork Variety	Presenting varied activities during seatwork

adage "Don't smile until Christmas," good teachers smiled more, joked more, and readily accepted student opinion and ideas (Emmer & Evertson, 1982).

Another component of a good teacher is *teaching*. For example, Leinhardt and her associates (Leinhardt & Seewald, 1981; Leinhardt, Zigmond, & Cooley, 1981) have reported some fascinating observational data on the actual amount of time teachers spend teaching and its relationship to student gains in reading. Leinhardt's major findings included: (a) students spend an average of only 16 minutes per day receiving instruction from the teacher as opposed to 21 minutes waiting for instruction and 34 minutes either preparing for or wrapping up a task; (b) small increases of 1–5 minutes in the amount of time spent in *silent* reading, but not oral reading, can lead to marked improvements in reading achievement; (c) one minute of teacher instruction increased student reading time by one minute; (d) although beginning readers must be taught to read, teachers spend only 1 minute per day explaining or modeling reading behavior (Leinhardt, et al., 1981). The implications of these findings suggest that school psychologists should assess and facilitate: (a) increases in the amount of time that students spend in silent reading, (b) reallocation of student time which is spent waiting and getting prepared for tasks, and (c) increases in the amount of time teachers spend instructing students (Witt & Bartlett, 1982).

School psychologists can be influential in improving the quality of teaching by assuming the role of knowledge–linker (Miller, 1978). Frequently, teachers are unaware of research such as Kounin's; school psychologists, on the other hand, are in a unique position to consume the research and then to make it available, in a practical format, to others in the educational system. Making teachers aware of their impact on the complex ecology of the classroom may be one of the most cost-effective, if not just plain effective, services a psychologist can provide.

CRITICAL DIMENSIONS IN THE CHOICE OF ALTERNATIVE TREATMENTS

Thus far this chapter has provided a brief overview of just a few of the interventions available for various problems. Given that there is an infinite number of possible problems and an almost equally great number of interventions (Yeaton & Sechrest, 1981), how does one begin to operationalize the process of deciding which treatment to apply to a given problem? The process of deciding *which* treatment implies that it is encumbant upon school psychologists to be knowledgeable of a number of different interventions. Further, it is important for school psychologists to have some criteria by which various treatments can be evaluated for their suitability in each particular situation.

A major underlying theme of this section is that the majority of interventions reported in journals or in textbooks could be made more useful to practicing school psychologists. Many have been developed through demonstration and/or research projects with resources far beyond what an individual school district can provide. For an intervention to be useful, it must be effective *and* it must be useable in the situation in which it is needed. We conceptualize this issue as related to four dimensions of the treatment itself: acceptability, effectiveness, cost, and treatment integrity.

Effectiveness

The first question most of us ask about a new treatment is, "Does it work?" The reason for asking this question has been stated succiently by Baer, Wolf, and Risley (1968): "If the application of behavioral techniques does not produce large enough effects for practical value, then application has failed. . . . Its practical value, specifically its powers in altering behavior enough to be socially important, is the essential criterion" (p. 96). For many years effectiveness has not only been the "essential" criterion, it has been almost the *sole* criterion. Strong, effective treatments which produce large effects are not necessary during the developmental stages of a science or technology because, in the beginning, any solution is better than none at all (Yeaton et al., 1981). Now, however, a number of very effective treatments exist for a variety of problems, and intervention agents can be more selective in choosing one which is not only effective but one which might meet other more specific demands of a situation.

In the selection of treatments, how do we know that a treatment will be effective? The answer is that we don't. We can not specify *in advance* whether a treatment will be effective for a given problem. One approach to this problem, however, is to select treatments which have been successful with similar problems in the past. In order to supplement human judgment in this process, Yeaton and Sechrest (1981) have proposed the development of treatment-effects norms. These norms would be developed by using the results of different studies with the same dependent variable. In essence, we now compare alternative treatment effects, but we conduct this process unsystematically. For example, if a teacher has a goal of improving both on-task behavior and assignment completion in a classroom, research previously cited in this chapter suggests that contingencies on academic behavior would accomplish both of these goals while contingencies on on-task behavior may not. Thus, the choice of treatment in this instance would be clear. The development of treatment-effect norms would facilitate this decision-making process for various treatments as they are applied to various problems.

A question related to effectiveness is, "How much change is enough?" The answer to this question is related to two factors: (a) developmental and environmental norms, and (b) the expectations of significant others in a child's environment. With respect to normative guidelines, Walker and Hops (1976) utilized normative peer data in an attempt to change behavior in line with environmental expectations. Target students and peers were observed in both an experimental and a regular classroom during baseline conditions. Following baseline, target subjects were provided token and social reinforcement for appropriate classroom behavior. The data (see Figure 5.2) show that the behavior of target students, which differed markedly from regular classroom peers during baseline, was very consistent with peers following treatment.

The use of normative data provides information not only on how much change is enough but also on how much change is too much. Winnett and Winkler (1972) chided the behavior modification establishment with an article entitled: "Current Behavior Modification in the Classroom: Be Still, Be Quiet, Be Docile." Their point was that many treatments were helping to maintain too much order and control when "it may be that learning can take place more effectively if it can be accompanied by singing and laughing and whistling and that a quiet, controlled, docile classroom may not be only unnecessary but destructive" (Winnett & Winkler, 1972, p. 500). Some treatments can result in behavior change beyond what is considered normal for the situation and may result in changes which are inconsistent with the goals of society as a whole. For example, Van Houten (1979) described the case of an unassertive boy who underwent therapy designed to increase the number of requests he made. Ini-

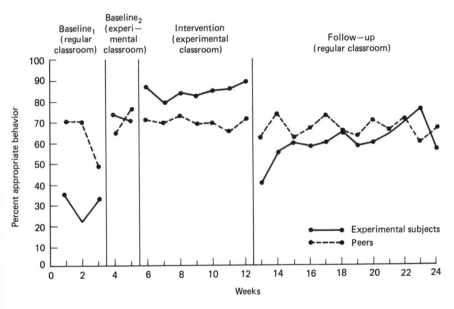

Figure 5.2. Normative peer data provide a means for evaluating "How much change is enough?" From Walker and Hops, 1976. Reprinted with permission of authors and publisher.

tially, the child increased to an acceptable frequency of requests but as treatment continued, the child began to make so many requests that he was considered a pest. Treatments which alter behaviors beyond some optimal level can thus become neither useful nor appropriate.

An evaluation of the effectiveness of treatment is important because there would appear to be a level of strength which is not too strong, and not too weak, but "just right." Treatments which are too weak may result in the problem being left more resistent to change than before (e.g., ineffectual punishment) and may reduce the motivational level of the people involved in the treatment. On the other hand, treatments which are too strong may be unnecessarily expensive or cause excessive disruption of the child's ecological system.

Acceptability

How would the parents of a child react after being told that their child would be treated for a learning disability by vigorous rubbing on the head? How would a teacher react to an intervention which required him or her to purchase $100.00 worth of reinforcers each week, at personal expense? In both of these cases, for various reasons, the response might be that the treatment was unacceptable. The acceptability of the treatment would determine whether it would be utilized.

Research on the acceptability of treatments suggests that individuals have relatively consistent ideas about what is an acceptable treatment; when choosing a treatment they consider such variables as: (a) whether the treatment is appropriate for a given problem, (b) whether it is fair, reasonable or intrusive, and (c) whether it is consistent with conventional notions of what a treatment should be (Kazdin, 1980a; 1981a). In general, acceptability is concerned with whether the ends justify the means.

The research on acceptability has taken two forms. First, there has been an interest in assessing nonprofessionals, lay persons, clients, and other potential consumers of treatments (Kazdin, 1981a). Because the courts have ruled various interventions unacceptable under certain circumstances (e.g., time-out), this type of acceptability has received increased attention. In general, findings have indicated that reinforcement procedures, such as reinforcement of incompatible behavior, are more acceptable than procedures such as time-out; that treatment efficacy is not related significantly to acceptability; that adverse side effects for particular interventions influence acceptability; and that the severity of a behavior problem affects acceptability in all treatments being judged as more acceptable for severe clinical cases (Kazdin, 1980a; 1981a).

Another line of research on acceptability has more direct application to educational settings. Specifically, teachers have been studied to determine the types of interventions which are acceptable to them (Witt & Elliott, in press). Here, acceptability reflects the extent to which interventions will actually be used by classroom teachers. Behavioral interventions are often criticized for being excessively complicated and awkward to administer.

The research by Witt, Elliott, and Martens (in press) has examined the criteria that teachers use to make judgements about the acceptability of interventions in educational settings. This research indicates that teachers are concerned about how much time an intervention will require, the risks it poses to a child, the amount of training required to implement an intervention, and the possible deleterious effects that the intervention might have on other children. Witt et al. also found that interventions which required more teacher time and which were more restrictive of student behavior were judged more acceptable when applied to moderate or severe behavior problems than to mild ones. Thus, time-out was judged more acceptable for destruction of other children's property than it was for daydreaming. Perhaps this is an extention of the "let the punishment fit the crime" notion.

Another line of research suggests that it is not only the treatment but also the results of treatment which influence acceptability. For example, Brickman and Zarantonello (1978) examined the procedures used in Milgram's classic research on obedience and found that those procedures were judged unacceptable only when they produced obedience.

The concept of acceptability is a complex one. What treatment would be recommended, for example, if children feel very positively about an intervention, but parents are unimpressed (Yeaton, Greene, & Bailey, 1981)? Further, what variables are related to the acceptance of an intervention by society as a whole? What factors determine whether a school will require an intervention or even *pay* for its implementation (Yeaton, et. al., 1981)?

Cost Considerations in the Use of Treatment

We will define cost in terms of the personnel resources, materials, and expense which can be attributed to a particular treatment. In most situations, all these components of cost will be important determiners of whether or not an intervention is utilized. The potential problems of excessive cost can be illustrated through an examination of the Program for Academic Survival Skills (PASS), a classroom management system developed by Greenwood, Hops, and Walker, Guild, Stokes, Young, Keleman, & Willardson, (1979). The program has been demonstrated to be very effective; however, implementation requires the following:

Participation of teachers in six two-hour training sessions

A minimum of 17 20-minute visits to the classroom by psychologists to assist in implementation and troubleshooting

Film-strip projector

Cassette recorder

Clock-and-light recording instrument

The numerous studies using PASS presumably have been conducted in atypical classrooms—as a practical matter, how many school districts could afford to purchase the materials, provide the release time for training, and allow psychologists to consult with any one classroom on such an extensive scale as is required to implement PASS? An intervention such as the home-based system of Witt et al. (in press) compares favorably with PASS on the dimension of cost because virtually no teacher time is required and reinforcers, which can be costly, were provided at home. An intervention which is not used is no intervention at all!

Treatment Integrity

Any particular intervention suggested to a teacher during a consultation session might elicit the response, "I already tried that (e.g., time-out, reinforcement of appropriate behavior, etc.) and it didn't work." The consultant immediately wonders exactly *how* the treatment was applied. Was it applied appropriately or was it applied in a careless or incomplete fashion without full knowledge of how it should be implemented. Treatments which are implemented as intended are said to have treatment integrity (Yeaton & Sechrest, 1981). The lack of treatment integrity has been related to the failure of numerous field-based interventions (Boruch & Gomez, 1977).

A prerequisite to insuring treatment integrity is knowing exactly how an intervention should be conducted. This is often difficult because reports of interventions do not always contain all of the information necessary to implement a treatment. In some cases, journal articles, a rich source of interventions, leave out important components. For example, many reports of relaxation training with children tell the therapist what to *say* but not what else to do (e.g., Michenbaum & Goodman, 1971). Various reports on the importance of physical positioning and posture during therapy would suggest that a description of where to sit would have been a helpful, and perhaps, an essential addition to the treatment description (Haase & Tepper, 1972).

As a general rule, treatment integrity appears to vary as an inverse function of treatment complexity. However, even the simplest of treatments must be monitored for integrity. Time-out, for example, should be implemented in a matter-of-fact manner with as little verbal or physical interaction with the child as possible. A psychologist may find it difficult to recommend this treatment to some parents because they may be likely to become emotional or shout at the child on the way to the time-out room. Other parents may be apt to apply time-out inconsistently. Both of these problems with treatment integrity could result in a loss of effectiveness.

A practical problem often experienced by school psychologists is the extent to which a treatment can be changed and still remain effective. Practical considerations often dictate that treatments be modified to meet the unique needs of a particular situation. Although some researchers have anticipated possible degradations of treatment packages and have tested alternative versions (Yeaton et al., 1981), most have not.

Certainly, more research is needed on issues related to treatment integrity. At this point, modifications to treatments are probably the rule rather than the exception. This point has been summarized by Yeaton and Sechrest (1981) as follows: "One is not surprised to discover that graduate students work diligently on their dissertation research when a nearly omnipotent major professor carefully supervises the quality and quantity of their efforts. Unless a similar contingency is arranged by a clinician, it is a poor bet to assume that parents, spouses, or even major professors would implement a treatment as planned" (Yeaton & Sechrest, 1981, p. 62). Clearly, research is needed on the consequences of altering various types of treatments.

EVALUATION OF INTERVENTION EFFECTIVENESS

The purpose of this chapter has been to provide a conceptual basis for the selection and implementation of successful interventions. But how do you know if an intervention is successful? In fact, how do you implement an intervention so that it can be evaluated? We will conclude this chapter by providing a model for the evaluation of psychological interventions. This model, which has been adapted from several sources (Phillips, 1982; Kazdin & Wilson, 1978; Yeaton et al., 1981), is in the form of a flow chart and is presented in Figure 5.3.

As can be seen, the first step, and for that matter what many authorities consider the most important step, is an operational definition of the problem (Gutkin & Curtis, 1982; Witt & Elliott, 1983). This objective has been discussed at length in the consultation chapter, so we will not dwell on it here. However, it is important to note that specifying behaviors in an operational manner is a prerequisite to most forms of evaluation. Ideally, problem definition should encompass not only problems with the child, but should also examine the entire ecological system as a source of discordance. Interventions which focus on system variables have a higher probability of becoming preventive in nature rather than merely reactions to acute crises.

A related problem is that of specifying the goals of an intervention. This chapter has provided some guidelines for selecting goals, namely the use of developmental norms, environmental norms, and the expectations of significant others. Additional guidelines for selecting target behaviors were proposed by Nelson and Hayes (1980). Priority should be given to: (a) behaviors dangerous to the client or others; (b) behaviors which maximize the natural reinforcers avail-

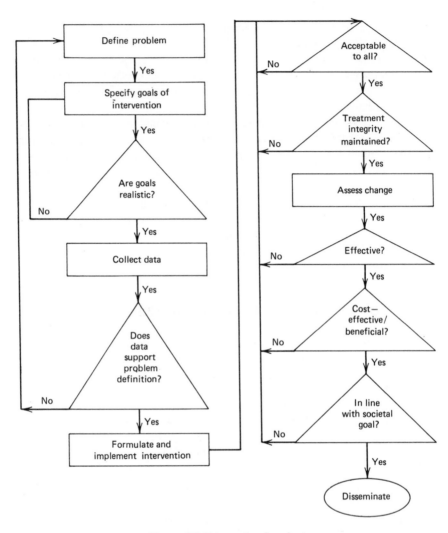

Figure 5.3. Intervention flowchart.

able in the environment; and (c) behaviors which are positive and in need of strengthening rather than negative behaviors in need of reduction.

The next step, collection of data, serves two functions. First, it provides evidence about whether or not a problem really exists. This is important in light of indications that human judgment does not always correspond with data from observations (Schnelle, 1974). Thus, it is possible that a teacher's perception that Johnny is out of his seat too much does not reflect the number of times Johnny is actually out of his seat. Instead, the teacher may be overly sensitive to either

Johnny himself or to out-of-seat behavior. The second reason for collecting data prior to intervention is that it provides a basis from which to determine how much the treatment affects behavior.

The collection of data is very often difficult to achieve because it may appear to be a nonessential component of treatment. Teachers, for example, may want to rely on their own subjective impressions of whether the target behavior or skill is improving. However, the subjective evaluation of a treatment can be problematic because some target behaviors change so slowly as to be almost imperceptible.

Data collection can be made more palatable by simplifying it as much as possible. It is unrealistic, for example, to require a teacher to utilize an interval recording system, as is typically applied in research studies, to observe every instance of out-of-seat behavior in a child who repeats this behavior 20 times per day. Teachers have a number of other activities which compete for their time and which have a higher priority. However, providing the teacher with an inexpensive wrist counter or a small abacus may simplify recording to the point that it is more likely to be utilized systematically. A second option would be to have the child monitor his or her own behavior. A pleasant side-effect of this procedure is that self-monitoring can produce therapeutic changes without any other external intervention (Connis, 1979). A third method of simplifying data collection is to "automate" the system. This can be accomplished by having workbook assignments or test scores serve as the criterion of interest. Since this type of information is already being scored and recorded, it can easily serve as a means to judge the effectiveness of treatment.

The selection of an intervention should be based upon the extent to which it is likely to be acceptable to those who use it and those on whom it is implemented, the extent to which it is cost effective, the extent to which treatment integrity can be predicted, the extent to which it is effective, and the extent to which it is likely to be accepted by society as a whole. Certainly, the preceived effectiveness of treatment should be a goal, but reports of effective interventions are so numerous that the selection of interventions must be made on a more discriminating basis.

When assessing the effects of a particular treatment, it is preferrable to obtain specific behavioral measures whenever possible. Evaluation of subjective criteria can obscure, bias, and distort judgments of actual treatment effects. For example, one can measure the number of contacts with other children more effectively than merely stating "doesn't get along with other children." Mischel (1973) summarized this point as follows:

> The focus shifts from attempting to compare and generalize about what individuals are like to an assessment of what they do—behaviorally and cognitively—in relationship to the psychological conditions in which they do it. The focus shifts from

describing situation-free people with broad adjectives to analyzing the specific in-teractions between conditions and the cognitions and behaviors of interest. (p. 265)

The "bottom line" in terms of assessing an intervention's effectiveness is the reduction of discordance between what is desired in the situation and what is actually occuring. Thus, in most practical situations, it is not necessary to require statistically or interocularly significant change in a target behavior. Perhaps some combination of small changes in the target behavior and teacher expectations will suffice. The final step in the evaluation process is to disseminate successful interventions. Dissemination typically occurs on a national level through journal articles describing intervention attempts. However, dissemination of information on a local level may provide a means for broadening the impact of individual practitioners. For example, a school psychologist and a teacher who consult together and develop an intervention may wish to write a one- or two-page description of the case and its outcome and then provide copies to other teachers in the school. This not only makes people aware of alternative interventions, but the intervention itself is presented in perhaps a more credible manner. In addi-tion, it provides information and feedback about what a school psychologist does, can do, and is doing.

An alternative method of dissemination has been suggested by Yeaton et al. (1981). We like the feeling of approaching a school administrator with data in hand and saying, "Here is a problem that we have been working on. These data suggest that we may be on to something. Would you be interested in backing a school-wide attack of this problem?" The emphasis here is on a proactive solu-tion to recurring problems. Such an approach would place us in an accountable and responsible position, but by continuing to use the evaluative model described here, ineffective solutions would simply be recycled and the process would begin again.

6

Legal and Ethical Issues

School psychology is affected by innumerable social, historical, and organizational factors. Perhaps the most conspicuous of these factors is the multitude of legal, ethical, and professional regulations. The practice of school psychology has become inextricably immersed in a complex array of laws and guidelines bearing on the daily practices of professional school psychologists. It is no longer appropriate to consider only what is "right" for a particular child because legal and ethical ramifications must also be weighed in decision making.

Consider the following examples:

1. A group of teachers and a school principal are concerned that a child is not receiving appropriate instruction in the regular classroom. They feel that the child should be placed in a special education program but have refrained from doing so because the child's parents do not want the child evaluated. The teachers urge the school psychologist to begin an evaluation anyway "because it is in the best interest of the child." As a child advocate, should the psychologist conduct an evaluation?

2. A 13-year-old girl drops into a psychologist's office and immediately blurts out that she has been having sexual contact with her boyfriend. She wants to obtain contraceptives but does not know where to search. She asks the psychologist for advice. Can the school psychologist provide such advice on the spot?

3. A young man of 15 wishes to begin counseling about some "personal problems" he is experiencing. However, before entering into such a relationship, he wants the school psychologist to assure him that everything he says will remain confidential. How should the school psychologist proceed?

4. A small school district is concerned about the expense required to hire school psychologists. Therefore, they decide to hire only one person where three are needed. In order to get the most service out of this one person, the district establishes explicit guidelines about what the psychologist can and cannot do. For example, the school psychologist is required to avoid contacting teachers or parents, to conduct evaluations using only an intelligence test, and to utilize a report format which consists of a checklist. The district's one psychologist is displeased with the guidelines but declines to fight the administration following a discussion in which he is told that he might be happier working in another district where the psychologists have the luxury of doing "nonessentials" such as administering achievement tests and conducting counseling sessions. Does a school psychologist in this situation have any recourse other than taking another position?

Cases such as those just described occur with some regularity in school districts across the country. Therefore, professionals must be knowledgable of the legal, ethical, and/or professional standards which apply in such cases because decisions about what to do in a given situation may have both personal and societal ramifications when scrutinized in the bright lights of a legal or ethical arena. This chapter will provide an introduction to major topics within legal and ethical realms that should influence professional psychologists' behavior. Included will be an examination of: (a) basic legal rights of all students, (b) legal regulation of testing, intervention, and research, and (c) professional ethics.

Before getting into specifics, we must note that the legal regulation of school psychology has increased geometrically during the past decade. Although most of the relevant actions taken by the nation's courts and legislatures were aimed primarily at the regulation of special and regular education rather than at the control of school psychology per se (Prasse, 1979), these actions have had a profound impact on the provision of school psychological services. It is possible that in an era of "deregulation" the pace of growth in this area may slacken in the 1980s; however, it seems inevitable that for the foreseeable future school psychologists will have to live with large numbers of substantive legal guidelines and restraints. Only through a knowledge of the societal, professional, ethical, and legal constraints can the individual school psychologist function in a reasoned, competent manner. Awareness of such guidelines and constraints is the first step.

Why the onslaught of legal regulations? Several factors present themselves. First, legislators have felt a genuine need to provide more services to the powerless and the unserved. High on the list of priorities were educational and psychological services for handicapped children, a group whose unmet needs were trumpeted to federal and state governments by parent advocacy groups, special educators, and psychologists alike. The late 1960s and early 1970s atmosphere of expanding governmental involvement in an ever increasing range of social programs made the passage of legislation at the federal and state levels a logical extention of previous governmental roles. Along with the millions of dollars of governmental aid for handicapped children came both the inevitable regulations limiting how those funds could be spent by educational institutions and the specification of rules governing the behavior of a wide range of personnel, including school psychologists. If anyone held the belief that governmental agencies might lend substantial support to the education of handicapped children without attaching "strings" to the package, they were indeed very naive.

A second factor leading to increased governmental involvement in the educational process was the mounting evidence that frequently schools were not acting in the best interests of the children they were serving. A series of law suits conducted independently around the nation highlighted the abuse of constitutional rights which both children and parents were suffering at the hands of school systems. Judges and legislators, in most instances, felt compelled to right the wrongs paraded before them. With each court case documenting additional legal problems with many traditional educational practices, the government's intrusion into, and control of, the public educational system became a bit more manifest.

It is important to emphasize that legal regulation, born out of a desire to help the underserved and the legally abused, is not necessarily a pernicious monster strangling school psychology with red tape and unnecessary bureaucratic nonsense. It could be argued, in fact, that much of the school psychologist's power to advocate for children and their parents, and to effect needed changes in resistant school systems, flows from the legal mandates set out in recent case and statutory law. Where problems exist with these regulations—and clearly there is no shortage of such problems—it is primarily because the rules and guidelines were established by politicians and bureaucrats who did not have, typically, the expertise or experience to effectively design educational and psychological service delivery systems.

Although all psychologists are regulated, and to some extent controlled, by state and federal laws, rules, and court decisions, school psychologists, by virtue of their intimate involvement with the two most pervasive institutions that influence children, schools and families, directly encounter societies' control more frequently and strongly. Much of the regulation has been directly precipitated by psychologists, either as a reaction to poor practice or a result of their proactive attempts to influence the development of regulation. Legalistic movement, (e.g., legislation and litigation) on behalf of children and their parents has thus been a two-edged sword. While it has vastly increased the flow of financial and professional resources, it has also restricted the flexibility with which these resources can be applied to presenting problems.

LEGAL RIGHTS OF STUDENTS

We begin our review with a discussion of the basic rights to which all children are entitled. Although our focus is on the rights of all children, we will concentrate on the rights of handicapped children for two reasons. First, handicapped children are a primary clientele of school psychologists. Second, and more important, children with good academic potential and appropriate classroom behavior have not typically encountered systematic denial of their educational rights. Usually, but not always, it has been minority children and/or those with handicaps whose rights have been abridged. Thus, the law discussed here pertains primarily to situations where children have been denied equal protection under the law.

Historically, the legal rights discussed here were virtually nonexistent during the early part of this century since the schools were viewed as functioning *in loco parentis* (i.e., in place of parents). As such, schools were given almost total freedom to educate and socialize children in any manner they saw fit. Some early court cases even allowed the school to exert influence over students while they were home during hours in which school was not in session (Overcast & Sales, 1982).

Perhaps the most significant development in the expansion of rights to children during the past half-century has been the extension of the principle of egalitarianism. Previously, children were not viewed as possessing the same rights and constitutional freedoms as adults in our society. Schools were free to expel students without procedural due process, to search students' lockers and personal effects, and even to deny students access to an education. The egalitarian trend has caused students in the public schools to be viewed as "persons," within the meaning of the Constitution, who have certain fundamental rights that schools must respect (Overcast & Sales, 1982). In general, the courts appear to have walked a fine line between granting students their constitutional rights and recognizing that schools must possess some latitude in imposing reasonable rules to maintain order and discipline so that the educational process can proceed in an orderly fashion (*Blackwell* v. *Issaquena County Board of Education*, 1966). Professionals have recognized broader rights of children as well (e.g., see Table 6.1).

The issues surrounding the legal rights of children can be categorized into twelve major areas (Overcast & Sales, 1982, Table 1): access to the educational

Table 6.1 The Rights of Children

1. We believe that handicapped children have the right to live and participate in settings that are as normal as possible, that they have the right to as much independence as we can help them to achieve.
2. We believe that the helping professions must recognize the needs of all, including the very young and the adult.
3. We believe that effective interventions for children can progress only if efforts cut across all of the disciplines in the helping professions—and into the community as well. We see our primary responsibility in improving instruction in all areas—personal, social, and vocational as well as academic. But we consider it foolish to argue over territorial rights, when we can accomplish more by working with other professionals in medicine, social services, and education.
4. We believe that professionals have for too long ignored the needs of the parents and families of children, treating them more as patients or adversaries than as clients, consumers of services, or co–workers. We believe that we have too often given the impression that parents were there to serve professionals, when in fact the opposite is more correct. We believe that no really successful intervention program can fail to involve parents who want to take part in their child's education.
5. We believe that teachers must demand effectiveness from their instructional approaches, and that the best way to evaluate instructional effectiveness is through direct observation and measurement of each child's performance of the skills being taught.
6. Finally, we are essentially optimistic about the futures of handicapped children. That is to say, we have enough confidence in their potentials to affirm that they can succeed in building fuller and more independent lives in the community. We believe that we have only begun to discover the ways to improve teaching, to increase learning, to prevent handicapping conditions, and to develop technology to compensate for handicaps. And while we make no predictions for the future, we are certain that we have not come as far as we can in helping children to help themselves.

Source: Adapted from Heward & Orlansky, 1980.

system, assignment, transportation, tuition and fees, compulsory attendance, classifications, school regulation of students, suspension and expulsion, graduation with a diploma, due process, right to privacy, and discipline and punishment. Knowledge of the law in each of these areas is important for all individuals who work within school systems; however, a complete discussion of each of the 12 areas is beyond the scope of this book. The interested reader is referred to Bersoff (1982) and Overcast and Sales (1982) for a more complete review. The treatment here will focus on the three areas most relevant to school psychologists: (a) access to the educational system, (b) due process, and (c) privacy rights. These are summarized in Table 6.2.

Table 6.2   Major Categories of Law Affecting Children in School

1. **Access to the Educational System:** Before a person may be said to have the rights of a student, he or she must obtain access to the school and achieve the status of "student." Schools may prescribe rules and regulations controlling access to their facilities. They may not attempt to restrict access based on a student's age, race, gender, residence, and physical or mental condition. Additionally, the school may not attempt to regulate attendance by married students and pregnant females.

2. **Assignment:** The school may have regulations regarding the assignment of students to particular schools or the transfer of students between schools.

3. **Transportation:** The school may or may not have a duty to provide transportation for the student between his or her home and the school. If it does have such a duty, the school may attempt to regulate the eligibility of students to make use of transportation facilities.

4. **Tuition and Fees:** Publicly supported schools generally may not charge tuition, but may assess incidental or supplemental fees. Special regulations may apply to nonresidents, indigent students, and students in institutions.

5. **Compulsory Attendance:** Almost all states generally require a certain number of years of compulsory education for their citizens. Some students may be excused from compulsory attendance because of religious reasons, and others may be able to take advantage of acceptable alternatives to compulsory attendance.

6. **Classifications:** Schools have the authority to assign students to particular grades or classes, and to establish criteria regarding promotion and demotion. Additionally, the school has control over the course of studies and the content of the curricula at each grade or class level.

7. **School Regulation of Students:** The school has the general power to regulate the behavior and conduct of students. At various levels of strength, this power exists regarding health regulations, and the behavior of students both during and outside school hours. During school hours the power exists over a wide variety of student behavior, including their freedom of speech and expression, their right to privacy, and the discipline and punishment assessed against their misconduct.

8. **Suspension and Expulsion:** For a variety of violations of school rules and regulations, a student may be suspended or expelled from school. The school must provide any of a number of procedural protections to help ensure the justice of such an action.

9. **Graduation and Diploma:** Upon completion of a program of education, the student is entitled to a diploma certifying his or her skills. In addition, the school may or may not be held accountable to the student for the quality of the education the student has received.

10. **Due Process:** Refers to the procedures which give parents and/or children the right to be informed about what is happening and the right to protest.

11. **Privacy Rights:** Concerns the freedom of individuals to pick and choose for themselves the time and circumstances under which and the extent to which their attitudes, beliefs, opinions, and behavior are to be shared or withheld from others.

12. **Discipline and Punishment:** Refers to the procedures, laws and regulations which affect how a child can be disciplined (e.g., corporal punishment).

230

Access to a Free and Appropriate Public Education

In Section I of the fourteenth amendment of the Constitution, the state is forbidden from denying "to any person within its jurisdiction the equal protection of the laws." Frequently referred to as the equal protection clause, this statement has been interpreted within educational circles as directing schools to provide equal educational opportunities to all students. By and large, school districts have not been bastions of benevolence proactively taking steps to ensure equal protection. Instead, schools have tended to extend equal educational opportunities to *all* children very reluctantly, usually only after being forced to do so by the courts or legislation.

The immense gains in making education accessable to all children are difficult to grasp when considered from the perspective of the highly structured and systematized educational programs available today. However, only 20 to 30 years ago, separate but unequal schools were the rule for black and white students, and mildly retarded children were denied access to an education because they were deemed unlikely to profit from public school classes (Cartwright, Cartwright, & Ward, 1981). The forces behind the extension of education to all children can be divided into two categories: court decisions and legislation. We will discuss these categories separately, beginning with a review of the major court cases impinging on the right to a free and appropriate public education. We will conclude this section by discussing P.L. 94-142 and other legislation pertaining to the rights of all children to an education.

Major Court Decisions Establishing a Free and Appropriate Public Education for all Students. Without question, the case of *Brown* v. *Board of Education* (1954) was the singlemost important step in opening the door such that all children could enjoy access to equal educational opportunity. *Brown* concerned discrimination against black students, but the basic logic of the decision has been utilized by litigants in a variety of areas. In *Brown,* the Court required schools to provide black students equal access to the same resources as white students. Thus, when any school resources are available to white students, those same resources must be available to black students. The reason that *Brown* is so important is that the Court supported the argument that students are a "class" of persons in our society. Further, all "members" of a "class" must be treated equally. When states required black students to attend segregated, usually inferior schools, the Court found that black students had been denied equal protection under the law on the basis of an unalterable and uncontrollable trait, their race (Turnbull & Turnbull, 1979). In subsequent court cases, *Brown* has been used as a precedent because handicapped and nonhandicapped students, for example, are all members of a single "class" of individuals in our society (i.e., students). Thus, when handicapped students were denied access to an education because of an unalterable and unchosen trait (i.e., their handicap), the courts ruled that handicapped students had been denied equal protection under the law.

The decisions of *PARC* v. *Commonwealth of Pennsylvania* (1972) and *Mills* v. *Board of Education of the District of Columbia* (1972) are generally credited as the ones most instrumental in making *Brown* meaningful for the handicapped. In *PARC*, the legal action focused on state laws that relieved "the state Board of Education from any obligation to educate a child whom a public school psychologist certified as uneducable and untrainable" and permitted "an indefinite postponement of admission to public school of any child who has not obtained a mental age of 5 years" (*PARC* v. *Commonwealth of Pennsylvania*, 1972, p. 282). The basic findings in *PARC* were as follows:

1. Expert testimony in this action indicates that . . . all mentally retarded persons are capable of benefiting from a program of education and training; that the greatest number of retarded persons, given such education and training, are capable of achieving self-sufficiency and the remaining few, with such education and training, are capable of achieving some degree of self-care; that the earlier such education and training begins, the more thoroughly and the more efficiently a mentally retarded person will benefit from it; and, whether begun early or not, that a mentally retarded person can benefit at any point in his life and development from a program of education and training.

2. The Commonwealth of Pennsylvania has undertaken to provide a free public education to all of its children between the ages of six and twenty-one years, and further, has undertaken to provide education and training for all of its mentally retarded children.

3. Having undertaken to provide a free public education to all of its children , including its mentally retarded children, the Commonwealth of Pennsylvania may not deny any mentally retarded child access to a free public program of education and training.

4. It is the Commonwealth's obligation to place each mentally retarded child in a free, public program of education and training appropriate to the child's capacity, within the context of the general educational policy that, among the alternative programs of education and training required by statute to be available, placement in a regular public school class is preferable to placement in a special public school class and placement in a special public school class is preferable to placement in any other type of program of education and training. (*PARC* v. *Commonwealth of Pennsylvania*, 1972)

In addition to guaranteeing a free and appropriate education to all retarded children, *PARC* also required the state (a) to locate all retarded children in the state, (b) to place retarded children in as normal an environment as possible, and (c) to protect the rights of each child through yearly reviews or, at parent request, due process hearings. Obviously, the provisions of *PARC* foreshadowed, and perhaps resulted in, several components of current state and federal legislation.

The *PARC* suit was followed closely by *Mills* v. *Board of Education of the District of Columbia* (1972). Unlike *PARC*, which focused exclusively on retarded children, *Mills* was considerably broader, covering children labeled as behavior problems. Interestingly, the defendants never disputed the facts of the case, nor did they deny that "they were under affirmative duty to provide plaintiffs . . . with publicly supported education suited to each child's needs. . . ." (*Mills*, 1972). Instead, the defendants argued that they lacked the financial resources to fulfill these obligations unless "the Congress of the United States appropriated millions of dollars to improve special education services . . . or the defendants divert millions of dollars from funds already specifically appropriated for other educational services" (Mills, 1972). Although the Court acknowledged that educating severely handicapped children can be a complex and expensive process, they were not persuaded by the defendant's arguments and ruled accordingly:

> If sufficient funds are not available to finance all of the services and programs that are needed and desirable in the system then the available funds must be expended equitably in such a manner that no child is entirely excluded from a publicly supported education consistent with his needs and ability to benefit therefrom. The inadequacies of the District of Columbia public school system, whether occasioned by insufficient funding or administrative inefficiency, certainly cannot be permitted to bear more heavily on the "exceptional" or handicapped child than on the normal child. (Mills, 1972)

As in *PARC*, the Court ruled that the District of Columbia was legally responsible for providing a free and appropriate education to all children within its jurisdiction regardless of a child's handicapping condition. Furthermore, before a child could be placed in special education, the district was required to notify the child's parents of the proposed placement and to inform them of their right to a formal hearing. The due process requirements for this notice and hearing were specified in considerable detail by the judge. Many of these regulations would ultimately find their way into federal legislation affecting handicapped children throughout the nation.

In addition to *PARC* and *Mills*, a wide variety of similar decisions were rendered throughout the nation in the early 1970s. Generally, these legal actions reinforced the *PARC* and *Mills* decisions. The interested reader is referred to Turnbull and Turnbull (1979) for a more detailed discussion of these other cases. For the purposes of this chapter, it is sufficient to note that although some school districts in the United States were providing appropriate educational programs for their handicapped students, many were not. A significant number of parents were told by the school to keep their handicapped children at home, that they were not the responsibility of the public schools, though these same parents were certainly required to continue paying their school tax! One now hears frequent complaints about federal intervention in local public schools. Few seem to re-member that a few short years ago not all handicapped children were allowed to go to school. Regulation by the courts and federal legislation have been neces-sary to ensure fair and equal treatment of all children in the schools.

Legislation Establishing a Free and Appropriate Education for all Students. In general, the accumulation of case law provides a strong impetus for develop-ment and enactment of legislation. What began as a small tributary with *Brown* in 1954 became a wide and powerful river in the early 1970s as court decision after court decision reinforced the notion that *all* children are entitled to an education. As a result of this accumulation of case law, the federal government increasingly became involved in legislating educational rights to all children. Beginning on a small scale with the enactment of the Mental Retardation Facili-ties and Community Mental Health Centers Act (1963), Congress has gradually increased the level of federal involvement. Other legislation, including the Voca-tional Education Amendments of 1968 and the Elementary and Secondary Edu-cation Act of 1969, culminated in the enactment of two major pieces of legisla-tion which have had enormous impact on the education of handicapped children: P.L. 94-142 (Education of All Handicapped Children Act, 1975) and Section 504 of the Rehabilitation Act of 1973.

Although P.L. 94-142 has often been referred to as landmark legislation, it actually contained very little in principle that could be considered new. Most of the major components of the law had already been firmly established by case law. The major contribution of P.L. 94-142 was to bring together in one compre-hensive bill all the major laws affecting handicapped children. Further, it com-mitted the power and resources of the federal government to treating handi-capped children with the same rights, privileges and financing as all other citizens.

Politically conservative politicians occasionally strike fear into the hearts of individuals whose employment is a function of P.L. 94-142 with debate concern-ing the repeal of this law. Such fear is unfounded for two reasons. First, there is widespread support among members of Congress for the law. The original bill passed by a margin of 404 to 7 in the House, and 87 to 7 in the Senate. Second, the repeal of P.L. 94-142 would not alter the existence of case law which established a free and appropriate public education as a constitutional right. Thus, while a repeal or alteration of the law may disrupt funding for a short period of time, the constitutional underpinnings will remain solidly in force. Many of the guarantees are present in other laws as well, such as Section 504 of the Vocational Rehabilitation Act.

P.L. 94-142 goes far beyond establishing each child's right to an education by operationalizing the process through which education must occur (e.g., an individualized education plan must be developed, children must be educated in the least restrictive environment, etc.). In addition, the law protects the rights of children and their parents by mandating nondiscriminatory assessment and by establishing due process procedures. The seven major provisions of P.L. 94-142 are summarized in Table 6.3. In the following paragraphs, we will discuss three of these provisions: related services, appropriate education, and individualized educational plan. Due to space limitations, only the most significant aspects of the law are discussed (see Appendix E).

Table 6.3   Major Provisions of P.L. 94-142

Free and Appropriate Public Education
All children are entitled to a free and appropriate public education, regardless of the
  nature or severity of their handicap.

Nondiscriminatory Assessment
Requires the establishment of procedures to assure that testing and evaluation materials
  and procedures utilized for the purposes of evaluation and placement of handicapped
  children will be selected and administered so as not to be culturally or racially
  discriminatory.

Development of an Individual Education Plan (IEP)
Requires the development of a written IEP for each handicapped child that will include
  a statement of current levels of educational achievement, annual and short-term
  goals, specific educational services to be provided, dates of initiation and duration
  of services, and criteria for evaluating the degree to which the objectives are
  achieved.

Due Process
Requires an opportunity to present complaints with respect to any matter relating to
  the identification, evaluation, or educational placement of a child. Specific due
  process procedures include: (a) written notification to parents before evaluation, (b)
  written notification when initiating or refusing to initiate a change in educational
  placement, (c) opportunity to obtain an independent evaluation of the child, and (d)
  an opportunity for an impartial due process hearing.

Privacy and Records
Requires that educational and psychological records pertaining to a child remain
  confidential except to those individuals who are directly involved in a child's
  education and who have a specific reason for reviewing the records. Further the law
  provides an opportunity for the parents or guardian of a handicapped child to
  examine all relevant records with respect to the identification, evaluation, and
  educational placement of the child.

Least Restrictive Environment
Requires to the maximum extent appropriate that handicapped children be educated
  with children who are not handicapped in as normal an environment as possible.

Related Services
Requires support services (e.g., psychological, audiology, occupational therapy, music
  therapy) are required to assist the handicapped child to benefit from special education.

On the most general level, all states and education agencies are required to provide appropriate special education and related services. Although regulations for implementation of P.L. 94-142 are enumerated in detail, room still exists for different interpretations of the meaning of such terms as "appropriate" and "related services." For example, with respect to the term appropriate, some individuals have interpreted an appropriate education as the *best* education available. Some agreement exists that a child is receiving appropriate education to the extent that he or she achieves commensurate with potential. However, it is often impossible to ascertain a child's true potential. Thus, schools have sometimes been saddled with the responsibility of paying for a parent's conception of "appropriate" rather than their own. For example, parents may ask that their child be sent to an expensive private school which offers *the* program for learning disabled children. The school may argue that such a placement is unnecessary since the district maintains a high quality learning disability program of its own. A hearing may be necessary to decide such cases. The ambiguity of the law contributes to misunderstandings, delays, and hard feelings between parents and school districts. At this point, the law is clear: An appropriate education does not necessarily equate with the best education and schools can fulfill their legal requirements to provide an appropriate education without necessarily providing the best possible education.

Within P.L. 94-142, the meaning of the phrase "related services" has also spawned interpretational problems. In general, related services are those such as speech pathology, audiology, and psychological services that are required to assist the handicapped child to benefit from special education. Again it is often difficult for a school district to decide where to draw the line. Should a school district bear the financial responsibility of sending a severely emotionally disturbed child to an out-of-state residential treatment facility? Should a school be responsible for assuming the medical and educational expenses for a child who must remain hospitalized for an indefinite period? It is not uncommon for a school district to pay in excess of $20,000 per year to educate a child in a residential placement, and it is not unheard of for a school to assume financial responsibility in excess of $100,000 for a child placed in a hospital setting because of an illness which precludes attending public school. More typically, however, schools have assumed only the cost of education while parents have been responsible for all expenses related to food, shelter, and medical supplies. As of the writing of this book, the question of what is covered and what is excluded under "related services" is actively being debated.

Another feature of P.L. 94-142 that has been somewhat problematic is the express requirement that each handicapped child have an individualized education plan (IEP). The IEP is a plan of action for each handicapped child and must contain at least the following information (also see Table 6.4):

1. A statement of the child's present levels of educational performance.
2. A statement of annual goals, including short-term instructional objectives.
3. A statement of the specific special education and related services to be provided to the child, and the extent to which the child will be able to participate in regular education programs.
4. The projected dates of initiation of services and the anticipated duration of the services.
5. Appropriate objective criteria and evaluation procedures for determining, on at least an annual basis, whether the short-term instructional objectives are being achieved.

The intent of the IEP requirement is laudable, but the actual implementation of these rules often leads to less than acceptable outcomes. For example, although the rules and regulations specifically state that educational personnel (e.g., teachers, psychologists, speech pathologists) will *not* be held accountable if annual IEP goals are not met, many school personnel are quite naturally concerned with the possible negative impact on their professional credibility with peers and parents if students fail to reach these annual goals. One way to avoid failures such as this is to set low standards of achievement for the student. Thus, in order to ensure success, at least on paper, IEPs are sometimes written with annual goals that require only the most minimal growth on the part of the student.

Another unforeseen problem has resulted from specifying that each IEP need be reviewed only on an annual basis. Although more frequent review is explicitly permitted, and even encouraged on an as-needed basis, the fact remains that IEP reviews are often called less frequently than may be optimal for the child because they require the time and effort of many different professionals. Clearly, the specification of at least an annual review is an improvement over the state of affairs before P.L. 94-142, when programs were rarely, if ever, reviewed. However, reviewing on only an annual basis is still too infrequent to have much impact on educational programming. Effective planning can be achieved only through a formative process where initial hypotheses and plans are revised continually in light of new data. Although P.L. 94-142 regulations call for the specification of "short-term instructional objectives," no mechanism exists by which the achievement of these short-term goals is monitored. It is quite possible that a child's failure to reach his or her short-term objectives will not be discovered until the end of the year at the annual IEP review. The IEP process would be more effective if it required some form of short-term follow-up consultation and evaluation.

In 1977, Section 504 of the Rehabilitation Act of 1973 was implemented. Section 504 is in most ways very similar to P.L. 94-142. This section is likely to

Table 6.4 A Sample Individual Education Program

Date January 5

(1) Student

Name: Joe S.
School: Tall Trees Elementary
Grade: 5–7
Current Placement: Regular class
Date of Birth: 11/4/64   Age:13-1

(2) Committee

Name	Position
Mr. Havlichek	Principal
Mr. White	Regular Teacher
Dr. Jones	School Psychologist
Mrs. Green	Resource Teacher
Mrs. S.	Parent

IEP From 1/20/84 To 6/1/84   Initial

(3) Present Level of Educational Functioning	(4) Annual Goal Statements	(5) Instructional Objectives	(6) Objective Criteria and Evaluation
MATH *Strengths* Can successfully compute 3-digit addition and subtraction facts without regrouping. Can complete an oral or written sequence of 4 digit numbers. *Weaknesses* Frequently makes computational errors on problems with which he has had a great deal of experience. Cannot successfully compute division problems.	*MATH* 1. To complete an oral or written sequence of 5-digit numbers with 0 in 10's, 100's or 1000's place. 2. To correctly add a 3-digit plus a 3-digit number with carrying in the 10's and 100's place.	*MATH* 1. Will complete oral and written sequence with 4, 5-digit number with no zeroes, with 90% accuracy. 2. Will complete oral and written sequence with 4-digit numbers with 0 in the 10's place and 0 in the 100's place, with 90% accuracy. 3. Will complete an oral and written sequence of 5-digit numbers with 0 in 10's place, 0 in 100's place and 0 in 1000's place. These tasks must be completed, with 90% accuracy.	*MATH* 1. Keymath at beginning and end of this 2-month period 2. Teacher-made CRT 3. Teacher observation

238

SOCIAL COMPETENCE
Strengths
Joins in team games with enthusiasm. Is able to cooperate with team members appropriately during team games.
Weaknesses
Demonstrates poor self-concept by making derogatory statements about himself.
Lacks respect for other classmates doing quiet work periods by talking out loud.
Demonstrates lack of self-discipline with out-of-seat behaviors during work periods.

SOCIAL COMPETENCE
1. Joe will develop desirable behaviors (good manners, responsibility & self-discipline) such that he is able to interact appropriately with teachers & peers.
2. Joe will increase positive interpersonal behavior such that he is able to make friends in his class.
3. Joe will develop a more positive self concept by increasing his success experiences.

4. Solves addition problems of 1-digit plus 2-digit numbers with carrying, with 90% accuracy.
5. Solves addition problems of 2-digit plus 2-digit numbers with carrying, with 90% accuracy.

SOCIAL COMPETENCE
1. Joe will give examples of and use socially acceptable language 90% of the time.
2. Joe will give rules of and practice etiquette in these situations: in the classroom, in cafeteria, on playground, as a guest, in a store, 90% of the time.
3. Joe will display self-discipline when placed in a tempting situation (e.g., finishing work before play, returning or reporting found articles) 90% of the time.
4. Joe will demonstrate that he can be trusted by successfully completing a task without delay or persuasion 90% of the time.
5. Joe will give 6 examples of good friendship while practicing new and positive behaviors toward peers during 80% of the school day.
6. Joe will discuss and give 5 examples of good and bad family relations between parents & children with 80% accuracy.

SOCIAL COMPETENCE
Observation
Teacher-made written tests
Discussion with teacher
Role play
Observation
Teacher-made tests
Role play and discussion.

(continued)

Table 6.4 *(Continued)*

(3) Present Level of Educational Functioning	(4) Annual Goal Statements	(5) Instructional Objectives	(6) Objective Criteria and Evaluation
READING *Strengths* Can identify the main idea of a paragraph from a 2nd grade reader. Comprehends written reading material at 2nd grade level. Reads 90% of words from Durrell Reading List at 2nd grade level. *Weaknesses* Cannot identify the meaning of certain words after having read them in a sentence. Unable to sound out an unknown word successfully when seeing it for the first time. Has difficulty with the comprehension skills of sequencing and inferring details when reading 2nd grade material.	*READING* 1. Joe will read paragraphs correctly and demonstrate comprehension skills. 2. Joe will demonstrate understanding of the visual clues to long & short vowel sounds by identifying correctly letters that are clues to vowel sounds.	*READING* 1. Given paragraphs and matching sets of multiple choice questions, he will complete the questions with 90% accuracy. 2. Given a 3-paragraph story, he will number the sentences in the order in which they sequentially occurred. 3. Given a paragraph containing clues to character's emotions, he will identify the emotions of the character correctly. 4. Will complete study sheets on *O*, *E*, and *Y* in final syllable or end of word, with 90% accuracy. 5. Will complete study sheets on *ai*, *ay*, *ea*, *ei*, *ie*, *oa*, and *oe* in the accented syllable, with 90% accuracy. 6. Will complete study sheets on identifying one consonant preceding a final *ie*, with 90% accuracy.	*READING* Teacher-made questions Teacher-made material Teacher-made material Teacher-made CRT Teacher-made CRT Teacher-made CRT

240

(7) Educational Services to Be Provided

Services Required	Date Initiated	Duration of Service	Individual Responsible for the Service
Regular Reading–Adapt	4/10/77	6/1/77	Mrs. Jones
Resource Room	4/10/77	6/1/77	Mrs. Green
Counselor Consultant	To be arranged		Not available at present

Extent of time in the regular education program: 60% increasing to 80%

Justification of the educational placement:

It is felt that the structure of the resource room can best meet the goals stated for Joe; especially coordinated with the regular classroom.

It is also felt that Joe could profit enormously from talking with a counselor: He needs someone with whom to talk and with whom he can share his feelings.

(8) I have had the opportunity to participate in the development of the Individual Education Program.

I agree with the Individual Education Program ( )

I disagree with the Individual Education Program ( )

_____

Parent's Signature

_____

Source: Adopted from Berdline & Blackhurst (1981). With permission of authors and publisher.

be recognized historically as the civil rights law which ensured the implementation of P.L. 94-142. Section 504 states that:

> no otherwise qualified handicapped individual in the United States . . . shall, solely by reason of his handicap, be excluded from the participation in, be denied the benefit of, or be subject to discrimination under any program or activity receiving Federal financial assistance. (Public Law 93-112, Section 504)

Like P.L. 94-142, Section 504 mandates a free, suitable education to each handicapped person, nondiscriminatory testing, placement in the least restrictive environment, and appropriate due process procedures. The primary differences between P.L. 94-142 and Section 504 are as follows:

1. Section 504 includes many categories of handicapped individuals not included in P.L. 94-142, such as those addicted to drugs or alcohol.
2. In order to receive funds under P.L. 94-142, a child must be assigned a diagnostic label such as "learning disabled." Under Section 504, a child does not necessarily have to be labeled; he or she need only be functionally handicapped.
3. Section 504 applies to all handicapped individuals regardless of age, while P.L. 94-142 is restricted to children between the ages of 3 and 21.
4. P.L. 94-142 pertains only to educational opportunities while Section 504 additionally prohibits discrimination in employment.

Procedural Due Process

Those who pioneered educational rights for children recognized that procedures for implementing the rights were as important as the rights themselves. Without a means for challenging any abridgement of these newly won rights, the victory would have been a hollow one indeed. Procedural due process (i.e., the right to protest or disagree in a systematic way) is an integral component for ensuring the educational rights of all children (Turnbull & Turnbull, 1979).

Procedural due process derives directly from the fourteenth amendment which forbids the state from depriving "any persons of life, liberty, or property without due process of law." Although education is not specifically mentioned in the Constitution, the Due Process Clause has been applied to educational settings in three ways. First, education has been viewed as a means for acquiring "property," "life," and "liberty" and, as such, an individual can not be denied access without the opportunity for due process of law (Turnbull & Turnbull, 1979). A second and slightly different view is that once a state extends a right, such as the right to an education, this is a property interest and cannot be withdrawn without affording the student the right to protest through appropriate due process procedures (Bersoff, 1982). A third application of the Due Process Clause concerns deprivations of liberty. The Supreme Court has interpreted the meaning of the term liberty very broadly and in *Goss* v. *Lopez* (1975) ruled: "Where a person's good name, reputation, honor, or integrity is at stake because of what the government is doing to him, the minimal requirements of the clause must be satisfied" (p. 574). Bersoff (1982) has summarized the implications of this principle for school psychology:

> This broad principle applied to school psychology means that schools cannot label children as handicapped unless there is some form of impartial hearing to substantiate the stigmatization that may result. While there may be some benefit to children to being labeled as retarded, emotionally disturbed, brain injured, or learning disabled in that they may fall under statutes granting rights to such persons, such labeling by school systems is considered to be an "official branding" by the state because of the many long-term potentially negative consequences that may result. For example, a record of impairment may prevent access to some forms of future employment, may increase insurance rates, or may be used as evidence of incompetence to make one's own decisions. The constitution thus prevents the school from unilaterally denominating children as handicapped. (p. 1045)

According to Turnbull and Turnbull (1979), due process procedures reaffirm "a belief widely held by lawyers—namely, that fair procedures will tend to produce acceptable, correct, and fair results" (pp. 171–172). Due process helps to create an equal partnership between the school and parents by ensuring that neither side makes changes in a child's educational program on a unilateral basis. This partnership is necessary because, in the past, schools typically have made most of the educational decisions, often on the basis of what the school could afford or what it considered to be in its own best interests. Now, however, due process is a means of assuring accountability so that educational systems perform as they are supposed to perform. Due process procedures consist of three key components: (a) prior notice and consent, (b) independent evaluation, and (c) due processing hearings.

Prior Notice and Consent. In order to play an active role in the decision-making concerning their child, parents must first be informed that an educational agency is contemplating a change. The pertinent provision of P.L. 94-142 is as follows:

> (a) Notice. Written notice . . . must be given to the parents of a handicapped child a reasonable time before the public agency:
> (1) Proposes to initiate or change the identification, evaluation, or educational placement of the child or the provisions of a free appropriate public education to the child, or
> (2) Refuses to initiate a change.

(b) Consent.
    (1) Parental consent must be obtained before:
        (i) conducting a preplacement evaluation; and
        (ii) initial placement of a handicapped child in a program providing special
        education and related services.

This notification must be provided in language understandable to the parents and must include a full description of the procedural safeguards available to the parents. Thus, in some school districts notification must be written in several languages in addition to English. Many school districts have prepared a brochure outlining the rights to which parents and their children are entitled.

In our experience, the prior notice requirement is often difficult for school districts to interpret. For example, it is not uncommon for school districts to establish a "screening" or "pre-referral" committee which provides ideas to teachers about how to handle students who are experiencing learning or behavior problems. This "brainstorming" of ideas is perfectly acceptable and even desirable, but often the committee will *decide* whether or no a child should be referred for evaluation and possible placement. If such a decision is made, the law is clear that parents should be notified. Certainly most school districts would inform the parents if the decision is made to evaluate the child. However, if the committee decides that evaluation would be inappropriate, many educational agencies routinely do not inform the parents of their refusal to initiate a change. According to law, parents must be notified of decisions which initiate or refuse to initiate a change of placement.

Another area of concern centers around the content and format of the prior notice. If a school were to indicate that it was considering changing a child's special education placement from E.H. resource room to an E.H. self-contained room, a parent might reasonably want to know the meaning of the terms "E.H.," "self-contained," and "resource." Educational agencies should strive to comply with the spirit of the law by communicating fully and completely what they are doing and may be doing with a child. A terse statement, phrased in educational jargon, concerning the change proposed by a school district will be meaningless to most parents. Even parents who understand the jargon must know the reasons for the changes and the other options that the district considered in arriving at its decision.

Independent Evaluation. Due process procedures entitle parents to have their child evaluated by a qualified individual who is not associated with the educational agency which is considering or refusing placement. In many cases, the cost of this evaluation must be assumed by the school district. The educational agency must take the results of the evaluation into consideration when deciding on an appropriate educational placement.

If the law did not allow for an outside evaluation, this would be akin to the state prosecutor's office not allowing a defense attorney to obtain an independent psychiatric evaluation for a client. Often an outside evaluation has many benefits to both the child and the school district because it allows for a more objective evaluation of not only the child but the setting. For example, if it is the teacher and not the child that is the problem, it may be much easier for an outside psychologist to identify and make this known than a district psychologist who must continue to work with the teacher who is at fault. Furthermore, if the parents are still shopping for a diagnosis, a second, confirming diagnosis may make it easier for the parents to accept what a school is telling them. Finally, psychologists who are concerned about their own findings should not hesitate to request a second opinion. To contain costs, districts may wish to exchange services. It is the ethical responsibility of a psychologist to get a second opinion. Parents should not have to initiate all requests for a second opinion. Psychologists themselves should ask for consultation.

Due Process Hearing. If parents, or in some cases the students themselves, do not agree with the educational agency's course of action, they are entitled to request an impartial due process hearing. Such hearings are conducted by individuals independent of the local school authorities and at a time and place convenient to the parent (Turnbull & Turnbull, 1979). The opportunity for an impartial hearing includes the right to review all relevant records in the possession of the school district, be represented by counsel, present evidence, cross-examine and compel the attendance of witnesses, and receive a complete and accurate account of the proceedings. Parties who are dissatisfied with the outcome of the due process hearing have the option of appeal to the state agency which administers education or to a state or federal court.

School psychologists often play a major role in due process hearings as expert witnesses. This can cause potential conflicts because, depending upon the specifics of a case, the school psychologist may be called as a witness for either the school district or the parents. In a number of hearings, psychologists find themselves in an adversarial relationship with another psychologist. The most useful form of preparation for a due process hearing is to document completely and thoroughly both the educational and psychological activities that have been attempted and the results of these activities.

Privacy Rights

The Family Educational Rights and Privacy Act (FERPA, 1976), commonly referred to as the Buckley Amendment, is the major federal legislative act regulating the treatment of educational records (see Appendix F). The act requires that all public educational institutions: (a) allow parents of students access to all official educational records related to their child, (b) provide parents an opportunity to challenge records which may be inaccurate or misleading, and (c) obtain the written consent of parents before releasing records to a third party. Basic to understanding regulations contained within FERPA is the legal definition of "educational records." Simply stated, educational records are any records that are maintained by an educational institution which are directly related to a student. Stated more succinctly by Trachtman (1972), a record is "anything put in writing for others to see" (p. 45).

Parental Rights to Inspect Educational Records. A major portion of FERPA specifies the rights of parents to inspect virtually all educational records pertaining to their child. Above and beyond the right to review these materials, the law obligates school systems to provide explanations and interpretations of these records in response to the reasonable requests of parents. Although the rules and regulations provide no definition of what constitutes a "reasonable request," it almost certainly includes parent's questions regarding psychological reports, observations, and/or test scores that are part of their child's educational record. A parent's right to inspect records also includes the right to a copy of the records *if* the school district's failure to provide a copy of these records would prevent a parent from exercising their rights of inspection. Thus, under those circumstances in which a parent's only opportunity to inspect their child's educational records would be to obtain a copy of those records, the school is obligated to provide copies.

The broad access to virtually all educational records granted to parents by FERPA raises some potential concerns regarding the ethical practice of school psychology. In particular, the ethical codes of APA and NASP state that psychologists are responsible for presenting psychological information to lay persons in a comprehensible manner. Since psychological records are accessible to parents, school psychologists must be careful to present the psychological data contained in educational records so as to minimize parental confusion and misinterpretation. One safeguard against misinterpretation is for school districts to require the presence of a school psychologist when parents inspect information of a psychological nature. Doing this would appear to be within both the legal letter and spirit of the law which states, "Nothing in . . . the Act . . . would preclude an educational agency . . . from adopting a policy which would require the presence of an official during the review and inspection of educational records, if that policy would not operate to effectively prevent the exercise of rights by the parent or student" (FERPA, 1976).

A significant question raised by FERPA is whether or not test protocols are accessable to parents. The law does enumerate several types of exempt materials including those records that "(i) are in the sole possession of the maker thereof, and (ii) are not accessible or revealed to any other individual except a substitute . . . . a 'substitute' means an individual who performs on a temporary basis the duties of the individual who made the record, and does not refer to an individual who permanently succeeds the maker of the record . . ." (FERPA, 1976, p. 24072).

Although the act does not specifically mention test protocols, many psychologists have argued that protocols do not fall within the category of educational records if they are maintained in the sole possession of a psychologist. Further, they argue that disclosing protocols would compromise test security. Although no definitive legal analysis of these arguments is available at this point in time (Bersoff, 1982), we must question their validity on several counts. First, test protocols are usually not in the sole possession of psychologists. Prasse (1979) pointed out that, at the very least, the student being tested helped to create this information and shares knowledge of it. Perhaps more significantly, selected pieces of test protocol data are shared routinely either in written or oral form at IEP and other team meetings. Furthermore, information from a test protocol is likely to emerge during due process hearings in which special education diagnoses or placement decisions are being disputed. Thus it is probable that test protocols do not meet the sole-possession criteria. Second, the intent of the "sole possession" exemption was to permit various professionals to exclude personal notes which they kept as memory aids. For example, while interviewing the student's mother, a psychologist might jot down a wide range of clinical impressions on a note pad. These rough notes are for the purposes of helping the psychologist remember the nuances and specifics of the interaction. If not shared with any other individual, in any way, they would not qualify as educational records. Test protocols, however, do not serve primarily as memory aids. Rather, they are a crucial source of information from which diagnostic/placement decisions are made. As a major intent of FERPA was to make available to parents documents that influence the decision-making process regarding their child, it is unlikely that the legislative intent of the sole possession exemption was to cover materials such as test protocols.

Parental Rights to Amend Educational Records. Above and beyond the right of access to educational records, FERPA also empowers parents to amend educational documents. The rules and regulations state that the "parent of a student . . . who believes that information contained in the educational records . . . is inaccurate or misleading or violates the privacy or other rights of the student can request that the educational agency . . . which maintains the records amend them" (FERPA, 1976, p. 24672). If the educational agency chooses not to comply with this parental request, it must inform the parents of this decision and advise them of their right to a hearing to contest the decision. At such a hearing, the parents have the right to be represented or assisted by other individuals, including an attorney, at their own expense. If, as a result of the hearing, the school system concurs with the parents that information in the student's educational records is inappropriate, the school is obligated to amend the record so as to remove its faulty aspects. If, on the other hand, the educational agency continues to believe that the contested record is neither inaccurate, misleading, or otherwise in violation of the student's rights, the parents must be given an opportunity to add to the educational record a statement explaining their objection(s) to that record. This parental comment must be maintained as long as the contested record is kept on file. Furthermore, the parental comment must be released along with the contested record if the contested record is ever disclosed to a third party.

Disclosure of Information. A final portion of FERPA is devoted to regulating the disclosure of educational records to a third party. Disclosure is defined as communication to *any* party of information in *any* form, including, but not limited to, oral, written, or electronic formats. Although there are some important exceptions, the rules and regulations state that "an educational agency . . . . shall obtain the written consent of the parent of a student . . . before disclosing . . . information from the educational records of a student . . ." (FERPA, 1976, p. 24573). The written consent must include: "(a) a specification of the records to be disclosed, (b) the purpose or purposes of the disclosure, and (c) the party or class of parties to whom the disclosure may be made" (FERPA, 1976, p. 24673). When disclosure of information to a third party requires parental consent, parents have the right to obtain a copy of the record(s) being disclosed.

Although these regulations appear at first to be all-encompassing, there are several important exceptions to these rules wherein educational records can be disclosed to third parties without obtaining parental consent. Disclosure of directory information (e.g., the student's name, address, telephone number, date and place of birth, weight and height, dates of attendance, and other similar information) is one example. Perhaps the most important exception for the school psychologist is that educational records may be disclosed to a third party without parental consent if they have a "legitimate educational interest" in the child. However, school districts must have a policy statement that specifies which parties are "school officials" and what the school system considers to be a "legitimate educational interest." It seems logical that school psychologists employed by a school district would be among those school officials considered to have a legitimate educational interest.

LEGAL REGULATION OF SCHOOL PSYCHOLOGY

In the previous section, we reviewed the most important court decisions and legislation affecting *all* children but particularly the handicapped. Using that information as a foundation, this section will further develop these basic legal underpinnings as they apply to the practice of school psychology. Specifically, it will describe the impact of the law on three areas in which school psychologists function: assessment, intervention, and research.

Before getting into these specific areas, it should be mentioned that *who* can practice school psychology is also governed by law. Most states have laws, standards, and regulations specifying the number and type of credits required to practice school psychology. The traditional entry level has been at the Master's Degree or certificate level. (Certificate level training is typically 60+ hours and subsumes a master's degree in school psychology). One of the hottest debates, if not *the* hottest debate, in school psychology over the last several years has been on the topic of entry level. Led by APA, many individuals have argued that a doctorate and some post-doctoral supervision should be required in order to be a professional school psychologist (i.e., one who does not require supervision). These individuals suggest that the complexities of working with children in a school setting mandate a well trained and diversified staff, and one which is appropriately supervised. The other side of this controversy is spear-headed by NASP, which insists that having a doctorate does not equate with competency. Further, it contends that training at the doctoral level makes an individual too expensive to be employed by most school districts. Unfortunately, there is a lack of data from both sides of this controversy, and the battle is likely to rage on.

The Legal Regulation of Testing and Evaluation

Of all the major activities in which school psychologists engage, testing is by far the most highly regulated. According to Bersoff (1982), however, most of the major court cases pertinent to testing are not so concerned with testing per se, but focus instead on tests as they are related to the identification and placement of disproportionate numbers of minority children in special classes. Although *Brown* created equal educational opportunities for all children, minority litigants have claimed that educational and psychological tests have been used as a means to circumvent the intent of *Brown* and to promote racial discrimination. In general, it has been argued that the blatant discrimination of the early 1950s has become progressively more sophisticated and subtle through the use of tests to classify students. As we review the major court decisions affecting testing, it may be useful to utilize racial discrimination as a conceptual organizer.

Stell v. Savannah–Chatham County Board of Education (1963). This case was one of the first in which tests such as the California Achievement Test and the California Test of Mental Maturity were utilized by an educational agency as evidence to support their claim that black children and white children should not be educated together. The tests were used as a basis to allege that black students' cognitive abilities were so inferior to those of white students that "to congregate children of such diverse traits . . . would seriously impair the educational opportunities of both white and Negro and cause them grave psychological harm" (p. 668). A recurrent theme in this and other cases is that the abilities measured by the tests are genetic and as such are not amenable to manipulation by educational programming. This case is not widely cited; however, it does illustrate the intention of a school district to circumvent the intent of *Brown* through the use of psychological and educational tests.

Hobson v. Hansen (1967). Schools have long worked under the principle that it is easier to manage six cats or six dogs separately than it is to manage three cats and three dogs together. Thus, schools have found it desirable to place students who learn more slowly in one group and their faster learning counterparts in another. Such systems have been referred to as "educational tracking" or more euphemistically, the bluebirds versus the robins. Tracking systems are appealing because, in classrooms with a diverse array of students, teachers who direct instruction at the "average" student often go too fast for the slower students and waste the time of the faster students. Educational agencies having an honest desire to see that each child performs up to his or her potential viewed tracking as an answer to their problem. At least they did prior to *Hobson*.

In *Hobson* the court ruled that the tracking system was "fatally defective." The ruling occurred despite the fact that the Washington, D.C. Public Schools were not intentionally using tracking as a means to discriminate and despite the district's "genuine attempt to remedy severe academic deficiencies of black children" (Bersoff, 1982, p. 1047). Along with its condemnation of tracking, the court was critical of the use of tests upon which the placements of individual children into tracks were based:

> The evidence shows that the method by which track assignments are made depends essentially on standardized aptitude tests which, although given on a system-wide basis, are completely inappropriate for use with a large segment of the student body. Because tests are standardized primarily on and are relevant to a white middle class group of students, they produce inaccurate and misleading test scores when given to lower class and Negro students (*Hobson*, 1967, p. 514).

The legal basis for the decision in *Hobson* was the equal protection clause of the fourteenth amendment. The reasoning was that poor and black children were not being treated equally or fairly because of their overrepresentation in the lower educational tracks. The fact that the court for the first time in *Hobson* condemned tests as racially biased started a chain reaction of litigation that has not yet ended.

Guadalupe v. Tempe Elementary School District (1972). Does it represent good psychological practice to administer a test which emphasizes English verbal skills to children whose primary language is *not* English? Is it fair to use the results of these intelligence tests as the primary criteria for placement of Mexican–American and Native American children in classrooms for the mentally retarded? Is it wise to leave parents out of the evaluation and placement process, and, in fact, fail to communicate with them in their native language? Most readers will answer "no" to each of these questions; some may even feel the questions are ludicrous. However, these were the very practices against which the Guadalupe Organization complained in September of 1971 in the Federal District Court for the district of Arizona.

The problems recounted in *Guadalupe* were simply bad practice from any perspective, be it psychological, social, legal, or psychometric. Table 6.5 presents the guidelines adopted by the State of Arizona to comply with the directives provided by the court in finding for the plaintiff. The policies enumerated in Table 6.5 correspond very closely with what is now standard operating procedure in many states. One wonders what current evaluation procedures and processes would look like if the courts had not intervened. Would school psychologists still be administering Stanford–Binets to Hispanic children with poor English skills?

Table 6.5   Regulations to Comply with Court Directives in *Guadalupe* v. *Tempe* Issued July 15, 1972 by the Arizona State Department of Education

1. All children whose primary language is determined to be other than English enrolled in programs for EMH and TMH be reevaluated at the earliest practical moment.
2. Before evaluation each child to be evaluated will be assessed to determine his primary language.
3. If a child's primary language is determined to be other than English, one or more of the following procedures will be used:
   a. A psychologist fluent in both the child's primary language and English.
   b. An interpreter to assist the psychologist both with language and testing.
   c. Test instruments which do not stress spoken language.
   d. Results and placement shall be explained to the parents in their primary language prior to placement and all information regarding mentally handicapped status shall be privileged and confidential.
4. A *recommendation* was made that no child be placed in a special education class if he/she scores higher than two standard deviations below the norm on an approved verbal intelligence test in the primary language of the home; or he/she scores higher than two standard deviations below the mean on an approved nonverbal intelligence test.
5. Intelligence tests shall not be either the exclusive or the primary screening device in considering a child for placement in classes for the handicapped.
6. Examination of adaptive behavior shall include, but not be limited to, a visit with the consent of the parent, to the child's home by an appropriate professional advisor who may be a physician, psychologist, professional social worker or school nurse, and interviews of members of the child's family at their home. If the language spoken in the home is other than English, such interviews shall be conducted in the language of the home.
7. On the basis of the evaluation carried out as prescribed above, provision for the child's educational needs shall be made by the school or schools concerned.

(continued)

Table 6.5—*Continued*

8. No child shall be considered for placement in classes for handicapped children unless the chief administrative official of the school district, or his designee have consulted, prior to placement, the following persons:
   a. A parent or guardian of the child.
   b. The school principal.
   c. A person responsible for administering or conducting special education courses in the school or school district.
   d. A teacher who currently has been instructing the child.
   e. An appropriate professional advisor.
   One person from each of the above categories shall meet together as an evaluation team to review the evaluation and placement of any child considered for placement in classes for handicapped children. The evaluation team shall recommend an appropriate educational program for all children considered for placement or placed in classes for exceptional children.
9. In addition to the written parental permission in the language of the home, the form shall describe the nature and content of the special programs offered, their prior effectiveness and the rate and time of return of children to regular classes. Such form shall also contain notice in both English and the primary language of the home of the right of the parent or guardian to *request a review of the placement once each semester*

Larry P. v. Riles. *Larry P.* is viewed as having had greater impact on the practice of testing than any case before or since. The suit was filed in behalf of black students who had been labeled as educably mentally retarded (EMR) and placed in special education classrooms. All of the students had been labeled EMR as a direct result of receiving a low score on a standardized intelligence test. The plaintiffs claimed that the intelligence tests were culturally biased, resulting in a disproportionate number of black children being classified as retarded (i.e., blacks represented 29% of the students in San Francisco schools but comprised 66% of all students in EMR programs).

According to Lambert (1981), the specific complaints concerning intelligence tests were as follows: (a) the items are drawn from white middle-class culture; (b) whites have more opportunities as young children, and this gives them an advantage on the test; (c) the language of black children may not be the same as the language of the test; (d) motivational factors, such as those that may be affected by the race of the examiner, may contribute to the poor performance of blacks; and (e) the tests are standardized basically on white samples, with only a token or representative number of blacks in the standardization sample. These claims were bolstered by statements from black psychologists who had retested the children using modifications of the same tests initially given to the plaintiffs. The modifications included the rewording of questions likely to be misunderstood by the children and the allowance of nonstandard but "culturally correct" answers. None of the children given the modified test scored in the EMR range.

A myriad of ancillary issues evolved in the case including whether being placed in an EMR classroom was beneficial or stigmatizing and whether intelligence tests measured acquired or innate abilities. Expert testimony continued for several months and, following the close of the trial, the court took an additional 17 months to synthesize all the information.

In the final analysis, the court ruled in favor of the plaintiffs. Without question, the most controversial feature of the ruling was the section which prevented the use of any intelligence test for the identification of black children for placement in EMR classrooms without first obtaining prior court approval. Additionally, the court ordered California to monitor and eliminate the placement of black children in EMR programs in numbers disproportionate to their representation in the total school population. The importance of the ruling to school psychologists has been summarized eloquently by Bersoff (1980), who noted that for the first time the court:

> permanently enjoined the use of the most hallowed, respected, and traditional tool of the professional psychologists trade—the individually administered intelligence test and, at the same time, may have signalled the end of self-contained classes for mildly retarded children whether populated by white or minority children. Judge Peckham called EMR classes "educational anachronisms" that focused on labels rather than individual needs, which isolated students and regulated them to inferior education instead of providing remedial training designed to return them to regular classes containing nonhandicapped students.

Some individuals, in analyzing the *Larry P.* decision, have argued that Judge Peckham's ruling appeared to ignore most of the scientific evidence presented during the trial and instead focused on the often emotional arguments presented by the plaintiffs (Condas, 1980; MacMillan & Meyers, 1980). Testimony presented by the plaintiffs portrayed the "culturally biased" intelligence test as the primary reason that black children were placed in "isolating," "inferior," "dead-end," and "stigmatizing" EMR classes. MacMillan and Meyers (1980) have questioned the logic of this statement and have faulted the court for not inquiring as to why so many black children are even brought into the referral process in the first place. Is it because these children are failing from the beginning and the schools lack sufficient educational options for remediating their deficits?

Reschly (1980) has questioned the manner in which test bias was evaluated at the trial. He argues that to evaluate test bias on purely subjective and intuitive grounds will lead to inaccurate conclusions. For example, empirical research has established that the widely criticized item from the WISC-R, "What is the thing to do if a boy (girl) much smaller than yourself starts to fight with you?'' may actually be easier for black children than for white children (Reynolds, 1981d, 1982b). Intuitively, one would think the item to be biased against poor children because turning your back on anyone who hits you in the ghetto or barrio would not be an intelligent thing to do. Such is the problem with nonempirical analyses.

Larry P. applied specifically to California and prevented the use of intelligence tests only in the identification of EMR children. The implications of the decision for other parts of the country are still unknown; however, it is known that reasonable persons can consider the same evidence and reach conclusions different from those of Judge Peckham.

PASE v. Hannon (1980). Less than one year after the decision was rendered for *Larry P.* in California, another Federal District Judge in Chicago, after hearing much of the same evidence and many of the same witnesses, arrived at a conclusion nearly opposite to Judge Peckham's. Namely, that intelligence tests essentially are not culturally biased against black children. The *PASE* decision has drawn nearly as much criticism from experts in test bias and retardation as did *Larry P.* Bersoff (1983) described the legal analysis conducted by Judge Grady in *PASE* as "scanty," "faulty," and "naive."

After hearing testimony from a series of expert witnesses (mostly psychologists), Judge Grady (*PASE,* 1980) concluded that none of the witnesses in the case "has so impressed me with his or her credibility or expertise that I would feel secure in basing a decision on his or her opinion" (p. 8). Then, after throwing out the years of accumulated experience and research by the expert witnesses, in an incredible display of subjectivity and questionable judgment, Judge Grady decided that it would be he who would examine each item of each test in question and rule as to whether the items were culturally biased or not. He thus proceeded to read each item of the tests and "decided." He found only a handful of the items on the Wechsler and Binet scales to be biased and ruled that the tests as a whole were unbiased. The entire decision was based upon only one person's subjective opinion concerning test bias.

Judge Peckham ruled that intelligence tests were culturally biased and Judge Grady ruled that they were not. Both cases were appealed and will likely end up in the Supreme Court. In the final analysis, however, it may actually have been Judge Grady in *PASE* who had the greater effect on invalidating the Wechsler and Binet scales (Bersoff, 1984). By reading each item of these two tests into the official court record, they were made available to public view. Given the proper legal citation, anyone may gain access to these "secure" tests, thus potentially invalidating them (a large number of tests are termed "secure" because to allow public access to them will make the results invalid).

Legislation Regulating Testing. The series of court decisions affecting testing did not go ignored by legislatures. Many of the major provisions of the various cases have been incorporated into statutory law at the federal level and in virtually every state. These provisions include requirements that a child be assessed in his native language, that tests be validated for the purposes for which they are used, and that evaluations include multiple measures collected in a multidisciplinary fashion. Table 6.6 lists the major requirements concerning testing contained within P.L. 94-142.

Table 6.6   Major Requirements Concerning Testing Contained within P.L. 94-142

1. Each State educational agency shall insure that each public agency establishes and implements procedures which meet the requirements of this law.
2. Testing and evaluation materials and procedures used for the purposes of evaluation and placement of handicapped children must be selected and administered so as not to be racially or culturally discriminatory.
3. Before any action is taken with respect to the initial placement of a handicapped child in a special education program, a full and individual evaluation of the child's educational needs must be conducted in accordance with the requirements of this law.
4. State and local educational agencies shall insure, at a minimum, that tests and other evaluation materials:
   a. Are provided and administered in the child's native language or other mode of communication, unless it is clearly not feasible to do so;
   b. Have been validated for the specific purpose for which they are used; and
   c. Are administered by trained personnel in conformance with the instructions provided by their producer.
5. Tests and other evaluation materials include those tailored to assess specific areas of educational need and not merely those which are designed to provide a single general intelligence quotient.
6. Tests are selected and administered so as best to ensure that when a test is administered to a child with impaired sensory, manual, or speaking skills, the test results accurately reflect the child's aptitude or achievement level or whatever other factors the test purports to measure, rather than reflecting the child's impaired sensory, manual, or speaking skills (except where those skills are the factors which the test purports to measure).
7. No single procedure is used as the sole criterion for determining an appropriate educational program for a child.
8. The evaluation is made by a multidisciplinary team or group of persons, including at least one teacher or other specialist with knowledge in the area of suspected disability.
9. The child is assessed in all areas related to the suspected disability, including, where appropriate, health, vision, hearing, social and emotional status, general intelligence, academic performance, communicative status, and motor abilities.

(continued)

Table 6.6—*Continued*

10. In interpreting evaluation data and in making placement decisions, each public
    agency shall:
    a. Draw upon information from a variety of sources, including aptitude and
       achievement tests, teacher recommendations, physical condition, social or
       cultural background, and adaptive behavior.
    b. Insure that information obtained from all of these sources is documented and
       carefully considered.
    c. Insure that the placement decision is made by a group of persons, including
       persons knowledgeable about the child, the meaning of the evaluation data,
       and the placement options.
    d. Insure that the placement decision is made in conformity with the least
       restrictive environment rules.
11. If a determination is made that a child is handicapped and needs special education
    and related services, an individualized education program must be developed for
    the child.

Legal Constraints on Therapy and Intervention

Once a decision is made to intervene in a student's life, a host of laws and
regulations are encountered concerning the involvement of parents, the procedures utilized, and the goals set. These constraints exist regardless of whether
counseling, behavior modification, or traditional psychotherapy are being considered. Indeed, consultative services may also be subject to regulation depending upon consultant intrusiveness and control. The issues of parental involvement are especially complex, particularly when adolescents seek psychological
services and desire that their parents not be informed.

The section will review briefly what we consider to be the two most
common legal problems surrounding intervention and therapy: parental consent
and confidentiality. For the most part, the law in these two areas, as it is
applicable to school psychologists, must be inferred from legislation and court
decisions in related areas such as clinical psychology and medicine.

Parental Permission to Participate in Intervention or Therapy. On any given
day, a school psychologist may encounter a pregnant teenager who wants counseling, a junior high student who is having problems with parents, or a teacher
who needs someone to talk to about a student having discipline problems. Perhaps none of these individuals wants to have parents involved. Do any or all of
these situations appear to require parental permission? Each of these examples
represents a difficult situation for the school psychologist because in each case
there is a desire to balance the need to help against any possible legal requirements. If the school psychologist requires parental permission, perhaps he or she

will lose a client. On the other hand, if permission is not obtained, the parents may instigate litigation.

Court decisions pertaining to this issue offer some guidance, but the decision as to when to seek parental permission is not clear cut. According to Bersoff (1982), there has been a general trend over the last 10 years for the courts to grant *adolescents* greater freedom to obtain medical and psychological assistance without parental permission. There is no question that the treatment of pre-adolescents should be undertaken only with the consent of parents.

Given that the courts have ruled that a pregnant minor can obtain an abortion (*Planned Parenthood of Central Missouri* v. *Danforth,* 1976) and/or purchase contraceptives (*Carey* v. *Population Services International, Inc.,* 1977) without parental permission, it is possible to infer that adolescents have the right to seek counseling without parental permission. However, the courts have tended to treat the abortion issue with much more sensitivity to the minor than to the parent. Thus, what the courts have done in abortion cases may not generalize to other situations. On most other topics, the Supreme Court has held consistently that minors are incompetent to make decisions for themselves and has voiced an overriding preference for parental control. For example, in *Parnham* v. *J.L.* (1979), which concerned the capacity of parents to admit their children to mental institutions, the Court held:

> The law's concept of the family rests on a presumption that parents possess what a child lacks in maturity, experience, and capacity for judgment required for making life's difficult decisions and . . . most children, even in adolescence, simply are not able to make sound judgments concerning many decisions, including their need for medical care or treatment. Parents can and must make those judgments. (pp. 602–603)

Thus, unless parents are making decisions or displaying actions which are harmful to their children (e.g., child abuse, denying needed blood transfusions), the court has come down strongly on the side of parental control.

What does this say for childrens' rights to seek therapeutic intervention from a psychologist? According to Bersoff (1982), "it is presently very risky for school psychologists to agree to see children for any kind of therapeutic purpose without their parents' consent" (p. 1068). Parents may be reluctant to have their children seen by a psychologist for several reasons. They may be concerned, for example, that a psychologist would communicate a different set of values to a child than those communicated by the parents. Alternatively, the parents may be concerned that a child would divulge private information about the family. It is our experience that obtaining parental permission is not overly bothersome to most students. In addition, the parents who seek out psychological assistance for their children far outnumber the parents who refuse such services.

Cases do arise in which parents refuse to give their permission for any type of intervention or assessment. In these cases, the law provides for something called a reverse due process hearing which is initiated by the school rather than the parents. If an impartial hearing officer agrees that it would be in the child's best interest to proceed with the provision of services, then a school district may proceed cautiously. Still, even after winning a due process hearing, the school may remain on questionable legal grounds. At this point, the legal ramifications of treating a child, under the auspices of the due process hearing but against parental permission, are unknown.

Confidentiality of Student Communications. The majority of the communications between school psychologists and their student clients should and can remain confidential. There are three important exceptions, however, and psychologists have the responsibility to tell students the limits of confidentiality. The first exception concerns information divulged by a student which suggests that a serious crime has been or will be committed or which indicates that a child is a danger to himself or to others. A rule of thumb is to evaluate the harm that will result to the student if the confidential information is revealed versus the danger to society which may result if a criminal act is committed. This rule derives from *Tarasoff* v. *Regents of California* (1974), in which the court concluded "that public policy favoring protection of the confidential character of patient-psychotherapist communication must yield to instances in which disclosure is essential to avert danger to others. The protective privilege ends where public peril begins" (p. 137).

A second exception to confidentiality may occur when a school psychologist is called to testify in court. Whether or not a school psychologist must reveal confidential information in court is a function of the laws of individual states. Some states stipulate that the communication between psychologist and client is privileged communication and cannot be disclosed in a legal proceeding without the permission of the client. Generally, psychologists who are not *licensed* to conduct private practive by a state can be forced to divulge confidential information. Most practicing school psychologists are *certified* by the state Department of Education as school psychologists, but they are not *licensed* as psychologists. Most state statutes do not view the communication between certified but unlicensed school psychologists and their clients as privileged; thus, many school psychologists must disclose confidential information in court if they are requested to do so.

A third possible exception to confidentiality may occur when a parent demands to know the details of the interactions that have occurred between their child and a psychologist. If the child is a minor, it is likely that the psychologist may be forced to tell if the issue ever came before a court. However, an explanation of the rationale for confidentiality may be sufficient. Parents may understand that a psychologist's ability to continue to help a child may depend upon the relationship remaining confidential. A psychologist may also satisfy a parent by agreeing to divulge the general goals of the therapy without jeopardizing the confidential details. If parent and psychologist agree on the goals, it is likely that a parent will not be as concerned with the means used to achieve the goal.

On first reading, these exceptions to confidentiality may appear very straightforward and clear. However, the application of these guidelines may cause some individual school psychologists a great deal of anguish. For example, what is the appropriate response if a 16-year-old boy discloses that he has been using marijuana? Since this represents a violation of the law, the correct and legal thing to do would probably be to inform his parents and call the police. However, by doing this, a psychologist would lose credibility with the boy and probably with many other students in the school once word got around. Thus, the psychologist's ability to help any student in the school would be greatly diminished. On the other hand, if the psychologist decided not to release the information and the student eventually informed his parents that the school psychologist had a longstanding knowledge of his drug use, the parents might be outraged. There is no easy solution to such cases. Each must be approached on an individual basis with full knowledge of the legal and ethical standards that apply. These situations are typically governed by state laws that can vary dramatically from state to state.

Legal Constraints on Research

The rules and guidelines most often used to regulate research with children in educational settings were developed by the U.S. Department of Health and Human Services (Federal Register, 1981, pp. 8366–8392). These guidelines require the development of a local committee to oversee and evaluate the merits of proposals to conduct research with children. According to Bersoff (1982), these committees should be concerned with four major aspects of the research:

1. Whether the risks to the subject are outweighed by both the benefit to the individual and the importance of the knowledge to be gained so as to warrant a decision to allow the subject to accept these risks.
2. Whether the rights and welfare of these persons, called "subjects at risk," will be adequately protected.
3. Whether legally effective informed consent can be obtained by appropriate and adequate methods.
4. Whether the design calls for periodic reviews of the research.

The guidelines go on to define a "subject at risk" as any individual, participating in research or pilot testing of new techniques, who may be subject to physical, psychological, or social injury. Many types of research conducted by school psychologists have been exempted from mandatory review because they pose no substantial risk. Specifically, the types of research that are exempt include:

> Research conducted in established or commonly accepted educational settings, involving normal educational practices, such as (a) research on regular or special education instructional strategies, or (b) research on the effectiveness among instructional techniques, curriculum, or classroom management.

> Research involving solely the use of standard educational diagnostic, aptitude, or achievement tests, if information taken from these sources is recorded in such a manner that subjects cannot be reasonably identified, directly or through identifiers linked to the subjects. (45 C.F.R. Section 46.101-124, 1981)

The reasoning behind the exemption of most types of educational research appears to be that such research poses very little, if any, risk to a child and may provide significant benefit to the individual research subject and/or society. Nothing in the guidelines, however, prevents local agencies from reviewing or preventing research on any topic, even those exempted by federal law.

Perhaps one of the most confusing and potentially troublesome decisions to be made by an educational or psychological researcher concerns when to obtain parental permission and provide informed consent to the children and/or their parents. In the situation where the research is of an archival nature and data collection consists of retrieving tests scores from a data bank in which individual students are not identified, parental permission is usually not warranted. On the other hand, informed consent must be obtained for any research in which individual children are singled out. The procedure for obtaining informed consent is as follows:

1. Fair explanation of the procedures to be followed, and their purposes, including identification of any procedures that are experimental.
2. Description of any attendant discomforts and risks reasonably to be expected.
3. Description of any benefits reasonably to be expected.
4. Disclosure of any appropriate alternative procedures that might reasonably be advantageous to the subject.
5. An offer to answer any inquiries concerning the procedure.
6. An instruction that the person is free to withdraw consent and to discontinue participating in the project or activity without prejudice.
7. Information regarding the availability of compensation for subjects injured as a result of participating in research. (Bersoff, 1982, p. 1069)

In cases in which consent is required, it must be affirmative written consent. This means that parents must approve of the research and say so in writing. It is not sufficient to send a letter home with a child and indicate, for example, ''If we do not hear from you in 10 days we will assume your cooperation, and will include your child in this program." In *Merriken* v. *Cressman* (1973), the court harshly criticized such letters by comparing them to a Book-Of-The-Month Club marketing strategy in which a failure to respond to such a notice is taken as an approval of or a request for the product.

ETHICS AND THEIR ROLE IN PROFESSIONAL PRACTICE

To begin our review of professional ethics it will be necessary to draw a distinction between legal and ethical issues. Ethics has been referred to as "the way a group of associates define their special responsibility to one another and to the rest of the social order in which they work" (Erickson, 1967, p. 367). APA and NASP ethical codes call for high professional and moral standards as well as the maintenance of high standards of competence to protect the welfare of society as well as the individual consumer. Of necessity, ethical guidelines are broad in nature and are construed to incorporate diverse models of psychological service (Bersoff, 1975). The abstract nature of ethical codes frequently makes it difficult to determine whether a particular act is unethical. Often the ethical guidelines of APA and NASP do not provide school psychologists with sufficient information so that the guidelines can be consulted proactively for guidance on how to proceed in an anticipated situation.

On the other hand, situations governed by law tend to be much more circumscribed, focusing on highly specific situations. Even though legal decisions have an impact on all similarly situated individuals, it is often difficult to know when another case is similar enough for the law to apply. For example, a court may prohibit the use of corporal punishment in a particular case because of a specific set of circumstances. Typically, this will result in a great deal of debate as to whether corporal punishment has been abolished in general or only in that specific situation.

Instances do occur in which ethical codes are in conflict with the law. For example, what should a school psychologist do when parents request to see the actual test protocol their child completed? To show the parents the protocol may violate ethical guidelines concerning the maintenance of test security. On the other hand, to refuse this request may infringe upon the legal rights of parents granted under the Buckley Amendment. The presence of conflict between ethical and legal directives, the ambiguity in both, and the problem of individual cases not "fitting," all add to the complexity of legal and ethical decision-making.

Specific Ethical Issues

A copy of the APA and NASP codes of ethics has been placed in the Appendixes to this volume. In this section we will take most of the major sections of the APA ethical code and amplify the relevance of each to the practice of school psychology. Our selection of the APA code, instead of the one advanced by NASP, was somewhat arbitrary, but the additional breadth and the recent revision of the APA code appealed to us from a heuristic standpoint.

Responsibility. The first section of APA's ethical code is concerned with psychologists' personal responsibility and states that "they accept responsibility for the consequences of their acts and make every effort to insure that their services are used appropriately." Of particular interest to school psychologists is the stipulation that membership in or employment by an organization does not abrogate individuals' responsibility for their own acts. In other words, if an administrator in a school district requests that all district psychologists discontinue talking with parents as part of the psychological evaluation process, the consequences of stopping this activity must be assumed by the school psychologist. The responsibility for providing substandard psychological services rests with the individual providing the service and cannot be blamed upon internal organizational problems.

How does one respond if employed by an organization which has policies that do not appear to reflect the best interests of the child? Three options exist. First, *before* being employed a prospective school psychologist should investigate an organization's procedures and policies concerning confidentiality of records (districts do differ markedly), referral processes, procedures for monitoring compliance with legal requirements, degree of parent involvement, psychologist/student ratio, and requirements concerning what psychologists can and cannot do. It may be possible to negotiate working conditions *before* accepting a position. A second option would be to seek employment with another school district. The third option is to do what Muriel Forrest did.

Muriel Forrest was a school psychologist who, for twelve years, was employed by the Edgemont Union Free School District in New York State. Her primary function was to conduct psychological evaluations of children referred for possible special education placement. Guided by her own conscience, ethical codes, and existing law, she often informed parents of their rights and advocated for them with the school district. Eventually the school district provided Ms. Forrest with a list of written rules concerning what she could and could not do in the process of evaluating students and working with their parents. These rules directed her to conduct shorter evaluations, to refrain from talking with parents, and to refrain from offering dissenting opinions and telling parents their legal options. Included was an astonishing statement from the local Board of Education:

> Employees of the District are agents of the District while they are carrying out the professional responsibilities inherent to their employment. Members of a Multi-disciplinary Team are professionals employed by the District to objectively evaluate

the educational needs of children. Advocates are persons who promote legal positions on behalf of a child and/or his or her parents during and after the evaluation and placement process and at hearings. No employee of the District shall act as an advocate for a child residing in the District who is or has been evaluated, nor shall an employee assume the role of advocate for the parent(s) who reside in the District. (cited by Prasse, 1982; p. 3)

Believing that the written directives from the school district violated the standards of her profession, Ms. Forrest refused to comply. As a result, she was dismissed by the district. Although the case is still in the courts at this writing, it is of interest to note that the American Psychological Association filed an amicus (i.e., friend of the court) brief on behalf of Ms. Forrest. The brief drew heavily on the APA ethics code as a defense for the actions taken by her. Specifically, "when the employer seeks to subordinate the interests of the client to those of the institution, psychologists have the duty to effect change by constructive action" (Amicus Brief in *Forrest* v. *Ambach*, pp. 12–13). The case has drawn intense national attention because the outcome will set an important precedent in instances where the professional standards of employees are in conflict with employer expectations.

Competence. The basic tenets of this ethical principle stipulate that psychologists maintain high standards of competence throughout their professional careers, that they engage in only those activities for which they are qualified, and that they accurately represent their skills to the public. This latter area concerning accurate representation of skills is one which may affect school psychologists more than other professional specialities. For example, certified school psychologists sometimes allow themselves to be referred to as just "psychologist." Simply leaving off the adjective *school* may represent a large difference in the eyes of the public and the law. One acquaintance of the authors allows herself to be referred to as "Dr." despite the fact that she does not hold a doctorate. Her reasoning is that people attach more credibility to what she says and are therefore more likely to take her advice seriously. Certainly holding the doctorate does not always equate with competency, and certainly it is an open question as to whether information delivered by a doctoral level individual is more effective than the same information spoken by a nondoctoral psychologist; however, the ethical code is quite specific that it is the right of the client to know a school psychologist's qualifications. Interns frequently have the same dilemma. Many fear the loss of credibility if people know they are an intern, "a mere student." However, parents with handicapped children have a great deal more at stake than the intern and have a right to make up their own minds concerning the weight given to the information supplied by the intern. Appropriate supervision of an intern adds credibility and enhances the quality of psychological services, thus providing a solution to an intern's title dilemma.

Another highly suspect activity which comes under the purview of this principle is the individual who uses doctoral training in school psychology as a back door into the private practice of clinical psychology. Most graduates of doctoral level school psychology training programs are eligible for licensure for the private practice of psychology. They engage in behavior which is perfectly ethical when they confine their practice to areas in which they have appropriate graduate education and supervised practice. The problem occurs when individuals who are prepared to work with children and families expand their practice to adult psychotherapy, hypnosis, sex therapy, or other areas in which they have had no supervised training.

School psychologists are not alone in misrepresenting their qualifications. It is not uncommon for a psychologist who is trained in adult clinical psychology to offer services in the area of school psychology. It is often difficult to determine whether a psychologist has the qualifications for a particular task and, because of this, individuals who witness incompetent practice often do not file complaints with the ethics committee of professional organizations or with their state Board of Psychological Examiners. It is often very frustrating for a school psychologist to hear a parent recount the naive recommendation provided by a clinical or counseling psychologist unprepared in school psychology. This is especially true since some states have laws which prevent the nondoctoral level psychologist from providing the public with what is perhaps a better service.

Moral and Legal Standards. Principle three of the ethical code stipulates that psychologists do not engage in or condone activities which are inhumane, unjustifiable, or which abridge the legal or civil rights of clients. One subsection of this principle points out that psychologists should be concerned with the development of legal and quasi-legal regulations to better serve the public interest. In his series on ethics in the APA Division 16 Newsletter, Martin has interpreted this section as a call for school psychologists to take a proactive role in changing organizational policies which are unfavorable to clients. For example, if a school district's program for gifted students discriminated against minority children, it would be unethical for a school psychologist to allow the practice to continue unabated.

Public Statements. Public statements include announcements of professional services, endorsements of products, and other activities such as psychological services provided through public media. This principle states that psychologists must make public statements which are factual and based upon objective information. One area in which this principle pertains to school psychology is in the already mentioned practice of calling oneself a psychologist versus a school psychologist. In advertisements by psychologists in private practice, use of the term school psychologist is preferred because it provides consumers with a more accurate representation of the types of services available. Some states, however, permit only the use of specific terms (e.g., psychologist), and may not allow the full term, school psychologist.

Another area of school psychology in which conservative interpreters of this principle may find fault is test advertising. It seems that nearly every test marketed offers something "revolutionary," implying that the test is truly unique. Psychologists have the responsibility to see that products bearing their name are marketed in a manner which is factually accurate and scientifically acceptable. Buros (1978) has asserted that the majority of tests are so technically inadequate that they should not even be on the market. Thus, it would seem that test advertisements that are in the public interest should discuss limitations as well as advantages (readers are referred to the *Technical Standards for Educational and Psychological Tests*).

Confidentiality. There are three areas in which the issue of confidentiality has important implications for school psychologists. First, children have the same rights to privacy and confidentiality as any adult. It goes without saying that discussions of the details of individual cases with others is inappropriate, except in situations where those individuals have a legitimate educational and professional role with the client. Second, it is the school psychologist's duty to discuss the limits of confidentiality before beginning assessment or evaluation activities. As discussed in the legal section, the limits of confidentiality include instances in which what the client says indicates a clear danger to the client or to others. In addition, nonlicensed psychologists may be forced to reveal confidential information when called to testify in court. Third, this principle calls for the proper maintenance and disposal of confidential records. School psychologists should work to establish policies which safeguard student records. Included here is the destruction of files which are dated and no longer reflective of a client's current strengths and weaknesses.

Welfare of the Consumer. This principle holds that the welfare of the consumer must be considered in preference to a psychologist's own personal needs or to the interests of the organization which employs the psychologist. The issues surrounding the Muriel Forrest case illustrate the types of conflicts which can occur between the interests of organizations and the welfare of the client. It is our experience that these conflicts can occur almost daily in the schools and other educational settings. For example, a child is identified as learning disabled, but all of the classrooms for learning disabled children are full. Occasionally, in this situation, children are illegally and unethically placed on a waiting list because of the expense involved in establishing another classroom. Both the applicable law and the ethics code are very clear that the needs of the client must be considered above organizational convenience.

Professional Relationships. Principle seven directs psychologists to "act with due regard for the needs, special competencies, and obligations of their colleagues in psychology and other professions.'' This is especially relevant to the multidisciplinary manner in which many school psychologists provide service. Ethical practice requires that we rise above the interprofessional jealousies and "turf guarding" which sometimes occurs and consider meeting the needs of the client as the primary goal.

This principle is particularly relevant to researchers in two ways. First, researchers who are allowed to conduct research in schools or other settings have an obligation to the agency, and to future researchers who may utilize the agency, to "ensure that host institutions receive adequate information about the research and proper acknowledgement for their contribution" (APA Ethics Code, Principle 7, Section E). Second, researchers are guided by this principle in the assignment of publication credit. Unfortunately the language concerning the determination of authorships is far too vague:

> Major contributions of a professional character made by several persons to a common project are recognized by joint authorship, with the individual who made the principal contribution listed first. Minor contributions of a professional character and extensive clerical or similarly nonprofessional assistance may be acknowledged in footnotes or in an introductory statement. (APA Ethics Code, Principle 7, Section F)

The question immediately arises as to what constitutes a major or minor contribution. This is an especially sensitive issue when students are involved with professors in research. Some professors assert that a student in training cannot possibly make a major contribution relative to an individual with a hundred publications and thus argue that a student should not be first author on any publication, even their own thesis or dissertation. Most individuals, however, assign authorship credit based upon a hierarchy of activities, regardless of the credentials of the person who performs the activity. Generally the idea for the publication, the writing of the publication, and contributions in the form of research design or statistics are considered in assigning authorship credit. Data collection and lesser mechanical activities are marginal in terms of earning authorship. For publications with more than one author, the individuals involved should discuss the order of authorship before getting started. If everyone carries out their responsibilities, then authorship order stays as decided.

Assessment Techniques. Detailed in this principle are ethical guidelines for the development, publication, and utilization of psychological assessment techniques. Every subsection of this principle directly impacts school psychologists. In general, ethical behavior includes making every effort to see that consumers are exposed to tests which were developed using established scientific procedures, that they know ahead of time the purpose of the test and what the results will be used for, that the test is administered so as to be fair to the special competencies or limitations of the client, and that the results be interpreted with all due caution and communicated clearly.

Research with Human Participants. The APA Code of Ethics follows very closely the laws pertaining to research which have already been discussed and will not be elaborated again here.

CONCLUDING COMMENTS

By now the reader has some appreciation of the complexities of the legal and ethical constraints under which school psychologists must work. Some individuals have voiced a concern that the profession is becoming over-regulated by outside influence and that this may interfere with efforts to provide the best services to teachers, parents, and children. Ysseldyke (1978), for example, has stated that "While school psychologists have sat around arguing their role and function, the courts, the legislature, and *special education administrators* have determined the destiny of their profession" (pp. 374–375). He goes on to suggest that "School psychology, as a profession, needs to exert itself to determine its own destiny, rather than being told what to do and how to do it" (p. 374). In large measure, we agree that school psychologists must take an active role in promoting and determining their future activities. However, we must not negate the many good things which have been initiated simply because we were not responsible for creating it. We feel that the evolving law and professional codes of ethics have actually enhanced the functioning of the professional school psychologist. We believe that the practice of the competent professional school psychologist is also the legal and ethical practice of psychology. The situation is analogous to the announcement that the 55 mph speed limit is "not only a good idea, it's the law." For the most part, the competent practice of school psychology is not only a good idea, it's the law.

CHAPTER 7

Research in School Psychology: Roles, Trends, and Methods

To the lay mind, the term research conjures up images of the absent-minded, if not naive, scientist working away in an isolated laboratory doing who knows what and caring perhaps very little about the usefulness of the outcome of research. It is unfortunate that research gives rise to such images and that, further, it creates, for many students and applied professionals, intense anxiety if not outright fear and intimidation. Research is a functional activity that is basic to the scientist–practitioner model of training applied psychologists espoused by organized psychology. Research is also central to theory building and the modeling of the relationships in psychology.

THE ROLE OF THEORY IN PRACTICE

"But that's just theory!"
"Don't give me theory, I want facts!"
In a particularly dramatic segment of his *Ascent of Man* series entitled "Knowledge or Certainty," Jacob Bronowski provides a most eloquent discussion of the fate of facts in the sense of absolute knowledge in science. Absolute knowledge, or more appropriately, the illusion of absolute knowledge, comes only through faith, eventually evolving into rigidly held dogma. Science has no absolute knowledge. Science is bound by error and directed by theory.

School psychologists are behavioral scientists who in the most applied setting imaginable are always carrying out research. The psychological assessment of a child is a small-scale research project, though one that may have dramatic and long range effects on the child. None of our tests provide us with facts about a child and why the child behaves in a particular manner. Tests only provide hypotheses about children, a fact we often forget. Some hypotheses eventually come to be viewed as fact if held widely enough for a sufficient period of time. For some time, and still in some last bastions of tradition, it was held that children exhibiting a Verbal–Performance IQ discrepancy of as much as 15 points were unquestionably learning disabled. However, we now know that about 1 in 4 normally functioning children between 4 and 16½ show such a discrepancy (Kaufman, 1979; Reynolds & Gutkin, 1981). Such a difference between verbal and performance levels of function may be part of the picture of a learning disability for a child, and it is an appropriate hypothesis to raise. Yet, further research into the child's functioning is necessary to determine whether the hypothesis is likely to be accurate. Still, one can never know with absolute certainty whether any hypothesis is correct. Every intervention project, every consultation carried out, involves research in some direct sense. While we are not often, if ever, able to apply the classic scientific method to problems involving humans, especially when taken individually, we do engage in certain principles of research on a daily basis. When testing, for example, we attempt to recreate a set of constant conditions under which to make our observations; in consultation, we first attempt to have all observers agree on the phenomenon being observed (the problem identification stage).

Once information has been gathered under a variety of conditions (i.e., the research has been done), meaning is given to these data according to some preconceived ideas. That is, we have guidelines to follow in interpreting data. These guidelines form a theory or a paradigm for viewing data and making sense out of it. Thus our practice is guided by research and theory. Some theories are certainly better than others, that is, more powerful, some are widely held, others are simply our own personal theories generated through years of experience and much trial and error. The power of a theory is very important and determines its degree of favor in the scientific community. Power in this sense means how well the theory is able to account for new and existing information. Can predictions from the theory be made about behavior and turn out to be relatively accurate? More so than with a competing theory? Most theories are wrong or unable to account for the data in a large number of cases yet, appropriately, they remain widely adopted and are actively promulgated. Why? A theory, even one that does not produce a lot of "hits" in its predictions, is not replaced until a more powerful theory is devised. Even weak theories tend to provide predictions that are at least better than a chance or random prediction.

An infinite number of hypotheses can be drawn regarding any particular problem encountered by the school psychologist. In order to function efficiently in practice, it is necessary for the psychologist to be able to select the most likely or most viable hypotheses quickly and accurately. This is the primary function of theory in practice: to guide our actions in a systematic fashion. Well-gounded, empirically evaluated theories of behavior enable one to make specific predictions regarding performance under a given set of ecological circumstances. Again, we must point out that one's theory will not always be correct, but a good theory will allow the psychologist to narrow the number of hypotheses to be entertained initially. Without a viable set of theories, one would be no more than a stimulus-bound technician relying on trial and error experience, anecdotal data, and illusionary relationships—more or less shooting in the dark when encountering a problem with a set of behavioral or organizational nuances not previously encountered.

RECIPROCAL DETERMINISM IN RESEARCH, THEORY, AND PROFESSIONALISM IN PRACTICE

"I want to work with kids, I don't need to know about research!"

At the same time that theory is providing guidelines for more efficacious practice, it is likewise directing research. Research is not conducted in a vacuous netherworld as an intellectual exercise. Research is focused toward the resolution of problems and the elaboration of theories related to those problems. The discovery of new knowledge is sometimes an objective; most often, the refinement of knowledge is the primary goal of research. Research is also best framed within the context of prior work, regardless of whether it supports or repudiates existing beliefs. While informing theory, research also builds an actuarial, empirical basis for practice. Practice at the same time is identifying new problems for research and elucidating the need for new or expanded theories adequately to explain, encompass, or account for some heretofore uninvestigated phenomenon. In this way, research, theory, and practice are always acting in concert with one another in the profession of psychology, where indeed our theories and our knowledge base are far from complete.

It often has been stated that half of what is taught in graduate and medical education at any given time later turns out to be wrong. The problem is that we do not know which half this will be. While this may be a disturbing thought to many, it should not be disconcerting or problematic to the scientist-professional school psychologist. What is standard, acceptable practice today may be the malpractice of tomorrow if one does not track new developments in one's profession. One need only examine the history of medicine to see a plethora of examples of changes in standard practice, many of recent origin. One of the best known and dramatic examples is the case of retrolental fibroplasia (RLF), once a leading cause of blindness and one that has now been almost completely eradicated. In the 1950s, standard medical practice for premature infants involved the administration of high concentrations of oxygen. This produced a fibrous growth of tissue behind the lens of the eye, not allowing it to attach properly, resulting in blindness. Only after extensive research was the primary cause of RLF uncovered. While the best informed professional could commit this error initially, a professional should not be frazzled by such a revelation nor be in danger of continuing misinformed actions once such information is available. To elaborate on this further requires a brief look at what makes up a professional, generally, and specifically in school psychology.

Discussing the professionalization of school psychology, Phillips (1981) defined a profession as an occupationally related social institution with:

> a high level of public trust that provides essential services to society . . . based on undergirding disciplines from which basic insights are drawn and applied knowledge and skill are obtained. There is also a body of knowledge specific to the profession . . . acquired through protracted training . . . accompanied by a strong service commitment and a *lifetime commitment to competence* [emphasis added]. The profession is organized into professional associations that . . . function to control standards for admissions to, and work and continuance in, the profession . . . accompanied by accountability to the profession rather than to the public, and relative freedom from *direct* on-the-job supervision." (p. 21)

The body of knowledge that supports a profession is developed in the scholarly literature of the profession. To maintain competence in a profession requires keeping current with this body of literature. Just locating and reading selectively in this literature is no mean feat. However, one must also read critically, evaluating the quality, relevance, and soundness of what is presented in the professional literature. These functions require solid training in basic research design and statistics. Commercial tests are proliferating at a considerable pace (Reynolds & Elliott, 1983), many without adequate empirical study of their psychometric characteristics. School psychologists need to be able to evaluate the current status of such tests and their supporting evidence and also to investigate the utility of new tests in the psychologist's own particular setting. Many other examples can be generated. These are all aspects of professionalism and they depend to a large extent on good research training. For the school psychologist, such training is an aspect of recognition as a professional rather than as a mere technician.

Frequently in the normal course of work in the school setting, the school psychologist will be called upon to carry out research projects at an individual or systems level requiring special psychological knowledge or familiarity with specialized research methods. This occurs most frequently when providing direct service to a child via the implementation of a behavioral treatment program. Many aspects of N of 1 research designs are brought to bear on such a problem. Baselines are established following the designation of target behaviors, interven-

BOX 7.1

Standard Practice and Research-in-Action

While standard practice serves a profession well, it must always be open to question, modification, and reevaluation. Circumstances change and what may have served well may lead to catastrophic results. Let us take a lesson from the processionary caterpillar.

Processionary caterpillars feed upon pine needles. They move through the trees in a long procession, one leading and the others following—each with his eyes half-closed and his head snugly fitted against the rear extremity of his predecessor.

Jean-Henri Fabre, the great French naturalist, after patiently experimenting with a group of the caterpillars, finally enticed them to the rim of a large flower pot. He succeeded in getting the first one connected up with the last one, thus forming a complete circle, which started moving around in a procession, with neither beginning nor end.

The naturalist expected that after a while they would catch on to the joke, get tired of their useless march, and start off in some new direction. But not so.

Through sheer force of habit, the living, creeping circle kept moving around the rim of the pot—around and around, keeping the same relentless pace for seven days and seven nights—and would doubtless have continued longer had it not been for sheer exhaustion and ultimate starvation.

Incidentally, an ample supply of food was close at hand and plainly visible, but it was outside the range of the circle so they continued along the beaten path.

They were following instinct—habit—custom—tradition—precedent—past experience—"standard practice"—or whatever you may choose to call it, but they were following it blindly.

They mistook activity for accomplishment. They meant well but got no place.

Source Unknown

The research-in-action perspective would have had much to offer the processionary caterpillars. Indeed, their survival depended upon it. Can school psychologists afford to blindly follow what has been taught for many years, to respond in a reflexive manner to the demands of the school system? Or, must we constantly be engaged in research, evaluating and modifying our actions accordingly, building an empirical basis for professional practice?

tions are made, and behavior tracked over time, with reversals conducted as may be appropriate. This is a legitimate research problem approached through the application of the scientific method; if the problem is unique or otherwise of interest to a large group of professionals, and significant documentation is maintained, it is publishable as case history research and can contribute to advancing knowledge in one's field. The *School Psychology Review,* official journal of NASP, regularly devotes space to the publication of just such research. School psychologists also become involved in systems level research as a function of their job. School psychologists employed in the public schools, for example, are doing very good work in the area of teacher stress and anxiety and its effects on children in the classroom. Some of these efforts have come about at the request of district administrative personnel while some have developed as a result of serious professional concern by school psychologists for what is seen to be a growing problem. Other interesting examples may be found in Snapp and Davidson (1982).

Research is a pervasive activity in the practice of school psychology as a profession. Knowledge and experience of research can not help but to make one a better functioning school psychologist. Our practice will in many ways influence the research that is being done and the development of the theories needed to provide paradigms for practice. At the same time, research is directed in many ways by theory, which is then modified based on the outcome of many research investigations, thereby changing conceptualizations of standard practice and presenting new problems for resolution through research.

A RESEARCH-IN-ACTION PERSPECTIVE

Phillips (1982) recently described a research-in-action perspective that we believe is relevant to all levels of school psychology practice. Phillips' perspective is predicated on the assumption that research should inform our actions as school psychologists—another point with which we are in total agreement. We would go further, however, to contend that research should allow the school psychologist to better inform the behaviors of those with whom direct contact is routine, such as teachers, principals, and special services coordinators. Research should be the basis for effective functioning by school psychologists.

Our view, and that of Phillips (1982), of the importance of research as a guide to practice in school psychology is not uniformly shared throughout the discipline. The role of research in practice is generally perceived to be relatively unimportant (Meacham & Peckham, 1978). Neither is research seen as effective in creating change in educational settings (Kratwohl, 1974), nor is it considered by many school administrators to be an important function of school psychologists (Kaplan, Clancy, & Chrim, 1977). Why then have we stressed research as such an important and pervasive function, and what is all of this about research-in-action?

As with most vocations related to public education, school psychology has been undergoing a severe crisis of confidence and trust over the last decade. Our knowledge, methods, and skills have been assailed and challenged in the media as well as in the courts. While the IQ controversy continues to get the greatest air time, declining SAT scores, learning that Johnny still can't read or write (and that Jane is doing little better), and putting labels on children to segregate them for inferior educational training continue to be discussed. Accountability has become the catchword for the public and the overseers of the budget. The demonstration of effectiveness has become a crucial issue for survival in the schools. In private practice a similar situation is brewing over health insurance payments.

Taking a research-in-action perspective can make the school psychologist a better problem solver and a more effective decision maker, leading to greater influence with other decision makers within the system. As Meehl (1954) and others (e.g., McDermott, 1982) have amply demonstrated, actuarial models of diagnostic decision making consistently are more accurate than clinical, intuitive, or logical approaches to such problems. From this research, it can be generalized that decision making in the public schools related to everyday problem-solving functions of the school psychologist are best accomplished through the empirical guides provided by research and theory. To be the most effective problem solver possible requires research knowledge and skills. We do not intend to imply through oversimplification that to be an effective school psychologist, one needs only to have great expertise in research, but rather that such knowledge and skills facilitate the school psychologist's becoming influential in creating the best possible learning circumstances in the schools. As we have noted throughout this volume, to achieve excellence as a professional school psychologist requires an understanding of the school as a social system and an organization. However, even the most influential and persuasive consultants will become impotent if the decisions which they make turn out repeatedly to be poorly derived and empirically unsound.

If we are to be effective and capable of demonstrating our positive impact on the educational system, we must place research into action as we practice our profession. In this regard, we must again agree strongly with the position of Phillips (1982) that, as professionals, school psychologists must assign a high priority to reading and evaluating pertinent research, regardless of whether actively engaged in conducting research within the system. Phillips (1982) also provided a useful framework for the evaluation of the quality and relevance of research in school psychology.

Other considerations are necessary in placing the research-in-action perspective into the professional practice of school psychology. When approaching problems in an educational setting, multiple solutions will typically be generated (e.g., see Chapter 4), several of which may be appropriate as an intervention. Knowledge gleaned from research, either from scholarly journals or internal to the system itself, may indicate the most effective intervention. While this is essential information in the decision-making process, the research-in-action perspective requires that we go further. We must go beyond the simpler process of locating and evaluating research relevant to the problem and consider the costs of implementing the suggested intervention or decision (Phillips, 1982). These costs may be incurred in cold hard cash, in time or services to other children, to the political and social influence of the school psychologist, or to other significant individuals within the system.

Making a cost-benefit analysis prior to the implementation of an intervention, at the individual or system level, recognizes the finite nature of the resources of the system, of its individual members, and of the parents and children themselves, who sometimes get overlooked in this process. Such analyses also emphasize the flexibility and reasonableness of the research-in-action perspective on decision making and avoid the facile approach of dustbowl empiricism that creates a rigidity not well liked by human participants. Conducting a cost-benefit analysis is rarely easy and depends to a large extent on behavioral specifications of the outcomes or objectives of the intervention or decision and on the quantification of as many relevant variables as possible. Even though difficult and typically crude (relative to other aspects of research), the cost-benefit analyses should be carried out and can be expected to have a favorable impact on implementation of the research-in-action perspective. Examples and further discussion of these issues may be found in several sources including Coffman, Slaikeu, and Iscoe (1979), Foreyt, Rockwood, Davis, Desrousges, and Hollingsworth (1975), Kazdin (1981b), and Phillips (1982). Other models such as cost-effectiveness might also be considered.

Phillips (1982) has also proposed that cost-benefit analysis be applied by school psychologists to reading and evaluating research in school psychology. Carried only a bit further, such an analysis could be applied to the entire research-in-action perspective. This process would be useful for individual school psychologists in determining whether to take a research-in-action perspective in their own professional practice. When doing so, one must be careful to include negative factors such as the cost of making wrong, poorly informed decisions that are affecting the lives of a large number of children.

School psychologists at all levels, but especially those in applied settings, will not always be in a position to carry out systematic research. Administrators frequently may not see the benefits over the short-term costs when re-evaluations are behind schedule or large numbers of referrals are awaiting some action by the school psychologist. School psychologists practicing in schools and other agencies are, however, frequently in a position to facilitate the research of others. A major barrier to research in school psychology is the lack of access to appropriate samples of children in the schools and to data which have already been gathered in the context of daily practice. Individuals who have the time, the motivation, and the computer access to do the necessary research are often university-based and thus need the assistance of a school-based psychologist to do research. Being a facilitator of research is thus a positive role and one that, as often as not, can lead to greater motivation to do research and perhaps greater acceptance of on-going research in school-based practice. By assisting others, one enhances his or her own practice through the information gained as well.

WHAT ARE WE RESEARCHING IN SCHOOL PSYCHOLOGY?

The principal goal of research in a professional discipline such as school psychology should be to provide an empirical basis for our actions and a nomothetic guide(s) to continued professional practice. This can proceed from a variety of perspectives. Experimental clinical research seeks to develop general laws or rules governing behavior and is thus obviously nomothetic. Idiographic research (i.e., $N = 1$ designs) provides verification of certain functional relationships mediating behavior but is at least covertly nomothetic since rarely is a single case of any particular problem presented in the literature. Rather, similar cases are studied with perhaps some variations until what was once $N = 1$ becomes $N = 1$, 2, . . . 7, 8 . . . k, leading to nomothetic verification, disconfirmations, or conclusions. Descriptive research also helps to verify nomothetic beliefs but provides an actuarial basis for decision making as well. Thus, a number of research strategies and designs contribute to our ultimate goals as scientists-practitioners. We must, however, also consider the content of our research. It is necessary to determine whether research is progressing in those areas that make it consistent with the needs of the professional school psychologist.

As noted in earlier chapters, there has been much written about the supposedly changing role of the school psychologist. There has been for some time a call for the school psychologist to be involved more in indirect service delivery (e.g., consultation) and less in such roles as the traditional psychometric one. Since it is our position that research guides practice, and that the needs of the practitioner should influence research in the discipline, we believe that an empirical base for practice must be provided in advance of changes in practice, to the extent feasible. Ideally, we strive toward a profession of empirical school psychology. Traditional roles remain, however, and must continue to be supported by research. Social change and simply the passage of time are important factors with regard to the external generalizability of research. What this means is that the results of behavioral science research may not be impervious to time. The primary implications, then, are that research results must be periodically tested and, where necessary, updated.

What are the primary areas of research covered in school psychology journals and do these areas reflect the activities in which school psychologists are primarily engaged? Has the content of school psychology research changed over the years and does it reflect a changing role for the school psychologist? These are complex questions which can not fully be answered. However, several studies have appeared which may be of assistance in devising responses to these questions. O'Callaghan (1974) traced the published issues and concerns appearing in the major school psychology journals from 1963 through 1973. Reynolds and Clark (in press) later conducted a similar survey of research trends in school psychology from 1974 through 1980.

In evaluating research trends in the field, O'Callaghan and later Reynolds and Clark surveyed all issues of the primary journals in school psychology: *Journal of School Psychology, Psychology in the Schools,* and the *School Psychology Digest/Review.* (The *School Psychology Digest* underwent a change of editorial policy in 1979 and changed its name to *School Psychology Review* the following year. While originally composed of all invited and condensed reprints of previously published articles, the *Review* now contains invited and unsolicited original works only.) Articles about school psychology appearing in two other major professional journals, *American Psychologist* and *Professional Psychology,* were included as well. Based on a content examination of the articles, O'Callaghan devised 16 content categories of research in school psychology which were also used by Reynolds and Clark. These categories of studies include the following areas:

1. Practice.
2. Professional preparation.
3. Professional identity.
4. Ethical and legal.
5. Early education.
6. Compensatory education.
7. Instrument development and validation.
8. Assessment and referral.
9. Research issues.
10. Current educational issues.
11. Clinical—personality.
12. Special education—exceptional children.
13. Classroom organization and management.
14. Social-educational psychology.
15. Instructional issues.
16. Higher mental processes.

These content areas appear to address a majority of the professional concerns of school psychologists. Narrative descriptions of these categories can be found in O'Callaghan's (1974) original article.

To look for trends in research across time and topics, it is necessary to classify all reviewed articles into one of these categories, a procedure followed in both studies. O'Callaghan grouped articles into three temporal categories from 1963 through 1973 as shown in Table 7.1; Reynolds and Clark (in press) reported on a year-by-year basis from 1974 through 1980. Significant changes in the

Table 7.1 Frequency of Publications in School Psychology Journals in 16 Content Categories

	'63–'66[a] N = 335			'67–'69[a] N = 336			'70–'73[a] N = 549			1974 N = 163			1975 N = 122		
	N[b]	RO[c]	%[d]	N[b]	RO[c]	%[d]	N[b]	RO[c]	%[d]	N[b]	RO[c]	%[d]	N[b]	RO[c]	%[d]
1. Practice	28	6	8	36	3	11	50	3	9	14	5	9	15	2	9
2. Professional preparation	12	11	4	14	11	4	22	12	4	10	8	7	7	8.5	6
3. Professional identity	52	1	16	23	7	7	35	10.5	6	30	1	18	8	7	5
4. Ethical and legal	7	14	2	2	15	1	3	16	1	12	6	7	9	5.5	1
5. Early education	0	16	0	0	16	0	4	14.5	1	0	16	0	1	16	1
6. Compensatory education															
a. Early	8	12.5	2	1	14	1	5	13	1	4	13.5	2	3	12.5	2
b. Later	0			2			0			0			0		
7. Instrument development and validation	44	2	13	36	3	11	85	1	15	20	2	12	22	1	18
8. Assessment and referral	15	9	4	20	10	6	45	4.5	8	15	12	3	3	12.5	2
9. Research issues	8	12.5	2	13	12	4	4	14.5	1	4	13.5	2	2	15	2
10. Current educational issues	16	8	5	22	8.5	7	35	10.5	6	7	10	4	3	12.5	2

11. Clinical-personality	37	3	11	26	6	8	43	7	8	11	7	7	9	5.5	7
12. Special education, exceptional child	24	7	7	22	8.5	7	39	8	7	3	15	2	3	12.5	2
13. Classroom organization and management	1	15	1	6	13	2	45	4.5	8	15	4	9	6	10	5
14. Social-educational															
a. Classroom ecology	11	10	4	30	5	10	32	6	8	4	9	6	10	3.5	10
b. Special group problems	3			2			12			5			2		
15. Instructional issues															
a. Teaching in schools	1	5		12			11			10			1		
b. Paraprofessionals	2	5	10	2	1	13	11	2	9	1	3	2	2	3.5	10
c. Learning theory and instructional methods	31			31			30		5	5			9		
16. Higher mental processes	35	4	10	36	3	11	38	9	7	6	11	4	7	8.5	6

(continued)

Table 7.1—*Continued*

	1976 N = 166			1977 N = 156			1978 N = 175			1979 N = 201			1980 N = 187			Total
	N^b	RO^c	$\%^d$	N^b	RO^c	$\%^d$	N^b	RO^c	$\%^d$	N^b	RO^c	$\%^d$	N^b	RO^c	$\%^d$	Total
1. Practice	9	9	5	7	9.5	4	24	2	14	16	6	8	20	3.5	11	219
2. Professional preparation	6	11.5	4	6	10.5	4	6	12	3	5	11.5	2	8	9	4	96
3. Professional identity	10	8	6	13	3	8	16	4.5	9	19	4	9	10	7.5	5	216
4. Ethical and legal	1	14.5	1	12	4.5	7	9	7.5	5	4	13	2	10	7.5	5	69
5. Early education	1	14.5	1	3	14	2	2	14.5	1	2	14	1	1	15	1	14
6. Compensatory education																
a. Early	0	16	0	0	16	0	1	16	1	1	15.5	4	0	16	0	25
b. Later	0			0			0			0			0			
7. Instrument development and validation	29	1	17	37	1	24	28	1	16	45	1	22	46	1	25	392
8. Assessment and referral	11	6	1	12	4.5	8	8	10	5	23	3	11	30	2	16	172
9. Research issues	2	13	1	1	15	1	2	14.5	1	1	15.5	4	2	15	1	39
10. Current educational issues	24	2	4	8	7.5	5	22	3	13	18	5	9	20	3.5	11	175

Category																
11. Clinical-personality	11	6	7	5	13	3	9	7.5	5	8	9.5	4	3	13	2	162
12. Special education, exceptional child	19	3.5	11	6	10.5	4	5	13	3	10	8	5	4	11.5	2	135
13. Classroom organization and management	19	3.5	11	20	2	13	16	4.5	9	25	2	12	11	6	6	164
14. Social-educational																
a. Classroom ecology	6	10	4	2	7.5	5	9	6	6	2	11.5	2	11	5	6	154
b. Special group problems	1			6		3	2			3			1			
15. Instructional issues																
a. Teaching in schools	1			1		1	1			1			1			
b. Paraprofessionals	1	6	7	1	6	6	0	10	5	1	9.5	4	0	11.5	2	198
c. Learning theory and instructional methods	9			2			7			6			2			
16. Higher mental processes	6	11.5	4	7	9.5	4	8	10	5	11	7	5	7	10	4	161

a From O'Callaghan (1974), other data from Reynolds and Clark (in press).
b Number of articles.
c Rank order.
d Percent of total number of articles.

frequency of articles published within each category occurred from year to year, and some obvious trends are evident. While broad and diverse interests are evident in all years considered, the research related to the traditional psychometric role of the school psychologist typically accounts for the largest percentage of articles published. Rank orders of the various categories show category 7 (Instrument development and validation) and category 8 (Assessment and referral) to have gradually increased in importance over the years, though category 7 is a relatively high frequency area of research for school psychologists across both decades. The changes in emphasis in school psychology research have been gradual but are nevertheless significant (Reynolds & Clark, in press). Rather than increasing in diversification, research published in school psychology's primary journals has slowly narrowed, tending to focus more rather than less on traditional psychometric practice.

It is possible that these results are an artifact of the classification system employed by O'Callaghan and by Reynolds and Clark. This system was devised in 1973 and, if the conceptual bases of research have changed enough, the classification system could be totally inappropriate. In order to assess this possibility and further delineate trends in school psychology research, we devised another scheme for classifying the articles which would perhaps reflect more current views of research in the discipline. We first divided research into 8 categories as follows: (a) *Roles and functions*, articles dealing with the activities of school psychologists; (b) *Consultative interventions*, articles regarding indirect service delivery by the school psychologist and related personnel; (c) *Other educational and psychological interventions*, primarily direct service delivery functions to children or nonconsultative interventions with other staff; (d) *Testing and measurement*, papers related to assessment functions or about tests or the measurement process; (e) *Legal and ethical issues*, articles debating, discussing, or clarifying legal and ethical problems related to any aspect of the school psychologist's function; (f) *Research and evaluation methods*, manuscripts dealing with the methods and techniques of research and evaluation or describing the outcome of an evaluation research study; (g) *Psychological theory*, articles specifically testing, evaluating, describing, or extending psychological or educational theories; and (h) *Other*, those papers not easily placed in any of the former categories.

The results of this analysis are reported in Table 7.2. In most respects, these results parallel those of Reynolds and Clark (in press), though the proportion of articles relating to theory is somewhat surprising. With the numerous calls for increasing consultative roles for school psychologists, the relatively small emphasis on consultation is disappointing, though not surprising. Even in this scheme of classification, the emphasis on the traditional role of testing in the research literature is as clear as it was in the earlier work of O'Callaghan (1974) and Reynolds and Clark (in press).

Table 7.2   Percent of School Psychology Articles Classified into One of Eight Current Broad Categories of Research

	Years							
	1974	1975	1976	1977	1978	1979	1980	Total
Roles and functions	19	8	5	9	11	9	7	10
Consultative interventions	5	7	9	2	9	6	9	7
Other educational and psychological interventions	21	15	27	18	14	15	17	18
Testing and measurement	21	26	21	32	26	37	32	28
Legal and ethical issues	10	8	5	14	10	9	10	9.5
Research and evaluation methods	3	2	4	3	6	4	6	4
Psychological theory	21	34	29	20	23	18	18	23
Other	0	.5	0	2	.5	.5	.5	.5

Based on surveys of school psychologists (e.g., Meacham & Peckham, 1978) and the continued call for increased involvement in nontraditional, indirect service delivery, one might have expected a decline of interest in traditional psychometric functions. Several societal factors may have been operating to influence research interests in the opposite direction. Research on test development and validation is well established and is an area of special competence developed in most school psychology training programs. Over the last 15 years, the social and legal aspects of testing have been highlighted in courts, legislatures, and the lay and scholarly presses; furthermore, concern for individual liberties and social justice reached peak concern. Thus the increased interest in publishing in these areas may reflect an appropriate concern and a focusing of attention during a time of public and legal questioning of much of the basis for the traditional practice of school psychology. On the other hand, the increasing emphasis on research related to testing denies the increased empirical support necessary to develop properly other areas of practice such as consultation. If, as we believe, research and empirical support should precede significant changes in practice, school psychologists who wish to alter the focus of psychological practice in the schools must pursue a greater research base for other areas of practice. Perhaps the role of the school psychologist has not changed as rapidly as we would like due to our own failure to provide the necessary empirical basis for such changes!

Of course, as we, O'Callaghan (1974), and Reynolds and Clark (in press) clearly recognized, the surveying of these journals does not encompass the publishing habits of all school psychologists. School psychologists publish in many scholarly outlets, particularly those journals noted in Appendix G. Yet the journals reviewed by these authors are the primary journals of the discipline of school psychology. These are the journals that should have the greatest impact on school psychology. It is always to its primary research journals that a discipline must look for scholarship, leadership, and direction through debate, empirical analysis, actuarial description, and the development of nomothetic guides to professional practice. For research to achieve its greatest impact on school psychologists, authors who would affect our discipline internally must opt for its primary scholarly outlets.

RESEARCH APPROACHES IN SCHOOL PSYCHOLOGY

As we have alluded to throughout the volume, school psychology research employs a variety of methods, strategies, and designs in the quest for knowledge that will help deal with the many complex facets of school psychological practice. Since training as a school psychologist involves basic training in research methods and design, we will not discuss such methods in detail here. Rather, we have chosen to highlight those methods of research often employed in research in school psychology. There are any number of ways of classifying research strategies as well, most of them equally problematic. The following classification has been devised for the convenience of the reader. The designs discussed briefly below are not unique to school psychology, or even psychology in general, but have broad applicability.

Descriptive Research

Much of the research in the social sciences is descriptive in nature. Indeed, before we can understand a phenomenon and make statements about its causes and effects, we must first obtain an accurate description. To many, descriptive research conjures up images of surveys collected through the mail; however, such methods of gathering information constitute only a very small part of what is considered to be descriptive research. Descriptive research includes not only the gathering of facts but the identification and clarification of relationships as well.

The primary distinction between descriptive and other research methods is that the investigator typically does not manipulate variables in the manner necessary to justify statements of cause and effect. Investigators may, and frequently do, discover correlational relationships in descriptive research and may, under conditions of natural observation, denote relationships between variables resulting in the formation of causal hypotheses to be tested under other types of designs. In descriptive research, the investigator has little if any control over any of the variables under study and is more concerned with describing the natural state of affairs. Though inferential statistics can be applied to descriptive data, this does not change the status of the research with regard to making causal inferences.

Descriptive research plays an important role in much school psychological practice. Psychological testing is a prime example of an application of descriptive research. The standardization and norming of a test or measurement device is the description of the performance of a selected group of individuals under a specified set of circumstances. Descriptive research thus plays a crucial role in decision making. Correlational studies of the relationship between IQ test performance and later academic achievement allow us to make predictions about the probability of academic failure for children at different IQ levels, thus assisting us greatly in deciding which children are in the greatest need of special educational services. Descriptive research can also prevent us from adhering to traditions based on unfounded assumptions or beliefs which create considerable error in the decision-making process. A classic example is Kaufman's (1976a, 1976b) studies of test scatter on the WISC-R.

For some time it was believed that Verbal–Performance IQ discrepancies of 12 to 15 points on the WISC-R were an almost certain indicator of a learning disability. A 15-point discrepancy in Wechsler IQs was the sole entrance criterion in some private schools for learning disabled children. Likewise, it was believed that the range of performance across the WISC-R subtests (the highest minus the lowest subtest score) was only 3 or 4 points for normal children. The average V-P IQ difference was guessed to be only 3 to 6 points. Kaufman (1976b) analyzed the frequency of occurrence of V-P differences for the WISC-R standardization sample of 2200 children and reported differences of 12 or more points occurring in about 33% of the sample and 15 or more points in about 25% of this group of essentially randomly selected children. A range of subtest scaled scores of up to 10 or 11 points was also found to fall within normal limits. Such descriptive information thus influences our decision making considerably, giving an empirical basis for judgments.

Case Studies and $N = 1$ Research Strategies

The case study is typically a comprehensive presentation of the history and the course of treatment for a single individual and is accompanied by whatever diagnostic data may be appropriate. The case study has played an important role in the development of clinical psychology and many areas of medicine and is currently receiving closer attention in school psychology. The properly reported case study can provide a much needed beginning in the description and understanding of any particular human behavior not carefully documented in the past. The case study can also serve an important function in the validation of treatment techniques for specific disorders. Though highly idiographic, a series of case studies can lead to nomothetic perspectives on behavior and to the discovery or establishment of functional relationships between internal and external events and behavior.

In the traditional case study, no experimental controls are available and causal and functional relationships always remain ambiguous. Some case studies are prepared in retrospect as well from records and other available case files and retrospective interviews. A single group of individuals with some common link may also be treated as a "case" for study and reporting in the literature. The larger the number of common circumstances that serve as antecedents to significant behavioral events, the more plausible causal relationships become; however, the ambiguities inherent to traditional case studies always leave some doubt. Case studies involving systems or organizational entities can also be quite useful in school psychology (e.g., see Snapp & Davidson, 1982).

Experimental designs in single case research are useful in establishing functional relationships in behavioral research. Such designs require considerable advance planning and preparation. Though presenting a number of methodological and interpretive problems (e.g., see Kazdin, 1978b), single case experimental designs have grown in popularity tremendously over the last decade. Some very complex designs may be devised; however, there are two basic research designs in single case experimentation that are applied to individuals or groups of individuals with some common characteristic. The reversal design, frequently denoted *ABA* or *ABAB* (where *A* represents the baseline phase and *B* the treatment phase) is the most often employed design, followed by the more complex multiple baseline design.

In the *ABAB* design, baseline data are collected in the beginning phase (A) of the experiment until a clear pattern of behavior emerges. In the next phase (B) some manipulation occurs, typically in the form of a behavioral intervention intended to affect the target behavior. Data are then collected following the introduction of the intervention. To clarify that the observed changes in behavior during phase *B* (if indeed any changes occur) are due to the newly introduced variable, the reversal phase (A) is made by returning to the prior status to see if behavior reverts to a pattern more similar to the baseline phase. Some investigators stop at this point, but more convincing designs re-introduce phase *B* to see if the previous changes in behavior recur. In *ABAB* designs, a single behavior is usually targeted for change.

In multiple baseline designs, several behaviors, individuals, or settings are selected and baselines established for each. Subsequently an intervention is applied to either the behavior, individual, or setting under investigation. A major advantage of such designs is that they avoid the need for a reversal phase that is often ethically questionable or frequently objectionable to practitioners.

Specialized statistical methods are available for analyzing a set of time-ordered observations of behavior in such designs. Significant variations of these strategies and their accompanying statistics fall under the general rubric of *time series design and analysis*. A time series design is essentially any set of K time-ordered observations of a process or event. Various designs, as well as the myriad of statistical procedures for analyzing these designs, may be found in Glass, Willson, and Gottman (1975), Kratochwill (1978), and McCleary and Hay (1980).

Traditional Experimental and Quasi-Experimental Designs

The term "experiment" was for some time reserved to indicate research in which the investigator had control over most if not all variables of interest. The researcher manipulated one set of variables to observe their effects on other variables under the conditions of random subject selection and assignment. Such a state rarely, if ever, exists in the social sciences. When less than satisfactory control of the pertinent variables is available, and when subjects are nonrandomly grouped, a quasi-experimental design should be employed. These distinctions and the specific benefits and liabilities of experimental and quasi-experimental designs are articulated in the now classic monograph of Campbell and Stanley (1963).

Experimental Design. In school psychology, there are typically three experimental designs that can be employed (although as we have seen above, other variations of experimental designs are possible). These are between-group designs, within-subject designs, and intrasubject-replication designs. The choice of design is dictated by a number of factors including the hypotheses to be addressed, as well as practical, legal, and ethical considerations, especially since we deal with humans. Researchers should be thoroughly familiar with the APA ethical codes regarding the conduct of research with human subjects.

The between-group design is probably the most well known, widely employed experimental research strategy. In this design a sample of subjects is randomly drawn from the population of interest and then randomly assigned to an experimental or treatment group or to a control group. With true random assignment, the two groups should be equivalent on all factors relevant to the experiment. As many groups may be created as there are experimental treatments. The treatment group(s) is then subjected to whatever experimental manipulation is to be made, and the groups are then compared with regard to their standing on an outcome or dependent variable. The between-group design is the simplest and most straightforward of all designs, although it is difficult to meet the condition of all random assignments. Its simplicity is a liability as well when evaluating extremely complex multidimensional behavior and its causes.

In the within-subject design strategy, subjects are drawn randomly from a population and each receives the experimental treatments. Subjects then serve as their own "control group" against which effects of the experimental manipulation are examined. The within-subjects design requires considerably fewer subjects than a between-group design but is also subject to more confounding.

Though presented separately, Kazdin (1981b) describes the intrasubject–replication design as a special case of the more general within-subject design. Most intrasubject–replication designs are similar to single case experimental designs employing *ABAB* reversal designs and/or time series analysis. These designs allow for intense, extensive study of individuals. The advantages, limitations, and variations of intrasubject–replication designs are discussed at length by Kazdin (1981b).

Quasi-Experimental Designs. When the investigator's control is limited and the standards for a true experimental design cannot be obtained, especially the condition of random selection and assignment of subjects, a quasi-experimental design typically results. Whereas the complexity of design in a true experiment is determined by the hypothesis under investigation, the complexity inherent to quasi-experimental designs is more likely to be demanded by the lack of control over potentially relevant variables and the inability to randomize subject selection and assignment. Many of the methods already discussed may become quasi-experimental designs, one of the prominent examples being time series experiments. Many specific designs for use under quasi-experimental conditions are detailed in Campbell and Stanley (1963), including the equivalent time samples design, the equivalent materials design, the nonequivalent control group design, and others.

In choosing a particular quasi-experimental design, the investigator must pay particular attention to the potential sources of error and invalidity generated by the lack of control over all relevant variables. Inherent to the identification of these sources of error is the knowledge of which specific variables might influence the outcome of the procedure that the investigator cannot control. While not allowing the elegance of inference available under the conditions of a true experiment, quasi-experimental designs are a powerful tool in the research armamentarium of the school psychologist in particular.

In the public schools, where most school psychological research is done, children are already grouped into classrooms. Random subject selection and assignment is very rarely a possibility and a host of subtle, and sometimes even quite obvious, factors operate to group children into specific classes. However, we are frequently interested in the academic or behavioral performance of children under different environmental circumstances. In order to make such comparisons in the schools, one must typically use intact groups which are frequently not equivalently distributed on any number of relevant variables. For this reason, the most popular of quasi-experimental designs, the nonequivalent control group design, is particularly important to causal research in school psychology, since it allows nonrandomly assigned children (i.e., existing classrooms of children) to be compared under different treatment conditions. Such designs may or may not use a pretest to determine the degree of equivalence of the groups or to establish covariates for later analysis. Specific examples of nonequivalent control group designs that are useful in research in the schools and analytical techniques for these designs can be found in a number of sources including Campbell and Stanley (1963) and Kazdin (1981b).

Since children are such complex organisms, learning such a poorly understood but basic process, and the school an equally complex social system, school psychologists are involved both with many different content areas of research and with a variety of settings. The preceeding discussions are not meant to delimit the research strategies appropriate for the profession but rather to introduce the most often encountered strategies. Many areas of research in which school psychologists have become involved in recent years are highly specialized and require specific training and knowledge of technical details, as well as research strategies specific to the area under investigation. With this diversity of interest in research by school psychologists, we see names familiar to us as school psychologists in a wide array of journals, many of a highly specialized nature. In addition to the Campbell and Stanley (1963) and Kazdin (1981b) references, school psychologists will also find the following recent works valuable in generating research strategies and appropriate analytical techniques: Achenbach (1978), Berk (1982), Edelbrock (in press), Kratochwill (1978), Maher (1978), and Reynolds and Gutkin (1982).

RESEARCH CENTERS IN SCHOOL PSYCHOLOGY

Research in school psychology is being conducted and reported in a variety of settings including the public schools, public and private institutions, occasionally in private practice, and in academic settings where research activity is considered to be a major responsibility of graduate faculty. Another facet of the Reynolds and Clark (in press) study discussed earlier in this chapter dealt with determining what universities, schools, or other agencies had been involved in major publishing roles in the primary school psychology journals during the period 1974 through 1980. At the outset, it must be made clear that this represents only research activities reported in school psychology journals. It is not known to what extent the findings reported by Reynolds and Clark (in press) would be affected if all publications of school psychology faculty or members of professional organizations in school psychology were used regardless of where their research appeared. However, we continue to believe that research published in school psychology journals should have the greatest impact on the discipline of school psychology and it is in this context that the Reynolds and Clark results should be viewed.

Reynolds and Clark tallied the number of times each agency or institution was represented in the school psychology literature. Multiple authorship from the same institution was counted as one representation. In the case of multiple authorship from different institutions, each received a point. A large number of agencies and institutions were found to contribute to the literature in school psychology. The top 10 contributing agencies, determined by frequency of representation, are shown in Table 7.3. More than 10 agencies appear each year because all tied ranks are included.

Table 7.3   Universities and Agencies Contributing the Largest Number of Articles to the School Psychology Research Literature 1974–1980.[a]

1974	1975
University of N.C.–Chapel Hill (6)	University of Texas–Austin (6)
Central Michigan University (5)	Ohio State University (6)
New York University (2)	University of Houston (4)
University of Arizona (2)	University of Arizona (3)
George Peabody College (2)	Worthington Public Schools (2)
California State–Long Beach (2)	Columbus Public Schools (2)
Indiana State (2)	University of Detroit (2)
University of Illinois (2)	College of the Mainland (2)
University of California–Berkeley (2)	California State–Stanislaus (2)
Boston University (2)	University of Iowa (2)
University of Texas–Austin (2)	University of Georgia (2)
Rutgers (2)	UCLA (2)
Gwinnette City Schools (2)	Temple University (2)
Malloy College (2)	Kent State (2)
University of N.C.–Greensboro (2)	University of California–Davis (2)
Virginia Polytechnic Institute (2)	University of Wisconsin–Madison (2)
Ohio State University (2)	Penn State (2)
University of Bridgeport (2)	Purdue University (2)
University of Hartford (2)	Georgia State (2)
Purdue University (2)	Indiana State (2)
University of Connecticut (2)	University of California–Berkeley (2)
SUNY–Albany (2)	University of Michigan (2)
South Illinois at Carbondale (2)	

1976	1977
UCLA (5)	Temple University (5)
University of Georgia (4)	University of N.C.–Chapel Hill (5)
University of Oregon (3)	Auburn (4)
University of Kansas (3)	University of Georgia (4)

Table 7.3 *(Continued)*

1976	1977
SUNY–Plattsburg (3)	Georgia State (4)
Temple University (3)	Central Michigan University (4)
University of California–Berkeley (3)	University of California–Davis (4)
University of Virginia (3)	University of Tennessee (3)
University of Rochester (3)	Arizona State (3)
University of Arizona (2)	University of California–Berkeley (3)
SUNY–Stony Brook (2)	University of Arizona (3)
Indiana State (2)	Bureau of Ed. for Handicapped (3)
University of Minnesota (2)	University of Rhode Island (3)
University of Western Ontario (2)	
University of Texas–Austin (2)	
Rutgers (2)	

1978	1979
University of South Carolina (5)	University of South Carolina (9)
University of Georgia (5)	University of Georgia (9)
Temple University (5)	University of Nebraska–Lincoln (8)
University of N.C.–Chapel Hill (4)	Temple University (7)
University of Arizona (4)	New York University (5)
George Reed for Teachers (3)	University of Iowa (5)
University of Minnesota (3)	Kent State (4)
Pacific State Res. Group–Neuropsychi-	Iowa State (4)
atric Institute (3)	Rutgers (4)
UCLA (3)	University of Nebraska–Omaha (4)
University of Kansas (3)	James Madison University (4)
	University of Minnesota (4)
	Penn State (4)
	University of Wisconsin–Madison (4)
	University of Pennsylvania (4)
	University of Arizona (4)

1980
University of Georgia (8)
University of South Carolina (6)
University of Nebraska–Lincoln (6)
Rutgers (6)
UCLA (5)
University of Arizona (5)
Southern Illinois–Carbondale (4)
University of Tennessee (4)
Kent State (4)
University of Minnesota (4)
University of Pittsburgh (4)

[a]The top ten schools are listed for each year with all ties included. The number of articles published is given in parentheses.

During the 1974–1980 period, considerable fluctuation occurs in membership among the 10 most frequently represented schools. Part of this fluctuation is undoubtedly due to the small number of times any given agency is represented; however, some interesting trends appear. The University of Arizona appears in every year and the University of Georgia in every year but the earliest of the analysis, 1974. Temple University is the next most frequently represented agency appearing in 5 of the 7 years. Other schools appearing in more than half of the years evaluated include Rutgers, UCLA, University of California–Berkeley, and the University of Minnesota. These schools generally have been recognized as "strongholds" of school psychology over the years.

Several interesting changes are also apparent in the rankings however. The University of South Carolina, unranked in 1974–1977, was one of the three most frequently represented schools in 1978–1980. Similarly, the University of Nebraska–Lincoln was not ranked in 1974–1978 but emerged as the second most frequently represented school in 1979 and in 1980. While certainly too early to draw any firm conclusions, such dramatic shifts may signal the emergence of new research centers offering their products to school psychology journals, as well as perhaps an increasing trend toward more diversification of doctoral level training in school psychology, a trend readily apparent from the substantial increase in doctoral school psychology programs accredited by the APA in recent years. Hopefully, this will prove beneficial to the discipline overall.

THE IMPORTANCE OF REPORTING RESEARCH IN SCHOOL PSYCHOLOGY

A research project or study is not complete until it has been communicated to one's scientific and professional peers. While this may not be true for "in-house" or privately funded projects designed to answer a specific question solely for the use of the sponsoring agent, this statement does hold as a basic tenet of science and invokes a specific responsibility on the part of researchers in all fields. Research in school psychology informs our actions as professionals. The communication process is thus crucial to the purpose of research in school psychology. If research is to improve both the services we provide and our decision-making capabilities, we certainly must have access to the products of research completed throughout the discipline. We have an ethical mandate to share our results with others in the discipline; it is a responsibility of being a professional in the field. The reporting of research through the peer review process of most scholarly journals has added benefits.

Journal Publication in School Psychology

The scholarly publication of research is at once a frustrating and a rewarding process. Frustration may at first arise over the length and often adversarial nature of the peer review process. Yet the intrinsic reward of a research project well accomplished and appearing in a journal read by one's colleagues can hardly be overestimated. To contribute to knowledge is not only the highest ideal of the scholar; it is rewarding in itself. Recognition from one's peers is likewise quite a rewarding element in the research publication process. Publication is itself recognition by one's colleagues of a significant accomplishment and contribution to the discipline. This is true due to the peer review process.

The peer review process, used by all three primary school psychology journals (see Appendix G), provides for a thorough qualitative appraisal of a researcher's work prior to being published. Meeting the criteria of design, relevance, and significance necessary for publication in a scholarly journal is no mean feat. In 1981 for example, more than 75% of the articles submitted to the primary school psychology journals were rejected for publication.

The peer review process may begin informally prior to the submission of a manuscript to a journal. While not a bad idea for even the most established researcher, the fledgling investigator is well advised to ask a former professor or a professional colleague for a critical reading of a paper before sending it to a journal editor. This can avoid the embarrassment of glaring errors being noted by the editor and journal reviewers when such errors could have been detected prior to submission. Once a general reading from a colleague has been obtained and his/her suggestions appropriately entertained, submission to the appropriate journal editor is the next step in the process. Editors usually require three high quality copies of the manuscript; if the copies are of sufficient quality, the original typescript may be retained. Journals which follow a peer review process will typically list the members of the editorial board, who serve as the editor's advisors, on the inside cover of the journal. This is also a likely place to locate the editorial policy of the journal. The latter states the scope and purpose of the journal and is most important in helping to select an appropriate journal for submitting your work.

Once the editor receives a manuscript, it is typically checked briefly for its style and for the appropriateness of its topic relative to the mission of the journal. During this review, the editor will decide which members of the review board have the greatest expertise in the subject area of the manuscript and will then ask them to rate the paper along a variety of dimensions and to make a recommendation regarding its suitability for publication in the journal. Most outright rejections occur due to inappropriate or inadequate research designs that do not allow the investigator to address the hypotheses of the study. If the questions asked by the study are important and the research design adequate, rarely will an outright rejection be received. Other facets of the paper may require substantial revision prior to publication; in such cases, the editor will ask for changes along the lines suggested by the reviewers, after which the revised manuscript will be given further consideration. While rarely is any manuscript accepted without some amount of revision, the changes required by the editor may range from some additional information on the subjects or small wording changes to major over-hauls and new literature reviews which might require months of additional work.

Both from our own experience as reviewers for more than 20 scholarly journals, as well as from the experience of others (e.g., Maher, 1978; Rabinowitz & Roberts, 1977) we have noted common, recurring errors in many papers that cause them to be rejected. These may be summarized as follows:

1. *Sampling from convenience rather than by design.* Frequently, re-searchers will accept any haphazard sample due to its availability or ease of use. Samples for research must be drawn in a manner representative of the population to which you wish to generalize. Convenience samples are seldom representative of any larger, meaningful population.

2. *Failure to randomly assign subjects to treatments.* Closely related to (1) above, this error occurs when groups are taken as intact entities, given differen-tial treatments, and compared on some outcome measure. Without random as-signment, it is imperative to show that no prior differences existed. In educa-tional research, intact classes are often taken for different treatments, yet we all know that classroom assignment is seldom, if ever, random or on the basis of some irrelevant variable.

3. *Inadequate numbers of subjects.* The power to detect differences is crucial to research. All too frequently, researchers will use such a small number of subjects in a study that the probability of detecting a difference, when one is present, is very small. With the introduction of multivariate statistics and the widespread availability of computer programs, another problem has emerged. Multivariate methods, in particular, variations of multiple regression (e.g., fac-tor analysis, discriminant analysis, canonical analysis, etc.), are maximizing procedures and take full advantage of chance relationships. Few realize the devastating effects of small sample sizes in multivariate research on the gener-alizability of results. Subject-to-variable ratios of at least 10 to 1 are needed. The dramatic distortions that can occur with small ratios, especially as they approach one-to-one, have been illustrated in Willson and Reynolds (1982).

4. *Inadequate control of the manipulation of the dependent variable.* When conducting an experiment, expectancy effects, experimenter effects, Hawthorne effects, and other factors intervene along with differing levels of expertise in the methods under study by the individual participants. As an example of the latter, suppose you are experimenting with the effects of three teaching methods in remediation of a specific type of reading disturbance; although each teacher receives the same amount of training with the particular method he or she will be using, teacher A achieved a higher level of expertise with his or her method than the other teachers did with their methods. Thus, the students in method A may learn more because of greater expertise of their teacher rather than greater effec-tiveness of the method; a mistaken conclusion could easily be drawn. Many problems exist with regard to controlling just how the manipulation of a dependent variable takes place and constant, careful scrutinizing is a necessity though, obviously, all factors cannot be completely ruled out.

5. *Failure to use appropriately sensitive or valid measures of the variables of interest.* In order to detect differences, a highly reliable measure must be used. This is most often a problem when homemade tests are developed without adequate reliability data, but it can also be common in other areas. In neuropsychological research, tests with reliability coefficients of .5 to .7 are common and have contributed to some confusion in the literature in this area (see Reynolds, 1982a). Validity evidence should also be available for any measure so that one can be certain just what is being assessed. Reliability and validity are always important, but especially so whenever a new measure is developed.

6. *Failure to use the appropriate statistical procedures.* A statistical procedure must be chosen that properly addresses the hypothesis under study. Occasionally the novice, and sometimes even the established, researcher will choose a statistical test that addresses a different hypothesis than that stated. One of the authors recently reviewed a paper that attempted to assess the difference in means for a variable measured twice by computing the correlation between scores at time one with scores at time two. Such a comparison tells nothing about equivalence of means but rather addresses the relative rank order of scores across occasions—a different question, and one that may be of interest, but not a test of means. The choice between univariate and multivariate methods must also be made. Careful consideration must be given to the selection of a statistical method and such decisions are best made prior to collecting data, while the entire project is in the planning stages.

It is better to iron out such problems as the above prior to attempts at publication. The journal review process will weed out most but not all of these problems prior to publication. However, we must read critically; for the consumer of research, our advice is *caveat emptor*. Box 7.2 presents a variety of general and specific points of concern that should be kept in mind when reading or writing research (Maher, 1978).

The review process, though certainly not without its flaws, provides a substantive service to the profession. Publication in a refereed journal testifies that at least several recognized scholars in the discipline have agreed on the significance of the problem being investigated, on the adequacy of the design and analysis to address the problem, and on the reasonableness of the presentation. Reviewers do not have to agree with the conclusions drawn by the investigator (a fact sometimes overlooked by reviewers) but only that the conclusions are reasonable and related to the data presented. Thus, certain qualitative decisions have been made regarding a research report before it is presented to the professional public. Not only does this process add credibility to the work, but it also reduces considerably the task of the reader, since many poorly executed studies will not have to be waded through to obtain appropriate information on a topic. This does not mean the reader can toss caution to the wind and accept whatever is written in a refereed journal. The professional consumer must continue to read with a critical and discerning eye, especially in highly controversial areas of research where many opposing views exist. As hard as science tries to exclude such factors, the researcher's attitudes, beliefs, and philosophy may inappropriately influence the conclusions drawn from a research project. Occasionally, poorly designed studies will find their way into the literature despite the peer review process, and the individual reader must be alert to such possibilities. Very good research, on the other hand, will sometimes be rejected for inappropriate reasons. The peer review process is far from perfect, too often adversarial, and too often tainted by the attitudes and beliefs of the participants. It is a good process nonetheless and one that serves the discipline well.

The journals listed in Appendix G employ the peer review process for the selection of articles. Hopefully, this list will be helpful in deciding on the most appropriate outlet for your own research. It is our hope that research intended to affect the practice and discipline of school psychology will first be offered to the primary journals of the field. It is to these journals that we must look for leadership and direction and here that we should expect to find the best that researchers in school psychology have to offer.

BOX 7.2

A Reader's, Writer's, and Reviewer's Guide to Assessing Research Reports

TOPIC CONTENT

1. Is the article appropriate to this journal? Does it fall within the boundaries mandated in the masthead description?

STYLE

1. Is the introduction as brief as possible given the topic of the article?
2. Are all of the citations correct and necessary, or is there padding? Are important citations missing? Has the author been careful to cite prior reports contrary to the current hypothesis?
3. Is there an explicit hypothesis?
4. Has the *origin* of the hypothesis been made explicit?
5. Was the hypothesis *correctly* derived from the theory that has been cited? Are other contrary hypotheses compatible with the same theory?
6. Is there an explicit rationale for the selection of measures, and was it derived logically from the hypothesis?

METHOD

1. Is the method so described that replication is possible without further information?
2. Subjects: Were they sampled randomly from the population to which the results will be generalized?
3. Under what circumstances was informed consent obtained?
4. Are there probable biases in sampling (e.g., volunteers, high refusal rates, institution population atypical for the country at large, etc.)?
5. What was the "set" given to subjects? Was there deception? Was there control for experimenter influence and expectancy effects?
6. How were subjects debriefed?
7. Were subjects (patients) led to believe that they were receiving "treatment"?
8. Were there special variables affecting the subjects, such as medication, fatigue, and threat that were not part of the experimental manipulation? In clinical samples, was "organicity" measured and/or eliminated?
9. Controls: Were there appropriate control groups? What was being controlled for?
10. When more than one measure was used, was the order counterbalanced? If so, were order effects actually analyzed statistically?
11. Was there a control task(s) to confirm specificity of results?
12. Measures: For both dependent and independent variable measures—was validity and reliability established and reported? When a measure is tailor-made for a study, this is very important. When validities and reliabilities are already available in the literature, it is less important.
13. Is there adequate description of tasks, materials, apparatus, and so forth?
14. Is there discriminant validity of the measures?
15. Are distributions of scores on measures typical of scores that have been reported for similar samples in previous literature?
16. Are measures free from biases such as
    a. Social desirability?
    b. Yeasaying and naysaying?
    c. Correlations with general responsivity?
    d. Verbal ability, intelligence?
17. If measures are scored by observers using categories or codes, what is the interrater reliability?
18. Was administration and scoring of the measures done blind?
19. If short versions, foreign-language translations, and so forth, of common measures are used, has the validity and reliability of these been established?
20. In correlational designs, do the two measures have theoretical and/or methodological independence?

(*continued*)

REPRESENTATIVE DESIGN

1. When the stimulus is a human (e.g., in clinical judgments of clients of differing race, sex, etc.), is there a *sample* of stimuli (e.g., more than one client of each race or each sex)?
2. When only one stimulus or a few human stimuli were used, was an adequate explanation of the failure to sample given?

STATISTICS

1. Were the statistics used with appropriate assumptions fulfilled by the data (e.g., normalcy of distributions for parametric techniques)? Where necessary, have scores been transformed appropriately?
2. Were tests of significance properly used and reported? For example, did the author use the *p* value of a correlation to justify conclusions when the actual size of the correlation suggests little common variance between two measures?
3. Have statistical significance levels been accompanied by an analysis of practical significance levels?
4. Has the author considered the effects of a limited range of scores, and so forth, in using correlations?
5. Is the basic statistical strategy that of a "fishing expedition;" that is, if many comparisons are made, were the obtained significance levels predicted in advance? Consider the number of significance levels as a function of the total number of comparisons made.

FACTOR ANALYTIC STATISTICS

1. Have the correlation and factor matrices been made available to the reviewers and to the readers through the National Auxiliary Publications Service or other methods?
2. Is it stated what was used for communalities and is the choice appropriate? Ones in the diagonals are especially undesirable when items are correlated as the variables.
3. Is the method of termination of factor extraction stated, and is it appropriate in this case?
4. Is the method of factor rotation stated, and is it appropriate in this case?
5. If items are used as variables, what are the proportions of yes and no responses for each variable?
6. Is the sample size given, and is it adequate?
7. Are there evidences of distortion in the final solution, such as singlet factors, excessively high communalities, obliqueness when an orthogo-

nal solution is used, linearly dependent variables, or too many complex variables?

8. Are artificial factors evident because of inclusion of variables in the analysis that are alternate forms of each other?

FIGURES AND TABLES

1. Are the figures and tables (a) necessary and (b) self-explanatory? Large tables of nonsignificant differences, for example, should be eliminated if the few obtained significances can be reported in a sentence or two in the text. Could several tables be combined into a smaller number?
2. Are the axes of figures identified clearly?
3. Do graphs correspond logically to the textual argument of the article? (E.g., if the text states that a certain technique leads to an *increment* of mental health and the accompanying graph shows a *decline* in symptoms, the point is not as clear to the reader as it would be if the text or the graph were amended to achieve visual and verbal congruence.)

DISCUSSION AND CONCLUSION

1. Is the discussion properly confined to the findings or is it digressive, including new post hoc speculations?
2. Has the author explicitly considered and discussed viable alternative explanations of the findings?
3. Have nonsignificant trends in the data been promoted to "findings"?
4. Are the limits of the generalizations possible from the data made clear? Has the author identified his/her own methodological difficulties in the study?
5. Has the author "accepted" the null hypothesis?
6. Has the author considered the possible methodological bases for discrepancies between the results reported and other findings in the literature?

Source: Acknowledgment is hereby given to Brendan A. Maher and the American Psychological Association. Reproduced from *Journal of Consulting and Clinical Psychology*, 1978, *46*, 835–838.

Presentations at Professional Meetings

Another means of communicating research findings to one's colleagues, and a means that can also serve as a preliminary sounding board prior to journal publication, is presentation at scholarly meetings. These are typically the annual meetings of a professional or scholarly society. In school psychology, the primary scholarly meetings are the annual conventions of the American Psychological Association and the National Association of School Psychologists. APA traditionally meets in late summer and NASP in late winter or early spring. Conventions of professional groups usually employ a peer review process for the selection of papers to be presented, though the process is almost always less stringent than for journal publication. The author of a selected paper agrees to attend the meeting and make an oral presentation of the paper and have copies of a prepared text available. Papers should not be read but presented in a relaxed but disciplined style. Presentation at a scholarly meeting has a number of advantages. It affords an excellent opportunity to meet and discuss the research with others having interests in the same or similar areas and provides instantaneous feedback about the impressions of your colleagues. Journal publication can lag from 12 to 18 months or even longer beyond the time an article is accepted by the journal. While APA and NASP are the primary national meetings in school psychology, a number of other groups share interests with our profession and frequently have school psychologists on their programs. These include the American Educational Research Association (AERA), American Orthopsychiatric Association (Ortho), Council for Exceptional Children (CEC), Association for Children with Learning Disabilities (ACLD), National Council on Measurement in Education (NCME), National Association for Gifted Children (NAGC), Society for Research in Child Development (SRCD), and others. Regional meetings such as the Annual Midwestern Conference on Psychology in the Schools, Eastern Psychological Association, Southwestern Educational Research Association, and Rocky Mountain Psychological Association can also afford excellent opportunities to meet colleagues and share information with them at considerably less expense than traveling to national conventions.

RETRIEVING INFORMATION IN SCHOOL PSYCHOLOGY

Nearly everyone is aware of the tremendous information explosion of the past quarter century. Information relative to school psychology is growing at an ever increasing rate. Even for the most tenacious individual, it is very difficult to keep up to date. For the professional practitioner, the problem is even more severe and has been likened to the "Rip Van Winkle Effect" (Quinnett, 1980), that is, waking up one day and finding that the profession has moved on, perhaps even beyond our ability to catch up. While no simple solutions exist, a number of information retrieval services are available which can assist greatly in obtaining most relevant and up-to-date material on particular problems encountered in school psychology.

One of the primary sources of information gathering or "searching" is *Psychological Abstracts,* a monthly publication indexing all recently published research of a psychological nature. The topical or subject indexing of this literature is most valuable in locating available research on any specific topic such as autism, dyslexia, or test bias, to give just a few examples. Virtually all college or university libraries regularly receive *Psychological Abstracts* and make it available for manual searching at the reference desk. Most will also have available, for a fee, computerized search capacities.

Another major resource for school psychologists attempting to locate detailed information on specific topics is the appropriate Educational Resources Information Clearinghouse (ERIC) publication. ERIC collects research reports in all educational fields and includes convention and conference papers, technical reports, and an indexing of published work related to education. Copies of otherwise difficult to obtain papers may frequently be purchased from ERIC for the cost of reproduction. While ERIC indexes can be searched manually, computerized searches are more typical and are available at most college and university libraries and some large school districts. For smaller, more specific bodies of literature, specialized sets of abstracts and indexes are available. The Society for Research in Child Development regularly publishes an index of research related to child development and the APA has recently initiated a series of smaller abstracts under the rubric of PsycSCAN that regularly indexes smaller segments of the psychology literature such as Learning Disabilities/Mental Retardation. For research on psychological tests, including critical reviews, the *Mental Measurement Yearbook* and the *Tests in Print* series of the Buros Institute of Mental Measurements are invaluable sources. Recently, *School Psychology Review* started publishing regular reviews of tests of interest to school psychologists.

School psychologists and other professionals would do well to establish a personal information gathering and storage system (see Phillips, 1982) or at least become involved in developing and maintaining a small library in the psychological services department of the school district. The three primary journals in the field should probably be subscribed to by all professional school psychologists, though this clearly does not occur. Other journals should be readily available as consultation materials. These are listed in Appendix G. Additionally, several major book series should be available in such a departmental library, including at a minimum *Advances in School Psychology, The Handbook of School Psychology,* Carmichael's *Manual of Child Psychology,* and the *Mental Measurement Yearbooks* and *Tests in Print.* Other series such as the Plenum Series on the

Psychology of Individual Differences, Buros-Nebraska Symposium on Measurement and Testing, the ETS Invitational Conference on Testing, and *Advances in Psychological Assessment,* among others, might also be considered.

RESEARCH FOR THE FUTURE OF SCHOOL PSYCHOLOGY: PERSONAL PERSPECTIVES

Some well-known and respected scholars in school psychology have contended that it is naive to believe that, as school psychologists, we control our own role and function, our destiny in the schools. The growth and development of school psychology as a profession should enhance our ability to control more directly our functioning in whatever employment settings in which we may find ourselves in the future. While not eschewing the political, social, and professional guild issues of control over the role of the school psychologist, we believe research in the discipline can and definitely should play a significant part in controlling our own behavior. To maintain recognition as a true profession we see no real alternative. Particularly, we see the research-in-action perspective (Phillips, 1982) as central to our continued viability in the public sector.

Research must form a basis for change in the evolution of school psychology. As we have noted, there has been considerable, and increasing, rhetoric regarding the role of the school psychologist and the need for change. In reality, little change has occurred in the past decade. One of many reasons is the lack of research to support changes in practice. To break out of a traditional mold that has become comfortable to administrators, we must be able clearly and convincingly to demonstrate the effectiveness of the behaviors to which we aspire. A principal example can be found in school-based psychological consultation. Consultation has been the most widely promoted of all the functions marked for increase by the profession, and appropriately so, we believe. Consultation appears to be an effective means of providing high quality services to children and to school staff, and at lower costs than presently incurred. Specific research on consultation, especially from the research-in-action perspective, is not yet sufficient to allow for the kind of convincing presentation to others that is called for in this regard. The most recent of major reviews of the consultation literature (Gutkin & Curtis, 1982; Medway, 1979; Meyers, 1981) not only demonstrate great promise for several approaches (also see chapter 3), but also show significant gaps in the research base of consultation practice.

Evaluation research on school psychological services as well as other aspects of the school system, should become an increasing area of serious attention by school psychologists. Evaluation of school psychological services on a component-by-component as well as a global basis can form a strong foundation for progressive change in the profession. This of course will have an impact on consultation, assessment, and all other aspects of the school psychologist's function. Evaluation research, properly construed, is a fascicle of research-in-action in that it should inform our actions as school psychologists, identifying the best and the worst of what we have to offer and pointing the way to maximization of our effectiveness.

Specific content areas will occupy much of school psychology research as it has in the past, though we detect a growing trend toward process-oriented research in school psychology. Assessment, diagnosis, and referral will likely always, and appropriately, occupy a central role in school psychology research. There are several very good reasons for this. School psychologists are generally well versed in psychometrics and assessment and have access to considerable amounts of data relative to assessment issues. School psychology developed out of the need to identify, evaluate, and intervene on the behalf of atypical children. Assessment changes as does society. There is no solid reason to believe that the results of research on assessment will be impervious to time and the social and political changes and the technological advances so rapidly occurring. With these changes comes the real need to reevaluate old, "tried and true" methods and to appraise new technologies spurred by advances in the parent field of psychology.

Two examples of the latter have recently come on the scene and will be occupying the research interests of a number of school psychologists for some time to come. The K-ABC (Kaufman & Kaufman, 1983) is a new cognitive measure, developed from advances in the last decade, of our understanding of human neuropsychological functioning. The K-ABC could not have been developed 10 years ago because the requisite theoretical underpinnings of the scale were insufficiently developed. Articulation of the relationship of performance on the K-ABC to intellectual integrity, academic skill, and the development of instructional programs remains a major research task, and one that admirably fits the research-in-action perspective.

Another specific research task in school psychological assessment will be the elaboration, evaluation, and application of Bergan's (1981) path-referenced assessment approach to evaluation and intervention with children experiencing academic difficulties. Bergan's approach is another good example of a new technology of assessment with important implications for school psychological practice. This approach stems from advances in related fields, measurement and statistics, in which a school psychologist was able to see the implications of new developments and understanding of structural modeling and regression for modifying curricula for learning problem children. These are important developments in school psychology that lend themselves ostensibly to a research-in-action perspective in which school psychologists in all types of settings can and should contribute.

Assessment will remain a necessary research interest of school psychologists due to the increasing scrutiny of the courts and legislatures and the curious if not sensational interest of the lay press. Assessment leads to decisions about individuals and will thus inherently remain controversial. Controversy should lead to a continued research effort in the field.

We could go on at some length listing specific areas of future research work for school psychologists, but it would be to little avail. Rather, we see more profit in promoting the more general model of the research-in-action perspective for school psychologists. The future of research in school psychology should be one of pragmatism, leading to a more informed practice, to better decision making, and to greater viability and impact on internal professional responsibility and control of school psychology.

CHAPTER 8

Syntheses and Future Challenges

This concluding chapter attempts to synthesize into a meaningful *gestalt* materials presented in prior chapters. Rather than provide a simple summary, the intent is to create an integrated perspective by examining the philosophical core of the profession and discussing some of its most critical future challenges. It is hoped that out of an understanding of these concepts will emerge insight into the trajectory of the profession.

WHAT IS SCHOOL PSYCHOLOGY?

A review of the school psychology literature, spanning the profession's first major conference (Thayer) (Cutts, 1955) to its most recent (Olympia) (Brown, Cardon, Coulter, & Meyers, 1982), reveals what can be characterized as virtually an obsession with questions pertaining to the definition of the field. Despite a great volume of articulate writing and the collective wisdom of the profession's best thinkers, the question still naggingly persists. What is school psychology?

In some ways, we can answer this question with dispatch. It is tempting to say that school psychology is simply the practice of psychology in the schools. While it is obvious that there is much validity to such a response, it is inadequate for a number of reasons. First, it makes little sense to define a profession by the setting in which its practitioners are employed. Clinical psychology, for example, has its roots in the VA hospital, but few (if any) would suggest that we define this field as "VA psychology." Likewise, counseling psychologists working in community mental health centers, private practice, and university counseling centers view themselves as "counseling psychologists" rather than, for example, as "private practice psychologists." For both clinical and counseling psychology, the words "clinical" and "counseling" denote a mindset held by practitioners and trainers in these areas. This mindset or mental paradigm is the primary definer of the profession, and it is one that practitioners and trainers carry with them irrespective of the specific setting that employs them at any given moment. Second, although the majority of school psychologists work in school settings, a sizable minority do not (Ramage, 1979). Among those receiving a doctorate in school psychology between the years 1975 and 1980 who chose not to work in a college or university, 35% were employed in settings other than schools, e.g., organized health care, business, government, private practice, non-profit agencies, etc. (Stapp & Fulcher, 1982). Several authors (e.g., Allen, Chinsky, Larcen, Lochman, & Lochman, 1976; Herron, Green, Guild, Smith & Kantor, 1970) have argued that all school psychologists, regardless of their place of employment, should focus a significant part of their energies on extra-school, community-based issues and problems. We are very sympathetic to this point of view, which is consistent with an ecological perspective of children, educational settings, and communities.

Another common approach to defining the field of school psychology has been to specify the roles performed by practicing school psychologists. A substantial number of national, regional, and local surveys have been conducted regarding this issue (e.g., Hughes, 1979; Lacayo, Sherwood, & Morris, 1981; Meacham & Peckham, 1978; Wright & Gutkin, 1981). The results of these and other similar analyses have been fairly uniform: School psychologists, as a group, spend the most time performing testing and testing-related activities. Consultation functions appear to be gaining in emphasis, although most surveys still find them lagging behind psychometric assessment. Direct intervention services consistently emerge in these surveys but typically are found to be receiving considerably less time than either testing or consultation. Finally, these data indicate that only a small percentage of school psychologists' time is being devoted to research endeavors. A recent survey of training programs in school psychology revealed parallel emphases, although unlike practice in the field, the research function appears to receive considerable attention during graduate training (Pfeiffer & Marmo, 1981). Taken together, these studies provide a reasonably clear picture of current job functions.

And yet the question persists. As this volume goes to press, significant debate, sparked by Bardon (1982), is occurring on the fundamental nature and future of the field (see the Future of School Psychology section of the December, 1982 issue of *Professional Psychology*). What is school psychology? To some extent, the lingering nature of this discussion reflects the dissatisfaction that many practitioners and academicians feel regarding the status quo. This phenomenon emerged rather clearly in the proceedings from both the Spring Hill (Ysseldyke & Weinberg, 1981) and Olympia (Brown et al., 1982) conferences. More significantly, a description of current practice and/or the setting in which it occurs does not provide an intellectually satisfying answer to the question. School psychology is more than a collection of activities currently being performed by practitioners in a particular setting and taught in university programs. At its most basic level, school psychology is a mindset; it is an integrated set of assumptions that can be used to order, understand, and modify the psychological and educational worlds of children and youth (Bardon, 1982). Rather than a literal, concrete reading of the profession's title, which leads to the conclusion that school psychology is psychology in the schools or the cumulative set of roles currently being performed by school psychologists, we favor a more open ended, symbolic interpretation. This latter approach leads us to focus on the assumptions and ideas which are implicitly behind the title "school psychology" and which comprise the philosophical core of the profession.

School psychology is an applied scientific discipline whose practitioners function within a scientist–practitioner model (Raimy, 1950). As such, knowledge gained from the scientific method is applied to presenting problems whenever possible, although it is recognized that the nomothetic nature of science precludes it from providing answers for all the idiographic questions confronting the practitioner (Bardon & Bennett, 1974). It is thus incumbent on school psychologists to read and evaluate research relevant to their practice. Of equal importance, it is crucial to incorporate as much of the scientific method as possible into one's daily professional activities. Conclusions drawn at any given point should be viewed as hypotheses, and as such, subject to revision in the light of new data. To the maximum extent possible, decision making should be premised on empirical phenomena and validated theory, even though these will often have to be tempered by personal experience as well as by professional and clinical judgment. As Reynolds (1982b) put it, "In God we trust, all others must have data" (p. 178).

Consistent with this view of school psychology as an applied science is its primary identification with the field of psychology—the scientific study of behavior. Even though school psychologists typically work in educational settings and are thus knowledgeable regarding the fields of regular and special education, they are psychologists first and foremost. This fact is reflected by the standards for the provision of school psychological services of both the American Psychological Association (APA) and the National Association of School Psychologists (NASP) (see Appendixes A and B in this volume). In their daily practice and research, school psychologists draw heavily upon the rich base of methodology and knowledge available from generic psychology, in addition to theories and data specific to school psychology.

School psychologists are primarily concerned with the welfare of children.

While the nature of the employment setting and the need for indirect services often results in a necessity to consider the school, teacher, or parent as the immediate client (Trachtman, 1981), we believe the bottom line is that school psychologists do what they do for the benefit of children. For example, during consultee-centered case consultation, in which school psychologists might focus most of their attention on bolstering a teacher's self-confidence or professional objectivity, the assumption behind this course of action is that self-confident, professionally objective teachers are better able to serve their students. Thus, while school psychologists' time, interactions, and interventions often center around a variety of adults, these actions are virtually always done with the intention of improving the lot of children.

Implicit in the term "school psychology" is the recognition that school psychologists are concerned about the "education" of children. Although this includes a deep and abiding interest in assisting children to attain their academic potential, it is by no means limited to this area. Rather, "education" is thought of in the broadest sense of the term. In fact, much of applied psychology, for both children and adults, can be understood in terms that are inherently "educational" in nature. Strupp (1978) writes,

> psychotherapy is a learning process and the role of the therapist is analogous to that of a teacher . . . Psychotherapy is based on the assumption that feelings, cognitions, attitudes, and behaviors are the product of a person's life experience—that is, they have been *learned*. If something has been learned, modification of the previous learning can occur. Where learning is impossible . . . psychotherapy has little to offer. (p. 4)

School psychology's interest in "education" reflects the belief that psychological growth and education are inextricably interwined, especially for children.

The profession's primary focus on school settings should thus be seen in light of the fact that many, if not most, significant "educational" experiences occur there for children ages 5 through 18. School settings present children with a living laboratory within which they "learn" how to function, at increasing levels of sophistication and independence, in the areas of both cognitive and social development. Much of what is psychologically meaningful in a child's life occurs at school within an "educational" context. From this point of view, however, it becomes clear that school psychologists may, indeed should, be involved in other "educational" settings as well, for example, home and other community agencies. School psychologists are interested more in a broad "psychology of schooling" (Bardon, 1982) than in a narrow application of psychology to schools.

An equally important but implicit concept contributing to the mindset of school psychology is the belief that psychological issues are best examined and dealt with in the client's natural environment. This is a logical outgrowth of the reciprocal determinism paradigm in which internal personal factors, behaviors, and environments are viewed as mutually and reciprocally interrelated. From this perspective, an individual can not be understood independent of the environment within which he or she functions. The environmental setting is viewed as a crucial part of the ecology of all presenting psychological problems and issues. Prevention, diagnosis, and intervention are thus most logically carried out *in vivo*. In this respect, school and community psychology have a great deal in common.

School psychologists are thus interested in functioning primarily in school settings because, along with the home, they are one of the two natural environments in which children spend most of their waking hours. Rather than working in the artificial world of the one-hour therapy session, school psychologists move freely through the natural environments of children. To a large extent, this minimizes the problems of stimulus generalization faced by psychologists working with clients in more restricted environments. Rather than worrying about whether therapeutic gains will transfer from the psychologist's office to the natural environment, school psychologists typically program changes and interventions into the natural environment, thus short-circuiting many generalization problems. As in the above analysis, this perspective leads to the conclusion that school psychologists may (should) work with children in other natural environments like the home or other community settings.

After reading the materials in this section, some might question whether "school psychology" is an appropriate name for the profession. In some ways it clearly is not, for a strictly literal interpretation of the term "school psychology" does not do justice to the breadth of the field. Bardon (1982) has suggested changing this title to either "applied educational psychology," "educator psychology," or "practitioner educational psychology" for the reasons cited in this chapter and others. We believe, however, that on balance the title "school psychology" should be maintained for a variety of reasons. First, it is descriptive of what the majority of school psychologists do, namely provide psychological services in school settings. Second, the field has established itself under this name both in the eyes of others (e.g., psychologists, educators, other helping professionals, parents, legislators, and the general public) and in terms of employment opportunities. To change the title at this point in the profession's history might risk or undo many of the accomplishments that have already been achieved (e.g., standards for the provision of school psychological services issued by APA and NASP). Finally, the title "school psychology" does uniquely represent most of what we have defined as the field of school psychology. If interpreted with appropriate flexibility, the term easily encompasses the major delimiters of the profession as a scientific discipline and as a specialty area within generic psychology whose primary focus is on the education of children (in the broadest sense of the term) within their natural environments.

FUTURE CHALLENGES FACING SCHOOL PSYCHOLOGY

Given a broad symbolic definition of the field, what are the challenges facing the profession in the near future? What are the most pressing unanswered questions which need to be resolved by school psychology in the next 5 to 15 years? At the most general level, the challenges facing school psychologists can be divided into two global spheres, for example, content and process.

Challenges in the Content Sphere: Operationalizing the Reciprocal Determinism Paradigm

The content sphere addresses the nature of interventions directly and indirectly undertaken by school psychologists. The challenge in this area is to improve upon the technology of the profession and thus serve children more effectively. There is literally no area of school psychology in which a state of technical perfection has been achieved and in which improvements are not needed. We have proposed in this volume that Bandura's reciprocal determinism paradigm is the most appropriate model for conceptualizing school psychological services. Knowledge of individual characteristics, human behavior, and environmental phenomena comprises the "content" of the profession. Our technology in many of these areas, however, is limited, and the profession has barely even begun to address the mutual and reciprocal interactions between each of these areas. Clearly, an exhaustive discussion of the content challenges facing the profession is beyond the scope of this chapter—it could easily be a book in and of itself. What follows is a brief analysis of a few of the most critical content challenges.

Assessment

Assessment of Individuals' Internal Characteristics. Substantial and well validated methodologies exist for assessing the individual characteristics of children. Page (1982) states, "the principles of good testing run like a gold core through school psychology; it is our best and most unique tool" (p. xii). But even here, a great deal of progress remains to be made. A review of *The Eighth Mental Measurements Yearbook* (Buros, 1978), for example, reveals that many, if not most, of the commercially available standardized tests are seriously inadequate either in terms of normative samples, reliability, validity, or some combination of these areas. Buros concluded, "At least half of the tests currently on the market should never have been published" (1978, p. xxxi). In a more detailed analysis of test quality, Mitchell (1984) concluded,

> it is regrettably true that there are still a surprising number of tests that are published without reliability evidence, validity evidence, or norms. . . . Twenty-two percent of the tests listed in *The Eighth Mental Measurements Yearbook* (1978) were without

any reliability data whatever. Eight and one-half percent had no validity data, and an additional 1% had neither reliability nor validity data for certain parts, levels, or editions. Five percent had no reliability data for certain scores, and 9% had no reliability data for certain grades, subtests, or forms. All together, some 41% of the tests listed in *The Eighth Mental Measurements Yearbook,* were lacking reliability and/or validity data in some important respect. . . . The data for norms were some-what better, but still not encouraging. Eleven per cent of the tests listed . . . had no norms whatever. Another 3% had no norms for certain scores, and 8% had norms only for certain subtests, forms, or parts of the standardization population. One percent had no description of the normative population, and for four percent the norms consisted only of means and standard deviations. All told, some 28% of the tests listed . . . were inadequately normed in some important respect.

It should not be concluded that the 41% of tests lacking in validity and/or reliability data or the 28% lacking in normative data were the result of very rigorous criteria applied. . . . As a matter of fact, any kind of correlation coefficient would usually serve to remove the accusing statement for either reliability or validity, and the situation for normative data was equally charitable. The standards for declaring such inadequacies in the descriptive entries were minimal at best.

Although it is recognized that the choice of measurement devices should not be made on the basis of any singular criteria, it is disturbing to note that the frequency with which many psychometric instruments are used appears to be determined primarily by factors other than their technical adequacy (Reynolds, 1979a; Wade & Baker, 1977; Ysseldyke, 1979; Ysseldyke, Algozzine, Regan, & Potter, 1980).

Ironically, and as noted previously by Page (1982), the science of norm-referenced assessment is among the profession's most highly developed and sophisticated bodies of knowledge. Problems in this area are primarily the result of inadequate application of measurement theory and data, rather than a lack of appropriate technology. Psychologists in general, and school psychologists in particular, must become more "intelligent" in their use of norm-referenced tests (Kaufman, 1979; Kaufman & Reynolds, 1983) if they are to silence the harsh internal and external criticisms resulting from the misuse and abuse of these instruments.

Assessment of Behavior. The challenges confronting school psychologists in the assessment of behavior are in some ways similar to those regarding the assess-ment of individuals' internal characteristics. In both instances, practitioners often make inadequate use of the technology that is available. Goh, Teslow, and Fuller (1981), for example, concluded from a national survey of assessment practices that although "most school psychologists do seem to realize the importance of looking at observable behaviors in conducting assessments . . . behavioral as-sessment has not become a frequent practice in the schools" (p. 705). The majority of school psychologists' time appears to be spent assessing the internal characteristics of children rather than their overt behavior. If one subscribes to a reciprocal determinism paradigm regarding the practice of school psychology, it is clear that a good deal of crucial assessment information is thus being missed. To the extent that a child's overt behavior is a significant element in the ecology of presenting problems, failure to assess these phenomena will lead to both inaccurate diagnoses and a high probability of inadequate treatment programs.

In the *Handbook of Behavioral Assessment,* Ciminero, Calhoun, and Adams (1977) include chapters on six methods of behavioral assessment, that is, direct observation, self-report schedules and inventories, self-monitoring procedures, behavioral interviews, analogue measures, and psychophysiological procedures. Due to space limitations, only a few of these approaches can be addressed in this chapter.

One of the most frequent techniques of behavioral assessment is the direct observation of behavior. Here a substantial literature and sophisticated technology already exist (e.g., Haynes, 1978). Among the most pressing research issues is a need for continued investigation of the psychometric qualities of direct observational methods. Unfortunately, many psychologists have assumed that questions of reliability and validity pertain only to test-based assessment and are somehow less pertinent for observational approaches. *The Standards for Educational and Psychological Tests* published by APA (1974), however, states that "the psychologist who counts examples of a specific type of response in a behavior–modification setting is as much responsible for the validity of his interpretations of change or the basic realibility of his observations as is any other test user" (p. 4). Without knowledge of the reliability and validity of observational procedures, the practitioner is unable to determine the extent to which observational data reflect reality versus measurement error. Unfortunately, there is relatively little research addressing this area (Keller, 1980). Excellent discussions of these issues can be found in Hersen and Barlow (1976), Kratochwill (1978), and the *Journal of Applied Behavior Analysis* (1977, issue 1).

A related need is for continued development of the statistical methods with which one can analyze observational data collected from single or small *N* applied interventions and research studies. While visual rather than statistical procedures have traditionally been accepted as adequate, Gottman and Glass (1978) make a potent argument for augmenting visual inspection with more refined statistical analyses capable of detecting subtle but real shifts in observational data that might easily be overlooked if one relied exclusively on visual analyses. In order to reinforce their point, they present data from Komechak (1974) (see Figure 8.1) and the following discussion.

> The data for Person A . . . shows a fairly erratic and stationary pattern of response.
> When analyzed with the proper statistical techniques . . . , the shift upward in the
> series at the point of intervention . . .—between the tenth and eleventh days—

proved to be highly statistically significant . . . But of the 13 judges, only 7 considered the observed shift to be statistically reliable for Person A. The findings are even more remarkable for Person B. This second series showed no statistically significant . . . shift at the point of intervention—between the ninth and tenth days—yet 11 of the 13 judges felt there was a significant upward shift in the series coincident with instituting rewards. . . . Clearly, the "eyeball test" gives results that vary from judge to judge and that can conflict sharply with the findings of statistical tests. (p. 199)

Probably the oldest and most frequently used method for assessing human behavior is the clinical/behavioral interview. Many psychologists take this technique for granted, not even considering it a formal method of assessment (Burke & DeMers, 1979). As a result, our empirical understanding of this extremely complex assessment tool is very limited. Linehan (1977) characterizes the absence of research in this area as "truly amazing" (p. 48). One of the most significant content challenges facing school psychology is the development of a science of interviewing. Which interviewer behaviors encourage the interviewee to report information both accurately and efficiently? Bergan and his colleagues (Bergan, 1977; Bergan & Neumann, 1980; Bergan & Tombari, 1975; Tombari &

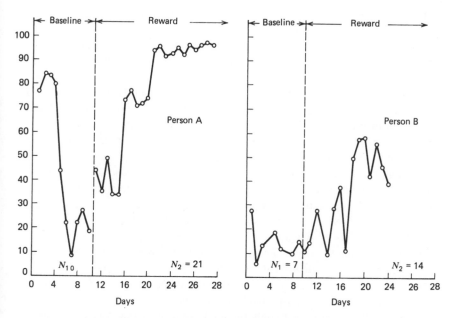

Figure 8.1. An example of behavioral data amenable to either visual or statistical analysis. (From J. M. Gottman & G. V. Glass, 1978. Reprinted by permission.)

Bergan, 1978) have begun to address this question by delineating the sequential stages of behavioral interviews (i.e., problem identification, problem analysis, plan implementation, and problem evaluation) and the salient dimensions of interviewer verbalizations (i.e., message source, message content, message process, and message control). Burke and DeMers (1979) have proposed a classification system for interview formats according to whether the interviewer uses a predetermined or unstandardized set of questions, the breadth of response options allowed to the interviewee, and the breadth of content areas explored during the interview. Given the extensive degree to which school psychologists rely on interview data for the assessment of child, teacher, and parent behaviors, it is imperative to develop and further refine the rudimentary technology that is currently available.

Assessment of Environments. The assessment of environments by school psychologists has received substantially less attention than the assessment of individual characteristics and behaviors (although behavior assessment frequently includes an analysis of contingencies occurring in the natural environment). In a national survey of school psychologists' assessment practices (Goh, Teslow, & Fuller, 1981), the assessment of classroom and organizational environments was completely overlooked. Virtually all of the profession's assessment practices appear to be child centered, that is, premised on a "psychology of individuals" (Sarason, 1971). From the perspective of a reciprocal determinism model, however, it is clear that environmental phenomena play a major role in the ecology of each child's experiences in school and other settings. The assessment of environments is thus an area needing extensive research and development in the immediate future.

Among the more significant factors impeding environmental assessments is the lack of a comprehensive, consensually accepted theory upon which to build assessment instruments and practices. Whether examining the state of the art at the classroom or organizational level, no clear paradigm emerges. Without a theory to provide guidance, researchers and practitioners alike are destined to be uncertain as to which environmental factors are crucial, thus warranting intensive assessment, and which are irrelevant, thus deserving of being ignored. A recent literature review regarding the impact on children and adults of the physical environment in classrooms (Weinstein, 1979) reflects the atheoretical nature of this area. Even though a variety of environmental phenomena were well reviewed (e.g., seating position, furniture arrangement, noise levels, open versus closed classrooms), no theoretical rationale was provided to explain why these, rather than other physical variables, were (or should be) singled out for intensive study. Similarly at the organizational level, much of the work has been atheoretical or the result of theories with only minimal explanatory power (Fullan, Miles, & Taylor, 1980). For example, while the organizational assessment work of Fox, Schmuck, Egmond, Ritvo, and Jung (1973) is based on social systems theory,

Figure 8.2. Subsystems of a school system. (From R. S. Fox, R. Schmuck, E. V. Egmond, M. Ritvo, & C. Jung, 1973. Reprinted by permission.)

the model upon which their practices is premised (see Figure 8.2) is primarily descriptive. Perhaps the most articulate environmental theory has been proposed by Barker (Barker, 1965, 1968; Barker & Associates, 1978). While his concept of "behavior settings" appears to be a step in the right direction, it has not yet been refined to the point where it can be routinely applied to the assessment of school, educational, and mental health environments.

Assessment of the Mutual and Reciprocal Interactions Among Individuals, Behaviors, and Environments. Clearly, the most difficult assessment challenge facing school psychology is the development of assessment techniques measuring the mutual and reciprocal interactions among individual characteristics, human behaviors, and environments. Most typically, school psychologists have been content to measure one or two of these phenomena, most often in isolation from each other. Little currently exists that captures in its full complexity the ecological nature of a child's psychological functioning. To accomplish this lofty goal will require a qualitative shift in the direction of contemporary assessment practice and research. Merely producing more and better versions of current techniques will likely be insufficient to attain this end. Assessment technologies are needed that capture the dynamic and continuous interplay between person, behavior, and environmental factors.

Diagnosis. A primary purpose of assessment is, of course, to gather sufficient data to enable psychologists and other professionals to reach a diagnosis of presenting problems with a reasonable degree of confidence. Diagnoses derived from the examination of assessment information may run the entire gamut from formal, molar diagnostic classifications (e.g., mental retardation) to informal, molecular diagnostic statements (e.g., Johnny's reading failure is due primarily to inadequate sight vocabulary). In every instance, however, diagnosis must be viewed as a means to an end rather than as an end in itself (Hobbs, 1975). Wolfensberger (1965) dramatically pointed out that psychoeducational diagnoses resulting in little or no additional services for children may often be worse than no diagnosis at all.

Despite the serious flaws that exist in current diagnostic systems, it is crucial to understand that the concept of formal diagnosis is of vital importance and value. As is the case for all scientifically based disciplines, school psychology requires formal systems for the classification of relevant events and phenomena if there are to be advancements in theory, research, and practice. Without diagnostic and categorical methods there can be no science. Like Hobbs, a noted critic of current diagnostic systems, we strongly disagree with those who call for the abolition of diagnosis. "Classification and labeling are essential to human communication and problem solving; without categories and concept designators, all complex communicating and thinking stop" (Hobbs, 1975, p. 5).

Diagnosis of Individuals. Many extremely complex challenges face the profession in the area of diagnosis, not the least of which is the development of comprehensive, reliable, and valid systems for diagnosing the characteristics of individuals. Most, if not all, of the formal diagnostic systems currently available to school psychologists have been severely criticized for a variety of reasons. Interestingly, school and other psychologists have had relatively little input into the genesis of current diagnostic systems. For example, the DSM series (American Psychiatric Association, 1952, 1968, 1980) and the GAP were formulated by psychiatrists, while the diagnostic categories of PL 94-142 were developed through a legislative process focusing on special education.

Philosophically, contemporary formal diagnostic systems have relied almost entirely on a medical model, internal pathology perspective. Over the decades, this reliance has served to focus the attention of psychologists on intrapsychic causes of psychological dysfunction to the exclusion of extrapersonal factors, and on the deficiencies and weaknesses of individuals rather than on their strengths. Both of these perspectives are inconsistent with the ecologically oriented, reciprocal determinism paradigm presented as most appropriate for school psychology and have been severely criticized by a substantial number of psychologists (e.g., McReynolds, 1979; Schacht & Nathan, 1977).

Above and beyond these conceptual problems, however, empirical shortcomings have also surfaced in a considerable variety of studies. Foremost among these difficulties is the apparent inadequacy of these systems in regard to interdiagnostician reliability. Simply stated, different clinicians examining the same information for the same client often reach highly divergent diagnoses.

In reference to the DSM II and the GAP system, Achenbach and Edelbrock (1978) summarize their review of the literature by stating,

> The reliability of both systems is mediocre, with agreement between diagnosticians averaging about 60% for major categories, such as psychotic versus neurotic disorders, and considerably less for specific disorders within these categories . . . However, the reliability estimates in all these studies would be lowered by corrections for chance agreements . . . Current drafts of the DSM III offer little hope of improvement in the child area. (p. 1276)

McDermott (1980), working with the etiological, descriptive, and prognostic diagnoses made by school psychologists, found the agreement among students, interns, and practitioners to be at or very near chance levels. He wrote,

> In general, it is important to note that while the present evidence indicates that the case for diagnostic congruence among school psychologists is certainly weak and no better than the case for congruence among other child specialties, the extent of incongruence among school psychologists seems no worse than that among associated disciplines . . . The research literature is replete with examples of definitive studies pointing to the lack of diagnostic congruence among clinical psychiatrists . . . , clinical psychologists . . . , mental health agencies . . . , public mental health workers . . . , and special educational placement teams. (pp. 21–22)

Even at the grossest level of discrimination (e.g., learning disabilities versus emotional disturbance, etc.), research has produced mixed results at best. Frame, Clarizio, Porter, and Vinsonhaler (1982) report diagnostic congruence among practicing school psychologists to be in the moderate range, with a phi coefficient varying from an average of .30 to .53, depending on whether one discounts the data provided by psychologists who choose no diagnostic classification for a simulated case. Epps, McGue, and Ysseldyke (1982) reported that judges were unable accurately to discriminate between LD and non-LD students. In a study conducted with the parents of actual special education children, Adleman (1978) concluded,

> a very large number of students with learning problems are being assigned more than one diagnostic label . . . there is relatively little agreement regarding the label that should be assigned, symptoms and signs used to arrive at one diagnostic label appear to be common to many other labels, . . . once a label is assigned it is difficult to know what it signifies other than a child with a problem. (p. 720)

Taken as a whole, this body of research indicates inadequate reliability for most, if not all, current systems of diagnosis in frequent use. Examination of the learning disabilities diagnosis as stated in PL 94-142 sheds light on the problems typically associated with current medical model and special education diagnoses.

> "Specific learning disability" means a disorder in one or more of the basic psychological processes involved in understanding or in using language, spoken or written, which may manifest itself in an imperfect ability to listen, think, speak, read, write, spell, or to do mathematical calculations. The term includes such conditions as perceptual handicaps, brain injury, minimal brain dysfunction, dyslexia, and developmental aphasia. The term does not include children who have learning problems which are primarily the result of visual, hearing, or motor handicaps, of mental retardation, or emotional disturbance, or of environmental, cultural, or economic disadvantage. (HEW, 1977, p. 42478)

Hammill (1976) summarizes the shortcomings of this definition (and by implication, the weaknesses of similar definitions for other diagnostic categories) as follows:

> While definitions like this one allow students to be described in broad, general terms, they are much too obscure, open-ended and subjective to be used as actual criteria for selecting individual students. Many of the words used in these definitions do not have any precise meanings and several of the ideas expressed or implied are currently surrounded by professional controversy. For example, what is a basic psychological process, a perceptual handicap, dyslexia, or minimal cerebral dysfunction? Professionals in psychology and education dispute hotly the existence, nature, and importance of the so-called "psychological processes." In addition experts in reading have never been able to reach a general agreement on the definition of dyslexia, much less on its diagnosis and treatment. And speech pathologists still argue about the concept of developmental aphasia. To this confusion may be added the observation that many of today's physicians consider terms like "minimal cerebral dysfunction" and "brain injury" to be ill-defined, waste-basket categories.
>
> Because the definitions are not very definitive, and therefore cannot be used to identify precisely the populations to be served, state education agencies have had to

design regulations in which the exact criteria to be used in operationalizing the definition are set forth in specific detail. For example, the intelligence quotient (IQ) restrictions, the degree of educational or linguistic deficiency, the kinds of tests to be used, the formula to be applied, etc., are usually specified in the regulations. These are then used by local education agencies for the purpose of identifying those students whose education will be supported financially under the "learning disabilities" label. Therefore, in any particular state, the nature of the students diagnosed as having a learning disability is actually a function of the regulations used to identify them rather than the definition used to describe them. For example, two states might adhere to the same definition but employ considerably divergent sets of regulations; in these instances, the characteristics of students identified as being learning disabled in one state might differ markedly from those identified in the other state. (pp. 29–30)

Given the myriad of problems already presented, it is important to note that significant progress is being made with the aid of multivatiate statistical approaches to classification. At the heart of this approach is the establishment of actuarial rules of classification based upon: (a) the psychometric characteristics of assessment devices, and (b) the relative efficacy of assessment data in making clinically relevant predictions and discriminations. McDermott (1982) has provided an excellent discussion of these techniques that is appropriate for the nonstatistician. Although we believe that this approach holds considerable potential, substantive methodological questions remain to be answered (Willson & Reynolds, 1982).

Diagnosis of Behavior. Related advances are also being made in the diagnosis of behavior. Here, multivariate techniques such as factor and cluster analysis are being used to identify empirically derived behavior syndromes, that is, groups of behaviors that occur together. After an extensive literature review, Quay and Werry (1979) identified four behavior syndromes, that is, conduct disorder, anxiety-withdrawal, immaturity, and socialized aggression, for which they believe there is "overwhelming evidence" (p. 36). The conduct disorder syndrome, for example, is characterized by "aggression, both verbal and physical, associated with generally 'disturbing' behavior and poor social relationships with both adults and peers" (p. 17). Among the 50 or so behaviors listed by Quay and Werry as those most frequently associated with conduct disorders are the following: fighting, temper tantrums, destruction of property, and stealing. Investigations of the reliability and validity of behavior syndromes have produced promising results (Achenbach & Edelbrock, 1978; Quay & Werry, 1979) but, as Edelbrock (1979) points out, much work remains to be done.

These . . . studies have produced a heterogeneous body of findings that can appear confusing, inconclusive, and even contradictory. Moreover, these studies have not yet resulted in a well differentiated empirical taxonomy of children's behavior disorders that is useful to researchers or practitioners. Yet, despite the diversity of theoretical persuasions, subject samples, sources of data, rating instruments, and methods of statistical analysis, there has been considerable convergence among these studies in identifying syndromes that characterize disturbed children. The identification of these syndromes is a necessary but not sufficient step toward the construction of empirically based classification systems. The next step, which has only begun, is the translation of these syndromes into categories for differentiating among individual children. (p. 356)

A discussion of other contemporary approaches to the diagnosis and classification of behavior can be found in Kratochwill (1982).

Diagnosis of Environments. Among the most significant gaps of knowledge confronting contemporary psychology is the absence of a system for classifying/diagnosing environments. Although the characteristics of behavior settings are viewed by many as among the most compelling forces shaping human behavior (Barker & Associates, 1978; Moos, 1976), there is little technology available with which to categorize specific environments. The concept of matching the individual strengths and weaknesses of students to particular educational environments is an idea that has had a great deal of intuitive appeal to many psychologists over a considerable period of time. Without a system for classifying environments, however, the probabilities of success in this endeavor are quite slim. Unfortunately, the technical advances in this area have not yet taken us much beyond common sense classification systems such as those empirically derived by Price and Blashfield (1975) and discussed by Carlson, Scott, and Eklund (1980), for example, elementary school settings, adult settings, family oriented settings, and government settings. A great deal of additional nosological work is obviously necessary if psychology is to develop a meaningful taxonomy of environments.

Diagnosis of the Mutual and Reciprocal Interactions Among Individuals, Behaviors, and Environments. With the development of a system for classifying environments, psychologists could begin to realize the full potential of the reciprocal determinism paradigm for the purposes of diagnosis. In its simplest form, such an approach would dictate the examination of diagnostic statements addressing the status of internal individual characteristics, behaviors, and environments, each independently derived through different nosological systems. This method would primarily be "additive" in nature, in that diagnostic insights gathered from each independent system would be looked at sequentially. Clearly, a higher form of nosology would be one that synthesized data from each aspect of the reciprocal determinism model, that is, individual characteristics, behavior, and environment, and yielded a diagnostic statement that reflected this integration. As opposed to the "additive" approach, this system would yield insights that were greater than the sum of its individual parts. Given the current state of the art in diagnosis, however, such a sophisticated system would not appear to be on the horizon.

Concluding Comments. Before leaving the topic of diagnosis, some comment is necessary regarding the relative merits of formal and informal diagnosis. The primary distinction between these approaches is the idiographic nature of the latter, and herein lies both its primary advantage and disadvantage. For example, in any given instance, a psychologist may believe that he or she has an excellent grasp of the reciprocal interactions among the individual, behavioral, and environmental components of a presenting problem. Lacking any formal nosological system with which to express these insights, he or she resorts to an informal diagnosis for the purposes of communication, for example, Billy's need to gain adult affection leads him to behave like a "class clown" during math class because the math class is structured in such a way as to prevent Billy from getting sufficient adult attention in the absence of this set of behaviors. If this statement accurately represents the problem, it may serve the practitioner well as a diagnostic formulation because it addresses the reciprocal interactions among the individual, behavioral, and environmental elements of the situation. From the perspective of advancing the science of school psychology, however, this statement leaves much to be desired. Informal diagnostic formulations are often too deeply rooted in the specifics of the particular presenting problem to be of much assistance for future problems involving different individual characteristics, behaviors, and environments. In brief, while informal diagnosis may be effective in terms of internal validity, it may prove to be inadequate in regard to external validity.

Treatment. For most practitioners, the *raison d'etre* for doing assessment and diagnosis is to determine a proper course of treatment. Underlying this common notion is the implicit assumption that there is a direct link between diagnosis and treatment; that is, certain treatments are more effective than others for problems classified under one diagnosis as opposed to another. This concept has its recent historical roots in Cronbach's 1957 presidential address to the APA convention and is typically referred to as aptitude (or trait) treatment interaction (ATI).

To give a rather simple example from the world of medicine, it is well known that patients diagnosed as diabetic (Diagnosis A) will react more favorably to insulin treatment (Treatment X) than to the administration of blood thinners (Treatment Y). On the other hand, individuals diagnosed as having blood clots (Diagnosis B) would be better treated with blood thinners (Treatment Y) than insulin (Treatment X) (see Figure 8.3). When viewed from this perspec-

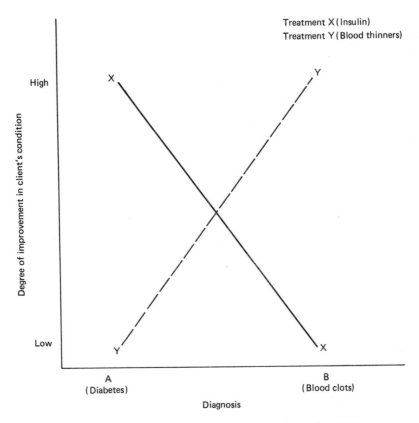

Figure 8.3. Example of an aptitude treatment interaction (ATI).

tive, it is easy to see the importance of determining an individual's diagnosis (i.e., whether they are suffering from diabetes or blood clots) because this piece of information directs the physician to the treatment of choice for the patient.

Unfortunately, despite a limited number of successes (Miller, 1981), the search for ATIs in educational psychology has generally been unsuccessful (Arter & Jenkins, 1979; Cronbach & Snow, 1977; Hessler & Sosnowsky, 1979; Tobias, 1976). For example, there are few, if any, treatments that have been proven to be more successful with learning disabled than emotional disturbed children and vice-versa. Similarly, research indicates that there is little factual basis to the assumption that children diagnosed as visual learners (Diagnosis A) necessarily do better with a visual (Treatment X) rather than an auditory (Treatment Y) curriculum and that children believed to be auditory learners (Diagnosis B) have better success with auditory (Treatment Y) rather than visual (Treatment X) teaching techniques (Arter & Jenkins, 1977; Ysseldyke, 1973).

To a large extent, psychology's inability to develop validated ATIs is predictable given the shortcomings of current assessment and diagnostic technology and theory. Perhaps even more significant, however, is the fact that almost all ATI research has been too narrow in its scope. Consistent with a medical model approach to applied psychology, the search for ATIs has been limited almost exclusively to studying the differential effects of various treatments on subjects varying along dimensions of individual characteristics (e.g., intelligence, personality, learning style). ATI effects attributable to behavior and/or environment variables have been almost entirely ignored, although Berliner and Cahen (1973) provide a limited discussion of the impact of teacher traits. If the reciprocal determinism paradigm is an accurate portrayal of reality, the search for ATIs will have to be redirected toward identifying the differential effects of treatments as they affect varying manifestations of individual, behavior, and environment interactions. Such a phenomenon might more accurately be termed a "*PBE* Treatment Interaction," where *P* stands for personological characteristics, *B* for behavior, and *E* for environment. Clearly, the identification of PBE Treatment Interactions is a task of both enormous methodological complexity and vital importance, and one which may take years, or perhaps even decades to address successfully.

Despite the lack of many clear, valid links between formal diagnosis and treatment, it is in the area of treatment that both generic and school psychology appear to have made the greatest forward strides. Intervention technologies have experienced rapid and consistent growth, although these advancements have come about relatively independent of diagnostic formulations.

Treatment of Internal Individual Characteristics. One of the greatest content challenges facing school psychologists regarding the treatment of internal individual characteristics would appear to be the development and refinement of short term therapies and crisis intervention techniques. With the ratio of school psychologists to children being roughly 1:4500 (Meacham & Peckham, 1978), the feasibility of long-term, traditional psychotherapy seems to be very limited. A primary goal for psychologists doing brief therapy interventions is to help children cope with the situationally-induced psychological stresses they face while growing up. A few of the many problems experienced by a large percentage of youth are: divorce; moving to new schools; death of parents, siblings, relatives, or friends; rejection; failure; etc. Successful resolution of psychological crises induced by events such as these are thought to result in positive psychological growth (Caplan, 1964).

While psychotherapists have traditionally looked askance at anything less comprehensive than long-term treatment designed to work through deep-seated intrapsychic dysfunctions, recent research comparing the effectiveness of time unlimited and brief therapy reveals "essentially no difference in results" (Butcher & Koss, 1978, p. 758). Those supporting short-term therapy approaches have argued that a great deal can be accomplished with brief treatments. This is thought to be true particularly when the patient is in a state of psychological crisis or disequilibrium, for this is hypothesized to be the point at which "the minimum intervention is likely to have the maximum effect" (Malan, 1976, p. 7).

An interesting example of large-scale crisis intervention is provided by Snapp and Davidson (1982). The first author was working as a school psychologist in a junior high school.

> One morning, apparently without provocation, an eighth grader came to school with a .22 caliber rifle. He walked into the classroom, within 10 feet of his teacher, and fired three shots. The teacher died instantly in front of 31 of the boy's classmates. (p. 866)

The authors go on to describe how crisis intervention and counseling were required for other teachers in the building as well as the deceased's peers and their parents.

Short-term, crisis intervention would appear to have a place among the school psychologist's roles (Barbanel, 1982). For one thing, it provides a vehicle for treating the internal characteristics of individuals, a function more traditionally left for the private therapy office. As a treatment approach that has only recently attracted substantial attention, however, there is a considerable need to more adequately define, refine, and research its theory, techniques, and outcomes.

Treatment of Behavior. Regarding the treatment of behavior, extremely advanced and sophisticated technologies exist for the purposes of intervention. "An overwhelming amount of empirical evidence has been amassed establishing the efficacy of operant techniques with clinical populations" (Kazdin, 1978b, p. 581). The major content question remaining in the area of behavioral programming relates to the issues of maintenance and of the transfer of gains made during treatment. Although a powerful, well researched technology has already been developed for the creation of behavior change, we know substantially less about how to maintain gains once behavioral interventions are terminated.

> Behavior modification programs have been extremely successful in altering behavior while the programs are in effect. Yet a major goal of most programs is response maintenance, that is, ensuring that the behaviors are maintained after the contingencies are withdrawn. Another goal is to achieve changes that transfer to situations and settings beyond those in which training was conducted. Response maintenance and transfer of training constitute critical issues for behavior modification programs in schools and indeed in other settings.
>
> In general, classroom behavior modification programs have demonstrated that reinforcement techniques markedly alter behavior but that the gains usually are lost once the program is withdrawn . . . Similarly, classroom programs usually show that

behaviors do not transfer beyond the setting in which the contingencies are implemented. The stimulus conditions controlling behavior often are quite narrow so that behavior changes are restricted to the specific setting in which the program has been carried out. (Kazdin, 1982a, p. 526)

Recently, a number of researchers have begun to focus on issues of generalization (Koegal, Russo, & Rincover, 1977; Stokes & Baer, 1977; Turkewitz, O'Leary, & Ironsmith, 1975). Among the most interesting approaches being taken is an increasing emphasis on the use of self-control techniques. It is reasoned that if subjects can be taught to control their own behaviors through the self-administration of therapy programs, then behavior changes may generalize more readily across time, settings, and behaviors. While experimental support for this hypothesis has not been compelling (Wahler, Berland, & Coe, 1979), it is too early to reach definite conclusions. Additional research is needed regarding this and a wide variety of other generalization techniques. The 1980s will likely serve as a decade in which the technology of behavior change maintenance and transfer receives a great deal of theoretical and experimental attention.

Treatment of Environments. The treatment of environments has primarily revolved around the concept of organization development. Many content challenges face school psychology in this area since it has received relatively little attention in the research literature. Although there have been a considerable number of documented successful interventions at the systems/organizational level by school psychologists (e.g., Meyers, Parsons, & Martin, 1979; Schmuck, Murray, Smith, Schwartz, & Runkel, 1975; Schmuck & Miles, 1971; Snapp & Davidson, 1982), few have reported their findings and methodology with enough precision to permit the isolation of effective versus inconsequential versus counterproductive aspects of these environmental treatments. The available technology in this area consists largely of a number of global techniques (e.g., survey feedback) and specific exercises (e.g., the Lake St. Clair Incident discussed in Chapter 3) which lack specificity regarding the circumstances and conditions under which they are effective or ineffective. Without this type of data, school psychologists are seriously hampered as they attempt to develop a science of organizational interventions.

Among the most effectively controlled studies on systems intervention was the one reported by Fairweather, Sanders, and Tornatzky (1974). The focus of this investigation was on variables affecting the adoption and diffusion of validated innovations made available to mental hospitals around the nation. For the purposes of this research project, they experimentally varied: (a) the hierarchical position of the original contact person in the mental hospital, (b) the manner in which the innovation was presented to the hospital staff, and (c) the type of support services offered during the adoption phase of the study. The impact of each of these and several other variables was measured in relationship to decisions to adopt the innovation, the degree of implementation of the innovation, and the diffusion of the innovation. The results of this study were a series of empirically derived principles for creating change in mental health organizations. Examples of Fairweather, Sanders, and Tornatzky's (1974) conclusions follow:

1. The Principle of Outside Intervention . . . the data confirm the concept that outside intervention is essential for change to occur . . . There is no evidence from the diffusion follow-up study that any appreciable degree of spontaneous adoption of innovation occurs in the absence of external stimulation . . . The experimental data from the implementation phase also indicate that the outside intervention must be active, personal, and often. (p. 185–186)

2. The Principle of Action-Oriented Intervention . . . intervention strategies oriented primarily toward cognitive awareness and attitudinal acceptance will be less effective than those oriented toward behavioral compliance and task accomplishment. (p. 187)

3. The Limitations of Formal Power Principle . . . entering the hospital organization at different levels in the status hierarchy yielded no significant differences in the number of hospitals that were persuaded to adopt the lodge . . . there is no evidence . . . that having an advocate of a high status in the hospital is of any advantage. (pp. 188–189)

4. The Principle of Participation. The clearest and most consistent finding . . . is the degree to which *involvement* across disciplines, across social status levels, and with more groups, produced greater change. (p. 190)

Findings such as these facilitate the development of a technology of organizational intervention. With the aid of additional research and experience, school psychologists should be able to expand substantially upon the body of knowledge currently available in this area.

There is, of course, also a need for a technology of environmental interventions at the individual classroom level. To some extent, we already know a great deal about this area as a result of research and experience with operant psychology/behavior modification. The contingent manipulation of rewards and punishments, however, is only a subset of possible environmental manipulations. Other important parameters such as the interpersonal, physical, pedagogical, and organizational environments of the classroom need investigation to determine their relationships to the educational and psychological growth of children, For example, what is the impact of open space and non-graded educational programs? It is reasonable to assume these approaches produce superior results for some students, some teachers, and some number of academic and social tasks. Unfortunately, we currently have little or no empirical basis for predicting which students, teachers, and tasks are best suited to such environments.

Treatment of the Mutual and Reciprocal Interactions Among Individuals, Behaviors, and Environments. Before leaving the area of treatment, it is important to note the recent advances and trends that have helped move psychology closer to realizing the potential of the reciprocal determinism paradigm. We refer specifically to cognitive behavioral interventions and family therapy. Both of these approaches address and provide treatment for the mutual and reciprocal interactions occurring among individuals, behaviors, and environments.

It is difficult to determine the precise beginnings of the cognitive behavior movement. Its different terminology notwithstanding, the early work of the Russian neuropsychologist, Luria, has greatly influenced the growth and development of what is now called cognitive behavior modification (e.g., Luria, 1961). Lazarus (1977), however, was among the first to note the need for expanding upon the behavioral approach to include information pertaining to the individual.

> Those who adhere to the more delimited meanings of "behavior therapy" tend to disregard significant "nonbehavioral" therapeutic developments. They also overlook convincing data demonstrating that in adult humans, conditioning is produced through cognitive mediation. Clinical exigencies demand that a therapist be able to account for events that the behavior therapy model cannot readily explain. Adoption of a more comprehensive (multimodal) framework is required. (p. 550)

Since this statement, a great deal of progress has been made in the area of cognitive behavioral treatments. A review of this body of literature can be found in the numerous books and articles addressing this topic (e.g., Foreyt & Rathjen, 1978; Kendall & Hollon, 1979; Meichenbaum, 1977; Meyers & Cohen, 1982). The field of cognitive behavioral interventions, according to Hollon and Kendall (1979), is at "a point of youthful maturity" (p. 452). Although much additional research is needed, its theory and clinical efficacy appear promising.

For the purposes of this discussion, the most important point is that cognitive behavioral theory and treatment represent a conceptual step forward because they meaningfully address more than one element of the reciprocal determinism triad, that is, the individual, his or her behavior, and his or her environment. Above and beyond this, the cognitive behavioral approach is an integrative rather than an additive model. It recognizes the mutual and reciprocal interactions occurring among an individual's cognitions and behaviors rather than simply examining each of these independently and "adding" them together without synthesis.

Family therapy approaches also hold considerable promise for operationalizing the reciprocal determinism paradigm. By conceptualizing the psychological difficulties of individuals within a systems theory framework, family therapists focus much of their attention on the mutual and reciprocal interactions among individuals, behaviors, and environments. As such, family therapy can be an undertaking of enormous subtlety and complexity. Petrie and Piersel (1982) note that "family therapy is presently more of an orientation than it is an agreed-on, commonly accepted set of principles and procedures" (p. 582). We believe, however, that this "orientation" is one of substantial theoretical and practical importance, even though a clearly focused discipline has yet to emerge. Interested readers are referred to Gurman and Kniskern (1978) for a comprehensive literature review of family therapy theory and research.

Summary. Clearly, the task of operationalizing the reciprocal determinism paradigm is one which, in many ways, remains to be accomplished. In every phase of practice, school psychologists face substantial content challenges. Much of the technology necessary for assessment, diagnosis, and treatment has yet to be developed and properly validated. Although significant progress is being made in each of these areas, the theory of reciprocal determinism is, essentially, ahead of the technology that is needed to implement it. This is, however, as it should be. As with any good theory, the reciprocal determinism model provides the profession with a conceptual framework, a "roadmap" leading to future advances in practice and research. While the gap between current knowledge and complete mastery of the paradigm may be humbling, it is not meant to engender professional insecurity or despair. Rather, the intent is to provide a vision of children and their worlds that is an accurate reflection of reality, in all its rich and frustrating complexity, and to abruptly bring to one's senses anyone complacent enough to believe that there is nothing new to be learned.

Challenges in the Process Sphere

Unlike the content sphere, which addresses *what* types of services are needed, the process sphere focuses on factors affecting *how* school psychological interventions are generated and carried out. Inattention to the process elements of presenting problems typically leads to inadequate and/or unimplemented treatment plans. Too often, school psychologists focus almost exclusively on the content aspects of professional problems (e.g., *What* interventions are needed to improve Johnny's reading skills?) and ignore the process aspects of the situation (e.g., *How* can I get Johnny's reading teacher to carry out correctly the program in question?).

Focus on Children Versus Adults. The delivery of school psychological treatments by school psychologists is deceptively complex. Among the most significant process issues is the fact that most of these interventions are indirect in nature. Specifically, school psychologists typically affect children through the activities of other adults. Although a great deal of time is spent in direct contact with children during the assessment phase of service delivery, the actual administration and execution of treatment is most frequently in the hands of teachers, parents, special educators, and school administrators, that is, other adults. The school psychologist makes recommendations, but only infrequently does the psychologist directly carry out these suggestions.

A paradox of considerable consequence seems to exist. The majority of school psychologists' time is spent focusing on children, while the impact school psychologists have is mediated and determined by the actions of other adults. While it is obviously important to continue the development and refinement of technology relating to assessment, diagnosis, and treatment of children, it could all be for naught if additional attention is not focused on the processes by which these content technologies and advances come to be implemented and/or ignored by adults.

Clearly, teachers, parents, and other adults are not passive consumers of school psychologists' content recommendations. It is very naive, for example, to assume that a teacher or parent will execute a psychologist's recommendation simply because that psychologist believes his or her ideas are in the best interests of the child. Gutkin and Curtis (1982) and Caplan (1970) have enumerated a few of the many possible reasons why teachers and other direct care persons might fail to execute a psychologist's recommendations: (a) they do not believe the intervention will work and thus do not wish to "waste their time," (b) they misunderstand the recommendations, (c) they lack knowledge necessary to implement the treatment, (d) they are deficient in a crucial skill, (e) they lack self-confidence, (f) they lack prerequisite resources, (g) they are unaware that they are implementing the program incorrectly, (h) they lack adequate time, (i) they are not sufficiently motivated, (j) they have lost their professional objectivity regarding a particular case, or (k) they have a hidden agenda and wish to see the treatment fail.

School psychology is thus a relatively unique field. Unlike physicians, lawyers, teachers, and most other professionals who directly "treat" their clients, school psychologists deliver services primarily with the aid of "intermediaries." It is critical for practitioners to realize, then, that the design of a "correct" treatment program for a child is, in most instances, only half the challenge needing to be met. Of equal importance, if school psychologists are to have meaningful impacts on the children they hope to serve, are the process issues that influence whether these "correct" treatments are implemented (Baer & Bushell, 1981; Stolz, 1981).

The following are a few of the many intriguing questions arising from this line of analysis. Are written psychological reports a viable means for producing behavior change in adults? Does the prudent use of psychological jargon decrease a psychologist's effectiveness as a result of reducing the clarity of his or her communications with other adults or increase effectiveness by elevating the psychologist's professional credibility in the eyes of others? What reinforcers/punishers are available to school psychologists to foster desired behaviors from teachers, parents, etc.? What styles of verbal communication are most effective with which types of teachers and under what sets of circumstances? Are there some types of interventions that teachers generally prefer over others (Witt & Elliott, in press; Witt, Elliott, & Hannafin, 1983)? If so, what are the relevant dimensions along which these interventions differ? In what way does the manner of data presentation influence decisions reached by multidisciplinery teams? Each of these, and many other related questions, are relevant to influencing the adults in each child's environment upon whom school psychologists depend for the implementation of psychological and educational programs.

From this perspective, school psychology can be reconceptualized as a field whose primary applied focus is on modifying the attitudes and behaviors of adults rather than on providing direct care and treatment to children. As such, our knowledge of how to influence professional, paraprofessional, and lay persons is crucial. Unfortunately, the psychology of interpersonal influence and other related areas of social psychology have gone relatively unnoticed in the school psychology literature. We suspect the practice of school psychology is also often done without adequate attention being paid to these and other associated issues.

Short-Term Follow-Up. All successful service delivery systems have mechanisms for feedback and corrective action. Even in the hard sciences, where technology is both extremely advanced and precise, the need for feedback systems and subsequent corrective action is obvious. We see a dramatic example of this in our space programs, in which "mid-course corrections" are the norm for virtually every flight. Despite the best efforts of the most highly trained and sophisticated aerospace professionals, everyone recognizes there will inevitably be a degree of error built into each mission. Failure to monitor and correct for this error can, of course, be disastrous.

The need for feedback and for mechanisms of corrective action would seem to be even greater in human service delivery systems than in areas such as space flight. First, it is clear that the technology of human service systems is not nearly as well refined as that for the hard sciences. For example, we have much more precise techniques for splitting an atom than we do for curing drug abuse. As a result, there will typically be fewer and less significant errors involved in projects such as the former when compared to the latter. Second, the cost of error in terms of human suffering can be exceedingly high when associated with major human service delivery systems such as medicine, education, and mental health.

Regarding school psychology in particular, the need for feedback and for mechanisms of corrective action would seem to be particularly high. As detailed in prior sections of this chapter, the technology currently available to the profession has many significant unresolved problems. Although advances continue to be made in the areas of assessment, diagnosis, and treatment, it is not yet possible to know, with any reasonable degree of certainty, which treatments are best for which clients under what sets of circumstances. Despite the best and most sincere efforts of the profession's most skillful individuals, the fruits of school psychology assessment and diagnosis must be viewed as *hypotheses* rather than as facts. In and of itself, this situation is not problematic, if a profession has access to systems for feedback and corrective action. In other words, appropriate service delivery processes can compensate for weaknesses in a profession's content and technology.

Unlike most other human service professions, however, school psychology faces an additional problem. As discussed previously, most school psychological treatments are carried out by adults other than school psychologists. If recommended treatments are failing, the school psychologist will not learn of this or be able to recommend corrective actions unless the adult administering the treatment communicates appropriate information to the psychologist. Given that less than 10% of the children placed in special education are typically returned to regular education (Gallagher, 1972), it is only logical to assume that many of the initial recommendations made by school psychologists and other special service personnel (e.g., LD specialists, speech pathologists) produce less than adequate results. Unlike the societal norms governing the relationships between physicians and nurses or physicians and parents, however, school psychologists are not routinely informed by direct-care personnel when treatment recommendations are failing.

Thus, the need for proactive, assertive short-term follow-up by school psychologists of their initial treatment recommendations is clear. Without it they can assume that a discomforting percentage of their efforts and ideas fail to have the intended impact on children.

It is hard to judge the adequacy of current short-term follow-up services in school psychology because few studies have directly addressed this question. Of course, this state of affairs in and of itself indirectly indicates that follow-up functions have received inadequate attention in the profession. One of the few studies that did directly address this topic was conducted by Goldwasser, Meyers, Christensen, and Graden (1981). They reported that 59% of the school psychologists responding to a national survey indicated only infrequent or no involvement in follow-up activities. Similarly, Ramage (1979) found that 51% of the nation's school psychologists were not providing "follow-up on students who have been referred and for whom recommendations have been made" (p. 156). Evidence of a more indirect nature reinforces the image of insufficient follow-up activities among many, if not most, school psychologists. As reported earlier in this chapter, national surveys of school psychologists' functions uniformly report the greatest portion of time is spent in testing related activities. Although consultation is the second most frequently cited role, it is reasonable to assume that much of this activity is of a pre-assessment nature rather than indicative of short-term follow-up. Finally, PL 94-142 and most states mandate revisions of IEPs on only an annual basis and assessment reevaluations on only a triannual basis. It is likely that with ratios of students to psychologists being higher than the profession desires (Meachan & Peckham, 1978; Ramage, 1979) and that with long case backlogs existing in many districts (Block, 1975), many psychologists are unable to do much more than perform the required reevaluations every three years. Parenthetically, it appears that these reevaluations are typically quite perfunctory and serve little real purpose in terms of program revision (Elliott, Piersel, & Galvin, 1983).

The picture that emerges regarding short-term follow-up activities is thus not one with which the field of school psychology should be content. Attention to this process issue would seem to be critical if the profession is to achieve its potential.

Power. We began this chapter by trying to answer the question "What is school psychology?" The fact that this question still needs to be asked at this point in the profession's history is indicative of a basic problem confronting the field. Specifically, up to this point in time, school psychology generally has lacked the power to shape its own future (Herron, et al., 1970). This has resulted, for example, in continuing calls from amidst the profession's ranks to broaden the roles and functions of school psychologists but with little real change in actual practice as it occurs in the field. School psychology, in many ways, has been relatively powerless regarding its ability to determine the nature and quality of its own services. The power issue is one of considerable complexity and one whose impact is felt on a day-to-day basis by most practitioners.

We suspect one reason this issue has not been dealt with adequately is the aversion of many persons in the human service professions toward the concept of "power." The word itself brings forth images of force, aggression, injustice, and insensitivity to the needs of people. Each of these is antithetical to the overarching philosophies of school psychologists who, as a group, undoubtedly view themselves and their roles in more humanistic terms. The important point is, however, that humanism and power are neither mutually exclusive nor antagonistic concepts. While power has been associated with some of the most heinous acts in history, it has also been responsible for some of our most noble moments. In its simplest terms, power is a means to an end. It allows one to accomplish predetermined goals. Without power one is impotent to do either good or evil.

On both a collective and an individual basis, all school psychologists should concern themselves with the issue of power. If the profession of school psychology fails to improve its current base of power, it shall be unable to bring about improved psychological services for children and will evidence increasing rates of practitioner burnout.

Public versus Private Sector. The fact that the overwhelming bulk of school psychological practice occurs in the public rather than the private sector has a profound impact on the power that school psychologists can exert over their own activities. Whether in public schools, public institutions, community mental health agencies, etc., the public practice of school psychology increasingly is under the control of a growing number of federal, state, and local laws (Bersoff, 1982; Kirp & Kirp, 1976). PL 94-142 is, of course, the most obvious example, although it is only one of many pieces of legislation affecting the public practice of psychology. Dilemmas caused by many of these laws can be quite significant. Lupiani (1978), for example, notes that some of this legislation requires psychologists to act in ways that are contrary to their codes of professional ethics.

Clearly, the public nature of school psychological practice restricts the profession's power and autonomy. To cope with this problem successfully school psychologists and their professional organizations must develop mechanisms for influencing those groups and individuals who determine public policy. At the national level, APA and its associated divisions, the Association for the Advancement of Psychology (AAP) and NASP all strive to have a substantive impact. In many ways, however, the most significant decisions affecting education and psychological services are made at the state and local levels. Here the burden of representing school psychology falls largely on state and local affiliates of NASP and APA and on individual practitioners. Currently a fairly strong network of state psychological and school psychological associations appears to exist. Ultimately, however, the greatest potential power may lie with the individual practitioner and the extent to which he or she articulates both the standards of the profession and the needs of children to persons in policy-making positions (e.g., state legislators, school board members, directors of special education and school psychological services). Data from a recent national survey indicate, however, that school psychologists perceive themselves to have little influence with boards of education and superintendents (Ramage, 1979). This state of affairs will have to change if school psychology is to control its own future.

Administration and Supervision of School Psychological Services. A most significant factor affecting the nature of school psychological services is the training of persons who administer and supervise these programs. Unfortunately, little or no survey data currently exist which directly address this critical issue (Murphy, 1981). Preliminary evidence indicates supervision and administration of school psychological services is often incongruent with APA standards (Wenger, 1982). From our personal experiences and those of our colleagues, it would appear that school psychological services only rarely are administered and directed by school psychologists. In public schools, the activities of school psychologists often fall under the control of regular and special education administrators.

Unfortunately, educational administrators rarely have training as professional psychologists and thus have little understanding of the art and science of psychology. The scientist-practitioner model, and the nuances and limitations of psychological practice are generally foreign to them. As a function of their teacher training and/or special education backgrounds, their goals for psycholog-ical services may not be at all congruent with those of school psychologists. Clearly, one reason the field of school psychology has been frustrated for several decades in its attempt to reshape itself has been that daily activities of its practi-tioners largely have been under the control of non-school psychologists (e.g., administrators).

The reader should not misinterpret the preceding remarks as a condemnation of educational administrators. First, many such individuals work hard to expand their base of information and thus become knowledgable of generic and school psychology. Even more significantly, it is the administrative systems rather than individuals that are at fault. It is no more reasonable to expect educational administrators to be expert school psychologists than it is to expect school psychologists to be expert speech pathologists.

If school psychology is to achieve its full potential, it will have to find vehicles by which to better control the administration of school psychological services and the supervision of its practitioners. Both APA (1981) and NASP (1978) provide guidelines for supervision and administration. It is, of course, up to school psychologists to assert themselves, both individually and collectively, by applying appropriate pressures to bring schools and other institutions into compliance with these guidelines. Above and beyond this, it would appear to be important for the profession to develop more school psychologists with admin-istrative skills. This might be done either by establishing a career ladder for current practitioners or an area of specialization open to students during graduate training.

Sources of Power. The profession of school psychology has many formal and informal sources of power at its disposal. A concerted and organized effort to use these would likely produce desirable and substantial results within a reasonable period of time.

NASP and APA, for example, are sources of considerable power and influ-ence. Although it may not be apparent to those practitioners whose sights are fixed at the local level, both these and other related organizations, for example, Association for the Advancement of Psychology (AAP), National Alliance of Pupil Service Organizations (NAPSO), National Association of State Consul-tants for School Psychological Services, Trainers of School Psychologists (TSP), Council of Directors of School Psychology Programs (CDSPP), have a consider-able impact on daily practice. The activities of these groups include, but are not limited to, the establishment of standards for graduate training, the provision of guidelines for practice, the development and enforcement of ethical codes, lob-bying efforts at both the national and state levels, providing funds and legal assistance for school psychologists striving to fulfill their professional respon-sibilities, creating opportunities for inservice and continuing education, and coordinating outreach to other national and state service organizations that benefit children.

If there is a tragedy in school psychology, it is that so much of the time and energies of both APA and NASP have been dissipated by struggles between them concerning such political issues as credentialing, title, and private practice. While progress has been made over the years for the good of the profession, these conflicts have resulted in school psychologists fighting among themselves, while the needs of clients receive less than the profession's full attention. It is our fervent hope that these issues can be resolved in the immediate future so that both APA and NASP can work together towards accomplishing the vast number of objectives and goals which they hold in common.

Recent graduates of training programs represent another potent source of potential for influencing the field. The reader should consider the following facts. As reported by state offices of education throughout the United States, in 1975–76 there were 12,226 persons employed as school psychologists (Meacham & Peckham, 1978). At roughly the same point in time (1976–77), there were 7,450 students enrolled in school psychology training programs and 2,263 graduates (Brown & Linstrom, 1978). The ratio of recent graduates to practitioners is thus quite high. Adding to the potential influence of recent graduates is the fact that the scope of their training typically has been substantially broader than what was available prior to the 1970s (Goh, 1977). In many ways, of course, knowledge is power!

The picture of school psychology emerging from these facts is one of a vital, dynamic field being infused with vast quantities of "new blood" and new ideas. Collectively, this new wave of school psychologists has substantial power to influence their own professional destinies, especially if they work together with more experienced members of the profession toward common goals. If, on the other hand, these new professionals allow themselves to become isolated from their colleagues and fail to participate in the professional networks at their disposal, the zeal and energy of this potentially powerful group will slowly ebb away. Graduate training programs, which produce the new school psychologists who may soon dominate the field, would seem to be working in everyone's best interests if they inculcate in their students knowledge regarding how to organize and facilitate systems-level changes (i.e., process skills) in addition to providing them with the more traditional child-centered bases of knowledge (i.e., content skills).

Perhaps the greatest source of power available to school psychologists is the quality of the services they provide to children, parents, school systems, and others. Unfortunately, unlike landing a man on the moon, building a new wing of a gymnasium, winning a football game, or increasing corporate profits, the benefits provided to society by school psychologists are often amorphous and intangible. The result is that services provided by school psychologists often go unnoticed and/or undervalued. Especially in times of declining budgets, it is imperative that the profession develop effective means for evaluating and documenting the quality of its contributions to the mental and educational health of children. While the issue of evaluation methodologies for school psychologists recently has begun to receive increased attention in the professional literature (e.g., Hoover, Maher, & Phillips, 1978; Maher, 1979, 1981; Payne, 1982), it is unclear whether this urgently needed set of skills has been acquired by the majority of practitioners. Rather than viewing the evaluation of school psychological services as a tedious or threatening task that is only peripherally related to school psychologists' main mission of serving children, we would argue that self-evaluation is an exciting avenue of professional growth and a major vehicle with which to establish and enhance our credibility in the eyes of parents, administrators, teachers, and other special service personnel. Ultimately, of course, it is precisely these and other similar adults whom school psychologists must influence if they are to serve children effectively.

Finally, as has been implied at each point of the discussion regarding sources of power, the bottom line in each and every instance will always be the individual school psychologist. Formal organizations, systems of evaluation, and the like, are only as good as the persons who stand behind them. If each practitioner has the initiative, resolve, and sophistication to move the profession forward, progress is inevitable. Unfortunately, inertia and the path of least resistance may prove to be more attractive for many. The track record of the profession in this regard has often left much to be desired. Too frequently we find school psychologists letting administrators, special educators, and legislators dictate both the general and specific nature of school psychological services, often overriding the better judgment of school psychologists themselves.

If those associated with school psychology wish to be accorded the status and privileges of a profession, it is incumbent on each individual school psychologist to behave in a manner that is consistent with this designation. While school psychology clearly possesses many of the requisite characteristics for a profession (e.g., there is an advanced body of knowledge held uniquely by persons in the field, there are ethical codes regulating practice), it has, in many instances, yet to attain a desired level of professional autonomy and control over its own daily practice, the hallmark of most professional groups. Power is the solution to this problem. The burden and challenge of amassing and exercising this power in an appropriate manner is one which we believe falls to each and every school psychologist.

CONCLUSION

It is difficult, if not impossible, to summarize the field of school psychology and the issues facing it in the few paragraphs that remain. As was true at prior points in the profession's history, it remains a field that has yet to stabilize along a variety of dimensions. From this instability may arise either chaos or a new order. Bardon (1976) postulates that the future of school psychology will serve as a bellwether for all applied fields of psychology as it attempts to walk the tightrope of pressures internal and external to the profession.

Much of the creative tension within school psychology arises from the potential breadth of the profession. Incorporating elements of educational, clinical, counseling, industrial/organizational, developmental, social, and community psychologies, the field has become an area fertile with tremendous potential for integration and growth. At times the profession appears to be verging on a new paradigm, combining each of these disciplines into a unique synthesis. At other moments, the field seems to be moving in multiple divergent and contradictory directions.

This chapter, and in many ways the entire book, was intended to give the reader a grasp of the historical, contemporary, and future ebb and flow of school psychology. Many serious content and process issues confront its practitioners and trainers, but it is precisely this complexity and potential for progress that intrigue those associated with it. School psychologists can be seminal individuals affecting the education and mental health of our nation's children. Few callings of a nobler nature would seem to exist.

References

Abeles, N. Psychodynamic theory. In H. M. Burks, Jr. and B. Steffke (Eds.), *Theories of counseling* (3rd ed.). New York: McGraw-Hill, 1979.

Abidin, R. R., Jr. A psychosocial look at consultation and behavior modification. *Psychology in the Schools,* 1972, *9,* 358–364.

Abidin, R. R., Jr. Operant behavioral consultations as conducted by master's and doctoral level psychologists in Virginia. *Journal of School Psychology,* 1977, *15,* 225–229.

Abramowitz, E. A. School psychology: A historical perspective. *School Psychology Review,* 1981, *10,* 121–126.

Achenbach, T. M. *Developmental psychopathology.* New York: The Ronald Press, 1974.

Achenbach, T. M. *Research is developmental psychology: Concepts, strategies, and issues.* New York: Free Press, 1978.

Achenbach, T. M. A junior MMPI? *Journal of Personality Assessment,* 1981, *45,* 332–333.

Achenbach, T. M., & Edelbrock, C. S. The classification of child psychopathology: A review and analysis of research efforts. *Psychological Bulletin,* 1978, *85,* 1275–1301.

Adelman, H. S. Diagnostic classification of learning problems: Some data. *American Journal of Orthopsychiatry,* 1978, *9,* 358–364.

Albee, G. W. Conceptual models and manpower requirements in psychology. *American Psychologist,* 1968, *23,* 317–320.

Algozzine, B., Ysseldyke, J., & Christenson, S. *The influence of teachers' tolerances for specific kinds of behaviors on their ratings of a third-grade student* (Research Report No. 74). Minneapolis: University of Minnesota, Institute for Research on Learning Disabilities, 1982.

Algozzine, B., Ysseldyke, J., Christenson, S., & Thurlow, M. *Teachers' intervention choices for children exhibiting different behaviors in school.* Minneapolis: University of Minnesota, Institute for Research on Learning Disabilities, 1982.

Allen, G. J., Chinsky, J. M., Larcen, S. W., Lochman, J. E., & Selinger, H. V. *Community psychology and the schools: A behaviorally oriented multilevel preventive approach.* Hillsdale, N.J.: Lawrence Erlbaum, 1976.

Allessi, G. J. Behavioral observation for the school psychologist: Responsive-discrepancy model. *School Psychology Review,* 1980, *9,* 31–45.

Alper, T. G., & Kranzler, G. D. A comparison of the effectiveness of behavioral and client-centered approaches for behavior problems of elementary school children. *Elementary School Guidance and Counseling,* 1970, *5,* 35–43.

Alpert, J. L. Conceptual bases of mental health consultation in the schools. *Professional Psychology,* 1976, *7,* 619–626.

Alpert, J. L. Some guidelines for school consultants. *Journal of School Psychology,* 1977, *15,* 308–319.

Alpert, J. L. Synthesis at Olympia Conference. *School Psychology Review,* 1982, *11,* 189–191.

Alpert, J. L., Ballentyne, D., & Griffiths, D. Characteristics of consultants and consultees and success in mental health consultation. *Journal of School Psychology,* 1981, *19,* 312–322.

Alpert, J. L., Ludwig, L. M., & Weiner, L. Selection of consultees in school mental health consultation. *Journal of School Psychology,* 1979, *17,* 59–66.

Alpert, J. L., & Trachtman, G. M. *School psychological consultation in the eighties.* Paper presented at the annual meeting of the National Association of School Psychologists, New York, March, 1978.

Alpert, J. L., Weiner, L. B., & Ludwig, L. M. Evaluation of outcome in school consultation. *Journal of School Psychology,* 1979, *17,* 333–338.

American Psychiatric Association. *Diagnostic and statistical manual of mental disorders.* Washington, D.C.: Author, 1952.

American Psychiatric Association, *Diagnostic and statistical manual of mental disorders* (2nd ed.). Washington, D.C.: Author, 1968.

American Psychiatric Association. *Diagnostic and statistical manual of mental disorders* (3rd ed.). Washington, D.C.: Author, 1980.

American Psychological Association. *Ethical principles in the conduct of research with human participants.* Washington, D.C.: Author, 1973.

American Psychological Association. *Standards for educational and psychological tests.* Washington, D.C.: Author, 1974.

American Psychological Association. *Standards for providers of psychological services.* Washington, D.C.: Author, 1977.

American Psychological Association. Specialty guidelines for the delivery of services by school psychologists. *American Psychologist,* 1981, *36,* 670–681.

Anastasi, A. *Psychological testing.* New York: Macmillan, 1957.

Anastasi, A. *Psychological testing* (4th Ed.). New York: Macmillan, 1976.

Anderson, C. S. The search for school climate: A review of the research. *Review of Educational Research,* 1982, *52,* 368–420.

Anderson, L. W. *Assessing affective characteristics in the schools.* Boston: Allyn & Bacon, 1981.

Anderson, T. A., Cancelli, A. A., & Kratochwill, T. R. *School Psychologists self-reported assessment views and practices.* Tucson: The University of Arizona. Manuscript submitted for publication, 1979.

Angoff, W. H. Scales, norms, and equivalent scores. In R. L. Thorndike (Ed.), *Educational Measurement.* Washington, D.C.: American Council on Education, 1971.

Arter, J. A., & Jenkins, J. R. Examining the benefits and prevalence of modality considerations in special education. *Journal of Special Education,* 1977, *11,* 281–298.

Arter, J. A., & Jenkins, J. R. Differential diagnosis—Prescriptive teaching: A critical appraisal. *Review of Educational Research,* 1979, *49,* 517–555.

Atkeson, B. M., & Forehand, R. Home-based reinforcement programs designed to modify classroom behavior: A review and methodological evaluation. *Psychological Bulletin,* 1979, *86,* 1298–1308.

Axline, V. *Play therapy.* New York: Ballantine Books, 1978.

Ayllon, T., & Azrin, N. H. *The token economy: A motivational system for therapy and rehabilitation.* New York: Appleton-Century-Crofts, 1968.

Ayllon, T., Garber, S., & Pisor, K. The elimination of discipline problems through a combined school-home motivational system. *Behavior Therapy,* 1975, *6,* 616–626.

Ayllon, T., & Roberts, M. D. Eliminating discipline problems by strengthening academic performance. *Journal of Applied Behavior Analysis,* 1974, *7,* 71–76.

Baer, D. M., & Bushell, D. The future of behavior analysis in the schools? Consider its recent past, and then ask a different question. *School Psychology Review,* 1981, *10,* 259–270.

Baer, D. M., Wolf, M. M., & Risley, T. R. Some current dimensions of applied behavior analysis. *Journal of Applied Behavior Analysis,* 1968, *1,* 91–97.

Bailey, J. S., Wolf, M. M., & Phillips, E. L. Home-based reinforcement and the modification of pre-delinquents' classroom behavior. *Journal of Applied Behavior Analysis,* 1970, *3,* 223–233.

Baker, H. L. Psychological services: From the school staff's point of view. *Journal of School Psychology,* 1965, *3,* 36–42.

Balow, B. Definitional and prevalence problems in behavior disorders of children. *School Psychology Review,* 1979, *8,* 348–354.

Bandura, A. Behavior theory and the models of man. *American Psychologist,* 1974, *29,* 859–869.

Bandura, A. Self-efficacy: Toward a unifying theory of behavioral change. *Psychological Review,* 1977, *84,* 191–215.

Bandura, A. The self-system in reciprocal determinism. *American Psychologist,* 1978, *33,* 344–358.

Barbanel, L. Short-term dynamic therapies with children. In C. R. Reynolds & T. B. Gutkin (Eds.), *The handbook of school psychology.* New York: Wiley, 1982.

Barbanel, L., & Hoffenberg-Rutman, J. Attitudes toward job responsibilities and training satisfaction of school psychologists: A comparative study. *Psychology in the Schools,* 1974, *11,* 424–429.

Barclay, J. R. Descriptive, theoretical and behavioral characteristics of subdoctoral school psychologists. *American Psychologist,* 1971, *26,* 257–280.

Bardon, J. I. (Ed.). Problems and issues in school psychology—1964; proceedings of a conference on "new directions in school psychology" sponsored by the National Institute of Mental Health. *Journal of School Psychology,* 1964–1965, *3,* 1–44.

Bardon, J. I. Overview of issue: Implications of the future of school psychology. *Journal of School Psychology*, 1972, *10*, 207–209.

Bardon, J. I. The state of the art (and science) of school psychology. *American Psychologist*, 1976, *31*, 785–791.

Bardon, J. I. *The consultee in consultation: Preparation and training*. Paper presented at the annual meeting of the American Psychological Association, San Francisco, August, 1977.

Bardon, J. I. Educational development as school psychology. *Professional Psychology*, 1979, *10*, 224–233.

Bardon, J. I. School psychology's dilemma: A proposal for its resolution. *Professional Psychology*, 1982, *13*, 955–968.

Bardon, J. I., & Bennett, V. C. *School Psychology*. Englewood Cliffs, N.J.: Prentice-Hall, 1974.

Bardon, J. I., & Wenger, R. D. Institutions offering graduate training in school psychology: 1973–1974. *Journal of School Psychology*, 1974, *12*, 70–83.

Bardon, J. I., & Wenger, R. D. School psychology training trends in the early 1970's. *Professional Psychology*, 1976, *7*, 31–37.

Barker, H. L. Psychological services: From the school staff's point of view. *Journal of School Psychology*, 1965, *3*, 36–42.

Barker, L. F. The first ten years of the National Committee for Mental Health, with some comments on the future. *Mental Hygiene*, 1918, *2*, 557–581.

Barker, R. G. Explorations in ecological psychology. *American Psychologist*, 1965, *20*, 1–14.

Barker, R. G. *Ecological psychology*. Stanford, Calif.: Stanford University Press, 1968.

Barker, R. G., & Associates. *Habitats, environments, and human behavior*. San Francisco: Jossey-Bass, 1978.

Barrios, B. A., Hartmann, D. P., & Shigetomi, C. Fears and anxieties in children. In E. J. Marsh & L. G. Terdal (Eds.), *Behavioral assessment of childhood disorders*. New York: Guilford Press, 1981.

Barrish, H. H., Sanders, M., & Wolf, M. M. Good behavior game: Effects of individual contingencies for group consequences on disruptive behavior. *Journal of Applied Behavior Analysis*, 1969, *2*, 119–124.

Barry, E. J. *Cultural retardation or shortcomings of assessment techniques*. Selected convention papers, 47th Annual International Convention of the Council for Exceptional Children, 1969, 35–43.

Barry, J. R. Criteria in the evaluation of consultation. *Professional Psychology*, 1970, *1*, 363–366.

Bar-Tal, D., & Bar-Zoher, Y. The relationship between perception of locus of control and academic achievement. *Contemporary Educational Psychology*, 1977, *2*, 181–199.

Baum, C. G., Forehand, R., & Zegiob, L. E. A review of observer reactivity in adult-child interactions. *Journal of Behavioral Assessment*, 1979, *1*, 167–178.

Bechtel, R. B. The study of man: Human movement and architecture. *Transaction*, 1967, *4*, 53–56.

Beckerman, T. M., & Good, T. L. The classroom ratio of high- and low-aptitude students and its effect on achievement. *American Educational Research Journal*, 1981, *18*, 317–327.

Beers, C. W. *A mind that found itself.* New York: Longmans, 1908.

Beisser, A. R., & Green, R. *Mental health consultation and education.* Palo Alto, Calif.: National Press Books, 1972.

Beitchman, J. H., Deilman, T. E., Landis, J. R., Benson, R. M., & Kemp, P. L. Reliability of the Group for the Advancement of Psychiatry diagnostic categories in child psychiatry. *Archives of General Psychiatry,* 1978, *35,* 1461–1466.

Bellack, A. S., & Hersen, M. *Behavior modification: An introductory textbook.* Baltimore, Md.: Williams and Wilkins, 1977.

Bennett, R. E. Methods for evaluating the performance of school psychologists. *School Psychology Monographs,* 1980, *4,* 45–59.

Bennett, V. C. Who is a school psychologist and what does he do? *Journal of School Psychology,* 1970, *8,* 166–171.

Bergan, J. R. *Behavioral consultation.* Columbus, Ohio: Charles E. Merrill, 1977.

Bergan, J. R. Path-referenced assessment in school psychology. In T. R. Kratochwill (Ed.), *Advances in school psychology* (Vol. 1). Hillsdale, N.J.: Lawrence Erlbaum, 1981.

Bergan, J. R., Byrnes, I. M., & Kratochwill, T. R. Effects of behavioral and medical models of consultation on teacher expectancies and instruction of a hypothetical child. *Journal of School Psychology,* 1979, *17,* 306–316.

Bergan, J. R., & Neumann, A. J. II. The identification of resources and constraints influencing plan design in consultation. *Journal of School Psychology,* 1980, *18,* 317–323.

Bergan, J. R., & Tombari, M. L. The analysis of verbal interactions occurring during consultation. *Journal of School Psychology,* 1975, *13,* 209–226.

Bergan, J. R., & Tombari, M. L. Consultant skill and efficiency and the implementation and outcomes of consultation. *Journal of School Psychology,* 1976, *14,* 3–14.

Berk, R. A. (Ed.). *Handbook of methods for detecting test bias.* Baltimore, Md.: Johns Hopkins University Press, 1982.

Berkowitz, I. H. (Ed.). *When schools care: Creative use of groups in secondary schools.* New York: Bruner/Mazel, 1975.

Berliner, D. C., & Cahen, L. S. Trait-treatment interactions and learning. In F. N. Kerlinger (Ed.), *Review of research in education.* Itasca, Ill.: Peacock Publishers, 1973.

Bersoff, D. N. Silk purses into sow's ears: The decline of psychological testing and a suggestion for its redemption. *American Psychologist,* 1973, *28,* 892–899.

Bersoff, D. N. Professional ethics and legal responsibilities: On the horns of the dilemma. *Journal of School Psychology,* 1975, *13,* 359–376.

Bersoff, D. N. *Larry P.* v. *Riles:* Legal perspective. *School Psychology Review,* 1980, *9,* 112–122.

Bersoff, D. N. The legal regulation of school psychology. In C. R. Reynolds & T. B. Gutkin (Eds.), *The handbook of school psychology.* New York: Wiley, 1982.

Bersoff, D. N. Social and legal influences on test development and usage. In B. Plake (Ed.), *Buros—Nebraska Symposium on Measurement and Testing* (Vol. 1). Hillsdale, N.J.: Lawrence Erlbaum, 1984.

Black, B. J. The teams gallop through the catchment areas. *Hospital and Community Psychology,* 1977, *28,* 917–918.

Blackhurst, A. E., & Berdline, W. H. *An introduction to special education*. Boston: Little, Brown, 1981.

Blackwell v. Issaquena County School Board of Education, 363 F. 2d 749 (1966).

Block, A. H. Personal communication, 1975.

Boruch, R. F., & Gomez, H. Sensitivity, bias, and theory in impact evaluation. *Professional Psychology*, 1977, *8*, 411–434.

Bossard, M. D., & Gutkin, T. B. The relationship of consultant skill and school organizational characteristics with teacher use of school-based consultation services. *School Psychology Review*, 1983, *12*, 50–56.

Bower, E. M. Reactions to the conference. *Journal of School Psychology*, 1965, *3*, 36–39.

Bower, E. M. Mental health. In R. Ebel (Ed.), *Encyclopedia of educational research* (4th ed.). New York: Macmillan, 1970.

Bowers, D. G. OD techniques and their results in 23 organizations: The Michigan ICL study. *Journal of Applied Behavioral Sciences*, 1973, *9*, 21–43.

Bowers, N. E. Some guidelines for the school psychologist in his attempts to intimidate the teacher during a conference. *Journal of School Psychology*, 1971, *9*, 357–361.

Brantley, J. C. Training programs in school psychology. *The School Psychology Digest*, 1977, *6*, 16–33.

Brantley, J. G., Reilly, D. H., Beach, N. L., Cody, W., Fields, R., & Lee, H. School psychology: The intersection of community, training institution and the school system. *Psychology in the Schools*, 1974, *11*, 28–31.

Brickman, L., & Zarantonello, M. The effects of deception and obedience on subjects' ratings of the Milgram study. *Personality and Social Psychology Bulletin*, 1978, *4*, 81–85.

Brophy, J., & Good, T. Brophy-Good system (Teacher-Child Dyadic Interaction). In A. Simon & E. G. Boyer (Eds.), *Mirrors for behavior*. Philadelphia: Research for Better Schools, 1974.

Broskowski, A. Concepts of teacher-centered consultation. *Professional Psychology*, 1973, *4*, 50–58.

Brown, D. T. Issues in the development of professional school psychology. In C. R. Reynolds & T. B. Gutkin (Eds.), *The handbook of school psychology*. New York: Wiley, 1982.

Brown, D. T., & Cardon, B. *Report of the joint NASP/APA task force on accreditation in school psychology*. Washington, D.C.: National Association of School Psychologists and American Psychological Association, November, 1979.

Brown, D. T., Cardon, B. W., Coulter, W. A., & Meyers, J. (Eds.), The Olympia proceedings. *School Psychology Review*, 1982, *9*(2).

Brown, D. T., & Hanson, D. *A historical analysis of school psychology*. James Madison University, unpublished manuscript, 1979.

Brown, D. T., & Horn, A. *Handbook of certification/licensure requirements for school psychologists* (3rd ed.). Washington, D.C.: National Association of School Psychologists, 1980.

Brown, D. T., & Lindstrom, J. P. The training of school psychologists in the United States: An overview. *Psychology in the Schools*, 1978, *15*, 37–45.

Brown, J. H., & Kelly, W. F. A conceptual model for home-school consultation. *Correc-*

tive and Social Psychiatry and Journal of Behavior Technology Methods and Therapy, 1976, *22,* 15–20.

Buktenica, N. A multidisciplinary training team in the public school. *Journal of School Psychology,* 1970, *8,* 220–225.

Brown v. *Board of Education,* 347 U.S. 438 (1954).

Buktenica, N. Special education and school psychology: Whither the relationship. *School Psychology Review,* 1980, *9,* 228–233.

Burgental, D. B., Whalen, C. K., & Henker, B. Causal attributions of hyperactive children and motivational assumptions of two behavior change approaches: Evidence for an interactionist position. *Child Development,* 1977, *48,* 874–884.

Burgess, R. L., & Conger, R. D. Family interaction in abusive, neglectful, and normal families. *Child Development,* 1978, *49,* 1163–1173.

Burke, J. P., & DeMers, S. T. A paradigm for evaluating assessment interviewing techniques. *Psychology in the Schools,* 1979, *16,* 51–60.

Buros, O. K. (Ed.). *The eighth mental measurements yearbook.* Highland Park, N.J.: The Gryphon Press, 1978.

Butcher, J. N., & Koss, M. P. Research on brief and crisis-oriented therapies. In S. L. Garfield & A. E. Bergin (Eds.), *Handbook of psychotherapy and behavior change* (2nd ed.). New York: Wiley, 1978.

Campbell, D. T., & Stanley, J. C. Experimental and quasi-experimental designs for research on teaching. In N. L. Gage (Ed.), *Handbook of research on teaching.* Chicago: Rand McNally, 1963.

Canfield, A. A., & Starr, D. D. *The Lake St. Clair Incident.* Ann Arbor, Mich.: Humanics Medra, 1978.

Caplan, G. *Principles of preventive psychiatry.* New York: Basic Books, 1964.

Caplan, G. *The theory and practice of mental health consultation.* New York: Basic Books, 1970.

Caplan, G. Types of mental health consultation. *American Journal of Orthopsychiatry,* 1963, *33,* 470–481.

Cardon, B. W., & Brown, D. T. *Report on the joint NASP/APA task force on accreditation in school psychology.* Washington, D.C.: National Association of School Psychologists and American Psychological Association, July, 1979.

Carey v. *Population Service Int'l Inc.,* 431 U.S. 678 (1977).

Carkhuff, R. R. *The art of problem-solving.* Amherst, Mass.: Human Resource Development Press, 1973.

Carlson, C. I., Scott, M., & Eklund, S. J. Ecological theory and method for behavioral assessment. *School Psychology Review,* 1980, *9,* 75–82.

Carter, B. D. School mental health consultation: A clinical social work interventive technique. *Clinical Social Work Journal,* 1975, *3,* 201–210.

Cartwright, G. P., Cartwright, C. A., & Ward, M. E. *Educating special learners.* Belmont, Calif.: Wadsworth, 1981.

Carver, F. D., & Sergiovanni, T. J. (Eds.), *Organizations and human behavior: Focus on schools.* New York: McGraw-Hill, 1969.

Catterall, C. D. Special education in transition—implications for school psychology. *Journal of School Psychology,* 1972, *10,* 91–98.

Centra, J. A., & Potter, D. A. School and teacher effects: An interrelational model. *Review of Educational Research,* 1980, *50,* 273–291.

Chambers, J. A., Barron, F., & Sprecher, J. W. Identifying gifted Mexican-American students. *Gifted Child Quarterly,* 1980, *24,* 123–128.

Chapman, H. B. *Organized research in education with special reference to the Bureau of Educational Research* (Bureau of Educational Research Monograph No. 7). Columbus, Ohio: State University Press, 1927.

Christenson, S., Algozzine, B., & Ysseldyke, J. E. *Probabilities associated with the referral-to-placement process* (Research report No. 60). Minneapolis: University of Minnesota, Institute for Research on Learning Disabilities, 1981.

Ciminero, A. R., Calhoun, K. S., & Adams, H. E. *Handbook of behavioral assessment.* New York: Wiley, 1977.

Ciminero, A. R., & Drabman, R. S. Current developments in the behavioral assessment of children. In B. B. Lahey & A. E. Kazdin (Eds.), *Advances in clinical child psychology* (Vol. 1). New York: Plenum, 1977.

Claiborn, C. D., & Strong, S. R. Group counseling in the schools. In C. R. Reynolds & T. B. Gutkin (Eds.), *The handbook of school psychology.* New York: Wiley, 1982.

Clair, T., & Kiraly, J. Accountability for the school psychologist. *Psychology in the Schools,* 1971, *8,* 318–321.

Clarizio, H. F. Primary prevention of behavioral disorders in the schools. *School Psychology Digest,* 1979, *8,* 434–445. (a)

Clarizio, H. F. School psychologists and the mental health needs of students. In G. D. Phye and D. J. Reschly (Eds.), *School psychology: Perspectives and issues.* New York: Academic Press, 1979. (b)

Clarizio, H. F., & McCoy, G. F. *Behavior disorders in children.* New York: Thomas Y. Crowell, 1976.

Clark, J. H., & Gutkin, T. B. *Perceptions of control and preferences for consultation: An experimental analysis.* Paper presented at the annual meeting of the American Psychological Association, Washington, D.C., 1982.

Clark, J. H., & Reynolds, C. R. *Research trends in school psychology: 1974–1980.* Paper presented to the annual meeting of the American Psychological Association, Los Angeles, August 1981.

Cleary, T. A., Humphreys, L. G., Kendrick, S. A., & Wesman, A. Educational uses of tests with disadvantaged students. *American Psychologist,* 1975, *30,* 15–41.

Clement, P., & Milne, D. C. Group play therapy and tangible reinforcers used to modify the behavior of 8-year-old boys. *Behavior Research and Therapy,* 1967, *5,* 301–312.

Coffman, D. A., Slaikeu, K. A., & Iscoe, I. An approach to cost accounting and cost-effectiveness in the delivery of campus mental health services. *Professional Psychology,* 1979, *10,* 656–665.

Coleman, R. G. A procedure for fading from experimenter-school-based to parent-home-based control of classroom behavior. *Journal of School Psychology,* 1973, *11,* 71–79.

Colligan, R. C., & McColgan, E. B. Perception of case conduct as a means of evaluating school psychological services. *Professional Psychology,* 1980, *11,* 291–297.

Comtois, R. J., & Clark, W. D. A framework for scientific practice and practitioner training. *JSAS Catalog of Selected Documents in Psychology*, 1977, *6*, 74–75 (Ms. No. 1301).

Condas, J. Personal reflections on the Larry P. trial and its aftermath. *School Psychology Review*, 1980, *9*, 154–158.

Cone, J. D. The relevance of reliability and validity for behavioral assessment. *Behavior Therapy*, 1977, *8*, 411–426.

Cone, J. D. The behavioral assessment grid (BAG): A conceptual framework and a taxonomy. *Behavior Therapy*, 1978, *9*, 882–888.

Conger, R. D. The assessment of dysfunctional family systems. In B. B. Lahey & A. E. Kazdin (Eds.), *Advances in clinical child psychology* (Vol. 4). New York: Plenum, 1981.

Connis, R. T. The effects of sequential pictorial cues, self-recording, and praise on the job task analysis of retarded adults. *Journal of Applied Behavior Analysis*, 1979, *12*, 355–362.

Conoley, J. C. (Ed.). *Consultation in schools: Theory, research, technology.* New York: Academic Press, 1980.

Conti, A., & Bardon, J. I. A proposal for evaluating the effectiveness of psychologists in the schools. *Psychology in the Schools*, 1974, *11*, 32–39.

Cook, V. J., & Patterson, J. G. Psychologists in the schools of Nebraska: Professional functions. *Psychology in the Schools*, 1977, *14*, 371–376.

Cornell, E. L. The psychologist in a school system. *Journal of Consulting Psychology*, 1942, *6*, 185–195.

Council for Exceptional Children. Minorities position policy statements. *Exceptional Children*, 1978, *45*, 57–64.

Cowen, E. L. Baby-steps toward primary prevention. *American Journal of Community Psychology*, 1977, *5*, 1–22.

Cowen, E. L., & Gesten, E. L. Community approaches to intervention. In B. B. Wolman, J. Egan, & A. O. Ross (Eds.), *Handbook of treatment of mental disorders in childhood and adolescence.* Englewood Cliffs, N.J.: Prentice-Hall, 1978.

Cowen, E. L., & Lorion, R. P. Changing roles for the school mental health professional. *Journal of School Psychology*, 1976, *14*, 131–138.

Cowen, E. L., Trost, M. A., Lorion, R. P., Dorr, D., Izzo, L. D., & Isaacson, R. *New ways in school mental health: Early detection and prevention of school maladaption.* New York: Human Sciences Press, 1975.

Critchley, D. L. The adverse influence of psychiatric diagnostic labels on the observation of child behavior. *Journal of Orthopsychiatry*, 1979, *49*, 157–160.

Cronbach, L. J. Coefficient alpha and the internal structure of tests. *Psychometrika*, 1951, *16*, 297–334.

Cronbach, L. J. The two disciplines of scientific psychology. *American Psychologist*, 1957, *12*, 671–684.

Cronbach, L. J. *Essentials of psychological testing* (3rd Ed.). New York: Harper & Row, 1970.

Cronbach, L. J. Test validation. In R. L. Thorndike (Ed.), *Educational Measurement* (2nd Ed.). Washington, D.C.: American Council on Education, 1971.

Cronbach, L. J., & Snow, R. E. *Aptitude and instructional methods: A handbook of research on interactions.* New York: Irvington, 1977.

Curtis, M. J., & Anderson, T. E. *Consulting in educational settings: A collaborative approach.* (slide/tape). Cincinnati: Faculty Resource Center, Univ. of Cincinnati, 1976.

Curtis, M. J., & Anderson, T. E. *Consulting in educational settings: Demonstrating collaborative techniques* (videotape). Cincinnati, Ohio: Faculty Resource Center, University of Cincinnati, 1977.

Curtis, M. J., & Watson, K. Changes in consultee problem clarification skills following consultation. *Journal of School Psychology,* 1980, *18,* 210–221.

Curtis, M. J., & Zins, J. E. Consultative effectiveness as perceived by experts in consultation and classroom teachers. In M. J. Curtis & J. E. Zins (Eds.), *The theory and practice of school consultation.* Springfield, Ill.: Charles C Thomas, 1981.

Cutts, N. E. (Ed.). *School psychologists at mid-century.* Washington, D.C.: American Psychological Association, 1955.

Dansinger, J. A five-year follow-up study of Minnesota school psychologists. *Journal of School Psychology,* 1969, *7,* 47–53.

Das, J. P., Kirby, J. R., & Jarman, R. F. *Simultaneous and successive cognitive processes.* New York: Academic Press, 1979.

Deffenbaugh, W. S. *Research bureaus in city school systems.* Washington, D.C.: Government Printing Office, 1922.

Dembinski, R. J., Schultz, E. W., & Walton, W. T. Curriculum intervention with the emotionally disturbed student: A psychoeducational perspective. In R. L. McDowell, G. W. Adamson, & F. H. Woods (Eds.), *Teaching emotionally disturbed children.* Boston: Little, Brown, 1982.

Deno, S. A consulting problem in which student behavior change is the focus. In C. A. Parker (Ed.), *Psychological consultation: Helping teachers meet special needs.* Reston, Va.: Council for Exceptional Children, 1975.

Department of Health, Education and Welfare. Implementation of Part B of the Education of the Handicapped Act. *Federal Register,* 1977, *42,* 42474–42517.

Dewey, J., & Bentley, A. F. *Knowing and the known.* Boston, Mass.: Beacon Press, 1949.

Dinkmeyer, D. J., & Carlson, J. *Consulting: Facilitating human potential and change processes.* Columbus, Ohio: Charles E. Merrill, 1973.

Dinkmeyer, D. J., & Dinkmeyer, D., Jr. Contributions of Adlerian psychology to school consulting. *Psychology in the Schools,* 1976, *13,* 32–38.

Doll, E. A. The divisional structure of APA. *American Psychologist,* 1946, *1,* 336–345.

Dorr, D. Some practical suggestions on behavioral consulting with teachers. *Professional Psychology,* 1977, *8,* 95–102.

D'Zurilla, T. J., & Goldfried, M. R. Problem solving and behavior modification. *Journal of Abnormal and Social Psychology,* 1971, *78,* 107–126.

Eaves, R. C., & McLaughlin, P. A systems approach for the assessment of the child and his environment: Getting back to basics. *Journal of Special Education.* 1977, *11,* 99–111.

Ebel, R. L. *Essentials of educational measurement.* Englewood Cliffs, N.J.: Prentice-Hall, 1972.

Ebert, D. W., Dain, R. N., Phillips, B. N. An attempt at implementing the diagnosis-intervention class model. *Journal of School Psychology,* 1970, *8,* 191–196.

Edelbrock, C. Empirical classification of children's behavior disorders: Progress based on parent and teacher ratings. *School Psychology Digest,* 1979, *8,* 355–369.

Edelbrock, C. Reading and evaluating research in childhood exceptionality. In R. T. Brown & C. R. Reynolds (Eds.), *Psychological Perspectives on Childhood Exceptionality.* New York: Wiley-Interscience, in press.

Eisenberg, L. School phobia: A study in the communication of anxiety. In E. P. Trapp & P. Himelstein, *Readings on the exceptional child.* New York: Appleton-Century-Crofts, 1972.

Eiserer, E. *The school psychologist.* New York: Center for Applied Research in Education, 1963.

Elkin, V. B. Structuring school psychological services: Internal and interdisciplinary considerations. In M. G. Gottsegen & G. B. Gottsegen (Eds.), *Professional school psychology.* New York: Grune & Stratton, Inc., 1963.

Elliott, S. N., & Gutkin, T. B. The interface between psychology and education: Services and treatments for exceptional children. In R. T. Brown & C. R. Reynolds (Eds.), *Psychological perspectives on childhood exceptionality.* New York: Wiley-Interscience, in press.

Elliott, S. N., & Piersel, W. C. Direct assessment of reading skills: An approach which links assessment to intervention. *School Psychology Review,* 1982, *11,* 267–280.

Elliott, S. N., Piersel, W. C., & Galvin, G. Psychological reevaluations: A survey of practices and perceptions of school psychologists. *Journal of School Psychology,* in press.

Elliott, S. N., & Witt, J. C. *Assessment of children's learning and behavior problems.* Boston: Little, Brown, in press.

Elliott, S. N., & Witt, J. C. *In-service training: An indirect educational intervention for children, continuing education for educators, and consultative role for school psychologists.* University of Nebraska-Lincoln, unpublished manuscript, 1981.

Emmer, E. T., & Evertson, C. M. Synthesis of research on classroom management. *Focus on Behaviorally Impaired,* 1982, *2,* 7–12.

English, R. W., & Higgens, T. E. Client-centered group counseling with pre-adolescents. *Journal of School Health,* 1971, *41,* 507–509.

Epps, S., McGue, M., & Ysseldyke, J. E. Interjudge agreement in classifying students as learning disabled. *Psychology in the Schools,* 1982, *19,* 209–220.

Erickson, K. P. A comment on disguised observation in sociology. *Social Problems,* 1967, *14,* 366–373.

Exner, J. E. Projective techniques. In I. B. Weiner (Ed.), *Clinical methods in psychology.* New York: Wiley-Interscience, 1976.

Eysenck, H. J. *The psychophysiology of intelligence.* Invited address to the annual meeting of the American Psychological Association, Montreal, August, 1980.

Fairchild, T. N. An analysis of the services performed by a school psychologist in an urban area: Implications for training programs. *Psychology in the Schools,* 1974, *11,* 275–281.

Fairchild, T. N. Accountability: Practical suggestions for school psychologists. *Journal of School Psychology,* 1975, *13,* 149–159.

Fairchild, T. N. School psychological services: An empirical comparison of two models. *Psychology in the Schools,* 1976, *13,* 156–162.

Fairweather, G. W., Sanders, D. H., & Tornatzky, L. G. *Creating change in mental health organizations.* New York: Pergammon, 1974.

Falik, L., Grimm, M., Preston, F., & Konno, T. Evaluating the impact of the counseling-learning team on the elementary school. *School Counselor,* 1971, *19,* 25–37.

Farling, W. H., & Agner, J. History of the National Association of School Psychologists: The first decade. *School Psychology Digest,* 1979, *8,* 140–152.

Farling, W. H., & Hoedt, K. C. *National, regional and state survey of school psychologists.* Washington, D.C.: U.S. Department of Health, Education and Welfare, 1971.

Federal Register. *Regulations implementing Education for All Handicapped Children Act of 1975 (Public Law 94-142).* Author, August 23, 1977, *42,* pp. 42474–42518.

Fein, L. G. *The changing school scene: Challenge to psychology.* New York: Wiley, 1974.

Feldman, R. E. Collaborative consultation: A process for joint professional consumer development of primary prevention programs. *Journal of Community Psychology,* 1979, *7,* 118–128.

Felton, G., & Bar-Zoher, Y. The relationship between perception of locus of control and academic achievement. *Contemporary Educational Psychology,* 1977, *2,* 181–199.

Felton, G., & Biggs, B. Psychotherapy and responsibility: Teaching internalization behavior to black low achievers through group therapy. *Small Group Behavior,* 1973, *4,* 147–155.

Felton, G., & Biggs, B. Teaching internalization behavior to collegiate low achievers in group psychotherapy. *Psychotherapy: Theory, Research and Practice,* 1972, *9,* 181–183.

Fenton, K. S., Yoshida, R. K., Maxwell, J. P., & Kaufman, M. T. Recognition of team goals: An essential step toward rational decision-making. *Exceptional Children,* 1979, *45,* 638–644.

Feuerstein, R. *The dynamic assessment of retarded performers: The learning potential assessment device, theory, instruments, and techniques.* Baltimore, Md.: University Park Press, 1979.

Finch, A. J., & Spirito, A. Use of cognitive training to change cognitive processes. *Exceptional Education Quarterly,* 1981, *1,* 31–39.

Fisher, B. A. *Small group decision-making, communication and the group process.* New York: McGraw-Hill, 1974.

Flaherty, E. W. Evaluation of consultation. In J. J. Pratt & R. J. Wicks (Eds.), *The psychological consultant.* New York: Grune & Stratton, 1979.

Flanders, N. *Interaction analysis in the classroom: A manual for observers* (rev. ed) Ann Arbor, Mich.: University of Michigan, 1966.

Flanders, N. *Analyzing teacher behavior.* Reading, Mass.: Addison-Wesley, 1970.

Ford, J. D., & Migles, M. The role of the school psychologist: Teachers' preferences as a function of personal and professional characteristics. *Journal of School Psychology,* 1979, *17,* 372–378.

Forehand, R., Breiner, J., McMahon, R. J., & Davies, G. Predictors of cross-setting behavior change in the treatment of child problems. *Journal of Clinical Child Psychology,* in press.

Foreyt, J. P., & Rathjen, D. P. (Eds.). *Cognitive behavior therapy: Research and application.* New York: Plenum, 1978.

Foreyt, J. P., Rockwood, C. E., Davis, J. C., Desvousges, W. H., & Hollingsworth, R. Benefit-cost analysis of a token economy program. *Professional Psychology*, 1975, *6*, 26–33.

Forrest v. Ambach, Supreme Court of the State of New York, 7715–80, 1980.

Foster, S. L., & O'Leary, K. D. Teacher attitudes toward educational and psychological services for conduct problem children. *Journal of Abnormal Child Psychology*, 1977, *5*, 101–111.

Fox, R. S., Luszki, M. B., & Schmuck, R. *Diagnosing classroom learning environments*. Chicago: Science Research Associates, 1966.

Fox, R. S., Schmuck, R., Egmond, E. V., Ritvo, M., & Jung, C. *Diagnosing professional climates of schools*. Fairfax, Va.: NTL Learning Resources Corporation, 1973.

Frame, R. E., Clarizio, H. F., Porter, A. C., & Vinsonhaler, J. R. Interclinician agreement and bias in school psychologists' diagnostic and treatment recommendations for a learning disabled child. *Psychology in the Schools*, 1982, *19*, 319–327.

Frampton, M. E., & Gall, E. D. *Special education for the exceptional*. Boston, Mass.: Porter Sargent, 1955.

Friedes, D. Review of the Stanford-Binet intelligence scale, third revision. In O. K. Buros (Ed.), *The seventh mental measurements yearbook*. Highland Park, N.J.: Gryphon Press, 1972.

Fry, M. A., & Lagomarsino, L. Factors that influence reading: A developmental perspective. *School Psychology Review*, 1982, *11*, 239–250.

Fullan, M., Miles, M. B., & Taylor, G. Organization development in schools: The state of the art. *Review of Educational Research*, 1980, *50*, 121–183.

Gallagher, J. J. The special education contract for mildly handicapped children. *Exceptional Children*, 1972, *38*, 527–535.

Gallagher, J. J. Psychology and special education—the future: Where the action is. *Psychology in the Schools*, 1969, *6*, 219–226.

Gallessich, J. Organizational factors influencing consultation in schools. *Journal of School Psychology*, 1973, *11*, 57–65.

Gallessich, J. Training the school psychologist for consultation. *Journal of School Psychology*, 1974, *12*, 138–149.

Gallessich, J., & Davis, J. Consultation: Prospects and retrospects. In J. C. Conoley (Eds.), *Consultation in schools: Theory, research, procedures*. New York: Academic Press, 1981.

Galton, F. *Hereditary genius: An inquiry into its laws and consequences*. New York: D. Appleton & Company, 1869.

Gaupp, P. S. Authority, influence and control in consultation. *Community Mental Health Journal*, 1966, *2*, 205–210.

Gerken, K. C., & Landau, S. Perceived effectiveness of school psychological services: A comparative study. *Journal of School Psychology*, 1979, *17*, 347–354.

Giaconia, R. M., & Hedges, L. V. Identifying features of effective open education. *Review of Educational Research*, 1982, *52*, 579–602.

Gibbins, S. Public Law 94–142: An impetus for consultation. *The School Psychology Digest*, 1978, *7*, 18–25.

Gibson, A. K., & Likert, R. *The profile of a school*. Ann Arbor, Mich.: Rensis Likert Associates, 1978.

Giebeink, J. W., & Ringness, T. A. On the relevancy of training in school psychology. *Journal of School Psychology*, 1970, *8*, 43–47.

Gilliam, J. E. Contributions and status rankings of educational planning committee participants. *Exceptional Children*, 1979, *45*, 466–468.

Gilmore, G. E. Models for school psychology: Dimensions, barriers, and implications. *Journal of School Psychology*, 1974, *12*, 95–101.

Gilmore, G. E., & Chandy, J. Teachers' perceptions for school psychological services. *Journal of School Psychology*, 1973, *11*, 139–147. (a)

Gilmore, G. E., & Chandy, J. Educators describe the school psychologist. *Psychology in the Schools*, 1973, *10*, 397–403. (b)

Glass, G. V., Willson, V. L., & Gottman, J. M. *Design and analysis of time series experiments*. Boulder, Colo.: Associated University Press, 1975.

Goh, D. S. Graduate training in school psychology. *Journal of School Psychology*, 1977, *15*, 207–218.

Goh, D. S., Teslow, C. J., & Fuller, G. B. The practice of psychological assessment among school psychologists. *Professional Psychology*, 1981, *12*, 696–706.

Goldfried, M. R. Behavioral assessment. In I. Weiner (Ed.), *Clinical methods in psychology*. New York: Wiley-Interscience, 1976.

Goldfried, M. R., & Kent, R. N. Traditional versus behavioral assessment: A comparison of methodological and theoretical assumptions. *Psychological Bulletin*, 1972, *77*, 409–420.

Goldman, R., & Cowan, P. Teacher cognitive characteristics, social system variables, and the use of consultation. *American Journal of Community Psychology*, 1976, *4*, 85–98.

Goldstein, S., Strickland, B., Turnbull, A. P., & Curry, L. An observational analysis of the IEP conference. *Exceptional Children*, 1980, *46*, 278–286.

Goldwasser, E., Meyers, J., Christenson, S., & Graden, J. A national survey of the impact of PL 94-142 on the practice of school psychology. *The School Psychologist*, 1981, *35*, 6.

Goodwin, D. L., & Coates, T. J. The Teacher-Pupil Interaction Scale: An empirical method for analyzing the interaction effects of teacher and pupil behavior. *Journal of School Psychology*, 1977, *15*, 51–59.

Goodwin, S. E., & Mahoney, M. J. Modification of aggression through modeling: An experimental probe. *Journal of Behavior Therapy and Experimental Psychiatry*, 1975, *6*, 200–202.

Goss v. Lopez, 419 U.S. 565 (1975).

Gottman, J. M., & Glass, G. V. Analysis of interrupted time-series experiments. In T. R. Kratochwill (Ed.), *Single subject research: Strategies for evaluating change*. New York: Academic Press, 1978.

Gottsegen, M. G., & Gottsegen, G. B. (Eds.). *Professional and school psychology*. New York: Grune & Stratton, 1963.

Gray, S. W. *The psychologist in the schools*. New York: Holt, 1963.

Greenwood, C. R., Hops, H., Walker, H. M., Guild, J. J., Stokes, J., Young, K. R., Keleman, K. S., & Willardson, M. Standardized classroom management program: Social validation and replication studies in Utah and Oregon. *Journal of Applied Behavior Analysis*, 1979, *12*, 235–253.

Grimes, J., & Reschly, D. J. *Standards and competencies for psychological assessment, intervention, and follow-up.* Paper presented to the Nebraska School Psychologists Association, Lincoln, Nebraska, September, 1980.

Gronlund, N. E. *Sociometry in the classroom.* New York: Harper, 1959.

Group for the Advancement of Psychiatry, Committee on Child Psychiatry: Psychopathological disorders in childhood: Theoretical considerations and a proposed classification. *GAP Report No. 62,* June 1966.

Guadalupe Organization v. *Tempe Elementary School District,* E.D. AZ., (1972).

Guidubaldi, J. (Ed.). Families: Current status and emerging trends. *School Psychology Review,* 1980, *9*(4).

Gurman, A. S., & Kniskern, D. P. Research on martial and family therapy: Progress, perspective and prospect. In S. L. Garfield & A. E. Bergin (Eds.), *Handbook of psychotherapy and behavior change.* New York: Wiley, 1978.

Gutkin, T. B. Teacher perceptions of consultative services provided by school psychologists. *Professional Psychology,* 1980, *11,* 637–642.

Gutkin, T. B. Relative frequency of consultee lack of knowledge, skill, confidence, and objectivity in school settings. *Journal of School Psychology,* 1981, *19,* 57–61.

Gutkin, T. B., & Ajchenbaum, M. *Consultee perceptions of control and attitudes towards consultation services.* Paper presented at the annual meeting of the National Association of School Psychologists, Toronto, 1982.

Gutkin, T. B., & Bossard, M. Impact of consultant, consultee, and organizational variables on teacher attitudes towards consultation services. *Journal of School Psychology,* in press.

Gutkin, T. B., & Curtis, M. J. School-based consultation: The indirect service delivery concept. In M. J. Curtis & J. E. Zins (Eds.), *The theory and practice of school consultation.* Springfield, Ill.: Charles C Thomas, 1981.

Gutkin, T. B., & Curtis, M. J. School-based consultation: Theory and techniques. In C. R. Reynolds & T. B. Gutkin (Eds.), *The handbook of school psychology.* New York: Wiley, 1982.

Gutkin, T. B., Singer, J. H., & Brown, R. Teacher reactions to school-based consultation services: A multivariate analysis. *Journal of School Psychology,* 1980, *18,* 126–134.

Gutkin, T. B., & Tieger, A. G. Funding patterns for exceptional children: Current approaches and suggested alternatives. *Professional Psychology,* 1979, *10,* 670–680.

Haase, R. F., & Tepper, D. T. Nonverbal components of empathetic communication. *Journal of Counseling Psychology,* 1972, *19,* 417–424.

Halpin, A. *Theory and research in administration.* New York: Macmillan, 1966.

Halpin, A., & Croft, D. *The organizational climate of schools.* Danville, Ill.: Interstate Printers and Publishers, 1963.

Hammill, D. D. Defining "LD" for programmatic purposes. *Academic Therapy,* 1976, *12,* 29–37.

Hardin, G. The cybernetics of competition: A biologist's view of society. In P. Shepard & D. McKinley (Eds.), *The subversive science: Essays toward an ecology of man.* Boston: Houghton-Mifflin, 1969.

Harper, R., & Balch, P. Some economic arguments in favor of primary prevention. *Professional Psychology,* 1975, *6,* 17–25.

Harris, J. *The evolution of school psychology.* Arizona State University, unpublished manuscript, 1980.

Harris, V. W., & Sherman, J. A. Use and analysis of the "Good Behavior Game" to reduce disruptive classroom behavior. *Journal of Applied Behavior Analysis,* 1973, *6,* 405–417.

Hart, S. Reactions to Olympia: School psychology takes the driver's seat. *School Psychology Review,* 1982, *11,* 186–188.

Hartlage, L. C., & Reynolds, C. R. Neuropsychological assessment and the individualization of instruction. In G. Hynd & J. Obrzut (Eds.), *Neuropsychological assessment and the school age child: Issues and procedures.* New York: Grune & Stratton, 1981.

Hartmann, D. P., Roper, B. L., & Bradford, D. C. Some relationships between behavioral and traditional assessment. *Journal of Behavioral Assessment,* 1979, *1,* 3–21.

Hausser, D. L., Pecorella, P. A., & Wissler, A. L. *Survey-guided development II: A manual for consultants.* La Jolla, Calif.: University Associates, 1977.

Hay, L. R., Nelson, R. O., & Hay, W. M. The use of teachers as behavioral observers. *Journal of Applied Behavior Analysis,* 1977, *10,* 345–348.

Haynes, S. N. *Principles of behavioral assessment.* New York: Gardner Press, 1978.

Haynes, S. N., & Horn, W. F. Reactivity in behavioral observation: A review. *Behavioral Assessment,* 1982, *4,* 369–385.

Haynes, S. N., & Wilson, C. C. *Behavioral assessment.* San Francisco: Jossey-Bass, 1979.

Hays, W. L. *Statistics for the social sciences.* New York: Holt, Rinehart, & Winston, 1973.

Hefferin, E. A., & Katz, A. H. Issues and orientation in the evaluation of rehabilitation programs. *Rehabilitation Literature,* 1971, *32,* 66–73.

Helton, G. B., Workman, E. A., & Matuszek, P. A. *Psychoeducational assessment: Integrating concepts and techniques.* New York: Grune & Stratton, 1982.

Heppner, P. P. A review of the problem-solving literature and its relationship to counseling process. *Journal of Counseling Psychology,* 1978, *25,* 366–375.

Herron, W., Green, M., Guild, M., Smith, A., & Kantor, R. *Contemporary school psychology.* Scranton, Pa.: International Textbook, 1970.

Hersen, M., & Barlow, D. H. *Single case experimental designs: Strategies for studying behavior change.* New York: Pergamon, 1976.

Hersen, M., & Bellack, A. S. *Behavioral assessment: A practical handbook.* New York: Pergamon, 1976.

Hersch, C. The discontent explosion in mental health. *American Psychologist,* 1968, *23,* 497–506.

Hessler, G. L., & Sosnowsky, W. P. A review of aptitude-treatment interaction studies with the handicapped. *Psychology in the Schools,* 1979, *16,* 388–394.

Heward, W. L., & Orlansky, M. D. *Exceptional children.* Columbus, Ohio: Charles E. Merrill, 1980.

Hewitt, F. M., & Forness, S. R. *Education of exceptional learners.* Boston: Allyn and Bacon, 1974.

Hildreth, G. H. *Psychological service for school problems.* Yonkers-on-Hudson, N.Y.: World Book Company, 1930.

Hilliard, A. G. Standardization and cultural bias as impediments to the scientific study and validation of "intelligence." *Journal of Research and Development in Education,* 1979, *12,* 47–58.

Hinkle, A., Silverstein, B., & Walton, D. M. A method for the evaluation of mental health consultation to the public schools. *Journal of Community Psychology,* 1977, *5,* 262–265.

Hobbs, N. *The futures of children.* San Francisco: Jossey-Bass, 1975.

Hobbs, N. (Ed.). *Issues in the classification of children* (Vol. I & II). San Francisco: Jossey-Bass, 1975.

Hobson v. *Hansen,* 269 F. Supp. 401 (D.C. 1967) *aff'd sub non., Smuck* v. *Hobson,* 408 f.2d 175 (D.C. Cir. 1969).

Hogensen, D. A multidisciplinary approach to the in-school management of acutely anxious and depressed students in a large urban senior high school setting. *Pupil Personal Services Journal,* 1973, *3,* 29–31.

Hollister, W. G., & Miller, F. T. Problem-solving strategies in consultation. *American Journal of Orthopsychiatry,* 1977, *47,* 445–450.

Hollon, S. D., & Kendall, P. C. Cognitive-behavioral interventions: Theory and practice. In P. C. Kendall & S. D. Hollon (Eds.), *Cognitive-behavioral interventions: Theory, research, and procedures.* New York: Academic Press, 1979.

Holt, F. D., & Kicklighter, R. H. (Eds.). *Psychological services in the schools: Readings in preparation, organization, and practice.* Dubuque, Iowa: William C. Brown, 1974.

Hook, C. M., & Rosenshine, B. V. Accuracy of teacher reports of their classroom behavior. *Review of Educational Psychology,* 1959, *49,* 171–176.

Hoover, J. G., Maher, C. A., & Phillips, B. N. (Eds.). School psychology and program evaluation. *Journal of School Psychology,* 1978, *16*(4).

Horrocks, J. E. State certification requirements for school psychologists. *American Psychologist,* 1946, *1,* 399–401.

Howell, K. W., Kaplan, J. S., O'Connell, C. Y. *Evaluating exceptional children.* Columbus, Ohio: Charles E. Merrill, 1979.

Hughes, J. N. Consistency of administrators' and psychologists' actual and ideal perceptions of school psychologists' activities. *Psychology in the Schools,* 1979, *16,* 234–239.

Humes, C. School psychologist accountability via PPBS. *Journal of School Psychology,* 1974, *12,* 40–45.

Hunt, J. M. Traditional personality theory in light of recent evidence. In E. P. Hollander & R. G. Hunt (Eds.), *Current perspectives in social psychology* (2nd ed.). New York: Oxford University Press, 1967.

Hunter, C., & Lambert, N. M. Needs assessment activities in school psychology program development. *Journal of School Psychology,* 1974, *12,* 130–137.

Hunter, J. E., Schmidt, F. L., & Rauschenberger, J. Methodological and statistical issues in the study of bias in mental testing. In C. R. Reynolds & R. T. Brown (Eds.), *Perspectives on bias in mental testing.* New York: Plenum, in press.

Hynd, G. (Ed.). Neuropsychology in the schools. Special issue of *School Psychology Review,* 1981, *10*(3), 321–393.

Hynd, G., & Obrzut, J. E. *Neuropsychological assessment and the school age child: Issues and procedures.* New York: Grune & Stratton, 1981.

Iscoe, I., Pierce-Jones, J., McGhearty, L., & Friedman, S. A. A brief description of a project and some preliminary results. In E. L. Cowan, E. Garner, & M. Zax (Eds.), *Emergent approaches to mental health problems.* New York: Appleton-Century-Crofts, 1967.

Jackson, D. N., & Messick, S. (Eds.). *Problems in human assessment.* New York: McGraw-Hill, 1967.

Jackson, P. W. *Life in classrooms.* New York: Holt, Rinehart & Winston, 1968.

Jackson, R. M., Cleveland, J. C., & Merenda, P. F. The longitudinal effects of early identification and counseling of underachievers. *Journal of School Psychology,* 1975, *13*, 119–128.

Jason, L. A., & Ferone, L. Behavioral versus process consultation interventions in school settings. *American Journal of Community Psychology,* 1978, *6*, 531–543.

Jason, L. A., Ferone, L., & Anderegg, T. Evaluating ecological behavioral and process consultation interventions. *Journal of School Psychology,* 1979, *17*, 103–115.

Jean, P. J., & Reynolds, C. R. *Sex and attitude distortion: The faking of liberal and traditional attitudes about changing sex roles.* Paper presented to the annual meeting of the American Educational Research Association, New York, March, 1982.

Jenkins, J. R., & Parry, D. Standardized achievement tests: How useful for special education? *Exceptional Children,* 1978, *7*, 448–453.

Jennings, F. G. (Ed.). Making change happen. *Teachers College Record,* 1976, *77*(3).

Jensen, A. R. *g:* Outmoded theory or unconquered frontier? *Creative Science and Technology,* 1979, *2*, 16–29.

Jensen, A. R. *Bias in mental testing.* New York: The Free Press, 1980. (a)

Jensen, A. R. Chronometric analysis of intelligence. *Journal of Social and Biological Structures,* 1980, *3*, 103–122. (b)

Johnson, D. W., Skon, L., & Johnson, R. Effects of cooperative, competitive, and individualistic conditions on children's problem-solving performance. *American Educational Research Journal,* 1980, *17*, 83–93.

Johnson, S. M., & Bolstad, O. D. Reactivity to home observation: A comparison of audio recorded behavior with observers present or absent. *Journal of Applied Behavior Analysis,* 1975, *8*, 181–187.

Kahl, L. J., & Fine, M. J. Teachers' perceptions of the school psychologist as a function of teaching experience, amount of contact, and socioeconomic status of the school. *Psychology in the Schools,* 1978, *15*, 577–582.

Kanfer, F. H., & Goldstein, A. P. *Helping people change.* New York: Pergamon, 1980.

Kanfer, F. H., & Phillips, J. S. *Learning foundations of behavior therapy.* New York: Wiley, 1970.

Kanfer, F. H., & Saslow, G. Behavioral diagnosis. In C. Franks (Ed.), *Behavior therapy: Appraisal and status.* New York: McGraw-Hill, 1969.

Kaplan, M. S., Clancy, B., & Chrin, M. Priority roles for school psychologists as seen by superintendents. *Journal of School Psychology,* 1977, *15*, 75–80.

Kaufman, A. S. A new approach to the interpretation of test scatter on the WISC-R. *Journal of Learning Disabilities,* 1976, *9*, 160–168. (a)

Kaufman, A. S. Verbal-Performance IQ discrepancies on the WISC-R. *Journal of Consulting and Clinical Psychology,* 1976, *9*, 160–168. (b)

Kaufman, A. S. *Intelligent testing with the WISC-R.* New York: Wiley-Interscience, 1979.

Kaufman, A. S. A review of almost a decade of research on the McCarthy Scales. In T. R. Kratochwill (Ed.), *Advances in School Psychology* (Vol. II). Hillsdale, N.J.: Lawrence Erlbaum, 1982.

Kaufman, A. S., & Kaufman, N. L. *Clinical evaluation of young children with the McCarthy Scales.* New York: Grune & Stratton, 1977.

Kaufman, A. S., & Kaufman, N. L. *Kaufman assessment battery for children.* Circle Pines, Minn.: American Guidance Service, 1983.

Kaufman, A. S., & Reynolds, C. R. Clinical evaluation of intellectual functioning. In I. Weiner (Ed.), *Clinical methods in psychology* (2nd ed.). New York: Wiley-Interscience, 1983.

Kaufman, R. A. A possible integrative model for the systematic and measurable improvement of education. *American Psychologist,* 1971, *26,* 250–256.

Kazdin, A. E. *History of behavior modification.* Baltimore: University Park Press, 1978. (a)

Kazdin, A. E. The application of operant techniques in treatment, rehabilitation and education. In S. L. Garfield & A. D. Bergin (Eds.), *Handbook of psychotherapy and behavior change.* New York: Wiley, 1978. (b)

Kazdin, A. E. Situational specificity: The two-edged sword of behavioral assessment. *Behavioral Assessment,* 1979, *1,* 57–75. (a)

Kazdin, A. E. Unobtrusive measures in behavioral assessment. *Journal of Applied Behavior Analysis,* 1979, *12,* 713–724. (a)

Kazdin, A. E. Acceptability of alternative treatment for deviant child behavior. *Journal of Applied Behavior Analysis,* 1980, *13,* 259–273. (a)

Kazdin, A. E. Acceptability of time-out from reinforcement procedures for disruptive child behavior. *Behavior Therapy,* 1980, *11,* 329–344. (b)

Kazdin, A. E. *Behavior modification in applied settings* (2nd ed.). Homewood, Ill.: Dorsey, 1980. (c)

Kazdin, A. E. Acceptability of child treatment techniques: The influence of treatment efficacy and adverse side effects. *Behavior Therapy,* 1981, *12,* 493–506. (a)

Kazdin, A. E. *Research design in clinical psychology.* Philadelphia: J. B. Lippincott, 1981. (b)

Kazdin, A. E. The token economy: A decade later. *Journal of Applied Behavior Analysis,* 1982, *15,* 331–446. (a)

Kazdin, A. E. Applying behavioral principles in the schools. In C. R. Reynolds & T. B. Gutkin, *The handbook of school psychology.* New York: Wiley, 1982. (b)

Kazdin, A. E., & Bootzin, E. R. The token economy: An evaluative review. *Journal of Applied Behavior Analysis,* 1972, *5,* 343–372.

Kazdin, A. E., & Cole, P. M. Attitudes and labeling biases toward behavior modification: The effects of labels, context, and jargon. *Behavior Therapy,* 1981, *12,* 56–58.

Kazdin, A. E., & Wilson, G. T. *Evaluation of behavior therapy.* Cambridge, Mass.: Balinger, 1978.

Keller, H. R. Behavioral consultation. In J. C. Conoley (Ed.), *Consultation in schools: Theory, research, procedures.* New York: Academic Press, 1981.

Keller, H. R. Issues in the use of observational assessment. *School Psychology Review,* 1980, *9,* 21–30.

Kendall, P. C., & Hollon, S. D. (Eds.). *Cognitive-behavioral interventions: Theory, research and procedures.* New York: Academic Press, 1979.

Kent, R. N., O'Leary, K. D., Dietz, A., & Diament, C. Comparison of observational recordings in vivo, via mirror, and via television. *Journal of Applied Behavior Analysis,* 1979, *12,* 517–522.

Keogh, B. K., Kukic, S. J., Becker, L. D., McLoughlin, R. J., & Kukic, M. B. School psychologists' services in special education programs. *Journal of School Psychology,* 1975, *13,* 142–148.

Kiresuk, T. J., & Sherman, R. Goal attainment scaling: A general method for evaluating comprehensive mental health programs. *Community Mental Health Journal,* 1968, *4,* 443–453.

Kirk, D. L., & Kirp, L. M. The legalization of the school psychologist's world. *Journal of School Psychology,* 1976, *14,* 83–89.

Kirschner, F. E. School psychology as viewed by supervisors of school psychological services. *Journal of School Psychology,* 1971, *9,* 343–346.

Koegal, R. L., Russo, D. C., & Rincover, A. Assessing and training teachers in the generalized use of behavior modification with autistic children. *Journal of Applied Behavior Analysis,* 1977, *10,* 197–205.

Komechak, M. G. *The effect of thought detection on anxiety responses.* Unpublished doctoral dissertation, North Texas State University, December, 1974.

Koocher, G. P., & Broskowski, A. Issues in the evaluation of mental health services for children. *Professional Psychology,* 1977, *8,* 583–592.

Koppitz, E. M. Personality assessment in the schools. In C. R. Reynolds & T. B. Gutkin (Eds.), *The handbook of school psychology.* New York: Wiley, 1982.

Korman, M. National conference on levels and patterns of professionals training in psychology. *American Psychologist,* 1974, *29,* 441–449.

Kornblau, B. W., & Keogh, B. K. Teachers' perceptions and educational decisions. *New Directions for Exceptional Children,* 1980, *1,* 87–101.

Kounin, J. S. *Discipline and group management in classrooms.* New York: Holt, Rinehart, & Winston, 1970.

Kramer, J. J., & Nagle, R. J. Suggestions for the delivery of psychological services in secondary schools. *Psychology in the Schools,* 1980, *17,* 53–59.

Kratochwill, T. R. (Ed.). *Single subject research: Strategies for evaluating change.* New York: Academic Press, 1978.

Kratochwill, T. R. (Ed.). *Advances in school psychology, Vol. I.* Hillsdale, N.J.: Lawrence Erlbaum, 1981.

Kratochwill, T. R. Advances in behavioral assessment. In C. R. Reynolds & T. B. Gutkin (Eds.), *The handbook of school psychology.* New York: Wiley, 1982. (a)

Kratochwill, T. R. (Ed.). *Advances in school psychology, Vol. II.* Hillsdale, N.J.: Lawrence Erlbaum, 1982. (b)

Kratochwill, T. R., & Bergan, J. R. Evaluating programs in applied settings through behavioral consultation. *Journal of School Psychology,* 1978, *16,* 375–386.

Kratochwill, T. R., & Severson, R. A. Process assessment: An examination of reinforcer effectiveness and predictive validity. *Journal of School Psychology,* 1977, *15,* 293–300.

Kratwohl, D. R. On analyses of the perceived ineffectiveness of educational research and some recommendations. *Educational Psychologist,* 1974, *11,* 73–86.

Kuehnel, J. Faculty, school, and organizational characteristics and schools' openness to mental health resources. *Dissertation Abstracts International*, 1975, *36*, 2716A (University Microfilms No. 75-24898).

Kurpuis, D. J. Defining and implementing a consultation program in schools. *School Psychology Digest*, 1978, *7*, 17.

Lacayo, N., Sherwood, G., & Morris, J. Daily activities of school psychologists: A national survey. *Psychology in the Schools*, 1981, *18*, 184–190.

Lachar, D., & Gdowski, C. L. *Actuarial assessment of child and adolescent personality: An interpretive guide for the Personality Inventory for Children*. Los Angeles, Calif.: Western Psychological Services, 1979.

Lachenmeyer, J. R. Mental health consultation and programmative change. In M. S. Gibbs, J. R. Lachenmeyer, & J. Sigal (Eds.), *Community psychology*. New York: Gardner Press, 1980.

Lambert, N. M. The school psychologist as a source of power and influence. *Journal of School Psychology*, 1973, *11*, 245–250.

Lambert, N. M. A school based consultation model. *Professional Psychology*, 1974, *5*, 267–276.

Lambert, N. M. Children's problems and classroom intervention from the perspective of classroom teachers. *Professional Psychology*, 1976, *7*, 507–517.

Lambert, N. M. School psychology training for the decades ahead, on rivers, streams, and creeks—currents and tributaries to the sea. *School Psychology Review*, 1981, *10*, 194–205.

Lambert, N. M., Sandoval, J., & Corder, R. Teacher perceptions of school-based consultants. *Professional Psychology*, 1975, *6*, 204–216.

Lambert, N. M., Yandell, W., & Sandoval, J. H. Preparation of school psychologists for school-based consultation: A training activity and a service to community schools. *Journal of School Psychology*, 1975, *13*, 68–75.

Larry P. et al. v. Wilson Riles et al. No. C 71 2270. United States District Court for the Northern District of California, San Francisco, October 1979, slip opinion.

Lauver, P. J. Consulting with teachers: A systematic approach. *Personnel and Guidance Journal*, 1974, *52*, 535–540.

Lazarus, A. A. Has behavior therapy outlived its usefulness? *American Psychologist*, 1977, *32*, 550–554.

Leinhardt, G., & Seewald, A. M. Overlap: What's tested, what's taught? *Journal of Educational Measurement*, 1981, *18*, 85–96.

Leinhardt, G., & Seewald, A. M. Student-level observation of beginning reading. *Journal of Educational Measurement*, 1981, *18*, 171–177.

Leinhardt, G., Zigmond, N., & Cooley, W. W. Reading instruction and its effects. *American Educational Research Journal*, 1981, *18*, 343–361.

Leithwood, K. A., & Montgomery, D. J. The role of the elementary school principal in program improvement. *Review of Educational Research*, 1982, *52*, 309–339.

Lemle, R. Primary prevention of psychological disorders in elementary and intermediate schools. *Journal of Clinical Child Psychology*, 1976, *5*, 26–32.

Lepper, M. R., Greene, D., & Nisbett, R. E. Undermining children's intrinsic interest with extrinsic reward: A test of the "overjustification" hypothesis. *Journal of Personality and Social Psychology*, 1973, *28*, 129–137.

Lesiak, W. J., & Lounsbury, E. Views of school psychological services: A comparative study. *Psychology in the Schools,* 1977, *14,* 185–188.

Levine, M., & Levine, A. *A social history of helping services.* New York: Appleton-Century-Crofts, 1970.

Lewin, K. *Field theory in the social sciences.* New York: Harper & Row, 1951.

Lewis, D. O., Balla, D. A., & Shanok, S. S. Some evidence of race bias in the diagnosis and treatment of the juvenile offender. *American Journal of Orthopsychiatry,* 1979, *49,* 53–61.

Lewis, D. O., Shanok, S. S., Cohen, R. J., Kligfeld, M., & Frisone, G. Race bias in the diagnosis and disposition of violent adolescents. *American Journal of Psychiatry,* 1980, *137,* 1211–1216.

Lindsey, O. R. (cited in Alessi, G. J.). Personal communication, 1971.

Lineham, M. M. Issues in behavioral interviewing. In J. D. Cone & R. P. Hawkins (Eds.), *Behavioral assessment: New directions in clinical psychology.* New York: Brunner/Mazel, 1977.

Lowry, L. G., & Smith, G. *The institute for child guidance: 1927–1933.* New York: Commonwealth Fund, 1933.

Lubin, B., Wallis, R. R., & Paine, C. Patterns of psychological test usage in the United States: 1935–1969. *Professional Psychology,* 1971, *2,* 70–74.

Luiten, J., Ames, W., & Ackerson, G. A meta-analysis of the effects of advance organizers on learning and retention. *American Educational Research Journal,* 1980, *17,* 211–218.

Lundquist, G. W. Needs assessment in organization development. In C. R. Reynolds & T. B. Gutkin (Eds.), *The handbook of school psychology.* New York: Wiley, 1982.

Lupiani, D. A. The practice of defensive school psychology. *Psychology in the Schools,* 1978, *15,* 246–251.

Luria, A. R. *The role of speech in the regulation of normal and abnormal behavior.* New York: Liveright, 1961.

Lysakowski, R. S., & Walberg, H. J. Instructional effects of cues, participation, and corrective feedback: A quantitative synthesis. *American Educational Research Journal,* 1982, *19,* 559–578.

Macht, J. *The slaying of the dragon within.* Denver: JEM Publishing Co., 1980.

MacMillan, B. L., & Meyers, C. E. Larry P: An educational interpretation. *School Psychology Review,* 1980, *9,* 136–148.

Maher, B. A. (Ed.). Methodological issues in clinical research. *Journal of Consulting and Clinical Psychology,* 1978, *46*(4), 595–638.

Maher, C. A. A synoptic framework for school program evaluation. *Journal of School Psychology,* 1978, *16,* 322–333.

Maher, C. A. Guidelines for planning and evaluating school psychology service delivery systems. *Journal of School Psychology,* 1979, *17,* 203–212.

Maher, C. A. Evaluation of special service delivery systems: An organizational domain-referenced approach. *Psychology in the Schools,* 1980, *17,* 60–69.

Majumder, R., Greever, K., Holt, P., & Friedland, B. Counseling techniques tested: Field study shows effective I/E counseling. *Journal of Rehabilitation,* 1973, *39,* 19–23.

Malan, D. H. *The frontier of brief psychotherapy.* New York: Plenum, 1976.

Manley, T. R., & Manley, E. T. A comparison of the personal values and operative goals of school psychologists and school superintendents. *Journal of School Psychology,* 1978, *16,* 99–109.

Mannino, F. V., & Shore, M. F. Effecting change through consultation. In F. V. Mannino, B. W. Maclennan, & M. F. Shore (Eds.), *The practice of mental health consultation.* New York: Gardner Press, 1975.

Marlowe, R. H., Madsen, C. H., Bowen, C. E., Reardon, R. C., & Logue, P. E. Severe classroom behavior problems: Teachers or counselors. *Journal of Applied Behavior Analysis,* 1978, *11,* 53–66.

Marsh, E. J., & Terdal, L. G. *Behavioral assessment of childhood disorders.* New York: Guilford Press, 1981.

Magary, J. F. (Ed.). *School psychological services in theory and practice, a handbook.* Englewood Cliffs, N.J.: Prentice-Hall, 1967.

Martens, E. *The organization of research bureaus in city school systems.* Washington, D.C.: Government Printing Office, 1924.

Martin, R. Expert and referent power: A framework for understanding and maximizing consultation effectiveness. *Journal of School Psychology,* 1978, *16,* 49–55.

McBride, R. In-service training. In C. R. Reynolds & T. B. Gutkin (Eds.), *The handbook of school psychology.* New York: Wiley, 1982.

McCafee, J. K., & Vergason, G. A. Parent involvement in the process of special education. *Focus on Exceptional Children,* 1979, *11,* 1–15.

McCarthy, D. *McCarthy scales of children's abilities.* New York: The Psychological Corporation, 1972.

McCleary, R., & Hay, R. A., Jr. *Applied time series analysis for the social sciences.* London: Sage, 1980.

McCoy, S. A. Clinical judgment of normal childhood behaviors. *Journal of Consulting and Clinical Psychology,* 1976, *44,* 710–714.

McDaniel, L. J., & Ahr, E. The psychologist as a resource person conducting inservice teacher education. *Psychology in the Schools,* 1965, *2,* 220–224.

McDermott, P. A. Actuarial assessment systems for the grouping and classification of school children. In C. R. Reynolds & T. B. Gutkin (Eds.), *The handbook of school psychology.* New York: Wiley, 1982.

McDermott, P. A. Congruence and typology of diagnoses in school psychology: An empirical study. *Psychology in the Schools,* 1980, *17,* 12–24.

McDowell, R. L., Adamson, G. W., & Wood, F. H. *Teaching emotionally disturbed children.* Boston: Little, Brown, 1982.

McNamara, J. R., & Woods, K. M. Confidentiality: Its effect on interviewee behavior. *Professional Psychology,* 1980, *11,* 714–721.

McReynolds, W. T. DSM-III and the future of applied social science. *Professional Psychology,* 1979, *10,* 123, 132.

Meacham, M. L., & Peckham, P. D. School psychologists at three-quarters century: Congruence between training, practice, preferred role and competence. *Journal of School Psychology,* 1978, *16,* 195–206.

Medway, F. J. Teacher's knowledge of school psychologist's responsibilities. *Journal of School Psychology,* 1977, *15,* 301–307.

Medway, F. J. Causal attributions for school-related problems: Teacher perceptions and teacher feedback. *Journal of Educational Psychology,* 1979, *71,* 809–818. (a)

Medway, F. J. How effective is school consultation: A review of recent research. *Journal of School Psychology*, 1979, *17*, 275–282. (b)

Medway, F. J., & Forman, S. G. Psychologists' and teachers' reactions to mental health and behavioral school consultation. *Journal of School Psychology*, 1980, *18*, 338–348.

Meehl, P. E. *Clinical versus statistical prediction: A theoretical analysis and a review of the evidence*. Minneapolis: University of Minnesota Press, 1954.

Mehrabian, A. *Public places and private spaces*. New York: Basic Books, 1976.

Meichenbaum, D. H. *Cognitive-behavior modification*. New York: Plenum, 1977.

Mercer, J. R. In defense of racially and culturally nondiscriminatory assessment. *School Psychology Digest*, 1979, *8*, 89–105.

Mercer, J. R., & Lewis, J. *Technical manual: SOMPA system multicultural pluralistic assessment*. New York: Psychological Corporation, 1979.

Merriken v. Cressman, 364 S. Supp. 913 (E.D. Pa 1973).

Messick, S. Test validity and the ethics of assessment. *American Psychologist*, 1980, *35*, 1012–1027.

Meyers, A. W., & Cohen, R. Cognitive-behavioral interventions for classroom and academic behaviors. *School Psychology Review*, 1982, *11*, 5–12.

Meyers, J. A consultation model for school psychological services. *Journal of School Psychology*, 1973, *11*, 5–15.

Meyers, J. Consultee-centered consultation with a teacher as a technique in behavioral management. *American Journal of Community Psychology*, 1975, *3*, 111–121.

Meyers, J. Mental health consultation. In T. R. Kratochwill (Ed.), *Advances in school psychology* (Vol. 1). Hillsdale, N.J.: Lawrence Erlbaum, 1981.

Meyers, J., Brown, D. T., & Coulter, W. A. Analysis of the action plans. *School Psychology Review*, 1982, *11*, 161–185.

Meyers, J., Friedman, M. P., & Gaughan, E. J., Jr. The effects of consultee-centered consultation on teacher behavior. *Psychology in the Schools*, 1975, *12*, 288–295.

Meyers, J., Parsons, R. D., & Martin, R. *Mental health consultation in the schools*. San Francisco: Jossey-Bass, 1979.

Meyers, J., Pitt, N. W., Gaughan, E. J., Jr., & Friedman, M. P. A research model for consultation with teachers. *Journal of School Psychology*, 1978, *16*, 137–145.

Meyers, J., Wurtz, R., & Flanagan, D. A national survey investigating consultation training occurring in school psychology programs. *Psychology in the Schools*, 1981, *18*, 297–302.

Michenbaum, D., & Burland, S. Cognitive behavior modification with children. *School Psychology Review*, 1979, *8*, 426–433.

Michenbaum, D., & Goodman, J. Training impulsive children to talk to themselves: A means of developing self-control. *Journal of Abnormal Psychology*, 1971, *77*, 115–126.

Miller, A. Conceptual matching models and interactional research in education. *Review of Educational Research*, 1981, *51*, 33–84.

Miller, C. D., Witt, J. C., & Finley, J. School psychologists perceptions of their work in the United States. *School Psychology International*, in press.

Miller, C. K., & Chansky, N. M. Psychologists' scoring of WISC protocols. *Psychology in the Schools*, 1972, *9*, 144–152.

Miller, C. K., Chansky, N. M., & Gredler, G. R. Rater agreement on WISC protocols. *Psychology in the Schools,* 1970, *7,* 190–193.

Miller, G. A. Psychology as a means of promoting human welfare. *American Psychologist,* 1969, *24,* 1063–1075.

Miller, J. N., & Engin, A. W. Performance based school psychology certification: Situational response testing. *Psychology in the Schools,* 1974, *11,* 422–424.

Miller, T. L., & Dyer, C. O. Role-model complements of school psychology with special education. In L. Mann & D. A. Sabatino (Eds.), *The fourth review of special education.* New York: Grune & Stratton, 1980.

Miller, W. E. A new role for the school psychologist—who needs it? *Psychology in the Schools,* 1978, *15,* 514–518.

Mills v. *Board of Education of District of Columbia,* 348 F. Supp. 866 (D. D.C. 1972).

Minor, M. W. Systems analysis and school psychology. *Journal of School Psychology,* 1972, *10,* 227–232.

Mischel, W. L. *Personality and assessment.* New York: Wiley, 1968.

Mischel, W. L. Toward a cognitive social learning reconceptualization of personality. *Psychological Review,* 1973, *80,* 252–283.

Mitchell, J. V., Jr. Testing and the Oscar Buros lament: From knowledge to implementation to use. In B. Plake (Ed.), *Social and technical issues in testing: Implications for test construction and usage.* Hillsdale, N.J.: Lawrence Erlbaum, 1984.

Monroe, V. Roles and status of school psychology. In G. D. Phye & D. J. Reachly (Eds.), *School psychology: Perspectives and issues.* New York: Academic Press, 1979.

Moos, R. H. *Environmental determinants of behavior: The human context.* New York: Wiley, 1976.

Moos, R. H. *Evaluating educational environments.* San Francisco: Jossey-Bass, 1979.

Moos, R. H., Insel, P., & Humphrey, B. *Preliminary manual for the Family Environment Scale.* Palo Alto, Calif.: Consulting Psychologists Press, 1974.

Morrison, G. M. Sociometric measurement: Methodological consideration of its use with mildly learning handicapped and nonhandicapped children. *Journal of Educational Psychology,* 1981, *73,* 193–201.

Moulin, E. K. The effects of client centered group counseling using play therapy media on the intelligence, achievement, and psycholinguistic abilities of underachieving primary school children. *Elementary School Guidance and Counseling,* 1970, *5,* 85–95.

Moustakos, C. *Children in play therapy.* New York: Ballantine Books, 1953.

Mowder, B. A. Legislative mandates: Implications for changes in school psychology training programs. *Professional Psychology,* 1979, *10,* 681–686.

Mullen, F. (Ed.). *The psychologist on the school staff: Report of the committee on reconsideration of the functions of the school psychologist.* American Psychological Association, 1958.

Murphy, G. *An historical introduction to modern psychology.* New York: Harcourt, Brace, 1929.

Murphy, J. P. Roles, functions, and competencies of supervisors of school psychologists. *School Psychology Review,* 1981, *10,* 417–424.

Nagle, R. J., & Medway, F. J. Issues in providing psychological services at the high school level. *School Psychology Review*, 1982, *11*, 359–369.

Nathan, P. E. Symptomatic diagnosis and behavioral assessment. In D. H. Barlow (Ed.), *Behavioral assessment of adult disorders*. New York: Guilford Press, 1981.

National Association of School Psychologists. *Standards for the provision of school psychological services*. Washington, D.C., 1978. (a)

National Association of School Psychologists. *Standards for training programs in school psychology; standards for credentialing of school psychologists; standards for field placement programs in school psychology*. Washington, D.C.: 1978. (b)

National Association of School Psychologists. *Membership Directory*, 1983.

National Education Association. Teacher Opinion Poll. *Today's Education*, 1979, *68*, 10.

Nelson, R. O., & Bowles, P. E. The best of two worlds—observations with norms. *Journal of School Psychology*, 1975, *13*, 3–9.

Nelson, R. O., Hay, L. R., & Hay, W. M. Comments on Cone's "The relevance of reliability and validity for behavioral assessment." *Behavior Therapy*, 1977, *8*, 427–430.

Nelson, R. O., & Hayes, S. C. Some current dimensions of behavioral assessment. *Behavioral Assessment*, 1980, *1*, 1–16.

Newland, T. E. Psychological assessment of exceptional children and youth. In W. M. Cruickshank (Ed.), *Psychology of exceptional children and youth* (4th ed.). Englewood Cliffs, N.J.: Prentice-Hall, 1980.

Ney, P. G., Palvesky, A. E., & Markley, J. Relative effectiveness of operant conditioning and play therapy in childhood schizophrenia. *Journal of Autism and Childhood Schizophrenia*, 1971, *1*, 337–349.

Nicholson, C. A. A survey of referral problems in 59 Ohio school districts. In F. D. Holt & R. H. Kicklighter (Eds.), *Psychological services in the schools*. Dubuque, Iowa: Wm. C. Brown Co., 1971.

Nunnally, J. *Psychometric theory*. New York: McGraw-Hill, 1978.

O'Callaghan, S. Publication trends in school psychology. *Journal of School Psychology*, 1974, *12*, 269–275.

Ojemann, R. H. Incorporating psychological concepts in the school curriculum. *Journal of School Psychology*, 1967, *5*, 195–204.

O'Leary, K. D., & Johnson, S. B. Psychological assessment. In H. C. Quay & J. S. Werry (Eds.), *Psychopathological disorders of childhood*. New York: Wiley, 1979.

O'Leary, K. D., & O'Leary, S. G. *Classroom management: The successful use of behavior modification* (2nd ed.). New York: Pergamon, 1977.

Ollendick, T. H., & Cerny, J. A. *Clinical behavior therapy with children*. New York: Plenum Press, 1981.

Olson, M. M. (Ed.). *Counseling children in groups: A forum*. New York: Holt, Rinehart, & Winston, 1973.

Osborn, A. *Applied imagination* (3rd ed.). New York: Scribners, 1963.

Overcast, T. D., & Sales, B. D. The legal rights of students in the elementary and secondary public schools. In C. R. Reynolds & T. B. Gutkin (Eds), *The handbook of school psychology*. New York: Wiley, 1982.

Owens, R. G. *Organizational behavior in schools*. Englewood Cliffs, N.J.: Prentice-Hall, 1970.

Owens, R. G., & Steinhoff, C. R. *Administering change in schools.* Englewood Cliffs, N.J.: Prentice-Hall, 1976.

Page, E. B. Foreword. In C. R. Reynolds & T. B. Gutkin (Eds.), *The handbook of school psychology.* New York: Wiley, 1982.

Paget, K., & Bracken, B. *The psychoeducational assessment of preschool children.* New York: Grune & Stratton, 1983.

Palmer, D. J. Factors to be considered in placing handicapped children in regular classes. *Journal of School Psychology,* 1980, *18,* 163–171.

Palmo, A. J., & Kuzniar, J. Modifications of behavior through group counseling and consultation. *Elementary School Guidance and Counseling,* 1972, *6,* 258–262.

PARC v. *Commonwealth of Pennsylvania,* 343 F. Supp. 279 (E.D. Pa 1972).

Parnes, S. J., & Meadow, A. Effects of "brainstorming" instructions on creative problem-solving by trained and untrained subjects. *Journal of Educational Psychology,* 1959, *50,* 171–176.

Parnes, S. J., Noller, R. B., & Biondi, A. M. *Guide to creative action.* New York: Scribners, 1977.

Parnham v. *J.L.,* 422 U.S. 584 (1979).

Parsons, R. *The investigation of consultation process: A small-N approach.* Paper presented at the annual meeting of the American Psychological Association, San Francisco, August, 1977.

PASE: Parents in action on special education et al. v. *Hannon et al.* No. c 74 3586. United States District Court for the Northern District of Illinois, Eastern Division, July 1980, slip opinion.

PASE v. *Hannon,* 506 F. Supp. 831 (N.D. Ill., 1980).

Payne, D. A. Portrait of the school psychologist as program evaluator. In C. R. Reynolds & T. B. Gutkin (Eds.), *The handbook of school psychology.* New York: Wiley, 1982.

Pennington, L. W. Provisions of school psychological services. *The School Psychology Digest,* 1977, *6,* 50–70.

Perkins, K. J. From identification to identity. *Journal of School Psychology,* 1964, *2,* 7–16.

Petrie, P., Brown, K., Piersel, W. C., Frinfrock, S.R., Schelble, M., LeBlanc, C. P., & Kratochwill, T. R. The school psychologist as behavioral ecologist. *Journal of School Psychology,* 1980, *18,* 222–233.

Petrie, P., & Piersel, W. C. Family therapy. In C. R. Reynolds & T. B. Gutkin (Eds.), *The handbook of school psychology.* New York: Wiley, 1982.

Pfeiffer, S. I. The school-based interprofessional team: Recurring problems and some possible solutions. *Journal of School Psychology,* 1980, *18,* 388–394.

Pfeiffer, S. I. The problems facing multidisciplinary teams: As perceived by team members. *Psychology in the Schools,* 1981, *18,* 330–333.

Pfeiffer, S. I., & Marmo, P. The status of training in school psychology and trends toward the future. *Journal of School Psychology,* 1981, *19,* 211–216.

Phillips, B. N. (Ed.). *Perspectives on school psychology.* Austin: University of Texas Press, 1966.

Phillips, B. N. The teacher-psychological specialist model. *Journal of School Psychology,* 1967, *6,* 67–71.

Phillips, B. N. The diagnostic-intervention class and the teacher-psychological specialist: Models for the school psychological services network? *Psychology in the Schools,* 1968, *5,* 135–139.

Phillips, B. N. School psychology in the 1980's: Some critical issues related to practice. In T. R. Kratochwill (Ed.), *Advances in school psychology* (Vol. I). Hillsdale, N.J.: Lawrence Erlbaum, 1981.

Phillips, B. N. Reading and evaluating research in school psychology. In C. R. Reynolds & T. B. Gutkin (Eds.), *The handbook of school psychology.* New York: Wiley, 1982.

Phye, G. D., & Reschly, D. J. (Eds.). *School psychology: Perspectives and issues.* New York: Academic Press, 1979.

Piersel, W. C., & Gutkin, T. B. Resistance to school-based consultation: A behavioral analysis of the problem. *Psychology in the Schools,* 1983, *30,* 311–320.

Planned Parenthood of Central Missouri v. *Danforth,* 428 U.S. 52 (1976).

Platt, J., & Spivack, G. *Workbook for training in interpersonal problem-solving thinking.* Philadelphia: Department of Mental Health Sciences, Hohnemann Community Mental Health/Mental Retardation Center, 1976.

Poland, S., Ysseldyke, J., Thurlow, M., & Mirkin, P. *Current assessment and decision-making practices in school settings as reported by directors of special education (Research Report No. 14).* Minneapolis: University of Minnesota, Institute for Research on Learning Disabilities, 1979.

Prasse, D. P. Privileged confidential communication: Who is protected? *Communique,* March 1979, 3–5.

Prasse, D. P. Professional standards versus system procedure: The decision of *Forrest v. Ambach. Communique,* March 1982, 3.

Price, R. H., & Blashfield, R. K. Explorations in the taxonomy of behavior settings: Analysis of dimensions and classification of settings. *American Journal of Community Psychology,* 1975, *3,* 335–351.

Pryzwansky, W. A reconsideration of the consultation model for delivery of school-based psychological services. *America Journal of Orthopsychiatry,* 1974, *44,* 579–583.

Pyle, R. R. Mental health consultation: Helping teachers help themselves. *Professional Psychology,* 1977, *8,* 192–198.

Quay, H. C. Special education: Assumptions, techniques, and evaluative criteria. *Exceptional Children,* 1973, *40,* 165–170.

Quay, H. C., & Werry, J. S. (Eds.). *Psychopathological disorders of childhood.* New York: Wiley, 1979.

Quinnett, P. Rip Van Winkle effect. *Professional Psychology,* 1980, *11,* 2–3.

Rabinowitz, W., & Roberts, D. Common flaws in research design. *National Association for Business Teacher Education Review,* 1977, *4,* 5–8.

Raffaniello, E. M. Competent consultation: The collaborative approach. In M. J. Curtis & J. E. Zins (Eds.), *The theory and practice of school consultation.* Springfield, Ill.: Charles C Thomas, 1981.

Raimy, V. (Ed.). *Training in clinical psychology.* Englewood Cliffs, NJ: Prentice-Hall, 1950.

Ramage, J. National survey of school psychologists: Update. *The School Psychology Digest,* 1979, *8,* 153–161.

Randolph, D. L., & Hardage, N. C. A comparison of behavioral consultation and behavioral consultation with model-reinforcement group counseling for children who are consistently off-task. *Journal of Educational Research*, 1973, *67*, 103–107.

Redfield, D. L., & Rousseau, E. W. A meta-analysis of experimental research on teacher questioning behavior. *Review of Educational Research*, 1981, *51*, 237–245.

Reger, R. *School psychology*. Springfield, Ill.: Charles C Thomas, 1965.

Reger, R. The medical model in special education. *Psychology in the Schools*, 1972, *9*, 8–12.

Reid, J. B. *Observation in home settings, II: A social learning approach to family intervention*. Eugene, Ore.: Castalia, 1978.

Reilly, D. H. A conceptual model for school psychology. *Psychology in the Schools*, 1974, *11*, 165–170.

Reinking, R. H., Livesay, G., & Kohl, M. The effects of consultation style on consultee productivity. *American Journal of Community Psychology*, 1978, *6*, 283–290.

Reisman, J. M. *A history of clinical psychology*. New York: Herlstead Press, 1976.

Reschly, D. J. School psychology consultation: "Frenzied, faddish, or fundamental?" *Journal of School Psychology*, 1976, *14*, 150–153.

Reschly, D. J. Psychological evidence in the Larry P. opinion: A case of right problem— wrong solution? *School Psychology Review*, 1980, *9*, 123–135.

Reschly, D. J., & Grimes, J. Standards and competencies for psychological assessment, intervention and follow-up. Paper presented at the *Nebraska School Psychologists Association*, Fall meeting, Lincoln, Nebraska, 1980.

Rettke, G. H. Psychological services: A developing model. In F. D. Holt & R. H. Kicklighter (Eds.), *Psychological services in the schools*. Dubuque, Iowa: Wm. C. Brown Co., 1971.

Reynolds, C. R. Factor structure of the Peabody Individual Achievement Test at five grade levels between grades one and twelve. *Journal of School Psychology*, 1979, *17*, 270–274. (a)

Reynolds, C. R. Should we screen preschoolers? *Contemporary Educational Psychology*, 1979, *4*, 175–181. (b)

Reynolds, C. R. Concurrent validity of what I think and feel: The Revised Children's Manifest Anxiety Scale. *Journal of Consulting and Clinical Psychology*, 1980, *48*, 774–775.

Reynolds, C. R. The neuropsychological assessment and the habilitation of learning: Consideration in the search for the aptitude x treatment interaction. *School Psychology Review*, 1981, *10*, 343–349. (a)

Reynolds, C. R. The neuropsychological basis of intelligence. In G. Hynd & J. Obrzut (Eds.), *Neuropsychological assessment and the school age child: Issues and procedures*. New York: Grune & Stratton, 1981. (b)

Reynolds, C. R. The fallacy of "two years below grade level for age" as a diagnostic criterion for reading disorders. *Journal of School Psychology*, 1981, *19*, 350–358. (c)

Reynolds, C. R. *Test bias: In God We Trust, all others must have data*. Invited address to the annual meeting of the American Psychological Association, Los Angeles, August, 1981. (d)

Reynolds, C. R. The importance of norms and other traditional psychometric concepts to assessment in clinical neuropsychology. In R. N. Malatesha & L. C. Hartlage (Eds.), *Neuropsychology and cognition* (Vol. 2). The Hague: Martinus Nijhoff Pub., 1982. (a)

Reynolds, C. R. The problem of bias in psychological assessment. In C. R. Reynolds & T. B. Gutkin (Eds.), *The handbook of school psychology*. New York: Wiley, 1982. (b)

Reynolds, C. R., & Brown, R. T. Bias in mental testing: An introduction to the issues. In C. R. Reynolds & R. T. Brown (Eds.), *Perspectives on bias in mental testing*. New York: Plenum, in press.

Reynolds, C. R., & Clark, J. H. Cognitive assessment of the preschool child. In K. D. Paget & B. Bracken (Eds.), *Psychoeducational assessment of the preschool and primary aged child*. New York: Grune & Stratton, 1983.

Reynolds, C. R., & Clark, J. H. Trends in school psychology research: 1974–1980. *Journal of School Psychology,* in press.

Reynolds, C. R., & Elliott, S. N. Trends in development and publication of educational and psychological tests. *Professional Psychology: Research and Practice,* 1983, *14,* 554–558.

Reynolds, C. R., & Gutkin, T. B. A multivariate comparison of the intellectual performance of blacks and whites matched on four demographic variables. *Personality and Individual Differences,* 1981, *2,* 175–181. (a)

Reynolds, C. R., & Gutkin, T. B. Test scatter on the WPPSI: Normative analyses of the standardization sample. *Journal of Learning Disabilities,* 1981, *14,* 460–464. (b)

Reynolds, C. R., & Gutkin, T. B. (Eds.). *The handbook of school psychology*. New York: Wiley, 1982.

Reynolds, C. R., & Richmond, B. O. What I think and feel: A revised measure of children's manifest anxiety. *Journal of Abnormal Child Psychology,* 1978, *6,* 271–280.

Reynolds, W. M. Psychological tests: Clinical usage versus psychometric quality. *Professional Psychology,* 1979, *10,* 324–429.

Rezmierski, V. E., Knoblock, P., Bloom, R. B. The psychoeducational model: Theory and historical perspective. In R. L. McDowell, G. W. Adamson, & F. H. Wood (Eds.), *Teaching emotionally disturbed children*. Boston: Little, Brown, 1982.

Rhodes, W. C. The illusion of normality. *Behavioral Disorders,* 1977, *2,* 122–129.

Rich, H. L. *Disturbed students*. Baltimore, Md.: University Park Press, 1982.

Rich, H. L., Beck, M. A., & Coleman, T. W. Behavior management: The psychoeducational model. In R. L. McDowell, G. W. Adamson, & F. H. Wood (Eds.), *Teaching emotionally disturbed children*. Boston: Little, Brown, 1982.

Rieke, S. L., & Curtis, M. J. The consistency between consultant performance during simulated and real-life consultation. In M. J. Curtis & J. E. Zins (Eds.), *The theory and practice of school consultation*. Springfield, Ill.: Charles C Thomas, 1981.

Riskin, J. Family interaction scales: A preliminary report. *Archives of General Psychiatry,* 1964, *11,* 484–494.

Ritter, D. R. Effects of a school consultation program upon referral patterns of teachers. *Psychology in the Schools,* 1978, *15,* 239–243.

Roback, A. A. *History of American psychology*. New York: Collier Books, 1964.

Roberts, R. D. Perceptions of actual and desired role functions of school psychologists by psychologists and teachers. *Psychology in the Schools,* 1970, *7,* 175–178.

Roberts, R. D., & Solomons, G. Perceptions of the duties and functions of the school psychologist. *American Psychologist,* 1970, *25,* 544–549.

Robin, A. L., Schneider, M., & Dolnick, M. The turtle technique: An extended case study of self-control in the classroom. *Psychology in the Schools,* 1976, *73,* 449–453.

Rogers-Warren, A., & Warren, S. F. *Ecological perspectives in behavior analysis.* Baltimore: University Park Press, 1977.

Ross, A. O. *Psychological disorders of children: A behavioral approach to theory, research, and therapy.* New York: McGraw-Hill, 1974.

Rubin, R. A., & Balow, B. Prevalence of teacher identified behavior problems: A longitudinal study. *Exceptional Children,* 1978, *45,* 102–111.

Russ, S. W. Group consultation: Key variables that effect change. *Professional Psychology,* 1978, *9,* 145–152.

Sabatino, D. A. School psychology—special education: To acknowledge a relationship. *Journal of School Psychology,* 1972, *10,* 99–105.

Sabatino, D. A. School psychology: An instrumental service for the handicapped. In T. R. Kratochwill (Ed.), *Advances in school psychology, Vol. I.* Hillsdale, N.J.: Lawrence Erlbaum, 1981.

Salvia, J., & Ysseldyke, J. E. *Assessment in special and remedial education* (2nd. ed.). Boston: Houghton Mifflin, 1981.

Sandoval, J. *The efficacy of school-based consultation.* Paper presented at the annual meeting of the American Psychological Association, San Francisco, September, 1977.

Sandoval, J., & Lambert, N. M. Instruments for evaluating school psychologists' functioning and service. *Psychology in the Schools,* 1977, *14,* 172–179.

Sandoval, J., Lambert, N. M., & Davis, J. M. Consultation from the consultee's perspective. *Journal of School Psychology,* 1977, *15,* 334–342.

Sandoval, J., & Love, J. A. School psychology in higher education: The college psychologist. *Professional Psychology,* 1977, *8,* 328–339.

Sarason, S. B. *The culture of the school and the problem of change.* Boston: Allyn & Bacon, 1971.

Sarason, S. B. Community psychology, networks, and Mr. Everyman. *American Psychologist,* 1976, *31,* 317–328.

Sarason, S. B., Levine, M., Goldenberg, I. I., Cherlin, D. L., & Bennett, E. *Psychology in community settings.* New York: Wiley, 1966.

Sattler, J. M. *Assessment of children's intelligence and special abilities* (2nd ed.). Boston: Allyn & Bacon, 1982.

Saudargas, R. W., Madsen, C. H., & Scott, I. W. Differential effects of fixed and variable time feedback on production rates of elementary school children. *Journal of Applied Behavior Analysis,* 1977, *10,* 673–678.

Schacht, T., & Nathan, P. E. But is it good for psychologists?: Appraisal and status of DSM-III. *American Psychologist,* 1977, *32,* 1017–1025.

Schein, E. H. *Process consultation: Its role in organization development.* Reading, Mass.: Addison-Wesley, 1969.

Schein, E. H. The role of the consultant: content expert or process facilitator? *The Personnel and Guidance Journal,* 1978, *56,* 339–343.

Schmuck, R. A. Organization development in the schools. In C. R. Reynolds & T. B. Gutkin (Eds.), *The handbook of school psychology.* New York: Wiley, 1982.

Schmuck, R. A., & Miles, M. B. (Eds.). *Organization development in schools.* Palo Alto, Calif.: National Press, 1971.

Schmuck, R. A., Murray, D. G., Smith, M. A., Schwartz, M., & Runkel, M. *Consultation for changing school structures: OD for multi-unit schools.* Eugene, Ore.: Center for Educational Policy and Management, 1975.

Schmuck, R. A., Runkel, P. J., Arends, J. H., & Arends, R. I. *The second handbook of organization development.* Palo Alto, Calif.: Mayfield Publishing, 1977.

Schnelle, J. F. A brief report on the invalidity of parent evaluations of behavior change. *Journal of Applied Behavior Analysis,* 1974, *7,* 341–343.

Schowengerdt, R. V., Fine, M. J., & Poggio, J. P. An examination of some bases of teacher satisfaction with school psychological services. *Psychology in the Schools,* 1976, *13,* 269–275.

Schroeder, C. S., & Miller, F. T. Entry patterns and strategies in consultation. In M. J. Curtis & J. E. Zins (Eds.), *The theory and practice of school consultation.* Springfield, Ill.: Charles C Thomas, 1981.

Schultz, D. *A history of modern psychology* (2nd ed.). New York: Academic Press, 1975.

Schweisheimer, W., & Walberg, H. J. A peer counseling experiment: High school students and small group leaders. *Journal of Counseling Psychology,* 1976, *23,* 398–401.

Scott, W. A. Reliability and content analysis: The case of nominal scale coding. *Public Opinion Quarterly,* 1955, *19,* 321–325.

Scriven, M. Evaluation perspectives and procedures. In W. J. Popham (Ed.), *Evaluation in education: Current applications.* Berkeley, Calif.: McCutcheon, 1974.

Sharpley, C. F. Elimination of vicarious reinforcement effects within an implicit reward situation. *Journal of Educational Psychology,* 1982, *74,* 611–617.

Shellenberger, S. Presentation and interpretation of psychological data in educational settings. In C. R. Reynolds & T. B. Gutkin (Eds.), *The handbook of school psychology.* New York: Wiley, 1982.

Shellenberger, S. (Ed.). Services to families and parental involvement with interventions. *School Psychology Review,* 1981, *10*(1).

Shorr, D. N., McClelland, S. E., & Robinson, H. B. Corrected mental age scores for the Stanford-Binet Intelligence Scale. *Measurement and Evaluation in Guidance,* 1977, *10,* 144–147.

Shumaker, J. B., Hovell, M. F., & Sherman, J. A. An analysis of daily report cards and parent-managed privileges in the improvement of adolescents' classroom performance. *Journal of Applied Behavior Analysis,* 1977, *10,* 449–464.

Simon, A., & Boyer, E. G. (Eds.). *Mirrors for behavior.* Philadelphia: Research for Better Schools, 1974.

Skinner, B. F. *Science and human behavior.* New York: Free Press, 1953.

Smith, C. R. Assessment alternatives: Non-standardized procedures. *School Psychology Review,* 1980, *9,* 46–57.

Smith, D. K. Classroom management and consultation: Implications for school psychology. *Psychology in the Schools,* 1981, *18,* 475–481.

Smith, M. L., & Glass, G. V. Meta-analysis of research on class size and its relationship to attitudes and instruction. *American Educational Research Journal,* 1980, *17,* 419–433.

Smith, R., Neisworth, J., & Greer, J. *Evaluating educational environments.* Columbus, Ohio: Charles E. Merrill, 1978.

Snapp, M., & Davidson, J. L. Systems intervention for school psychologists: A case study approach. In C. R. Reynolds and T. B. Gutkin (Eds.), *The handbook of school psychology.* New York: Wiley, 1982.

Spielberger, C. D. *Manual for the state-trait anxiety inventory for children.* Palo Alto, Calif.: Consulting Psychologists Press, 1973.

Spivack, G., Platt, J. J., & Shure, M. B. *The problem-solving approach to adjustment.* San Francisco: Jossey-Bass, 1976.

Stapp, J., & Fulcher, R. The employment of 1979 and 1980 doctorate recipients in psychology. *American Psychologist,* 1982, *37,* 1159–1185.

Steinberg, M., & Chandler, G. Coordinating services between a mental health center and public schools. *Journal of School Psychology,* 1976, *14,* 355–362.

Stell v. Savannah - Chatham Board of Education, 220 F. Supp. 667 (S.B. Ga. 1963), rev'd 333 F. 2d 55 (5th cir. 1963), *cert. denied,* 379 U.S. 933 (1964).

Stokes, T. F., & Baer, D. M. An implicit technology of generalization. *Journal of Applied Behavior Analysis,* 1977, *10,* 349–367.

Stolz, S. B. Adoption of innovations from applied behavior research: "Does Anybody Care?" *Journal of Applied Behavior Analysis,* 1981, *14,* 491–505.

Stone, F. B. Behavior problems of elementary school children. *Journal of Abnormal Child Psychology,* 1981, *9,* 407–418.

Strupp, H. H. Psychotherapy research and practice: An overview. In S. L. Garfield & A. E. Bergin (Eds.), *Handbook of psychotherapy and behavior change* (2nd ed.). New York: Wiley, 1978.

Stuart, R. B. *Trick or treatment: How and when psychotherapy fails.* Champaign, Ill.: Research Press, 1970.

Styles, W. A. Teachers' perceptions of the school psychologist's role. *Journal of School Psychology,* 1965, *3,* 23–27.

Sulzer-Azaroff, B., & Mayer, G. R. *Applying behavior-analysis procedures with children and youth.* New York: Holt, Rinehart, & Winston, 1977.

Sundberg, N. D., Tyler, L. E., & Taplin, J. R. *Clinical psychology: Expanding horizons* (2nd ed.). Englewood Cliffs, N.J.: Prentice-Hall, 1973.

Suran, B. G., & Rizzo, J. V. *Special children: An integrative approach.* Dallas: Scott, Foresman, 1979.

Swap, S. M. Prieto, A. G., & Harth, R. Ecological perspectives of the emotionally disturbed child. In R. L. McDowell, G. W. Adamson, & F. H. Wood (Eds.), *Teaching emotionally disturbed children.* Boston: Little, Brown, 1982.

Symonds, P. M. The school psychologist—1942. *Journal of Consulting Psychology,* 1942, *6,* 173–176.

Szasz, T. S. The myth of mental illness. *American Psychologist,* 1960, *15,* 113–118.

Szmuk, M. I. C., Docherty, E. M., & Ringness, T. A. Behavioral objectives for psychological consultation in the school as evaluated by teachers and school psychologists. *Psychology in the Schools,* 1979, *16,* 143–148.

Tageson, C. W., & Corazzini, J. G. A collaborative model for consultation and paraprofessional development. *Professional Psychology*, 1974, *5*, 191–197.

Tarasoff v. *Regents of University of California*, 13 C. 3d 177, 529 P. 2d 533, 118 Cal.
Rptr. 120 (1974).

Tarter, R. E., Templer, D. I., & Hardy, C. Reliability of the psychiatric diagnosis.
Diseases of the Nervous System, 1975, *36*, 30–31.

Thomas, A., Chess, S., Birch, H. G. *Temperament and behavior disorders in children.*
New York: New York University Press, 1968.

Thombs, M. R., & Muro, J. J. Group counseling and the sociometric status of second-
grade children. *Elementary School Guidance and Counseling*, 1973, *7*, 194–197.

Thurlow, M. L. What is a typical team meeting? In J. E. Ysseldyke, B. Algozzine, & M.
Thurlow (Eds.), *A naturalistic investigation of special education team meetings.*
(Research Report No. 40). University of Minnesota: Institute for Research on Learn-
ing Disabilities, 1980.

Thurlow, M. L., & Ysseldyke, J. E. Current assessment and decision-making practices in
model LD programs. *Learning Disability Quarterly*, 1979, *2*, 15–24.

Tidwell, R. Informal assessment to modify the role and image of the school psychologist.
Psychology in the Schools, 1980, *17*, 210–215.

Tindall, R. H. School psychology: The development of a profession. In G. D. Phye & D.
J. Reschly (Eds.), *School psychology: Perspectives and issues.* New York: Academic Press, 1979.

Tobias, S. Achievement treatment interactions. *Review of Educational Research*, 1976,
46, 61–74.

Tobiessen, J., & Shai, A. A comparison of individual and group mental health consultation with teachers. *Community Mental Health Journal*, 1971, *7*, 218–226.

Tombari, M. L., & Bergan, J. R. Consultant cues and teacher verbalizations, judgments,
and expectancies concerning children's adjustment problems. *Journal of School
Psychology*, 1978, *16*, 212–219.

Tomlinson, J. R. Accountability procedures for psychological services. *Psychology in the
Schools*, 1973, *1*, 42–47.

Tomlinson, J. R. Functional analysis and accountability of psychological services. *Psychology in the Schools*, 1974, *2*, 291–294.

Trachtman, G. M. Doing your thing in school psychology. *Professional Psychology*,
1971, *2*, 377–381.

Trachtman, G. M. Pupils, parents, privacy, and school psychologists. *American Psychologist*, 1972, *17*, 32–45.

Trachtman, G. M. On such a full sea. *School Psychology Review*, 1981, *10*, 138–181.

Trachtman, G. M. What have we accomplished? *School Psychology Review*, 1982, *11*,
192–194.

Traxler, A. J. State certification of school psychologists. *American Psychologist*, 1967,
22, 660–666.

Trickett, E. J., & Moos, R. H. The social environment of junior high and high school
classrooms. *Journal of Educational Psychology*, 1973, *65*, 93–102.

Turkewitz, H., O'Leary, K. D., & Ironsmith, M. Generalization and maintenance of
appropriate behavior. *Journal of Consulting and Clinical Psychology*, 1975, *43*,
577–583.

Turnbull, H. R., & Turnbull, A. P. *Free appropriate public education: Law and implementation*. Denver: Love Publishing Co., 1979.

Tyler, F. B., & Gatz, M. Development of individual psychosocial competence in a high school setting. *Journal of Consulting and Clinical Psychology*, 1975, *43*, 441–449.

Ullman, L., & Krasner, L. *A psychological approach to abnormal behavior*. Englewood Cliffs, N.J.: Prentice-Hall, 1969.

Vallett, R. E. *The practice of school psychology: Professional problems*. New York: Wiley, 1963.

Vallett, R. E. A formula for providing psychological services. *Psychology in the Schools*, 1965, *11*, 326–329.

VanHouten, R. Social validation: The evolution of standards of competency for target behaviors. *Journal of Applied Behavior Analysis*, 1979, *12*, 581–591.

Vernberg, E. M., & Medway, F. J. Teacher and parent causal perceptions of school problems. *American Educational Research Journal*, 1981, *18*, 29–37.

Vernon, P. A. *Speed of information processing and general intelligence*. Unpublished doctoral dissertation, University of California-Berkeley, 1981.

Wade, T. C., & Baker, T. B. Opinions and use of psychological tests: A survey of clinical psychologists. *American Psychologist*, 1977, *32*, 874–882.

Wade, T. C., Baker, T. B., Morton, T. L., & Baker, L. J. The status of psychological testing in clinical psychology: Relationships between test use and professional activities and orientations. *Journal of Personality Assessment*, 1978, *42*, 3–10.

Wahler, R. G., Berland, R. M., & Coe, T. D. Generalization processes in child behavior change. In B. B. Lahey & A. E. Kazdin (Eds.), *Advances in clinical child psychology* (Vol. 2). New York: Plenum, 1979.

Wahler, R., House, A., & Stambaugh, E. *Ecological assessment of child problem behavior: A clinical package for home, school, and institutional setting*. New York: Pergamon Press, 1976.

Walker, H. M., & Hops, H. Use of normative peer data as a standard for evaluating classroom treatment effects. *Journal of Applied Behavior Analysis*, 1976, *9*, 159–168.

Walker, H. M., Hops, H., & Fiegenbaum, E. Deviant classroom behavior as a function of combinations of social and token reinforcement and cost contingency. *Behavior Therapy*, 1976, *7*, 76–88.

Walker, J., & Zinober, J. W. Issues in evaluating children's mental health services. In R. Coursey (Ed.) *Program evaluation for mental health*. New York: Grune & Stratton, 1977.

Wallace, G. Interdisciplinary efforts in learning disabilities: Issues and recommendations. *Journal of Learning Disabilities*, 1976, *9*, 59–65.

Walter, R. The functions of a school psychologist. *American Educator*, 1925, *29*, 167–170.

Warren, S., & Brown, W. Examiner scoring errors on individual intelligence tests. *Psychology in the Schools*, 1973, *10*, 118–122.

Watson, R. I. *The great psychologists* (3rd ed.). Philadelphia: J. B. Lippincott, 1971.

Wechsler, D. *Wechsler preschool and primary scale of intelligence*. New York: The Psychological Corporation, 1967.

Wechsler, D. *Wechsler intelligence scale for children—revised.* New York: The Psychological Corporation, 1974.

Wechsler, D. *Wechsler adult intelligence scale—revised.* New York: The Psychological Corporation, 1981.

Weinstein, C. S. The physical environment of the school: A review of the research. *Review of Educational Research,* 1979, *49,* 577–610.

Wenger, R. D. Teacher response to collaborative consultation. *Psychology in the Schools,* 1979, *16,* 127–131.

Wenger, R. D. *Results of a survey of the implementation of the specialty guidelines for the delivery of services by school psychologists.* Paper presented to the annual meeting of the American Psychological Association, Washington, D.C., August, 1982.

White, M. A., & Harris, M. *The school psychologist.* New York: Harper, 1961.

Whyte, W. H. How to cheat on personality tests. In D. Jackson & S. Messick (Eds.), *Problems in human assessment.* New York: McGraw-Hill, 1967.

Wilcox, M. R. Variables affecting group mental health consultation for teachers. *Professional Psychology,* 1980, *11,* 728–732.

Willems, E. P. Behavioral technology and behavioral ecology. *Journal of Applied Behavior Analysis,* 1974, *7,* 151–165.

Williams, D. L. Consultation: A broad flexible role for school psychologists. *Psychology in the Schools,* 1972, *9,* 16–21.

Williams, R. C., Wall, C. C., Martin, W. M., & Berchin, A. *Effecting organizational renewal in schools: A social systems perspective.* New York: McGraw-Hill, 1974.

Willson, V. L., & Reynolds, C. R. Methodological and statistical problems in discerning membership in clinical populations. *Clinical Neuropsychology,* 1982, *4,* in press.

Wing, H., & Sarsley, V. The rehabilitation staffing conference in an extended care facility. *Geriatrics,* 1971, *26,* 144–147.

Winnett, R. A., & Winkler, R. C. Current behavior modification in the classroom: Be still, be quiet, be docile. *Journal of Applied Behavior Analysis,* 1972, *5,* 499–504.

Winnicott, D. W. *Therapeutic consultation in child psychiatry.* New York: Basic Books, 1971.

Wirt, R. D., Lachar, D., Kleindinst, J. K., & Seat, P. D. *Multidimensional description of child personality: A manual for the Personality Inventory for Children.* Los Angeles: Western Psychological Services, 1977.

Witt, J. C., & Bartlett, B. J. School psychologists as knowledge-linkers in the solution of children's reading problems. *School Psychology Review,* 1982, *11,* 221–229.

Witt, J. C., & Elliott, S. N. The response cost lottery: A time efficient and effective classroom intervention. *Journal of School Psychology,* 1982, *20,* 155–161.

Witt, J. C., & Elliott, S. N. Assessment in behavioral consultation: The initial interview. *School Psychology Review,* 1983, *12,* 42–49.

Witt, J. C., & Elliott, S. N. Acceptability of classroom management procedures. In T. R. Kratochwill (Ed.), *Advances in School Psychology,* vol. III, Hillsdale, NJ: Erlbaum, in press.

Witt, J. C., Elliott, S. N., & Hannifin, M. J. *Acceptability of behavioral interventions used in classrooms: The influence of amount of teacher time, severity of the problem behavior, and type of intervention.* Paper presented to the annual meeting of the American Educational Research Association, Montreal, Canada, April, 1983.

Witt, J. C., Elliott, S. N., & Martens, B. K. The influence of amount of teacher time, severity of behavior problem, and type of intervention on teacher judgments of intervention acceptability. *Behavioral Disorders,* in press.

Witt, J. C., Hannafin, M. J., & Martens, B. K. Home-based reinforcement: Behavioral covariation between academic performance and inappropriate behavior. *Journal of School Psychology,* in press.

Witt, J. C., & Martens, B. K. Assessing the acceptability of behavioral interventions. *Psychology in the Schools,* in press.

Witt, J. C., Martens, B. K., & Elliott, S. N. Factors affecting teacher judgements pertaining to the acceptability of behavioral intervention: Teacher time involvement, behavior problem severity, and type of intervention. *Behavior Therapy,* in press.

Witt, J. C., & Miller, C. D. *An ecological approach to classroom misbehavior.* Unpublished manuscript, University of Nebraska-Lincoln.

Witt, J. C., Miller, C. D., McIntyre, B., & Smith, D. Effect of parent participation, staffing length, and staffing size on parental satisfaction with staffings. *Exceptional Children,* in press.

Wolf, M. M. Social validity: The case for subjective measurement or how applied behavior analysis is finding its heart. *Journal of Applied Behavior Analysis.* 1978, *11,* 203–214.

Wolfensberger, W. Diagnosis diagnosed. *Journal of Mental Subnormality,* 1965, *11,* 62–70.

Wolman, B. B. (Ed.) *Handbook of clinical psychology.* New York: McGraw-Hill, 1965.

Woodcock, R. W. *Woodcock reading mastery tests.* Circle Pines, Minn.: American Guidance Service, 1973.

Woods, K. M., & McNamara, J. R. Confidentiality: Its effect on interviewee behavior. *Professional Psychology,* 1980, *11,* 714–121.

Wright, B. J., & Isenstein, V. R. *Psychological tests and minorities.* Rockville, Md.: NIMH, DHEW Publication # (ADM) 78-482, 1977.

Wright, D., & Gutkin, T. B. School psychologists' job satisfaction and discrepancies between actual and desired work functions. *Psychological Reports,* 1981, *49,* 735–738.

Yeaton, W. H., Greene, W. H., & Bailey, J. S. Behavioral community psychology strategies and tactics for teaching community skills to children and adolescents. In B. B. Lahey & A. E. Kazdin (Eds.), *Advances in Child Clinical Psychology.* New York: Plenum Press, 1981.

Yeaton, W. H., & Sechrest, L. Critical dimensions in the choice and maintenance of successful treatment: Strength, integrity, and effectiveness. *Journal of Consulting and Clinical Psychology,* 1981, *49,* 156–167. (a)

Yeaton, W. H., & Sechrest, L. Empirical approaches to effect size estimation in health research. In P. M. Wortman (Ed.), *Estimating effect size.* Beverly Hills, Calif.: Sage, 1981. (b)

Yoshida, R. K. Multidisciplinary decision-making in special education: A review of issues. *School Psychology Review,* 1980, *9,* 221–227.

Yoshida, R. K., Fenton, K. S., Maxwell, J. P., & Kaufman, M. J. Group decision-making in the planning team process: Myth or reality? *Journal of School Psychology,* 1978, *16,* 237–244.

Ysseldyke, J. E. Diagnostic prescriptive teaching: The search for aptitude-treatment interactions. In L. Mann and D. Sabatino (Eds.), *The first review of special education*, Vol. 1. Philadelphia: J.S.E. Press, 1973.

Ysseldyke, J. E. Remediation of ability deficits in adolescents: Some major questions. In L. Mann, L. Goodman, & J. L. Widerholt (Eds.), *The learning disabled adolescent*. Boston: Houghton Mifflin, 1978. (a)

Ysseldyke, J. E. Who's calling the plays in school psychology? *Psychology in the Schools*, 1978, *15*, 373–378. (b)

Ysseldyke, J. E. Issues in psychoeducational assessment. In G. Phye & D. J. Reschly (Eds.), *School psychology: Perspectives and issues*. New York: Academic Press, 1979.

Ysseldyke, J. E. The Spring Hill Symposium on the future of psychology in the schools. *American Psychologist*, 1982, *37*, 547–552.

Ysseldyke, J. E., Algozzine, B., Regan, R., & McGue, M. The influence of test scores and naturally occurring pupil characteristics on psychoeducational decision-making with children. *Journal of School Psychology*, 1981, *19*, 167–177.

Ysseldyke, J. E., Algozzine, B., Regan, R. R., & Potter, M. Technical adequacy of tests used in simulated decision making. *Psychology in the Schools*, 1980, *17*, 202–209.

Ysseldyke, J. E., Algozzine, B., & Thurlow, M. (Eds.). *A naturalistic investigation of special education team meetings*. (Research Report No. 40). Minneapolis: University of Minnesota, Institute for Research on Learning Disabilities, 1980.

Ysseldyke, J. E., & Mirkin, P. K. The use of assessment information to plan instructional interventions: A review of the research. In C. R. Reynolds and T. B. Gutkin (Eds.), *The handbook of school psychology*. New York: Wiley, 1982.

Ysseldyke, J. E., & Weinberg, R. Editorial comment: An introduction to the Spring Hill Symposium. *School Psychology Review*, 1981, *10*, 116–120.

Zegiob, L. E., & Forehand, R. Parent-child interactions: Observer effects and social class differences. *Behavior Therapy*, 1978, *9*, 118–123.

Zins, J. E., & Curtis, M. J. Using data-based evaluation in developing school consultation services. In M. J. Curtis & J. E. Zins (Eds.), *The theory and practice of school consultation*. Springfield, Ill.: Charles C Thomas, 1981.

Zubin, J. Classification of behavior disorders. *Annual Review of Psychology*, 1967, *18*, 373–406.

The National Association of School Psychologists Standards for the Provision of School Psychological Services

I. DEFINITIONS

1.1 A School Psychologist is a professional psychologist and educator who has met all requirements for credentialing according to NASP credentialing standards. This credential is based on completion of a NCATE accredited training program for school psychologists. A School Psychologist is deemed capable of providing services in the public or private sector.

1.2 Professional standards govern the *training (NASP Standards for Training Programs), field placement (NASP Standards for Field Placement), professional credentialing (NASP Standards for Credentialing of School Psychologists)*, and *ethical practice (NASP Principles for Professional Ethics)* of school psychology, in addition to the following standards for *services*.

1.3 Children, wherever used in the text, are those individuals who are served by an educational agency, public or private.

1.4 A Supervisor of School Psychological Services is a professional psychologist and educator who has met NASP requirements for credentialing as a school psychologist, has completed three years of successful experience as a school psychologist, as evaluated by a professional school psychologist supervisor, and who has been designated by an employing agency as the administrator/supervisor responsible for the school psychological services of the agency.

II.   FEDERAL LEVEL

2.1   *Organization*

The federal educational agency should employ a School Psychologist eligible for supervisory status as indicated in 1.4 in order to accomplish the following objectives:

2.2.1   To provide professional leadership assistance to the federal educational agency and state educational agencies in regard to standards, policies, and procedures for program delivery and for utilization, funding, training and inservice education of school psychological services personnel.

2.1.2   To participate in the administration of federal programs providing funding for school psychological services in state, intermediate and local education agencies.

2.1.3   To provide evaluation, research, and dissemination activities to determine the effectiveness of school psychological services programs, to determine needed changes, and to identify and communicate exemplary practices and resources to training and service units.

2.2.1   The Congress of the United States should ensure that the rights of parents and children are protected by the creation and modification of laws which provide for the services of School Psychologists, which include but are not limited to evaluation, intervention, and consultation for individuals, groups and systems. These services are provided to all children.

2.2.2   The Congress should ensure that such school psychological services are provided in a free and appropriate way to all children in need of such services.

2.2.3   The Congress should ensure that federal laws recognize the appropriate involvement of School Psychologists in educational programs and that federal funding is made available for the training, services, and continuing professional development of School Psychologists in order to guarantee appropriate and effective services.

2.2.4   The Congress should create no laws which effectively prohibit the credentialed School Psychologist from the ethical and legal practice of his/her profession in the service of children.

2.3   *Regulations*

2.3.1   All federal agencies should utilize the services of the federal educational agency School Psychologist in developing and implementing regulations pursuant to all relevant federal laws.

2.3.2   All federal agencies should seek the advice and consultation of the National Association of School Psychologists prior to the adoption of regulations pursuant to any federal law which involves or should reasonably involve the profession of school psychology.

III. STATE LEVEL

3.1 *Organization*

Each state educational agency (SEA) should employ a School Psychologist eligible for supervisory status as indicated in 1.4 in order to accomplish the following objectives:

3.1.1 To provide professional leadership assistance to the SEA and local educational agencies (LEAs) in regard to standards, policies, and procedures for program delivery and for the utilization, funding, training, and inservice education of school psychological services personnel.

3.1.2 To administer state and federal programs providing funding for school psychological services in intermediate and local educational agencies and for the training of School Psychologists.

3.1.3 To provide evaluation, research, and dissemination activities to determine the effectiveness of school psychological training and service programs, to determine needed changes, and to identify and communicate exemplary practices and resources to training and service units.

3.2 *Laws*

3.2.1 All state legislative bodies should ensure that the rights of parents and children are protected by the creation and modification of laws which provide for the services of School Psychologists for all children, including, but not limited to evaluation, intervention, and consultation for individuals, groups, and systems. These services are provided to all children.

3.2.2 The state legislature should ensure that such school psychological services are provided in a free and appropriate way to all children in need of such services.

3.2.3 The state legislature should ensure that state laws recognize the appropriate involvement of School Psychologists in educational programs and that adequate funding is made available for the training, services, and continuing professional development of School Psychologists in order to guarantee appropriate and effective services.

3.2.4 The state legislature should create no laws which prohibit the credentialed School Psychologist from the ethical and legal practice of his/her profession in the service of children.

3.2.5 The state legislature should ensure that there are sufficient numbers of adequately prepared and credentialed School Psychologists to provide services consistent with NASP Standards for the Provision of School Psychological Services. In most settings, this will require *at least* one School Psychologist for each 1000 children served by the LEA.

3.3 *Rules*

3.3.1 All state agencies should utilize the services of the SEA School Psychologist in developing and implementing administrative rules pursuant to all relevant state laws, federal laws, and regulations.

3.3.2 All state agencies should seek the advice and consultation of the state School Psychologists professional association prior to the adoption of rules pursuant to any state law, federal law, or regulation which involves or should reasonable involve the profession of school psychology.

3.3.3 All state educational agencies should utilize the services of the SEA School Psychologist in the SEA review and approval of school psychology training programs.

3.3.4 All state educational agencies shall utilize the services of the SEA School Psychologist in developing and implementing administrative rules for credentialing of School Psychologists. Such rules shall be consistent with the credentialing standards of the National Association of School Psychologists.

IV. LOCAL LEVEL

4.1 *Organization*

4.1.1 School psychological services are organized such that:

    4.1.1.1 Where two or more School Psychologists are employed, a coordinated system of school psychological services is in effect and is supervised by a Supervisor of School Psychological Services, as defined in 1.4.

    4.1.1.2 A credentialed School Psychologist who has completed an NCATE accredited program and three years of satisfactory service as a School Psychologist, at least one of which must have been in the employing agency, supervises each six or fewer school psychology interns employed by the local educational agency.

    4.1.1.3 School psychological services personnel may supervise/coordinate or share the responsibility for supervising/coordinating system/community mental health programs.

    4.1.1.4 School Psychologists may serve as administrators and coordinators of pupil services units, psychological services, interdisciplinary teams for exceptional and non-exceptional pupils, innovative programs for culturally different or disadvantaged populations, and the screening and assessment programs designed for these groups. These roles involve special skills and comprehensive knowledge of:

        a. interpersonal and group functioning

        b. administrative management techniques

    c. state and federal policies and laws

    d. district, community, and state resources

    e. procedures to facilitate optimal matching of pupil needs and human resources

    f. knowledge of budgeting techniques and funding source requirements

    g. personnel management techniques

    h. organization and implementation of remediation programs

4.1.2 School Psychologists may provide services to and be attached to any administrative or program unit within the school district.

4.2 Policies

The local educational agency shall adopt policies specifying that:

4.2.1 The function of the School Psychologist shall be to provide within legal and recognized professional standards an organizational and service framework within which efficient and appropriate school psychological services are provided to children, parents, and school staff.

4.2.2 The School Psychologist shall be responsible and accountable for school psychological services delivered to the administration of all programs served; shall be responsible for development, implementation, professional supervision, and articulation of psychological services to the programs of the agency, and shall report to the designated agency administrator regarding the organization and effectiveness of the services.

4.2.3 The School Psychologist must continue his/her professional training and development of professional skills in order to maintain eligibility for state or federal categorical aids reimbursement. He/she is responsible for obtaining professional growth experiences through participation in approved schooling, related workshops and seminars, and through investigating exemplary practices and projects (consistent with the NASP Program for Continuing Professional Development).

4.2.4 The school psychological services staff shall be responsible and accountable for the development, implementation, and evaluation of the following, through one or more of its staff members:

    4.2.4.1 A comprehensive continuum of coordinated psychological services for all children who are experiencing educational and/or behavioral problems, including those with suspected or identified handicaps and others whose needs can best be met within regular education, through parent consultation, and the utilization of community based resources.

    4.2.4.2 School psychological services as a part of a comprehensive interdisciplinary assessment and program planning procedure for children with suspected handicaps or for alternative planning when it is determined that the child does not have a handicap.

4.2.4.3 Non-biased intellectual, personality, emotional, and adaptive assessment of children utilizing individually administered informal and standardized assessment techniques.

4.2.4.4 Psychological prevention, intervention, and consultation for children, parents, and staff with regard to the educational, social, emotional, and behavioral needs of children.

4.2.4.5 Specialized resources to meet the identified needs of children.

4.2.4.6 Inservice education and continuing professional development activities with respect to identification, non-biased evaluation, programming, screening, and other procedures relevant to individuals with and without handicaps in relationship to educational programs.

4.2.4.7 Liaison with appropriate community agencies with regard to children whose special needs require such community agency assistance.

4.2.4.8 Other service and program obligations consistent with state and federal laws, rules, and regulations.

4.2.4.9 Evaluation and research with regard to the effectiveness of services.

4.2.4.10 All psychological services plans and report forms as required by the state educational agency and federal programs.

4.2.5 Assessment and Program Planning

4.2.5.1 The availability of standardized assessment techniques for use in determining the manner in which students might be helped to achieve educational success is in the best interests of the student.

4.2.5.2 The following minimum standards and practices shall be required to insure non-biased assessment and educational programming for all children:

4.2.5.2.1 An interdisciplinary team shall be involved in assessment and program decision making.

4.2.5.2.2 The interdisciplinary team shall include a fully trained and credentialed School Psychologist.

4.2.5.2.3 All members of the interdisciplinary team shall regularly review the ethical standards of their profession and shall act in a manner consistent with them.

4.2.5.2.4 The School Psychologist shall communicate a minority position to all involved when in disagreement with the interdisciplinary team position.

4.2.5.2.5 Assessment procedures and program recommendations shall be chosen to maximize the student's opportunities to be successful in the general culture.

4.2.5.2.6 Multi-faceted assessment batteries shall be used which focus on the student's strengths and needs.

4.2.5.2.7 All student information shall be interpreted in the context of the student's socio-cultural background.

4.2.5.2.8 Assessment techniques shall be used only by personnel professionally trained in their use.

4.2.5.2.9 School Psychologists shall do everything possible to promote the development of objective, valid, and reliable assessment techniques.

4.2.5.2.10 Informed written consent of parents and/or student shall be required for assessment and special program implementation.

4.2.5.2.11 The parents and/or student shall be invited to participate in decision-making meetings.

4.2.5.2.12 Upon request by the parents and/or student, an advocate of the same socio-cultural background as that of the student shall participate in conferences focusing on assessment results and program recommendations.

4.2.5.2.13 A record of meetings regarding assessment results and program recommendations shall be available to all directly concerned.

4.2.5.2.14 Educational programs shall maximize the strengths of diverse backgrounds in achieving success in the general culture.

4.2.5.2.15 The School Psychologist shall be directly involved in determining options in and revisions of educational programs to insure that they are adaptive to the needs of students.

4.2.5.2.16 The School Psychologist shall follow up on the efficacy of his/her recommendations.

4.2.5.2.17 Student needs shall be given priority over administrative efficiency in determining educational programs.

4.2.5.2.18 Specific educational prescriptions shall result from the assessment team's actions.

4.2.5.2.19 Where a clear determination of the student's needs does not result from assessment, a diagnostic teaching program should be offered.

4.2.5.2.20 Regular review of the student's program shall be conducted and shall be followed by necessary program modifications.

4.2.6 *Professional Ethics of the National Association of School Psychologists:* All school psychological services personnel are required to know and adhere to the Principles for Professional Ethics.

4.2.7 School Psychological Records

4.2.7.1 The local agency policy on student records shall be consistent with state and federal law and shall specify the types of data developed by the School Psychologist which are classified as school or pupil records. Test protocols, observation and interview notes, and psychological treatment notes shall not be shared with others and shall be classified as personal notes of the School Psychologist. As such, these personal notes are the sole property of the School Psychologist and are not classified as school or pupil records. While parents of handicapped children may inspect and review any personally identifiable data relating to their child which were collected, maintained, or used in identifying, locating, and evaluating their child's handicap, such personally identifiable data contained in personal notes may not be copied without the permission of the School Psychologist.

4.2.7.2 Access to psychological records is restricted to those permitted by law who have legitimate educational interest in the records. School Psychologists are required to interpret school psychological records to those seeking access.

4.2.7.3 School psychological records are only created where the information is necessary and relevant to legitimate educational program needs and where parents have given their informed consent for the creation of such a record. This consent shall be based upon the parent's full knowledge of the purposes for which the information is sought and the personnel who will have access to it.

4.2.7.4 School psychological records are purged in keeping with relevant federal and state laws and in order to protect children from decisions based on incorrect or misleading data.

4.3 *Plans*

4.3.1 The School Psychologist shall be involved in the preparation of local agency plans required by state and/or federal laws dealing with the educationally disadvantaged, handicapped, gifted, delinquent, linguistic minorities, and mental health needs.

4.3.2 Plans for the involvement of School Psychologists in local programs shall be developed by the School Psychologist in cooperation with appropriate staff of the local agency.

4.3.3 Each year's specific objectives for school psychological services are written in measurable terms in reference to the planned effects on:
   a. the school system as a whole
   b. specific staff groups
   c. specific student groups
   d. parent groups
   e. community action related to education

4.3.4 Specific objectives are written in measurable terms by each School Psychologist for each of the following:
   a. students
   b. staff members
   c. parents
   d. schools

4.4 *Procedures*

4.4.1 The recruitment of school psychological services personnel by local agencies shall be conducted with the advice and assistance of credentialed and experienced School Psychologists. Selection of the Psychological services staff members shall be consistent with the needs of the local agency and the population to be served. Professional school psychological services staff members shall meet state certification requirements, based upon NASP credentialing standards, and be graduates of programs accredited by NCATE (National Council for Accreditation of Teacher Education).

4.4.2 Each School Psychologist regularly evaluates his/her effectiveness in reaching objectives personally set and keeps records of his/her efforts and the results from those efforts on all cases in which said person is involved. (Such records identify and tabulate all forms of involvement, not just formal individual pupil study.)

4.4.3 Staff records (graphs, charts, tables, etc.) are kept on diagnosis-intervention-result relationships.

4.4.4 The activities of school psychological services staff are in accord with the existing ethical standards of the profession of school psychology (and in keeping with state educational agencies recommendations for these services) which are clearly communicated to and fully understood by each School Psychologist.

4.4.5 School Psychologists develop and implement procedures leading to the maintenance and improvement of the effectiveness of school psychological services.

4.4.6 The school psychological services staff meets regularly during the school year to evaluate progress toward its objectives and make necessary procedural-directional modifications related to its efforts.

V. PRACTITIONER LEVEL

5.1 *Practices*

5.1.1 School Psychologists study individuals to determine their needs through individual and group procedures in a manner consistent with the following points:

5.1.1.1 A clearly stated referral system is in writing and is communicated to parents, staff members and students (to facilitate self-referral).

5.1.1.2 School Psychologists participate in determining to whom their services will be offered.

5.1.1.3 Informed parental and/or student consent is always gained for formal individual evaluation.

5.1.1.4 School psychological services personnel have and make appropriate use of opportunities to study educational, medical, psychological and social history data, confer with involved others (staff, parents, peers, etc.), and observe the pupils of concern in a variety of settings for the purpose of early identification and subsequent evaluation, individually and/or in groups.

5.1.1.5 Individual evaluation, as conducted by the School Psychologist, includes consideration for the areas of personal-social adjustment, intelligence-scholastic aptitude, adaptive behavior, educational readiness, academic achievement, sensory and perceptual-motor functioning, and environmental/cultural influences.

5.1.1.6 Individual evaluation results in the School Psychologist being able to conceptualize and communicate the pupil's present functioning characteristics, strengths, and needs.

5.1.2 School Psychologists insure the development, implementation, and follow-up of psycho-educational intervention plans for helping specific children.

5.2.2.1 The School Psychologist insures that consideration is given to present and potential resources in the school, home, and community.

5.1.2.2 Intervention plans are cooperatively developed in conferences by the School Psychologist, those who referred the child, and those who in all likelihood will be required to implement them.

5.1.2.3 The School Psychologist is skilled in selection and in implementation of intervention techniques and materials.

5.1.2.4 The School Psychologist is involved in the design and development of specialized procedures to be employed in the amelioration of the child's learning or behavioral handicap.

5.1.2.5 Follow-up procedures (involving a time sequence for reports from those working with a child, follow-up conference or conferences and, if necessary, re-evaluations) are planned at the conclusion of or during intervention plan development.

5.1.2.6 Evaluation results, intervention plans, implementation procedures, and follow-up plans are clearly communicated to all involved on a "need to know" basis during an acknowledged period of usefulness.

5.1.3 School Psychologists provide direct services to pupils through:

5.1.3.1 Counseling, behavior management, and psychological therapy, serving as an agent for educational and/or personal change on both an individual and group basis.

5.1.3.2 Remediation (e.g., providing direct assistance to individuals in both regular and exceptional programs).

5.1.4 School Psychologists serve children through serving staff and parents.

5.1.4.1 School psychological services staff provide individual/group counseling services to staff and parents.

5.1.4.2 School psychological services staff design and develop specialized procedures for preventing disorders and for improving children's learning and/or behavioral functioning.

5.1.4.3 Consultative services, in addition to those associated with individual pupil study, are provided to school staff and parents.

5.1.4.4 Training experiences are provided to school staff, parents, and others in the community in regard to general issues of human learning, development and behavior.

5.1.5 School Psychologists serve children through taking part in school program decision-making activities.

5.1.5.1 The school psychological services team has members on formal and informal committees responsible for decisions in areas having system-wide implications (e.g., a system-wide curriculum; integration of special education and general education programs; educational philosophy, objectives, and goals; staff development).

5.1.5.2 The school psychological services team is involved in the continual evaluation of school programs, comparing student behavior to stated objectives, and the making of recommendations for modifying programs based on the results of such evaluations.

5.1.6 School Psychologists provide liaison and consulting services to the community and its agencies in areas of psychological/mental health nature.

5.1.6.1 School Psychologists communicate frequently with community and state agencies and professionals (e.g., child guidance and/or community mental health centers; family services agencies; welfare agencies; community doctor, psychologists and psychiatrists.)

5.1.6.2 A School Psychologist is informed of and has the opportunity to participate in community agency staffings in cases involving students.

5.1.6.3 Community agency personnel are invited to participate in school system conferences concerning children with whom they are involved.

5.1.6.4 School Psychologists are given responsibilities for recommending referral to and communication with community and state agencies and personnel.

5.1.7 The School Psychologist provides leadership services.

5.1.7.1 The School Psychologist is presently and observably working to insure that:

a. instruction is appropriately individualized;

b. special and general education program are integrated;

c. norm-referenced evaluation is complemented by criterion-referenced evaluation;

d. parents are regularly informed of their child's progress in criterion-referenced terms;

e. each child experiences success and that systems of regularly failing students are abolished;

f. preventive programs (early identification, counseling, individualizing programs, etc.) are given more emphasis than remedial programs;

g. early childhood education programs are effected;

h. family life, sex education, and life adjustment programs are cooperatively developed and implemented by school, parents, and community;

i. the emphasis is on the assessment of individual needs and not on indiscriminate assignment of children to categorical programs;

    j. each student is relating personally, at a one-to-one level, with one or more school staff members;

    k. students are helped to achieve maturity of judgment by being given, by a defined sequence, increasing responsibility for decision-making;

    l. the protection of the human and civil rights of all pupils is advocated.

5.1.8 The School Psychologist designs, conducts, and utilizes the results of research of a psychological nature.

    5.1.8.1 Applied and/or basic research should be pursued, focusing on:

        a. Psychological functioning of human beings.

        b. Psycho-educational assessment tools and procedures.

        c. Educational programs and techniques applied to individual cases and groups of various sizes.

        d. Educational processes and milieu.

        e. Social system interactions and patterns within and associated with school communities.

    5.1.8.2 Involvement ranges from support or advisory services, to major direct responsibility in any of the following aspects of research:

        a. Planning

        b. Data Collection

        c. Data Analysis

        d. Dissemination

        e. Translating research into practical applications within the school community.

5.1.9 School Psychologists perform other duties in an accountable manner, by keeping records of these efforts, evaluating their effectiveness, and modifying their practices as needed.

5.1.10 Each School Psychologist practices in full accordance with the code of professional ethics of the National Association of School Psychologists.

APPENDIX **B**

Specialty Guidelines for the Delivery of Services by School Psychologists

The Specialty Guidelines that follow are based on the generic *Standards for Providers of Psychological Services* originally adopted by the American Psychological Association (APA) in September 1974 and revised in January 1977 (APA, 1974b, 1977b). Together with the generic *Standards,* these Specialty Guidelines state the official policy of the Association regarding delivery of services by school psychologists. Admission to the practice of psychology is regulated by state statute. It is the position of the Association that licensing be based on generic, and not on specialty, qualifications. Specialty guidelines serve the additional purpose of providing potential users and other interested groups with essential information about particular services available from the several specialties in professional psychology.

Professional psychology specialties have evolved from generic practice in psychology and are supported by university training programs. There are now at least four

Source: These Specialty Guidelines were prepared through the cooperative efforts of the APA Committee on Standards for Providers of Psychological Services (COSPOPS) and the APA Professional Affairs Committee of the Division of School Psychology (Division 16). Jack I. Bardon and Nadine M. Lambert served as the school psychology representatives of COSPOPS, and Arthur Centor and Richard Kilburg were the Central Office liaisons to the committee. Durand F. Jacobs served as chair of COSPOPS, and Walter B. Pryzwansky chaired the Division 16 committee. Drafts of the school psychology Guidelines were reviewed and commented on by members of the Executive Committee of Division 16, representatives of the National Association of School Psychologists, state departments of education, consultants in school psychology, and many professional school psychologists in training programs and in practice in the schools.

recognized professional specialties—clinical, counseling, school, and industrial/organizational psychology.

The knowledge base in each of these specialty areas has increased, refining the state of the art to the point that a set of uniform specialty guidelines is now possible and desirable. The present Guidelines are intended to educate the public, the profession, and other interested parties regarding specialty professional practices. They are also intended to facilitate the continued systematic development of the profession.

The content of each Specialty Guideline reflects a consensus of university faculty and public and private practitioners regarding the knowledge base, services provided, problems addressed, and clients served.

Traditionally, all learned disciplines have treated the designation of specialty practice as a reflection of preparation in greater depth in a particular subject matter, together with a voluntary limiting of focus to a more restricted area of practice by the professional. Lack of specialty designation does not preclude general providers of psychological services from using the methods or dealing with the populations of any specialty, except insofar as psychologists voluntarily refrain from providing services they are not trained to render. It is the intent of these Guidelines, however, that after the grandparenting period, psychologists not put themselves forward as *specialists* in a given area of practice unless they meet the qualifications noted in the Guidelines (see Definitions). Therefore, these Guidelines are meant to apply only to those psychologists who wish to be designated as *school psychologists*. They do not apply to other psychologists.

These Guidelines represent the profession's best judgment of the conditions, credentials, and experience that contribute to competent professional practice. The APA strongly encourages, and plans to participate in, efforts to identify professional practitioner behaviors and job functions and to validate the relation between these and desired client outcomes. Thus, future revisions of these Guidelines will increasingly reflect the results of such efforts.

These Guidelines follow the format and, wherever applicable, the wording of the generic *Standards*.[1] The intent of these Guidelines is to improve the quality, effectiveness, and accessibility of psychological services. They are meant to provide guidance to providers, users and sanctioners regarding the best judgment of the profession on these matters. Although the Specialty Guidelines have been derived from and are consistent with the generic *Standards,* they may be used as a separate document. *Standards for Providers of Psychological Services* (APA, 1977b), however, shall remain the basic policy statement and shall take precedence where there are questions of interpretation.

Professional psychology in general and school psychology in particular have had a long and difficult history of attempts to establish criteria for determining guidelines for the delivery of services. In school psychology, state departments of education have traditionally had a strong influence on the content of programs required for certification and on minimum competency levels for practice, leading to wide variations in requirements among the many states. These national Guidelines will reduce confusion, clarify important dimensions of specialty practice, and provide a common basis for peer review of school psychologists' performance.

The Committee on Professional Standards established by the APA in January 1980 is charged with keeping the generic *Standards* and the Specialty Guidelines responsive to the needs of the public and the profession. It is also charged with continually reviewing, modifying, and extending them progressively as the profession and the science of psychology develop new knowledge, improved methods, and additional modes of psychological services.

The Specialty Guidelines for the Delivery of Services by School Psychologists have been established by the APA as a means of self-regulation to protect the public interest. They guide the specialty practice of school psychology by specifying important areas of quality assurance and performance that contribute to the goal of facilitating more effective human functioning.

PRINCIPLES AND IMPLICATIONS OF THE SPECIALTY GUIDELINES

These Specialty Guidelines have emerged from and reaffirm the same basic principles that guided the development of the generic *Standards for Providers of Psychological Services* (APA, 1977b):

1. These Guidelines recognize that admission to the practice of school psychology is regulated by state statute.
2. It is the intention of the APA that the generic *Standards* provide appropriate guidelines for statutory licensing of psychologists. In addition, although it is the position of the APA that licensing be generic and not in specialty areas, these Specialty Guidelines in school psychology should provide an authoritative reference for use in credentialing specialty providers of school psychological services by such groups as divisions of the APA and state associations and by boards and agencies that find such criteria useful for quality assurance.
3. A uniform set of Specialty Guidelines governs school psychological service functions offered by school psychologists, regardless of setting or source of remuneration. All school psychologists in professional practice recognize and are responsive to a uniform set of Specialty Guidelines, just as they are guided by a common code of ethics.
4. School psychology Guidelines establish clearly articulated levels of training and experience that are consistent with, and appropriate to, the functions performed. School psychological services provided by persons who do not meet the APA qualifications for a professional school psychologist (see Definitions) are to be supervised by a professional school psychologist. Final responsibility and accountability for services provided rest with professional school psychologists.
5. A uniform set of Specialty Guidelines governs the quality of services to all users of school psychological services in both the private and the public sectors. Those receiving school psychological services are protected by the same kinds of safeguards, irrespective of sector; these include constitutional guarantees, statutory regulation, peer review, consultation, record review, and staff supervision.
6. These Guidelines, while assuring the user of the school psychologist's accountability for the nature and quality of services specified in this document, do not preclude the school psychologist from using new methods or developing innovative procedures for the delivery of school psychological services.

These Specialty Guidelines for school psychology have broad implications both for users of school psychological services and for providers of such services:

1. Guidelines for school psychological services provide a foundation for mutual understanding between provider and user and facilitate more effective evaluation of services provided and outcomes achieved.

2. Guidelines for school psychological services are essential for uniformity of regulation by state departments of education and other regulatory or legislative agencies concerned with the provision of school psychological services. In addition, they provide the basis for state approval of training programs and for the development of accreditation procedures for schools and other facilities providing school psychological services.

3. Guidelines give specific content to the profession's concept of ethical practice as it applies to the functions of school psychologists.

4. Guidelines for school psychological services have significant impact on tomorrow's education and training models for both professional and support personnel in school psychology.

5. Guidelines for the provision of school psychological services influence the determination of acceptable structure, budgeting, and staffing patterns in schools and other facilities using these services.

6. Guidelines for school psychological services require continual review and revision.

The Specialty Guidelines presented here are intended to improve the quality and the delivery of school psychological services by specifying criteria for key aspects of the service setting. Some school settings may require additional and/or more stringent criteria for specific areas of service delivery.

Systematically applied, these Guidelines serve to establish a more effective and consistent basis for evaluating the performance of individual service providers as well as to guide the organization of school psychological service units.

DEFINITIONS

Providers of school psychological services refers to two categories of persons who provide school psychological services:

A. Professional school psychologists.[2,3] Professional school psychologists have a doctoral degree from a regionally accredited university or professional school providing an organized, sequential school psychology program in a department of psychology in a university or college, in an appropriate department of a school of education or other similar administrative organization, or in a unit of a professional school. School psychology programs that are accredited by the American Psychological Association are recognized as meeting the definition of a school psychology program. School psychology programs that are not accredited by the American Psychological Association meet the definition of a school psychology program if they satisfy the following criteria:

1. The program is primarily psychological in nature and stands as a recognizable, coherent organizational entity within the institution.

2. The program provides an integrated, organized sequence of study.
3. The program has an identifiable body of students who are matriculated in that program for a degree.
4. There is a clear authority with primary responsibility for the core and specialty areas, whether or not the program cuts across administrative lines.
5. There is an identifiable psychology faculty, and a psychologist is responsible for the program.

Patterns of education and training in school psychology[4] are consistent with the functions to be performed and the services to be provided, in accordance with the ages, populations, and problems found in the various schools and other settings in which school psychologists are employed. The program of study includes a core of academic experience, both didactic and experiential, in basic areas of psychology, includes education related to the practice of the specialty, and provides training in assessment, intervention, consultation, research, program development, and supervision, with special emphasis on school-related problems or school settings.[5]

Professional school psychologists who wish to represent themselves as proficient in specific applications of school psychology that are not already part of their training are required to have further academic training and supervised experience in those areas of practice.

B. All other persons who offer school psychological services under the supervision of a school psychologist. Although there may be variations in the titles and job descriptions of such persons, they are not called school psychologists. Their functions may be indicated by use of the adjective *psychological* preceding the noun.

1. A *specialist in school psychology* has successfully completed at least 2 years of graduate education in school psychology and a training program that includes at least 1,000 hours of experience supervised by a professional school psychologist, of which at least 500 hours must be in school settings. A specialist in school psychology provides psychological services under the supervision of a professional school psychologist.[6]
2. Titles for others who provide school psychological services under the supervision of a professional school psychologist may include *school psychological examiner, school psychological technician, school psychological assistant, school psychometrist,* or *school psychometric assistant.*

School psychological services refers to one or more of the following services offered to clients involved in educational settings, from preschool through higher education, for the protection and promotion of mental health and the facilitation of learning.[7]

A. Psychological and psychoeducational evaluation and assessment of the school functioning of children and young persons. Procedures include screening, psychological and educational tests (particularly individual psychological tests of intellectual functioning, cognitive development, affective behavior, and neuropsychological status), interviews, observation, and behavioral evaluations, with explicit regard for the context and setting in which the professional judgments based on assessment, diagnosis, and evaluation will be used.

B. Interventions to facilitate the functioning of individuals or groups, with concern for how schooling influences and is influenced by their cognitive, conative, affective, and social development. Such interventions may include, but are not limited to, recommending, planning, and evaluating special education services; psychoeducational therapy; counseling; affective educational programs; and training programs to improve coping skills.[8]

C. Interventions to facilitate the educational services and child care functions of school personnel, parents, and community agencies. Such interventions may include, but are not limited to, in-service school-personnel education programs, parent education programs, and parent counseling.

D. Consultation and collaboration with school personnel and/or parents concerning specific school-related problems of students and the professional problems of staff. Such services may include, but are not limited to, assistance with the planning of educational programs from a psychological perspective; consultation with teachers and other school personnel to enhance their understanding of the needs of particular pupils; modification of classroom instructional programs to facilitate children's learning; promotion of a positive climate for learning and teaching; assistance to parents to enable them to contribute to their children's development and school adjustment; and other staff development activities.

E. Program development services to individual schools, to school administrative systems, and to community agencies in such areas as needs assessment and evaluation of regular and special education programs; liaison with community, state, and federal agencies concerning the mental health and educational needs of children; coordination, administration, and planning of specialized educational programs; the generation, collection, organization, and dissemination of information from psychological research and theory to educate staff and parents.

F. Supervision of school psychological services (see Guideline 1.2, Interpretation).

A *school psychological service unit* is the functional unit through which school psychological services are provided; any such unit has at least one professional school psychologist associated with it:

A. Such a unit provides school psychological services to individuals, a school system, a district, a community agency, or a corporation, or to a consortium of school systems, districts, community agencies, or corporations that contract together to employ providers of school psychological services. A school psychological service unit is composed of one or more professional school psychologists and, in most instances, supporting psychological services staff.

B. A school psychological service unit may operate as an independent professional service to schools or as a functional component of an administrative organizational unit, such as a state department of education, a public or private school system, or a community mental health agency.

C. One or more professional school psychologists providing school psychological services in an interdisciplinary or a multidisciplinary setting constitute a school psychological service unit.

D. A school psychological service unit may also be one or more professional psychologists offering services in private practice, in a school psychological consulting firm, or in a college- or university-based facility or program that contracts to offer school psychological services to individuals, groups, school systems, districts, or corporations.

Users of school psychological services include:

A. Direct users or recipients of school psychological services, such as pupils, instructional and administrative school staff members, and parents.

B. Public and private institutions, facilities, or organizations receiving school psychological services, such as boards of education of public or private schools, mental health facilities, and other community agencies and educational institutions for handicapped or exceptional children.

C. Third-party purchasers—those who pay for the delivery of services but who are not the recipients of services.

D. Sanctioners—such as those who have a legitimate concern with the accessibility, timeliness, efficacy, and standards of quality attending the provision of school psychological services. Sanctioners may include members of the user's family, the court, the probation officer, the school administrator, the employer, the facility director, and so on. Sanctioners may also include various governmental, peer review, and accreditation bodies concerned with the assurance of quality.

Guideline 1

Providers

1.1 *Each school psychological service unit offering school psychological services has available at least one professional school psychologist and as many additional professional school psychologists and support personnel as are necessary to assure the adequacy and quality of services offered.*

Interpretation: The intent of this Guideline is that one or more providers of psychological services in any school psychological service unit meet the levels of training and experience of the professional school psychologist specified in the preceding definitions.

When a professional school psychologist is not available on a full-time basis to provide school psychological services, the school district obtains the services of a professional school psychologist on a regular part-time basis. Yearly contracts are desirable to ensure continuity of services during a school year. The school psychologist so retained directs the psychological services, supervises the psychological services provided by support personnel, and participates sufficiently to be able to assess the need for services, review the content of services provided, and assume professional responsibility and accountability for them. A professional school psychologist supervises no more than the equivalent of 15 full-time specialists in school psychology and/or other school psychological personnel.

Districts that do not have easy access to professional school psychologists because of geographic considerations, or because professional school psychologists do not live or work in the area employ at least one full-time specialist in school psychology and as many more support personnel as are necessary to assure the adequacy and quality of services. The following strategies may be considered to acquire the necessary supervisory services from a professional school psychologist:

A. Employment by a county, region, consortium of schools, or state department of education of full-time supervisory personnel in school psychology who meet appropriate levels of training and experience, as specified in the definitions, to visit school districts regularly for supervision of psychological services staff.

B. Employment of professional school psychologists who engage in independent practice for the purpose of providing supervision to school district psychological services staff.

C. Arrangements with nearby school districts that employ professional school psychologists for part-time employment of such personnel on a contract basis specifically for the purpose of supervision as described in Guideline 1.

The school psychologist directing the school psychological service unit, whether on a full- or part-time basis, is responsible for determining and justifying appropriate ratios of school psychologists to users, to specialists in school psychology, and to support personnel, in order to ensure proper scope, accessibility, and quality of services provided in that setting. The school psychologist reports to the appropriate school district representatives any findings regarding the need to modify psychological services or staffing patterns to assure the adequacy and quality of services offered.

1.2 *Providers of school psychological services who do not meet the requirements for the professional school psychologist are supervised directly by a professional school psychologist who assumes professional responsibility and accountability for the services provided. The level and extent of supervision may vary from task to task so long as the supervising psychologist retains a sufficiently close supervisory relationship to meet this Guideline. Special proficiency training or supervision may be provided by a professional psychologist of another specialty or by a professional from another discipline whose competency in the given area has been demonstrated.*[9]

Interpretation: Professional responsibility and accountability for the services provided require that the supervisor review reports and test protocols; review and discuss intervention strategies, plans, and outcomes; maintain a comprehensive view of the school's procedures and special concerns; and have sufficient opportunity to discuss discrepancies among the views of the supervisor, the supervised, and other school personnel on any problem or issue. In order to meet this Guideline, an appropriate number of hours per week are devoted to direct face-to-face supervision of each full-time school psychological service staff member. In no event is this supervision less than one hour per week for each staff member. The more comprehensive the psychological services are, the more supervision is needed. A plan or formula for relating increasing amounts of supervisory time to the complexity of professional responsibilities is to be developed. The amount and nature of supervision is specified in writing to all parties concerned.

1.3 *Wherever a school psychological service unit exists, a professional school psychologist is responsible for planning, directing, and reviewing the provision of school psychological services.*

Interpretation: A school psychologist coordinates the activities of the school psychological service unit with other professionals, administrators, and community groups, both within and outside the school. This school psychologist, who may be the director, coordinator, or supervisor of the school psychological service unit, has related responsibilities including, but not limited to, recruiting qualified staff, directing training and research activities of the service, maintaining a high level of professional and ethical practice, and ensuring that staff members function only within the areas of their competency.

To facilitate the effectiveness of services by raising the level of staff sensitivity and professional skills, the psychologist designated as director is responsible for participating in the selection of staff and support personnel whose qualifications are directly relevant to the needs and characteristics of the users served.

In the event that a professional school psychologist is employed by the school psychological service unit on a basis that affords him or her insufficient time to carry out full responsibility for coordinating or directing the unit, a specialist in school psychology is designated as director or coordinator of the school psychological services and is supervised by a professional school psychologist employed on a part-time basis, for a minimum of 2 hours per week.

1.4 *When functioning as part of an organizational setting, professional school psychologists bring their backgrounds and skills to bear on the goals of the organization, whenever appropriate, by participating in the planning and development of overall services.*

Interpretation: Professional school psychologists participate in the maintenance of high professional standards by serving as representatives on, or consultants to, committees and boards concerned with service delivery, especially when such committees deal with special education, pupil personnel services, mental health aspects of schooling, or other services that use or involve school psychological knowledge and skills.

As appropriate to the setting, school psychologists' activities may include active participation, as voting and as office-holding members, on the facility's executive, planning, and evaluation boards and committees.

1.5 *School psychologists maintain current knowledge of scientific and professional developments to preserve and enhance their professional competence.*

Interpretation: Methods through which knowledge of scientific and professional developments may be gained include, but are not limited to, (a) the reading or preparation of scientific and professional publications and other materials, (b) attendance at workshops and presentations at meetings and conventions, (c) participation in on-the-job staff development programs, and (d) other forms of continuing education. The school psychologist and staff have available reference material and journals related to the provision of school psychological services. School psychologists are prepared to show evidence periodically that they are staying abreast of current knowledge in the field of school psychology and are also keeping their certification and licensing credentials up-to-date.

1.6 *School psychologists limit their practice to their demonstrated areas of professional competence.*

Interpretation: School psychological services are offered in accordance with the providers' areas of competence as defined by verifiable training and experience. When extending services beyond the range of their usual practice, school psychologists obtain pertinent training or appropriate professional supervision. Such training or supervision is consistent with the extension of functions performed and services provided. An extension of services may involve a change in the theoretical orientation of the practitioner, in the techniques used, in the client age group (e.g., children, adolescents, or parents), or in the kinds of problems addressed (e.g., mental retardation, neurological impairment, learning disabilities, family relationships).

1.7 *Psychologists who wish to qualify as school psychologists meet the same requirements with respect to subject matter and professional skills that apply to doctoral training in school psychology.* [10]

Interpretation: Education of psychologists to qualify them for specialty practice in school psychology is under the auspices of a department in a regionally accredited university or of a professional school that offers the doctoral degree in school psychology, through campus- and/or field-based arrangements. Such education is individualized, with due credit being given for relevant course work and other requirements that have previously been satisfied. In addition to the doctoral-level education specified above, appropriate doctoral-level training is required. An internship or experience in a school setting is not adequate preparation for becoming a school psychologist when prior education has not been in that area. Fulfillment of such an individualized training program is attested to by the awarding of a certificate by the supervising department or professional school that indicates the successful completion of preparation in school psychology.

1.8 *Professional school psychologists are encouraged to develop innovative theories and procedures and to provide appropriate theoretical and/or empirical support for their innovations.*

Interpretation: A specialty of a profession rooted in science intends continually to explore, study, and conduct research with a view to developing and verifying new and improved methods of serving the school population in ways that can be documented.

Guideline 2

Programs

2.1 *Composition and organization of a school psychological service unit:*
2.1.1 *The composition and programs of a school psychological service unit are responsive to the needs of the school population that is served.*

Interpretation: A school psychological service unit is structured so as to facilitate effective and economical delivery of services. For example, a school psychological service unit serving predominantly low-income, ethnic, or racial minority children has a staffing pattern and service programs that are adapted to the linguistic, experiential, and attitudinal characteristics of the users. Appropriate types of assessment materials and norm reference groups are utilized in the practice of school psychology.

2.1.2 *A description of the organization of the school psychological service unit and its lines of responsibility and accountability for the delivery of school psychological services is available in written form to instructional and administrative staff of the unit and to parents, students, and members of the community.*

Interpretation: The description includes lines of responsibility, supervisory relationships, and the level and extent of accountability for each person who provides school psychological services.

2.1.3 *A school psychological service unit includes sufficient numbers of professional and support personnel to achieve its goals, objectives, and purposes.*

Interpretation: A school psychological service unit includes one or more professional school psychologists, specialists in school psychology, and other psychological services support personnel. When a professional school psychologist is not available to provide services on a full- or part-time basis, the school psychological services are conducted by a specialist in school psychology, supervised by a professional school psychologist (see Guideline 1.2).

The work load and diversity of school psychological services required and the specific goals and objectives of the setting determine the numbers and qualifications of professional and support personnel in the school psychological service unit. For example, the extent to which services involve case study, direct intervention, and/or consultation will be significant in any service plan. Case study frequently involves teacher and/or parent conferences, observations of pupils, and a multi-assessment review, including student interviews. Similarly, the target populations for services affect the range of services that can be offered. One school psychologist, or one specialist in school psychology under supervision, for every 2,000 pupils is considered appropriate.[11]

Where shortages in personnel exist, so that school psychological services cannot be rendered in a professional manner, the director of the school psychological service unit informs the supervisor/administrator of the service about the implications of the shortage and initiates action to remedy the situation. When this fails, the director appropriately modifies the scope or work load of the unit to maintain the quality of services rendered.

2.2 *Policies:*

2.2.1 *When the school psychological service unit is composed of more than one person or is a component of a larger organization, a written statement of its objectives and scope of services is developed, maintained, and reviewed.*

Interpretation: The school psychological service unit reviews its objectives and scope of services annually and revises them as necessary to ensure that the school psychological services offered are consistent with staff competencies and current psychological knowledge and practice. This statement is discussed with staff, reviewed by the appropriate administrators, distributed to instructional and administrative staff and school board members, and when appropriate, made available to parents, students, and members of the community upon request.

2.2.2 *All providers within a school psychological service unit support the legal and civil rights of the users.*[12]

Interpretation: Providers of school psychological services safeguard the interests of school personnel, students, and parents with regard to personal, legal, and civil rights. They are continually sensitive to the issue of confidentiality of information, the short-term and long-term impacts of their decisions and recommendations, and other matters pertaining to individual, legal, and civil rights. Concerns regarding the safeguarding of individual rights of school personnel, students, and parents include, but are not limited to, due-process rights of parents and children, problems of self-incrimination in judicial proceedings, involuntary commitment to hospitals, child abuse, freedom of choice, protection of minors or legal incompetents, discriminatory practices in identification and placement, recommendations for special education provisions, and adjudication of domestic relations disputes in divorce and custodial proceedings. Providers of school psychological services take affirmative action by making themselves available to local committees, review boards, and similar advisory groups established to safeguard the human, civil, and legal rights of children and parents.

2.2.3 *All providers within a school psychological service unit are familiar with and adhere to the American Psychological Association's* Standards for Providers of Psychological Services, Ethical Principles of Psychologists, Standards for Educational and Psychological Tests, Ethical Principles in the Conduct of Research With Human Participants, *and other official policy statements relevant to standards for professional services issued by the Association.*

Interpretation: A copy of each of these documents is maintained by providers of school psychological services and is available upon request to all school personnel and officials, parents, members of the community, and where applicable, students and other sanctioners.

2.2.4 *All providers within a school psychological service unit conform to relevant statutes established by federal, state, and local governments.*

Interpretation: All providers of school psychological services are familiar with and conform to appropriate statutes regulating the practice of psychology. They also are informed about state department of education requirements and other agency regulations that have the force of law and that relate to the delivery of school psychological services (e.g., certification of, eligibility for, and placement in, special education programs). In addition, all providers are cognizant that federal agencies such as the Department of Education and the Department of Health and Human Services have policy statements regarding psychological services. Providers of school psychological services are familiar as well with other statutes and regulations, including those addressed to the civil and legal rights of users (e.g., Public Law 94-142, The Education for All Handicapped Children Act of 1975), that are pertinent to their scope of practice.

It is the responsibility of the American Psychological Association to maintain files of those federal policies, statutes, and regulations relating to this section and to assist its members in obtaining them. The state psychological associations, school psychological associations, and state licensing boards periodically publish and distribute appropriate state statutes and regulations.

2.2.5 *All providers within a school psychological service unit inform themselves about and use the network of human services in their communities in order to link users with relevant services and resources.*

Interpretation: School psychologists and support staff are sensitive to the broader context of human needs. In recognizing the matrix of personal and societal problems, providers make available to clients information regarding human services such as legal aid societies, social services, health resources like mental health centers, private practitioners, and educational and recreational facilities. School psychological staff formulate and maintain a file of such resources for reference. The specific information provided is such that users can easily make contact with the services and freedom of choice can be honored. Providers of school psychological services refer to such community resources and, when indicated, actively intervene on behalf of the users. School psychologists seek opportunities to serve on boards of community agencies in order to represent the needs of the school population in the community.

2.2.6 *In the delivery of school psychological services, providers maintain a cooperative relationship with colleagues and co-workers in the best interest of the users.*

Interpretation: School psychologists recognize the areas of special competence of other psychologists and of other professionals in the school and in the community for either consultation or referral purposes (e.g., school social workers, speech therapists, remedial reading teachers, special education teachers, pediatricians, neurologists, and public health nurses). Providers of school psychological services make appropriate use of other professional, research, technical, and administrative resources whenever these serve the best interests of the school staff, children, and parents and establish and maintain cooperative and/or collaborative arrangements with such other resources as required to meet the needs of users.

2.3 *Procedures:*

2.3.1 *A school psychological service unit follows a set of procedural guidelines for the delivery of school psychological services.*

Interpretation: The school psychological service staff is prepared to provide a statement of procedural guidelines in written form in terms that can be understood by school staff, parents, school board members, interested members of the community, and when appropriate, students and other sanctioners. The statement describes the current methods, forms, case study and assessment procedures, estimated time lines, interventions, and evaluation techniques being used to achieve the objectives and goals for school psychological services.

This statement is communicated to school staff and personnel, school board members, parents, and when appropriate, students or other sanctioners through whatever means are feasible, including in-service activities, conferences, oral presentations, and dissemination of written materials.

The school psychological service unit provides for the annual review of its procedures for the delivery of school psychological services.

2.3.2 *Providers of school psychological services develop plans appropriate to the providers' professional practices and to the problems presented by the users. There is a mutually acceptable understanding between providers and school staff, parents, and students or responsible agents regarding the goals and the delivery of services.*

Interpretation: The school psychological service unit notifies the school unit in writing of the plan that is adopted for use and resolves any points of difference. The plan includes written consent of guardians of students and, when appropriate, consent of students for the services provided. Similarly, the nature of the assessment tools that are to be used and the reasons for their inclusion are spelled out. The objectives of intervention(s) of a psychological nature as well as the procedures for implementing the intervention(s) are specified. An estimate of time is noted where appropriate. Parents and/or students are made aware of the various decisions that can be made as a result of the service(s), participate in accounting for decisions that are made, and are informed of how appeals may be instituted.

2.3.3 *Accurate, current, and pertinent documentation of essential school psychological services provided is maintained.*

Interpretation: Records kept of psychological services may include, but are not limited to, identifying data, dates of services, names of providers of services, types of services, and significant actions taken. These records are maintained separately from the child's cumulative record folder. Once a case study is completed and/or an intervention begun, records are reviewed and updated at least monthly.

2.3.4 *Each school psychological services unit follows an established record retention and disposition policy.*

Interpretation: The policy on maintenance and review of psychological records (including the length of time that records not already part of school records are to be kept) is developed by the local school psychological service unit. This policy is consistent with existing federal and state statutes and regulations.

2.3.5 *Providers of school psychological services maintain a system to protect confidentiality of their records.*

Interpretation: School psychologists are responsible for maintaining the confidentiality of information about users of services, from whatever source derived. All persons supervised by school psychologists, including nonprofessional personnel and students, who have access to records of psychological services maintain this confidentiality as a condition of employment. All appropriate staff receive training regarding the confidentiality of records.

Users are informed in advance of any limits for maintenance of confidentiality of psychological information. Procedures for obtaining informed consent are developed by the school psychological service unit. Written informed consent is obtained to conduct assessment or to carry out psychological intervention services. Informing users of the manner in which requests for information will be handled and of the school personnel who will share the results is part of the process of obtaining consent.

The school psychologist conforms to current laws and regulations with respect to the release of confidential information. As a general rule, however, the school psychologist does not release confidential information, except with the written consent of the parent or, where appropriate, the student directly involved or his or her legal representative. Even after consent for release has been obtained, the school psychologist clearly identifies such information as confidential to the recipient of the information. When there is a conflict with a statute, with regulations with the force of law, or with a court order, the school psychologist seeks a resolution to the conflict that is both ethically and legally feasible and appropriate.

Providers of school psychological services ensure that psychological reports which will become part of the school records are reviewed carefully so that confidentiality of pupils and parents is protected. When the guardian or student intends to waive confidentiality, the school psychologist discusses the implications of releasing psychological information and assists the user in limiting disclosure to only that information required by the present circumstance.

Raw psychological data (e.g., test protocols, counseling or interview notes, or questionnaires) in which a user is identified are released only with the written consent of the user or his or her legal representative, or by court order when such material is not covered by legal confidentiality, and are released only to a person recognized by the school psychologist as competent to use the data.

Any use made of psychological reports, records, or data for research or training purposes is consistent with this Guideline. Additionally, providers of school psychological services comply with statutory confidentiality requirements and those embodied in the American Psychological Association's *Ethical Principles of Psychologists* (APA, 1981).

Providers of school psychological services remain sensitive to both the benefits and the possible misuse of information regarding individuals that is stored in large computerized data banks. Providers use their influence to ensure that such information is managed in a socially responsible manner.

Guideline 3

Accountability

3.1 *The promotion of human welfare is the primary principle guiding the professional activity of the school psychologist and the school psychological service unit.*
Interpretation: School psychological services staff provide services to school staff members, students, and parents in a manner that is considerate and effective.

School psychologists make their services readily accessible to users in a manner that facilitates the users' freedom of choice. Parents, students, and other users are made aware that psychological services may be available through other public or private sources, and relevant information for exercising such options is provided upon request.

School psychologists are mindful of their accountability to the administration, to the school board, and to the general public, provided that appropriate steps are taken to protect the confidentiality of the service relationship. In the pursuit of their professional activities, they aid in the conservation of human, material, and financial resources.

The school psychological service unit does not withhold services to children or parents on the basis of the users' race, color, religion, gender, sexual orientation, age, or national origin. Recognition is given, however, to the following considerations: (a) the professional right of school psychologists, at the time of their employment, to state that they wish to limit their services to a specific category of users (e.g., elementary school children, exceptional children, adolescents), noting their reasons so that employers can make decisions regarding their employment, assignment of their duties, and so on; (b) the right and responsibility of school psychologists to withhold an assessment procedure when not validly applicable; (c) the right and responsibility of school psychologists to withhold evaluative, psychotherapeutic, counseling, or other services in specific instances in which their own limitations or client characteristics might impair the effectiveness of the relationship; and (d) the obligation of school psychologists to seek to ameliorate through peer review, consultation, or other personal therapeutic procedures those factors that inhibit the provision of services to particular users. In such instances, it is incumbent on school psychologists to advise clients about appropriate alternative services. When appropriate services are not available, school psychologists inform the school district administration and/or other sanctioners of the unmet needs of clients. In all instances, school psychologists make available information, and provide opportunity to participate in decisions, concerning such issues as initiation, termination, continuation, modification, and evaluation of psychological services. These Guidelines are also made available upon request.

Accurate and full information is made available to prospective individual or organizational users regarding the qualifications of providers, the nature and extent of services offered, and where appropriate, the financial costs as well as the benefits and possible risks of the proposed services.

Professional school psychologists offering services for a fee inform users of their payment policies, if applicable, and of their willingness to assist in obtaining reimbursement when such services have been contracted for as an external resource.

3.2 *School psychologists pursue their activities as members of the independent, autonomous profession of psychology.* [13]

Interpretation: School psychologists are aware of the implications of their activities for the profession of psychology as a whole. They seek to eliminate discriminatory practices instituted for self-serving purposes that are not in the interest of the users (e.g., arbitrary requirements for referral and supervision by another profession) and to discourage misuse of psychological concepts and tools (e.g., use of psychological instruments for special education placement by school personnel or others who lack relevant and adequate education and training). School psychologists are cognizant of their responsibilities for the development of the profession and for the improvement of schools. They participate where possible in the training and career development of students and other providers; they participate as appropriate in the training of school administrators, teachers, and paraprofessionals; and they integrate, and supervise the implementation of, their contributions within the structure established for delivering school psychological services. Where appropriate, they facilitate the development of, and participate in, professional standards review mechanisms.

School psychologists seek to work with other professionals in a cooperative manner for the good of the users and the benefit of the general public. School psychologists associated with special education or mental health teams or with multidisciplinary settings support the principle that members of each participating profession have equal rights and opportunities to share all privileges and responsibilities of full membership in the educational or human service activities or facilities and to administer service programs in their respective areas of competence. (Refer also to Guideline 2.2.5, Interpretation.)

3.3 *There are periodic, systematic, and effective evaluations of school psychological services.*

Interpretation: When the psychological service unit representing school psychology is a component of a larger organization (e.g., school system, county or state regional district, state department of education), regular evaluation of progress in achieving goals is provided for in the service delivery plan, including consideration of the effectiveness of school psychological services relative to costs in term of use of time and money and the availability of professional and support personnel.

Evaluation of the school psychological service delivery system is conducted internally and, when possible, under independent auspices as well. This evaluation includes an assessment of effectiveness (to determine what the service unit accomplished), efficiency (to determine the costs of providing the services), continuity (to ensure that the services are appropriately linked to other educational services), availability (to determine the appropriateness of staffing ratios), accessibility (to ensure that the services are readily available to members of the school population), and adequacy (to determine whether the services meet the identified needs of the school population).

It is highly desirable that there be a periodic reexamination of review mechanisms to ensure that these attempts at public safeguards are effective and cost efficient and do not place unnecessary encumbrances on the providers or impose unnecessary expenses on users or sanctioners for services rendered.

3.4 *School psychologists are accountable for all aspects of the services they provide and are responsive to those concerned with these services.*
Interpretation: In recognizing their responsibilities to users, sanctioners, and other-providers, and where appropriate and consistent with the users' legal rights and privileged communications, school psychologists make available information about, and provide opportunity to participate in, decisions concerning such issues as initiation, termination, continuation, modification, and evaluation of school psychological services.

Guideline 4

Environment

4.1 *Providers of psychological services promote development in the school setting of a physical, organizational, and social environment that facilitates optimal human functioning.*
Interpretation: Federal, state, and local requirements for safety, health, and sanitation are observed.

As providers of services, school psychologists are concerned with the environment of their service units, especially as it affects the quality of service, but also as it impinges on human functioning in the school. Attention is given to the privacy and comfort of school staff, students, and parents. Parent and staff interviews are conducted in a professional atmosphere, with the option for private conferences available. Students are seen under conditions that maximize their privacy and enhance the possibility for meaningful intervention; for example, they should have the opportunity to leave their classroom inconspicuously and should be free from interruptions when meeting with the psychologist. Physical arrangements and organizational policies and procedures are conducive to the human dignity, self-respect, and optimal functioning of school staff, students, and parents and to the effective delivery of service.

Footnotes

[1]The footnotes appended to these Specialty Guidelines represent an attempt to provide a coherent context of earlier APA policy statements and other documents regarding professional practice. The Guidelines extend these previous policy statements where necessary to reflect current concerns of the public and the profession.

[2]There are three categories of individuals who do not meet the definition of *professional school psychologist* but who can be considered professional school psychologists if they meet certain criteria.

The following two categories of professional psychologists who met the criteria indicated below on or before the adoption of these Specialty Guidelines on January 31, 1980, are considered professional school psychologists: Category 1—those who completed (a) a doctoral degree program primarily psychological in content, but not in school psychology, at a regionally accredited university or professional school and (b) 3 postdoctoral years of appropriate education, training, and experience in providing school psychological services as defined herein, including a minimum of 1,200 hours in school settings; Category 2—those who on or before September 4, 1974, (a) completed a master's degree from a program primarily psychological in content at a regionally accredited university or professional school and (b) held a license or certificate in the state in which they practiced, conferred by a state board of psychological examiners, or the endorsement of a state psychological association through voluntary certification, and who, in addition, prior to January 31, 1980, (c) obtained 5 post-master's years of appropriate education, training, and experience in providing school psychological services as defined herein, including a minimum of 2,400 hours in school settings.

After January 31, 1980, professional psychologists who wish to be recognized as professional school psychologists are referred to Guideline 1.7.

The APA Council of Representatives passed a "Resolution on the Master's-Level Issue" in January 1977 containing the following statement, which influenced the development of a third category of professional school psychologists:

> The title "Professional Psychologist" has been used so widely and by persons with such a wide variety of training and experience that it does not provide the information the public deserves.
>
> As a consequence, the APA takes the position and makes it a part of its policy that the use of the title "Professional Psychologist," and its variations such as "Clinical Psychologist," "Counseling Psychologist," "School Psychologist," and "Industrial Psychologist" are reserved for those who have completed a Doctoral Training Program in Psychology in a university, college, or professional school of psychology that is APA or regionally accredited. In order to meet this standard, a transition period will be acknowledged for the use of the title "School Psychologist," so that ways may be sought to increase opportunities for doctoral training and to improve the level of educational codes pertaining to the title. (Conger, 1977, p. 426)

For the purpose of transition, then, there is still another category of persons who can be considered professional school psychologists for practice in elementary and secondary schools. Category 3 consists of persons who meet the following criteria on or before, but not beyond, January 31, 1985: (a) a master's or higher degree, requiring at least 2 years of full-time graduate study in school psychology, from a regionally accredited university or professional school; (b) at least 3 additional years of training and experience in school psychological services, including a minimum of 1,200 hours in school settings; and (c) a license or certificate conferred by a state board of psychological examiners or a state educational agency for practice in elementary or secondary schools.

Preparation equivalent to that described in Category 3 entitles an individual to use the title *professional school psychologist* in school practice, but it does not exempt the individual from meeting the requirements of licensure or other requirements for which a doctoral degree is prerequisite.

[3]A professional school psychologist who is licensed by a state or District of Columbia board of examiners of psychology for the independent practice of psychology and who has 2 years of supervised (or equivalent) experience in health services, of which at least 1 year is postdoctoral, may be listed as a "Health Service Provider in Psychology" in the *National Register of Health Service Providers in Psychology:*

> A Health Service Provider in Psychology is defined as a psychologist, certified/licensed at the independent practice level in his/her state, who is duly trained and experienced in the delivery of direct, preventive, assessment and therapeutic intervention services to individuals whose growth, adjustment, or functioning is actually impaired or is demonstrably at high risk of impairment. (Council for the National Register of Health Service Providers in Psychology, 1980, p. xi)

[4]The areas of knowledge and training that are a part of the educational program for all professional psychologists have been presented in two APA documents, *Education and Credentialing in Psychology II* (APA, 1977a) and *Criteria for Accreditation of Doctoral Training Programs and Internships in Professional Psychology* (APA, 1979). There is consistency in the presentation of core areas in the education and training of all professional psychologists. The description of education and

training in these Guidelines is based primarily on the document *Education and Credentialing in Psychology II*. It is intended to indicate broad areas of required curriculum, with the expectation that training programs will undoubtedly want to interpret the specific content of these areas in different ways depending on the nature, philosophy, and intent of the programs.

[5]Although specialty education and training guidelines have not yet been developed and approved by APA, the following description of education and training components of school psychology programs represents a consensus regarding specialty training in school psychology at this time.

The *education* of school psychologists encompasses the equivalent of at least 3 years of full-time graduate academic study. While instructional formats and course titles may vary from program to program, each program has didactic and experiential instruction (a) in scientific and professional areas common to all professional psychology programs, such as ethics and standards, research design and methodology, statistics, and psychometric methods, and (b) in such substantive areas as the biological bases of behavior, the cognitive and affective bases of behavior, the social, cultural, ethnic, and sex role bases of behavior, and individual differences. Course work includes social and philosophical bases of education, curriculum theory and practice, etiology of learning and behavior disorders, exceptional children, and special education. Organization theory and administrative practice should also be included in the program. This list is not intended to dictate specific courses or a sequence of instruction. It is the responsibility of programs to determine how these areas are organized and presented to students. Variations in educational format are to be expected.

The *training* of school psychologists includes practicum and field experience in conjunction with the educational program. In addition, the program includes a supervised internship experience beyond practicum and field work, equivalent to at least 1 academic school year, but in no event fewer than 1,200 hours, in schools or in a combination of schools and community agencies and centers, with at least 600 hours of the internship in the school setting. An appropriate number of hours per week should be devoted to direct face-to-face supervision of each intern. In no event is there less than 1 hour per week of direct supervision. Overall professional supervision is provided by a professional school psychologist. However, supervision in specific procedures and techniques may be provided by others, with the agreement of the supervising professional psychologist and the supervisee. The training experiences provided and the competencies developed occur in settings in which there are opportunities to work with children, teachers, and parents and to supervise others providing psychological services to children.

[6]In order to implement these Specialty Guidelines, it will be necessary to determine in each state which non-doctoral-level school psychologists certified by the state department of education are eligible to be considered professional school psychologists for practice in elementary and secondary schools. A national register of all professional school psychologists and specialists in school psychology would be a useful and efficient means by which to inform the public of the available school psychological services personnel.

[7]Functions and activities of school psychologists relating to the teaching of psychology, the writing or editing of scholarly or scientific manuscripts, and the conduct of scientific research do not fall within the purview of these Guidelines.

[8]Nothing in these Guidelines precludes the school psychologist from being trained

beyond the areas described herein (e.g., in psychotherapy for children, adolescents, and their families in relation to school-related functioning and problems) and, therefore, from providing services on the basis of this training to clients as appropriate.

[9]In some states, a supervisor's certificate is required in order to use the title *supervisor* in the public schools. Supervision of providers of psychological services by a professional school psychologist does not mean that the school psychologist is thereby authorized or entitled to offer supervision to other school personnel. Supervision by the school psychologist is confined to those areas appropriate to his or her training and educational background and is viewed as part of the school psychologist's professional responsibilities and duties.

The following guideline for supervision has been written by the Executive Committee of the Division of School Psychology:

> In addition to being a professional school psychologist, the person who supervises school psychological services and/or school psychological personnel shall have the following qualifications: broad understanding of diagnostic assessment, consultation, programming, and other intervention strategies; skills in supervision; the ability to empathize with supervisees; and commitment to continuing education. The supervising school psychologist also shall have had the equivalent of at least 2 years of satisfactory full-time, on-the-job experience as a school psychologist practicing directly in the school or dealing with school-related problems in independent practice.

[10]This Guideline follows closely the statement regarding "Policy on Training for Psychologists Wishing to Change Their Specialty" adopted by the APA Council of Representatives in January 1976. Included therein was the implementing provision that "this policy statement shall be incorporated in the guidelines of the Committee on Accreditation so that appropriate sanctions can be brought to bear on university and internship training programs that violate [it]" (Conger, 1976, p. 424).

[11]Two surveys of school psychological practice provide a rationale for the specification of this Guideline (Farling & Hoedt, 1971; Kicklighter, 1976). The median ratios of psychologists to pupils were 1 to 9,000 in 1966 and 1 to 4,000 in 1974. Those responding to Kicklighter's survey projected that the ratio of psychologists to pupils would be 1 to 2,500 in 1980. These data were collected before the passage of Public Law 94-142, the Education for All Handicapped Children Act of 1975. The regulations for implementing this act require extensive identification, assessment, and evaluation services to children, and it is reasonable in 1981 to set an acceptable ratio of psychologists to pupils at 1 to 2,000.

[12]See also *Ethical Principles of Psychologists* (APA, 1981), especially Principles 5 (Confidentiality), 6 (Welfare of the Consumer), and 9 (Research With Human Participants), and *Ethical Principles in the Conduct of Research With Human Participants* (APA, 1973). Also, in 1978 Division 17 approved in principle a statement on "Principles for Counseling and Psychotherapy With Women," which was designed to protect the interests of female users of counseling psychological services.

[13]Support for the principle of the independence of psychology as a profession is found in the following:

> As a member of an autonomous profession, a psychologist rejects limitations upon his [or her] freedom of thought and action other than those imposed by his [or her] moral, legal, and social responsibilities. The Association is always prepared to provide appropriate assistance to any responsible member who becomes subjected to unreasonable limitations upon his [or her] opportunity to function as a practitioner, teacher, researcher, administrator, or consultant. The Association is always prepared to cooperate with any responsible professional organization in

opposing any unreasonable limitations on the professional functions of the members of that organization.

This insistence upon professional autonomy has been upheld over the years by the affirmative actions of the courts and other public and private bodies in support of the right of the psychologist—and other professionals—to pursue those functions for which he [or she] is trained and qualified to perform. (APA, 1968, p. 9)

Organized psychology has the responsibility to define and develop its own profession, consistent with the general canons of science and with the public welfare.

Psychologists recognize that other professions and other groups will, from time to time, seek to define the roles and responsibilities of psychologists. The APA opposes such developments on the same principle that it is opposed to the psychological profession taking positions which would define the work and scope of responsibility of other duly recognized professions. (APA, 1972, p. 333)

REFERENCES

American Psychological Association. *Psychology as a profession.* Washington, D.C.: Author, 1968.

American Psychological Association. Guidelines for conditions of employment of psychologists. *American Psychologist,* 1972, *27,* 331–334.

American Psychological Association. *Ethical principles in the conduct of research with human participants.* Washington, D.C.: Author, 1973.

American Psychological Association. *Standards for educational and psychological tests.* Washington, D.C.: Author, 1974. (a)

American Psychological Association. *Standards for providers of psychological services.* Washington, D.C.: Author, 1974. (b)

American Psychological Association. *Education and credentialing in psychology II.* Report of a meeting, June 4–5, 1977. Washington, D.C.: Author, 1977. (a)

American Psychological Association. *Standards for providers of psychological services* (Rev. ed.). Washington, D.C.: Author, 1977. (b)

American Psychological Association. *Criteria for accreditation of doctoral training programs and internships in professional psychology.* Washington, D.C.: Author, 1979 (amended 1980).

American Psychological Association. *Ethical principles of psychologists* (Rev. ed.). Washington, D.C.: Author, 1981.

Conger, J. J. Proceedings of the American Psychological Association, Incorporated, for the year 1975: Minutes of the annual meeting of the Council of Representatives. *American Psychologist,* 1976, *31,* 406–434.

Conger, J. J. Proceedings of the American Psychological Association, Incorporated, for the year 1976: Minutes of the annual meeting of the Council of Representatives. *American Psychologist,* 1977, *32,* 408–438.

Council for the National Register of Health Service Providers in Psychology. *National register of health service providers in psychology.* Washington, D.C.: Author, 1980.

Farling, W. H., & Hoedt, K. C. *National survey of school psychologists.* Washington, D.C.: Department of Health, Education, and Welfare, 1971.

Kicklighter, R. H. School psychology in the U.S.: A quantitative survey. *Journal of School Psychology,* 1976, *14,* 151–156.

APPENDIX C

American Psychological Association Ethical Principles of Psychologists[1,2] (1981 Revision)

PREAMBLE

Psychologists respect the dignity and worth of the individual and strive for the preservation and protection of fundamental human rights. They are committed to increasing knowledge of human behavior and of people's understanding of themselves and others and to the utilization of such knowledge for the promotion of human welfare. While pursuing these objectives, they make every effort to protect the welfare of those who seek their services and of the research participants that may be the object of study. They use their skills only for purposes consistent with these values and do not knowingly permit their misuse by others. While demanding for themselves freedom of inquiry and commu-

[1]Approved by the Council of Representatives (January 1981).

[2]These Ethical Principles apply to psychologists, to students of psychology and others who do work of a psychological nature under the supervision of a psychologist. They are also intended for the guidance of non-members of the Association who are engaged in psychological research or practice.

Source: Copyright © American Psychological Association, Inc. Reprinted by permission.

This version of the Ethical Principles of Psychologists (formerly entitled: Ethical Standards of Psychologists) was adopted by the American Psychological Association's Council of Representatives on January 24, 1981. The Ethical Principles of Psychologists (1981 Revision) contains both substantive and grammatical changes in each of the nine ethical principles which comprised the Ethical Standards of Psychologists previously adopted by the Council of Representatives in 1979, plus a new tenth principle entitled: Care and Use of Animals. Inquiries concerning the Ethical Principles of Psychologists should be addressed to the Administrative Officer for Ethics; American Psychological Association; 1200 Seventeenth Street, N.W.; Washington, D.C. 20036.

nication, psychologists accept the responsibility this freedom requires: competence, objectivity in the application of skills, and concern for the best interests of clients, colleagues, students, research participants and society. In the pursuit of these ideals, psychologists subscribe to principles in the following areas: 1. Responsibility, 2. Competence, 3. Moral and Legal Standards, 4. Public Statements, 5. Confidentiality, 6. Welfare of the Consumer, 7. Professional Relationships, 8. Assessment Techniques, 9. Research with Human Participants, and 10. Care and Use of Animals.

Acceptance of membership in the American Psychological Association commits the member to adherence to these principles.

Psychologists cooperate with duly constituted committees of the American Psychological Association, in particular, the Committee on Scientific and Professional Ethics and Conduct, by responding to inquiries promptly and completely. Members also respond promptly and completely to inquiries from duly constituted state association ethics committees and professional standards review committees.

PRINCIPLE 1: RESPONSIBILITY

In providing services, psychologists maintain the highest standards of their profession. They accept responsibility for the consequences of their acts and make every effort to insure that their services are used appropriately.

a. As scientists, psychologists accept responsibility for the selection of their research topics and the methods used in investigation, analysis, and reporting. They plan their research in ways to minimize the possibility that their findings will be misleading. They provide thorough discussion of the limitations of their data, especially where their work touches on social policy or might be construed to the detriment of persons in specific age, sex, ethnic, socioeconomic or other social groups. In publishing reports of their work, they never suppress disconfirming data, and they acknowledge the existence of alternative hypotheses and explanations of their findings. Psychologists take credit only for work they have actually done.

b. Psychologists clarify in advance with all appropriate persons and agencies the expectations for sharing and utilizing research data. They avoid relationships which may limit their objectivity or create a conflict of interest. Interference with the milieu in which the data are collected is kept to a minimum.

c. Psychologists have the responsibility to attempt to prevent distortion, misuse, or suppression of psychological findings by the institution or agency of which they are employees.

d. As members of governmental or other organizational bodies, psychologists remain accountable as individuals to the highest standards of their profession.

e. As teachers, psychologists recognize their primary obligation to help others acquire knowledge and skill. They maintain high standards of scholarship by presenting psychological information objectively, fully, and accurately.

f. As practitioners, psychologists know that they bear a heavy social responsibility because their recommendations and professional actions may alter the lives of others. They are alert to personal, social, organizational, financial, or political situations and pressures that might lead to misuse of their influence.

PRINCIPLE 2: COMPETENCE

The maintenance of high standards of competence is a responsibility shared by all psychologists in the interest of the public and the profession as a whole. Psychologists recognize the boundaries of their competence and the limitations of their techniques. They only provide services and only use techniques for which they are qualified by training and experience. In those areas in which recognized standards do not yet exist, psychologists take whatever precautions are necessary to protect the welfare of their clients. They maintain knowledge of current scientific and professional information related to the services they render.

a. Psychologists accurately represent their competence, education, training, and experience. They claim as evidence of educational qualifications only those degrees obtained from institutions acceptable under the Bylaws and Rules of Council of the American Psychological Association.

b. As teachers, psychologists perform their duties on the basis of careful preparation so that their instruction is accurate, current, and scholarly.

c. Psychologists recognize the need for continuing education and are open to new procedures and changes in expectations and values over time.

d. Psychologists recognize differences among people, such as those that may be associated with age, sex, socioeconomic, and ethnic backgrounds. When necessary, they obtain training, experience, or counsel to assure competent service or research relating to such persons.

e. Psychologists responsible for decisions involving individuals or policies based on test results have an understanding of psychological or educational measurement, validation problems, and test research.

f. Psychologists recognize that personal problems and conflicts may interfere with professional effectiveness. Accordingly, they refrain from undertaking any activity in which their personal problems are likely to lead to inadequate performance or harm to a client, colleague, student, or research participant. If engaged in such activity when they become aware of their personal problems, they seek competent professional assistance to determine whether they should suspend, terminate, or limit the scope of their professional and/or scientific activities.

PRINCIPLE 3: MORAL AND LEGAL STANDARDS

Psychologists' moral and ethical standards of behavior are a personal matter to the same degree as they are for any other citizen, except as these may compromise the fulfillment of their professional responsibilities, or reduce the public trust in psychology and psychologists. Regarding their own behavior, psychologists are sensitive to prevailing community standards and to the possible impact that conformity to or deviation from these standards may have upon the quality of their performance as psychologists. Psychologists are also aware of the possible impact of their public behavior upon the ability of colleagues to perform their professional duties.

a. As teachers, psychologists are aware of the fact that their personal values may affect the selection and presentation of instructional materials. When dealing with topics that may give offense, they recognize and respect the diverse attitudes that students may have toward such materials.

b. As employees or employers, psychologists do not engage in or condone practices that are inhumane or that result in illegal or unjustifiable actions. Such practices include but are not limited to those based on considerations of race, handicap, age, gender, sexual preferences, religion, or national origin in hiring, promotion, or training.

c. In their professional roles, psychologists avoid any action that will violate or diminish the legal and civil rights of clients or of others who may be affected by their actions.

d. As practitioners and researchers, psychologists act in accord with Association standards and guidelines related to the practice and to the conduct of research with human beings and animals. In the ordinary course of events psychologists adhere to relevant governmental laws and institutional regulations. When federal, state, provincial, organization, or institutional laws, regulations, or practices are in conflict with Association standards and guidelines, psychologists make known their commitment to Association standards and guidelines, and wherever possible work toward a resolution of the conflict. Both practitioners and researchers are concerned with the development of such legal and quasi-legal regulations as best serve the public interest, and they work toward changing existing regulations that are not beneficial to the public interest.

PRINCIPLE 4: PUBLIC STATEMENTS

Public statements, announcements of services, advertising, and promotional activities of psychologists serve the purpose of helping the public make informed judgments and choices. Psychologists represent accurately and objectively their professional qualifications, affiliations, and functions, as well as those of the institutions or organizations with which they or the statements may be associated. In public statements providing psychological information or professional opinions or providing information about the availability of psychological products, publications, and services, psychologists base their statements on scientifically acceptable psychological findings and techniques with full recognition of the limits and uncertainties of such evidence.

a. When announcing or advertising professional services, psychologists may list the following information to describe the provider and services provided: name, highest relevant academic degree earned from a regionally accredited institution, date, type and level of certification or licensure, diplomate status, APA membership status, address, telephone number, office hours, a brief listing of the typ of psychological services offered, an appropriate presentation of fee information, foreign languages spoken, and policy with regard to third-party payments. Additional relevant or important consumer information may be included if not prohibited by other sections of these Ethical Principles.

b. In announcing or advertising the availability of psychological products, publications, or services, psychologists do not present their affiliation with any organization in a manner that falsely implies sponsorship or certification by that organization. In particular and for example, psychologists do not state APA membership or fellow status in a way to suggest that such status implies specialized professional competence or qualifications. Public statements include, but are not limited to, communication by means of periodical, book, list, directory, television, radio, or motion picture. They do not contain: (i) a false, fraudulent, misleading, deceptive, or unfair statement; (ii) a misinterpretation of fact, or a statement likely to mislead or deceive because in context it makes only a partial disclosure of relevant facts; (iii) a testimonial from a patient regarding the quality of a psychologist's services or products; (iv) a statement intended or likely to create false or unjustified expectations of favorable results; (v) a statement implying unusual, unique, or one-of-a-kind abilities; (vi) a statement intended or likely to appeal to a client's fears, anxieties, or emotions concerning the possible results of a failure to obtain the offered services; (vii) a statement concerning the comparative desirability of offered service; (viii) a statement of direct solicitation of individual clients.

c. Psychologists do not compensate or give anything of value to a representative of the press, radio, television, or other communication medium in anticipation of or in return for professional publicity in a news item. A paid advertisement must be identified as such, unless it is apparent from the context that it is a paid advertisement. If communicated to the public by use of radio or television, an advertisement shall be prerecorded and approved for broadcast by the psychologist, and a recording of the actual transmission shall be retained by the psychologist.

d. Announcements or advertisements of "personal growth groups," clinics, and agencies give a clear statement of purpose and a clear description of the experiences to be provided. The education, training, and experience of the staff members are appropriately specified.

e. Psychologists associated with the development or promotion of psychological devices, books, or other products offered for commercial sale make reasonable efforts to insure that announcements and advertisements are presented in a professional, scientifically acceptable, and factually informative manner.

f. Psychologists do not participate for personal gain in commercial announcements or advertisements recommending to the public the purchase or use of proprietary or single-source products or services when that participation is based solely upon their identification as psychologists.

g. Psychologists present the science of psychology and offer their services, products, and publications fairly and accurately, avoiding misrepresentation, through sensationalism, exaggeration, or superficiality. Psychologists are guided by the primary obligation to aid the public in developing informed judgments, opinions, and choices.

h. As teachers, psychologists insure that statements in catalogs and course outlines are accurate and not misleading, particularly in terms of subject matter to be covered, bases for evaluating progress, and the nature of course experiences. Announcements, brochures, or advertisements describing workshops, seminars, or other educational programs accurately describe the audience for which the program is intended as well as eligibility requirements, educational objectives, and nature of the materials to be covered. These announcements also accurately represent the education, training, and experience of the psychologists presenting the programs, and any fees involved.

i. Public announcements or advertisements soliciting research participants in which clinical services or other professional services are offered as an inducement, make clear the nature of the services as well as the costs and other obligations to be accepted by the participants of the research.

j. Psychologists accept the obligation to correct others who represent that psychologist's professional qualifications, or associations with products or services, in a manner incompatible with these guidelines.

k. Individual diagnostic and therapeutic services are provided only in the context of a professional psychological relationship. When personal advice is given by means of public lecture or demonstration, newspaper or magazine articles, radio or television programs, mail, or similar media, the psychologist utilizes the most current relevant data and exercises the highest level of professional judgment.

l. Products that are described or presented by means of public lectures or demonstrations, newspaper or magazine articles, radio or television programs, or similar media meet the same recognized standards as exist for use in the context of a professional relationship.

PRINCIPLE 5: CONFIDENTIALITY

Psychologists have a primary obligation to respect the confidentiality of information obtained from persons in the course of their work as psychologists. They reveal such information to others only with the consent of the person or the person's legal representative, except in those unusual circumstances in which not to do so would result in clear danger to the person or to others. Where appropriate, psychologists inform their clients of the legal limits of confidentiality.

a. Information obtained in clinical or consulting relationships, or evaluative data concerning children, students, employees, and others, are discussed only for professional purposes and only with persons clearly concerned with the case. Written and oral reports present only data germane to the purposes of the evaluation and every effort is made to avoid undue invasion of privacy.

b. Psychologists who present personal information obtained during the course of professional work in writings, lectures, or other public forums either obtain adequate prior consent to do so or adequately disguise all identifying information.

c. Psychologists make provisions for maintaining confidentiality in the storage and disposal of records.

d. When working with minors or other persons who are unable to give voluntary informed consent, psychologists take special care to protect these persons' best interests.

PRINCIPLE 6: WELFARE OF THE CONSUMER

Psychologists respect the integrity and protect the welfare of the people and groups with whom they work. When there is a conflict of interest between a client and the psychologist's employing institution, psychologists clarify the nature and direction of their loyalties and responsibilities and keep all parties informed of their commitments. Psychologists fully inform consumers as to the purpose and nature of an evaluative, treatment, educational or training procedure, and they freely acknowledge that clients, students, or participants in research have freedom of choice with regard to participation.

a. Psychologists are continually cognizant of their own needs and of their potentially influential position vis-a-vis persons such as clients, students, and subordinates. They avoid exploiting the trust and dependency of such persons. Psychologists make every effort to avoid dual relationships which could impair their professional judgment or increase the risk of exploitation. Examples of such dual relationships include but are not limited to research with and treatment of employees, students, supervisees, close friends, or relatives. Sexual intimacies with clients are unethical.

b. When a psychologist agrees to provide services to a client at the request of a third party, the psychologist assumes the responsibility of clarifying the nature of the relationships to all parties concerned.

c. Where the demands of an organization require psychologists to violate these Ethical Principles, psychologists clarify the nature of the conflict between the demand and these principles. They inform all parties of psychologists' ethical responsibilities, and take appropriate action.

d. Psychologists make advance financial arrangements that safeguard the best interests of and are clearly understood by their clients. They neither give nor receive any remuneration for referring clients for professional services. They contribute a portion of their services to work for which they receive little or no financial return.

e. Psychologists terminate a clinical or consulting relationship when it is reasonably clear that the consumer is not benefitting from it. They offer to help the consumer locate alternative sources of assistance.

PRINCIPLE 7: PROFESSIONAL RELATIONSHIPS

Psychologists act with due regard for the needs, special competencies, and obligations of their colleagues in psychology and other professions. They respect the prerogatives and obligations of the institutions or organizations with which these other colleagues are associated.

a. Psychologists understand the areas of competence of related professions. They make full use of all the professional, technical, and administrative resources that serve the best interests of consumers. The absence of formal relationships with other professional workers does not relieve psychologists of the responsibility of securing for their clients the best possible professional service nor does it relieve them of the obligation to exercise foresight, diligence, and tact in obtaining the complementary or alternative assistance needed by clients.

b. Psychologists know and take into account the traditions and practices of other professional groups with whom they work and cooperate fully with such groups. If a person is receiving similar services from another professional, psychologists do not offer their own services directly to such a person. If a psychologist is contacted by a person who is already receiving similar services from another professional, the psychologist carefully considers that professional relationship and proceeds with caution and sensitivity to the therapeutic issues as well as the client's welfare. The psychologist discusses these issues with the client so as to minimize the risk of confusion and conflict.

c. Psychologists who employ or supervise other professionals or professionals in training accept the obligation to facilitate the further professional development of these individuals. They provide appropriate working conditions, timely evaluations, constructive consultation and experience opportunities.

d. Psychologists do not exploit their professional relationships with clients, supervisees, students, employees, or research participants sexually or otherwise. Psychologists do not condone nor engage in sexual harassment. Sexual harassment is defined as deliberate or repeated comments, gestures, or physical contacts of a sexual nature that are unwanted by the recipient.

e. In conducting research in institutions or organizations, psychologists secure appropriate authorization to conduct such research. They are aware of their obligation to future research workers and insure that host institutions receive adequate information about the research and proper acknowledgment of their contributions.

f. Publication credit is assigned to those who have contributed to a publication in proportion to their professional contribution. Major contributions of a professional character made by several persons to a common project are recognized by joint authorship, with the individual who made the principal contribution listed first. Minor contributions of a professional character and extensive clerical or similar nonprofessional assistance may be acknowledged in footnotes or in an introductory statement. Acknowledgement through specific citations is made for unpublished as well as published material that has directly influenced the research or writing. A psychologist who compiles and edits material of others for publication publishes the material in the name of the originating group, if appropriate, with his/her own name appearing as chairperson or editor. All contributors are to be acknowledged and named.

g. When psychologists know of an ethical violation by another psychologist, and it seems appropriate, they informally attempt to resolve the issue by bringing the behavior to the attention of the psychologist. If the misconduct is of a minor nature and/or appears to be due to a lack of sensitivity, knowledge, or experience, such an informal solution is usually appropriate. Such informal corrective efforts are sensitive to any rights to confidentiality involved. If the violation does not seem amenable to an informal solution, or is of a more serious nature, psychologists bring it to the attention of the appropriate local, state, and/or national committee on professional ethics and conduct.

PRINCIPLE 8: ASSESSMENT TECHNIQUES

In the development, publication, and utilization of psychological assessment techniques, psychologists make every effort to promote the welfare and best interests of the client. They guard against the misuse of assessment results. They respect the client's right to know the results, the interpretations made and the bases for their conclusions and recommendations. Psychologists make every effort to maintain the security of tests and other assessment techniques within limits of legal mandates. They strive to assure the appropriate use of assessment techniques by others.

a. In using assessment techniques, psychologists respect the right of clients to have a full explanation of the nature and purpose of the techniques in language that the client can understand, unless an explicit exception to this right has been agreed upon in advance. When the explanations are to be provided by others, the psychologist establishes procedures for insuring the adequacy of these explanations.

b. Psychologists responsible for the development and standardization of psychological tests and other assessment techniques utilize established scientific procedures and observe the relevant APA standards.

c. In reporting assessment results, psychologists indicate any reservations that exist regarding validity or reliability because of the circumstances of the assessment or the inappropriateness of the norms for the person tested. Psychologists strive to insure that the results of assessments and their interpretations are not misused by others.

d. Psychologists recognize that assessment results may become obsolete. They make every effort to avoid and prevent the misuse of obsolete measures.

e. Psychologists offering scoring and interpretation services are able to produce appropriate evidence for the validity of the programs and procedures used in arriving at interpretations. The public offering of an automated interpretation service is considered as a professional-to-professional consultation. The psychologist makes every effort to avoid misuse of assessment reports.

f. Psychologists do not encourage or promote the use of psychological assessment techniques by inappropriately trained or otherwise unqualified persons through teaching, sponsorship, or supervision.

PRINCIPLE 9: RESEARCH WITH HUMAN PARTICIPANTS

The decision to undertake research rests upon a considered judgment by the individual psychologist about how best to contribute to psychological science and human welfare. Having made the decision to conduct research, the psychologist considers alternative directions in which research energies and resources might be invested. On the basis of this consideration, the psychologist carries out the investigation with respect and concern for the dignity and welfare of the people who participate, and with cognizance of federal and state regulations and professional standards governing the conduct of research with human participants.

a. In planning a study, the investigator has the responsibility to make a careful evaluation of its ethical acceptability. To the extent that the weighing of scientific and human values suggests a compromise to any principle, the investigator incurs a correspondingly serious obligation to seek ethical advice and to observe stringent safeguards to protect the rights of human participants.

b. Considering whether a participant in a planned study will be a "subject at risk" or a "subject at minimal risk," according to recognized standards, is of primary ethical concern to the investigator.

c. The investigator always retains the responsibility for insuring ethical practice in research. The investigator is also responsible for the ethical treatment of research participants by collaborators, assistants, students, and employees, all of whom, however, incur similar obligations.

d. Except for minimal risk research, the investigator establishes a clear and fair agreement with the research participants, prior to their participation, that clarifies the obligations and responsibilities of each. The investigator has the obligation to honor all promises and commitments included in that agreement. The investigator informs the participant of all aspects of the research that might reasonably be expected to influence willingness to participate, and explains all other aspects of the research about which the participant inquires. Failure to make full disclosure prior to obtaining informed consent requires additional safeguards to protect the welfare and dignity of the research participant. Research with children or participants who have impairments which would limit understanding and/or communication, requires special safeguard procedures.

e. Methodological requirements of a study may make the use of concealment or deception necessary. Before conducting such a study, the investigator has a special responsibility to: (i) determine whether the use of such techniques is justified by the study's prospective scientific, educational, or applied value; (ii) determine whether alternative procedures are available that do not utilize concealment or deception; and (iii) insure that the participants are provided with sufficient explanation as soon as possible.

f. The investigator respects the individual's freedom to decline to participate in or to withdraw from the research at any time. The obligation to protect this freedom requires careful thought and consideration when the investigator is in a position of authority or influence over the participant. Such positions of authority include but are not limited to situations when research participation is required as part of employment or when the participant is a student, client, or employee of the investigator.

g. The investigator protects the participants from physical and mental discomfort, harm, and danger that may arise from research procedures. If risks of such consequences exist, the investigator informs the participant of that fact. Research procedures likely to cause serious or lasting harm to a participant are not used unless the failure to use these procedures might expose the participant to risk of greater harm, or unless the research has great potential benefit and fully informed and voluntary consent is obtained from each participant. The participant should be informed of procedures for contacting the investigator within a reasonable time period following participation should stress, potential harm, or related questions or concerns arise.

h. After the data are collected, the investigator provides the participant with information about the nature of the study and attempts to remove any misconceptions that may have arisen. Where scientific or humane values justify delaying or withholding information, the investigator incurs a special responsibility to monitor the research and to assure that there are no damaging consequences for the participant.

i. Where research procedures result in undesirable consequences for the individual participant, the investigator has the responsibility to detect and remove or correct these consequences, including long-term effects.

j. Information obtained about the research participant during the courses of an investigation is confidential unless otherwise agreed upon in advance. When the possibility exists that others may obtain access to such information, this possibility, together with the plans for protecting confidentiality, is explained to the participant as part of the procedure for obtaining informed consent.

PRINCIPLE 10: CARE AND USE OF ANIMALS

An investigator of animal behavior strives to advance our understanding of basic behavioral principles and/or to contribute to the improvement of human health and welfare. In seeking these ends, the investigator insures the welfare of the animals and treats them humanely. Laws and regulations notwithstanding, the animal's immediate protection depends upon the scientist's own conscience.

a. The acquisition, care, use, and disposal of all animals is in compliance with current federal, state or provincial, and local laws and regulations.

b. A psychologist trained in research methods and experienced in the care of laboratory animals closely supervises all procedures involving animals and is responsible for insuring appropriate consideration of their comfort, health, and humane treatment.

c. Psychologists insure that all individuals using animals under their supervision have received explicit instruction in experimental methods and in the care, maintenance, and handling of the species being used. Responsibilities and activities of individuals participating in a research project are consistent with their respective competencies.

d. Psychologists make every effort to minimize discomfort, illness, and pain to the animals. A procedure subjecting animals to pain, stress, or privation is used only when an alternative procedure is unavailable and the goal is justified by its prospective scientific, educational, or applied value. Surgical procedures are performed under appropriate anesthesia: techniques to avoid infection and minimize pain are followed during and after surgery.

e. When it is appropriate that the animal's life be terminated, it is done rapidly and painlessly.

National Association of School Psychologists Principles for Professional Ethics

Standards for professional conduct, usually referred to as ethics, recognize the obligation of professional persons to provide services and to conduct themselves so as to place the highest esteem on human rights and individual dignity. A code of ethics is an additional professional technique which seeks to ensure that each person served will receive the highest quality of service. Even though ethical behavior involves interactions between the professional, the person served, and the employing institution, responsibility for ethical conduct must rest with the professional.

School psychologists are a specialized segment within a larger group of professional psychologist. The school psychologist works in situations where circumstances may develop which are not clearly dealt with in other ethical guidelines. This possibility is heightened by intense concern for such issues as "due process," protection of individual rights, record keeping, accountability, and equal access to opportunity.

The most basic ethical principle is that of the responsibility of a professional person to perform only those services for which that person has acquired a recognized level of competency. In practice, recognition must be made of the uncertainties associated with delivery of psychological services in a situation where rights of the student, the parent,[1] the school, and society may conflict.

The intent of these guidelines is to supply clarification which will facilitate the delivery of quality psychological services in the schools. Thus they acknowledge the fluid and expanding functions of the school. In addition to these ethical standards, there is the ever present necessity to differentiate between legal mandate and ethical responsibility. The school psychologist is urged to become familiar with applicable legal requirements.

[1]Parent refers to legal guardian.

The ethical standards in this guide are organized into several sections representing the multifaceted concerns with which school psychologists must deal. The grouping arrangement is a matter of convenience, and principles discussed in one section apply also to other areas and situations. The school psychologist should consult with other experienced psychologists and seek advice from the professional organization when a situation is encountered for which there is no clearly indicated course of action.

PROFESSIONAL COMPETENCY

In addition to mastery of professional psychological skills, the school psychologist prepares for this special area of functioning by becoming knowledgeable of the organization, objectives, and methods of the school. This is a basic requirement for rendering competent psychological service in the school.

    a.   The school psychologist strives to maintain the highest standards of service by an objective collecting of appropriate data and information necessary to effectively work with the student. In conducting a psychological evaluation, due consideration is given to individual integrity and individual differences by the selection and use of appropriate procedures and assessment techniques.

    b.   The school psychologist is guided by an awareness of the intimate nature of the process which may entail an examination of the personal aspects of the life of an individual. The school psychologist uses an approach which reflects a humanistic concern for dignity and personal integrity.

    c.   The school psychologist is prudently aware of the possible influence personal biases and professional limitations impose on the ability to serve a student, and of the continuing obligation for protecting the privacy and confidence of the student.

PROFESSIONAL RESPONSIBILITY

The school psychologist is committed to the application of professional expertise for promoting improvement in the quality of life available to each person. This objective is pursued in ways that protect the dignity and rights of persons served. Professional skills, position, and influence are applied only for purposes which are consistent with these values.

    a.   The school psychologist defines the direction and the nature of personal loyalties, objectives, and competencies, and advises and informs all persons concerned of these commitments. Students are faithfully and objectively represented to teachers, parents, and other professionals as well as to the student.

    b.   The school psychologist insists upon collecting data for an evaluation in a manner that lends itself to maximum verification, includes relevant information, and is based on assessment techniques which are appropriate for the client.

    c.   When reporting data which are to be representative of the student, the school psychologist makes certain that the information is in such form and style as to assure that the recipient of the report will be able to give maximum assistance to the client. The emphasis is on the interpretation and organization rather than the simple passing along of test scores, and will include a professional appraisal of the degree of reliance which can be placed on the information.

   d.   Where a situation occurs in which there are divided or conflicting interests (as parent–school–student), the school psychologist is responsible for working out a pattern of action which assures mutual benefit and protection of rights for all concerned.

PROFESSIONAL RELATIONSHIPS WITH STUDENTS

Informing the student of all aspects of the potential professional relationship prior to continuing psychological services to the student is challenging but necessary. Special professional skill is demanded to overcome possible difficulties associated with the student's normal dependent relationship with adults, lack of language facility, and limited experiences.

   a.   The school psychologist recognizes the obligation to the student, and respects the student's right of choice to enter, or to participate from (sic) services voluntarily.

   b.   The school psychologist explains to the student who the psychologist is, what the psychologist does, and why the student is being seen. The explanation includes the uses to be made of information obtained, procedures for collecting the information, persons who will receive specific information, and any obligation the psychologist has for reporting specified information. This explanation should be in language understood by the student.

   c.   The school psychologist informs the student of the rationale of sharing information. The course of action proposed takes into account the rights of the student, the rights of the parent, the responsibilities of the school personnel, and the expanding self-independence and mature status of the student.

   d.   The school psychologist discusses with the student all contemplated changes in status and plans which are suggested as a result of psychological study. The discussion includes positive and negative consequences and an account of alternatives available to the student.

   e.   The student is referred when a condition is identified which is outside the treatment competencies or scope of the school psychologist. Such referrals are made on the basis of assistance being available at the referral source.

PROFESSIONAL RELATIONSHIPS WITH THE SCHOOL

The school psychologist recognizes that a working understanding of the goals, processes, and legal requirements of the educational system is essential for an effective relationship with the school. Familiarization with the organization, instructional materials, and teaching strategies of the school are basic for the psychologist to contribute to the common objective for fostering maximum self-development opportunities for each student.

   a.   The school psychologist interprets professional services provided in order to ensure a realistic picture of what psychological services entail.

b. The school psychologist's concern for protecting the interests and rights of students is communicated to the school administration and staff.

c. The school psychologist communicates findings and recommendations in language readily understood by the school staff. These communications describe possible favorable and unfavorable consequences associated with the alternative proposals.

d. The school psychologist is obligated to ascertain that psychoeducational information reaches responsible and authorized persons and is adequately interpreted for their use in helping the pupil. This involves establishing procedures which safeguard the personal and confidential interests of those concerned.

PROFESSIONAL RELATIONSHIPS WITH PARENTS

Parental involvement is a significant influence on efforts to improve a student's capacity for coping with demands. Failure to obtain parental support may compound pressures acting on the student and increase adjustment and learning difficulties. Conferences with parents are characterized with (sic) candor and in language understood by the parent. The discussion includes recommendations suggested by psychoeducational findings. The school psychologist strives to find a set of alternatives which match the skills, values, and possibilities inherent in each parent as an individual personality capable of helping the student.

a. The school psychologist recognizes the importance of parental support and seeks to obtain this by assuring that there is parent contact prior to seeing the student. The school psychologist secures continuing parental involvement by a frank and prompt reporting to the parent of findings obtained in the evaluation of the student.

b. The school psychologist continues to work with the parent when the parent objects to their child receiving psychological services. Alternatives are described which will enable the child to get needed help.

c. The school psychologist insures that recommendations and plans for assisting the child are discussed with the parent. The discussion includes probabilities and alternatives associated with each set of plans. The parents are advised as to sources of help available at school and those available in the community.

d. The school psychologist informs the parent of the nature of records made of parent conferences and evaluations of the child. The advisement includes what information goes into reports, who will receive the reports, and what safeguards are used for protecting the information.

PRINCIPLES GOVERNING RELATIONSHIPS WITH OTHER PROFESSIONS

The school psychologist avoids narrow or vested professional interests so as to work in full cooperation with other professional disciplines in a relationship based on mutual respect and recognition of joint proficiency in some common technical skills.

a. The school psychologist explains and interprets professional competencies of the school psychologist to other professionals so that assignment of services can be made clearly and unambiguously.

b. The school psychologist maintains the skills and ethics of the profession while cooperating with other professionals.

c. The school psychologist is obligated to have prior knowledge of the competency and qualifications of the referral resource.

d. The school psychologist recognizes that various techniques and methods are shared with other professional groups.

PRINCIPLES PERTAINING TO RELATIONSHIPS WITH THE COMMUNITY

Although enjoying professional identity as a psychologist, the school psychologist is also a citizen, thereby, accepting the same responsibilities and duties expected of all members of society. Pursuing dual roles of citizen-psychologist or psychologist-citizen can pose conflicts.

a. The school psychologist acts as a resource person to establish and maintain the availability of adequate psychological services, and also, recognizes the right of individuals to avail themselves of such services at their own discretion and free of coercion.

b. As a citizen, the school psychologist may use customary procedures and practices for bringing about social change. Such activities are conducted as an involved citizen and not as a representative of school psychologists.

c. When a school psychologist suspects existence of detrimental or unethical psychological practices, the professional organization should be consulted.

ADDITIONAL RESOURCES

Ethical issues are not always clearcut. Other sources include:

a. Standards for Educational and Psychological Tests and Manuals, Washington, D.C. APA, AERA, & NCME, 1973.

b. "The Responsible Use of Tests: A Position Paper of AMEG, APGA, and NCME." Measurement and Evaluation in Guidance, Vol. 5, No. 2, July 1972, p. 385–388.

c. Ethical Principles in the Conduct of Research with Human Participants, Washington, D.C.: American Psychological Assoc., Inc. 1973.

d. The School Psychology Digest: Vol. 3, No. 1, Washington, D.C.: The National Assoc. of School Psychologists, 1974.

APPENDIX E

Abridged Rules and Regulations for the Implementation of P.L. 94–142 (The Education for All Handicapped Children Act of 1975)

SUBPART A—GENERAL

Purpose, Applicability, and General Provisions Regulations

§ 300.1 Purpose.   The purpose of this part is:

   (a) To insure that all handicapped children have available to them a free appropriate public education which includes special education and related services to meet their unique needs.

   (b) To insure that the rights of handicapped children and their parents are protected.

   (c) To assist States and localities to provide for the education of all handicapped children, and

   (d) To assess and insure the effectiveness of efforts to educate those children.

§ 300.2 Applicability to State, Local, and Private Agencies

   (a) *States.* This part applies to each State which receives payments under Part B of the Education of the Handicapped Act.

   (b) *Public agencies within the State.* The annual program plan is submitted by the State educational agency on behalf of the State as a whole. Therefore, the provisions of this part apply to all political subdivisions of the State that are involved in the education of handicapped children. These would include: (1) The State educational agency, (2) local educational agencies and intermediate educational units, (3) other State agencies and schools (such as Departments of Mental Health and Welfare and State schools for the deaf or blind), and (4) State correctional facilities.

   (c) *Private schools and facilities.* Each public agency in the State is responsible for

426

insuring that the rights and protections under this part are given to children referred to or placed in private schools and facilities by that public agency.

Comment. The requirements of this part are binding on each public agency that has direct or delegated authority to provide special education and related services in a State that receives funds under Part B of the Act, regardless of whether that agency is receiving funds under Part B.

§ 300.4 Free Appropriate Public Education. As used in this part, the term "free appropriate public education" means special education and related services which:

(a) Are provided at public expense, under public supervision and direction, and without charge.

(b) Meet the standards of the State educational agency, including the requirements of this part,

(c) Include preschool, elementary school, or secondary school education in the State involved, and

(d) Are provided in conformity with an individualized education program which meets the requirements under §§300.340–300.349 of Subpart C.

§ 300.5 Handicapped Children

(a) As used in this part, the term "handicapped children" means those children evaluated in accordance with §§300.530–300.534 as being mentally retarded, hard of hearing, deaf, speech impaired, visually handicapped, seriously emotionally disturbed, orthopedically impaired, other health impaired, deaf-blind, multi-handicapped, or as having specific learning disabilities, who because of those impairments need special education and related services.

(b) The terms used in this definition are defined as follows:

(1) "Deaf" means a hearing impairment which is so severe that the child is impaired in processing linguistic information through hearing, with or without amplification, which adversely affects educational performance.

(2) "Deaf-blind" means concomitant hearing and visual impairments, the combination of which causes such severe communication and other developmental and educational problems that they cannot be accommodated in special education programs solely for deaf or blind children.

(3) "Hard of hearing" means a hearing impairment, whether permanent or fluctuating, which adversely affects a child's educational performance but which is not included under the definition of "deaf" in this section.

(4) "Mentally retarded" means significantly subaverage general intellectual functioning existing concurrently with deficits in adaptive behavior and manifested during the developmental period, which adversely affects a child's educational performance.

(5) "Multihandicapped" means concomitant impairments (such as mentally retarded-blind, mentally retarded-orthopedically impaired, etc.), the combination of which causes such severe educational problems that they cannot be accommodated in special education programs solely for one of the impairments. The term does not include deaf-blind children.

(6) "Orthopedically impaired" means a severe orthopedic impairment which adversely affects a child's educational performance. The term includes impairments caused

by congenital anomaly (e.g., clubfoot, absence of some member, etc.), impairments caused by disease (e.g. poliomyelitis, bone tuberculosis, etc.), and impairments from other causes (e.g., cerebral palsy, amputations, and fractures or burns which cause contractures).

(7) "Other health impaired" means limited strength, vitality or alertness, due to chronic or acute health problems such as a heart condition, tuberculosis, rheumatic fever, nephritis, asthma, sickle cell anemia, hemophilia, epilepsy, lead poisoning, leukemia, or diabetes, which adversely affects a child's educational performance.

(8) "Seriously emotionally disturbed" is defined as follows:

(i) The term means a condition exhibiting one or more of the following characteristics over a long period of time and to a marked degree, which adversely affects educational performance:

(A) An inability to learn which cannot be explained by intellectual, sensory, or health factors;

(B) An inability to build or maintain satisfactory interpersonal relationships with peers and teachers;

(C) Inappropriate types of behavior or feelings under normal circumstances;

(D) A general pervasive mood of unhappiness or depression; or

(E) A tendency to develop physical symptoms or fears associated with personal or school problems.

(ii) The term includes children who are schizophrenic or autistic. The term does not include children who are socially maladjusted, unless it is determined that they are seriously emotionally disturbed.

(9) "Specific learning disability" means a disorder in one or more of the basic psychological processes involved in understanding or in using language, spoken or written, which may manifest itself in an imperfect ability to listen, think, speak, read, write, spell, or to do mathematical calculations. The term includes such conditions as perceptual handicaps, brain injury, minimal brain disfunction, dyslexia, and developmental aphasia. The term does not include children who have learning problems which are primarily the result of visual, hearing, or motor handicaps, of mental retardation, or of environmental, cultural, or economic disadvantage.

(10) "Speech impaired" means a communication disorder, such as stuttering, impaired articulation, a language impairment, or a voice impairment, which adversely affects a child's educational performance.

(11) "Visually handicapped" means a visual impairment which, even with correction, adversely affects a child's educational performance. The term includes both partially seeing and blind children.

§ 300.9 Native Language.   As used in this part, the term "native language" has the meaning given that term by section 703(a)(2) of the Bilingual Education Act, which provides as follows:

The term "native language", when used with reference to a person of limited English-speaking ability, means the language normally used by that person, or in the case of a child, the language normally used by the parents of the child.

Comment. Section 602(21) of the Education of the Handicapped Act states that the term "native language" has the same meaning as the definition from the Bilingual Education Act. In using the term, the Act does not prevent the following means of communication:

(1) In all direct contact with a child (including evaluation of the child), communication would be in the language normally used by the child and not that of the parents, if there is a difference between the two.

(2) If a person is deaf or blind, or has no written language, the mode of communication would be that normally used by the person (such as sign language, braille, or oral communication).

§ 300.13 Related Services

(a) As used in this part, the term "related services" means transportation and such developmental, corrective, and other supportive services as are required to assist a handicapped child to benefit from special education, and includes speech pathology and audiology, psychological services, physical and occupational therapy, recreation, early identification and assessment of disabilities in children, counseling services, and medical services for diagnostic or evaluation purposes. The term also includes school health services, social work services in schools, and parent counseling and training.

(b) The terms used in this definition are defined as follows:

(1) "Audiology" includes:

(i) Identification of children with hearing loss;

(ii) Determination of the range, nature, and degree of hearing loss, including referral for medical or other professional attention for the habilitation of hearing;

(iii) Provision of habilitative activities, such as language habilitation, auditory training, speech reading (lip-reading), hearing evaluation, and speech conservation;

(iv) Creation and administration of programs for prevention of hearing loss;

(v) Counseling and guidance of pupils, parents, and teachers regarding hearing loss; and

(vi) Determination of the child's need for group and individual amplification, selecting and fitting an appropriate aid, and evaluating the effectiveness of amplification.

(2) "Counseling services" means services provided by qualified social workers, psychologists, guidance counselors, or other qualified personnel.

(3) "Early identification" means the implementation of a formal plan for identifying a disability as early as possible in a child's life.

(4) "Medical services" means services provided by a licensed physician to determine a child's medically related handicapping condition which results in the child's need for special education and related services.

(5) "Occupational therapy" includes:

(i) Improving, developing or restoring functions impaired or lost through illness, injury, or deprivation.

    (ii) Improving ability to perform tasks for independent functioning when functions are impaired or lost; and

    (iii) Preventing, through early intervention, initial or further impairment or loss of function.

(6) "Parent counseling and training" means assisting parents in understanding the special needs of their child and providing parents with information about child development.

(7) "Physical therapy" means services provided by a qualified physical therapist.

(8) "Psychological services" include:

    (i) Administering psychological and educational tests, and other assessment procedures;

    (ii) Interpreting assessment results;

    (iii) Obtaining, integrating, and interpreting information about child behavior and conditions relating to learning.

    (iv) Consulting with other staff members in planning school programs to meet the special needs of children as indicated by psychological tests, interviews, and behavioral evaluations; and

    (v) Planning and managing a program of psychological services, including psychological counseling for children and parents.

(9) "Recreation" includes:

    (i) Assessment of leisure function;

    (ii) Therapeutic recreation services;

    (iii) Recreation programs in schools and community agencies; and

    (iv) Leisure education.

(10) "School health services" means services provided by a qualified school nurse or other qualified person.

(11) "Social work services in schools" include:

    (i) Preparing a social or developmental history on a handicapped child;

    (ii) Group and individual counseling with the child and family;

    (iii) Working with those problems in a child's living situation (home, school, and community) that affect the child's adjustment in school; and

    (iv) Mobilizing school and community resources to enable the child to receive maximum benefit from his or her educational program.

(12) "Speech pathology" includes:

    (i) Identification of children with speech or language disorders;

    (ii) Diagnosis and appraisal of specific speech or language disorders;

    (iii) Referral for medical or other professional attention necessary for the habilitation of speech or language disorders;

    (iv) Provisions of speech and language services for the habilitation or prevention of communicative disorders; and

    (v) Counseling and guidance of parents, children, and teachers regarding speech and language disorders.

(13) "Transportation" includes:

    (i) Travel to and from school and between schools,

    (ii) Travel in and around school buildings, and

    (iii) Specialized equipment (such as special or adapted buses, lifts, and ramps), if required to provide special transportation for a handicapped child.

Comment. There are certain kinds of services which might be provided by persons from varying professional backgrounds and with a variety of operational titles, depending upon requirements in individual States. For example, counseling services might be provided by social workers, psychologists, or guidance counselors; and psychological testing might be done by qualified psychological examiners, psychometrists, or psychologists, depending upon State standards.

§ 300.14 Special Education

    (a)(1) As used in this part, the term "special education" means specially designed instruction, at no cost to the parent, to meet the unique needs of a handicapped child, including classroom instruction in physical education, home instruction, and instruction in hospitals and institutions.

    (2) The term includes speech pathology, or any other related service, if the service consists of specially designed instruction, at no cost to the parents, to meet the unique needs of a handicapped child, and is considered "special education" rather than a "related service" under State standards.

    (3) The term also includes vocational education if it consists of specially designed instruction, at no cost to the parents, to meet the unique needs of a handicapped child.

    (b) The terms in this definition are defined as follows:

    (1) "At no cost" means that all specially designed instruction is provided without charge, but does not preclude incidental fees which are normally charged to non-handicapped students or their parents as a part of the regular education program.

    (2) "Physical education" is defined as follows:

    (i) The term means the development of:

    (A) Physical and motor fitness;

    (B) Fundamental motor skills and patterns; and

    (C) Skills in aquatics, dance, and individual and group games and sports (including intramural and lifetime sports).

    (ii) The term includes special physical education, adapted physical education, movement education, and motor development.

    (3) "Vocational education" means organized educational programs which are directly related to the preparation of individuals for paid or unpaid employment, or for additional preparation for a career requiring other than a baccalaureate or advanced degree.

Comment. (1) The definition of "special education" is a particularly important one under these regulations, since a child is not handicapped unless he or she needs special education. (See the definition of "handicapped children" in section 300.5) The definition of "related services" (section 300.13) also depends on this definition, since a related service must be necessary for a child to benefit from special education. Therefore, if a child does not need special education, there can be no "related services," and the child (because not "handicapped") is not covered under the Act.

SUBPART C—SERVICES

Free Appropriate Public Education

§ 300.300 Timelines for Free Appropriate Public Education

(a) *General.* Each State shall insure that free appropriate public education is available to all handicapped children aged three through eighteen within the State not later than September 1, 1978, and to all handicapped children aged three through twenty-one within the State not later than September 1, 1980.

(b) *Age ranges 3–5 and 18–21.* This paragraph provides rules for applying the requirement in paragraph (a) of this section to handicapped children aged three, four, five, eighteen, nineteen, twenty, and twenty-one:

(1) If State law or a court order requires the State to provide education for handicapped children in any disability category in any of these age groups, the State must make a free appropriate public education available to all handicapped children of the same age who have that disability.

(2) If a public agency provides education to non-handicapped children in any of these age groups, it must make a free appropriate public education available to at least a proportionate number of handicapped children of the same age.

(3) If a public agency provides education to 50 percent or more of its handicapped children in any disability category in any of these age groups, it must make a free appropriate public education available to all of its handicapped children of the same age who have that disability.

(4) If a public agency provides education to a handicapped child in any of these age groups, it must make a free appropriate public education available to that child and provide that child and his or her parents all of the rights under Part B of the Act and this part.

(5) A State is not required to make a free appropriate public education available to a handicapped child in one of these age groups if:

(i) State law expressly prohibits, or does not authorize, the expenditure of public funds to provide education to non-handicapped children in that age group; or

(ii) The requirement is inconsistent with a court order which governs the provision of free public education to handicapped children in that State.

§ 300.305 Program Options.

Each public agency shall take steps to insure that its handicapped children have available to them the variety of educational programs and services available to non-handicapped children in the area served by the agency, including art, music, industrial arts, consumer and homemaking education; and vocational education.

§ 300.306 Nonacademic Services

(a) Each public agency shall take steps to provide nonacademic and extracurricular services and activities in such manner as is necessary to afford handicapped children an equal opportunity for participation in those services and activities.

(b) Nonacademic and extracurricular services and activities may include counseling services, athletics, transportation, health services, recreational activities, special interest groups or clubs sponsored by the public agency, referrals to agencies which provide assistance to handicapped persons, and employment of students, including both employment by the public agency and assistance in making outside employment available.

§ 300.307 Physical Education

(a) *General.* Physical education services, specially designed if necessary, must be made available to every handicapped child receiving a free appropriate public education.

(b) *Regular physical education.* Each handicapped child must be afforded the opportunity to participate in the regular physical education program, available to non-handicapped children unless:

(1) The child is enrolled full time in a separate facility; or

(2) The child needs specially designed physical education, as prescribed in the child's individualized education program.

(c) *Special physical education.* If specially designed physical education is prescribed in a child's individualized education program, the public agency responsible for the education of that child shall provide the services directly, or make arrangements for it to be provided through other public or private programs.

(d) *Education in separate facilities.* The public agency responsible for the education of a handicapped child who is enrolled in a separate facility shall insure that the child receives appropriate physical education services in compliance with paragraphs (a) and (c) of this section.

Priorities in the Use of Part B Funds

§ 300.320 Definitions of "First Priority Children" and "Second Priority Children"

For the purposes of §§300.321–300.324, the term:

(a) ''First priority children'' means handicapped children who:

(1) Are in an age group for which the State must make available free appropriate public education under §300.300; and

(2) Are not receiving any education.

(b) ''Second priority children'' means handicapped children, within each disability, with the most severe handicaps who are receiving an inadequate education.

Comment. After September 1, 1978, there should be no second priority children, since States must insure, as a condition of receiving Part B funds for fiscal year 1979, that all handicapped children will have available a free appropriate public education by that date.

New ''First priority children'' will continue to be found by the State after September 1, 1978 through on-going efforts to identify, locate, and evaluate all handicapped children.

§ 300.321 Priorities

(a) Each State and local educational agency shall use funds provided under Part B of the Act in the following order of priorities:

(1) To provide free appropriate public education to first priority children, including the identification, location, and evaluation of first priority children.

(2) To provide free appropriate public education to second priority children, including the identification, location, and evaluation of second priority children.

§ 300.323 Services to Other Children

If a state or a local educational agency is providing free appropriate public education to all of its first priority children, that State or agency may use funds provided under Part B of the Act:

(a) To provide free appropriate public education to handicapped children who are not receiving any education and who are in the age groups not covered under §300.300 in that State; or

(b) To provide free appropriate public education to second priority children; or

(c) Both.

§ 300.324 Application of Local Educational Agency to Use Funds for the Second Priority

A local educational agency may use funds provided under Part B of the Act for second priority children, if it provides assurance satisfactory to the State educational agency in its application (or an amendment to its application):

(a) That all first priority children have a free appropriate public education available to them;

(b) That the local educational agency has a system for the identification, location, and evaluation of handicapped children, as described in its application; and

(c) That whenever a first priority child is identified, located, and evaluated, the local educational agency makes available a free appropriate public education to the child.

Individualized Education Programs

§ 300.340 Definition.

As used in this part, the term "individualized education program" means a written statement for a handicapped child that is developed and implemented in accordance with §§300.341–300.349.

§ 300.341 State Educational Agency Responsibility

(a) *Public agencies.* The State educational agency shall insure that each public agency develops and implements an individualized education program for each of its handicapped children.

(b) *Private schools and facilities.* The State educational agency shall insure that an individualized education program is developed and implemented for each handicapped child who:

(1) Is placed in or referred to a private school or facility by a public agency; or

(2) Is enrolled in a parochial or other private school and receives special education or related services from a public agency.

§ 300.342 When Individualized Education Programs Must Be in Effect

(a) On October 1, 1977, and at the beginning of each school year thereafter, each public agency shall have in effect an individualized education program for every handicapped child who is receiving special education from that agency.

(b) An individualized education program must:

(1) Be in effect before special education and related services are provided to a child; and

(2) Be implemented as soon as possible following the meetings under §300.343.

§ 300.343 Meetings

(a) *General.* Each public agency is responsible for initiating and conducting meetings for the purpose of developing, reviewing, and revising a handicapped child's individualized education program.

(b) *Handicapped children currently served.* If the public agency has determined that a handicapped child will receive special education during school year 1977–1978, a meeting must be held early enough to insure that an individualized education program is developed by October 1, 1977.

(c) *Other handicapped children.* For a handicapped child who is not included under paragraph (b) of this action, a meeting must be held within thirty calendar days of a determination that the child needs special education and related services.

(d) *Review.* Each public agency shall initiate and conduct meetings to periodically review each child's individualized education program and if appropriate revise its provisions. A meeting must be held for this purpose at least once a year.

Comment. The dates on which agencies must have individualized education programs (IEPs) in effect are specified in §300.342 (October 1, 1977, and the beginning of each school year thereafter). However, except for new handicapped children (i.e., those evaluated and determined to need special education after October 1, 1977), the timing of meetings to develop, review, and revise IEPs is left to the discretion of each agency.

In order to have IEPs in effect by the dates in §300.342, agencies could hold meetings at the end of the school year or during the summer preceding those dates. In meeting the October 1, 1977 timeline, meetings could be conducted up through the October 1 date. Thereafter, meetings may be held any time throughout the year, as long as IEPs are in effect at the beginning of each school year.

The statute requires agencies to hold a meeting at least once each year in order to review, and if appropriate revise, each child's IEP. The timing of those meetings could be on the anniversary date of the last IEP meeting on the child, but this is left to the discretion of the agency.

§ 300.344 Participants in Meetings

(a) *General.* The public agency shall insure that each meeting includes the following participants: (1) A representative of the public agency, other than the child's teacher, who is qualified to provide, or supervise the provision of, special education.

(2) The child's teacher.

(3) One or both of the child's parents, subject to §300.345.

(4) The child, where appropriate.

(5) Other individuals at the discretion of the parent or agency.

(b) *Evaluation personnel.* For a handicapped child who has been evaluated for the first time, the public agency shall insure:

(1) That a member of the evaluation team participates in the meeting; or

(2) That the representative of the public agency, the child's teacher, or some other person is present at the meeting, who is knowledgeable about the evaluation procedures used with the child and is familiar with the results of the evaluation.

§ 300.345 Parent Participation

(a) Each public agency shall take steps to insure that one or both of the parents of the handicapped child are present at each meeting or are afforded the opportunity to participate, including:

(1) Notifying parents of the meeting early enough to insure that they will have an opportunity to attend; and

(2) Scheduling the meeting at a mutually agreed on time and place.

(b) The notice under paragraph (a)(1) of this section must indicate the purpose, time, and location of the meeting, and who will be in attendance.

(c) If neither parent can attend, the public agency shall use other methods to insure parent participation, including individual or conference telephone calls.

(d) A meeting may be conducted without a parent in attendance if the public agency is unable to convince the parents that they should attend. In this case the public agency must have a record of its attempts to arrange a mutually agreed on time and place such as:

(1) Detailed records of telephone calls made or attempted and the results of those calls.

(2) Copies of correspondence sent to the parents and any responses received, and

(3) Detailed records of visits made to the parent's homes or place of employment and the result of those visits.

(e) The public agency shall take whatever action is necessary to insure that the parent understands the proceedings at a meeting, including arranging for an interpreter for parents who are deaf or whose native language is other than English.

(f) The public agency shall give the parent, on request, a copy of the individualized education program.

§ 300.346 Contents of Individualized Education Program.

The individualized education program for each child must include:

(a) A statement of the child's present levels of educational performance;

(b) A statement of annual goals, including short term instructional objectives;

(c) A statement of the specific special education and related services to be provided to the child, and the extent to which the child will be able to participate in regular educational programs;

(d) The projected dates for initiation of services and the anticipated duration of the services; and

(e) Appropriate objective criteria and evaluation procedures and schedules for determining, on at least an annual basis, whether the short term instructional objectives are being achieved.

§ 300.349 Individualized Education Program—Accountability.

Each public agency must provide special education and related services to a handicapped child in accordance with an individual education program. However, Part B of the Act does not require that any agency, teacher, or other person be held accountable if a child does not achieve the growth projected in the annual goals and objectives.

Comment. This section is intended to relieve concerns that the individualized education program constitutes a guarantee by the public agency and the teacher that a child will progress at a specified rate. However, this section does not relieve agencies and teachers from making good faith efforts to assist the child in achieving the objectives and goals listed in the individualized education program. Further, the section does not limit a parent's right to complain and ask for revisions of the child's program, or to invoke due process procedures, if the parent feels that these efforts are not being made.

SUBPART D—PRIVATE SCHOOLS

Handicapped Children in Private Schools Placed or Referred by Public Agencies

§ 300.401 Responsibility of State Educational Agency. Each State educational agency shall insure that a handicapped child who is placed in or referred to a private school or facility by a public agency:

(a) Is provided special education and related services:

(1) In conformance with an individualized education program which meets the requirements under §§300.340–300.349 of Subpart C;

(2) At no cost to the parents; and

(3) At a school or facility which meets the standards that apply to State and local educational agencies (including the requirements in this part); and

(b) Has all of the rights of a handicapped child who is served by a public agency.

§ 300.403 Placement of Children by Parents

(a) If a handicapped child has available a free appropriate public education and the parents choose to place the child in a private school or facility, the public agency is not required by this part to pay for the child's education at the private school or facility. However, the public agency shall make services available to the child as provided under §§300.450–300.460.

(b) Disagreements between a parent and a public agency regarding the availability of a program appropriate for the child, and the question of financial responsibility, are subject to the due process procedures under §§300.500–300.514 of Subpart E.

Handicapped Children in Private Schools Not Placed or Referred by Public Agencies

§ 300.452 Local Educational Agency Responsibility

(a) Each local educational agency shall provide special education and related services designed to meet the needs of private school handicapped children residing in the jurisdiction of the agency.

(b) Each local educational agency shall provide private school handicapped children with genuine opportunities to participate in special education and related services consistent with the number of those children and their needs.

§ 300.453 Determination of Needs, Number of Children, and Types of Services. The needs of private school handicapped children, the number of them who will participate under this part, and the types of special education and related services which the local educational agency will provide for them must be determined after consultation with persons knowledgeable of the needs of these children, on a basis comparable to that

used in providing for the participation under this part of handicapped children enrolled in public schools.

SUBPART E—PROCEDURAL SAFEGUARDS

Due Process Procedures for Parents and Children

§ 300.500 Definitions of "Consent," "Evaluation," and "Personally identifiable." As used in this part: "Consent" means that:

(a) The parent has been fully informed of all information relevant to the activity for which consent is sought, in his or her native language, or other mode of communication;

(b) The parent understands and agrees in writing to the carrying out of the activity for which his or her consent is sought, and the consent describes that activity and lists the records (if any) which will be released and to whom; and

(c) The parent understands that the granting of consent is voluntary on the part of the parent and may be revoked at any time.

"Evaluation" means procedures used in accordance with §§300.530–300.534 to determine whether a child is handicapped and the nature and extent of the special education and related services that the child needs. The term means procedures used selectively with an individual child and does not include basic tests administered to or procedures used with all children in a school, grade, or class.

"Personally identifiable" means that information includes:

(a) The name of the child, the child's parent, or other family member;

(b) The address of the child;

(c) A personal identifier, such as the child's social security number or student number; or

(d) A list of personal characteristics or other information which would make it possible to identify the child with reasonable certainty.

§ 300.502 Opportunity to Examine Records. The parents of a handicapped child shall be afforded, in accordance with the procedures in §§300.562–300.569 an opportunity to inspect and review all education records with respect to:

(a) The identification, evaluation, and educational placement of the child, and

(b) The provision of a free appropriate public education to the child.

§ 300.503 Independent Educational Evaluation

(a) *General.* (1) The parents of a handicapped child have the right under this part to obtain an independent educational evaluation of the child, subject to paragraphs (b) through (e) of this section.

(2) Each public agency shall provide to parents, on request, information about where an independent educational evaluation may be obtained.

(3) For the purposes of this part:

    (i) "Independent educational evaluation" means an evaluation conducted by a qualified examiner who is not employed by the public agency responsible for the education of the child in question.

    (ii) "Public expense" means that the public agency either pays for the full cost of the evaluation or insures that the evaluation is otherwise provided at no cost to the parent, consistent with §300.301 of Subpart C.

(b) *Parent right to evaluation at public expense.* A parent has the right to an independent educational evaluation at public expense if the parent disagrees with an evaluation obtained by the public agency. However, the public agency may initiate a hearing under §300.506 of this subpart to show that its evaluation is appropriate. If the final decision is that the evaluation is appropriate, the parent still has the right to an independent educational evaluation, but not at public expense.

(c) *Parent initiated evaluations.* If the parent obtains an independent educational evaluation at private expense, the results of the evaluation:

(1) Must be considered by the public agency in any decision made with respect to the provision of a free appropriate public education to the child, and

(2) May be presented as evidence at a hearing under this subpart regarding that child.

(d) *Requests for evaluations by hearing officers.* If a hearing officer requests an independent educational evaluation as part of a hearing, the cost of the evaluation must be at public expense.

(e) *Agency criteria.* Whenever an independent evaluation is at public expense, the criteria under which the evaluation is obtained, including the location of the evaluation and the qualifications of the examiner, must be the same as the criteria which the public agency uses when it initiates an evaluation.

§ 300.504 Prior Notice: Parent Consent

(a) *Notice.* Written notice which meets the requirements under §300.505 must be given to the parents of a handicapped child a reasonable time before the public agency:

(1) Proposes to initiate or change the identification, evaluation, or educational placement of the child or the provision of a free appropriate public education to the child, or

(2) Refuses to initiate or change the identification, evaluation, or educational placement of the child or the provision of a free appropriate public education to the child, or

(b) *Consent* (1) Parental consent must be obtained before:

(i) Conducting a preplacement evaluation; and

(ii) Initial placement of a handicapped child in a program providing special education and related services.

(2) Except for preplacement evaluation and initial placement, consent may not be required as a condition of any benefit to the parent or child

(c) *Procedures where parent refuses consent.* **(1)** Where State law requires parental consent before a handicapped child is evaluated or initially provided special education and related services. State procedures govern the public agency in overriding a parent's refusal to consent.

(2)(i) Where there is no State law requiring consent before a handicapped child is evaluated or initially provided special education and related services, the public agency may use the hearing procedures in §§300.506–300.508 to determine if the child may be evaluated or initially provided special education and related services without parental consent.

(ii) If the hearing officer upholds the agency, the agency may evaluate or initially provide special education and related services to the child without the parent's consent, subject to the parent's rights under §§300.510–300.513.

Comment. **1.** Any changes in a child's special education program, after the initial placement, are not subject to parental consent under Part B, but are subject to the prior notice requirement in paragraph (a) and the individualized education program requirements in Subpart C.

2. Paragraph (c) means that where State law requires parental consent before evaluation or before special education and related services are initially provided, and the parent refuses (or otherwise withholds) consent, State procedures, such as obtaining a court order authorizing the public agency to conduct the evaluation or provide the education and related services, must be followed.

If, however, there is no legal requirement for consent outside of these regulations, the public agency may use the due process procedures under this subpart to obtain a decision to allow the evaluation or services without parental consent. The agency must notify the parent of its actions, and the parent has appeal rights as well as rights at the hearing itself.

§ 300.505 Content of Notice

(a) The notice under §300.504 must include:

(1) A full explanation of all of the procedural safeguards available to the parents under Subpart E;

(2) A description of the action proposed or refused by the agency, an explanation of why the agency proposes or refuses to take the action, and a description of any options the agency considered and the reasons why those options were rejected;

(3) A description of each evaluation procedure, test, record, or report the agency uses as a basis for the proposal or refusal; and

(4) A description of any other factors which are relevant to the agency's proposal or refusal.

(b) The notice must be:

(1) Written in language understandable to the general public, and

(2) Provided in the native language of the parent or other mode of communication used by the parent, unless it is clearly not feasible to do so.

(c) If the native language or other mode of communication of the parent is not a written language, the State or local educational agency shall take steps to insure:

(1) That the notice is translated orally or by other means to the parent in his or her native language or other mode of communication;

(2) That the parent understands the content of the notice, and

(3) That there is written evidence that the requirements in paragraph (c) (1) and (2) of this section have been met.

§ 300.506 Impartial Due Process Hearing

(a) A parent or a public educational agency may initiate a hearing on any of the matters described in §300.504(a)(1) and (2).

(b) The hearing must be conducted by the State educational agency or the public agency directly responsible for the education of the child, as determined under State statute, State regulation, or a written policy of the State educational agency.

(c) The public agency shall inform the parent of any free or low-cost legal and other relevant services available in the area if:

(1) The parent requests the information; or

(2) The parent or the agency initiates a hearing under this section.

§ 300.507 Impartial Hearing Officer

(a) A hearing may not be conducted:

(1) By a person who is an employee of a public agency which is involved in the education or care of the child, or

(2) By any person having a personal or professional interest which would conflict with his or her objectivity in the hearing.

(b) A person who otherwise qualifies to conduct a hearing under paragraph (a) of this section is not an employee of the agency solely because he or she is paid by the agency to serve as a hearing officer.

(c) Each public agency shall keep a list of the persons who serve as hearing officers. The list must include a statement of the qualifications of each of those persons.

§ 300.508 Hearing Rights

(a) Any party to a hearing has the right to:

(1) Be accompanied and advised by counsel and by individuals with special knowledge or training with respect to the problems of handicapped children;

(2) Present evidence and confront, cross-examine, and compel the attendance of witnesses;

(3) Prohibit the introduction of any evidence at the hearing that has not been disclosed to that party at least five days before the hearing;

(4) Obtain a written or electronic verbatim record of the hearing;

(5) Obtain written findings of fact and decisions. (The public agency shall transmit those findings and decisions, after deleting any personally identifiable information, to the State advisory panel established under Subpart F).

(b) Parents involved in hearings must be given the right to:

(1) Have the child who is the subject of the hearing present; and

(2) Open the hearing to the public.

§ 300.509 Hearing Decision: Appeal.
A decision made in a hearing conducted under this subpart is final, unless a party to the hearing appeals the decision under §300.510 or §300.511.

§ 300.510 Administrative Appeal: Impartial Review

(a) If the hearing is conducted by a public agency other than the State educational agency, any party aggrieved by the findings and decision in the hearing may appeal to the State educational agency.

(b) If there is an appeal, the State educational agency shall conduct an impartial review of the hearing. The official conducting the review shall:

(1) Examine the entire hearing record;

(2) Insure that the procedures at the hearing were consistent with the requirements of due process;

(3) Seek additional evidence if necessary. If a hearing is held to receive additional evidence, the rights in §300.508 apply;

(4) Afford the parties an opportunity for oral or written argument, or both, at the discretion of the reviewing official;

(5) Make an independent decision on completion of the review; and

(6) Give a copy of written findings and the decision to the parties.

(c) The decision made by the reviewing official is final, unless a party brings a civil action under §300.512.

§ 300.511 Civil Action.
Any party aggrieved by the findings and decision made in a hearing who does not have the right to appeal under §300.510 of this subpart, and any party aggrieved by the decision of a reviewing officer under §300.510 has the right to bring a civil action under section 615(e)(2) of the Act.

§ 300.512 Timeliness and Convenience of Hearings and Reviews

(a) The public agency shall insure that not later than 45 days after the receipt of a request for hearing:

(1) A final decision is reached in the hearing; and

(2) A copy of the decision is mailed to each of the parties.

(b) The State educational agency shall insure that not later than 30 days after the receipt of a request for a review:

(1) A final decision is reached in the review; and

(2) A copy of the decision is mailed to each of the parties.

(c) A hearing or reviewing officer may grant specific extensions of time beyond the periods set out in paragraphs (a) and (b) of this section at the request of either party.

(d) Each hearing and each review involving oral arguments must be conducted at a time and place which is reasonably convenient to the parents and child involved.

§ 300.513 Child's Status During Proceedings

(a) During the pendency of any administrative or judicial proceeding regarding a complaint, unless the public agency and the parents of the child agree otherwise, the child involved in the complaint must remain in his or her present educational placement.

(b) If the complaint involves an application for initial admission to public school, the child, with the consent of the parents, must be placed in the public school program until the completion of all the proceedings.

Comment. Section 300.513 does not permit a child's placement to be changed during a complaint proceeding, unless the parents and agency agree otherwise. While the placement may not be changed, this does not preclude the agency from using its normal procedures for dealing with children who are endangering themselves or others.

§ 300.514 Surrogate Parents

(a) *General.* Each public agency shall insure that the rights of a child are protected when:

(1) No parent (as defined in §300.10) can be identified;

(2) The public agency, after reasonable efforts, cannot discover the whereabouts of a parent; or

(3) The child is a ward of the State under the laws of that State.

(b) *Duty of public agency.* The duty of a public agency under paragraph (a) of this section includes the assignment of an individual to act as a surrogate for the parents. This must include a method

(1) for determining whether a child needs a surrogate parent, and

(2) for assigning a surrogate parent to the child.

(c) *Criteria for selection of surrogates.*

(1) The public agency may select a surrogate parent in any way permitted under State law.

(2) Public agencies shall insure that a person selected as a surrogate:

(i) Has no interest that conflicts with the interests of the child he or she represents; and

(ii) Has knowledge and skills, that insure adequate representation of the child.

(d) *Non-employee requirement; compensation.*

(1) A person assigned as a surrogate may not be an employee of a public agency which is involved in the education or care of the child.

(2) A person who otherwise qualifies to be a surrogate parent under paragraph (c) and (d)(1) of this section is not an employee of the agency solely because he or she is paid by the agency to serve as a surrogate parent.

(e) *Responsibilities.* The surrogate parent may represent the child in all matters relating to:

(1) The identification, evaluation, and educational placement of the child, and

(2) The provision of a free appropriate public education to the child.

Protection in Evaluation Procedures

§ 300.530 General

(a) Each State educational agency shall insure that each public agency establishes and implements procedures which meet the requirements of §§300.530–300.534.

(b) Testing and evaluation materials and procedures used for the purposes of evaluation and placement of handicapped children must be selected and administered so as not to be racially or culturally discriminatory.

§ 300.531 Preplacement Evaluation.

Before any action is taken with respect to the initial placement of a handicapped child in a special education program, a full and individual evaluation of the child's educational needs must be conducted in accordance with the requirements of §300.532.

§ 300.532 Evaluation Procedures.

State and local educational agencies shall insure, at a minimum, that:

(a) Tests and other evaluation materials:

(1) Are provided and administered in the child's native language or other mode of communication, unless it is clearly not feasible to do so;

(2) Have been validated for the specific purpose for which they are used; and

(3) Are administered by trained personnel in conformance with the instructions provided by their producer;

(b) Tests and other evaluation materials include those tailored to assess specific areas of educational need and not merely those which are designed to provide a single general intelligence quotient;

(c) Tests are selected and administered so as best to ensure that when a test is administered to a child with impaired sensory, manual, or speaking skills, the test results accurately reflect the child's aptitude or achievement level or whatever other factors the test purports to measure, rather than reflecting the child's impaired sensory, manual, or speaking skills (except where those skills are the factors which the test purports to measure):

(d) No single procedure is used as the sole criterion for determining an appropriate educational program for a child; and

(e) The evaluation is made by a multidisciplinary team or group of persons, including at least one teacher or other specialist with knowledge in the area of suspected disability.

(f) The child is assessed in all areas related to the suspected disability, including, where appropriate, health, vision, hearing, social and emotional status, general intelligence, academic performance, communicative status, and motor abilities.

§ 300.533 Placement Procedures

(a) In interpreting evaluation data and in making placement decisions, each public agency shall:

(1) Draw upon information from a variety of sources, including aptitude and achievement tests, teacher recommendations, physical condition, social or cultural background, and adaptive behavior;

(2) Insure that information obtained from all of these sources is documented and carefully considered;

(3) Insure that the placement decision is made by a group of persons, including persons knowledgeable about the child, the meaning of the evaluation data, and the placement options; and

(4) Insure that the placement decision is made in conformity with the least restrictive environment rules in §§300.550–300.554.

(b) If a determination is made that a child is handicapped and needs special education and related services, an individualized education program must be developed for the child in accordance with §§300.340–300.349 of Subpart C.

§ 300.534 Reevaluation. Each State and local education agency shall insure:

(a) That each handicapped child's individualized education program is reviewed in accordance with §§300.340–300.349 of Subpart C, and

(b) That an evaluation of the child, based on procedures which meet the requirements under §300.532 is conducted every three years or more frequently if conditions warrant or if the child's parent or teacher requests an evaluation.

Least Restrictive Environment

§ 300.550 General

(a) Each State educational agency shall insure that each public agency establishes and implements procedures which meet the requirements of §§300.550–300.556.

(b) Each public agency shall insure:

(1) That to the maximum extent appropriate, handicapped children, including chil-

dren in public or private institutions or other care facilities, are educated with children who are not handicapped, and

(2) That special classes, separate schooling or other removal of handicapped children from the regular educational environment occurs only when the nature or severity of the handicap is such that education in regular classes with the use of supplementary aids and services cannot be achieved satisfactorily.

§ 300.551 Continuum of Alternative Placements

(a) Each public agency shall insure that a continuum of alternative placements is available to meet the needs of handicapped children for special education and related services.

(b) The continuum required under paragraph (a) of this section must:

(1) Include the alternative placements listed in the definition of special education under §300.13 of Subpart A (instruction in regular classes, special classes, special schools, home instruction, and instruction in hospitals and institutions), and

(2) Make provision for supplementary services (such as resource room or itinerant instruction) to be provided in conjunction with regular class placement.

§ 300.552 Placements. Each public agency shall insure that:

(a) Each handicapped child's educational placement:

(1) Is determined at least annually,

(2) Is based on his or her individualized education program, and

(3) Is as close as possible to the child's home;

(b) The various alternative placements included under §300.551 are available to the extent necessary to implement the individualized education program for each handicapped child;

(c) Unless a handicapped child's individualized education program requires some other arrangement, the child is educated in the school which he or she would attend if not handicapped; and

(d) In selecting the least restrictive environment, consideration is given to any potential harmful effect on the child or on the quality of services which he or she needs.

Comment. It should be stressed that, where a handicapped child is so disruptive in a regular classroom that the education of other students is significantly impaired, the needs of the handicapped child cannot be met in that environment. Therefore regular placement would not be appropriate to his or her needs. . ."

Confidentiality of Information

§ 300.560 Definitions. As used in this subpart:

"Destruction" means physical destruction or removal of personal identifiers from information so that the information is no longer personally identifiable.

"Education records" means the type of records covered under the definition of "education records" in Part 99 of this title (the regulations implementing the Family Educational Rights and Privacy Act of 1974).

"Participating agency" means any agency or institution which collects, maintains, or uses personally identifiable information, or from which information is obtained, under this part.

§ 300.561 Notice to Parents.

(a) The State educational agency shall give notice which is adequate to fully inform parents about the requirements under § 300.128 of Subpart B, including:

(1) A description of the extent to which the notice is given in the native languages of the various population groups in the State;

(2) A description of the children on whom personally identifiable information is maintained, the types of information sought, the methods the State intends to use in gathering the information (including the sources from whom information is gathered), and the uses to be made of the information;

(3) A summary of the policies and procedures which participating agencies must follow regarding storage, disclosure to third parties, retention, and destruction of personally identifiable information; and

(4) A description of all of the rights of parents and children regarding this information, including the rights under section 438 of the General Education Provisions Act and Part 99 of this title (the Family Educational Rights and Privacy Act of 1974, and implementing regulations).

(b) Before any major identification, location, or evaluation activity, the notice must be published or announced in newspapers or other media, or both, with circulation adequate to notify parents throughout the State of the activity.

§ 300.562 Access Rights

(a) Each participating agency shall permit parents to inspect and review any education records relating to their children which are collected, maintained, or used by the agency under this part. The agency shall comply with a request without unnecessary delay and before any meeting regarding an individualized education program or hearing relating to the identification, evaluation, or placement of the child, and in no case more than 45 days after the request has been made.

(b) The right to inspect and review education records under this section includes:

(1) The right to a response from the participating agency to reasonable requests for explanations and interpretations of the records;

(2) The right to request that the agency provide copies of the records containing the information if failure to provide those copies would effectively prevent the parent from exercising the right to inspect and review the records; and

(3) The right to have a representative of the parent inspect and review the records.

(c) An agency may presume that the parent has authority to inspect and review records relating to his or her child unless the agency has been advised that the parent does not have the authority under applicable State law governing such matters as guardianship, separation, and divorce.

§ 300.563 Record of Access.
Each participating agency shall keep a record of parties obtaining access to education records collected, maintained, or used under this part (except access by parents and authorized employees of the participating agency), including the name of the party, the date access was given, and the purpose for which the party is authorized to use the records.

§ 300.564 Records on More Than One Child.
If any education record includes information on more than one child, the parents of those children shall have the right to

inspect and review only the information relating to their child or to be informed of that specific information.

§ 300.565 List of Types and Locations of Information. Each participating agency shall provide parents on request a list of the types and locations of education records collected, maintained, or used by the agency.

§ 300.567 Amendments of Records at Parent's Request

(a) A parent who believes that information in education records collected, maintained, or used under this part is inaccurate or misleading or violates the privacy or other rights of the child, may request the participating agency which maintains the information to amend the information.

(b) The agency shall decide whether to amend the information in accordance with the request within a reasonable period of time of receipt of the request.

(c) If the agency decides to refuse to amend the information in accordance with the request it shall inform the parent of the refusal, and advise the parent of the right to a hearing under § 300.568.

§ 300.568 Opportunity for a Hearing. The agency shall, on request, provide an opportunity for a hearing to challenge information in education records to insure that it is not inaccurate, misleading, or otherwise in violation of the privacy or other rights of the child.

§ 300.571 Consent

(a) Parental consent must be obtained before personally identifiable information is:

(1) Disclosed to anyone other than officials of participating agencies collecting or using the information under this part, subject to paragraph (b) of this section; or

(2) Used for any purpose other than meeting a requirement under this part.

(b) An educational agency or institution subject to Part 99 of this title may not release information from education records to participating agencies without parental consent unless authorized to do so under Part 99 of this title.

(c) The State educational agency shall include policies and procedures in its annual program plan which are used in the event that a parent refuses to provide consent under this section.

§ 300.572 Safeguards

(a) Each participating agency shall protect the confidentiality of personally identifiable information at collection, storage, disclosure, and destruction stages.

(b) One official at each participating agency shall assume responsibility for insuring the confidentiality of any personally identifiable information.

(c) All persons collecting or using personally identifiable information must receive training or instruction regarding the State's policies and procedures under § 300.129 of Subpart B and Part 99 of this title.

(d) Each participating agency shall maintain, for public inspection, a current listing of the names and positions of those employees within the agency who may have access to personally identifiable information.

§ 300.573 Destruction of Information

(a) The public agency shall inform parents when personally identifiable information collected, maintained, or used under this part is no longer needed to provide educational services to the child.

(b) The information must be destroyed at the request of the parents. However, a permanent record of a student's name, address, and phone number, his or her grades, attendance record, classes attended, grade level completed, and year completed may be maintained without time limitation.

Comment. Under section 300.573, the personally identifiable information on a handicapped child may be retained permanently unless the parents request that it be destroyed. Destruction of records is the best protection against improper and unauthorized disclosure. However, the records may be needed for other purposes. In informing parents about their rights under this section, the agency should remind them that the records may be needed by the child or the parents for social security benefits or other purposes. If the parents request that the information be destroyed, the agency may retain the information in paragraph (b).

SUBPART G—ALLOCATION OF FUNDS; REPORTS

Allocations

§ 300.701 State Entitlement; Formula

(a) The maximum amount of the grant to which a State is entitled under section 611 of the Act in any fiscal year is equal to the number of handicapped children aged three through 21 in the State who are receiving special education and related services, multiplied by the applicable percentage, under paragraph (b) of this section, of the average per pupil expenditure in public elementary and secondary schools in the United States.

(b) For the purposes of the formula in paragraph (a) of this section, the applicable percentage of the average per pupil expenditure in public elementary and secondary schools in the United States for each fiscal year is:

(1) 1978—5 percent,

(2) 1979—10 percent,

(3) 1980—20 percent,

(4) 1981—30 percent, and

(5) 1982, and for each fiscal year after 1982, 40 percent.

(c) For the purposes of this section, the average per pupil expenditure in public elementary and secondary schools in the United States, means the aggregate expenditures during the second fiscal year preceding the fiscal year for which the computation is made (or if satisfactory data for that year are not available at the time of computation, then during the most recent preceding fiscal year for which satisfactory data are available) of all local educational agencies in the United States (which, for the purpose of this section, means the fifty States and the District of Columbia), plus any direct expenditures by the State for operation of those agencies (without regard to the source of funds from which either of those expenditures are made), divided by the aggregate number of children in average daily attendance to whom those agencies provided free public education during that preceding year.

§ 300.702 Limitations and Exclusions

(a) In determining the amount of a grant under § 300.701 of this subpart, the Commissioner may not count:

(1) Handicapped children in a State of the extent that the number of those children is greater than 12 percent of the number of all childred aged five through 17 in the State;

(3) Handicapped children who are counted under section 300. of the Elementary and Secondary Education Act of 1965.

(b) For the purposes of paragraph (a) of this section, the number of children aged five through 17 in any State shall be determined by the Commissioner on the basis of the most recent satisfactory data available to him.

§ 300.707 Local Educational Agency Entitlements; Formula.

From the total amount of funds available to all local educational agencies, each local educational agency is entitled to an amount which bears the same ratio to the total amount as the number of handicapped children aged three through 21 in that agency who are receiving special education and related services bears to the aggregate number of handicapped children aged three through 21 receiving special education and related services in all local educational agencies which apply to the State educational agency for funds under Part B of the Act.

AMENDED LEARNING DISABILITIES REGULATIONS

§ 300.5 Handicapped Children

(b) . . .

(9) "Specific learning disability" means a disorder in one or more of the basic psychological processes involved in understanding or in using language, spoken or written, which may manifest itself in an imperfect ability to listen, think, speak, read, write, spell, or to do mathematical calculations. The term includes such conditions as perceptual handicaps, brain injury, minimal brain dysfunction, dyslexia, and developmental aphasia. The term does not include children who have learning problems which are primarily the result of visual, hearing, or motor handicaps, of mental retardation, of emotional disturbance, or of environmental, cultural, or economic disadvantage.

Additional Procedures for Evaluating Specific Learning Disabilities

§ 300.540 Additional Team Members.

In evaluating a child suspected of having a specific learning disability, in addition to the requirements of § 300.532, each public agency shall include on the multidisciplinary evaluation team:

(a) (1) The child's regular teacher; or

(2) If the child does not have a regular teacher, a regular classroom teacher qualified to teach a child of his or her age; or

(3) For a child of less than school age, an individual qualified by the State educational agency to teach a child of his or her age; and

(4) At least one person qualified to conduct individual diagnostic examinations of children, such as a school psychologist, speech-language pathologist, or remedial reading teacher.

§ 300.541 Criteria for Determining the Existence of a Specific Learning Disability

(a) A team may determine that a child has a specific learning disability if:

(1) The child does not achieve commensurate with his or her age and ability levels in one or more of the areas listed in paragraph (a) (2) of this section, when provided with learning experiences appropriate for the child's age and ability levels; and

(2) The team finds that a child has a severe discrepancy between achievement and intellectual ability in one or more of the following areas:

    (i) Oral expression;

    (ii) Listening comprehension;

    (iii) Written expression;

    (iv) Basic reading skill;

    (v) Reading comprehension;

    (vi) Mathematics calculation; or

    (vii) Mathematics reasoning.

(b) The team may not identify a child as having a specific learning disability if the severe discrepancy between ability and achievement is primarily the result of:

(1) A visual, hearing, or motor handicap;

(2) Mental retardation;

(3) Emotional disturbance; or

(4) Environmental, cultural or economic disadvantage.

§ 300.542 Observation

(a) At least one team member other than the child's regular teacher shall observe the child's academic performance in the regular classroom setting.

(b) In the case of a child of less than school age or out of school, a team member shall observe the child in an environment appropriate for a child of that age.

§ 300.543 Written Report

(a) The team shall prepare a written report of the results of the evaluation.

(b) The report must include a statement of:

(1) Whether the child has a specific learning disability;

(2) The basis for making the determination;

(3) The relevant behavior noted during the observation of the child;

(4) The relationship of that behavior to the child's academic functioning;

(5) The educationally relevant medical findings, if any;

(6) Whether there is a severe discrepancy between achievement and ability which is not correctable without special education and related services; and

(7) The determination of the team concerning the effects of environmental, cultural, or economic disadvantage.

(c) Each team member shall certify in writing whether the report reflects his or her conclusion. If it does not reflect his or her conclusion, the team member must submit a separate statement presenting his or her conclusions.

Rules and Regulations for P. L. 93-380 Implementing Section 438 (The Family Educational Rights and Privacy Act)

SUBPART A—GENERAL

§ 99.1 Applicability of Part

(a) This part applies to all educational agencies or institutions to which funds are made available under any Federal program for which the U.S. Commissioner of Education has administrative responsibility, as specified by law or by delegation of authority pursuant to law.

(b) This part does not apply to an educational agency or institution solely because students attending that nonmonetary agency or institution receive benefits under one or more of the Federal programs referenced in paragraph (a) of this section, if no funds under those programs are made available to the agency or institution itself.

(c) For the purposes of this part, funds will be considered to have been made available to an agency or institution when funds under one or more of the programs referenced in paragraph (a) of this section: (1) Are provided to the agency or institution by grant, contract, subgrant, or subcontract, or (2) are provided to students attending the agency or institution and the funds may be paid to the agency or institution by those students for educational purposes, such as under the Basic Educational Opportunity Grants Program and the Guaranteed Student Loan Program (Titles IV-A-1 and IV-B, respectively of the Higher Education Act of 1965, as amended).

(d) Except as otherwise specifically provided, this part applies to education records of students who are or have been in attendance at the educational agency or institution which maintains the records.

§ 99.2 Purpose. The purpose of this part is to set forth requirements governing the protection of privacy of parents and students under section 438 of the General Education Provisions Act, as amended.

§ 99.3 Definitions. As used in this Part:

"Act" means the General Education Provisions Act, Title IV of Pub. 1.90-247, as amended.

"Attendance" at an agency or institution includes, but is not limited to: (a) attendance in person and by correspondence, and (b) the period during which a person is working under a work-study program.

"Commissioner" means the U.S. Commissioner of Education.

"Directory information" includes the following information relating to a student: the student's name, address, telephone number, date and place of birth, major field of study, participation in officially recognized activities and sports, weight and height of members of athletic teams, dates of attendance, degrees and awards received, the most recent previous educational agency or institution attended by the student, and other similar information.

"Disclosure" means permitting access or the release, transfer, or other communication of education records of the student or the personally identifiable information contained therein, orally or in writing, or by electronic means, or by any other means to any party.

"Educational institution" or "educational agency or institution" means any public or private agency or institution which is the recipient of funds under any Federal program referenced in §99.1(a). The term refers to the agency or institution recipient as a whole, including all of its components (such as schools or departments in a university) and shall not be read to refer to one or more of these components separate from that agency or institution.

"Education records" (a) means those records which: (1) Are directly related to a student and (2) are maintained by an educational agency or institution or by a party acting for the agency or institution.

(b) The term does not include:

(1) Records of instructional, supervisory, and administrative personnel and educational personnel ancillary thereto which:

    (i) Are in the sole possession of the maker thereof, and

    (ii) Are not accessible or revealed to any other individual except a substitute. For the purpose of this definition a "substitute" means an individual who performs on a temporary basis the duties of the individual who made the record, and does not refer to an individual who permanently succeeds the maker of the record in his or her position.

(2) Records of a law enforcement unit of an educational agency or institution which are:

    (i) Maintained apart from the records described in paragraph (a) of this definition;

    (ii) Maintained solely for law enforcement purposes, and

    (iii) Not disclosed to individuals other than law enforcement officials of the same jurisdiction; *Provided,* That education records maintained by the educational agency or institution are not disclosed to the personnel of the law enforcement unit.

(3) (i) Records relating to an individual who is employed by an educational agency or institution which:

(A) Are made and maintained in the normal course of business;

(B) Relate exclusively to the individual in that individual's capacity as an employee, and

(C) Are not available for use for any other purpose.

(ii) This paragraph does not apply to records relating to an individual in attendance at the agency or institution who is employed as a result of his or her status as a student.

(4) Records relating to an eligible student which are:

(i) Created or maintained by a physician, psychiatrist, psychologist, or other recognized professional or paraprofessional acting in his or her professional or paraprofessional capacity, or assisting in that capacity;

(ii) Created, maintained, or used only in connection with the provision of treatment to the student, and

(iii) Not disclosed to anyone other than individuals providing the treatment; *Provided,* That the records can be personally reviewed by a physician or other appropriate professional of the student's choice. For the purpose of this definition, "treatment" does not include remedial educational activities or activities which are part of the program of instruction at the educational agency or institution.

(5) Records of an educational agency or institution which contain only information relating to a person after that person was no longer a student at the educational agency or institution. An example would be information collected by an educational agency or institution pertaining to the accomplishments of its alumni.

"Eligible student" means a student who has attained eighteen years of age, or is attending an institution of post-secondary education.

"Financial Aid," as used in §99.31 (a) (4), means a payment of funds provided to an individual (or a payment in kind of tangible or intangible property to the individual) which is conditioned on the individual's attendance at an educational agency or institution.

"Institution of postsecondary education" means an institution which provides education to students beyond the secondary school level; "secondary school level" means the educational level (not beyond grade 12) at which secondary education is provided, as determined under State law.

"Panel" means the body which will adjudicate cases under procedures set forth in §§99.65–99.67.

"Parent" includes a parent, a guardian, or an individual acting as a parent of a student in the absence of a parent or guardian. An educational agency or institution may presume the parent has the authority to exercise the rights inherent in the Act unless the agency or institution has been provided with evidence that there is a State law or court order governing such matters as divorce, separation or custody, or a legally binding instrument which provides to the contrary.

"Party" means an individual, agency, institution or organization.

"Personally identifiable" means that the data or information includes (a) the name of the student, the student's parent, or other family member, (b) the address of the student, (c) a personal identifier, such as the student's social security number or student number, (d) a list of personal characteristics which would make the student's identity easily traceable, or (e) other information which would make the student's identity easily traceable.

"Record" means any information or data recorded in any medium, including, but not limited to: handwriting, print, tapes, film, microfilm, and microfiche.

"Secretary" means the Secretary of the U.S. Department of Health, Education, and Welfare.

"Student" (a) includes any individual with respect to whom an educational agency or institution maintains education records.

(b) The term does not include an individual who has not been in attendance at an educational agency or institution. A person who has applied for admission to, but has never been in attendance at a component unit of an institution of postsecondary education (such as the various colleges or schools which comprise a university), even if that individual is or has been in attendance at another component unit of that institution of postsecondary education, is not considered to be a student with respect to the component to which an application for admission has been made.

§ 99.4 Student Rights

(a) For the purposes of this part, whenever a student has attained eighteen years of age, or is attending an institution of postsecondary education, the rights accorded to and the consent required of the parent of the student shall thereafter only be accorded to and required of the eligible student.

(b) The status of an eligible student as a dependent of his or her parents for the purposes of §99.31(a)(8) does not otherwise affect the rights accorded to and the consent required of the eligible student by paragraph (a) of this section.

(c) Section 438 of the Act and the regulations in this part shall not be construed to preclude educational agencies or institutions from according to students rights in addition to those accorded to parents of students.

§ 99.5 Formulation of Institutional Policy and Procedures

(a) Each educational agency or institution shall, consistent with the minimum requirements of section 438 of the Act and this part, formulate and adopt a policy of—

(1) Informing parents of students or eligible students of their rights under §99.6;

(2) Permitting parents of students or eligible students to inspect and review the education records of the student in accordance with §99.11, including at least:

(i)   A statement of the procedure to be followed by a parent or an eligible student who requests to inspect and review the education records of the student;

(ii) With an understanding that it may not deny access to an education record, a description of the circumstances in which the agency or institution feels it has a legitimate cause to deny a request for a copy of such records;

(iii) A schedule of fees for copies, and

(iv) A listing of the types and locations of education records maintained by the educational agency or institution and the titles and the addresses of the officials responsible for those records;

(3) Not disclosing personally identifiable information from the education records of a student without the prior written consent of the parent of the student or the eligible student, except as otherwise permitted by §§99.31 and 99.37; the policy shall include, at least: (i) A statement of whether the educational agency or institution will disclose personally identifiable information from the education records of a student under §99.31 (a) (1) and, if so, a specification of the criteria for determining which parties are "school officials" and what the educational agency or institution consider to be a "legitimate educational interest," and (ii) a specification of the personally identifiable information to be designated as directory information under §99.37;

(4) Maintaining the record of disclosures of personally identifiable information from the education records of a student required to be maintained by §99.32, and permitting a parent or an eligible student to inspect that record;

(5) Providing a parent of the student or an eligible student with an opportunity to seek the correction of education records of the student through a request to amend the records or a hearing under Subpart C, and permitting the parent of a student or an eligible student to place a statement in the education records of the student as provided in §99.21(c);

(b) The policy required to be adopted by paragraph (a) of this section shall be in writing and copies shall be made available upon request to parents of students and to eligible students.

§ 99.6 Annual Notification of Rights

(a) Each educational agency or institution shall give parents of students in attendance or eligible students in attendance at the agency or institution annual notice by such means as are reasonably likely to inform them of the following:

(1) Their rights under section 438 of the Act, the regulations in this part, and the policy adopted under §99.5; the notice shall also inform parents of students or eligible students of the locations where copies of the policy may be obtained; and

(2) The right to file complaints under §99.63 concerning alleged failures by the educational agency or institution to comply with the requirements of section 438 of the Act and this part.

(b) Agencies and institutions of elementary and secondary education shall provide for the need to effectively notify parents of students identified as having a primary or home language other than English.

§ 99.7 Limitations on Waivers

(a) Subject to the limitations in this section and §99.12, a parent of a student or a student may waive any of his or her rights under section 438 of the Act or this part. A waiver shall not be valid unless in writing and signed by the parent or student, as appropriate.

(b) An educational agency or institution may not require that a parent of a student or student waive his or her rights under section 438 of the Act or this part. This paragraph does not preclude an educational agency or institution from requesting such a waiver.

(c) An individual who is an applicant for admission to an institution of postsecondary education or is a student in attendance at an institution of postsecondary education may waive his or her right to inspect and review confidential letters and confidential statements of recommendation described in §99.12(a)(3) except that the waiver may apply to confidential letters and statements only if: (1) The applicant or student is, upon request, notified of the names of all individuals providing the letters or statements; (2) the letters or statements are used only for the purpose for which they were originally intended, and (3) such waiver is not required by the agency or institution as a condition of admission to or receipt of any other service or benefit from the agency or institution.

(d) All waivers under paragraph (c) of this section must be executed by the individual, regardless of age, rather than by the parent of the individual.

(e) A waiver under this section may be made with respect to specified classes of: (1) Education records, and (2) persons or institutions.

(f)(1) A waiver under this section may be revoked with respect to any actions occurring after the revocation.

(2) A revocation under this paragraph must be in writing.

(3) If a parent of a student executes a waiver under this section, that waiver may be revoked by the student at any time after he or she becomes an eligible student.

§ 99.8 Fees

(a) An educational agency or institution may charge a fee for copies of education records which are made for the parents of students, students, and eligible students under section 438 of the Act and this part; *Provided,* That the fee does not effectively prevent the parents and students from exercising their right to inspect and review those records.

(b) An educational agency or institution may not charge a fee to search for or to retrieve the education records of a student.

SUBPART B—INSPECTION AND REVIEW OF EDUCATION RECORDS

§ 99.11 Right to Inspect and Review Education Records

(a) Each educational agency or institution, except as may be provided by §99.12, shall permit the parent of a student or an eligible student who is or has been in attendance at the agency or institution, to inspect and review the education records of the student. The agency or institution shall comply with a request within a reasonable period of time, but in no case more than 45 days after the request has been made.

(b) The right to inspect and review education records under paragraph (a) of this section includes:

(1) The right to a response from the educational agency or institution to reasonable requests for explanations and interpretations of the records; and

(2) The right to obtain copies of the records from the educational agency or institution where failure of the agency or institution to provide the copies would effectively prevent a parent or eligible student from exercising the right to inspect and review the education records.

(c) An educational agency or institution may presume that either parent of the student has authority to inspect and review the education records of the student unless the agency or institution has been provided with evidence that there is a legally binding instrument, or a State law or court order governing such matters as divorce, separation or custody, which provides to the contrary.

§ 99.12 Limitations on Right to Inspect and Review Education Records at the Postsecondary Level

(a) An institution of postsecondary education is not required by section 438 of the Act or this part to permit a student to inspect and review the following records:

(1) Financial records and statements of their parents or any information contained therein;

(2) Confidential letters and confidential statements of recommendation which were placed in the education records of a student prior to January 1, 1975; *Provided,* That:

(i) The letters and statements were solicited with a written assurance of confidentiality, or sent and retained with a documented understanding of confidentiality, and

(ii) The letters and statements are used only for the purposes for which they were specifically intended;

(3) Confidential letters of recommendation and confidential statements of recommendation which were placed in the education records of the student after January 1, 1975:

(i) Respecting admission to an educational institution;

(ii) Respecting an application for employment, or

(iii) Respecting the receipt of an honor or honorary recognition; *Provided,* That the student has waived his or her right to inspect and review those letters and statements of recommendation under §99.7(c).

(b) If the education records of a student contain information on more than one student, the parent of the student or the eligible student may inspect and review or be informed of only the specific information which pertains to that student.

§ 99.13 Limitation on Destruction of Education Records.

An educational agency or institution is not precluded by section 438 of the Act or this part from destroying education records, subject to the following exceptions:

(a) The agency or institution may not destroy any education records if there is an outstanding request to inspect and review them under §99.11;

(b) Explanations placed in the education record under §99.21 shall be maintained as provided in §99.21(d), and

(c) The record of access required under §99.32 shall be maintained for as long as the education record to which it pertains is maintained.

SUBPART C—AMENDMENT OF EDUCATION RECORDS

§99.20 Request to Amend Education Records

(a) The parent of a student or an eligible student who believes that information contained in the education records of the student is inaccurate or misleading or violates the privacy or other rights of the student may request that the educational agency or institution which maintains the records amend them.

(b) The educational agency or institution shall decide whether to amend the education records of the student in accordance with the request within a reasonable period of time of receipt of the request.

(c) If the educational agency or institution decides to refuse to amend the education records of the student in accordance with the request it shall so inform the parent of the student or the eligible student of the refusal, and advise the parent or the eligible student of the right to a hearing under §99.21.

§ 99.21 Right to a Hearing

(a) An educational agency or institution shall, on request, provide an opportunity for a hearing in order to challenge the content of a student's education records to insure that information in the education records of the student is not inaccurate, misleading or otherwise in violation of the privacy or other rights of students. The hearing shall be conducted in accordance with §99.22.

(b) If, as a result of the hearing, the educational agency or institution decides that the information is inaccurate, misleading or otherwise in violation of the privacy or other rights of students, it shall amend the education records of the student accordingly and so inform the parent of the student or the eligible student in writing.

(c) If, as a result of the hearing, the educational agency or institution decides that the information is not inaccurate, misleading or otherwise in violation of the privacy or other rights of students, it shall inform the parent or eligible student of the right to place in the education records of the student a statement commenting upon the information in the education records and/or setting forth any reasons for disagreeing with the decision of the agency or institution.

(d) Any explanation placed in the education records of the student under paragraph (c) of this section shall:

(1) Be maintained by the educational agency or institution as part of the education records of the student as long as the record or contested portion thereof is maintained by the agency or institution, and

(2) If the education records of the student or the contested portion thereof is disclosed by the educational agency or institution to any party, the explanation shall also be disclosed to that party.

§ 99.22 Conduct of the Hearing.   The hearing required to be held by §99.21(a) shall be conducted according to procedures which shall include at least the following elements:

(a) The hearing shall be held within a reasonable period of time after the educational agency or institution has received the request, and the parent of the student or the eligible student shall be given notice of the date, place and time reasonably in advance of the hearing;

(b) The hearing may be conducted by any party, including an official of the educational agency or institution, who does not have a direct interest in the outcome of the hearing;

(c) The parent of the student or the eligible student shall be afforded a full and fair opportunity to present evidence relevant to the issues raised under §99.21, and may be assisted or represented by individuals of his or her choice at his or her own expense, including an attorney;

(d) The educational agency or institution shall make its decision in writing within a reasonable period of time after the conclusion of the hearing; and

(e) The decision of the agency or institution shall be based solely upon the evidence presented at the hearing and shall include a summary of the evidence and the reasons for the decision.

SUBPART D—DISCLOSURE OF PERSONALLY IDENTIFIABLE INFORMATION FROM EDUCATION RECORDS

§ 99.30 Prior Consent for Disclosure Required

(a)(1) An educational agency or institution shall obtain the written consent of the parent of a student or the eligible student before disclosing personally identifiable information from the education records of a student, other than directory information, except as provided in §99.31.

(2) Consent is not required under this section where the disclosure is to (i) the parent of a student who is not an eligible student, or (ii) the student himself or herself.

(b) Whenever written consent is required, an educational agency or institution may presume that the parent of the student or the eligible student giving consent has the authority to do so unless the agency or institution has been provided with evidence that there is a legally binding instrument, or a State law or court order governing such matters as divorce, separation or custody, which provides to the contrary.

(c) The written consent required by paragraph (a) of this section must be signed and dated by the parent of the student or the eligible student giving the consent and shall include:

(1) A specification of the records to be disclosed,

(2) The purpose or purposes of the disclosure, and

(3) The party or class of parties to whom the disclosure may be made.

(d) When a disclosure is made pursuant to paragraph (a) of this section, the educational agency or institution shall, upon request, provide a copy of the record which is disclosed to the parent of the student or the eligible student, and to the student who is not an eligible student if so requested by the student's parents.

§ 99.31 Prior Consent for Disclosure Not Required

(a) An educational agency or institution may disclose personally identifiable information from the education records of a student without the written consent of the parent of the student or the eligible student if the disclosure is—

(1) To other school officials, including teachers, within the educational institution or local educational agency who have been determined by the agency or institution to have legitimate educational interests;

(2) To officials of another school or school system in which the student seeks or intends to enroll, subject to the requirements set forth in §99.34;

(3) Subject to the conditions set forth in §99.35, to authorized representatives of:

(i)   The Comptroller General of the United States,

(ii) The Secretary,

(iii) The Commissioner, the Director of the National Institute of Education, or the Assistant Secretary for Education, or

(iv) State educational authorities;

(4) In connection with financial aid for which a student has applied or which a student has received; *Provided,* That personally identifiable information from the education records of the student may be disclosed only as may be necessary for such purposes as:

(i) To determine the eligibility of the student for financial aid,

(ii) To determine the amount of the financial aid,

(iii) To determine the conditions which will be imposed regarding the financial aid, or

(iv) To enforce the terms or conditions which will be imposed regarding the financial aid, or

(5) To State and local officials or authorities to whom information is specifically required to be reported or disclosed pursuant to State statute adopted prior to November 19, 1974. This subparagraph applies only to statutes which require that specific information be disclosed to State or local officials and does not apply to statutes which permit but do not require disclosure. Nothing in this paragraph shall prevent a State from further limiting the number or type of State or local officials to whom disclosures are made under this subparagraph:

(6) To organizations conducting studies for, or on behalf of, educational agencies or institutions for the purpose of developing, validating, or administering predictive tests, administering student aid programs, and improving instruction; *Provided,* That the studies are conducted in a manner which will not permit the personal identification of students and their parents by individuals other than representatives of the organization and the information will be destroyed when no longer needed for the purposes for which the study was conducted; the term "organizations" includes, but is not limited to, Federal, State, and local agencies, and independent organizations;

(7) To accrediting organizations in order to carry out their accrediting functions;

(8) To parents of a dependent student as defined in section 152 of the Internal Revenue Code of 1954;

(9) To comply with a judicial order or lawfully issued subpoena; *Provided,* That the educational agency or institution makes a reasonable effort to notify the parent of the student or the eligible student of the order or subpoena in advance of compliance therewith; and

(10) To appropriate parties in a health or safety emergency subject to the conditions set forth in §99.36.

(b) This section shall not be construed to require or preclude disclosure of any personally identifiable information from the education records of a student by an educational agency or institution to the parties set forth in paragraph (a) of this section.

§ 99.32.   Record of Disclosures Required to be Maintained

(a) An educational agency or institution shall for each request for and each disclosure of personally identifiable information from the education records of a student, maintain a record kept with the education records of the student which indicates:

(1) The parties who have requested or obtained personally identifiable information from the education records of the student, and

(2) The legitimate interests these parties had in requesting or obtaining the information.

(b) Paragraph (a) of this section does not apply to disclosures to a parent of a student or an eligible student, disclosures pursuant to the written consent of a parent of a student or an eligible student when the consent is specific with respect to the party or parties to whom the disclosure is to be made, disclosures to school officials under §99.31(a)(1), or to disclosures of directory information under §99.37.

(c) The record of disclosures may be inspected;

(1) By the parent of the student or the eligible student,

(2) By the school official and his or her assistants who are responsible for the custody of the records, and

(3) For the purpose of auditing the recordkeeping procedures of the educational agency or institution by the parties authorized in, and under the conditions set forth in §99.31(a)(1) and (3).

§ 99.33 Limitation on Redisclosure

(a) An educational agency or institution may disclose personally identifiable information from the education records of a student only on the condition that the party to whom the information is disclosed will not disclose the information to any other party without the prior written consent of the parent of the student or the eligible student, except that the personally identifiable information which is disclosed to an institution, agency or organization may be used by its officers, employees and agents, but only for the purposes for which the disclosure was made.

(b) Paragraph (a) of this section does not preclude an agency or institution from disclosing personally identifiable information under §99.31 with the understanding that the information will be redisclosed to other parties under that section; *Provided,* That the recordkeeping requirements of §99.32 are met with respect to each of those parties.

(c) An educational agency or institution shall, except for the disclosure of directory information under §99.37, inform the party to whom a disclosure is made of the requirement set forth in paragraph (a) of this section.

§ 99.34 Conditions for Disclosure to Officials of Other Schools and School Systems

(a) An educational agency or institution transferring the education records of a student pursuant to §99.31(a)(2) shall:

(1) Make a reasonable attempt to notify the parent of the student or the eligible student of the transfer of the records at the last known address of the parent or eligible student, except:

(i) When the transfer of the records is initiated by the parent or eligible student at the sending agency or institution, or

(ii) When the agency or institution includes a notice in its policies and procedures formulated under §99.5 that it forwards education records on request to a school in which a student seeks or intends to enroll; the agency or institution does not have to provide any further notice of the transfer;

(2) Provide the parent of the student or the eligible student, upon request, with a copy of the education records which have been transferred; and

(3) Provide the parent of the student or the eligible student, upon request, with an opportunity for a hearing under Subpart C of this part.

(b) If a student is enrolled in more than one school, or receives services from more than one school, the schools may disclose information from the education records of the student to each other without obtaining the written consent of the parent of the student or the eligible student; *Provided,* That the disclosure meets the requirements of paragraph (a) of this section.

§ 99.35 Disclosure to Certain Federal and State Officials for Federal Program Purposes

(a) Nothing in section 438 of the Act or this part shall preclude authorized representatives of officials listed in §99.31(a)(3) from having access to student and other records which may be necessary in connection with the audit and evaluation of Federally supported education programs, or in connection with the enforcement of or compliance with the Federal legal requirements which relate to these programs.

(b) Except when the consent of the parent of a student or an eligible student has been obtained under §99.30, or when the collection of personally identifiable information is specifically authorized by Federal law, any data collected by officials listed in §99.31(a)(3) shall be protected in a manner which will not permit the personal identification of students and their parents by other than those officials, and personally identifiable data shall be destroyed when no longer needed for such audit, evaluation, or enforcement of or compliance with Federal legal requirements.

§ 99.36 Conditions for Disclosure in Health and Safety Emergencies

(a) An educational agency or institution may disclose personally identifiable information from the education records of a student to appropriate parties in connection with an emergency if knowledge of the information is necessary to protect the health or safety of the student or other individuals.

(b) The factors to be taken into account in determining whether personally identifiable information from the education records of a student may be disclosed under this section shall include the following:

(1) The seriousness of the threat to the health or safety of the student or other individuals;

(2) The need for the information to meet the emergency;

(3) Whether the parties to whom the information is disclosed are in a position to deal with the emergency; and

(4) The extent to which time is of the essence in dealing with the emergency.

(c) Paragraph (a) of this section shall be strictly construed.

§ 99.37 Conditions for Disclosure of Directory Information

(a) An educational agency or institution may disclose personally identifiable information from the education records of a student who is in attendance at the institution or agency if that information has been designated as directory information (as defined in §99.3) under paragraph (c) of this section.

(b) An educational agency or institution may disclose directory information from the education records of an individual who is no longer in attendance at the agency or institution without following the procedures under paragraph (c) of this section.

(c) An educational agency or institution which wishes to designate directory information shall give public notice of the following:

(1) The categories of personally identifiable information which the institution has designated as directory information;

(2) The right of the parent of the student or the eligible student to refuse to permit the designation of any or all of the categories of personally identifiable information with respect to that student as directory information; and

(3) The period of time within which the parent of the student or the eligible student must inform the agency or institution in writing that such personally identifiable information is not to be designated as directory information with respect to that student.

SUBPART E—ENFORCEMENT

§ 99.60 Office and Review Board

(a) The Secretary is required to establish or designate an office and a review board under section 438(g) of the Act. The office will investigate, process, and review violations, and complaints which may be filed concerning alleged violations of the provisions of section 438 of the Act and the regulations in this part. The review board will adjudicate cases referred to it by the office under the procedures set forth in §§99.65–99.67.

(b) The following is the address of the office which has been designated under paragraph (a) of this section: The Family Educational Rights and Privacy Act Office (FERPA), Department of Health, Education, and Welfare, 330 Independence Ave. SW., Washington, D.C. 20201.

§ 99.61 Conflict with State or Local Law.
An educational agency or institution which determines that it cannot comply with the requirements of section 438 of the Act or of this part because a State or local law conflicts with the provisions of section 438 of the Act or the regulations in this part shall so advise the office designated under §99.60(b) within 45 days of any such determination, giving the text and legal citation of the conflicting law.

§ 99.62 Reports and Records.
Each educational agency or institution shall (a) submit reports in the form and containing such information as the Office of the Review Board may require to carry out their functions under this part, and (b) keep the records and afford access thereto as the Office or the Review Board may find necessary to assure the correctness of those reports and compliance with the provisions of sections 438 of the Act and this part.

§ 99.63 Complaint Procedure

(a) Compliants regarding violations of rights accorded parents and eligible students by section 438 of the Act or the regulations in this part shall be submitted to the Office in writing.

(b)(1) The Office will notify each complainant and the educational agency or institution against which the violation has been alleged, in writing, that the complaint has been received.

(2) The notification to the agency or institution under paragraph (b)(1) of this section shall include the substance of the alleged violation and the agency or institution shall be given an opportunity to submit a written response.

(c) (1) The Office will investigate all timely complaints received to determine whether there has been a failure to comply with the provisions of section 438 of the Act or the regulations in this part, and may permit further written or oral submissions by both parties.

(2) Following its investigation the Office will provide written notification of its findings and the basis for such findings, to the complainant and the agency or institution involved.

(3) If the Office finds that there has been a failure to comply, it will include in its notification under paragraph (c) (2) of this section, the specific steps which must be taken by the agency or educational institution to bring the agency or institution into compliance. The notification shall also set forth a reasonable period of time, given all of the circumstances of the case, for the agency or institution to voluntarily comply.

(d) If the educational agency or institution does not come into compliance within the period of time set under paragraph (c) (3) of this section, the matter will be referred to the Review Board for a hearing under §§99.64–99.67, inclusive.

§ 99.64 Termination of Funding. If the Secretary, after reasonable notice and opportunity for a hearing by the Review Board, (1) finds that an educational agency or institution has failed to comply with the provisions of section 438 of the Act, or the regulations in this part, and (2) determines that compliance cannot be secured by voluntary means, he shall issue a decision, in writing, that no funds under any of the Federal programs referenced in §99.1(a) shall be made available to that educational agency or institution (or, at the Secretary's discretion, to the unit of the educational agency or institution affected by the failure to comply) until there is no longer any such failure to comply.

§ 99.65 Hearing Procedures

(a) *Panels.* The Chairman of the Review Board shall designate Hearing Panels to conduct one or more hearings under §99.64. Each Panel shall consist of not less than three members of the Review Board. The Review Board may, at its discretion, sit for any hearing or class of hearings. The Chairman of the Review Board shall designate himself or any other member of a Panel to serve as Chairman.

(b) *Procedural rules* (1) With respect to hearings involving, in the opinion of the Panel, no dispute as to a material fact the resolution of which would be materially assisted by oral testimony, the Panel shall take appropriate steps to afford to each party to the proceeding an opportunity for presenting his case at the option of the Panel (i) in whole or in part in writing or (ii) in an informal conference before the Panel which shall afford each party: (A) Sufficient notice of the issues to be considered (where such notice has not previously been afforded); and (B) an opportunity to be represented by counsel.

(2) With respect to hearings involving a dispute as to a material fact the resolution of which would be materially assisted by oral testimony, the Panel shall afford each party an opportunity, which shall include, in addition to provisions required by subparagraph (1)(ii) of this paragraph, provisions designed to assure to each party the following:

(i) An opportunity for a record of the proceedings:

(ii) An opportunity to present witnesses on the party's behalf; and

(iii) An opportunity to cross-examine other witnesses either orally or through written interrogatories.

§ 99.66 Hearing before Panel or a Hearing Officer.

A hearing pursuant to §99.65(b)(2) shall be conducted, as determined by the Panel Chairman, either before the Panel or a hearing officer. The hearing officer may be (a) one of the members of the Panel or (b) a nonmember who is appointed as a hearing examiner under 5 U.S.C. 3105.

§ 99.67 Initial Decision; Final Decision

(a) The Panel shall prepare an initial written decision, which shall include findings of fact and conclusions based thereon. When a hearing is conducted before a hearing officer alone, the hearing officer shall separately find and state the facts and conclusions which shall be incorporated in the initial decision prepared by the Panel.

(b) Copies of the initial decision shall be mailed promptly by the Panel to each party (or to the party's counsel), and to the Secretary with a notice affording the party an opportunity to submit written comments thereon to the Secretary within a specified reasonable time.

(c) The initial decision of the Panel transmitted to the Secretary shall become the final decision of the Secretary, unless, within 25 days after the expiration of the time for receipt of written comments, the Secretary advises the Review Board in writing of his determination to review the decision.

(d) In any case in which the Secretary modifies or reverses the initial decision of the Panel, he shall accompany that action with a written statement of the grounds for the modification or reversal, which shall promptly be filed with the Review Board.

(e) Review of any initial decision by the Secretary shall be based upon the decision, the written record, if any, of the Panel's proceedings, and written comments or oral arguments by the parties, or by their counsel, to the proceedings.

(f) No decision under this section shall become final until it is served upon the educational agency or institution involved or its attorney.

APPENDIX G

Journals of Major Interest to School Psychologists

This appendix presents three categories of journals of interest to school psychologists. The primary category includes those journals that the authors of this book consider central to the academic and professional disciplines of school psychology and should be read regularly by anyone in the field. The secondary category includes those journals regularly publishing articles bearing on the practice of school psychology; however, the primary focus of these journals is not in the field of school psychology. School psychologists should regularly examine these journals for articles of interest. The tertiary category includes journals that are somewhat peripheral to school psychology yet periodically publish articles that will interest school psychologists. These journals should be read occasionally for articles that bear on school psychology. All of these journals should be available at any major university library. The category of primary journals should be made available in the library of any school psychology training program and the psychological services office of most school districts. Not all journals that should ever be read by school psychologists are included in this appendix. A number of journals of high quality have not been listed due to space requirements. Some journals have not been listed because of qualitative judgments made by the authors. We hope that this list will prove helpful to school psychologists in locating research and opinion central to their field.

PRIMARY JOURNALS[1]

Journal of School Psychology

Publishes articles on research, opinions, and practice in school psychology aimed toward fostering the continued development of school psychology as a scientific and professional

---

[1]A new primary journal, *Professional School Psychology*, will begin publication in 1985, and will be sponsored by APA Division 16. This journal will be of major interest to the field.

specialty. First published in 1963. Published quarterly. Circulation 2500. Nine articles per average issue. Articles for publication should be submitted in triplicate to Thomas A. Oakland, Editor, Department of Educational Psychology, the University of Texas, Austin, Texas 78712.

Psychology in the Schools

Contains papers on the application of psychology to schools; evaluation and assessment; educational practices and problem; and strategies in behavioral change. First published in 1965. Published quarterly. Circulation 2500. Twenty-five articles per average issue. Special rates available for students. Articles for publication should be submitted in triplicate to Gerald B. Fuller, Editor, Department of Psychology, Central Michigan University, Mt. Pleasant, Michigan 48859.

School Psychology Review

(Formerly *School Psychology Digest*.) Publishes original research, reviews of theoretical and applied topics, and descriptions of intervention techniques of interest to school psychologists. Has special theme issues. First published in 1972. Published quarterly. Circulation 8500. Ten articles per average issue. Official journal of the National Association of School Psychologists. Articles for publication should be submitted in triplicate to Steve N. Elliott, Editor, Department of Psychology, Louisiana State University, Baton Rouge, Louisiana 70803.

SECONDARY JOURNALS

American Journal of Orthopsychiatry

Publishes articles related to research, theory, and practice in mental health and human development from a multidisciplinary perspective. Clinical, research, or expository papers are accepted.

Contemporary Educational Psychology

Contains articles that demonstrate the application of psychological methods and skills to the educational process. Classroom and laboratory studies are accepted especially when the emphasis of the study is on problem solving. Occasional reviews and critiques are published.

Educational and Psychological Measurement

Publishes empirical research and methodological and statistical papers relevant to the broad field of measurement. Validity studies of tests included. Computer programs also published.

Exceptional Children

Includes significant research findings, current issues and trends in administration, curriculum, and classroom management for children who are blind, partially sighted, handicapped, deaf or hard of hearing, gifted, retarded, and emotionally disturbed.

Journal of Abnormal Child Psychology

Devoted to research and theory concerned with psychopathology in childhood and adolescence emphasizing original experimental and correlational research.

Journal of Clinical Child Psychology

A problem-oriented journal publishing a wide range of articles on creative programs, models, service patterns, research, actions, and ideas that promote the well-being of children and youth.

Journal of Clinical Psychology

Contains objective research studies in clinical psychology areas of psychodiagnosis, psychodynamics, psychopathology, clinical judgment, objective tests, personality tests, projective tests, and the handling of psychological cases.

Journal of Consulting and Clinical Psychology

Concerned with research in the development, validity, and use of techniques of diagnosis and treatment of disordered behavior, studies of personality and of its assessment and development where these have bearing on problems of consulting and clinical psychology; the etiology and characteristics of psychopathological states; or case studies.

Journal of Educational Measurement

Contains reports and research articles of applications of measurement in an educational context; solicited reviews of current standardized educational and psychological tests and of other important measurement works.

Journal of Educational Psychology

Publishes investigations and theoretical papers dealing with problems of learning, teaching, and psychological development, relationships, and adjustment of the individual. Preference is given to studies of the more complex types of behavior, especially in or relating to educational settings.

Journal of Educational Research

Publishes the results of original research on a wide range of topics in education: teaching strategies, curriculum, tests and measurement, teacher education, student personnel services, administration.

Journal of Learning Disabilities

Publishes clinical applications, research, and theoretical articles on specific learning disabilities. The journal is a multidisciplinary, international exchange of information, covering disciplines that contribute to the study of the nature and remediation of specific learning disabilities.

Journal of Personality Assessment

For the study and advancement of projective and other assessment techniques; research articles, reviews of literature, case studies, new tests, theoretical studies, comments, rebuttals, and book reviews related to personality assessment.

Journal of Psychoeducational Assessment

Contains articles related to all aspects of psychoeducational assessment including current and future trends in assessment and occasional position papers. Journal studies focus on important assessment domains including behavior, intellect, personality, achievement, neuropsychology, perception, motor, language, and adaptive abilities. Includes cross-cultural/ethnic studies and reports on various exceptional populations.

Journal of Special Education

Contains articles of research, theory, opinion, and review regarding special education and areas of special concern to general education.

Measurement and Evaluation in Guidance

Concerned with measurement and testing, manuscripts that deal with theoretical and other problems of the measurement specialist to those directed to the administrator, counselor, or personnel worker, having clearly described implications for the practitioner in measurement and evaluation.

Professional Psychology

Covers the range of psychology as a profession, particularly in the areas of applications of research, standards of practice, teaching practices, interprofessional relations, delivery of services, and innovative approaches to training.

TERTIARY JOURNALS

American Journal of Community Psychology

Focuses on research and theory concerned with interactions between individuals and communities, organizations, institutions, and human groups.

American Educational Research Journal

Carries original reports of empirical and theoretical studies in education.

American Journal of Education

Among the more sophisticated education journals publishing works of both a theoretical and an empirical nature.

American Journal of Mental Deficiency

Concerned with contributions to knowledge of mental retardation and the characteristics of mentally retarded persons.

American Psychologist

Publishes articles on current issues in psychology as well as empirical, theoretical, and practical articles on broad aspects of psychology.

Applied Psychological Measurement

Publishes empirical research on the application of techniques of psychological measurement to substantive problems in all areas of psychology and related disciplines (sociology, political science, etc.).

Behavior Modification

Publishes research and clinical papers in applied behavior modification. Assessment and modification techniques for problems in psychiatric, clinical, educational, and rehabilitation settings are appropriate. Occasional case studies.

Child Development

A publication outlet for research, theoretical articles, or reviews that have theoretical implications for developmental research.

Child Study Journal

A publication medium for theory and research on child and adolescent development with particular attention to articles devoted to the educational and psychological aspects of human development.

Clinical Neuropsychology

Publishes research bearing on the practice of clinical neuropsychology. Open peer commentary, case studies, exchanges of information, and book and test reviews are regularly included.

Educational Research Quarterly

Publishes findings of original research, development and models, or conceptual designs that focus on issues relevant to all dimensions of education.

Educational Review

Contains articles dealing with research, descriptions of experimental work in schools, critical reviews of teaching methods or curriculum content in schools; articles on administrative problems, tests and measurement, child growth and development and the relation of schools to the community.

Elementary School Journal

Contains articles concerned with research, school subjects, innovative classroom practice, teacher education, child development, supervision, school and social change, and administration.

Harvard Educational Review

A forum for research, analysis, and discussion of vital issues in educational theory, education, policy, and practice.

Journal of Abnormal Psychology

Devoted to research and theory in the broad field of abnormal behavior, its determinants, and its correlates.

Journal of Applied Behavioral Science

Publishes articles related to substantive and methodological issues that can lead to changes in the quality of human life. Articles are focused on using the behavioral sciences to understand and affect the processes of social innovation and change.

Journal of Applied Behavior Analysis

Publishes reports of experimental research involving the application of the experimental analysis of behavior to problems of social importance. Technical papers on research and issues arising from behavioral applications also presented.

Journal of Autism and Childhood Schizophrenia

Articles include reports of experimental research, critical reviews of important areas of treatment, and information on the severe psychopathologies of childhood as related to psychology, psychiatry, special education, and related disciplines.

Journal of Community Psychology

Empirical articles devoted to research, evaluation; assessment, intervention and review articles that deal with human behavior in community settings.

Journal of Counseling Psychology

Publication medium for theory and research on counseling and related activities carried on by counselors and personnel workers; emphasis on empirical studies of the counseling process, evaluation of counseling, and counseling methods.

Journal of Experimental Education

Contains articles on the mathematics and methodology of educational research and statistics.

Multivariate Behavioral Research

Contains articles on research results and methods in psychology, educational psychology, and related disciplines using a multivariate analysis approach.

Psychological Bulletin

Publishes reviews of research literature in psychology and interpretations of substantive and methodological issues; reports original research only when aimed at the solution of some particular research problem in psychology of sufficient breadth to interest a wide readership.

Review of Educational Research

Publishes integrative reviews and interpretations of educational research literature on substantive and methodological issues.

School Review

Seeks to develop and maintain a lively forum for the communication and discussion of vital issues in education; interested in all levels of education, psychology, sociology.

Young Children

Articles related to the needs, development, and education of children from birth to eight years. Focus is on early education, teacher training, curriculum ideas, and research.

Application for Membership in the American Psychological Association as a Student in Psychology

#

1983 APPLICATION AND ENDORSEMENT BLANK FOR STUDENT AFFILIATE

INSTRUCTIONS TO APPLICANT: Fill out the portion of the blank labeled "Application." Have the part labeled "Endorsement" filled out by a Member or Fellow of the APA. The director of your graduate studies or the chair of your department of psychology would be a suitable endorser. Your application and endorsement blank, accompanied by a check or money order, should then be sent to the American Psychological Association at the address given below. Your fee will be returned if your application is not approved.

APPLICATION
(Please print or type)

Name in full_____

               (Last)   *(First)*   *(Middle Initial)*

Mailing address _____

_____

_____

          City   State   Zip Code

ACADEMIC HISTORY

		Major Field		Minor Field			
Institution	Years	Subject	Sem. Hrs.	Subject	Sem. Hrs.	Degree	Date of Degree

Institution you are now attending _____

Date _____ Signature_____

ORDER BLANK FOR JOURNALS

As a Student Affiliate, you are eligible to subscribe to APA journals at the rates paid by members. Listed below are the journals published by the APA. The annual fee is $10.00. WRITE THE SUBSCRIPTION PRICES OPPOSITE THOSE TO WHICH YOU WISH TO SUBSCRIBE. Total the subscription prices, subtract the discount, add the $10.00 fee, and enter the amount due on the line marked "**Total Amount Payable.**" Further details about subscriptions are on the reverse side of this sheet.

Publications	Prices	1983 Subscriptions
American Psychologist (Monthly)	$ 5.00	AP
Contemporary (Monthly)	$ 20.00	CT
Abnormal (Quarterly)	$ 20.00	AB
Applied (Quarterly)	$ 20.00	AL
Comparative — Both Journals	$ 29.00	CM
Behavioral Neuroscience (Bimonthly)	$ 20.00	NE
Comparative Psychology (Quarterly)	$ 9.00	BH
Consulting & Clinical (Bimonthly)	$ 30.00	CS
Educational (Bimonthly)	$ 25.00	ED
Bulletin (Bimonthly)	$ 25.00	BU
Counseling (Quarterly)	$ 15.00	CO
Review (Quarterly)	$ 15.00	RV
Personality & Social (Monthly)	$ 45.00	PS
Developmental (Bimonthly)	$ 20.00	DV
Professional (Bimonthly)	$ 30.00	PR

Publications	Prices	1983 Subscriptions
Experimental (JEP): All Four Journals	$ 60.00	XJ
JEP: General (Quarterly)	$ 15.00	XG
JEP: Learning, Memory, & Cognition		
(Quarterly)	$ 20.00	XL
JEP: Human Perception (Bimonthly)	$ 20.00	XP
JEP: Animal Behavior (Quarterly)	$ 10.00	XA
Psychological Documents (Quarterly)	$ 10.00	JS
Psychological Abstracts (Issues only, monthly)	$200.00	P1
Psychological Abstracts, Issues (Monthly),		
Indexes (S-annual)	$300.00	P2
PsycSCAN: Clinical (Quarterly)	$ 10.00	P3
PsycSCAN: Developmental (Quarterly)	$ 10.00	P4
PsycSCAN: Applied (Quarterly)	$ 10.00	P5
PsycSCAN: LD/MR (Quarterly)	$ 10.00	P6

SPECIAL 10% DISCOUNT ON 1983 APA JOURNALS

TOTAL SUBSCRIPTIONS .... $ _____
Multiply subscription total by .10 .... $ _____
Discounted total .... $ _____
FEE .... $ **$10.00**
TOTAL AMOUNT PAYABLE .... $ _____

Signed ....

ENDORSEMENT

To the best of your knowledge, is the information given by the applicant correct?

The applicant is a graduate or undergraduate student in psychology or_____ at_____

                              (write in other field)   (name of institution)

Date _____ Signature of Endorser_____

                            (Fellow, Member of APA) underline one

For your convenience, one check or money order in payment of both your fee and your subscriptions may be written. *Make your remittance payable in U.S. dollars to the American Psychological Association.*

Mail to: AMERICAN PSYCHOLOGICAL ASSOCIATION
1200 Seventeenth Street, N.W.
Washington, D.C. 20036

9/82

Application for Membership in the National Association of School Psychologists

NASP APPLICATION FOR MEMBERSHIP

(Fiscal and Membership Year: July 1 - June 30)

Applicant Name _____
(As Desired on Certificate of Membership)
Number and Street _____

City _____ State_____ Zip_____

Job Title_____

Check where appropriate to your application:

( ) Regular Membership   ( ) Student Membership

Membership Category (please check one):

____ A. Currently functioning as school
psychologist.

____ B. Trained as a school psychologist, but
currently functioning as a consultant or
supervisor in psychological services.

____ C. Primarily engaged in training school
psychologists at a college or university.

____ D. Certified as a school psychologist under
the laws of a state.

____ E. Student.

Degrees held_____

Year Obtained_____ University _____

Professional organizations to which you belong:
National: APA ( ), APGA ( ), CEC ( ), NEA ( ),

Others:_____

How did you hear about NASP? _____

Years of experience: with present employer: _____; in the field of school psychology _____; in the field of
education other than school psychology _____; school psychology _____.

Are you currently engaged in private practice (please check): ( ) No   ( ) Part Time   ( ) Full Time

Date_____ Applicant Signature _____

NOTE: Your Professional Status must be verified by enclosing a copy of your State Certification or your
Supervisor's signature signed below. Our official address is still in Washington, D.C., but all fiscal and
membership matters should be directed to:

NASP • P. O. BOX 184 • KENT, OHIO 44240

_____   _____
(Signature of Supervisor or Advisor verifying above.)   (Employer)

Make check payable to NASP

MEMBERSHIP DUES

	Regular	Student
July, Aug., Sept......	$45.00	$15.00
October 1	40.00	13.50
November 1	35.00	12.00
December 1	30.00	10.00
January 1	25.00	8.00
February 1	20.00	8.00
March 1.............	15.00	8.00
At Convention or		
April, May, June	45.00*	15.00*

*Dues paid until June 30 of next fiscal year.

APPENDIX J

A Guide to Resources for Handicapped Children

Many of the organizations listed below have been dealing with the special problems of low incidence handicapping conditions for many years. By definition, these disorders are infrequent and until recently were even more rarely seen in the public schools. These conditions pose special problems with which you are likely to have quite limited if any experience. Most of these organizations are devoted to assisting parents and professionals work more effectively with these children as well as providing help for the children themselves. Whenever you do encounter one of these disabling conditions, you will find the materials provided through these groups helpful to you as well as the child, parent, and other school staff. This listing is not exhaustive but includes those organizations and publications we know about and have found helpful. If you know of others, please send them along to the senior author for inclusion in the next edition.

- Al-Anon Family Group Headquarters
  P.O. Box 182
  Madison Square Station
  New York, NY 10010

- American Foundation for the Blind
  15 W. 16th Street
  New York, NY 10011

- American Printing House for the Blind
  1839 Frankfort Avenue
  P.O. Box 6085
  Louisville, KY 40206

- Cystic Fibrosis Foundation
  6000 Executive Blvd.
  Suite 309
  Rockville, MD 20852

- Epilepsy Foundation of America
  1838 L Street, N.W.
  Washington, DC 20036

- Juvenile Diabetes Foundation
  23 East 26th St.
  New York, NY 10010

- Muscular Dystrophy Association, Inc.
  810 27th Street
  New York, NY 10019

- National Association for Down's
  Syndrome
  P.O. Box 63
  Oak Park, IL 60303

- National Association for Visually
  Handicapped
  305 East 24th St.
  New York, NY 10010

- National Center for Education
  Materials and Media for the
  Handicapped
  Ohio State University
  Faculty for Exceptional Children
  Columbus, OH 43210

- National Institute of Health
  Building 31, Room 8A16
  Bethesda, MD 20205

- National Migraine Foundation
  5214 Northwestern Ave.
  Chicago, IL 60625

- National Multiple Sclerosis Society
  205 East 42nd St.
  New York, NY 10017

- National Reyes's Syndrome Foundation
  8293 Homestead Road
  Benzonia, MI 49616

- National Spinal Cord Injury
  Foundation
  369 Elliott St.
  Newton Upper Falls, MA 02169

- National Society for Autistic Children
  1234 Massachusetts Ave., N.W.
  Suite 1017
  Washington, DC 20005

- National Tay-Sachs and Allied Disease
  Association
  122 E. 42nd St.
  New York, NY 10017

- Shriners Hospitals of Crippled Children
  P.O. Box 25356
  Tampa, FL 33623

- Synanon Foundation, Inc.
  P.O. Box 786
  Marshall, CA 94949

- United Cancer Council
  1803 N. Meridian St., Room 202
  Indianapolis, IN 46202

- United Cerebral Palsy Association, Inc.
  66 E. 34th Street
  New York, NY 10016

Author Index

Abeles, N., 107
Abidin, R. R., Jr., 22, 82, 107
Abramowitz, E. A., 12
Achenbach, T. M., 144, 186, 187, 199, 289, 317, 319
Ackerson, G., 162
Adams, H. E., 164, 312
Adamson, G. W., 191, 195
Adleman, H. S., 318
Agner, J., 3, 10
Ahr, E., 22
Ajchenbaum, M., 81, 109
Albee, G. W., 43, 49, 107
Algozzine, B., 63, 143, 186, 200, 311
Allen, G. J., 36, 46, 306
Allessi, G. J., 155, 157, 158
Alper, T. G., 200
Alpert, J. L., 15, 79, 81, 82, 83, 108, 109, 110
American Psychiatric Association, 30, 316
American Psychological Association, 17, 37, 41, 52, 59, 68, 312, 334
Ames, N., 162
Anastasi, A., 5, 143
Anderegg, T., 113
Anderson, C. S., 160, 169
Anderson, L. W., 143

Anderson, T. A., 159
Anderson, T. E., 80, 82, 87, 88, 109
Angoff, W. H., 121
Arends, J. H., 86, 101, 103, 112, 170
Arends, R. I., 86, 101, 103, 112, 170
Arter, J. A., 199, 322
Atkeson, B. M., 205, 207
Axline, V., 199
Ayllon, T., 202, 203, 204, 205, 206, 213
Azrin, N. H., 204

Baer, D. M., 216, 325, 329
Bailey, J. S., 206, 219
Baker, H. L., 27, 109
Baker, L. J., 159
Baker, T. B., 159, 311
Balch, P., 109
Balla, D. A., 179
Ballantyne, D., 109, 110
Balow, B., 187, 192
Bandura, A., 32, 85, 209
Barbanel, L., 24, 48, 199, 324
Barclay, J. R., 27
Bardon, J. I., 2, 3, 17, 21, 22, 23, 24, 25, 28, 30, 50, 56, 71, 80, 110, 200, 201, 306, 307, 308, 309, 336
Barker, L. F., 6

Subject Index